Napoleon's Wars

CHARLES ESDAILE

Napoleon's Wars

An International History, 1803–1815

ALLEN LANE
an imprint of
PENGUIN BOOKS

ALLEN LANE

Published by the Penguin Group
Penguin Books Ltd, 80 Strand, London WC2R ORL, England
Penguin Group (USA) Inc., 375 Hudson Street, New York, New York 10014, USA
Penguin Group (Canada), 90 Eglinton Avenue East, Suite 700, Toronto, Ontario, Canada M4P 2Y3
(a division of Pearson Penguin Canada Inc.)
Penguin Ireland, 25 St Stephen's Green, Dublin 2, Ireland
(a division of Penguin Books Ltd)
Penguin Group (Australia), 250 Camberwell Road, Camberwell, Victoria 3124, Australia
(a division of Pearson Australia Group Pty Ltd)
Penguin Books India Pvt Ltd, 11 Community Centre, Panchsheel Park, New Delhi – 110 017, India
Penguin Group (NZ), 67 Apollo Drive, Rosedale, North Shore 0632, New Zealand
(a division of Pearson New Zealand Ltd)
Penguin Books (South Africa) (Pty) Ltd, 24 Sturdee Avenue, Rosebank, Johannesburg 2196, South Africa

Penguin Books Ltd, Registered Offices: 80 Strand, London WC2R ORL, England

www.penguin.com

First published 2007
1

Copyright © Charles Esdaile, 2007

The moral right of the author has been asserted

Set in PostScript Adobe Sabon
Typeset by Rowland Phototypesetting Ltd, Bury St Edmunds, Suffolk
Printed in England by Clays Ltd, St Ives plc

A CIP catalogue record for this book is available from the British Library

978-0-713-99715-6

www.greenpenguin.co.uk

For my mother, Elizabeth Alice Ellen Esdaile, with much love

Contents

List of Illustrations

List of Maps

Preface and Acknowledgements

Conqueror or liberator? Aggressor or victim? Sinner or saint? Man of blood or martyr? For two hundred years the argument with regard to Napoleon and his foreign policy has rumbled on unabated: it shows no sign of coming to an end, let alone being resolved. The reasons are perfectly clear. Throughout his career Napoleon had an eye on posterity, whilst his exile to the tiny island of St Helena provided him with ample opportunity literally to make history. Through his edited table-talk, through the interviews that he conceded to passing guests and travellers, and through the memoirs that he encouraged his companions to write, he reached out beyond the confines of grave and exile, and established a version of events which historians have found impossible to ignore.

More than any other figure in history, meanwhile, Napoleon has had the capacity to inspire a loyal band of followers to spend their lives in a crusade to defend his historical reputation. Armed with the 'holy scripture' handed down on the mount of St Helena, and aided by a variety of political and historical fellow travellers, these latterday soldiers of the *grande armée* have for generation after generation variously sought to persuade the world that their hero desired only to defend the honour of France, to preserve the French Revolution, to liberate the rest of Europe from the chains of the *ancien régime* and even to create a united Europe that would have been a precursor of the current European Union. By constantly returning to the charge, they have kept the debate alive and, amongst other things, made this book possible. Indeed, not just possible but essential: their arguments are so powerful and attractive that they have in effect won the battle for the public mind. People who have never heard of Brumaire, Marengo, Austerlitz or Wagram, nevertheless 'know' that Napoleon somehow stands for liberty, progress and the advancement of the 'little man'. Hence the triumph of Napoleon as brand name, and the prominence his figure has achieved in the world of advertising (and perhaps the cinema: Napoleon is not just one of the most written about personalities in history, but is also reputed to be the one that, after Jesus Christ, has been the most portrayed on film).

The idea that any one book could possibly reverse this situation is laughable, but for all that the attempt must be made. Thus the Napoleon who stands so tall in the public mind, the Napoleon who to this day exerts so great a pull on the public imagination, is the Napoleon that the emperor himself wished us to see, the Napoleon who first emerged in the propaganda of a hundred imperial bulletins and a thousand copies of *Le Moniteur* and was then enshrined for all time in the legend of St Helena. By the same token, all the arguments that have been used – and are still used – to create a positive image of the emperor are in effect the arguments of Napoleon himself. Each and every one of those arguments, however, is open at the very least to serious question, and there are now few academic historians who accept them at anything like face value. Yet academic historians rarely attract the audience that they deserve, and the first purpose of this book is therefore to synthesize their work and insert it into a debate from which it is all too often absent.

But *Napoleon's Wars* is not just one more contribution to the Napoleon controversy. It is also an attempt to approach the subject from a very different perspective. Hitherto the subject of the Napoleonic Wars has almost always been handled through one or other of two prisms: either as a biography of Napoleon or as a study of his campaigns. As historical genres there is nothing wrong with either of these approaches, but they do have certain limitations in that they concentrate on a story that is distinctly unidimensional and, worse, retell a story that has been told over and over again. In consequence, a survey of the historiography of the Napoleonic Wars cannot but leave the observer with a sense of dissatisfaction. What we have is invariably a litany of Napoleon's battles, but the Napoleonic Wars did not solely consist of Napoleon's battles, but were also waged in a series of theatres – the Iberian Peninsula, Italy, the Balkans, Scandinavia – which the emperor either never graced with his presence at all or only visited very briefly. Of these other theatres of war, all of them situated on the peripheries of the Continent, only the first has received detailed treatment (and even then in a fashion that has been just as skewed). We therefore come to the second purpose of *Napoleon's Wars*: to write a history of the Napoleonic Wars that reflects their pan-European dimension and is not just francocentric. In doing so I have had to fill in many gaps, and the result is sometimes somewhat curious; I have had to expend far more ink on the Serbian revolt of 1804 than on the battle of Austerlitz, for example. But if this is the case I make no apologies; there would be neither merit nor point in wasting words on narratives that are already two a penny.

Connected with this issue is the third aim of *Napoleon's Wars*. Although this is anything but clear from the conventional historiography, Napoleon did not just exist in a vacuum. Like the French Revolution before him, he rather emerged in a Europe whose international history was dominated by events, not in the West, but rather in the East. The focus of attention at the time was above all on Poland and the Ottoman Empire, and the manoeuvring that centred on these two states – the one defunct by 1800 and the other already the proverbial 'sick man' of Europe, albeit a sick man that was currently making real efforts to fight off his disease. These foci did not alter either for the events of 1789 or for those of 1799. What this book also attempts to do, then, is to place the Napoleonic Wars in their true context. The idea, admittedly, is not an original one: in 1995, Paul Schroeder's magisterial *Transformation of European Politics* attempted much the same task. But this present work represents the first attempt to look at the Napoleonic Wars alone. Whilst Schroeder does the same thing, and doubtless much more elegantly, he does so in the context of a study that ranges all the way from 1763 to 1848, almost concealing the fact that it is one of the most important twentieth-century contributions to the Napoleon controversy.

So much, then, for rationale and justification. As ever, my debts are many. At the top of the list must stand my agent, Bill Hamilton, whose suggestion that I should write 'a big book on Napoleon' sparked off the process of thought that eventually led me to where I am today. Next in line come my editor at Penguin Books, Simon Winder, who has been the soul of faith, patience and encouragement alike, and his assistant, Chloe Campbell, who is truly one of the jewels in Penguin's crown. This work being in many respects a synthesis, I should next add the staff of the British Library, the Biblioteca Nacional in Madrid, and finally the Sydney Jones Library at the University of Liverpool, much technical assistance also having been received from Cecilia Mackay, who carried out all the picture research, and Jane Robertson whose careful copy-editing has greatly enhanced the text. Then, too, there are my colleagues, and especially my many co-workers in the field of Napoleonic history. Graced as I am by a particularly distinguished peer group, I should here especially like to mention Marianne Elliot, Alan Forrest, Tim Blanning, Michael Broers, Rory Muir, Christopher Hall, Michael Rowe, Janet Hartley, Jeremy Black, Paul Schroeder, Enno Kraehe, Clive Emsley, Malcolm Crook, Desmond Gregory, Michael Duffy, John Lynn, Stuart Woolf, David Gates, Alexander Grab, Geoffrey Ellis, Donald Horward, Owen Connelly, Harold Parker, Jean Tulard, Phillip Dwyer, Brendan Simms, Rick Schneid and, last but not least, Gunther Rothenburg and David Chandler, both of whom sadly passed away shortly before the manuscript of *Napoleon's Wars* was completed. For reasons of space, I am unable to acknowledge my many borrowings from them (and, indeed, many other scholars) in proper form, but I am none the less grateful to them all, and am well aware that without their efforts this book could probably never have been written; from many of them, too, I have received the warmest friendship, the best of company and the kindest of support and encouragement. Finally, there is my family. Camp-followers as heroic and long suffering in their way as any of the poor souls who trudged along in the wake of Napoleon's armies, Alison, Andrew, Helen, Maribel and Bernadette have walked with me every step of the long road that has led from Amiens to Waterloo and, like their predecessors, deserve much in the way of recognition.

Lastly, a word on technicalities. All quotations have been put into modern English in terms of punctuation and spelling, whilst outdated anglicisms have in general also been eschewed (so that Saragossa, for example, is rendered 'Zaragoza', Leghorn 'Livorno' and Gothenburg 'Göteborg'). By contrast, in the many instances in Scandinavia, Eastern Europe and the Balkans where foreign names have changed in the wake of twentieth-century shifts in frontiers, ethnicities and political allegiances, foreign names have for the most part been left in the form most likely to be familiar to readers of Napoleonic history: for the modern form, please see the glossary at the end of the book. There are, however, a few exceptions. To refer to Alexandria, Prague, Warsaw and Moscow by any other names would be both affected and unhelpful, whilst one or two very small places have completely defeated all efforts to discover the modern version. One such is Pläswitz, the Silesian village where an armistice was agreed between Napoleon and his Russian and Prussian opponents in June 1813: indeed, there is no agreement even on the

German name for this place: 'Pläswitz' is only the most common element in a list which includes Parchwitz, Plaeswitz, Pleiswitz, Plasswitz and Pleschwitz. For all such inadequacies and inconsistencies, not to mention the factual errors – all my own – that the text may contain, I can only offer my apologies.

Charles Esdaile
Liverpool
2 July 2006

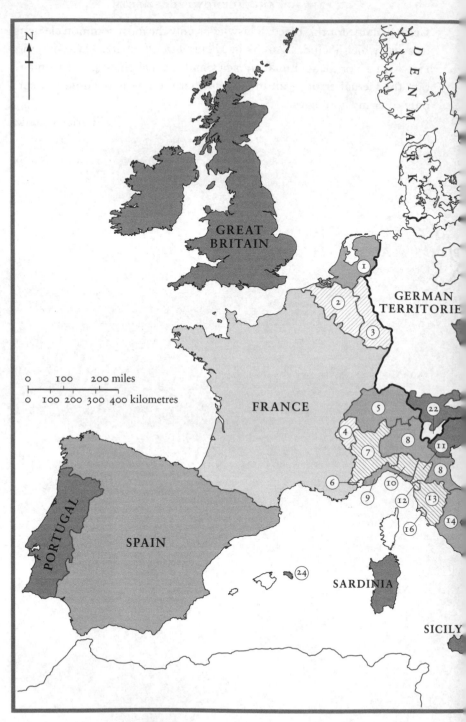

N

GREAT
BRITAIN

D E N M A R K

GERMAN
TERRITORIE

FRANCE

PORTUGAL

SPAIN

SARDINIA

SICILY

0   100   200 miles

0   100 200 300 400 kilometres

①
②
③
⑤
④
⑦
⑥
⑧
⑨
⑩
⑫
⑬
⑯
⑪
⑧
⑭
㉒
㉔

Europe, January 1799

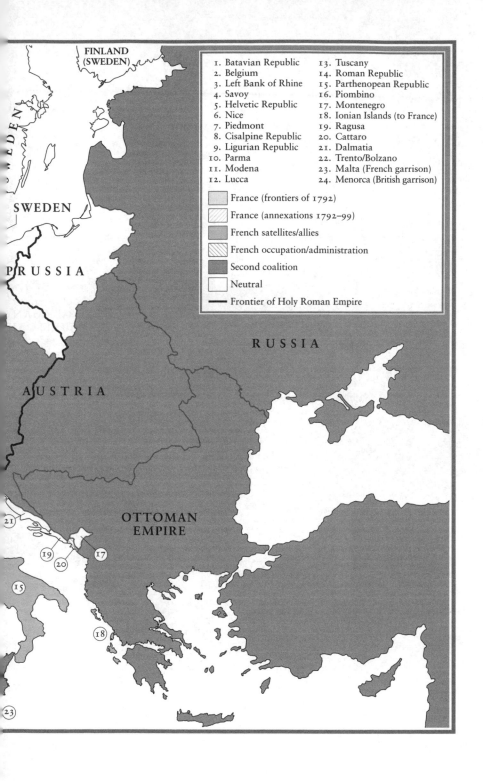

FINLAND
(SWEDEN)

SWEDEN

PRUSSIA

AUSTRIA

RUSSIA

OTTOMAN
EMPIRE

1. Batavian Republic
2. Belgium
3. Left Bank of Rhine
4. Savoy
5. Helvetic Republic
6. Nice
7. Piedmont
8. Cisalpine Republic
9. Ligurian Republic
10. Parma
11. Modena
12. Lucca
13. Tuscany
14. Roman Republic
15. Parthenopean Republic
16. Piombino
17. Montenegro
18. Ionian Islands (to France)
19. Ragusa
20. Cattaro
21. Dalmatia
22. Trento/Bolzano
23. Malta (French garrison)
24. Menorca (British garrison)

France (frontiers of 1792)

France (annexations 1792–99)

French satellites/allies

French occupation/administration

Second coalition

Neutral

Frontier of Holy Roman Empire

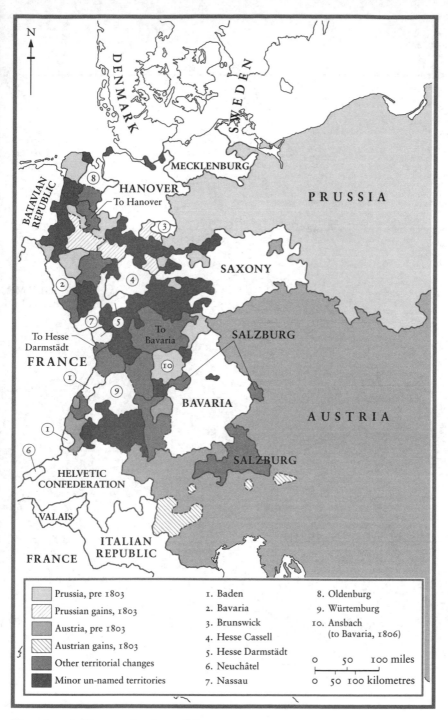

Napoleon's Reorganization of Germany, 1803

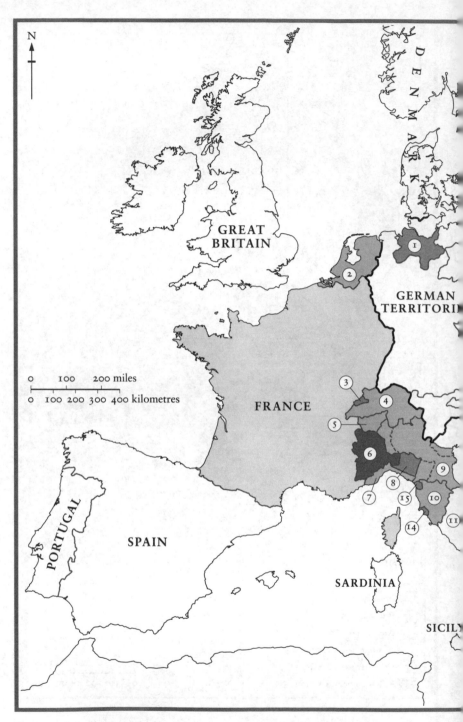

N

GREAT
BRITAIN

D E N M A R K

GERMAN
TERRITORI

FRANCE

PORTUGAL

SPAIN

SARDINIA

SICILY

0   100   200 miles
0   100 200 300 400 kilometres

Europe, July 1803

FINLAND
(SWEDEN)

1. Hanover/Hamburg etc.
2. Batavian Republic
3. Neuchâtel
4. Helvetic Confederation
5. Republic of the Valais
6. Piedmont
7. Ligurian Republic
8. Parma
9. Italian Republic (showing
   territory gained since 1799)
10. Kingdom of Etruria
11. Papal States
12. Montenegro
13. Republic of the
    Seven Islands
14. Piombino
    (French occupied)
15. Lucca
16. Ragusa
17. Cattaro
18. Dalmatia
19. Malta (British garrison)

France (frontiers of 1801)
France (annexations 1800–3)
French satellites
French occupation/administration
Frontier of Holy Roman Empire

SWEDEN

RUSSIA

RUSSIA

AUSTRIA

OTTOMAN
EMPIRE

NAPLES

N

GREAT
BRITAIN

DENMARK

CONF. OF THE RHINE

FRANCE

PORTUGAL

SPAIN

SARDINIA

SICIL

0   100   200 miles
0   100 200 300 400 kilometres

Europe, September 1806

SWEDEN

PRUSSIA

SAXONY

AUSTRIA

RUSSIA

OTTOMAN
EMPIRE

NAPLES

1. Holland
2. Minor German territories excluded from Confederation of the Rhine
3. Bayreuth
4. Neuchâtel
5. Helvetic Confederation
6. Republic of the Valais
7. Kingdom of Italy
8. Parma
9. Ligurian Republic
10. Lucca
11. Piombino
12. Kingdom of Etruria
13. Papal States
14. Istria/Dalmatia
15. Ragusa (to France 1807)
16. Montenegro
17. Tyrol/Vorarlberg (to Bavaria, 1805)
18. Venetia (to Kingdom of Italy, 1805)
19. Hanover (to Prussia, 1806)
20. Hamburg/Lubeck
21. Salzburg (to Austria, 1805)
22. East Friesland (Prussia)
23. Munster/Paderborn (Prussia)
24. Republic of the Seven Isles
25. Malta (British garrison)

France (frontiers of 1803)

France (annexations 1803–6)

French occupation/administration

French satellites/allies

Fourth coalition

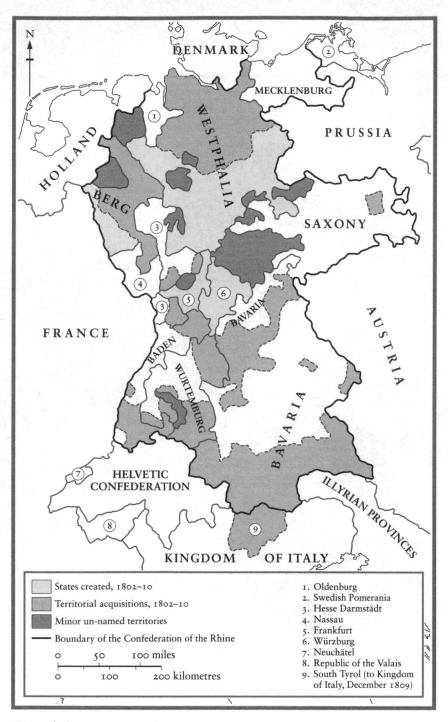

DENMARK

MECKLENBURG

PRUSSIA

HOLLAND

WESTPHALIA

① 1

BERG

SAXONY

③ 3

FRANCE

④ 4

⑤ 5

⑥ 6

BAVARIA

AUSTRIA

③ 3

BADEN

WURTEMBURG

BAVARIA

HELVETIC
CONFEDERATION

⑦ 7

ILLYRIAN PROVINCES

⑧ 8

⑨ 9

KINGDOM   OF ITALY

▢ States created, 1802–10	1. Oldenburg
▨ Territorial acquisitions, 1802–10	2. Swedish Pomerania
▨ Minor un-named territories	3. Hesse Darmstädt
— Boundary of the Confederation of the Rhine	4. Nassau
	5. Frankfurt
0 50 100 miles	6. Würzburg
0 100 200 kilometres	7. Neuchâtel
	8. Republic of the Valais
	9. South Tyrol (to Kingdom of Italy, December 1809)

Central Europe, September 1809

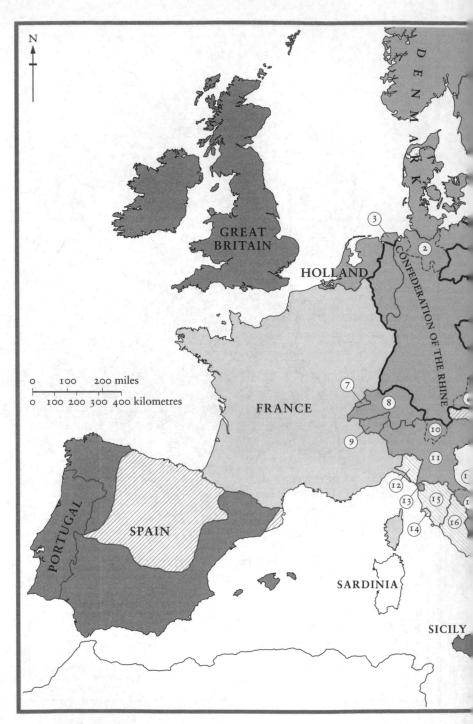

N

0   100   200 miles
0 100 200 300 400 kilometres

Europe, March 1810

1. Swedish Pomerania	13. Lucca
2. Hanover/Hanseatic States (to Westphalia, 1810)	14. Piombino
	15. Kingdom of Etruria
3. East Friesland (to Holland)	16. Rome
4. Western Galica (to Grand Duchy of Warsaw, 1810)	17. Marches (to Kingdom of Italy, 1808)
5. Danzig (French occupation)	18. Habsburg territory lost to Illyrian Provinces
6. Salzburg/Ried (to Bavaria, 1809)	19. Illyrian Provinces
7. Neuchâtel	20. Montenegro
8. Helvetic Confederation	21. Tarnopol (to Russia, 1809)
9. Republic of the Valais	22. Bialystok (to Russia, 1807)
10. South Tyrol/Trentino (to Kingdom of Italy, December, 1809)	23. Finland (to Russia, 1809)
	24. Ionian Islands (disputed)
	25. Aaland Islands (to Russia)
11. Kingdom of Italy	26. Malta (British garrison)
12. Parma	

France (frontiers of 1806)

France (annexations 1806–9)

French occupation/administration

French satellites/allies

Great Britain and allies/dependencies

—— Frontier of Confederation of the Rhine

SWEDEN

PRUSSIA

GRAND DUCHY
OF WARSAW

RUSSIA

AUSTRIA

OTTOMAN
EMPIRE

NAPLES

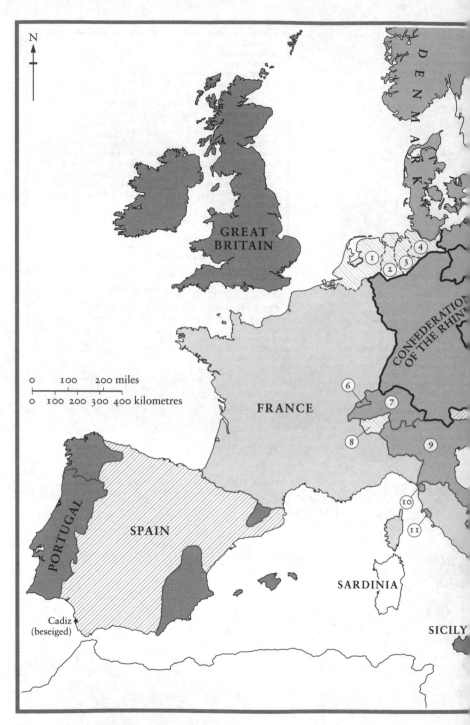

N

GREAT
BRITAIN

DENMARK

①
②
③
④

CONFEDERATION
OF THE RHINE

FRANCE

⑥
⑦
⑧
⑨

0   100   200 miles
0   100 200 300 400 kilometres

PORTUGAL

SPAIN

⑩
⑪

SARDINIA

Cadiz
(beseiged)

SICILY

Europe, May 1812

1. Holland
2. Berg (part)
3. Oldenburg
4. Westphalia (part)
5. Danzig
6. Neuchâtel
7. Helvetic Confederation
8. Republic of the Valais
9. Kingdom of Italy
10. Lucca
11. Piombino
12. Illyrian Provinces
13. Montenegro
14. Bessarabia (to Russia, 1812)
15. Ionian Islands (disputed)
16. Swedish Pomerania
17. Malta

France (frontiers of December 1809)

France (annexations 1810–12)

French occupation/administration

French satellites/allies

Great Britain and dependencies

Frontier of Confederation of the Rhine

SWEDEN

PRUSSIA

GRAND DUCHY
OF WARSAW

RUSSIA

AUSTRIA

OTTOMAN
EMPIRE

NAPLES

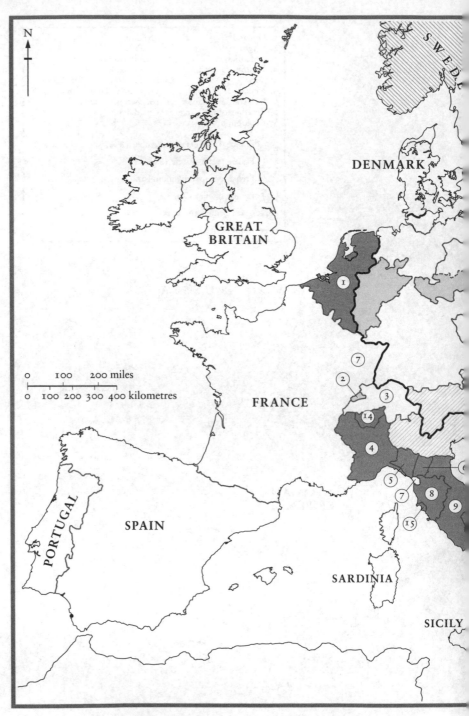

N

0   100   200 miles
0   100 200 300 400 kilometres

GREAT
BRITAIN

DENMARK

S·WEDE

FRANCE

PORTUGAL

SPAIN

SARDINIA

SICILY

① ⑦ ② ③ ⑭ ④ ⑤ ⑦ ⑧ ⑨ ⑮ ⑥

Europe after the Congress of Vienna

1. United Netherlands
2. Neuchâtel (to Prussia)
3. Helvetic Confederation
4. Piedmont/Genoa (to Sardinia)
5. Parma
6. Modena
7. Lucca
8. Tuscany
9. Papal States
10. Naples (to Sicily)
11. Tarnopol (to Austria)
12. Montenegro
13. Ionian Islands (British protectorate)
14. Valais (to Helvetic Confederation)
15. Piombino (to Tuscany)
16. Malta (to Great Britain)
17. Danzig (to Prussia)

Territorial restorations and acquisitions

Prussia Austria Russia

Sweden Other

Frontier of German confederation

RUSSIA

PRUSSIA

CONGRESS
POLAND

AUSTRIA

OTTOMAN
EMPIRE

Introduction
The Napoleonic Wars in Historical Perspective

Writing of the outbreak of the Napoleonic Wars in 1803, John Holland Rose once remarked, 'The history of Napoleon now becomes, for twelve momentous years, the history of mankind.'[1] Such a remark today seems like a relic of a bygone era. At the time that Britain and France were coming to blows, Robert Fulton was inventing the steamship, Richard Trevithick building the first steam locomotive, and William Jessop engineering the first public railway in the world. In North America, Lewis and Clark were on the brink of becoming the first white men to make it all the way from the eastern seaboard to the Pacific Ocean; in Africa the Sokoto caliphate was in the process of islamicizing the Hausa people of what is today northern Nigeria; and in China the so-called 'White Lotus' sect was leading a series of anti-Manchu revolts that discredited the ruling Qing dynasty and helped pave the way for its subsequent disintegration. As for the world of ideas, new currents were starting to emerge that would have horrified most of the men of 1789 (let alone Napoleon): while Saint-Simon was at work on the ideas of proto-socialism, Madame de Staël, Mary Wollstonecroft and a number of other writers were explicitly raising the banner of female emancipation. The history of Napoleon, then, was never the history of the world. Was it, though, the history of Europe? It is this question that this book seeks to answer, at least from the perspective of international relations. Was the French ruler a prime mover in events? Was Napoleonic Europe, in short, proof of the 'great-man' theory of history? Or was he rather caught up in processes that had been set in train without any intervention on his part? The emperor himself seems to have been in two minds. At one time he remarked, 'I have always commanded; from the moment that my life began I was filled with power, and such were my circumstances and my strength alike that from the moment that I came to prominence I

I

recognized neither masters nor laws.'[2] Yet at another what occurred in Europe between 1803 and 1815 he put down to something very different: 'I have never really been my own master; I have always been governed by circumstances.'[3] Whatever the truth, one thing is clear: the France of Napoleon was not acting in a vacuum. Even if the course of international relations does prove to have been bent to his will, the other powers in Europe had strategic and diplomatic goals that long predated Napoleon, and did not cease to play their own games just because they successively came under ever greater threat from Paris. Hence the need for a work on the international aspects of Napoleonic Europe that is something other than just one more life of Napoleon Bonaparte, or one more recitation of his campaigns.

Let us begin by discussing what we mean when we say the Napoleonic Wars. Hostilities broke out on 18 May 1803 when Britain, pushed beyond endurance by repeated acts of aggression and hostility, declared war on France and her new ruler, the so-called First Consul, Napoleon Bonaparte. For the next two years there was little in the way of land conflict, but amidst much naval manoeuvring on the high seas which led, amongst other things, to Spain joining forces with France in 1804, a large French army massed on the French coast and menaced Britain with invasion. No fleet of landing craft set sail, however, and in August 1805 the danger receded altogether: whereas in 1803 Britain had stood alone, the summer of 1805 had seen a powerful anti-French coalition come together. Alongside Britain there now stood Austria, Russia, Sweden and Naples, and so the French armies were soon marching east to deal with the new threat. A Franco-Spanish fleet was destroyed at Trafalgar, but the Austrians were defeated at Ulm and the Russians at Austerlitz. Badly beaten, Austria made peace and for a brief moment it appeared that Britain and Russia might follow her example. Even had this happened, it is unlikely Europe would have been able to keep the peace: following the outbreak of a revolt in Serbia in 1804, the Ottoman Empire was rapidly sliding towards war with Russia, such a conflict eventually breaking out in the autumn of 1806. But all chances of peace with France were soon at an end: neither Britain nor Russia was able to obtain the compromise peace that they sought, or at least not in an acceptable form, and then in September an increasingly desperate Prussia attacked Napoleon. There followed further great battles: the Prussians were crushed at Jena and Auerstädt, whilst a French invasion of Poland led in February 1807 to the terrible slaughter on the blizzard-swept field of Eylau. For a moment Napoleon was checked, but the coming of summer saw a new offensive that led to another French triumph at Friedland, whereupon the Tsar of Russia, Alexander I, decided to make peace.

This settlement was a turning point. Following the victories of the past two years, Napoleon was at the height of his power. Crowned emperor of France in December 1804, he now presided over a vast empire. Over the past few years the satellite republics inherited from the 1790s had been joined by new territories, and the whole now constituted a series of monarchies ruled by one or other of Napoleon's many brothers and sisters. These principalities included Holland, the German states of Westphalia and Berg, the Kingdom of Italy (roughly speaking, the valley of the river Po) and Naples. Many other areas, meanwhile – Belgium, the Rhineland, Piedmont – had been annexed to France and varying degrees of control were also enjoyed in Germany, where the old Holy Roman Empire had been replaced by a new Confederation of the Rhine, and Poland, part of which had been organized into yet another satellite state known as the Grand Duchy of Warsaw. With Spain a loyal ally and Russia in effect persuaded to join Napoleon in his war against Britain, the way was open for final victory, to achieve which the emperor instigated a continent-wide embargo on British trade that is generally referred to as the Continental System.[4]

Napoleon completely failed to exploit this opportunity and it is often said that in 1808 he made the greatest mistake of his career by turning on his Spanish allies and overthrowing the Bourbon monarchy in favour of his brother, Joseph Bonaparte. Such an assessment, however, is short-sighted. The Spanish adventure may have plunged France into a long and devastating war which was to see-saw back and forth in the Iberian Peninsula for the next five years, but in itself this was not a disaster. Exerting a greater degree of control in Spain made sense in terms of both Napoleon's war against Britain and the partition of the Ottoman Empire, which he was certainly considering by 1808, whilst the war there was by no means unwinnable. The real error was Napoleon's treatment of the rest of the Continent. Such was the loathing and distrust with which Britain was regarded in Germany, Italy, Scandinavia, Austria and Russia that a policy of conciliation and respect might well have won the emperor the active support of the whole of Europe, and made it very

3

difficult for Britain to continue the war. From the beginning, however, the Napoleonic imperium showed itself to be bent on nothing more than exploitation; even the reforms that it brought in amounted to little more than attempts to produce more men and money. And for the other powers it was clear that what faced them was in effect complete subjugation to Paris. Realizing this, Austria, like Prussia before her, made a last-ditch attempt to assert her independence in 1809, only to be defeated at Wagram. This victory, the last of Napoleon's great triumphs, was not enough to restore France's authority, however. Increasingly restive, Russia broke with Napoleon at the end of 1810 and mobilized her army. To the very end, conflict in the East could have been avoided, but the French ruler would not compromise with Alexander over any of the matters at issue, and in June 1812 a gigantic French army invaded Russia. This proved disastrous for Napoleon. His hold on the rest of Europe was jeopardized by the need to mass as large a force as possible against Russia, whilst the army that marched into Lithuania and ultimately ended up in Moscow was completely destroyed by a combination of stubborn Russian resistance and the rigours of the Russian climate.

There followed a terrible endgame. In a decision of crucial importance, Alexander resolved not to stop at the Russian frontier, but to invade Germany and the Grand Duchy of Warsaw so as to deal Napoleon such a blow that his dreams of glory would finally be brought to an end. This led Prussia to rise up against the French, whilst further posturing on the emperor's part brought in the Austrians and many of the German states. After months of bitter fighting the new army that Napoleon had managed to improvise in the wake of the Russian disaster was destroyed at Leipzig, leaving the French ruler no option but to evacuate Germany and retreat to the river Rhine. Offered several peace deals that would have left him on the throne of France, Napoleon resolved to fight on in the hope that the alliance against him might fall apart, but his situation was now desperate. Not only was France in revolt at the endless demands for more conscripts, but, having overthrown the Bonaparte Kingdom of Spain at the battle of Vitoria in June 1813, the Anglo-Portuguese army had crossed the Pyrenees. In a campaign of great brilliance, Napoleon held out for a few more weeks, but by early April it was quite clear that the situation was hopeless, and the emperor was in the end forced to abdicate by his own generals.

With the exception of a further episode of violence the following year, when Napoleon escaped from the petty kingdom he had been awarded on the Italian island of Elba, seized power in Paris and once more went to war, only to be defeated at the battle of Waterloo, the Napoleonic Wars were over. What, though, are we to make of them as a historical episode? The first thing to note is that the conflict of 1803–15 has often been regarded as a continuation of the nine years of war that had followed the outbreak of hostilities between Revolutionary France and varying combinations of the other states of Europe in April 1792. At first France had only been faced by Austria and Prussia, but then in 1793 the increasingly radical tenor of events in France led many other countries to join the struggle against her. For a year or more it was a question of the French versus the rest, but very soon a variety of factors led state after state to fall away and even to make alliances with France against Britain. By 1797 all that was left were Britain and Austria, and in that year even Austria was brought down by a string of victories gained by Napoleon – then plain General Bonaparte – in Italy. As was to be the case ten years later, Britain stood all but alone, but on this occasion too French aggression played into her hands. Led by Napoleon, a French army invaded Egypt and this prompted Austria, Russia, Naples and the Ottoman Empire to go to war. However, from this struggle Napoleon – from November 1799 ruler of France – emerged victorious. Austria and Naples were defeated and forced to make peace; Russia was persuaded in effect to change sides; and Britain was left with no option but to secure such terms as she could in the Treaty of Amiens.

It is often argued that this long sequence of wars was the fruit of an ideological clash between France and the *ancien régime*, that the principles of the French Revolution were so shocking to the rulers and statesmen of the rest of Europe that they embarked on a crusade against them that could have no end until they had been crushed and the Bourbons restored to the throne of France. Equally, convinced that there was no other option, and that it was, indeed, their duty, successive rulers of France strove to export the principles of the Revolution to the ends of the earth. This idea has been much exaggerated. There was certainly much loathing of 'Jacobinism' in Europe's *salons*, courts and chancelleries, while the conflict was accompanied by sustained propaganda campaigns of a like never been seen before. But in the end few governments or rulers were genuinely committed to the cause of what would later be known as regime change and still fewer enthusiastic at the idea

5

of the restoration of the Bourbon monarchy as it had existed in 1789. Even in the 1790s there had been plenty of states willing to essay a policy of détente with France, and others who had joined her in pursuit of long-standing foreign policy interests of one sort or another, while by the time of Austerlitz, Jena and Friedland there was in practice no state that could not have lived with Napoleon provided that he accepted certain limits to France's power. Indeed, to imagine that the French Revolution and its successors somehow set aside the main issues in international relations would be most short-sighted: one of the reasons why France achieved as much as she did was because most of the powers that faced her continued until 1812 or later to pursue other concerns. Russia is a good example. In 1791 and again in 1794 Russia's troops were fighting not the French but the Poles, while during the Napoleonic Wars Alexander I did not hesitate to get involved in conflicts not just in the Balkans but also in the Baltic and central Asia. Equally, in 1814 Sweden's forces were to be found not battling Napoleon, but rather concentrating on the conquest of Norway.

If Europe was not divided along ideological lines, what did the long period of conflict that gripped her between 1792 and 1815 stem from? In the end, as we shall see, the prime mover was Napoleon's own aggression, egomania and lust for power, but one cannot ignore other factors that are essentially structural or systemic. The most important of these were, first, the issue of what to do about Eastern Europe and, in particular, how to fill the vacuum left by the decline of Sweden, Poland and the Ottoman Empire, and the second, the endemic colonial and commercial conflict that had for most of the past century charac-terized the relationship between Britain and France. Indeed, with respect to the first issue, it is even possible to argue that the French Revolutionary Wars were precipitated by, and part of, a much wider crisis that began in Eastern Europe in 1787. Rather than imagining the French Wars as a new type of conflict that foreshadowed the total wars of the twentieth century, it is more sensible to think of them in terms of the dynastic wars of the eighteenth century. As far as Napoleon is concerned, the most obvious parallel is Louis XIV. King of France between 1643 and 1715, in 1667 Louis embarked on a programme of conquest that, on the surface, foreshadowed that of Napoleon. First of all, a series of conflicts with Holland and other powers brought France an important slice of the Spanish Netherlands and the region of Alsace, and then in

1700 the death without issue of King Charles II of Spain opened up the possibility of acquiring for France – or at least a suitable 'cat's-paw' in the person of Louis's grandson, Philippe – the whole of the inheritance of the Spanish Habsburgs. Had this ploy succeeded, Louis would have ended up with a sphere of influence encompassing Spain, Naples, Sicily, Sardinia, Lombardy and the Spanish Netherlands, not to mention a colonial empire that would have incorporated much of North and South America.

With France effectively propelled to superpower status, her domination of Western Europe would have been total, and thus it was that a broad coalition of powers arose to challenge Louis in the War of the Spanish Succession. On the one side were France, Spain (where Philippe had quickly established himself as Felipe V) and a few minor German states that had fallen out with Austria; and on the other, Britain, Holland, Denmark, Austria and most of the states of the Holy Roman Empire. The following struggle was for its time at least as demanding as the Napoleonic Wars. The armies raised by the combatants were very substantial. In 1710 Louis XIV's army amounted to 255,000 men and that of Queen Anne of Britain to about 58,000; indeed, one estimate places the figure for the French army as high as 360,000. At first sight these figures appear quite small, and certainly much smaller than the armies that were fielded in the Napoleonic period, but then, the population base was much lower. In 1700 France had about 20 million inhabitants, whereas by 1800 the figure had risen to some 33 million, the equivalent figures for Britain being 5 million and 16 million. With general prosperity and especially levels of agricultural prosperity at a lower level, warfare was also a far greater burden on society. And for France in particular the War of the Spanish Succession represented a veritable calvary. As Louis was unable to maintain a presence in either Germany or Italy, the entire weight of the struggle fell on his unfortunate subjects. Conscription was very heavy – between 1701 and 1713 455,000 men were called up – and still more men were periodically pressed to dig fortifications, with the result that agricultural production experienced a significant fall, thereby forcing up bread prices. Larger armies, an obsession with the attack and defence of fortresses and the ever greater prominence of cannon all made the cost of the fighting enormous. Between 1700 and 1706 government expenditure amounted to 1,100 million francs, while between 1708 and 1715 it rose to 1,900 million. Then in 1709 there came natural catastrophe. France had already been ravaged by epidemics of dysentery and other scourges, but in that year she was struck by one of the worst winters ever recorded. With the harvest completely destroyed, the populace succumbed to famine. No one knows how many died, but so apocalyptic are the descriptions that have come down to us that the figure certainly ran to many hundreds of thousands, and possibly several millions.

Elsewhere things were not quite so desperate (though some of the German states almost certainly put a greater proportion of their men under arms than they ever had to in the Napoleonic period), and it might, too, be pointed out that battles were by no means as frequent as they were a hundred years later. This was an important distinction, but when the rival armies did meet the results were still spectacular. In the first place, the field armies of the period were not that much smaller than their Napoleonic counterparts. At Blenheim, for example, 60,000 French and Bavarian troops faced 56,000 Allies; at Malplaquet Marlborough had 110,000 troops and Villars 80,000; at Oudenarde 80,000 Allies fought 85,000 French; and at Ramillies the two sides had 50,000 men apiece. This gives an average of 142,000 combatants in each battle, which does not compare unfavourably with the figures for the Napoleonic epoch quoted below. In the second place, the slaughter was just as bad as anything seen on the battlefields of Napoleon, Wellington and the Archduke Charles. At Almansa, for example, the Allies lost 17,000 casualties out of the 22,000 men they had engaged, while at Blenheim the losses of the French and Bavarians came to 38,000. Bloodiest of all these combats, however, was Malplaquet where the losses of the two sides combined reached 42,000. On a number of occasions, then, the War of the Spanish Succession saw battle reach a pitch of intensity that was the equal of anything seen in the Napoleonic Wars.

Nor could the Napoleonic Wars lay claim to being unique in their geographical reach. Whilst they were fought out on a stage that was truly worldwide – not counting the serious conflicts that were sparked off in both North and South America, minor forces of the combatants directly clashed with one another as far afield as Java, the Cape of Good Hope, Buenos Aires and the West Indies – the Seven Years War of 1756–63 witnessed colonial campaigns of a scope that the struggle of 1803–15 had nothing to match. Indeed, it might even be said that if there was a great leap forward in warfare at this time, it came not in

1803 nor even in 1792, but rather in 1756: whereas the major conflicts of the reign of Louis XIV and the forty years that followed had all been largely European affairs, it was the Seven Years War that turned Europe's colonies in Asia, Africa and the New World into a battlefield – indeed, on occasion, the main battlefield.

What, then, marks out the Napoleonic Wars from what had gone before? Head of the list must come the idea that, just as the Seven Years War made conflict in Europe a global affair, so the struggle that began in 1803 was the first one waged by nations-in-arms. This concept had been invented by the French in 1793, but it now took its place on the other side of the lines as well: universal conscription was introduced in Spain in 1808, Sweden in 1812 and Prussia in 1813, while in Britain the continual absence of conscription to the army was countered by a number of Acts of Parliament laying down that all men should tender some form of military service even if it was only in part-time reserve forces designed to meet the needs of home defence. And even in states whose systems of recruitment remained unreformed – a good example here is Russia – the demand for men was at times so great that it is difficult to believe that many more troops could have been called up even had a French-style system been introduced. Hence, in part at least, the new stress on the role of propaganda, and hence too the fact that field armies suddenly got much bigger. In testimony to the War of the Spanish Succession's somewhat exceptional character, the number of combatants in the twelve battles of the Seven Years War fought by Frederick the Great amounted to an average of 92,000 men, while, somewhat surprisingly, the same figure for the six greatest battles of the French Revolutionary Wars comes to only 87,000. Yet put together the battles of Austerlitz, Jena, Eylau, Friedland, Tudela, Aspern-Essling and Wagram – the combats that established Napoleon's hegemony in the period 1805–1809 – and the same total comes to 162,000. And looking at the battles of the years of Napoleon's decline in 1812–13 – Borodino, Lutzen, Bautzen, Dresden and Leipzig – produces another leap forward to 309,400.

The military consequences of this development were immense. Whereas in the eighteenth century the considerable investment represented by the individual soldier ensured that the generals of Europe sought wherever possible to avoid battle and to win their campaigns by manoeuvre, it was now possible to fight far more battles. In the War of the Spanish Succession, it is possible to come up with perhaps a dozen major battles, but in the Napoleonic Wars the number is at least forty. Meanwhile, the armies had become so large that they could no longer function as single units but had to be broken down into permanent sub-units. Known as divisions, these had first appeared in the French Revolutionary Wars, but it had soon become apparent that there were serious flaws with the initial steps that were taken in this direction. The divisions created in the Armies of the North, the Sambre and Meuse, the Eastern Pyrenees, Italy and the rest were often too small to sustain themselves for very long, while the decision that they should be self-supporting led to the cavalry and artillery being split up into 'penny-packets' that were of little use to anyone. What was needed was something rather different, and in 1804 this was found in the form of Napoleon's new corps system. Henceforward the basic formation in the emperor's forces was the corps, each of which was usually made up of three or four divisions of infantry and a division of cavalry, each division being made up of two brigades of infantry or cavalry and a battery of artillery. In addition, a corps commander might enjoy the services of a couple of extra batteries of artillery, but the bulk of the guns, and especially the heavy twelve-pounders that delivered the main punch, were held back at army level as a special reserve that could be deployed wherever the general in command of the army – in the case of the main French forces Napoleon himself – saw fit. Also held back at army level might be one or more corps made up of nothing but heavy cavalry and horse artillery, the role of these troops generally being to exploit a breakthrough in the enemy line and turn defeat into complete rout. With various differences in detail and nomenclature, by 1812 this model of organization had become standard in all the armies of Europe, and with it battle had been transformed. Although it still happened – Waterloo is the obvious example – a decisive victory was no longer likely to be obtained in a single day. Instead, battles were now fought out over several days by commanders attempting to control operations from some farmstead a mile or more to the rear (again Waterloo is an exception here). In short, we see the passing of an era, and the first dim stirrings of a new age of war.

One might here, too, touch on the participation of the civilian populace in the struggle. As is well known, the Napoleonic Wars gave the world the word 'guerrilla', and the fact is that in Italy, the Tyrol, the

Iberian Peninsula and Russia the civilian populations were drawn into the struggle in considerable numbers as irregular combatants. This development should not be exaggerated: the famous Spanish guerrillas, for example, have in recent years been shown to have had strong links with the regular forces, just as the real basis of irregular resistance in Russia was not the peasantry but the Cossacks. Furthermore it was not entirely new: in the War of the Spanish Succession, for example, bands of desperate peasants had regularly taken arms in an attempt to save their homes and crops from destruction or requisition. Yet sufficient was the reality that it is possible to argue that it was the Napoleonic Wars that formalized the concept of asymmetrical warfare. At the same time, such was the effort that they were calling forth from their unfortunate inhabitants that none of the powers of Europe found themselves able to avoid at least a measure of engagement with public opinion. For the first time, we enter an era in which propaganda and news management became an integral part of the war effort, as well as one in which the populace on all sides was urged to hate the enemy. In addition, if the people were expected to fight, then they had to be given something to fight for, the result being that in various parts of the Continent, most notably Prussia and Spain, the example set by France in September 1793 was copied via the introduction of various measures of political and social reform. And, last but not least, the development of the modern state was given a sharp boost: with the huge demands now involved in making war, many administrations found themselves introducing new methods of administration, fostering the emergence of modern bureaucracies, and exploiting new sources of revenue, all of which drove a further nail into the coffin of the *ancien régime*.

The Napoleonic Wars, then, marked a watershed in the history of warfare and Europe alike. Let us conclude this introduction, however, by returning to the rulers of the eighteenth century and, in particular, Louis XIV. Even if he did not go to war himself after 1673, the 'Sun King' always remained a military monarch. The court at Versailles was very much the headquarters of successive French war efforts, and Louis's leading male courtiers were invariably also prominent military commanders. There was, too, a strong fixation with martial glory: even as an old man Louis had himself depicted in full armour in his paintings, while Versailles was full of reminders of the glories of French arms. If Louis embarked on a series of wars as soon as he had assumed effective control of his dominions in 1661, it was in part because he saw war-making as a central part of the business of kingship, as the chief means, perhaps, by which a ruler could augment his status. There was, as we shall see, much here that was to be repeated a hundred years later, but there were also a number of crucial differences. Never entirely insensible to the horrors of war, Louis was capable of recognizing that there were moments when discretion was the better part of valour. Driven from Germany and Italy and forced to make war solely on the basis of France's own resources and, for the most part, on her very soil, from 1706 Louis was desperate to end the War of the Spanish Succession. To his ever more generous proposals, however, the Allied response was to offer peace terms that were utterly unreasonable: France was not only to be stripped of many important border cities and forced to destroy many fortresses, but to send French troops to eject Felipe V from Spain should he refuse to abdicate voluntarily. In consequence, Louis deemed it was better to fight on; as he observed, if he must wage war, he would prefer not to do so against his own grandson. Indeed, it is quite clear that the 'Sun King' had never wanted war in the first place: the earlier Nine Years War of 1688–97 having already placed a serious strain on France's resources, Louis would have been prepared to split the Spanish inherit-ance between Philippe and his Austrian rival even though the Bourbon dynasty had the stronger claim. And even in earlier years Louis's ambitions were strictly limited: what he wanted was not an empire but simply secure borders.

Louis XIV may stand as a model for almost all the monarchs of eighteenth-century Europe. All were quite prepared to make use of war as an instrument of policy and to employ military success as the foundation and measure of their prestige, but, with the possible excep-tion of Charles XII of Sweden, all set reasonable limits to their campaigns of conquest. If we take the case of Frederick the Great of Prussia, for example, the object of his wars with Austria was first to take and then to retain control of the province of Silesia, it being none of his business to conquer Bohemia or Hungary, nor still less topple the Habsburgs from their throne. Except for a very brief period in 1792 when the Brissotin leaders of the French Revolution were led by a rush of blood to the head to promise liberation to all the peoples of Europe, this principle of limited warfare was followed even in the French Revolution-ary Wars of 1799: the Directory no more aspired to 'jacobinize' the

whole of the Continent than the powers they were fighting were interested in turning the clock back to 1789. But Napoleon was different. At
the end of his life Louis XIV is supposed to have lamented that he had
loved war too well. This may or may not be true, but no such remark
may be found in the annals of Napoleon's exile on St Helena, and it is
hard to imagine the emperor ever giving voice to such a sentiment.
Napoleon Bonaparte was not just the ultimate warlord – a man who
would have been nothing without war and conquest – but he was never
capable of setting the same limits on himself as the rulers and statesmen
who had waged the conflicts of the eighteenth century. There are those
who would argue that this was not of his doing – that he was in effect
impelled to embark on the road of universal conquest because of the
refusal of Great Britain, especially, to allow France her just deserts. This
is another debate, but it seems most unlikely that the 'Sun King' would
ever have gone down such a path. In any case, the matter is irrelevant:
however the Napoleonic Wars are explained, it was the emperor's determination to eschew compromise, to flex his muscles on every possible
occasion and to push matters to extremes that made them what they
were.

Whatever the causes of the Napoleonic Wars, they left in their wake
both a very different Europe and a very different world. Prior to 1789
France had been unquestionably the strongest of the great powers.
Though temporarily in eclipse thanks to defeat in the Seven Years War
and the financial difficulties that stemmed from her support of the
thirteen colonies in the War of American Independence, she was still
wealthier than any of her continental competitors and possessed of the
best army in Europe. Meanwhile, in alliance with Spain, she was able to
exert at least a partial curb on British domination of the wider world
and at the same time to participate in the benefits of the colonial trade.
By 1815, however, all this had been swept aside. France's domestic
resources remained very great, but the establishment of a new German
confederation – the creation, it may be said, of a German nation – had
ensured that the capacity to dominate the 'third Germany' that had been
central to the Napoleonic imperium (and had in fact been Louis XIV's
only hope of winning the War of the Spanish Succession) was no more.
Across the seas, meanwhile, much of France's colonial empire had been
swept away, together with Spanish control of the mainland of Central
and South America. Ironically, then, the greatest hero in French history

had presided over nothing less than a total collapse in France's international position, leaving Britannia to rule the waves and the rest of Europe to contend with the emergence of what would ultimately become an even greater threat to its security than France had been. In short, the year 1815 was both an end and a beginning.

I

The Origins of the Napoleonic Wars

It has already been made clear that this work is not a biography of Napoleon Bonaparte. For this there are a number of very good reasons. As was hinted at in the preface, the story of the life of this most famous of French rulers has generally not been told in a helpful way. A sense of chronology is established, certainly, but most of the authors are so concerned to rush from one battle or love interest to the next that they leave themselves with little space to place the battle of Austerlitz or Napoleon's marriage to Marie Louise in their full political and diplomatic context. Still worse, as biography of Napoleon succeeds biography of Napoleon, very few advance understanding or even the historical record. With such works often highly derivative, we are left with the same old story, and what is more, a story in which a single highly coloured figure stands out against a background of murky monochromists. There are, it is true, rival works that take the opposite view and demonize Napoleon, but these too do little to explore the complexities of the situation in which he operated and tend rather to concentrate on the flaws of his character and the iniquities of his behaviour. This is not, however, the way to expound the story of Napoleon. Even if it is the case that the history of Europe between 1803 and 1815 could be reduced to such personal dimensions (which it cannot), the other actors and perspectives in the drama must needs be explored in their own right rather than simply existing as foils for the hero or villain. Biography still has its place, but it is noticeable that those biographies which are most useful as works of history – good examples are those of Lefebvre and Tulard – are the ones which are the thinnest in terms of their treatment of the details of Napoleon's battles, loves and personal life.

Yet, for all that, we cannot entirely dispense with biographical detail. As is the case with many 'great men', the details that we have of

Napoleon's early life are not entirely reliable. Let us start, however, with what we know. Baptized as Napoleone Buonaparte, the future emperor of France was born in the Corsican capital of Ajaccio to a family of the petty nobility on 15 August 1769. Tales of the family's poverty have probably been exaggerated: the house where Napoleon spent his early years was a substantial one and his mother, Letizia Remolino, brought his father, Carlo, a prominent legal official, a reasonable dowry. Money was not superabundant, but there was property and status: for two centuries the Buonapartes had been substantial members of the local oligarchy and in recent years they had acquired further weight by taking a leading role in the regime of Pasquale Paoli (see below). On St Helena, indeed, Napoleon was quite specific that his was not exactly a rags-to-riches story:

In my family . . . we spent practically nothing on food, except of course such groceries as coffee, sugar and rice, which did not come from Corsica. We grew everything else. The family owned a . . . mill to which all the villagers brought their flour to be milled, and they paid for this with a certain percentage of flour. We also had a communal bakehouse, the use of which was paid in fish . . . There were two olive groves in Ajaccio . . . One belonged to the Bonaparte family and the other to the Jesuits . . . The family also made its own wine.[1]

Even foreign conquest did not shake this prosperity. Carlo Buonaparte had no difficulty in ingratiating himself with the French when they annexed the island in 1768, not only retaining his various legal offices but also establishing himself as something of an interlocutor between his countrymen and their new masters. Though his children were numerous – Napoleon was the second of eight brothers and sisters, not to mention five more who died as infants or at a very early age – there was therefore no difficulty in procuring an adequate education for at least the five boys and, beyond that, the promise of service with the Bourbon state (indeed, even Elise, the eldest daughter, was found a place at an exclusive college outside Paris).

So much for the bare facts, but what of the young boy himself? Inevitably, no sooner had Napoleon risen to power, than all sorts of stories were going the rounds about his childhood, and from this distance it is quite impossible to separate fact from fiction. But from all the tales of the boy-tyrant who bullied everyone and vandalized every object that came to hand, the boy-general who led his playmates in mock-battle, the boy-womanizer who walked to school hand-in-hand with pretty girls, and the boy-patriot who criticized his father for not having followed Paoli into exile – tales, we are told, at which he 'used to laugh heartily'[2] – various things do stand out. First of all, Napoleon seems to have been starved of love by his parents (though affectionate enough, his father was often absent on official business, while his mother was a singularly austere woman, who treated her children with considerable harshness). Secondly, desperate for the approval and attention for which he had to compete with his numerous siblings, Napoleon expressed his frustration by turning to violence in an attempt to secure first place amongst them, the chief victim of this campaign being his unfortunate elder brother, Joseph. Thirdly, this same desire for recognition led to an ambition and hunger for success that was remarked on by all who met him. Fourthly, frequent beatings reinforced this obsession with power and at the same time encouraged him to become a habitual liar. And lastly, dissatisfaction and insecurity produced a dreamer: from an early age fascinated by history, there seems little doubt that Napoleon was a 'loner' who often retired for long periods to his room to indulge his love of reading and at the same time indulge himself with dreams of escape and heroism. To quote Chaptal:

His mother often told me that . . . Napoleon never took part in the games played by other children of his age, and that he on the contrary took pains to avoid them. Given a little room of his own whilst still very young on the third floor of the house, he would often shut himself up on his own. Not even coming down to eat with the family, he would read constantly, and especially works of history.[3]

Was anything added to this volatile mixture by Napoleon's Corsican background? According to some accounts the answer is very clearly 'yes'. Napoleon, we learn, grew up imbued with a deep sense of honour and a prodigious love of display that owed their origins to an obsession with status typical of Corsican society. To this was added a fierce clan loyalty that inspired him constantly to seek the advancement of his family and, in addition, to feel a responsibility for the welfare of each of its individual members, not to mention a deep-seated spirit of adventure that had led many Corsicans to seek their fortunes by turning corsair or soldier of fortune. And finally there were the linked issues of egalitarianism and justice for all: in Corsica, even noble families such as the Buonapartes were not set so very far apart from the mass of the populace, while poor and not so poor alike could justifiably feel deep resentment at the island's long history of conquest, exploitation and neglect. However, there is little here that fills the observer with much confidence. Much more important is the issue of the Paoli regime of 1755–69. As a possession of the Republic of Genoa, Corsica had by the early eighteenth century become affected by a variety of grievances, and in 1729 the island rose in revolt. Long years of stalemate followed and by the middle years of the century it appeared that the Corsican cause was spent. Early in 1755, however, Pasquale Paoli, a junior officer in the Neapolitan army who was the younger brother of one of the chief leaders of the insurrection, returned to the island. By all accounts a remarkable figure, Paoli quickly placed himself at the head of the revolt and managed to rekindle his feuding and disunited countrymen's enthusiasm for the struggle. Military victory was not obtained – the Genoese could never be eradicated from the main coastal fortresses – but Paoli did succeed in creating a functioning state and, what is more, a state that for a short time secured the admiration of many of the leading figures of the age. Inspired by the writings of Montesquieu, the Corsican leader promulgated a written constitution that proclaimed the sovereignty of the people, established a parliament that was in part elected by universal manhood suffrage, in part elected by the clergy, and in part chosen by Paoli himself; and greatly restricted his authority as de facto president. But if he could in this fashion establish Corsica's political credentials as the home of liberty, and thereby win the admiration of such figures as Jean-Jacques Rousseau and James Boswell, he could not save Corsica from conquest: in 1768 Genoa ceded control of the island to France, and within a year Bourbon troops had crushed all resistance.

What, if anything, did all this give Napoleon? In terms of youthful inspiration, at least, a great deal. The involvement of his father with Paoli – he had risen to be his secretary and accompanied him in his desperate defence of the island against the French – was a source of pride to the young Corsican, as well as an object lesson in how to make personal capital from an age of political turmoil. At the same time, too, it both sharpened his own dreams of glory and provided him with a focus for his ambition. Yet more important than anything else was the figure of Pasquale Paoli himself, who Napoleon undoubtedly viewed as an important role model: according to Las Cases, the Corsican leader 'for a long time inspired something of a cult in him'.[4] As the future emperor told his schoolfriend, Bourrienne, 'Paoli was a great man; he loved his country.'[5] Many years later, he was to use almost the same words, telling one of his visitors on St Helena that he was 'a fine character' who was 'always for his country'.[6] But Paoli was not just a patriot. An intensely charismatic figure, a gallant soldier and a wise legislator, he won the devotion of his followers, the respect of his enemies and the plaudits of the *philosophes*. At the same time Paoli was the archetypal saviour-figure: the great man who had come from nowhere to save the Corsican rebellion, lead it to glory and finally go down to defeat in the face of overwhelming odds. But, above all, the Corsican leader was also a man who manipulated his status as national hero for his own ends, stealthily increasing his own power while appearing at all times to be operating within the pseudo-democratic traditions of the insurrection which he headed. Even if much of this was not apparent to the young Napoleon until later years, it was, beyond doubt, a heady mix. Asked whether Paoli was a good general by one of his masters, the then schoolboy is supposed to have replied, 'He is, sir, and I want to grow up like him.'[7]

Thus far, it has been difficult to write of the French ruler with much certainty. As his secretary later observed, 'Each of us . . . without ceasing to be honest, can show a different Napoleon.'[8] Beyond the early years, however, the story becomes clearer. In December 1778 he left his native island for the first time and sailed to France, where, after four months spent learning French at a clerical school at Autun, he entered the military academy at Brienne. Albeit largely in retrospect, at this point his life begins to be observed in more detail. His first chronicler was his fellow student, Louis de Bourrienne, who was to go on to serve Napoleon as his military secretary between 1798 and 1802. Like many memoirs of the period, Bourrienne's recollections are notoriously unreliable, being not only ghostwritten but marred by personal enmity (dismissed from his position for embezzlement, Bourrienne developed a deep sense of resentment towards his former master). Published under the Bourbons, the memoirs were also marked by a desire to secure the favour of the Restoration and expunge the stain of service with Napoleon. Yet the picture that Napoleon's schoolfellow paints of the boy who arrived at

Brienne in May 1779 has a certain ring of truth to it, and all the more so as it is in large part confirmed by several less well-known memoirs. Relatively poor – he was only at the academy at all because his father had used his contacts with the occupying authorities to obtain a government bursary – intense, physically unprepossessing, desperately homesick and barely able to speak French, Napoleone Buonaparte was a classic outsider. Nor did he help his own case, adopting a prickly manner and flying to the defence of the Corsican cause at the slightest provocation. 'His conversation,' wrote Bourrienne, 'almost always bore the appearance of ill humour, and he was certainly not very sociable.'[9] Hardly surprisingly, the result was that he was at first the butt of a great deal of insensitivity and bullying. Few of his teachers took much interest in him as a scholar and he was forever being teased. Nor was there any escape: not only were the students all boarders, but the six-year course was devoid of holidays. Whether the young Corsican really led his fellow students in a great snowball fight conducted on the lines of a mock-battle, or took on single-handed a group of older cadets who had trampled a vegetable garden he had cultivated, or threw a violent tantrum rather than submit to a particularly brutal punishment, or was sacked from the command of a company in the college's cadet corps for his haughty demeanour, is beside the point. All that really matters is that once again we see a Napoleon for whom struggle was a psychological necessity, a Napoleon who was completely cut off from both his family and the outside world, and a Napoleon who sought solace in books which assuaged his bitterness and frustration. To quote Bourrienne again, 'Bonaparte was not liked by his companions . . . He associated but little with them, and rarely took part in their amusements . . . During play-hours he withdrew to the library, where he read with great eagerness works of history, particularly Polybius and Plutarch.'[10]

All this made the Brienne years an important period in Napoleon's early life. Only at mathematics did he really shine as a scholar, but his voracious reading gave him sufficient general knowledge to acquire a certain sense of superiority over his classmates. Added to this, of course, was the fact that he was a Corsican, and therefore in his eyes a cut above the rest of humanity. For this we must thank Rousseau and Boswell, both of whom he devoured enthusiastically, but these were not the only authors who shaped his adolescent thinking. Fascinated by the ancients, he read all the works on Greece and Rome that he could find and, thanks in part to the works of Plutarch, became more and more impressed by the caesars. Dazzled by the concept of absolute power – significantly, he is recorded as having regarded the murderers of Julius Caesar not as heroes but as traitors – he also became obsessed by the concept of patriotism, as expounded by the French dramatist Corneille. It was very much the stuff of dreams, and the result was a youthful messiah complex: in company with Paoli, whom he still idolized, Napoleon would return to Corsica and free it from the hated French. But if he did so, it would not be as a believing Catholic: though taught by priests, the future emperor increasingly came to challenge their doctrines. What sense, for example, could be made of a creed that automatically condemned the great men of Greece and Rome to eternal damnation? Was the result of this loss of faith, as some have argued, a void that Napoleon needed to fill with some other deity? If so, then the fatherland was an obvious candidate, and all the more so given his exposure to Rousseau's notions of the 'general will'. But to argue that the young Corsican needed an ideal seems foolhardy: already a confirmed misanthrope by the time that he graduated from Brienne in 1784, he had all the stimulus he needed in his own ambition and sense of self-worth.

Brienne was followed by just under a year at the École Royale Militaire in Paris. This academy was the very pinnacle of *ancien régime* military education and at the same time an institution which gave very strong preference to the sons of army officers and denied entry to anyone who could not prove that their forebears had been noble for at least four generations. The issue of nobility was not a problem – the Buonapartes had excellent credentials – but that of service in the officer corps was quite another, and as such it seems likely that here at least the legend is true: as Buonaparte senior had never been an officer, his son can be assumed to have obtained his position at the École Militaire by means of his intellectual prowess alone. As with his years at Brienne, Napoleon's experiences in Paris are shrouded in legend. All that is known for certain is that the young Corsican's father died of stomach cancer a few months after he was admitted to the École Militaire, and that, with his family now in some financial difficulty, he decided to attempt to cram the normal two full years of study into just one (a fact that may explain why he eventually graduated as the forty-second in his class). But, if many of the anecdotes told about this period are again distinctly dubious, there seems little doubt that the impact of Napoleon's early years went unredeemed. If his father died, for example, it merely heightened his ambition: distrusting the easy-going Joseph – the 'gentle Buonaparte' – he saw the loss as an opportunity to take over the role of head of the household and restore the fortunes of his family. As obsessed with the cause of Corsican independence as ever – apart from anything else, support for his homeland was a useful means of expressing the instinctive desire of any sixteen-year-old to revolt against his father – he also remained the butt of both official disapproval and much coarse humour. Nor did it help that there was little improvement in either his looks or his stature: if the highly unreliable Laure Permon is to be believed, he looked so ridiculous that she nicknamed him 'Puss-in-Boots'. As for the product of all this, it was a mixture of frustration, arrogance, pride, hauteur and ambition. And there was still the same brooding introversion: a young woman who met him on a felucca sailing between Ajaccio and Toulon in 1788 remembered 'an ungracious little fellow' with 'an unpleasant face' who had his nose stuck in a book the whole time and was so rude that a fellow passenger remarked that he should be thrown into the sea.[11] Also present was a barely suppressed violence: apparently fancying himself as a man of letters, Napoleon wrote a series of stories in which gruesome murders alternated with wholesale bloodbaths. Lust after fame on the battlefield though he might, he was not just, to paraphrase Wilfred Owen, a young man eager for some desperate glory, but also a young man filled with hatred and resentment.

Whatever the impact of his years as a cadet may have been on his psychology, by the time that Napoleon was commissioned in the artillery as a sub-lieutenant in the autumn of 1785, he had fallen under the sway of the vague political radicalism that was beginning to grip much of educated opinion in France. After all, as a junior officer and a scion of the petty nobility, he was a member of not one but two groups that had serious concerns regarding their prospects and status in the France of the *ancien régime*, while, if only because of the Genevan writer's eulogization of Paoli's Corsica, he was also an avid reader of Jean-Jacques Rousseau. Yet, still possessed of the closest ties with his homeland – in the three and a half years that passed before the coming of the Revolution, he had spent almost two on leave with his family – Napoleon remained a Corsican revolutionary rather than a French one, and was inclined to interpret reform in a way that reflected the needs of his homeland. For France, then, he cared not a whit except to the extent that revolution in Paris would spell freedom in Ajaccio. Nor were the so-called principles of 1789 of much concern to him. What mattered was rather the power of the state. In brief, to be free, Corsica would have to be strong, and if she wished to be strong, then she would also have to have a reformed administration in the style of that of Paoli, for only thus could she be guaranteed the men and resources necessary to defend herself. So much for Corsica, but what of Napoleon? In the short term he would fulfil the role of the ageing leader's right-hand man, but Paoli would not live for ever – he had been born in 1725 – and it is not difficult to see the direction in which the young artilleryman's thoughts were heading. Napoleon would not just restore *il babbo* – 'the grand-father' – as he was called, but supplant him and even become him. In short, what really attracted him to the cause of revolution was the linked figures of the saviour and the enlightened absolutist: as the one, he would return in triumph to Corsica and liberate her from the rule of Paris, and as the other he would preside over a new regime that would put all to rights, in which guise he would rule as a benevolent dictator. Power, of course, was not to be abused – the new messiah would rule in accordance with a constitution and never exercise his might other than in the service of the people as a whole. But these disclaimers do not carry much weight: for all his denunciations of despotism, his heroes – aside from Paoli – remained Frederick the Great of Prussia, Julius Caesar and the Athenian soldier-statesman, Alcibiades. And, if he had indeed read and admired Rousseau, it is worth pointing out that the Genevan writer could be read as an apostle of darker creeds than democracy: implicit in the notion of the general will is a vision of absolute power that could not but appeal to a would-be saviour.

When revolution came in 1789, then, Napoleon saw it primarily as a moment when history might be rolled back and Corsica freed. Obtaining yet another leave of absence from his regiment's headquarters at Auxonne, where he had been on duty for the last ten months, in September 1789 he therefore again set off for Ajaccio. On reaching home, he found the island's politics in confusion. For some of his compatriots – for the most part men who came from clans that had found themselves excluded from favour in the years of de facto independence – the way forward lay in the extension to Corsica of the same rights obtained by the metropolis in July 1789, and they therefore rallied to the Revolution, being eventually rewarded by a decree that made the island one with the rest of France. But for others, the answer rather lay in the return of the exiled Paoli and, by extension, a fresh revolt. On top of all this, the introduction in Corsica of the same system of local government as that which now made its appearance on the mainland provoked a furious outburst of intrigue and faction fighting. Through all this Napoleon negotiated his way with considerable opportunism, but rather less success. While his aim remained national independence, simply to raise the standard of revolt was unthinkable, and so Napoleon chose a more pragmatic course. Under his leadership the Bonapartes would seize control of the levers of power in Corsica while at the same time playing the part of Paris's chief agents in Corsica and using this position of trust to petition for the return of Paoli. This last was soon obtained, and on 14 July *il babbo* landed near Bastia, and was then quickly elected both to the command-in-chief of the Corsican national guard and to the presidency of the council of the department of France which the island now constituted. At this point, however, things went wrong. Already alienated by Napoleon's commission in the army, the old leader was deeply offended when Napoleon made some trenchant public criticisms of his defence of Corsica against the French in 1769. Far from becoming Paoli's right-hand man, Napoleon found himself out in the cold, the result being that in February 1791 he had no option but to return to his regiment at Auxonne.

Back in France Napoleon played the part of the tribune of the people, and so exasperated his royalist commanding officer that he had him transferred to another unit at Valence. Here he continued his revolutionary activities, becoming secretary of the local Jacobin club, taking a prominent part in a variety of public ceremonies, and encouraging the purchase of the *biens nationaux*. But all this was at best a manoeuvre designed to keep his options open: beneath the surface Napoleon had not abandoned his hopes of securing the patronage of Paoli. His erstwhile hero spurned his advances, however, and thus it was that in the autumn of 1791 Napoleon again applied for leave and returned home, where he set about securing a commission in the famous 'volunteers of 1791'. In April 1792 success was achieved in the shape of a lieutenant-colonelcy in the second battalion raised in Corsica (albeit not without the assistance of a certain degree of bribery and ballot-rigging). Meanwhile, Joseph had become mayor of Ajaccio's town council. But acceptance by

Paoli remained as far off as ever and Napoleon knew that his continued absence in Corsica was jeopardizing his commission in the regular army. When the local Jacobins decided to stage a showdown with their political opponents, he therefore had little option but to lend them the support of his troops. However, the plan failed and, with the radicals forced to back down, Napoleon had to restore his position in the metropolis. As he had now been suspended from the army list, this meant heading for Paris, especially as his political opponents in Corsica were busily engaged in pretending that he was somehow a counter-revolutionary. In the end everything was resolved: pardoned for his actions and reinstated as a regular officer, Napoleon was promoted to captain and given permission to return to Corsica yet again, this time on the pretext that he had to escort his sister Elise back to her homeland after the closure of the ladies' academy she had been attending in the capital.

Napoleon had clearly played his cards sufficiently well to keep in with Paris. But that did not mean that he was happy. On the contrary, his visit to the capital had coincided with the violent risings of 20 June and 10 August 1792, and these understandably left him not only with a deep fear of popular violence, but also convinced him that the Jacobins were playing with fire. As he wrote to Joseph, 'The Jacobins are fools who have no common sense.'[12] In short, the future ostensibly lay with Corsica, but Napoleon was more out of favour there than ever, for Paoli was increasingly alarmed by the direction events were taking. To advance the interests of his family, his erstwhile admirer therefore had no option but to take the side of the Jacobin party in the island, and all the more so as the Jacobins were now in control in Paris. In doing so, however, he does not appear to have deceived his own family. 'I have always descried in Napoleon,' wrote his brother Lucien, 'an ambition that, whilst not wholly egotistic, surpasses his love of the public good ... Given a [fresh] revolution, Napoleon would strain every nerve to maintain his position, whilst I even believe him capable of turning his coat if that is what is required to make his fortune.'[13] As the future emperor later reminisced, it was 'a fine time for an enterprising young man'.[14]

Whatever the truth may have been, from here it was but a short step to a breach with Paoli. According to Napoleon's own account, the Corsican leader was now scheming with the British to deliver the island into their hands. No such plot was afoot – there seems to have been no contact between Paoli and the British until April 1793 and even then the approach came not from Paoli but the British. As for the idea that Paoli suggested the future emperor should seek a career in the British army, this is pure invention. If relations between the two were very frosty, it was rather because Paoli had increasingly fallen under the influence of traditional rivals of the Bonapartes, of which the most notable was the Pozzo di Borgo clan. Following an unsuccessful expedition against Sardinia, a territory of the hostile state of Piedmont, the resentment on both sides finally exploded. On the one hand, Napoleon hinted that Paoli had deliberately sabotaged the expedition, while on the other Paoli accused the Jacobins of forcing him into ordering a hopeless attack in order to provide a pretext for his arrest and execution. Whatever the reality of the situation, the affair plunged Corsica into open conflict. In this situation the Bonapartes and their allies had no chance. Increasingly the weaker faction in Corsican politics, the Jacobins were routed, leaving Napoleon and his entire family no option but to flee to the French mainland.

The breach with Paoli, and with it the loss of his family estates, ended Napoleon's Corsican dreams for good. Henceforward he would be French and, for the moment at least, a Jacobin: only weeks after his arrival in France he was penning *Le Souper de Beaucaire*, an imagined conversation between himself and a number of local civilians in which he expatiated on the evils of the so-called federalist revolt that was then gripping much of France, and defended the actions of the government forces that had just stormed Avignon. As for Corsica and its ruler, all loyalty to them was expunged: Napoleon never returned to his homeland and rarely spoke of it except with disdain, while *Le Souper de Beaucaire* and a previous pamphlet published virtually simultaneously with his flight into exile heaped scorn upon his sometime idol and accused him of treason, thereby exonerating the Bonaparte clan of the charge of betrayal.

This vehemence, however, is all too transparent. On one level, it was a classic instance of how love can turn overnight to hatred: there is no reason to doubt that Napoleon's failure in Corsica came as a very severe blow to his ego, while at the same time causing him real sadness. At the same time, if Napoleon was now a Frenchman and a Jacobin, it was simply because he had nowhere else to go, and no other way of advancing his career – a career, incidentally, that seemed likely to be greatly boosted by the large numbers of army officers who had fled France since 1789.

Set against this is the fact that he had been espousing radical political views since his days as an officer cadet. Yet, as we have seen, those closest to him never trusted his sincerity in this respect, whilst to the very end he seems to have believed that he could win over Paoli to his way of thinking. One is left then with a picture of the most cynical calculation: love of Corsica was replaced not by love of France but love of Napoleon. For the moment that meant there must be much play-acting. Like most other works of their sort, the memoirs of Paul de Barras are not wholly to be trusted. Even so the picture that he paints of his first meeting with Napoleon is certainly plausible:

Bonaparte offered me a few copies of a pamphlet recently written by him, which he had had printed at Avignon, at the same time begging my per-mission to distribute it among the officers and privates of the Republican army. Carrying a huge bundle of them, he remarked while handing them round, 'This will show you whether or not I am a patriot! Can any man be too much of a revolutionist? Marat and Robespierre are my saints!'[15]

Whatever the truth of this story, there is no doubt that Napoleon's tactics worked. Fortunately for him, one of the three *représentants en mission* whom the Convention had elected to send to the Marseilles area in the summer of 1793 was Antoine-Christophe Saliceti. An old friend of Joseph who had represented Corsica in the National Assembly, he had become the de facto leader of the island's Jacobins. Operating very much in the spirit of Corsican clan loyalty, he now befriended the Bonapartes. At his urging the Convention voted the family substantial financial compensation, while Joseph was found a post as an assistant commissary on the staff of the army that had been sent to subdue the Midi under General Carteaux. As for Napoleon, his efforts as a propagandist were lauded to the skies in Saliceti's dispatches to Paris and on 16 September he was given command of the guns supporting the army besieging Toulon. Of the famous episode that followed, it is necessary to say very little in so far as the actual fighting is concerned, though Napoleon undoubtedly not only showed both courage and decision, but also considerably hastened the fall of the city. What does deserve comment is the egocentrism that he displayed in the course of the affair. Napoleon, it seems, knew best, and lost no time in letting his opinions be known. Thanks to his complaints, the first commander of the besieging army, General Carteaux, was replaced and imprisoned, while his successor, General Dugommier, eventually became so irritated by his constant interventions that he had to order him to mind his own business and confine his attention to the artillery. Coupled with all this were clear signs of a desire to play to the gallery. Napoleon appeared amidst his gunners to direct their fire in person, slept on the ground wrapped up in a cloak, made a particularly gallant sergeant an officer on the spot (the man in question was the future General Junot), cultivated the friendship of a small 'band of brothers' that included such men as Victor, Marmont and Duroc, and finally proved his physical courage by taking part in the final assault on horseback, when his place as commander of the artillery was rather in the rear. Whether he deserved the renown that he won in the course of the fighting is debatable, but the truth hardly mattered. Hero or not, he had made his name.

It was at Toulon that my reputation began. All the generals, representatives and soldiers who had heard me give my opinions in the different councils three months before the taking of the town, anticipated my future military career ... In the Army of the Pyrenees, Dugommier was always talking about his commander of artillery at Toulon, and his high opinion was impressed on the minds of all the generals and officers who afterwards went ... to the Army of Italy.[16]

Well, perhaps. According to Bourrienne, 'The news of the taking of Toulon caused a sensation ... throughout France, the more lively as such success was unexpected and almost unhoped for.'[17] But Napoleon's new comrade-in-arms, Marmont, thought very differently. As he later wrote, '[Napoleon] had made his name through his actions, but the latter did not possess sufficient *éclat* for his reputation to be carried beyond the ranks of the army in which he was serving; if his name was spoken of with esteem and respect, it was unknown in Paris and even Lyon.'[18] And the aftermath was not as flattering to Napoleon as he would have liked. He was promoted to the rank of brigadier, but the French propaganda machine heaped praise not upon him but rather on Saliceti, while if Dugommier, Saliceti and Robespierre's brother Augustin (like Saliceti a *représentant en mission* in the Midi) all lauded him to the skies in their dispatches, he was not accorded the prominence in operations that he felt he deserved. Nor were his plans for future operations adopted. Though still only formally second-in-command of artillery of the Army of Italy, the new general was eager to obtain a major role in the formation to which he was attached and bombarded Paris with schemes for an offensive against the Piedmontese. At the same time he did everything he could to secure the favour of Augustin Robespierre and his colleague, Ricord. To quote Barras:

From the time Bonaparte joined the first Army of Italy . . . he desired and systematically sought to get to the top of the ladder by all possible means. Fully convinced that women constituted a powerful aid, he assiduously paid court to the wife of Ricord, knowing that she exercised great influence over Robespierre the Younger . . . He pursued Madame Ricord with all kinds of attentions, picking up her gloves, holding her fan, holding with profound respect her bridle and stirrup when she mounted her horse, accompanying her in her walks hat in hand, and seeming to tremble continually lest some accident befall her.[19]

To return to the military situation, such politicking did Napoleon no good. In the first months of 1794 the most pressing danger was not the Piedmontese, but the large Spanish army that had crossed the eastern Pyrenees and was occupying southern Roussillon. To move against this force, Napoleon claimed, would be a mistake, but his reasons for taking this line – the supposed danger of a national insurrection and the logistical and geographic difficulties posed by operations in Spain – are difficult to accept at face value in view of what was to occur in 1808. To quote Barras again, 'Bonaparte . . . while engrossed entirely with his own interests, believed he was merely anxious for the public weal.'[20] As it became clear that all Napoleon cared about was glory, no account was taken of his arguments; on the contrary, the Army of the eastern Pyrenees was reinforced and ordered to expel the Spaniards from French soil and march on Barcelona. With the aid of plans worked out by Napoleon, some success was achieved on the Italian frontier in a series of minor campaigns that culminated in a victory over the Piedmontese at Dego, but there was neither the will nor the men to sustain the advance, and at the end of September the invaders fell back to their start line.

For Napoleon, then, success at Toulon was followed by frustration. His opportunistic schemes to advance his career had been blocked and, worse, he had fallen from favour in Paris. At the time of the battle of Dego, he had not even been with the French forces. The reason for this transformation in his fortunes was the fall of Robespierre in July 1794.

Thanks to the fact that the *représentant en mission* attached to the Army of Italy happened to be Augustin Robespierre and, further, that the latter had taken him under his wing as a rising star, Napoleon had become more closely associated with the Terror than was wise. For this he now paid the price. First to move against him was his patron Saliceti, who was attached to the Army of the Alps rather than the Army of Italy and seems to have become eager to cut his protégé down to size. Terrified by the manner in which many southern towns were erupting against anyone linked with the Robespierres – there were massacres in Marseilles, Aix and Nimes – the Corsican seized on the fact that Napoleon had just participated in a secret mission to the neutral Republic of Genoa as an excuse to arrest him, the mere fact that he had crossed the frontier being sufficient to suggest that he must be involved in some foreign plot. That there was no case against Napoleon is beside the point and for a few days he was in deadly danger. In the end Saliceti relented and proclaimed his innocence, apparently on the grounds that having his sometime friend and client executed would not win him any favours with the new government in Paris, but Napoleon was not allowed to rejoin the army. Instead, he was given the thankless and in the end futile task of drawing up plans for an invasion of Corsica. Even in love he was unsuccessful, a bid to make the daughter of a wealthy local nobleman his wife being firmly rejected on the grounds of lack of prospects.

Frustration, then, was heaped on frustration, and all the more so as 1794 had been a year in which France had triumphed on all fronts. Aided by a series of great victories, her armies had cleared the Spaniards from Roussillon, occupied the northern fringes of Catalonia, seized the Rhineland and definitively reconquered Belgium. With some of the forces involved in these campaigns very large indeed, Toulon was beginning to look like very small beer. And, of course, it was yesterday's news: the heroes of the hour were now not Napoleon, but Pichegru and Jourdan. At the beginning of 1795, then, Napoleon was a bitterly frustrated man.

A second romance – this time with the sister of Joseph Bonaparte's wife, Julie Clery – was making no better progress than the first one, while the expedition to Corsica was dispersed by a British naval squadron. On top of this there then came a posting to command the artillery of the Army of the West in distant Brittany. For the time being relatively quiet, the west was hardly a welcome billet for a soldier of fortune, and

Napoleon therefore immediately set off for Paris to attempt to secure something better. However, the Minister of War was a moderate who had not forgiven Napoleon his association with the Robespierres, and the only response was a switch to an infantry brigade. In response to this demotion, Napoleon claimed that he was ill – on sick leave he would at least be able to remain in Paris and cast around for something better. By all accounts it was a miserable time. The cost of living was very high, and Napoleon was forced to live very frugally in the most miserable of lodgings; indeed, he would not have been able to survive at all had not Joseph, who had retained his post in the commissariat, sent him occasional remittances. Privation and worry, meanwhile, told on his physical appearance. The future General Thiébault, for example, remembered him as 'a little man . . . looking nothing but a victim [whose] untidy dress, long, lank hair and . . . worn-out dress . . . betrayed his straits', whilst Laure Junot's memories were very similar.

At this point in his life Napoleon was ugly . . . His skin was so yellow . . . and he looked after himself so little, that, with his uncombed and badly powdered hair, he had a disagreeable aspect. His small hands . . . were thin . . . and grimy . . . Whenever I compare the picture that I have of Napoleon entering the courtyard of the Hotel de la Tranquillité . . . with an awkward and uncertain step, wearing a cheap round hat rammed down over his eyes, from which two 'spaniels ears' of unkempt hair fell over the collar of the same iron-grey overcoat that later became so glorious a banner . . . and boots that were as poorly made as they were cared for, with the one which I saw later on, I can scarcely believe that I am seeing the same man.[21]

Not for the first time in his career, Napoleon was soon contemplating suicide. Something of his misery comes across in the account of Bourrienne, with whom he now took up once again.

It was with pain that he resolved to wait patiently the removal of the prejudices which men in power had entertained against him, and he hoped that in the perpetual changes that were taking place power would at length pass into the hands of those who would be disposed to consider him with favour . . . He now became thoughtful, frequently melancholy and disturbed, and he . . . envied the good fortune of his brother, Joseph, who had just married Mademoiselle Clery, the daughter of a rich and respectable merchant at Marseilles . . . Meanwhile, time passed away, but nothing was done:

his projects were unsuccessful, and his applications unattended to. This injustice embittered his spirit, and he was tormented with the desire to do something. To remain in the crowd was intolerable. He resolved to leave France, and the favourite idea . . . that the east was the most certain path to glory, inspired him with the desire to proceed to Constantinople, and to make a tender of his services to the [sultan].[22]

All this produced growing levels of resentment. On the one hand Napoleon reminisced fondly about Toulon and talked wildly of his 'star', while on the other he broke out in tirades against Saliceti, whom he held to be the cause of all his ills, and muttered about the posturing dandies known as *incroyables* who filled the streets. To all the other stimuli driving Napoleon forward there was therefore now added the desire for revenge, whether it was on the civilian politicians who had held back his career or on the society that had seemed so fickle in its appreciation of him. The urge was not necessarily personal: Saliceti, for example, was later treated with great generosity by Napoleon, who not only intervened to save him from imprisonment after the coup of 18 Brumaire, but gave him a series of important political and diplomatic appointments in Italy. But of his desire for vindication, there was no doubt: one day, he swore, he would command the streets of Paris, streets that were meanwhile quickly killing off what little was left of his youthful idealism. In the wake of the fall of puritanical Robespierre, monied society had been gripped by a wave of relief that manifested itself in hedonism, ostentation and a visible loosening of sexual mores. Costume became extravagant in the extreme, while men and women alike positively gloried in their promiscuity. 'At this time,' wrote a young army officer, 'the disorganization of society reached its height. Rank had disappeared; wealth had changed hands. As it was still dangerous to boast of one's birth . . . the new-rich . . . set the fashion, and to all the oddities of a faulty upbringing these people joined the absurdities of a patronage devoid of dignity . . . This taste for the arts . . . had the result of affecting the fashions, and even the habits, of the capital with the most bare-faced licence . . . One would not have believed it, unless one had seen it oneself, but charming women of good education and birth wore flesh-coloured trousers and . . . dresses of transparent muslin with their bosoms bare and their arms naked to the shoulder, and so appeared in public places.'[23] Meanwhile, with the defence of property the chief order of the day, its acquisition became a matter that was only slightly less pressing: speculation and corruption knew no bounds. With all this going on against a background of the most utter misery, the effect was to promote the most far-reaching cynicism: liberty, fraternity and equality might still be paid lip service, but it was clear that, at best, they had become mere slogans. Nor was any of this lost on Napoleon. To quote a letter he wrote to Joseph, 'There is only one thing to do in this world, and that is to keep acquiring money and more money, power and more power. All the rest is meaningless.'[24]

Be that as it may, it was not long before Napoleon's faith in his star was rewarded. Exactly what happened is unclear, but, one way or another, in September 1795 Napoleon found himself on the staff of the army's Bureau Topographique, the embryonic general staff established in 1793 by Lazare Carnot. In this capacity he was immediately put forward as the head of a military mission to Ottoman Turkey, but there was some delay in ratifying the appointment and Napoleon himself was therefore still in Paris when on 3 October the city erupted in revolt against the new executive government, known as the Directory, that had just been installed in the capital by virtue of the freshly promulgated Constitution of 1795. The Vendémiaire rising, as it became known, was a serious military threat, involving thousands of disaffected members of the National Guard. Hastily placed under the command of the leading politician, Paul de Barras, as the Army of the Interior, the defenders were outnumbered and disorganized, and for a moment it seemed that they might be overwhelmed. However, all the men available for action were concentrated around the Tuileries palace, and when the insurgents attacked they were met by the famous 'whiff of grapeshot'. Among the defenders was Napoleon, who appears to have come forward to offer his services to Barras, and then been given the position of his aide-de-camp or, possibly, second-in-command. As such he displayed much courage and energy. According to Thiébault, 'From the first his activity was astonishing: he seemed to be everywhere at once . . . He surprised people further by his laconic, clear and prompt orders, imperative to the last degree. Everybody was struck also by the vigour of his arrangements, and passed from admiration to confidence, from confidence to enthusiasm.'[25] Yet it is clearly not true that he directed the resistance, or that, in Carlyle's phrase, he was commandant to Barras's commandant's cloak: even by his own account, for example, it was not himself but

Barras who took the initiative in ordering up the cannon that dispersed the rebels.

But this is scarcely to the point. Within a very short time, the impression had spread that it was the young Corsican who had saved the Revolution. In this development Barras himself played a considerable role, for it suited him to justify his earlier support for Napoleon. Also helpful was Louis Fréron, a leading Thermidorian who had cooperated with Barras in the pacification of the south in 1793 and was now pursuing the beautiful Pauline Bonaparte. Meanwhile, Napoleon himself played his cards with considerable skill, on the one hand affecting an air of modesty and reluctance when the officers who had defeated the revolt were presented to the Convention, and on the other attaching himself firmly to Barras, through whom he was to secure an entrée to the most fashionable salons of Paris. Nor did he at this point cultivate the air of a conqueror. 'I can still see his little hat,' reminisced Thiébault, 'surmounted by a chance plume badly fastened on, his tricolour sash more than carelessly tied, his coat cut anyhow, and a sword which in truth did not seem the sort of weapon to make his fortune.'[26] Vendémiaire became his salvation. With Barras elected to the presidency of the Directory, on 26 October Napoleon was appointed to the command of the Army of the Interior with the rank of major-general. To quote Bourrienne, Vendémiaire 'brought Bonaparte forward and elevated him above the crowd'.[27]

At the same time, the 'whiff of grapeshot' was formative in another sense. From the very beginning of the Revolution it is clear that Napoleon was contemptuous of the crowd as a political force. In his eyes it was a mere mob, lacking in organization, that could easily be overawed by an opponent possessed of military discipline and firm leadership. Had Louis XVI appeared on horseback to defend the Tuileries in 1792, he told Joseph, the palace would never have fallen. But the principle was political as much as it was military: the mob *had* to be defeated. Uncivilized and brutal, in Napoleon's eyes it would inevitably run amok the moment the bounds of order and discipline were relaxed. Indeed, as an eyewitness to the storming of the Tuileries in August 1792 he had seen the ferocity of which it was capable all too clearly – the defenders had in many cases literally been hacked to pieces. Gratuitous defilement and mutilation had been very much the order of the day, and within a few days further horrors had come in the terrible atrocities known as the September massacres. Already the product of a society in which fear of peasant insurrection and banditry was endemic, Napoleon could not but recoil in disgust. All these feelings, needless to say, were confirmed by Vendémiaire. On the one hand, the crowd had been crushed: faced by 25,000 insurgents, 8,000 government troops had broken the uprising in little more than twenty-four hours of serious fighting with the loss of perhaps 100 casualties. And, on the other, most of the insurgents had not taken part in the actual fighting but given themselves over to drunkenness and pillage. If they had been called on to the streets at all, meanwhile, it was the result of a political factionalism born solely of what Napoleon saw as selfish ambition. As he had written to his brother Lucien in 1792, 'Those at the top are poor creatures . . . Everyone wants to succeed at the price of no matter what horror and calumny; intrigue is as base as ever.'[28] What Vendémiaire showed, then, was not just that the rabble could and should be kept in check, but also that the powerful state created by the Revolution that Napoleon so admired was threatened not just in the streets but in the corridors of power – that the new elites, in short, had to be kept under tutelage as well.

If there was much material to ponder here, there is no evidence that the hero of Vendémiaire was considering a bid for power at this time. All the same, by the end of 1795 we see a Napoleon who had almost overnight become a key player in the politics of revolutionary Paris, a wealthy man with an official residence on the Place Vendôme, and a regular visitor to the most fashionable *salons* of the capital. In March 1796 there followed his marriage to the thirty-two-year-old Creole widow, Rose de Beauharnais ('Josephine' was the name given her by Napoleon, who had the curious habit of rebaptizing all his female conquests). Was this, too, just one more piece of calculation? For many historians this has been an act of faith. As Josephine had until very recently numbered Paul de Barras amongst her many lovers, and was still highly regarded by him, marrying her may have seemed a good way of retaining the ear of one of the most powerful men in France. Equally, Josephine's first husband having been a nobleman executed in the Terror, the young general may have believed that he was securing the acceptance that had been denied him at Brienne. In the words of his close friend, Marmont, 'Bonaparte's *amour-propre* was flattered. The ideas of the Old Order had always attracted him a great deal, and, although he played the republican, he was still susceptible to . . . all sorts of aristocratic prejudice.'[29] And, finally, money may also have played a role, the artful Josephine having given Napoleon the quite erroneous impression that she was extremely rich. Yet other historians have insisted either that he was simply besotted with her, or, alternatively, that it was the hopelessly indebted Josephine herself who took the lead, seducing him into a marriage that was not only highly advantageous to her, but the only way out of a situation in which the looks that were her only asset were already starting to fade. Whatever the reason, by all accounts Josephine was wooed with considerable vigour, as witness Hortense de Beauharnais's recollection of a dinner *chez* Barras, which proved to be the first time that she met her future stepfather:

Barras's guest-list proved to be very numerous: the only people I knew were Tallien and his wife. At table I found myself placed between my mother and a general, who, in order to talk to her, thrust himself across me with such force and persistence that I grew tired of him and pushed my chair back. Despite myself, however, I could not but notice that he had a good figure and an expressive face, albeit one of a remarkable pallor. He talked with great spirit and appeared to be interested in nothing other than my mother. The general turned out to be Bonaparte.[30]

Was Napoleon acting solely with an eye to his future career? The matter is impossible to fathom, but whatever the reason for the marriage, the young general now possessed a wife of an avaricious bent whom he had, it seems, promised she would be 'rolling in gold'.[31]

Napoleon married Josephine on 9 March 1796. Two days later he left Paris for the frontiers of Piedmont, having the previous month been appointed to the command of the Army of Italy. For the overly cynical, this was 'Barras's dowry' – Napoleon's reward for having relieved the Director of his old mistress. But this is clearly to go too far. The plan of campaign for 1796 for the first time involved an offensive in Italy, and in this theatre of war the Corsican general was the French army's chief expert: indeed, the few weeks he had spent in the Bureau Topographique had largely been spent in drawing up fresh plans for operations there. Furthermore, although he had gained a substantial victory at Loano on 23–4 November 1795, the current commander of the Army of Italy, General Schérer, was opposed to any further advance. That said, however, Napoleon was eager for a field command. In the first place, as he said himself, 'A general twenty-five years of age cannot stay for long at the head of an army of the interior.'[32] Apart from sheer love of glory, his sudden emergence from obscurity had yet to be matched by the respect of many of his fellow generals, some of whom, at least, were now his declared enemies (one such was the equally young and energetic Lazare Hoche, who had just won great renown by pacifying the Vendée and was also another former lover of Rose de Beauharnais). And, though by no means too proud to reject his patronage, Napoleon clearly disliked Barras. He later remarked, 'Barras . . . had neither the talent of leadership, nor the habit of work . . . Having left the service as a captain, he had never made war, whilst he possessed nothing in the way of military knowledge. Elevated to the Directory by the events of Thermidor and Vendémiaire, he did not have any of the qualities necessary for such a post.'[33] The feeling was mutual – according to the Director, his protégé was an 'oily-tongued wheedler'[34] – but for the time being the alliance persisted and Barras urged his fellow Directors to give Napoleon the Italian command. For a particularly interesting slant on the situation, we may turn to the memoirs of Lavallette, who was soon to become one of Napoleon's aides-de-camp:

The duties of commander-in-chief in Paris conferred great power on General Bonaparte . . . but soon the government felt annoyed and even humiliated by the yoke imposed on them by the young general. As a matter of fact he only acted on his own initiative, concerning himself with everything, making every decision himself, and only acting as he himself thought best. The activity and wide range of his mind, the domineering quality of his character would not lend themselves to obedience on any matter at all. The Directory still wished to handle the Jacobins with tact; the general ordered the hall in which they met to be closed, and the government only heard that this had been done when it was about to debate the question. The residence in Paris of members of the former nobility appeared to be dangerous. The Directory wanted to expel them, but the general protected them. The government had to yield. He issued regulations, recalled certain generals who had been disgraced, dismissed every impulsive suggestion summarily, ruffled the vanity of all, set all hatreds at defiance, and stigmatized as clumsiness the slow and uncertain policy of the government. And when the Directory made up their minds to protest mildly, he . . . explained his ideas and his plans so clearly and easily, and with such eloquence, that there was no answering him, and two hours afterwards everything he had said was carried out. However, if the Directory was tired of him, General Bonaparte was no less tired of life in Paris, which offered no scope for his ambition, no opportunity for glory such as his genius craved. A long time ago he had made plans for the conquest of Italy. A lengthy period of service with the Army of Nice [*sic*] had given him the time necessary to mature his schemes, to calculate all difficulty and to weigh all hazards; he applied to the government for the command of that army, for money and for troops. He was appointed commander-in-chief and was given the troops, but only the moderate sum of a hundred thousand crowns. It was with such meagre resources that he was to conquer Italy at the head of an army which had not been paid for six months and was without shoes. But Bonaparte knew his own strength, and, embracing a tremendous future with exhilaration, he bade farewell to the Directory, which watched him go with secret pleasure, happy to be rid of a man whose character mastered them, and whose vast schemes were merely, in the eyes of most of its members, the impulse of a young man full of pride and effrontery.[35]

In March 1796, then, the personal history of Napoleon Bonaparte at last meshed with the march of international relations. Before engaging with the conflict in which he became a combatant, however, it would be advisable to take a step back and survey the picture that has emerged from this discussion of the future emperor's early years. Let us first be entirely honest. The years from 1769 to 1796 are extremely difficult to chronicle: unpublished primary material is in short supply, while such memoirs that exist, not to mention the recollections of Napoleon himself, are uniformly partisan and in some instances little better than inventions. Nor is this an end to the problem, for much of the material that we have is so ambiguous that it is susceptible to entirely contradictory interpretations. No Napoleon, then, is in the end likely to be anything more than a reflection of the personal inclinations of its creator. Yet it does remain much harder to accept the image of Napoleon the idealist than it does that of Napoleon the opportunist. Whether it was the neglected child born to a mother who had suffered a difficult pregnancy, the scion of a family of inveterate social climbers, the second son engaged in endless rivalry with his elder brother, Joseph, the despised outsider at Brienne, the gawky officer cadet teased by girls as 'Puss-in-Boots', the failed Corsican politician, the exiled refugee, the hero of the hour deprived of his rightful glory, the penniless brigadier touting frantically for a post in Paris, the 'Vendémiaire general' in debt to the despicable Barras, or the young husband enamoured of a wife who was as ardent as she was grasping – a whole succession of Napoleons conspired to produce a genuinely frightening figure. To use the word 'megalomaniac' at this stage would probably be unwise, but all the same what we see is a man filled by loathing of the mob, contemptuous of ideology, obsessed by military glory, convinced that he had a great destiny and determined to rise to the top. Added to this was jealousy of the many generals who had won far more laurels on the battlefield than he had, and, in particular, of General Hoche. 'It is a fact,' wrote Barras, 'that of all the generals Hoche was the one who most absorbed Bonaparte's thoughts ... On arriving in Italy he asked all new-comers, "Where is Hoche? What is Hoche doing?" '[36] It was a dangerous combination. Marmont recalled his first meeting with Napoleon after Vendémiaire, when the new commander radiated 'extraordinary aplomb', while being marked by 'an air of grandeur that I had not noted before'. As to the question of whether he could be kept under control, this seemed doubtful: 'This man who knew how to command so well could not possibly be destined by Providence to obey.'[37]

Such was the young man who in 1796 found himself at the head of the Army of Italy. What, though, of the conflict, or rather series of conflicts, into which he was now plunged? Let us begin by making one thing very clear. The French Revolutionary Wars were not a struggle between liberty on the one hand and tyranny on the other. As we have seen, indeed, they were not wholly about the French Revolution at all. Of course, this does not mean that ideology played no role in the spread of conflict: on various occasions, it intensified tension. But it was not the chief cause of trouble. The diplomatic history of the 1790s (and indeed, the 1800s) suggests that few of the great powers of Europe had any problems with the concept of peace with France, or even an alliance with her. Nor did the 1790s bring any real change in the aims of the great powers, who in each case pursued goals that would have been comprehensible to rulers of fifty or even a hundred years before. This should not be taken to mean that these goals were fixed. Every state at one time or another had choices to make in terms of their priorities and partners, or felt that it had no option but to sacrifice one goal in favour of another. Much the same was true of the structures within which they operated: the dynamic of international relations in Europe altered very considerably over the course of the eighteenth century, and continued to change after 1789. But until the beginning of the nineteenth century, at least, the general range of those choices remained substantially the same, the implication being, of course, that the French Revolution did not suddenly engage the exclusive attention of every *ancien-régime* chancellory and ministry of war.

One might with some justice go well beyond this. Not until 1814 did the powers finally set aside their differences and concentrate all their forces and energies in a fight to the finish with Napoleon. For the time being, though, our priority must rather be to examine the age of conflict that formed the eighteenth-century context. For over a hundred years before 1789 there had hardly been a year when the whole of Europe had been at peace. Why this was so is again a question that need not detain us here for too long. However, in brief, for all the monarchies of Europe the battlefield was at one and the same time a gauge of their power and a theatre for their glorification and, by extension, an important means of legitimizing their power at home where they were frequently challenged by feudal aristocracies and powerful religious hierarchies. Meanwhile, war bred more war. To some extent the ever greater demands which it imposed – for the eighteenth century was an age when armies and navies grew steadily bigger and more demanding in terms of their equipment – could be financed by internal reform. Hence the 'enlightened absolutism' which was so characteristic of the period from 1750 to 1789 and beyond, not to mention the efforts of both Britain and Spain to exploit their American colonies more effectively. But a variety of problems, including not least the resistance of traditional elites – a factor that could in itself generate armed conflict – meant that there were only limited advantages to be derived from such solutions, and thus it was that most rulers looked at one time or another to territorial gains on their frontiers or the acquisition of fresh colonies. This, of course, implied war in Europe (which given its cost in turn implied territorial gain or at the very least financial compensation). No major state would ever have agreed to relinquish even the smallest province voluntarily and, while the weaker ones could sometimes be overawed into doing so, a unilateral gain for one monarch was not acceptable to any of the others: if, say, Sweden took over Norway, Russia would have expected to take over a slice of Poland. Nor was this an end to the problem. To go to war successfully, it was necessary to possess allies, and allies in turn expected to be paid for their services, either in money or in land. As this set off a fresh chain of demands for compensation, many of the conflicts of the eighteenth century turned into truly continental affairs that drew in states from Portugal to Russia and from Sweden to Sicily. Nor, by the same token, could any peace settlement ever be definitive. Thus, no war was ever fought with the aim of obtaining total victory. Aside from the question of cost, no dynastic monarch would ever have sought to beggar another altogether, if only because the ruler concerned might prove a useful ally in the next crisis. Yet this in turn meant that the loser of any conflict was almost always in a position to seek to overturn the result of one war by seeking victory in another, and so a game that was essentially pointless continued to fascinate and mesmerize.

Many factors, then, conspired to make war endemic in eighteenth-century Europe. However, the pressures that led to conflict were increasing, not least through changes in the structure of international relations. Very, very gradually, foreign policy was moving from being an affair of dynasties to being an affair of nations. This development must not be exaggerated: indeed, it affected only a few states and made limited progress even in them. Yet, for all that, it cannot be completely ignored. In a very vague and general sense it was everywhere understood that there ought to be a connection between foreign policy and the well-being of the subject, but in most cases little more than lip service was paid to the idea, while there was no sense that the populace had a right either to be consulted on the issue of war or peace or to expect concrete benefits in the event of victory. The peoples of Europe were in effect mere pawns to be mobilized or called to endure suffering exactly as their rulers thought fit. Starting in England in the seventeenth century, however, a new pattern began to emerge in that we see the first stirrings of public opinion. As early as the 1620s, for example, Charles I caused outrage among many of his subjects by failing to intervene effectively in favour of the Protestant cause in the Thirty Years War. In this instance, the stimulus was religious, but as the establishment of the American colonies, the penetration of India and Africa and the slave trade brought wealth to Britain, so the issue shifted rather to matters of commerce, the state increasingly being expected to use its power to protect the investments of the oligarchy (and beyond them the well-being of a much broader section of society). In practice, of course, the British state did not need much in the way of urging when it came to defending its colonial possessions and increasing their extent, but it would now find it much harder to back away from doing so. Similar pressures, meanwhile, had been generated in the United Provinces, France and, to a lesser extent, Spain, while elsewhere particular groups had emerged that remained too isolated from the rest of society to deserve the label 'public opinion' and yet had a considerable stake in foreign policy (a good example is the Russian nobility's strong interest in the Baltic trade with Britain).

Though by no means unimportant, these issues were outweighed by other more pressing matters. Particularly for the eastern powers, there was the issue of the rising costs of their military establishments. As the eighteenth century advanced, so their armies increased: Russia and Prussia more than doubled the size of their armies between 1700 and 1789, with Austria not far behind. What had mattered in the early part of the century had been dynastic prestige and in particular the question of which reigning families should rule the many states that were bedevilled by succession crises. But beginning with Frederick II of Prussia's invasion of Silesia in 1740 what mattered now was territory. Conquest was essential, and because this was the case all considerations of legality and morality began to go by the board. But so long as all the major states in Europe were playing the same game, it was held (at least by many of their rulers and statesmen) that universal conquest brought with it universal good. The weaker states of the Continent would suffer, certainly, but as none of the great powers would lose out in relation to one another, the net result would be a balance of power that made for general security. To put it another way, conquest was a moral duty from which all would benefit, and war, by extension, an act of benevolence. Nor did war seem especially threatening. In 1789 the standing armies of Europe may have been much bigger than they had been in 1700, but new crops, better transport, improved bureaucracies, more productive fiscal systems, harsher discipline and tighter procedures in the field all ensured that the horrors of the Thirty Years War, in which masses of unpaid men had simply surged from one side of Germany to the other, living off the country and denying the authority of political masters that had lost all ability to pay and supply them, would not be repeated. At the same time, war was also less costly in another sense. Thanks to developments in the art of generalship, it was assumed that battle would be less frequent. Enemy armies would be manoeuvred out of their positions, and their commanders – products of an age of reason – would tamely accept the logic of their position and march away, leaving their opponents to move in unopposed. If battles could largely be avoided, sieges, too, would become less of an endurance test, for it was widely accepted that once a fortress had had its walls breached, its governor would capitulate without further resistance so as to save the lives of both the townsfolk and his men.

But in reality Europe was no more getting safer than she was becoming more civilized. Given that every possible territorial solution that could be worked out for the Continent of Europe was bound to upset one or other of the great powers, continual conquest led not to perpetual peace but rather perpetual war, and therefore produced not security, but insecurity. As the Seven Years War had shown, as the stakes grew ever higher, so rulers with their backs against the wall would habitually resort to battle rather than simply accepting the logic of superior numbers or generalship, just as they would be inclined to put fortress governors under great pressure to resist the enemy to the utmost: this was the conflict that gave rise to the phrase *'pour encourager les autres'*. As the War of the Bavarian Succession had shown, late eighteenth-century regular armies were much less likely than those, say, of the War of the Spanish Succession to be able to pull off the sort of feats of manoeuvre that would have been required to decide the issue of wars without a battle: Marlborough's march to the Danube in 1704 could never have been replicated seventy years later. And there was certainly no diminution in the sufferings of the civilian population, nor in the damage which an army's passage could inflict on a district. On the wilder fringes of warfare – the Balkans, the frontiers of the American colonies – torture and massacre were very much the order of the day while large parts of Germany had been devastated by the Seven Years War. The overall picture is a grim one: war may not have been the monster of the seventeenth century, but it was still a savage beast. Many rulers and statesmen were well aware of this reality, and a few even tried to back away from the traditional power game. But in the end they were helpless, for the only weapon they could fall back upon was the same mixture of alliance and armed force that had caused the problem in the first place.

Indeed, the situation was even worse than this suggested. By the mid-1780s a major conflagration was in the making. Let us begin by

considering France. Once mighty, since 1763 she had suffered a series
of major catastrophes and humiliations. In the East the first partition of
Poland of 1772 gravely weakened her chief allies in Eastern Europe.
Stripped of her enormous American territories in the Seven Years War,
she had gained a certain degree of revenge by assisting the nascent United
States of America in the American War of Independence, only to find
that this action had shattered her financial position beyond repair. And
finally, without money, Louis XVI was repeatedly humbled, being forced
both to accept a profoundly unfavourable commercial treaty by the
British and to stand by helplessly while Prussian forces crushed the
pro-French regime established by the Dutch revolution of 1785–7. To
say that on the eve of the Revolution France was bent on a war that
could reverse these disasters would be a wild over-statement – her
statesmen were actually pursuing a variety of courses, some of them
quite contradictory – but nevertheless this was certainly an option that
was being kept open and prepared for. While a massive programme of
military reform transformed the army and prepared it for offensive
operations, French diplomats sought to bolster the position of Austria
– France's chief ally – by seeking an alliance with Persia that might make
Russia think twice about going on the offensive in the West. At the same
time, efforts were made to dissuade Vienna from embarking on military
adventures in the Balkans and also to build up the Turks against Russia.
As for Britain, she too was threatened by French alliances with the rulers
of Egypt (in theory, a province of the Ottoman Empire, but in practice
a quasi-independent dominion), Oman and Hyderabad.

It was not just France that was threatening to overthrow the status
quo, however. Among the eastern powers, too, there were worrying
stirrings. In Austria, Joseph II had been engaged in an aggressive attempt
to build a powerful, centralized state, but he had run into increasing
opposition and was inclined to seek redress not only in plans that would
have involved taking over Bavaria in exchange for giving her rulers the
Austrian Netherlands (i.e. the western half of present-day Belgium), but
in launching an attack on the Ottoman Empire alongside Russia. Also
contemplated was a renewed war with Prussia, which had been asking
for trouble in recent years by frustrating a series of Austrian attempts
to reinforce her position in the Holy Roman Empire, and was also no
longer ruled by the mighty Frederick the Great, who had died in 1786.
Yet, now under Frederick William II, the Prussians were also on the

move. Their gains in the first partition of Poland had been much smaller than those obtained by either Russia or Austria and failed to include a number of key objectives. Still worse, while Russia had gone on to make further gains in the Russo-Turkish war of 1768–74, the War of the Bavarian Succession of 1778 had brought Prussia precisely nothing. In the first place, the means used were to be peaceful ones – like Vienna, Potsdam was quite capable of working out fanciful plans for territorial exchanges and Frederick William II himself was no warlord – but it is clear that there was to be no drawing back. In Sweden there was a situation parallel to that of Austria in that a reformist monarch – in this case Gustav III – had run into serious opposition at home, and wished to reinforce the power of the throne by a flight to the front vis-à-vis Russia. And last but not least there was the Russia of Catherine the Great, which was proving so aggressive in its interpretation of the treaty that had ended the previous war with Turkey that Constantinople was being pushed ever closer towards a counter-stroke.

This is not the place to retell the long and complicated story of the events that followed. In brief the inevitable crisis exploded in August 1787 when Turkey attacked Russia. This in turn provoked a general war in Eastern Europe with Austria and Russia pitched against Turkey, Sweden pitched against Russia, and Denmark pitched against Sweden. By 1790 most of the fighting had died down, but in the midst of the general confusion revolution had broken out in Poland where a reformist faction was anxious to restore her fortunes and build a modern state. Until now, events in France had for the most part been ignored, but in the course of 1791 she too was dragged into the crisis on account of Leopold II of Austria's desperate attempts to stave off a further round of hostilities and, in particular, a further partition of Poland. There was no desire for war with the French Revolution per se – indeed, in Leopold's case there was no desire for war at all – but in April 1792 clumsy Austrian tactics combined with political manoeuvrings in France herself initiated the French Revolutionary Wars. Initially, the belligerents were limited to France on the one hand and Austria and Prussia on the other, but within a year events had drawn most of the states of Europe into a great coalition against France. But this was no counter-revolutionary crusade: none of the powers that fought France had any desire to restore the *ancien régime* as it had existed in 1789, and many either limited their commitment to the struggle or dropped out of it altogether; within

a short time of Napoleon taking over the Army of Italy, indeed, Spain
was actually fighting on France's side. For most powers, in fact, the war
against the Revolution was either subordinated to long-standing foreign
policy aims or waged in accordance with those aims. Thus Russia and
Prussia always put the acquisition of territory in Poland (which was
completely wiped off the map by two further partitions in 1792 and
1795) before the struggle against France, while in Prussia's case she only
entered the conflict at all because she thought that it would bring her
territorial gains in Germany. Austria was still thinking in terms of the
'Bavarian exchange'. And as for Britain, she went to war to prevent
France from taking over the Low Countries, did so all the more willingly
because war with Paris offered her a way out of the diplomatic isolation
that had made her so vulnerable in the American War of Independence,
and for much of the time prosecuted the struggle by means of tactics
that gave a further boost to her colonial and maritime superiority. This
was not to say that ideology was lacking. No ruler wanted revolution at
home – there was, indeed, genuine horror at the events of 1792–4 – and
many governments clamped down hard on freedom of debate. At the
same time, the defence of the *ancien régime* or the international order
was made use of as a handy means of legitimizing the war effort, just as
counter-revolution was employed – most notably, by the British – as a
means of stirring up revolt inside France. But engaging in a total war to
restore Louis XVIII (Louis XVI's successor) was quite another matter.
A Bourbon on the throne of France might be a good thing in many
respects, but in the end it was something that could be sacrificed to
expediency, especially as the belligerents were divided as to what 'restoration' should actually mean, with the British, at least, advocating some
sort of constitutional settlement and others looking to a reconstituted
absolutism.

In France the concept of an ideological war was certainly much
stronger than elsewhere. In 1791–2 there had been real fears of a
counter-revolutionary crusade, while the Brissotins – the radical faction
that had championed the cause of war – had accompanied their demands
with much talk of sweeping the tyrants from their thrones. But appearances are deceptive. In large part the fears of foreign intervention were
a deliberate creation of the Brissotins, for whom war was primarily a
political tool designed to consolidate the Revolution and further their
personal ambition. And, despite their rhetoric, when France went to war

in April 1792, she did so only against Austria. Every effort was made to avoid conflict with Prussia, and get the Prussians to turn on their old enemies. The war the Brissotins got, then, was not at all the one they really wanted. With France hopelessly unprepared for such a struggle – her army was in disarray and the famous Volunteers of 1791 and 1792 a distinctly unreliable weapon – revolutionizing the Continent now gained real importance. But it was not just this: to some extent Brissot and his own followers simply became carried away with their own speech-making and drunk with vainglory; hence the glorious abandon with which they declared war on country after country in early 1793. Yet in the end their crusade amounted to very little. Late 1792 saw France offer to give help to any people who wished to recover their liberty, denounce the principles that lay behind such acts as the partition of Poland, and set up a variety of foreign legions whose task it was to raise the peoples of their home countries in revolt. But there were plenty of clear-sighted realists in Paris who realized that this was hopelessly impractical and unlikely to achieve anything in the way of results. Amongst them was Robespierre, and so practically the first act of the Committee of Public Safety was to make it quite clear that its watchword was France and France alone: amongst those who died under the guillotine in the summer of 1793 were a number of over-enthusiastic foreign revolutionaries. Under the Thermidorian regime and the Directory the pendulum swung back in the direction of aggression, but liberation was now but a word, albeit a useful one that allowed France's rulers to prove their revolutionary credentials. In Belgium and the left bank of the Rhine, it was code for annexation, and in Holland, where the first of a series of satellite republics were established, a euphemism for political, military and economic exploitation. And if revolution was supported elsewhere, most notably in Ireland, it was clearly little more than a device to weaken and disrupt the enemy. As for the specific goals of French policy, it was clear that many of them fitted in very closely with goals that had been enunciated at one time or another under the *ancien régime*. Also visible was an intellectual structure that had nothing revolutionary about it at all. At least one member of the Directory – Reubell – saw Belgium and the left bank of the Rhine simply as France's compensation for the gains made by the eastern powers in Poland. Ideological commitment to expansion was not completely dead: inside the Directory Reubell was challenged by the fiery Larevellière-Lépeaux, who was not only an erstwhile Brissotin, but the deputy who on 19 November 1792 had introduced the decree promising assistance to any people that wished to recover its liberty. But in general the watchword was calculation. Indeed, it is Schroeder's contention that, under the influence of the prime realist Carnot, the Directory wanted not a continuation of the war, but rather a general peace settlement: so anxious was the 'architect of victory' for this outcome, that he was even ready to forsake the Rhine frontier.

If peace was to be obtained, however, at the beginning of 1796 it appeared that it was going to have to be by force of arms, for Austria and Britain – the twin linchpins of opposition to the Republic – were by no means ready to make peace. Although under serious financial pressure, Austria was not yet desperate enough to consider a separate peace. In many ways this made sense: aside from the need to escape impending bankruptcy, by 1796 Austria's chief war aim was the acquisition of Bavaria in exchange for her territories in the Low Countries, and this, as Schroeder has shown, was more likely to be achieved through a deal with France than by any other means. But in reality, dropping out of the war was impossible. Should peace talks with France fail and Britain find out about Austria's double-dealing, Vienna could probably bid farewell to both British support for the so-called Bavarian exchange and, more importantly, a large loan she was currently trying to negotiate with London. Nor would a successful deal with France be much help: Austria might rationalize her frontiers in the west, but in doing so she would almost certainly risk war with Prussia and Russia, who were both likely to press for territorial compensation. In the circumstances then, fighting on, which in any case meshed with the personal fear and antipathy felt by the Austrian chancellor, Thugut, for the Revolution, seemed by far the safest option, for it at least locked in the Russians – also theoretically at war with France – into their alliance with Vienna, and thereby protected the gains Austria had made from the recent partitions of Poland and helped dissuade the Prussians from joining France (a real possibility that was certainly pursued by French diplomacy in the wake of Prussia's signature of a peace treaty with France in 1795). As for Britain, despite growing domestic unrest and the personal desire for peace of the prime minister, William Pitt, she too had no option but to fight on: secret contacts held with France in 1795 having suggested that, Carnot notwithstanding, the Directory would never abandon the Low

Countries unless absolutely forced to do so, anything but victory would signal complete humiliation.

So, with neither Britain nor Austria capable of taking the offensive at this point, the initiative lay with France, who could in any case afford to attack given the withdrawal of Prussia and Spain from the First Coalition in 1795. Napoleon naturally wanted to win the war on the Italian front – Barras claims that he bombarded 'the Directorate and Ministers with demands for men, money and clothing'.[38] This help was not forthcoming, for the Directory intended its main blows against the enemy to be rather a major invasion of Ireland and an offensive in southern Germany. Yet Napoleon still came to the fore. The expedition to Ireland was turned back by a 'Protestant wind', and the invasion of Germany defeated by the Austrians. In Italy, however, matters were very different: striking across the frontier from its base at Nice in April 1796, within a few short months Napoleon's ragged little army – at the beginning of the campaign he had only some 40,000 men, who Marmont describes as 'dying of hunger and almost without shoes'[39] – had forced Piedmont, Tuscany, Modena and the Papal States to make peace, over-run northern Italy, and beaten a succession of Austrian armies. With Vienna itself threatened with occupation, the badly shaken Austrians asked for an armistice, and an initial peace settlement was duly signed at Leoben on 18 April 1797.

By this time, moreover, Napoleon had become much more than a simple general. Very early on in the campaign, success in battle, the devotion of his troops, and a growing sense of his own power convinced him that he was a man of destiny. After the battle of Lodi – a relatively small action fought on 10 May 1796 in which Napoleon's forces launched a heroic attack across a narrow bridge defended by large numbers of Austrians – he claimed to have been filled with the sudden realization that 'I could well become . . . a decisive actor in our political scene'.[40] At the same time, French failures elsewhere – to which his own victories provided a vivid contrast – reinforced his importance to the Directory, and thus his political independence. Stimulated by the need to provide his small army with a secure base for its operations, not to mention a desire to play to the gallery and discredit his more pragmatic superiors, Napoleon therefore deliberately encouraged republican feeling, the result being the formation of, first, the temporary Cispadane and Transpadane Republics in October 1796 (which eight months later were united with still more territory as the Milan-based Cisalpine Republic) and then the Genoa-based Ligurian Republic in June 1797. With the initiative firmly in his hands, Napoleon was also effectively left to offer the Austrians peace terms of his own making, these finally being agreed in the Treaty of Campo Formio of 17 October 1797.

Though badly defeated militarily, Austria did remarkably well out of this settlement, gaining the bishopric of Salzburg and large parts of the old Venetian Republic, which was partitioned between her, the Cisalpine Republic and France (who took the Ionian islands). Indeed, Vienna's only loss other than Lombardy – the chief basis of the Cisalpine Republic – and such territories as she controlled on the left bank of the Rhine, was the Austrian Netherlands. Furthermore, the pill was sweetened by two important promises. First, Austria was to receive compensation in Germany, and second, Prussia was to be excluded from this settlement (to accommodate this position, Napoleon unilaterally renounced France's claim to all Prussia's Rhenish territories). Characteristically, however, Napoleon's magnanimity was the fruit of calculation: knowing that his rivals Hoche and Moreau were on the brink of a fresh invasion of Germany, the future emperor was desperate to stop the war before they stole some of his glory. As he told the Italian nobleman Miot de Melito in the summer of 1797, 'If I leave the signing of peace treaties to another man, he would be placed higher in public opinion than I am by my victories.'[41] Still worse, Campo Formio ran directly counter to the Directory's policy in Italy, which had been to use any territory gained there only as a bargaining tool that could be exchanged for Belgium and the left bank of the Rhine (the latter of which it failed to secure).

Campo Formio was not the only evidence of Napoleon's independence. Without telling Paris, for example, he approached the defeated Piedmontese with the offer of a military alliance in an attempt to swell his forces. And, in respect of Rome, whereas the Directory wanted a punitive peace settlement that would have seen the abolition of the Inquisition and the nullification of all the bulls the Church had issued anathematizing the Revolution, Napoleon chose rather to impose a more moderate treaty that cost the papacy much territory and a large indemnity but allowed it to keep most of its ideological pretensions. As for the clergy, while paying lip-service to Paris's rampant anti-clericalism, Napoleon flattered the local bishops and refrained from persecuting the many French priests who had fled to northern Italy. But in the face of this behaviour those members of the Directory who recognized the danger – and it should be remembered not all of them did so – were helpless. In May 1796, for example, an attempt to divide the Army of Italy into two separate forces was scotched by the threat of resignation, while in November a general dispatched by Carnot to force Napoleon to make an armistice with the Austrians was dealt with by the rather more subtle method of co-opting the officer concerned. Back in France, meanwhile, the Corsican general enjoyed a prominence that was hitherto unprecedented. Writing of his journey to take up his post with the Army of Italy, for example, Lavallette remarked:

I heard the name of Bonaparte everywhere as I went along; each day brought the name of a victory. His letters to the government, his proclamation worded in such lofty style and with such remarkable eloquence, went to everyone's heads. The whole of France shared the enthusiasm of the army for so much glory ... The names of Montenotte, of Milesimo, of Lodi, Milan, Castiglione, were repeatedly mentioned with a noble pride, together with those of Jemappes, of Fleurus and of Valmy.[42]

To quote Madame de Staël, 'In Paris General Bonaparte was being spoken of a great deal: the superiority of his spirit ... and his talents as a commander had given his name an importance superior to that acquired by any other individual since the start of the Revolution.'[43] And last but not least, the tutor of Napoleon's new step-daughter, Hortense de Beauharnais, was positively gushing: 'Did you know that your mother was going to unite her fortune with that of so extraordinary a man? What talents! What valour! Every instant a fresh conquest.'[44]

All this admiration was in large part a creation of Napoleon himself. Whether he really did suddenly have a vision of himself as ruler of France after the battle of Lodi will never be known, but what is clear is that from very early on in the campaign he threw himself into the task of winning the favour of public opinion. One plank in this policy was to appear a model of civic virtue. 'Bonaparte, who still wears the woollen epaulettes of his first years of military life, preserves up to this time the outward garb of modesty both in his utterances and his habiliments; 'tis in the name of liberty he issues his proclamations.'[45] Another was to placate the Directory with loot. This ploy operated at two levels. In the first place, Paris's increasingly desperate need for money was assuaged by the imposition of a variety of fines and levies that had by the end of 1796 alone netted well over 45 million francs in cash and another 12 million in terms of plate and jewels. And, in the second, the Revolution's cultural pretensions were flattered by the dispatch of large numbers of pictures, statues and other artistic treasures. Finally, there was also the issue of propaganda. For the first time the young general found himself in a position in which he could manipulate his public image: hence the famous painting he commissioned in the wake of the battle of Arcola with its suggestion of both conquering hero and man of the future, and hence, too, his establishing of no fewer than three newspapers whose sole task it was to sing his praises.

If propaganda was important, so also was man-management. No sooner had he been appointed to the Italian command, than Napoleon surrounded himself with a band of officers who could be relied upon as talented and trusted henchmen. Among these men were Jean Andoche Junot and Auguste Marmont, who had both met Napoleon at Toulon and later shared the lean months of 1795 with him; another Toulon veteran named Charles Leclerc, who was in June 1797 picked out as a suitable husband for Napoleon's sister, Pauline; Guillaume Brune, a brigade commander who had distinguished himself in the Vendémiaire affair; Jean-Baptiste Bessières, a Gascon cavalryman recommended to him by Joachim Murat; and lastly Murat himself, the officer responsible for bringing up the guns that had actually fired the 'whiff of grapeshot'. To this group were added many of the existing commanders of the Army of Italy – Berthier, Augereau, Masséna, Lannes, Sérurier – whose initial resentment and suspicion of the 'political' general sent to lead them was overcome by a mixture of cajolery, bribery and sheer force of character. Following the example of Napoleon himself, who beyond doubt became a rich man as a result of his victories, the generals were also permitted to feather their own nests: both Masséna and Augereau developed a particular reputation for rapaciousness, while Marmont was seemingly reproved for not having taken full advantage of the opportunities open to him.

But building up the Army of Italy as a powerbase was not just a question of packing it with his friends or winning the loyalty of a few leading officers. As comes over from the memoirs of General Thiébault, the net was cast much wider.

Bonaparte . . . did his utmost to appeal in every possible way to the imagination of his soldiers. His phrases, no less fortunate, than full of meaning, were repeated with enthusiasm; his familiarities gave rise to many anecdotes . . . Promotions were showered upon the army, plenty prevailed in it, and he took infinite pains to be every man's pride and hope. But all this seemed insufficient for him, and he employed ridicule to amuse his soldiers, while making them despise their enemy. Thus . . . the barracks and cantonments were flooded with a squib, comically imagined and wittily composed. The soldiers read it and repeated it with shouts of laughter. It contained the humble remonstrance of the grenadiers of the Army of Italy to the high, mighty and invincible Emperor of Austria, who was designated by any number of absurd titles and epithets. It began by thanking him for the young volunteers whom he had been so kind as to send from Vienna, and by asking him for more, while complaining that the pantaloons he gave his soldiers were too scanty and the cloaks too short . . . that the soldiers never had any money in their pockets, and that none of them had a watch . . . It was only mess-room chaff, but the soldiers found it excellent, and that was what was wanted.[46]

Clever though his use of humour was, the real key to Napoleon's success was logistics. Sadly, the famous proclamation that he issued to the Army of Italy when he took command on the eve of the campaign is now generally recognized to be a later fabrication. At the same time outright marauding was forbidden, albeit more because it was a threat to military efficiency and discipline than because it was reprehensible in itself (not that this did much to reduce the problem). Yet it is clear that the promises supposedly made by Napoleon to his men were honoured: the soldiers were quite literally fed, clothed and, most importantly, paid from their conquests. Directly or indirectly, the loyalty of the soldiers was won through an appeal to their self-interest whereas hitherto the language used in proclamations and battlefield harangues had been very much that of patriotism and civic virtue. On top of all this, they were constantly flattered as men who had over and over again triumphed against all odds, not to mention men whom their general was counting on in person. Given that Napoleon also took care to appear to share their dangers, whether it was by aiming a battery of cannon under enemy fire at Lodi or taking part in an assault on a crucial bridge at Arcola, there emerged the makings of the strong bond between Napoleon and his soldiers that was to sustain the French army right through to 1815. By the middle of 1797, in fact, the Army of Italy no longer served France but Napoleon, who in consequence felt safe to employ the most ambiguous bombast: 'Mountains separate us from France, but were it necessary to uphold the constitution, to defend liberty, to protect the government and the Republicans, then you would cross them with the speed of an eagle.'[47]

Through a combination of brilliant generalship and his skill as a leader of men, Napoleon had acquired a position of extraordinary power in the French body politic. As hostilities with Austria drew to a close this was confirmed in dramatic fashion. In the spring of 1797 the government suffered a severe defeat in partial general elections. What all this meant in political terms is very complicated, but it certainly did not portend, as many lives of Napoleon have claimed, a major threat to the Republic. Assisted by British patronage, a number of committed royalists were active in France and their propaganda activities may well have done something to increase the scale of the government's defeat. But, the activities of a minority of extremists notwithstanding, royalism as such was not a problem. Very few royalists were outright absolutists, and the election result was above all the reflection of a growing desire for peace, political reconciliation and social stability. What threatened the Revolution was therefore not restoration but compromise, but for all those who calculated that their best interests lay in a continuation of the war this was quite bad enough. Very soon, then, a coup was being contemplated by the three members of the Directory committed to a continuation of the war, and in this they immediately received the support of both Napoleon and Hoche. One might, indeed, go further here. The radical faction in the Directory were active participants in the drama, certainly, but they were also in no doubt whatsoever as to the line that Napoleon expected them to take. On 14 July he issued a proclamation to his troops, calling on them to make ready to defend the Republic against its internal enemies, while the next day he sent a letter to the Directory threatening to resign unless it took immediate action against the royalists. With their position buttressed by the fortuitous arrival outside the capital of 10,000 men from Hoche's army who were being transferred to the Channel coast, the radicals needed no further urging. Napoleon's subordinate, Augereau, was appointed to take command of the garrison of the capital, and on 4 September (18 Fructidor) the axe finally fell. The moderates in the Directory – Carnot and a new appointment named Barthélemy – were arrested and the Assembly purged. Though Napoleon had not acted alone, the message was clear enough: France was ruled by the bayonet. Nor was this an end to it: Hoche had for some time been a sick man, and on 19 September he died at Wetzlar. If the bayonet ruled France it was Napoleon who ruled the bayonet.

If the victor of Lodi, Arcola and Rivoli was starting to develop concrete ambitions on the political front, it was hardly surprising. If the opportunity was there, so too was the experience. As soon as active campaigning ended, Napoleon had installed himself in the sumptuous Mombello palace outside Milan, and here he established what can only be described as a private court. Old friends such as Bourrienne, who had been favoured with appointment as his secretary, found themselves reduced to the role of minions: 'Here ceased my intercourse with him as equal to equal, companion with companion, and those relations commenced in which I saw him great, powerful and surrounded with homage and glory. I no longer addressed him as formerly; I was too well aware of his personal importance.'[48] De facto ruler of the Cisalpine Republic, he gave himself the airs of a hereditary prince, such an impression being strengthened by the appearance at his headquarters of not just Josephine, but her children, Eugène and Hortense, his mother and several of his sisters. For a taste of the atmosphere that prevailed, let us turn to Miot de Melito:

I was received by Bonaparte . . . in the midst of a brilliant court rather than the usual army headquarters I had expected. Strict etiquette already reigned around him. Even his aides-de-camp and his officers were no longer received at his table, for he had become fastidious in the choice of guest whom he admitted to it. An invitation was an honour eagerly sought, and obtained only with great difficulty . . . He was in no wise embarrassed . . . by these excessive honours, but received them as though he had been accustomed to them all his life. His reception . . . rooms were constantly filled with a crowd of generals, administrators and the most distinguished gentlemen of Italy, who came to solicit the favour of a momentary glance or the briefest interview. In a word, all bowed before the glory of his victories and the haughtiness of his demeanour. He was no longer the general of a triumphant republic, but a conqueror on his own account.[49]

An important point is hit on here. Like many of his classical heroes, Napoleon found himself, as Miot de Melito remarks, in the role not just of general but of law-maker, for the Cisalpine Republic had to be provided with a constitution and a code of law. To advise him, there came flocking all the leading literati of Lombardy, while like any enlightened absolutist of the century that was about to close, Napoleon patronized the arts and interested himself in agriculture, education and public works. To naked ambition, then, there was added self-delusion: almost overnight, the Corsican adventurer had become in his own eyes the benefactor of humanity.

All this, it is safe to say, turned Napoleon's head completely. As he remarked, 'I have tasted supremacy and I can no longer renounce it.'[50] Meanwhile, his flights of fancy became ever more extreme: 'What I have done so far is nothing. I am only at the beginning of the course that I must run. Do you think that I am triumphing in Italy merely to . . . found a republic?'[51] By the middle of 1797, in fact, Napoleon was thinking of seizing control of the French government: he openly spoke of not wanting to leave Italy unless it was to play 'a role in France resembling the one I have here', and further remarked, 'The Parisian lawyers who have been put in charge of the Directory understand nothing of government. They are mean-minded men . . . I very much doubt that we can remain in agreement much longer.'[52] If the Directors were 'mean-minded' they were also utterly corrupt, as, in fact, was much of the civilian administration. A certain caution is needed here: after 18 Brumaire Napoleon had every reason to exaggerate the crimes of his predecessors and his lead has naturally been followed by all those who have sought to propagate his legend, but in the end the Directory will only bear a certain degree of refurbishment: such figures as Barras and Talleyrand really were deeply venal. And this, of course, could only encourage Napoleon. In Bourrienne's words, 'He despised the Directory, which he accused of weakness, indecision, extravagance, and a perseverance in a system degrading to the national glory.'[53]

Napoleon would not just rule France, then, but also save her, this dream being strengthened still further by the situation that he found when he finally returned to France early in December 1797 after inaugurating the Congress of Rastatt. The paper money which had been keeping France going since the Revolution had become so worthless that it had

had to be suppressed, hard currency was in short supply, and the urban poor were being ravaged by bread prices that were almost as high as those which had brought the crowd on to the streets in 1789. On top of this, while the Directory could hardly avoid giving Napoleon a hero's welcome, it was clear that beyond its ranks the general enjoyed immense popularity. According to Laure Permon:

However great the vanity of Bonaparte, it cannot but have been satisfied by the manner in which people of every class gathered . . . to greet his return to the fatherland. The populace cried, 'Long live Bonaparte! Long live the victor of Italy! Long live the peace-maker of Campo Formio!' The bourgeoisie exclaimed, 'God keep him! May he save us from the *maximum* and the directors!' And the upper classes . . . flocked with enthusiasm to the young man who in one year had gone from the battle of Montenotte to the treaty of Leoben. Faults . . . he may well have committed, but at that moment he was a colossus of glory as great as it was pure![54]

Also interesting here is Germaine de Staël, who was a witness to the great reception which the Directory arranged for Napoleon in the Luxembourg Palace.

No room would have been big enough to accommodate the crowds that turned up: there were spectators at every window and on every roof. Dressed in Roman costume, the five Directors were placed on a dais at one end of the courtyard, and nearby the members of the two councils, the high courts and the institute. If this spectacle had taken place before the National Assembly had bowed the knee to military despotism on 18 Fructidor, it might have been thought very grand: a fine band was playing patriotic airs, and flags recalling our great victories draped the dais of the Directory. Bonaparte arrived dressed very simply and followed by his aides-de-camp: all of them were taller than the general, but such was the humility of their demeanour that they seemed to be dwarfed by him. As for the elite of France there present, they deluged him with applause: republicans, royalists and everyone alike saw their present and future in terms of the support of his powerful hand.[55]

Predictably enough, all this did little to assuage Napoleon's contempt for civilian politicians and personal ambition. On the contrary, as Gohier noted:

Far from being satisfied with the solemn reception which he was accorded on his return from Italy ... Bonaparte saw in the pomp in which it was couched nothing more than the desire of the Directory to parade itself in all its glory ... To satisfy his vanity, it would have been necessary to allow him to present himself to the people all by himself in a triumphal chariot.[56]

At all events, having returned to Paris, Napoleon lost no time in sounding out a variety of contacts with regard to realizing his ambitions (a process he had in fact embarked upon before he had even left Italy). His initial plan was to get himself elected to the Directory and then seize power in conjunction with one or more of its members prior to rewriting the constitution so as to give much greater weight to the executive power (and with it, needless to say, himself). But in this he was unsuccessful. No one who mattered was willing to throw themselves on his mercy at this point and some of those to whom he turned as old allies, such as Barras, were now increasingly fearful of him. For the time being, then, there was nothing to do but embark on a search for still more glory. Action, in fact, was essential, for, as he remarked, 'In Paris nothing is remembered for long. If I remain doing nothing ... I am lost.'[57] To suggest that this restless energy and ambition now became the only factor in the determination of French policy would be incorrect, but the fact was that Napoleon had already had a massive impact on France's relations with the rest of Europe and imparted a direction to the international history of the Continent that would otherwise have been lacking. At the beginning of 1796 the Directory had been set on a course that saw it bent on the military defeat of Britain and Austria and their remaining allies, most of which were to be found amongst the minor states of Italy. With Prussia out of the war, Russia little interested in the affairs of Western Europe and Spain on the brink of becoming a French ally, there was every reason to expect that France's goal – the formal abandonment of the Bourbons and the confirmation of her acquisition of the Rhineland and the left bank of the Rhine – would be achieved through the exhaustion of her enemies alone. Austria was almost bankrupt, and even Britain was finding the demands of the war difficult to bear. Individual members of the Directory may have taken a different line, but no general plan of conquest – or, if it is preferred, liberation – was under consideration. And, when conquests were suddenly showered on Paris (from a totally unexpected direction), the plan was still to use them as bargaining counters that could be exchanged for France's real aims. What changed all this was Napoleon. By embarking on a course of republicanization in Italy, while at the same time cynically partitioning the neutral Republic of Venice with Austria, he set off a chain reaction. As Vienna could not now be bought off by the return of Lombardy, she would instead have to be offered territory in Germany. But, given the Austrian insistence – acceded to by Napoleon – that Prussia should have no part in these proceedings, France was now risking war with Potsdam. In the event this danger was avoided, for at Rastatt the French delegation demanded the whole of the left bank of the Rhine, which in turn implied giving Prussia her place at the German trough. Yet all this meant was the probability of fresh trouble in Italy, where the Habsburgs resented the loss of Mantua, and were likely to respond to Prussian expansion in Germany with demands for the relevant strip of Lombardy.

For reasons that were not solely the fault of Napoleon, France was now also committed to further expansion. As the Cisalpine Republic now had to be protected, the occupation of Switzerland, or to put it another way, the direct route between Paris and Milan, had become an immediate necessity. All over Italy patriots were in a state of ferment. And in Paris the men associated with the coup of 18 Fructidor were in the first place terrified by the spectre of military intervention, in the second greedy for more gold, and in the third committed to a Jacobinism for whose social aspects they had no enthusiasm whatsoever. Whether it was to satisfy the generals, line their own pockets and those of the bankrupt French treasury, or live up to the radical image conjured up in the defeat of Carnot and the 'royalists', there was only one way forward. Within a few months, a new republic had been established in Rome, but all this did was to make some Austrian counterstroke more likely, and all the more so as Vienna's agreement to territorial change in Germany was certain to strip it of most of its main supporters in the Holy Roman Empire and, by extension, likely to lead it to seek compensation in greater control in Italy. Also gone was the possibility of a compromise settlement with Britain: early in 1797 the British had opened peace negotiations with the Directory, but they had collapsed in the wake of Fructidor, while the radicalism of the next few months persuaded Pitt and his ministers that France was once again in the grip of a criminal regime that was quite beyond the pale. There was now, as the British politician William Windham noted, no probability of 'any good settlement with France, except by means of civil war aided by war from without'.[58]

It is possible to go too far here. Peace might well have been obtained with Britain in 1797, but it can be argued that, so long as there was no willingness to set aside centuries of Anglo-French rivalry, it would have been inherently unstable. By the same token, meanwhile, limiting France's ambitions to the Rhine frontier would not necessarily have bought peace in Germany. But that is by-the-by, the fact being that Fructidor and Campo Formio perpetuated the war with Britain, and made a resumption of conflict with Austria much more likely. Thanks in large part to Napoleon, the threat of active opposition also now began to emerge from still another direction. Hitherto Russia had in effect stayed out of the war with France. Though ruled by a monarch who was ferocious in her denunciation of the Revolution and theoretically a member of the First Coalition, she had done nothing: rather than fighting France, what mattered had been consolidating Moscow's gains in Poland. In 1796, the bellicose and ruthlessly expansionist Catherine II died and was replaced by her son, Paul I, whose reputation as a military martinet cloaked a strong desire for a pacific foreign policy that would allow him to concentrate on domestic reform. In a variety of ways, however, Napoleon's actions had seriously jeopardized this de facto neutrality. Simply by conquering northern Italy, he had greatly alarmed Catherine, who by 1796 had Poland completely under control, and it is highly probable that, had she lived, Russian troops would have been dispatched to the Alps or the Adriatic. From this problem Napoleon was saved by the demise of Catherine, but he continued to dice with the danger, not the least of the risks that he took here being to feign the role of a patron of Polish independence. Although the Directory had for obvious reasons set its face against such a scheme (the formation of some sort of army in exile had, in fact, been advocated on several occasions by Polish refugees who had reached Paris), in 1797 Napoleon recruited a large number of Polish prisoners of war into a special force which was put at the disposal of the Cisalpine Republic. Known as the Polish Auxiliary Legion, this soon became the size of a small division – at its greatest size it might have consisted of some 6,000 men – while, to add insult to injury, it was placed under the command of a hero of the revolt of 1794 named Dabrowski. Needless to say, Napoleon was utterly uninterested in liberating Poland – aside from gaining a few more men, his chief interest seems rather to have lain in providing the Cisalpine Republic with a disciplined force of veteran soldiers who could be relied upon to uphold the regime – but that did not stop him from allowing Dabrowski to issue a revolutionary manifesto calling all his fellow countrymen to arms. Moreover, the Legion adopted uniforms of a traditional Polish cut and were guaranteed the right to return to Poland in the event that their countrymen had need of them.

Having upset Russia in one direction, Napoleon now proceeded to do so in another. For a variety of reasons, Greece and the eastern Mediterranean had long been an area of Russian interest. Under the influence of Prince Grigori Potemkin, Catherine II had seriously considered establishing a satellite state in Greece on the ruins of the Ottoman Empire. In the end this scheme had not been implemented, but it had not been fully set aside either: for the time being Greece might remain Turkish, but no one was in any doubt that, when the time came to expel the Turks from Europe, it would be Russia that had first claim on the Hellenic world. Napoleon, however, had other ideas. For reasons that are not quite clear, at some point during the Italian campaign the French commander's eyes turned east. Egypt certainly crossed his mind as his next objective – he raised the idea several times in letters to the Directory – and it was undoubtedly to this end that he suddenly proposed that France should seize Malta. Why, though, should he have decided to take the Ionian islands – the most notable are Corfu, Zante and Cephalonia – as France's share in the rape of Venice? Like Malta, they were useful naval bases, but, unlike Malta they were also birds in the hand – an important consideration given the need to find an immediate home for the Venetian navy (which Napoleon had been careful to secure for France). At the same time they were useful territories that might be ceded to Constantinople in return for the surrender of Egypt, or, alternatively, employed as a focus for Greek nationalism that might put pressure on the Turks. Then again, their acquisition allowed Napoleon once more to play the liberator, while ensuring that Austria was denied unrestricted access to the Adriatic and guaranteeing France a share in the Ottoman Empire should it be partitioned. Yet another argument, and one advanced by Napoleon himself, was that they were important to France's trade as stepping stones for the importation of Egyptian cotton. And, finally, they were simply *there*: presented with the opportunity to bait the Russian bear, the French commander could not resist the opportunity to do so.

Whatever the reason for Napoleon's actions with regard to the Ionian islands, there is no doubt that they deeply upset Russia. In themselves, however, they were not sufficient to persuade Paul I to go to war. What counted here was the Egyptian campaign of 1798. In some accounts this too has been laid at the door of Napoleon, but in fact this is unfair: the future emperor was not the scheme's only backer, and in some ways not even its most important one. Nevertheless, the usual pride and ambition played a part. Ordered to take command of preparations for the invasion of Britain favoured by the Directory as its next move in the conflict, early in 1798 Napoleon took one look at the scheme's prospects and refused point-blank to have anything to do with it, there being no way that he was prepared to risk seeing his reputation lost with all hands in some watery grave in the English Channel; or, for that matter, cool his heels in Calais or Boulogne for the long months that would pass before an invasion could even be attempted. Eager for some sphere of action, at this point he promptly revived the scheme for the invasion of Egypt which he had mentioned the previous summer: 'An expedition could be made into the Levant which would threaten the commerce of India.'[59]

In acting in this fashion, Napoleon was in part responding to some romantic lure of the East. To quote Bourrienne, 'The east presented a field of conquest and glory on which his imagination delighted to brood. "Europe", said he, "is but a molehill – all the great reputations have come from Asia."'[60] Yet Napoleon's own words suggest something rather different:

The seductions of an oriental conquest turned me aside from thoughts of Europe more than I would have believed . . . In Egypt I found myself freed from the obstacles of an irksome civilization. I was full of dreams . . . I saw myself founding a religion, marching into Asia, riding an elephant, a turban on my head, and in my hand the new Koran that I would have composed to suit my needs. In my undertakings I would have combined the experiences of the two worlds, exploiting for my own profit the theatre of all history . . . The time I spent in Egypt was the most beautiful of my life.[61]

In short, the dreams of becoming a new Alexander the Great came only *after* Napoleon had arrived in Egypt and not before. What mattered in the first weeks of 1798 were rather more mundane considerations, as chronicled by Germaine de Staël:

Bonaparte was always looking for means of engaging men's imagination, and so far as this was concerned he knew exactly how they may be governed when one is not born to a throne. An invasion of Africa, a war waged in a country that was almost fabulous, as was the case with Egypt, could not but work on every spirit. Meanwhile, it would be easy to persuade the French that they would derive great benefit from a Mediterranean colony, and that one day it would offer them some means of attacking the establishments of the English in India. As for the project, it was laden with glory, and would add further lustre to the name of Bonaparte. If he had stayed in France, by contrast, the Directory would have hurled . . . calumnies without number at him and tarnished his reputation . . . Bonaparte would have been broken to smithereens before the thunderbolt had even struck him. In consequence, he had good reason to want to make himself the stuff of poetry rather than leave himself exposed to Jacobin tittle-tattle.[62]

On top of all this, Napoleon was desperate for action for its own sake. 'This city of Paris,' he complained, 'weighs down on me as if I was covered by a lead blanket.'[63] As he later told Claire de Rémusat, 'I do not know what would have become of me had I not had the happy idea of going to Egypt.'[64]

But was going to Egypt really a 'happy idea'? If the country could have been run by France for her own benefit as some sort of dependency, then the gains would doubtless have been enormous. Equally, choosing Egypt as his goal was a clever stroke on Napoleon's part, as it allowed him to pose as a patron of the arts: with interest growing in Egypt's ancient past, this fresh adventure from the start had a veneer of cultural respectability that the Corsican general was careful to strengthen by drafting the services of a select band of intellectuals. From a tactical point of view, however, getting a large army from one end of the Mediterranean to the other would be some task: the British might not have had any ships in the Mediterranean at the beginning of 1798 (they had withdrawn their squadron from the theatre in 1796), but they were present in strength at Gibraltar and could get a powerful fleet to the area around Malta and Sicily within a few days. But supposing the French reached Egypt, what then? Should the British choose to do so, they could easily cut the invaders off from France: the French record at sea was less than spectacular, and there was no reason to suppose that the Toulon fleet's thirteen ships of the line would be able to fight off a substantial British attack (several of the ships were in poor condition and there was a serious shortage of trained crewmen). And if this was so, how could Egypt be exploited as a source of cotton and other colonial produce? In any event, the country would first have to be conquered and this would not be easy. The troops would be operating in a climate to which they were utterly unaccustomed and would be exposed to the ravages of disease of every sort. In addition, Egypt was an enormous country composed in large part of barren deserts and mountains, while its defenders, however pitifully armed and organized by European standards, heavily outnumbered Napoleon's forces. Alexandria and Cairo could be taken easily enough, but what about Upper Egypt or the Red Sea coast? At risk was a long and costly campaign in which the French could expect little in the way of reinforcements.

Let us say, however, that conquest was achieved. What then? As Egypt was of no importance to Britain in commercial terms the mere fact of seizing her was not much of a blow to her trade. What mattered was India, but this simply raised fresh problems. A march on India in the style of Alexander the Great's advance to the Indus was hopelessly impractical, but other schemes made little sense either. A maritime invasion, for example, would have required the construction of a fleet of warships and transports on the other side of Egypt on a coast that lacked adequate port facilities and in a sea whose only exit could easily be blockaded by the Royal Navy (it is pointless here to talk of the Suez Canal *avant la lettre* that was spoken of by Napoleon's instructions: even if the country was pacified overnight, such a project would have required years to complete). Then there was the possibility of commerce raiding. However, in this respect, too, the prospects were hardly glowing. A few privateers might somehow have been fitted out from local shipping, and Suez or Qusseir established as a new base for the French raiders already operating in the Indian Ocean, but the Red Sea was an inconvenient spot from which to operate, and it is hard to see how the cost of invading Egypt would have justified the marginal gains in operating capacity that would have been added to the possibilities already offered by the French island of Mauritius. And, finally, if the gains were likely to be marginal, there was also the issue of international relations. The Turks, it was supposed, would not fight – though nominally subject to Turkish suzerainty, Egypt was in practice self-governing and brought in very little profit to Constantinople – and, even if they did so, they were not much of a threat. But it was not just a question of the Turks: invading the eastern Mediterranean would almost certainly bring in Russia – Paul I had just given notice of his intention to take a stand by declaring himself to be the protector of Malta or, more precisely, its rulers, the Knights of St John – and this in turn might easily persuade Austria to push for more territory in Italy.

Invading Egypt, then, was rank madness, for success was dependent on the near impossibility of Britain declining to take substantial action in response to the French move. Indeed, only one strategy would have made it worthwhile: were the Royal Navy to be seriously distracted by the stab at Egypt – in other words, if the Cabinet panicked in the face of the lobbying that could be expected from the East India Company – it is just possible that an invasion army might have been rushed across the Channel. Yet no steps were taken to organize such an expedition. To look upon the expedition in conventional terms therefore seems unwise, and it is in fact perfectly possible to find other explanations. Beginning with Napoleon, the plan seems to have been that he would get his army to Egypt, send the French fleet back to safety in Corfu, secure some immediate victories and then slip back to France in a fast frigate so as to exploit the fruits of his apparent triumph. In short, to quote Marmont, 'Finding opportunities to keep his name in the spotlight ... was the limit of his thought.'[65] But what of the scheme's other main sponsor, the French Foreign Minister, Charles-Maurice de Talleyrand? He, one suspects, was playing an even subtler game. Desperate to secure international acceptance of the new France, it seems probable that his aim was to divert the Republic's aggression and in particular the lust for glory of its most famous commander, into areas that would not cause the powers simply to throw up their hands in horror. What he aimed at, in short, was to initiate the partition of the Ottoman Empire and thereby draw Austria and Russia into a de facto coalition with France. Britain, meanwhile, would be isolated and wild talk of revolutionizing Europe would fade from the scene. As for the problem of Napoleon, Talleyrand's thinking is clear enough. He had originally seen him as a potential ally in his campaign to restore order and international respectability to France but this belief had been badly shaken by the conquest of Italy. Despite attempts to argue otherwise, the inference seems to be that he was betting that the general would not be able to get back to France in the short term. And, of course, he might go down to ruinous defeat, in which case Talleyrand would still come out on top, for a defeated Napoleon would be a useful scapegoat for the foreign minister himself and a 'busted flush' who would have lost all credibility in Paris with a Directory that had never been entirely happy with the expedition.

Whatever the thinking behind it, on 19 May 1798 the great expedition sailed for Egypt. In naval and military terms, there is little need to go into what happened next. Having quickly captured Malta, Napoleon dodged Nelson's fleet and reached Egypt safely, whereupon the French forces occupied Cairo to the accompaniment of the dazzling victory of the Pyramids. But at this point things went wrong. The French fleet was destroyed at the battle of Aboukir; Turkey, Naples, Austria and Russia all went to war; the French were driven from most of Italy; short-lived success in Naples, which had been transformed into the so-called Parthenopaean Republic in January 1799, was cancelled out in a welter of blood-letting and peasant revolt; and Napoleon himself was for some time precluded from returning to France by the need to rescue his reputation from the loss of his ships. In their different ways, then, both Napoleon and Talleyrand were foiled. Yet the former, at least, remained undaunted. Although an invasion of Palestine failed before the walls of Acre, Napoleon clinched the glory that he needed by literally wiping out a Turkish army of 9,000 men in the second battle of Aboukir (25 July 1799), at which point he fortuitously obtained a packet of European newspapers. Suggesting as these did that France was on the brink of complete defeat, this was all Napoleon needed, and less than a month later he secretly took ship for France, accompanied only by a small group of trusted cronies. With Egypt seemingly securely in the hands of the French and a string of fresh victories under his belt, there were just enough grounds for him to be able to affect the role of conquering hero once again. Bolstered by the arrival just prior to his surprise reappearance of a series of official dispatches that glossed over the failure in the Holy Land, painted the French position in the most roseate of hues and exaggerated the scale of his battlefield triumphs, Napoleon was greeted with great excitement. Hence the scenes witnessed when Napoleon made landfall at Fréjus on 9 October:

An officer rowed to the beach in a boat. We could see him quite clearly. Some men came to meet him, but scarcely had a few seconds passed than we perceived a great commotion: people were running towards the town, and soon the beach was covered by a huge crowd. Boats were loaded with passengers, and . . . a horde of people quickly climbed through the portholes into the ship . . . Soon there was no possibility of the general being mistaken as to the feelings of the entire population. 'You only can save France,' they cried to him on all sides. 'Without you she perishes. You are sent by Heaven: take up the reins of government!'[66]

Nor did things change thereafter. 'Our journey from Fréjus to Paris', wrote Napoleon's stepson, Eugène de Beauharnais, 'was a triumphal progress. One single sentiment animated the entire French people and indicated to Napoleon what he should do. At Lyons, especially, the joy of the inhabitants reached the pitch of delirium.'[67] As for the capital, here too spirits were high. To quote one of the future emperor's most enthusiastic collaborators:

On his arrival Bonaparte took up his residence at the little house that he had bought in the Rue Chantereine . . . This was soon thronged with all the leading personalities of the government, the legislature, the army and the Institute, together with all those who exercised some degree of personal influence . . . Every heart was so overflowing with joy, admiration and love at the return of the hero that, whilst nobody actually acknowledged the fact that he possessed supreme power, everybody recognized this to be the case.[68]

The reasons for this excitement are understandable. For men of property the domestic situation had become increasingly intolerable. The economy was in ruins; law and order had in many rural areas almost completely broken down due to the immense numbers of men who had been forced into brigandage by poverty and conscription; there had been a resumption of revolt in the Vendée and further trouble in Belgium; and the great military crisis of 1799 was only resolved by once more resorting to measures that recalled the Terror of 1793. To deal with these problems, it was felt that France needed a greatly reinforced executive power, the Directory having proved not just corrupt but incapable of imposing the required degree of authority. Meanwhile, for a much wider spectrum of society, what mattered was peace and with it cheap bread and an end to forced military service. And for rich and poor alike there was the further need for victory, and with it the consolidation of the gains they had made since 1789. The result was inevitable. As Napoleon's future Minister of the Interior, Jean Antoine Chaptal wrote:

In this state of affairs, it was announced that General Bonaparte had disembarked at Fréjus. The news spread with the speed of light. Hope was reborn in every heart. All the parties rallied to him. The remembrance of his brilliant campaign in Italy, the memorable achievements of his armies in Egypt, did not permit any other choice. He was carried in triumph from Fréjus to Paris, and some days later proclaimed First Consul.[69]

This, of course, is much too simplistic. Modern scholars recognize that France's condition was by no means as dark as it was painted by Napoleon's later apologists and collaborators. In reality, the Directory had introduced a variety of salutary reforms that in principle gave the Republic a much stronger army and a more effective fiscal system. Meanwhile, a series of good harvests had reduced food prices very considerably, while the twin menace of rebellion and military defeat had been overcome. At the same time, one should neither be too deterministic about the consulate nor forget that the plot that brought Napoleon to power was the work, not of *l'italique*, but of a group of civilian politicians who were not even thinking of Napoleon as the 'sword' that could execute their will – had he not fallen at the battle of Novi, the general in command would probably have been Joubert, whilst Sieyès was supposedly actually engaged in the task of persuading Moreau to accept the role when he received the news that the conqueror of Egypt had landed. The arrival of a Napoleon bent on establishing himself in power completely changed the situation however. It was a decisive moment, and one that finally brought Napoleon to the top. As Germaine de Staël recalled, 'It was the first time since the Revolution that one heard one name in every mouth. Until then it had always been "the Constituent Assembly, the people, the Convention". Now, however, nobody spoke of anyone except the man who was going to take the place of everyone else and render the human race anonymous.'[70]

In a sense, then, we are back where we started. Although we have yet to examine the process by which this occurred, France was in the hands of a single towering personality. Given what we have seen of the evolution of Napoleon's character, there can be no doubt what this portended. For all the claims of his apologists, a critical review of the new

French ruler's early years produces a picture of a man who was very far from being the hero and liberator of legend. So far as Napoleon was concerned, by 1799 ideology was something that he had jettisoned long ago. Moreover, even when it had been a genuine part of his life, it seems clear that it was never there for its own sake. Let us take, for example, Napoleon's Corsican nationalism. Fierce though this was, in the end it was at heart an affectation. In his schoolboy years a means of asserting his personality, it very quickly became merely a vehicle for his family interests and vaunting personal ambition, and was jettisoned as soon as it became clear that the Bonaparte clan had lost the battle to secure control of its native island. Much the same applies, meanwhile, to Napoleon's Jacobinism. Privately disgusted by the excesses of the Revolution, he very quickly became convinced that the radical politicians who egged on such scenes were no more than self-seeking demagogues. Yet recognizing the power of their ideas and, above all, their importance in the army, which remained the element in French society most devoted to the radicalism of 1792–3, he made use of them to establish an unassailable powerbase in its ranks. But throughout, ideology was a matter of secondary importance to him. In northern Italy he defied government policy to set up the Ligurian and Cisalpine Republics, but this overtly liberationist behaviour was countered by his refusal to impose a peace on the Papal States that would have shattered the temporal power of the papacy, and his cession of much of Venice to the Habsburgs. In Egypt, too, the same cavalier attitude was apparent. Napoleon was – personally speaking – deeply irreligious, and yet in Cairo he flirted with Islam and proclaimed his intention of governing in accordance with the Koran in the vain hope that this would win the cooperation of the local elite and stave off the threat of Turkish intervention. In the same way, in Italy he had flattered the local bishops and pretended that he was a friend of the Catholic Church. As he famously remarked in August 1800, 'It was by declaring myself to be Catholic that I finished the war in the Vendée, by declaring myself to be Muslim that I established myself in Egypt, in declaring myself to be ultramontane that I won over the hearts of the Italians. If I governed a nation of Jews, I would re-establish the Temple of Solomon.'[71]

According to Napoleon's apologists, this cynicism was only apparent: all he wanted was to govern all men as they wished to be governed and to treat all religions with equal respect. Such arguments, however, are at best disingenuous. For Napoleon all that really mattered was the pursuit of power and his own glorification. He sought to bind these in with ideas of the national interest and the defence of the Revolution, but in the end they were simply to be enjoyed for their own sake. In the words of one embittered politician, 'Bonaparte has never known anything but absolute power ... It is so gratifying to find oneself surrounded, solicited, flattered; to be able to distribute benefits amongst one's family and friends; to conquer ever more opulence and grandeur.'[72] What did this mean for international relations? In later years Napoleon always attempted to minimize the impact of his activities from 1796 to 1799. The Directory, he argued, needed war and, in consequence, he had simply been its instrument. However, whilst war brought much plunder to France, it also caused such difficulties on the home front that peace became a prerequisite of political and social stability. But for Napoleon it seems quite clear that such a peace might have been obtained in 1797, for Austria was defeated militarily and Britain willing to come to terms. Equally, although he was not the only actor in the drama, without Napoleon there would have been no breach with Russia in 1798, still less any resumption of hostilities with Austria and Naples. Interwoven in this was what seemed at the time to be a revolution in international politics: having single-handedly committed France to a major change of policy in Italy, Napoleon embarked on a unilateral partition of the Ottoman Empire, which had the extraordinary result of uniting St Petersburg and Constantinople. This is not to say that traditional foreign policy interests did not survive, nor that they had been overturned by the Revolution: if Russia fought alongside the Ottoman Empire in 1798, for example, it was in part to keep it safe for partition on her own terms at a later date. None the less a disturbing new element – a personal ambition so great that it could not be constrained within the boundaries of the European states system – had entered international relations.

2

From Brumaire to Amiens

By the middle of November 1799, Napoleon had made himself ruler of France. Escaping from Egypt, he returned to a country assailed by political intrigue, internal unrest and economic crisis. Skilfully exploiting the situation to his own advantage, Napoleon emerged from the turmoil as de facto ruler of France, his official title being First Consul. In so far as the international history of Europe is concerned, a number of questions immediately come to mind. How was Napoleon perceived in the capitals of Britain, Austria, Russia and the other states that made up the Second Coalition? To what extent did perceptions of the new French ruler affect foreign attitudes towards France? And what did the First Consul himself intend to do with the power that he had won at Brumaire? All this, meanwhile, gives rise to further reflections. Was Europe at a turning point in her history – a moment when the destinies of an entire continent were transformed by a single adventurer? Or was the international situation essentially unchanged, the factors that condemned Europe to a long period of conflict having already been set in stone? Before these questions can be answered, we must once again turn to the man who came to power in 1799 and, more particularly, to his relationship with the French state.

Let us begin with the issue of Napoleon's personal power. Very soon this was as great as that of any monarch. Thus the negotiations that produced the new Constitution from which Napoleon formally derived his authority as First Consul were concluded by the middle of December 1799. The civilian conspirators who had precipitated the fall of the Directory had needed a 'sword', but the one they had settled upon proved impossible to sheathe. At the heart of their councils was Emmanuel Sieyès. A priest from Chartres who had won fame in 1789 by penning the famous pamphlet *Qu'est-ce que c'est le Tiers Etat?* and playing a leading role in the National Assembly, Sieyès had become a member of the Directory in 1799. Seen as a spiritual father of the Republic, he was also its leading authority in the realms of constitutional theory. Like his fellow conspirators, what the veteran revolutionary leader wanted was a system that would safeguard the interests of the propertied elite that dominated the Republic against Jacobins and royalists alike. To achieve this he planned to establish a complicated system of checks and balances whose end result would be to guarantee stable and effective government while at the same time ensuring that no political faction could seize the machinery of state for its own ends. As a part of this arrangement, the power of the executive was to be strengthened and that of the legislature reduced, but in no way was France to become a dictatorship. While a ceremonial 'grand elector' acted as head of state, responsibility for home and foreign affairs would be split and each of these areas assigned to an independent 'consul'. To get him out of the way, meanwhile, Napoleon would be offered the virtually powerless 'grand electorate'. Sieyès's general would not have any truck with this, however. No sooner had discussions begun on the new constitution presaged by Brumaire than the 'oracle', as Sieyès was known, found himself hopelessly outclassed. As he reputedly observed, 'Gentlemen, you have a master! This man knows everything, wants everything and can do anything!'[1]

Within a very few days, Sieyès's plans lay in ruins. Napoleon was happy to accept the structure that was put forward for the legislature, which was left all but devoid of real power, and he was also quite content to see the principle of universal manhood suffrage rendered null and void by making elections not only indirect but presentational (i.e. the electorate did not choose deputies per se, but rather lists of potential deputies from which the executive made its own selection via a 'conservative senate' appointed from above). But he refused point-blank to accept the position of Grand Elector and insisted that the executive should be united. Let France, then, suggested Sieyès, be ruled by a three-man consulate whose members would share power with one another on an equal basis. Yet this, too, was unacceptable: as far as Napoleon was concerned, one man alone should rule. The implications of this should perhaps have been clear. But, as ever, the conqueror of Italy played his hand with consummate skill. In complete contrast to the style that he was to affect just a few weeks later, he dressed in civilian clothes, assuming an air of reason and moderation, and taking great care to pander to the sensibilities of his fellow temporary consuls, Sieyès and Ducos (aside from respecting them in procedural matters, Napoleon also offered Sieyès in particular the presidency of the senate). Two other factors were on his side. First of all, there was simple common sense: if the Directory had not worked, why should anything better be expected from a three-man carbon copy? And there was Napoleon's own stamina: able to concentrate on matters of detail for hour after hour, he prolonged discussion to such an extent that the commission established to discuss the new constitution would have been prepared to accept virtually anything. Given Napoleon's prestige – as far as educated opinion was concerned, he was the only man who could save France – the result was inevitable. There would be three consuls, certainly, but one of them would be 'first'. Nor did this mean *primus inter pares*. In control would be the First Consul – Napoleon, of course – and while the Second and Third Consuls had the right to be consulted, they had no power of veto and for good measure were appointed for shorter periods than the ten years allotted to Napoleon.

There is no need to expatiate here upon the many means which Napoleon had at his disposal to exercise his personal power as a result of the Constitution of Year VIII. The fact of the matter is quite simple: *la grande nation* was Napoleon's to do with as he wished. And what he would do with it ought to have been all too obvious. To quote Chaptal, 'Only military glory had brought him to supreme power. That same glory was all that associated him with hope and enthusiasm. And it would be that same glory that sustained him to the end.'[2] From the beginning, then, it was war and military glory that were placed at the centre of the regime and Napoleon's formal entry into the Tuileries on 17 February 1800 was in large measure a celebration of conquest:

At one o'clock precisely, Bonaparte left the Luxembourg . . . Three thousand picked men, among whom was the superb regiment of the guides, were assembled for the occasion. All marched in the finest order with their bands playing . . . The consular carriage was drawn by six white horses . . . These beautiful horses had been presented to the First Consul by the Emperor of Germany after the treaty of Campo Formio. Bonaparte also wore the magnificent sabre which had been given to him by the Emperor Francis . . . The approaches to the Tuileries were lined by the [Consular Guard] . . . The troops being drawn up in the [Place du Carrousel], the First Consul, alighting from his carriage . . . leaped on his horse, and reviewed the troops . . . The First Consul prolonged the review for some time, passed between the lines, addressing flattering expressions to the commanders of corps. He then placed himself near the entrance to the Tuileries, having Murat on his right, Lannes on his left and behind him a numerous staff of young warriors, whose faces were browned by the suns of Egypt and of Italy . . . When he saw pass before him the colours of the ninety-sixth, the forty-third and the thirtieth *demi-brigades*, as these standards presented only a bare pole surmounted by some tatters, perforated by balls and blackened with gunpowder, he took off his hat and bowed to them in token of respect. This homage of a great captain . . . was hailed by a thousand acclamations, and, the troops having defiled, the First Consul, with a bold step, entered the Tuileries.[3]

The days that followed were along very much the same lines, as the well-placed Antoine Thibaudeau records:

The First Consul in his early days resembled rather a general than a civil magistrate . . . Day by day on horse or on foot the First Consul passed through the files of his troops, getting to know familiarly the officers and men, and being sure that they became acquainted with him. He entered into the most minute details of their equipment, arms and drill, and inquired carefully into their wants and wishes. Acting in his double capacity of general and magistrate he distributed, in the name of the nation, praise and blame, promotion and rewards. In this way also he aroused emulation among the different corps, and made the army the finest spectacle to be seen in Paris by visitors from the country or abroad. It was easy to see how completely at home the First Consul felt among his soldiers: he took genuine pleasure in remaining for hours in their midst . . . All this gave the First Consul splendid opportunities of exhibiting to the world his indefatigable energy and mastery of the art of war.[4]

What we see here, perhaps, is merely the response of a parvenu ruler to a situation in which, overnight, he had to gain acceptance by the crowned heads of Europe. Arguing that Napoleon was merely trying to secure the recognition of the rulers of Austria, Prussia and Russia does not acquit him of the charge of being addicted to war, however. For the First Consul, glory was not just important as a manifestation of monarchy. Victory on the battlefield had brought him to power and, as he well knew, victory on the battlefield was in the end what would keep him there. Commenting on the possibility of Napoleon making peace in 1800, for example, Madame de Staël remarked:

Nothing was more contrary to his nature . . . He could only live in agitation, and . . . only breathe freely in a volcanic atmosphere. Any man who becomes the sole head of a great country by means other than heredity can only maintain himself in power if he gives the nation either liberty or military glory – if he makes himself, in short, either a Washington or a conqueror. But it would have been hard for Bonaparte to be more different from Washington than was actually the case, and so it was impossible for him to establish . . . an absolute power except by bemusing reason [and] by every three months presenting the French people with some new spectacle.[5]

Yet for all that, surrounded though he was by soldiers – according to Hortense de Beauharnais, his personal suite had 'the air of a general staff'[6] – Napoleon came to power as a peacemaker. Virtually all shades of French opinion were heartily sick of war by 1799 and the new First Consul's great advantage was that he seemed to be able to combine peace with the protection of the Revolutionary settlement. As he rode into Paris immediately following the coup, his way lined by cheering crowds, his response was to proclaim, 'Frenchmen! You want peace; your government wants it even more than you!'[7] Virtually the first action of consular diplomacy was therefore the dispatch of appeals to both George III of England and Francis II of Austria for an end to the war (strictly speaking, Francis was at this time Francis II of the Holy Roman Empire; however, when this collapsed he took the title 'Emperor of Austria', becoming Francis I). These, however, were hardly serious. On one level they were a useful means of gaining time: at the beginning of 1800 Napoleon was preoccupied with the need to suppress the ever troublesome Vendée which had once again risen in revolt. And, as Talleyrand, who was now once again France's Foreign Minister, wrote, they 'had a happy effect upon the internal peace of the country'.[8] But, as Napoleon well knew, the Second Coalition was hardly likely to accept them. On the contrary, at this time it still had strong hopes of victory: the Bourbons had been restored to the throne of Naples, powerful Austrian forces had occupied the Cisalpine Republic, Piedmont and southern Germany, and Britain was supreme at sea and had isolated the army left behind by Napoleon in Egypt.

But in reality the allied position was far less strong than all this suggested. As Lord Hawkesbury recognized, there were deep differences within the coalition:

Our connections with foreign powers are still subject to great uncertainty and embarrassment. Though the emperor of Russia is cordially connected with Great Britain in all that relates to the war, he does not agree, nor can he be made to agree, with . . . the emperor of Germany. The emperor of Russia pursues the war on the simple principle of restoring . . . all ancient governments. The court of Vienna will look to nothing else but the aggrand-isement of . . . the house of Austria, and will not adopt any ancient principle, or support any former system, except so far as it does not interfere with their ambitious views.[9]

Not surprisingly, the response to Napoleon's overtures was fiercely hostile, but this was exactly what the First Consul wanted. As he later wrote:

If France had made peace at that time under existing circumstances, she would have made it after a campaign of disasters; indeed, she would have drawn back in consequence of a single campaign. This would have been dishonourable, and would only have encouraged princes to form new coalitions against her. All the chances of the campaign of 1800 were in her favour: the Russian armies were leaving the theatre of war; the pacification of the Vendée placed a new army at the disposal of the Republic; in the interior, factions were overruled and the chief magistrate possessed the entire confidence of the nation. It behoved the Republic not to make peace until after restoring the equilibrium of Italy; she could not, without abandoning her destiny, consent to a peace less advantageous than . . . Campo Formio. At this period peace would have ruined the Republic: war was necessary to it for the maintenance of energy and union in the state, which was ill organized, whilst the people would have demanded a great reduction in taxes and the disbanding of the army; in consequence, after a peace of two years, France would have taken the field again under great disadvantages. War was necessary to me. The campaigns of Italy, the peace of Campo Formio, the campaigns of Egypt, the transactions of 18 Brumaire, the unani-mous voices of the people for raising me to the supreme magistracy had undoubtedly placed me very high, but a treaty of peace derogatory to that of Campo Formio . . . would have destroyed my influence over the imaginations of the people and deprived me of the means of putting an end to the anarchy of the Revolution by establishing a definitive and permanent system.[10]

Napoleon, then, was not acting in good faith. Having thrown the responsibility for continuing the war upon his enemies, he could now seek further victories that would augment his glory and allow him to dictate peace on his own terms. To put it another way, in the words of a proclamation he had addressed to the army on 18 Brumaire, 'Liberty, victory and peace will reinstate the French Republic in the rank which she held in Europe.'[11]

But was there any alternative to war? Amongst admirers of Napoleon, it is axiomatic that the picture he faced at the beginning of 1800 was one of universal foreign hostility and, further, that the powers of Europe were determined to restore the Bourbons and, with them, absolute monarchy. This view is misleading in the extreme. Britain and Austria, certainly, were inclined to continue the war, but they were not much interested in the cause of Louis XVIII, who had been treated by them with considerable disrespect. Ordered about from place to place and afforded only a precarious degree of financial support, his authority had never once been proclaimed on the infrequent occasions when the Allies found themselves in control of French territory. Getting the Bourbons back on the throne was certainly favoured by some British statesmen, but it was not the centrepiece of Britain's war aims, for the simple reason that the territorial and maritime security on which they were centred could always be achieved by other means, and probably better ones at that. Britain had gone to war in 1793 to prevent France from riding roughshod over treaties and frontiers as she thought fit and, more particularly, taking over the whole of the Channel coast (a worry that in 1795 was greatly reinforced by the Republic's conquest of Holland). She had made use of French royalism, certainly. Supporting the various insurgents and conspirators associated with the Bourbons was a useful diversion that on occasion tied down large numbers of troops and caused considerable disruption in Paris. At the very time that Napoleon came to power, British arms were being supplied to a major royalist insurrection that had just broken out in Brittany and the Vendée. At the same time many British politicians, including, of course, most of those who made up the administrations of the 1790s, feared the principles of the French Revolution, and supported Pitt's clampdown on domestic radicalism. But a Bourbon restoration was quite another matter. Some politicians and statesmen – most notably, the Foreign Secretary, Lord Grenville, and his acolyte, William Windham – continued to believe in a 'strategy of overthrow' whereby peace would be restored and Jacobinism stamped out by the liberation of France, but the Secretary of State for War and the Colonies, Henry Dundas, and many others, distrusted such visionary schemes. While Grenville argued for a march on Paris, the sceptics favoured a colonial and economic struggle that would allow the British simply to outlast the French. Inherent in this strategy was the possibility of a compromise peace based on the restoration of the frontiers of 1792, and this in turn was strengthened by growing disillusionment with French royalism as a military and political force (and, for that matter, with its chief supporters: arrogant and overbearing, Grenville was not good at carrying opinion with him, and Windham was notorious for his lack of realism and poor judgement). Meanwhile, even the most hardline members of the Grenville faction were not fighting a war for feudalism. On the contrary, in their view France should be allowed to enjoy her own 1688 and end up as some sort of constitutional monarchy, and in most quarters even this limited goal was qualified by the recognition that any solution reached in France would have to be the work not of foreign arms, but of her own politicians.

By the beginning of 1800, then, there had emerged the basis of a more moderate position than the one encompassed by the Grenvillites. If France could be hedged about in such a way that she could not export the Revolution, she could safely be left to her own devices, thereby obviating the need for a change of regime. Whatever use was made of royalism, Britain's aim in the Second Coalition was centred on a plan that was to form the keystone of her European policy until the end of the Napoleonic Wars. France was to be confined to the frontiers of 1792 and shut in by a series of buffer states which would be backed up by a quadruple alliance of the great powers. Thus far there was no difference from Grenville's stategy: indeed, the scheme was in origin his. But, whereas for the Foreign Secretary, the great cordon sanitaire would set the seal on total victory, for men of a more temperate disposition it was a substitute for this end. If the regime in France proved unable to sustain itself, all well and good, but its overthrow was no longer a necessity. With the advent of Napoleon, meanwhile, a further complication emerged. On the one hand his record suggested that he was a warlord and adventurer who was no more to be trusted than his predecessors, and yet on the other there were reports that he was aping the forms of the monarchy and planning to introduce a moderate constitution that would protect men of property. Grenville claimed that Brumaire made no difference, but the Prime Minister, William Pitt, took a more flexible line than is often allowed. For the time being, Britain must be cautious: with France in control of Belgium, for example, there could be no question of peace negotiations, but the possibility of a treaty was not ruled out, and a Corsican secret agent was dispatched to Paris with the explicit brief of finding out more. As for the Bourbons, they could not be allowed to stand in the way of British national interest: nothing should be done that would bar Britain from considering whether continuing the war was more damaging to her situation than negotiating a peace settlement. To this end Pitt stressed that it was vital that no commitment should be made to the restoration of Louis XVIII per se. Indeed, the question might be asked, why should Britain fight for Louis XVIII when Louis XIV had one hundred years before been posing much the same danger to Britain's interests?

Although the rejection of Napoleon's peace overtures was accompanied by much ferocious rhetoric – in a Commons debate on 3 February 1800, Pitt not only savaged the whole course of French policy since 1792, but accused the First Consul personally of being behind all the worst of France's actions – Britain was by no means committed to a war to the death in 1800. And, if this was true of Britain, it was also true of Austria. Like many of his British counterparts, the Austrian chancellor, Thugut, loathed the French Revolution, while he clearly saw the conflict as a clash of ideologies in which Austria 'must fight a nation which has not only become utterly fanatical, but which tries to drag along with it other peoples, and which has prepared its current efforts for a long time in all of Europe through the voices of its prophets'.[12] However, there were important nuances in his position. In 1791 he had written:

If the democratic regime ever acquires any consistency and starts to spread the misfortune with which Europe is threatened, I would not hesitate to give all my support to the most vigorous means to pull this evil up by the roots, to make of these scoundrels an example that would dissuade forever those tempted to imitate it, and profit at the same time by the opportunity to deprive France of its former preponderance that it has so often abused *vis-à-vis* the other European courts.[13]

From this two things are apparent. First, if the Revolution could be contained, it need not actually be destroyed. France would have to be defeated, certainly, but there was no need for total victory and with it the overthrow of the Republic: like Pitt, in fact, Thugut dreamed of sealing off France with a cordon sanitaire whose basis would be territorial changes on the French borders that would place all the major fortresses of the region in the hands of Austria, Prussia and a much expanded Bavaria. Even if the Austrian army did eventually have to appear before the Tuileries, it would not be with the intention of opening the gates to a Bourbon who had, in the old phrase, learned nothing and forgotten nothing, for to do so would simply be to run the risk of a second 1789 and with it a second war.

To return to the views Thugut expressed in 1791, the second issue they raise is that making war on the Revolution was linked to wider issues of foreign policy. One of these was simply keeping France weak, which was in some ways a situation that suited Austria very well. But another – and one left unsaid – is the issue of 'compensation'. Though Austria did in the end gain some territory from the elimination of Poland from the map of Europe between 1793 and 1795, the partition of the Polish state was a major catastrophe for the Habsburgs that greatly weakened their position in Eastern Europe. Not only was the territory they obtained of only limited intrinsic worth, but Russia was now in a position to march straight across the frontier. Particularly in the period after the second partition in 1793, when it seemed that Austria was going to get nothing at all in the face of major gains for Russia and Prussia, Vienna had to fight on, for only thus could it obtain the new territory that would even the balance. In 1797, however, it had suddenly been presented with that territory in the form of most of the Republic of Venetia, whereupon Thugut had rather grudgingly made peace. The principles of the French Revolution were still anathema, but Austria had at last gained something from the conflict. With public opinion in Vienna openly war-weary – Thugut was jeered whenever he appeared in the streets – neither Britain nor Russia able or willing to do much to support the Austrians, the treasury bankrupt and the army utterly unable to resist the attacks of Napoleon, an end to the war might at least be tried.

The very favourable impression made on Thugut by the political power exercised by the victor of Arcola and Rivoli also helped, the fact being that a peace settlement negotiated by Napoleon might just stick – that Napoleon was a man with whom he could do business.

It is quite clear, however, that Thugut did not like the treaty that resulted. In his eyes, the French problem was quite unresolved, and he had only really made peace because the alternative was military catastrophe. Nor was the acquisition of most of Venetia much of a sop, for almost twice as many people lived in the lost lands of Belgium and Lombardy as had been gained at Campo Formio. Still worse, French behaviour in the months that intervened between the original armistice at Leoben and the signature of the treaty itself and in the short period of peace that had followed, suggested, first, that there was no intention of acting in good faith towards Vienna and, second, that the Revolution would continue its onward march. Before the French had handed over Venetia, for example, they had stripped it of many resources and encouraged the growth of revolutionary feeling, while the creation of republics in Genoa, Rome and Switzerland and the sudden expansion of French demands with regard to the left bank of the Rhine to include the territory of not just Austria but everyone else as well, convinced Thugut that the goal was indeed universal upheaval. Nor was the behaviour of the ambassador France now sent to Vienna much better: a notoriously vain, unpleasant and ambitious man of a strongly Jacobin persuasion, General Bernadotte adopted an air that was as swaggering as it was insolent, and cultivated the acquaintance of a variety of malcontents.

Yet the conviction that France was a danger to every monarchy in Europe – even to the whole of European civilization – did not mean that Thugut was bent on a perpetual war to the death. In the end the only hope was military victory, but the Austrian statesman knew full well that even a compromise peace could only be achieved by means of a grand alliance of all the powers that was absolutely solid and determined to subordinate everything else to the defeat of France. But of this there was no sign. Even if she joined a coalition, Prussia could be trusted neither to fight the French nor to refrain from stabbing Austria in the back in Germany. Britain was more reliable, perhaps, but even she had made overtures to France in 1797, while her ability to contribute to a land war – the only type of conflict that Thugut valued – was extremely limited; as for 'Pitt's gold', it was only forthcoming in limited amounts that came not as outright grants but rather loans that were repayable at an exorbitant rate of interest (an issue which in the period 1797–8, in particular, made relations between London and Vienna very frosty). And, last but not least, the Russia of Paul I was not necessarily to be trusted either: setting aside the tsar's own stability – though he was probably not mad (as is often claimed), the Russian ruler was extraordinarily prickly and capricious – there was also the question how Russia could intervene effectively on the battlefields of Germany and Italy and whether the Russian army was capable of taking on France.

All this meant that, far from rushing into a renewed war with France at the earliest possible opportunity, Thugut had actually held back and tried to appease Paris. Indeed, he had only gone to war at all once it was clear that the French would be opposed by a substantial coalition. In the event, however, the coalition had proved to be substantial only in the number of states that it could initially put into the field. Initial success had been squandered in disagreements over strategy, and the Russian forces, in particular, had proved of dubious reliability and far fewer in numbers than had been promised. By the end of 1799, pragmatism led Thugut to adopt a different line and all the more so given his private hopes that Napoleon would be able to suppress faction – the real motor, it was felt, of French aggression – and thereby create the conditions for a lasting peace settlement. The peace overture of January 1800 was therefore rejected, but the terms of the Austrian response were by no means as scathing as those of its British counterpart, and the next few months were marked by an exchange of letters with Talleyrand in which Thugut appears to have made a genuine attempt to sound out the chances of a deal. In short, the Thugut of 1800 does not appear to be the ideological warrior of earlier years, but rather a traditional eighteenth-century statesman whose response to the French challenge was a search for territorial acquisitions – the chief targets were Lombardy, Piedmont and the erstwhile papal territories of Bologna and Ferrara – that would make Austria a stronger state. Until negotiation or victory on the battlefield secured these fresh lands, Austria would not make peace. But the object was no longer – if it ever had been – the overthrow of the Revolution, while it was not just France that concerned Thugut, but also Russia and Prussia.

The impression that Napoleon could have bought off Austria in 1800 is strengthened by a consideration of the views and character of the

Emperor Francis and his brother, the Archduke Charles. For Francis, dislike of the French Revolution was as axiomatic as it was for Thugut, and he had responded to the discovery of a series of half-baked 'Jacobin' conspiracies in 1794 by executing the ringleaders. In the same vein, his rule was associated with ever tighter censorship, with the exploitation of the Church as an instrument of counter-revolutionary propaganda, the establishment of a powerful secret police and the widespread use of spies and informers. And in 1792 he had certainly been keener on war with France than his predecessor, Leopold II. That said, he had always considered the conflict with France to be a defensive struggle, and was not at all inclined to sanction a march on Paris. Moreover, he genuinely hated war (whose horrors he had experienced in person in Flanders in 1794 in the course of a visit to the troops) and, as a man who was both deeply cautious and habitually pessimistic, was much opposed to foreign adventures. As a result, the 'war baron', Thugut, could never wholly count on his support, while by 1800 the emperor was uncertain that carrying on the war against France was anything other than futile. As for his younger brother, the Archduke Charles, he may have been Austria's finest general, but he was even more convinced than the emperor that the Austrian army could not hope to beat the French, harboured a deep personal hatred for Thugut and in both 1797 and 1798 had been a leading member of the substantial peace party that emerged in the Austrian court.

Beneath the surface, then, in 1800 Austria was ambivalent about the war with France and little interested in the overthrow of Napoleon. What of the other eastern powers? Prussia, of course, was not in the war at all in 1800. Deeply hostile to Austria – in the wake of Prussia's withdrawal from the war in France in 1795, a number of Frederick William II's advisers floated the idea of going to war against her – Potsdam had no desire whatsoever to fight France, nor, still less, to offer Vienna assistance. Indeed, rather than risk becoming embroiled with France, at the end of 1795 the Prussians voluntarily renegotiated the southern frontier of the sphere of influence which they had been accorded in northern Germany in reward for pulling out of the war. In 1798 a serious attempt was made to get Prussia to join the Second Coalition, but this had foundered, first on the general hatred of Austria, and second on the nature of King Frederick William III, who had come to the throne the previous year and was as pacific as he was irresolute.

According to the self-appointed spokesman of the most reactionary elements among the *junkers*, Ludwig von de Marwitz, 'He was by nature averse to action', while the liberal Hermann von Boyen lamented:

His powers of analysis were at times, in periods of tranquillity, nothing short of acute, but only if it was a question of discovering the weaknesses of a thing or a person; in this respect he possessed a truly remarkable facility . . . But directly the matter to be adjudged required serious decisions which might lead to complications, his powers of discernment became confused, and on those occasions he became anxious whenever possible to avoid responsibility.[14]

But it was not just a case of pusillanimity. Even more so than Francis II, the Prussian monarch genuinely hated armed conflict. As he told his uncle, Prince Henry, 'Everybody knows that I abhor war and that I know of nothing greater on earth than the preservation of peace and tranquillity as the only system suited to the happiness of human kind.'[15] Like Francis II too, he also disliked any vestige of militarism, and, so far was he removed from holding to the old adage that Prussia was less a state with an army than an army with a state, in 1798 he had issued a sharp reproof to his officer corps in which he enjoined them to remember that the well-being of the army depended on that of civilian society rather than the other way about. Setting aside the king's personal proclivities, there were many other factors that suggested that the best course was to remain neutral. War would have meant huge expenditure at a time when the treasury – never very full given the poverty of much of Prussia's territory – was almost bankrupt and the king anxious to make amends in this respect, while it would also have cost the Prussian army serious losses and thereby put Potsdam at risk of Austrian *revanche* in Silesia and even Poland. And, finally, in a war against France victory would at best be uncertain, for Prussia's scattered lands were wide open to attack from the west, while the prescient Frederick William suspected that the Prussian army was not in a fit state to go to war: its performance in 1793–5 had not been good and there was a growing clamour for reform even in its own ranks.

But why go to war with France at all? In the first place, France seemed to pose no threat: relations with her were reasonably friendly; the Prussian sphere of influence in northern Germany established by means of the treaty of Basel in 1795 had essentially been respected; and there was no sign of revolutionary ideas spreading to Frederick William's dominions. In the second, by pursuing negotiations with France Prussia had already secured cast-iron promises of compensation for the lands she had lost on the left bank of the Rhine in the form of territories taken from the petty states of central Germany, and could hope for still more gains in the form of Hanover. And, in the third, neutrality posed no risk to Prussia's wider diplomacy should the situation change: Britain and Austria would need Prussia as much in 1805 or 1810 as they had in 1795 and 1800. Set against all this, the idea of a crusade against France carried little weight even in the relatively favourable circumstances of 1799. While an anti-French line had its supporters, including, most notably, the chief minister Heinrich Christian von Haugwitz, who was becoming increasingly convinced that France was so insatiable a force that she would inevitably one day turn on Prussia, the majority of the king's advisers continued to advocate neutrality. If Frederick William was one of the first rulers in Europe to congratulate Napoleon in the wake of 18 Brumaire, it is therefore hardly surprising.

So in 1800 Napoleon knew he had nothing to fear from Prussia. Of Frederick William III, indeed, he was openly contemptuous. As he later remarked, 'As a private citizen, the King of Prussia is a loyal, good and honest man, but in his political capacity, he is a man by nature governed by necessity who is at the mercy of anyone who is possessed of force and is prepared to raise his hand.'[16] And, if he had nothing to fear from Potsdam, the same was true of St Petersburg. At first sight, this is somewhat surprising. Ruler of Russia since 1796, Paul I was an extremely volatile figure who was notorious for his outbursts of uncontrollable rage, his fascination from boyhood for all things military and his determination to transform Russia's somewhat ramshackle armed forces. 'The palace', wrote the future Foreign Minister, Prince Czartoryski, 'was converted into a guardhouse: everywhere you heard the heavy tramp of officers' boots and the clink of spurs.'[17] Nor was Paul just the very model of a modern major-general. On the contrary, he was also a bitter opponent of the French Revolution. Though he was not actually insane, everything we know about his personality suggests that he was suffering from what has been described as an obsessive-compulsive personality disorder. For such people, everything must be ordered and they themselves wholly in control, and the Revolution therefore appeared to Paul as an immense affront. It was not just that it threatened the principle of monarchy. Still worse was the fact that it precipitated debate, disorder and uncertainty. In consequence, he was even more intense in his fulminations against events in France than his mother, Catherine the Great. Unlike her, however, he was from the first disposed to take military action against France, and, by the same token, disgusted when Russia in the end did nothing: so great was his anger, that from 1792 onwards he severed all ties with the empress and virtually confined himself to his private estate.

Curiously, none of this makes Paul I a warmonger so far as the French Revolution was concerned. Indeed, his very first act of foreign policy on coming to the throne in December 1796 was to cancel the military aid that Catherine had eventually decided to extend to the First Coalition. What had started to take over were pragmatic motives. France might well be an ideological danger, but she was now so strong that sending troops against her would merely be to squander precious military resources. As for Britain and Austria, their record as opponents of the French was at best patchy and at worst singularly discouraging. In consequence, they were urged to make peace, while Paul professed himself willing to recognize the Republic and see France retain Savoy, Nice, Belgium and the Austrian sections of the left bank of the Rhine. None of this is to say that the ideological menace was discounted, but Paul's answer to it was now very different. France might have her natural frontiers, but beyond that she must not be allowed to go, to which end he seems to have envisaged a permanent league of Britain, Prussia, Russia and Austria that would be able to keep the tricolour in check.

Yet despite this pacific beginning, by the end of 1798 Russia was formally at war with France. According to some historians, Paul had only been buying time for his military reforms to take effect and had never abandoned the cause of legitimism (as witness the manner in which he gave shelter to both Louis XVIII and Pope Pius VI in the winter of 1797–8). It is, then, possible that conflict would have followed anyway, but this is something that we can never know. In the world of concrete fact, what changed matters was Napoleon's acquisition of the Ionian islands and the subsequent conquest of, first, Malta and then Egypt. Paul had no desire to follow his mother's example by conquering yet more of the Ottoman Empire, but in 1797 he had declared himself to be the protector of the Knights of St John – a decision that was quickly rewarded with the position of Grand Master – while neither he nor any other tsar could have tolerated a substantial French military presence in the eastern Mediterranean. Russia's war aims, then, were ultimately strategic rather than ideological, though in practice the tsar agreed with the British Grenvillites that the only hope of a permanent solution to the problem was a march on Paris and the overthrow of the Republic. Very soon, however, Paul was disillusioned. In the crucial Italo-Swiss theatre, he found that his expeditionary force was too weak to do anything other than go along with Austrian strategy and, still worse, that the Austrians had set other goals before the invasion of France, the result of which was that the Russian corps commanded by General Korsakov suffered a crushing defeat at Zurich. In the Mediterranean, Russia fell out with Britain over the future of Malta; in Italy, Russia fell out with Austria over the question of whether or not the latter should be able to compensate herself for her territorial losses elsewhere with lands taken from Naples and Piedmont; and, finally, in Holland, which had been invaded by an Anglo-Russian expeditionary force, Russia fell out with Britain over the latter's failure to exploit an initial allied advantage and eventual negotiation of a convention with the French. And, to cap it all, in neither Italy, Switzerland nor Austria had the Russian army performed well: not only had the discipline of the troops broken down, but Paul's attempt to revive the Frederician manner largely abandoned by Catherine the Great had not proved much of an answer on the battlefield. Just as Paul had feared in 1796, war had proved a futile expedient: Austria and Britain were not to be relied on as partners, and Russia was unable to fight a war in Western Europe by herself and could in the attempt do no more than waste men and money.

By the end of 1799, an angry and disappointed Paul had broken off military cooperation with Austria. Formally speaking, Russia was still in the war, but in the course of 1800 a variety of factors combined to change the situation still further. Not the least of these were quarrels with the British over the subsidy which Russia had been promised in exchange for joining in the attack on France. But far more important were the changed perceptions of France brought about by the advent of Napoleon. Thus, for Paul, Brumaire transformed matters completely. Championing Louis XVIII when he had been the only possible figurehead of the cause of legitimism – the only representative of peace and order – in France had been all very well, but now there was a much more dynamic and attractive alternative. In short, Napoleon's pursuit of the trappings of monarchy had worked: in the new French ruler Paul saw a Corsican upstart, certainly, but a Corsican upstart who would put France to rights, and with her the whole of Europe. Friendly intimations were soon being received from Paris via Berlin, the gist of them being that France was prepared to make peace on reasonable terms and recognize Russia's interests in Germany and the Mediterranean. There were other gestures yet to come – most notably the generous treatment accorded by Napoleon to the Russian prisoners captured in Holland and the promise that Malta would be restored to the Knights of St John – but by the summer of 1800 all the forces Paul had sent to Western Europe were on their way home. Nor was Russia simply withdrawing from the coalition. Implicit in the French cultivation of St Petersburg was an attempt to secure an alliance: indeed, in January 1800 a deal had been proposed whereby Russia and France would between them despoil the Ottoman Empire of Egypt, Greece, Constantinople, the Balkans and the Greek islands; establish an independent Poland under a Russian prince; and compensate Prussia for the loss of her Polish territories with fresh lands in Germany and Silesia. Meanwhile, a variety of elements in the Russian court, including, most importantly, Chancellor Rostopchin, had in turn come to the conclusion that such an alliance would suit Russia very well. On 29 December 1800, then, Paul wrote to Napoleon in person in the friendliest terms, proposing a Franco-Russian alliance that would result in a general peace. To back this letter up a Russian emissary was dispatched to Paris. This démarche, meanwhile, was accompanied by important changes inside Russia, including the dismissal of the pro-British deputy chancellor, Panin, and the expulsion of Louis XVIII and all his followers.

It is important to note that this Franco-Russian rapprochement was deeply flawed. For Napoleon, Paul I was a mere tool, a weapon that he could deploy against Britain and Austria. Thus, in 1800 what he was particularly interested in was the Russian navy, and also the possibility that Paul might be inveigled into launching an overland attack on India. In fact Paul was anything but a mere tool; he was someone who had very concrete aims in allying himself with the First Consul. Not the least of these might have been expected to be further Russian aggrandizement in the Balkans where Rostopchin, at least, hoped for French support in obtaining modern-day Rumania and Bulgaria. Yet nothing could have been further from Paul's mind, the fact being that he enjoyed good relations with the Turks. And, while happy in a general sense to put pressure on Britain, he was not interested in an attack on India. A force of Don Cossacks was ordered to advance into the khanate of Bokhara, certainly, but while this territory straddled the route to India, the move rather stemmed from a quite separate crisis that had developed on Russia's southern frontier. The flashpoint here was the trans-Caucasian state of Georgia. Until 1795 the latter had been an independent Christian kingdom, but in that year it had been invaded by the then Shah of Persia, Aga Mohamed, and forced to accept his suzerainty. This was a challenge that Paul could not allow to pass and in January 1801 he decreed Georgia's annexation and sent an army to drive out the Persians, who were now ruled by Aga Mohamed's son, Fath Ali. Persia being a powerful opponent, the presence of troops in Bokhara is best explained as an attempt to open up a second front against her. But what, then, did Paul want from a deal with Napoleon? Britain was certainly an issue here: Paul resented her maritime pretensions and was much concerned that a British expedition to Egypt might result in a permanent British presence in the eastern Mediterranean. But checking Britain was not Paul's only aim. An alliance with France was also the best means of negotiating a French evacuation of Egypt. And at the same time there was also the issue of protecting Russian interests in Europe: here the tsar not only had numerous dynastic connections amongst the smaller German states, but also wished to extend Russian influence by posing as the protector of the weak against the strong. This had been given particular urgency, first by Austria's determination to secure territorial compensation in Italy at the expense of Piedmont and Tuscany, and second by the major reorganization of the Holy Roman Empire that was clearly on the way. In short, Russian policy cut two ways at once. Napoleon could expect Russian support against Britain and Austria, but he too was going to be expected to show restraint in Germany and Italy, and even to draw back in the Mediterranean. In the short term Russia's desires in part coincided with those of France, then, but in the long term matters would be very different.

But as yet these discrepancies remained hidden beneath the surface, the chief point being that Napoleon was not facing the unremitting enmity of the whole of Europe. On the contrary, the Continent was deeply divided, thanks to sharp conflicts of interest between Prussia and Russia in Poland, Russia and Austria in the Balkans, and Austria and

Prussia in Germany. And at the same time, fears of Britain kept Spain, for one, firmly in the French camp. In consequence, the First Consul's only enemies at the beginning of 1800 were Britain and Austria, whose commitment to the struggle were at best limited, but who would yet have to be thoroughly beaten before they would make peace. The struggle that followed, then, was hardly a desperate lunge to stave off overwhelming odds in the style of, say, the Waterloo campaign of 1815. Nevertheless, it did not begin well for Napoleon. Seizing the initiative, the Austrians attacked in Italy with 97,000 men, drove back the outnumbered French and besieged their adversaries in Genoa, which, defended with great courage by Masséna, held out till 4 June. Despite being taken by surprise, Napoleon's response was dramatic: while Moreau crossed the Rhine and defeated the Austrians at Stockach on 3 May, the First Consul led the newly created Army of Reserve across the Alps and descended on the Austrian rear, winning a very narrow victory at Marengo on 14 June. As even Napoleon's admirers admit, this was not his finest hour. The strategy of crossing the Alps was sound – brilliant even – but having reached Milan, he badly misjudged his Austrian opponent, Melas. Believing that Melas would simply fall back on newly conquered Genoa, he dispersed his forces in a cordon designed to trap the whitecoats. Melas, however, had more fight in him than Napoleon suspected, and suddenly rounded on the forces accompanying the First Consul himself with odds of over two to one. In a battle which saw the French driven back five miles, their new ruler was all but beaten, but in the nick of time General Desaix appeared with fresh troops and launched a counter-attack that caught the weary and over-extended Austrians off balance and drove them back in rout (though not before Desaix had been killed at the moment of victory).

The campaign of Marengo was badly bungled by Napoleon's standards. Nevertheless, sufficient damage had been done to the Austrians to persuade them to evacuate their Italian conquests in exchange for an armistice. In response to a renewed appeal for a peace settlement sent to Francis II from the battlefield of Marengo, an emissary was even dispatched to Paris. The terms on offer were not ungenerous – Austria was offered the same terms as she had been at Campo Formio. Nor was this surprising: Napoleon had no moral commitment to these terms or any other, and was only interested in a rapid settlement with Austria that would allow him to turn all his strength against Britain, force her to make peace and thereby rescue France's control of Malta and Egypt (Malta had been invaded by the British and Egypt was wide open to attack). Reflecting the doubts felt by many observers in Vienna, the Austrian envoy, St Julien, duly agreed to Napoleon's terms but, bolstered by the fact that six days after the battle of Marengo Britain had signed a treaty of subsidy with Austria whereby she agreed to pay her an interest-free loan of £2 million, Thugut succeeded in persuading Francis to reject the agreement. However, hard pressed as they were by the forces of General Moreau, the Austrians now requested an armistice in Germany, where they withdrew to the line of the river Inn, apart from the invested garrisons of Ulm, Ingoldstädt and Phillippsburg. Having in this fashion acquired some useful hostages – the French promised to allow the troops concerned to be revictualled every ten days, but insisted that only ten days' food would be allowed in on each occasion – Napoleon now tried to secure his goals in Egypt by other means. Thus, Thugut having floated the counter-proposal of a general peace conference, the French ruler suggested that the armistice be extended to Britain as well. When the Pitt administration jibbed at this demand on the grounds that, while Britain was happy to take part in the congress proposed by Thugut, an armistice with France meant above all a cessation of hostilities at sea, and, by extension, giving the French access to Egypt, Napoleon responded by threats of an immediate resumption of hostilities. Realizing that Austria had little chance of withstanding the French, Britain proposed a compromise that would have given the First Consul the right to send periodic food convoys to Egypt. This, too, was unacceptable to Napoleon, and the result was fresh terms that increased the pressure still further: in order to save the Austrian armistice, the Allies would now have to permit a strong frigate squadron to sail for Egypt and surrender the German fortresses. Desperate to buy even a few more days' respite, Francis II ordered his garrisons to surrender, but the British suspected – quite rightly – that the frigates would be crammed not just with food but with considerable troop reinforcements, while they knew full well that the ships themselves would be put to the task of defending the Egyptian coast. A suspension of hostilities being one thing and the French being permitted to entrench themselves on the Nile quite another, this was the end of the road and the British duly broke off negotiations, leaving the Austrians no option but to follow suit.

Was Napoleon sincere in his pursuit of peace in the wake of Marengo?

This is certainly the view of his admirers. So charitable a view is hard to sustain, however. To make a lasting peace with Austria, it would have been necessary to offer her a series of concessions that respected her interests as a great power. This would have involved the restoration of Italy as an Austrian sphere of influence – a move that would have entailed pulling the French forces of occupation back to the Alps and abandoning the Cisalpine Republic – the acceptance of Austrian territorial gains at the expense of Bavaria and France (who would have had to surrender the Adriatic ports and islands she had seized at Campo Formio), and the abandonment of any designs that France may have had with regard to the control of Germany. Yet none of these concessions were forthcoming. Nor, indeed, was anything else to be expected. The territories that would have had to be given up in the south – Piedmont, Lombardy, the Legations, Cisalpine Venetia and Venetian Dalmatia – had all fallen under France's sway by virtue of personal conquest on the part of Napoleon and could not have been given up without seriously damaging his prestige, while in Germany, to have accepted an Austrian advance would have been seen as jeopardizing the Rhine frontier. If Napoleon wanted peace, it was peace through victory, rather than peace through compromise.

Hostilities, then, were soon resumed. Pleased though Napoleon would have been to drive Britain and Austria apart, the First Consul was only too willing to embark on a further continental campaign. Nor was this surprising: in the aftermath of Marengo, the populace had erupted in transports of joy:

The First Consul . . . continued a few days longer at Milan to settle the affairs of Italy, and then set out on his return to Paris . . . I shall say but little of the manifestations of joy and admiration with which Bonaparte met throughout his journey . . . On arriving at Lyons we alighted at the Hotel des Celestins, where the acclamations of the people were so great and the multitude so numerous . . . that Bonaparte was obliged to show himself at the balcony . . . We left Lyons in the evening, and continued our journey by Dijon, and there the joy of the inhabitants amounted to frenzy.[18]

At the same time, if the events of 14 June 1800 did not in themselves bring the First Consul any extra power in France, they did shatter all chance that the various politicians who had found themselves outmanoeuvred in the aftermath of Brumaire might put the Napoleonic jack back in its box. While Napoleon had been away on campaign, Sieyès had been conspiring with Fouché and others to overthrow him. With command of the Army of the Interior in the hands of Bernadotte – an almost equally ambitious figure who married jealousy of Napoleon with, on the surface at least, pronounced Jacobinism – defeat at Marengo would have sealed Napoleon's fate. In the aftermath of victory, however, the situation was very different. Not only did a variety of malcontents rally to Napoleon's standard, but Sieyès sank into obscurity, while talk began of making Napoleon First Consul for life. As he remarked to Bourrienne, 'Well, a few more events like this campaign and I may perhaps go down to posterity.'[19] Nor did one have to be a member of his intimate circle to observe the fresh development in his ambitions. In the words of Bertrand Barère – an erstwhile member of the Convention who was numbered among the first batch of proscribed Jacobins to be amnestied by Napoleon:

The tyrannical consul was not forgotten in the victorious general, especially as he now displayed a haughty selfishness, utterly incompatible with devotion to his country, and . . . had removed the gilded bronze letters which were placed over the principal entrance of the palace of the Tuileries. When it was seen that the words 'French Republic' were an eyesore to the First Consul, the more than royal ambition of the Corsican, and the destruction of the Republic, could no longer be doubted.[20]

What made the idea of fresh victories against Austria still more attractive was the fact that as First Consul Napoleon had access to far greater means of propaganda than had ever been the case before. Although the French ruler hid behind the fact that it coincided with the anniversary of the fall of the Bastille, his return to Paris was celebrated with great pomp and ceremony, while the campaign had already been marked by the creation of an entirely false image of Napoleon as romantic hero doing personal battle with the forces of nature. As a bulletin of 24 May proclaimed, 'The First Consul descended from the top of the St Bernard by sliding on the snow . . . and leaping over precipices.'[21] In reality, Napoleon had made the crossing in much more prosaic fashion, mounted on a mule, just as his troops trudged along not precipitous goat-tracks but a reasonably serviceable highway. Yet such details did not stop him from embellishing his alpine adventure still further. Thus, in one of a series of paintings commissioned after Marengo, the First Consul is depicted by David in the act of waving on his troops while mounted on a mettlesome charger. Carved on the rocks in the foreground, appear three names: Bonaparte, Hannibal and Carolus Magnus (i.e. Charlemagne). As for the forces of nature, they remain present in the vicious wind that is whipping Napoleon's voluminous cloak from around his body. Implicit in this image are a variety of claims: next to Alexander the Great, Hannibal was the greatest hero of the ancient world, while Charlemagne's kingdom encompassed both France and Italy. Less well known but just as interesting is the painting that was produced of Marengo by Lejeune: Desaix is present in the picture – indeed, he is shown in the act of falling dead at the head of his victorious troops – but he is portrayed as a tiny figure deep in the middle distance, whereas the chief focus of the picture is Napoleon, who is pictured riding forward with his staff and directing operations. Nor is this an end to the story: at first sight, the First Consul appears to be riding to the rescue of his subordinate rather than the other way about.

A fresh campaign on the Continent, then, was not unwelcome to Napoleon. But on this occasion he was denied the glory to which he so aspired. Still in Paris when hostilities broke out on 22 November, Napoleon seems to have intended to head for Italy and take control of the 90,000 French troops concentrated on the river Mincio under General Brune. In the event there was to be no third Italian campaign, for the Austrians again seized the initiative and thereby precipitated a chain of events that left the First Consul out in the cold. This time, however, the onslaught came in Bavaria, where the forces of the Archduke John turned Moreau's left flank and launched a drive on Munich. In theory, the plan was a good one, for the French might have been trapped against the Bavarian Alps, but John was an inexperienced commander while the French had the advantage of interior lines. The result was disaster for the allied cause. Pouncing on the Austrians at the village of Hohenlinden on 3 December, Moreau shattered John's army beyond repair, before breaking through to the Danube and marching deep into Austria. With Hohenlinden in some respects a greater victory than Marengo – in the earlier action the Austrians lost thirty-three guns whereas at Hohenlinden they lost fifty – Napoleon was furious at being deprived of his share of the glory, all the more so as Moreau was a staunch Republican as well as a long-term rival. Years afterwards he was still inclined to run down the general's achievement:

[Hohenlinden] was one of those great battles that are born of chance and won without any planning. Moreau did not show enough decision: that was why he chose to remain on the defensive. In the end it was a mere scuffle: the enemy was struck in the very midst of his operations and defeated by troops they had cut off and should have destroyed. All the merit belonged to the ordinary soldiers and to the commanders of the divisions which found themselves in most danger, all of whom fought like heroes.[22]

Yet, however irritated the First Consul may have been, Hohenlinden secured his strategic objectives. Demoralized and exhausted, Vienna sued for peace, and on 8 February 1801 her representatives duly signed the treaty of Lunéville, by which Austria was again forced to accept France's annexation of Belgium and the left bank of the Rhine and to recognize the independence of the various satellite states. But now there were also further conditions. Austria had to agree to destroy a number of fortresses on the right bank of the Rhine, and to give up the Habsburg-ruled duchies of Modena and Tuscany, together with some of the territory she had acquired from Venice in 1797 (of these territories, Modena and the Venetian lands went to the Cisalpine Republic, and, in a gesture intended to conciliate Spain, Tuscany was given to the son of the Duke of Parma – a son-in-law of Charles IV – as the Kingdom of Etruria). As if all this was not bad enough, the Austrians were also made to agree that the Duke of Tuscany should receive compensation in Germany, from which it followed that the ecclesiastical states that made up Vienna's chief powerbase in the Holy Roman Empire should be put up for 'secularization' or annexation. In principle, Austria had already agreed to this process at Campo Formio in that she had accepted that the rulers of the territories lost in France's annexation of the left bank of the Rhine should also be compensated from within the Empire. But what Lunéville meant was that the reorganization of Germany was now likely to be wholesale rather than partial, for such was Austria's need for compensation that the Prussians would have to be drawn in too. Add to this Vienna's failure to impose any clause in the treaty to the effect that the emperor – i.e. Francis II – should have a controlling interest in the settlement of the new frontiers, still less that foreign powers should be excluded, and it can be seen that Austria had suffered a shattering blow. As Metternich later lamented, 'With the conclusion of the Peace of Lunéville, the weakness and vacillation of the Austrian cabinet reached their height . . . The German empire visibly approached its dissolution.'[23] And, in effect, gone too was Austrian influence in Naples. In the words of the commander of the Neapolitan army that had invaded central Italy, Comte Roger de Damas:

The Queen . . . was in Vienna. The moment that the question arose of an armistice between the Austrian and the French armies she secured an official promise in writing that the ministry would consent to no treaty that did not include her army and her states. The emperor owed this return to the King of Naples after the active support that the latter had given him. However . . . before the ink was dry [he] put his name to an armistice that entirely ignored us. M. de Bellegarde wrote to me, 'I have just concluded an armistice in which you do not appear [and could] only obtain a promise that you should not be attacked. You know how these people keep their promises: take precautions.'[24]

This warning could not have been more timely. A Neapolitan foray into Tuscany was duly defeated at Siena on 14 January 1801, and Ferdinand IV was left with no option but to sue for peace. Dictated by Damas's French counterpart, Joachim Murat, the terms of the resultant treaty of Florence were predictably harsh: Naples had to cede Elba, Piombino and several small enclaves of territory that she held in Tuscany to the Kingdom of Etruria; to pay an indemnity of 120,000 ducats within three months; to close her ports to British ships; to amnesty and restore the property of all those who had been involved in the short-lived Parthenopaean Republic of 1798; to allow the occupation of the Adriatic coast for the duration of the war with Britain by a French army that would be paid and supplied by the Neapolitans themselves; and to surrender, again until peace was signed with London, three frigates to the French navy. Only narrowly did Ferdinand IV manage to retain the services of his chief minister, Baron Acton, an English soldier of fortune who had secured the favour of the Neapolitan court in the 1770s and ever since then played a leading role in its politics (the French, of course, regarded him as a British agent and were determined to get rid of him). All that could be said of the arrangement was that it might have been worse. Indeed, as Damas admitted, the peace terms 'were by no means as bad in proportion as the terms to which Austria was obliged to submit'.[25]

This insouciance, however, was not shared in Naples, where Acton

had gone to great lengths to avoid personal responsibility for the negotiations: indeed, the diplomat who had actually been sent to Florence was
publicly disgraced and banished from the court for three years. This
reflected the deep impact the whole affair had on Queen Maria Carolina,
the Austrian princess who was the de facto ruler of the country given
the lack of interest in public affairs evinced by her slow-witted husband,
Ferdinand IV. A violent opponent of the French Revolution, who had
been horrified by the execution of Louis XVI and Marie-Antoinette, she
had been a leading advocate of war in 1793, lamented the treaty of
peace that had been signed with France in 1796, and welcomed the
resumption of hostilities in 1798. Yet she was always ambivalent about
Napoleon:

Personally I abhor the part that Bonaparte serves and plays. He is the Attila,
the scourge, of Italy, but I have a genuine esteem and deep admiration for
him. He is the greatest man several centuries have produced. His force,
constancy, activity and talent have won my admiration . . . My sole regret
is that he serves so detestable a cause. I should like the fall of the Republic,
but the preservation of Bonaparte . . . I hope that his plans will miscarry and
his enterprises fail [but] at the same time I wish for his personal happiness
and glory so long as it is not at our expense . . . If he dies they should reduce
him to powder and give a dose of it to each ruling sovereign, and two to
each of their ministers, [and] then things would go better.[26]

For Maria Carolina, then, Napoleon himself was not so great an issue
so long as he left Naples alone. Her hatred of France, meanwhile, was
further dissipated by the campaign of 1800. It was not just that Austria
had let Naples down in the aftermath of Hohenlinden. Caught by Napoleon's passage of the Alps at Livorno en route to Vienna, whither she
was going in a personal attempt to secure Naples' interests in central
Italy against Thugut's determination to secure territorial compensation
for Austria, she was able to observe defeat at close quarters. To quote a
letter that she wrote to the Neapolitan ambassador in Vienna on 28 June,
'The fugitives of the Austrian army arrive here in a pitiful state. You see
them dying in the streets without clothes or shirts, and they no longer
look human. The ill will of the generals and admirals is as incredible as
their talk. They all want peace and repose. If all the emperor's troops
are like those I see, I advise him to make peace and never again think of
war.'[27] On 2 July, she put her views even more clearly:

I swear that once the peace is settled it will be an expert in cunning who can catch me again except in the case of aggression against our country . . . The rest of Europe may be on fire, Thugut emperor and Fox King of England, but even so I would not be drawn from a permanent system of neutrality, or, to be more precise, of nullity. I only aspire to repose.[28]

Despair at Austria's war-making capacity, meanwhile, was presently joined by irritation at Britain's actions in the Mediterranean, the bone of contention here being the island of Malta. After a long siege in which the Neapolitan armed forces were heavily involved, the French garrison of Valetta was forced to surrender on 5 September 1800. While this was welcome, there was great irritation in Palermo at the manner in which the Neapolitans had been excluded from the peace negotiations. With relations already strained by the manner in which the notoriously complacent Sir William Hamilton had been replaced as ambassador by the much more forceful Arthur Paget, the queen was much distressed:

The French are driven out and that is all to the good, but . . . we were keenly mortified to have had no part in the capitulation considering our troops, munitions [and] artillery, and our positive rights to the island . . . It is all the more painful to be so completely duped and receive an injury from a friend. We are such fast friends of England that we are delighted that this great ally should keep a fortress which dominates Sicily, but her method of procedure, this contemptuous treatment after all our care, cordiality, assistance and enormous expense – these are galling indeed.[29]

This dissatisfaction was to have repercussions later. In the meantime, only the Ottoman Empire and Britain remained for Napoleon to deal with. Of these, the Turks were impossible to knock out of the war, although Napoleon did his best to lure them into peace negotiations. Even so, they were not much of a threat: not only were they preoccupied with a series of internal disorders, but on 20 March 1800 an army they had sent to reconquer Egypt by land had been heavily defeated at Heliopolis. With the Turks effectively out of the battle, the French were free to concentrate on Britain. In order to ensure that Egypt hung on as long as possible – although Napoleon had hinted to the Turks that he might evacuate the province, in reality he hoped to keep it – troop reinforcements were dispatched to Alexandria and the Army of the Orient encouraged to fight to the death. Meanwhile, the pressure on

London was increased by getting Spain to launch an attack on Portugal – Britain's last ally in Europe – in May 1801. This conflict, the so-called War of the Oranges, was less than satisfactory from Napoleon's point of view. According to the original plan, large areas of Portugal were to have been occupied and held as bargaining counters that could be exchanged for Malta and the various colonial territories and other possessions that Britain had seized from France, Spain and Holland. Fifteen thousand French troops were to be involved in the fighting. These were to be sent across the Pyrenees and by early May had got as far as the border fortress of Ciudad Rodrigo. And, finally, Portugal's ports were to be closed to British shipping (a major blow, for Lisbon was a vital port-of-call for the Royal Navy and Portugal an important trading partner for British merchants). At the same time, the First Consul would be assured of a further slice of military glory at a time when his arms elsewhere in Europe were at rest. Setting aside the minor bait thrown to the Spaniards, the British would be left with no option but to disgorge one of the keys to Napoleon's schemes in the east.

In the event these plans were all foiled. Much concerned at the prospect of a strong French presence in the Iberian Peninsula, King Charles IV and his court favourite, Manuel de Godoy, joined with the Portuguese in securing a rapid end to the war before Napoleon's plans could be put into practice. After some token skirmishes Lisbon agreed to cede a small slice of Extremadura to Spain, to pay an indemnity to France and to close her ports to Britain, but in exchange the Spaniards withdrew from Portugal and eschewed any further threat to her territorial integrity. For reasons of his own, the First Consul's personal representative, Lucien Bonaparte, went along with this arrangement, but Napoleon was enraged. Determined to secure his original goals, he refused to ratify the resultant treaty of Badajoz, and ordered a resumption of hostilities, but Godoy refused point-blank to give way and even went so far as to threaten a separate peace with Britain. Utterly furious, Napoleon demanded to know whether the Bourbons had tired of reigning. But in the end the affair blew over, as by the autumn of 1801 the international situation had changed enormously.

Before looking at this fresh situation, it is worth considering what we know of Napoleon's war aims as they stand revealed by the events of 1801. If one thing is clear, it is that his aims were not just limited to retaining France's natural frontiers, together with the sphere of influence she had carved out in Holland and northern Italy. On the contrary, implicit in the First Consul's dealings with Spain and Portugal is the assumption not just that Egypt could be held until a general peace settlement was reached, but also that it could be retained thereafter. Nor was France simply to enjoy an oriental empire. On the contrary, Napoleon was also looking to the western hemisphere. Peace with England was quite clearly expected to restore to France her 'sugar islands' in the West Indies. But beyond that there was also the question of the vast territory of Louisiana. Ceded to Spain in 1762 at the close of the Seven Years War, this stretched from the Gulf of Mexico to the present-day Canadian frontier and from the river Mississippi to the Rocky Mountains. Although largely unexplored, and colonized by Europeans only in the extreme south, where New Orleans was a major port and the centre of a plantation economy based on rice, sugar and cotton, it was clear that this vast region was potentially of immense importance. A valuable source of colonial produce, it was also a convenient source of food and raw materials for France's colonies in the West Indies. As for the interior, who knew what wonders it concealed, Napoleon having undoubtedly been much impressed by the gold and silver brought to Spain by her older territories in the New World. And last but not least, there was the issue of global strategy, for a base in the American West would allow Napoleon to put pressure on the British in Canada and to threaten the United States.

In fairness to Napoleon, it should be noted that, as with Egypt, he was not the only Frenchman to look to Louisiana. In 1795 the peace negotiations with Spain that produced the treaty of Basel had seen an attempt to get hold of the territory, while in 1796–7 the Directory had repeatedly sought to persuade Godoy to consider the idea, of which Talleyrand was a prominent supporter. On top of this, the 1790s had shown that the United States was not the friend and ally of France that might have been supposed. Despite the Franco-American treaty of amity of 1778, George Washington had declared the United States to be neutral, and refused point-blank to tolerate the attempts of the French ambassador to use the United States as a base for privateering or, still more dramatically, the conquest of Louisiana by a privately recruited army of frontier toughs. When the British began to impound American ships trading with France and her colonies, Washington responded not by declaring war but by negotiating a treaty that effectively accepted

Britain's right to block all trade with France in exchange for the payment of compensation in respect of any American ships or cargoes seized by the British. In retaliation, the French first declared that they would treat all American ships as fair game themselves, and, second, imposed a code of practice that was even more stringent than that operated by the British. With losses mounting, the French privateers behaving little better than pirates and no compensation forthcoming whatsoever, in 1798 President Adams in effect declared war on France. Plans were mooted for an attack on Louisiana, Florida and France's remaining islands in the Caribbean, while a small navy was fitted out and sent out to do battle against the Directory's warships and privateers. Greatly alarmed at the threat to Louisiana, within a year the French were backing away from further conflict. Conciliatory messages were sent to Adams, and Napoleon had scarcely come to power before he had repudiated the decrees that had wrought such havoc with American shipping. Thanks to a variety of political circumstances in the United States, including, not least, the manner in which the war was tending to strengthen the position of Adams's enemies, the Federalists, these moves achieved the desired effect. Diplomatic relations were restored and a peace settlement was elaborated that effectively annulled the treaty of 1778 – thereby cementing the principle of American neutrality – in exchange for the rejection of Britain's claims with regard to neutral shipping and the de facto surrender of United States claims for compensation for the losses inflicted on her shipping since 1793. For the time being, all was quiet, but such were the contradictions between the French and American positions that further trouble was likely. In short, the acquisition of Louisiana remained essential. At the very time, then, that negotiations were moving towards the agreement of 30 September 1800 – the treaty of Mortefontaine – parallel talks were being held with Spain with regard to Louisiana. There was little difficulty in obtaining the retrocession: the Spanish government regarded Louisiana as more trouble than it was worth and was happy to see France take it over and especially so if it guaranteed the establishment of the Spanish-ruled Kingdom of Etruria in Italy. On 1 October 1800, then, the treaty of San Ildefonso handed Louisiana back to France, but for the time being the new arrangement remained secret and for a variety of reasons the actual transfer of power did not take effect until 15 October 1802.

In the circumstances, this was just as well. Had Napoleon's American schemes been revealed, it is almost certain that Britain would never have made peace. As it was, British commitment to the war was rapidly falling away. Britain was supreme at sea, certainly: Malta, as we have seen, was seized from the French; the Spaniards were defeated in a number of skirmishes; and the Danes beaten at Copenhagen (see below). And, of course, since nothing could break the dominance of the Royal Navy, nothing could stop the British from seizing the colonial and other off-shore territories of her opponents: by 1800 her prizes included Tobago, St Pierre et Miquelon, Pondicherry, Martinique, St Lucia, the Saints, Mariegalante, Deseada, the Dutch East Indies, Ceylon, Malacca, Deme-rara, Essequibo, Berbice, Trinidad, Madagascar, Surinam, Goree, Cura-çao, Menorca and Corsica (although this last had only been held from 1793 to 1796). That same seapower could also strike at the French position in Egypt: in December 1800 a large British expeditionary force sailed from Gibraltar for Alexandria under Sir Ralph Abercromby. By the end of March 1801, the British had established a firm bridgehead on the Mediterranean coast, heavily defeated the French at the second battle of Aboukir, and closed in on Alexandria. Buoyed up by hopes of relief – to the very end Napoleon kept trying to get fresh troops across the Mediterranean – the garrison held on into the summer, but Cairo surrendered in June without a fight. If the Egyptian adventure was all but over, in India too the British had met with complete success. From 1798 onwards, a series of campaigns had shattered a series of rulers friendly to France and pushed back the frontiers of British rule and in the process made the name of a hitherto unknown officer named Arthur Wellesley.

There were, then, plenty of voices pressing for a continuation of the war. One was that of Lord Malmesbury, the experienced diplomat who had undertaken the peace negotiations of 1797. As he confided to his diary in March 1801:

I fear Ministers have shown too much eagerness for negotiation. Bonaparte will avail himself of it either to be insolent (if he feels strong in his seat) or to betray them into a bad peace by an affected complaisance (if he is insecure in it). There is reason to suppose the distant French armies are not disposed to be very obedient, and that those who command them consider themselves as possessing as good claims to govern France as the First Consul. He dare not, therefore, bring them back into France, and is by no means sure that they will keep the countries they are now in possession of for him and his purposes. I dread a naval armistice: if we accede to it, it will be like the foremost jockey giving time for the others to come up with him while the race is running. But this, and concessions as to the claims of the neutral nations, and probably some boon or act of complaisance to Paul will, I apprehend, be proposed to us, and my best hope is that Bonaparte, giddy with success and vanity and reckoning too much on our easy compliance, will convey these proposals in such overbearing and insolent language as even the present pacific enduring Ministers will be offended at.[30]

Yet, Britain's prospects were limited: troops were in short supply – Abercromby's army was only assembled at the cost of abandoning all hope of defending Portugal – and there was little chance of using an army successfully in Europe. Despite the most inflated claims by its supporters in London, French royalism showed no signs of generating the sort of armed rising that might have justified a landing in France, while attacks on naval bases such as Cádiz, Ferrol and Brest proved uniformly unsuccessful. Something might be attempted against Spain's possessions in the Americas by means of seapower – there was, in particular, much talk of the conquest of Cuba – but in the short term it was hard to see how such operations could make much difference in Europe, nor still less how the Royal Navy alone could reverse French dominance or prevent the French from closing more and more ports to British trade. And, last but not least, France was clearly making considerable strides in terms of the organization and power of the state. Whereas in the 'Jacobin' France of the 1790s, chaos had seemed to be the norm, brigandage was now gradually being extinguished, conscription rendered more productive and stability restored to the administration.

Not surprisingly, then, there was plenty of gloom to set alongside the optimism of the diehards. To quote a letter written by Lord Auckland to Lord Wellesley, who was then Governor-General of India:

We can no longer conceal from ourselves that the war is likely to end without any settlement of the independence of Europe, and with great accessions to the colonial dominion of France. I do not even think that the sudden disappearance of Bonaparte from the scene of action would give any essential turn to affairs. He would probably be succeeded by Berthier, Moreau or Masséna, or some other *dux* . . . would take the reins. In short, strange and unforeseen terms may take place, but, I must confess, we see nothing within the line of fair calculation and probability that tends to enable us either to push the war with effect, or to make a peace with safety.[31]

Meanwhile, at home Britain faced a growing economic crisis, and with it widespread popular unrest. The harvests of 1799 and 1800 had both failed, much to the detriment of the price of bread. In consequence, domestic demand for consumer products fell at the very moment that French success on the Continent was reducing the number of outlets for British exports. As a result, many textile factories, in particular, went bankrupt, and attempts to ease the problem by importing extra grain from Prussia – already the source of half the annual supply of this commodity – were blocked by that state's decision to join the League of Armed Neutrality (see below). Also cut off thanks to the new development was Britain's chief source of naval supplies, while trade was hit very badly by Prussia's decision not only to close her own ports to British trade, but to occupy Hanover (which controlled the rivers Elbe and Weser). As if all this was not enough, the increasingly hungry populace now found themselves exposed to the impact of the notorious Combination Law, a measure that had been introduced in 1799 to check the growth of trade unions. Despite the defeat of the rising of 1798, Ireland, too, remained restive. And finally, a sick man worn out by heavy drinking, the Prime Minister William Pitt was weary and despondent.

Peace, then, was essential. How, though, was this to be achieved? With Pitt at the helm, Paris would be unlikely to respond favourably to any peace overtures, so demonized had the Prime Minister become across the Channel. It was, in consequence, most fortuitous that just at this point a major dispute should have broken out over Catholic emancipation. Put forward by Pitt as a means of conciliating Ireland, this measure was fiercely denounced by George III, whereupon the Prime Minister resigned. So convenient was his departure that it has been suggested that the whole affair was deliberately manufactured so as to clear the way for peace talks. If this theory is correct – and the evidence is not wholly conclusive – then it is certainly strengthened by the outgoing Prime Minister's recommendation of the Speaker of the House of Commons, Henry Addington, as his successor. As Pitt knew full well, Addington was absolutely committed to an early peace, the very first act of the new Cabinet being to announce that it was ready to come to terms.

In keeping with his image of the reluctant warrior, Napoleon was content to entertain these overtures. With the French garrison clearly doomed, a peace treaty was the only means of salvaging anything from the Egyptian fiasco. Napoleon had also recently suffered a severe blow in the diplomatic field. At the end of 1799, as we have seen, Russia had withdrawn her troops from operations against the French following differences with Britain and Austria, the First Consul being quick to take advantage of the breach in the hope of further disconcerting his remaining opponents. Paul I was therefore wooed with promises of the return of 7,000 prisoners then in French hands, and of the cession of Malta, which at this point was still held by the French. Much impressed with this generosity, Paul allowed himself to be persuaded that an alliance with France was in the Russian interest, and by the late autumn of 1800 he was mobilizing an army on the Austrian frontier. On top of this, he also organized an alliance of the Baltic states – Russia, Sweden, Prussia and Denmark – to put pressure on Britain through the so-called League of Armed Neutrality. The Baltic powers had grown increasingly irritated by Britain's constant interference with their shipping, and the aim of this new alliance was to put pressure on London to grant them the freedom of the seas by threatening the use of armed force. For Napoleon these events were highly promising, for Russia and the Baltic states could boast considerable naval resources. But on 23 March 1801 Paul was murdered in a palace coup and replaced by his son, Alexander I, a ruler who, while friendly to Napoleon, wished in the first instance to shun foreign adventures in favour of a programme of domestic reform. And hard on the heels of this event, a British squadron under Sir Hyde Parker attacked and defeated the Danish fleet at Copenhagen. Although the Prussians remained in occupation of Hanover, which they had invaded in accordance with their treaty obligations under the League, all hope of really striking against the British was suddenly gone. In consequence, there was simply no point in the First Consul taking hostilities any further, especially as France remained as war-weary as ever, and the British seemed likely to accept whatever terms they were offered (to ensure that they did so, Napoleon made a great show of preparing an invasion fleet). At the same time, peace offered further advantages, for the French navy could be rebuilt and Germany brought further under France's sway. In short, it was very much in France's interests to offer terms, the result being, first, the Preliminaries of London of 1 October 1801, and then the Treaty of Amiens of 25 March 1802. As Turkey signed a separate peace on 9 October 1801, for the first time since April 1792 the whole of Europe was at peace.

To obtain peace Britain had to offer terms that were extremely generous. France's natural frontiers were recognized, along with the various satellite republics, and her colonial losses restored, together with the Dutch possessions of the Cape, Surinam, Curaçao, Malacca and the Spice Islands, Britain retaining only Spanish Trinidad and Dutch Ceylon. At the same time, Menorca was returned to Spain and Malta to the Knights of St John, guarantees also being given that the British army would be called home from Egypt. As for France, all she had to do was agree to withdraw all her forces from her surviving satellites, which were henceforth to be treated as independent states. Even here, however, there was a measure of defeat: the Cisalpine Republic, the Helvetic Republic and the Batavian Republic might all be stripped of their French troops, but the British were obliged to accept their new form of government and, by extension, accept the fact that they would remain firmly within the French sphere of influence. Strictly speaking, it ought to be noted that Napoleon had agreed to give up Egypt, but in the circumstances this was no concession at all, for France's dreams of a new colonial empire on the Nile had over the last few months been completely overcome, while evacuation was made contingent on Britain's surrender of Malta. Only on two small points was there much consolation, and neither of these was the fruit of direct negotiations with France. When Napoleon formally made peace with Russia on 8 October 1801 he had been forced to abandon his claim to the Ionian archipelago and to recognize the new political organization in the form of the 'Republic of the Seven Islands'. And on 6 November, Frederick William III ordered the evacuation of Hanover on the grounds that to keep it would entail complications with Britain of a sort that could only be sustained if she was at war with France.

Other than peace itself, Britain had therefore gained almost nothing, and the treaty was greeted in some quarters with alarm and disquiet. According to William Windham, for example, 'The country has received its death blow.'[32] For Grenville, it was a 'much-to-be-lamented business' and 'an act of weakness and humiliation'.[33] And for Canning, it was 'most disgraceful and calamitous'.[34] Such comments have often been used as evidence that Britain – or at least the British establishment – was never serious in its acceptance of the peace settlement and only wanted a breathing space. But Windham and the rest were all either 'ultras' who saw the war in terms of a clash of ideologies or men who had personal reasons of various sorts for hating Addington. All the evidence suggests that they were very much in a minority in their wholesale rejection of the treaty. There was a degree of wariness, certainly, but from George III downwards a range of figures could be found who were prepared to give peace a try. As for those who opposed the settlement, the fact that William Pitt supported it as the best arrangement that Addington could have obtained completely undermined their position: to have gone against the treaty and sought to overthrow the government on a ticket of renewed war would in effect have been to cast aside their great hero. It would at the same time run counter to a public opinion that greatly welcomed an end to hostilities and had a degree of sympathy with the ideas of the French Revolution. To quote Lord Malmesbury again:

On the twelfth [of October, 1801] a Frenchman called Lauriston, occasional aide-de-camp to Bonaparte, brought over the ratification. A Jacobin saddler in Oxford Road saw him pass . . . He assembled the mob, persuaded them he was Bonaparte's brother, and Lauriston was drawn about by them in a hackney coach to all his visits. Government . . . treated it very lightly, yet it was a most disgraceful circumstance and a sad precedent.[35]

Could peace have lasted in 1802? At first sight, the answer must be 'no'. Britain and France were prepared to come to terms, but neither had relinquished their essential war aims. While Britain still desired security in Europe, Napoleon was equally concerned to preserve French hegemony, and the two goals soon proved to be incompatible. But this is almost certainly too deterministic. Britain was most unlikely to renew the war in the immediate future: not only was most political opinion against such a move, but those who did wish to fight on were hopelessly undermined by the contradictions of their position. Moreover, given that Napoleon was already showing signs of reneging on the arrangements decided on in the Preliminaries of London even before the definitive peace was signed at Amiens, it is hard not to conclude that British interest in the Continent had been set aside. And if French hegemony in Western Europe was not under threat from London, it was certainly not under threat from anywhere else. The new emperor of Russia was very much leaning towards Napoleon, while Prussia was content with its dominance of northern Germany and Austria anxious to avoid a fight, even groping towards disengagement from Germany and Italy in favour of an advance in the Balkans. On top of that, French success had been quite extraordinary: the 'natural' frontiers having been achieved at no cost even to France's colonial empire; Louis XIV himself could not have asked for more.

Nor was the settlement itself so very bad as a basis for an end to the 'age of war' that had characterized the eighteenth century. As Schroeder points out, the settlement reached in the period 1801–2 was in fact remarkably realistic in global terms. Britain, France and Russia were effectively recognized as the three leading powers of Europe, and each of them was accorded dominance in one particular sphere. Britain was allowed to retain her supremacy at sea: even Napoleon did not demand the dismantling of the Royal Navy, and this meant that France's colonial presence was one that existed on sufferance and could always be closed down. France stood supreme in Western Europe and was bolstered by much enlarged frontiers and an unassailable sphere of influence in Italy and Germany. And Russia was seemingly assured that the Ottoman Empire would be her exclusive preserve, and that she would have a major voice in the reorganization of Germany that now loomed. As for Austria and Prussia, while clearly less well favoured than Britain, France and Russia, they too might hope for compensation in Germany. And if it was theoretically the case that no one power would be allowed to dominate Germany – one possible bone of contention amongst the powers – a similar situation was reached in the Mediterranean: France had her base at Toulon, Britain hers at Gibraltar, and Russia hers – at least potentially – in the Ionian islands, while Malta was denied to everybody. In short, what we see is a compromise settlement that was no more unstable than earlier general European peace treaties, and we must therefore find other reasons for its failure to produce anything other than a mere truce. What, though, should we make of the war that had just terminated? Put in a nutshell, what it showed was that France was so strong in the wake of the Revolution and, more particularly, the coming of Napoleon Bonaparte, that there was no way that she could be contained except by a general alliance amongst the powers. For that to be workable, Britain would have to accept a continental commitment, Austria and Prussia set aside their endless rivalry over Germany, and

Russia lift her eyes from Poland and the Ottoman Empire. In other words, the powers would have to evolve a new approach to international relations that was based on common interest rather than mutual rivalry and the pursuit of traditional ambitions. In 1802, however, this development was still far away, blocked by obstacles so entrenched that only the most cataclysmic of forces could have swept them aside. But what did Napoleon Bonaparte with all his genius, his dynamism, his daring and his ruthlessness represent but just such a force? Embedded in the very triumphs of Marengo and Hohenlinden, Lunéville and Amiens were the seeds of France's downfall.

3

The Peace of Amiens

On 25 March 1802 Europe's guns fell silent for the first time since April 1792. For ten years bar one month the powers of Europe had been caught up in a confused series of campaigns that only barely approximated to the struggle of the French versus the rest of legend. From these campaigns the French had emerged victorious: long years of international impotence had been reversed, the 'natural frontiers' obtained, and Holland, Switzerland and northern Italy incorporated into a de facto empire in which Paris's word was law. Though thwarted in Egypt and undermined in India, France had also recovered her colonial possessions, at least in title, and regained a presence on the mainland of North America. Yet there was an element of balance in the situation that makes it possible to argue that Amiens might have produced a general and lasting peace, especially as all the powers of Europe were either deeply war-weary – Britain, France and Austria – or preoccupied with domestic issues – Russia and Prussia. What was required, self-evidently, was restraint and good will on all sides, coupled with a recognition, first, that all the powers had legitimate interests, and, second, that the conduct of international relations had to be instilled with a spirit of compromise. For peace to last, therefore, much would depend upon Napoleon. At the very least, the First Consul would have to withdraw his troops from Holland, Switzerland and Italy, respect the integrity and independence of the Cisalpine, Ligurian, Helvetic and Batavian Republics, and generally restrain his actions on the Continent of Europe. A liberal policy towards British trade would have been advisable, not to mention progress towards the trade agreement called for – though not stipulated – at Amiens, while it was imperative that the French curb their activities in the wider world. Given Napoleon's character, ambition and ever more inflated view of his own abilities, however, this was most unlikely, and thus it was that within fourteen months conflict resumed.

Once again, then, we return to the personal history of Napoleon Bonaparte. The First Consul always maintained in later years that he saw Amiens as a lost opportunity: 'At Amiens I honestly believed that the fates of France, Europe and myself had all been fixed, and the war brought to an end . . . As far as I was concerned, I was going to give myself over to the administration of France alone, and I believe that I would have given birth to prodigies . . . Of what lustre was I deprived.'[1] Given the context of these words was the elaboration of the legend of St Helena, they are impossible to accept at face value, but even the most committed sceptic cannot deny that Napoleon's personality did not find its only outlet on the battlefield. On the contrary, the First Consul came to power steeped in a view of the ancient world that saw the ideal classical hero as a man who was not only a military commander, but also a law-giver. Beginning with the debate on the new constitution, from his first days in office he therefore flung himself into the business of civil government:

In the four years of his Consulate he held several councils every day. In these meetings all the objects of administration, of finance, of justice, were successively examined. And, as he was possessed of great perception, there often escaped his lips the most profound interjections and the most judicious reflections, and these astounded men who were much better versed in these affairs. The meetings often continued until five o'clock in the morning.[2]

For a similar impression we can turn to the memoirs of Antoine Thibaudeau, an erstwhile member of the Convention, who in September 1800 was appointed as a member of the Council of State:

When Napoleon was raised to the chief magistracy he already enjoyed a great reputation. But great as his reputation already was, all the world was astonished by the ease with which he grasped the reins and mastered those parts of the administration with which he was totally unfamiliar. Still greater surprise was felt at the manner in which he treated matters which were entirely strange to him . . . He presided over nearly all the sittings of the Council of State during which the Civil Code was being discussed, and took a very active part in the debates, beginning, sustaining, directing and reanimating them by turns. Unlike some of the professional orators in the

Council, he made use of no rhetorical efforts; he never sought for well-rounded periods or fine words; he spoke without any preparation, embarrassment or affectation . . . He was never inferior . . . in knowledge . . . to any member of the Council; he usually equalled the most experienced of them in the facility with which he got to the root of a question, in the justice of his ideas, and in the force of his arguments. He often surpassed them all by the turn of his sentences and the originality of his expressions.[3]

Napoleon, then, was genuinely enthusiastic in his new role of 'chief magistrate'. As the years of fighting petered out, so a certain change of atmosphere became apparent. The First Consul began to represent himself as a civilian ruler – 'Why, there is not a man in France', he thundered, 'who is more of a civilian than I am'[4] – to appear in public in civilian dress and to have painters such as Ingres and Gros depict him not in the blue uniform of a general but rather in the red costume that had been accorded him in his capacity as head of the French state. General Bonaparte, too, was as often as not 'Citizen Bonaparte', and the French ruler spent much time patronizing the arts and visiting factories and workshops. 'During the autumn of 1802,' wrote Bourrienne, 'there was held at the Louvre . . . an exhibition of the products of industry which was highly gratifying to the First Consul. He seemed proud of the high degree of perfection the industrial arts had attained in France.'[5]

The idea that Napoleon had been reborn as a man of peace is wide of the mark, however. In reality, a number of factors combined to ensure that, if he was not actually bent on war, then he was at the very least prepared to take serious risks. In the first place, there were the pressures generated by his own character. The First Consul, as we have seen, was obsessed with the concept of power. As Mathieu Molé, a young nobleman who in 1806 became one of the Council of State's secretaries, put it, 'The more I saw of him, the greater was my conviction that he . . . thought only of satisfying his own desires and adding incessantly to his own . . . greatness.'[6] At the same time, Napoleon was a man of both immense vanity and immense ambition. While they certainly reflect a hostile view, the words of the erstwhile Director, Gohier, are most interesting:

Behind a façade of simplicity that was used to impose on the multitude, he hid an excessive vanity, an *amour propre* without limits. If he habitually disdained finery in a court that was more richly adorned than ever before, it was in order to fix everyone's gaze upon him . . . In effect, by affecting an appearance that was more than modest while at the same time insisting that nobody could appear before him without being covered in gold, embroidery, ribbons and gems of every sort, Bonaparte was saying: 'Although I am the only one who merits it, I am the only person here who has no need of ornament. As far as everyone else is concerned, they owe their lustre solely to the light that I cast on all those who surround me.' The glory . . . that is often taken to have been his dominant passion, was in fact itself dominated by his insatiable desire to achieve. The renown to which all our greatest captains have aspired was for him his point of departure rather than the goal which he hoped to attain. The base of his character was a reflex audacity whose object was the satisfaction of an ambition without limits.[7]

And, if the goal was supremacy, war was the means – at times the only means – by which it could be attained and safeguarded. War, however, did not just fulfil a basic need in Napoleon's character. At the same time, the First Consul always realized that military glory was bound up with his political survival, just as war had been inseparably linked with his rise to prominence. As he said on one occasion in 1803, 'The First Consul does not resemble those kings by the grace of God who consider their states as a heritage. He needs brilliant actions and therefore war.'[8] And in 1802 Napoleon was quite explicit as to his intentions: 'Victories which are past soon cease to strike the imagination . . . My intention certainly is to multiply the works of peace. It may be that in the future I shall be better known by them than by my victories, but for the present nothing is so resonant as military success.'[9]

Nor was the question purely a matter of guaranteeing Napoleon's personal prestige in the eyes of his fellow rulers or of stamping his authority upon the Continent of Europe. Fearing the mob as he did, he seems also to have regarded war as a means of disciplining his subjects and curbing French volatility. As he said, 'Even in the midst of war, I have never neglected the establishment of useful institutions and the promotion of peace and order at home. There still remains much to be done, and I shall certainly never rest from my labours. But is not military success still more necessary to dazzle or to content our people?'[10] At the same time, although the French ruler was in no sense its prisoner, there was also the question of the army. Exactly as had been the case under the Republic, the sheer size of the French military establishment was a spur to a forward policy. Economics aside, Napoleon had to ensure that its aspirations were met, and all the more so given its rapid evolution from the Jacobin 'army of virtue' to an 'army of honour' led by senior commanders who could potentially become 'over-mighty subjects'. To quote Pasquier:

The army necessarily became the object of his most serious concerns. It might have been thought that it would have been satisfied to see a general placed at the head of the government at last, and this ought in fact to have been the case, and yet it was in its ranks that there were to be found the greatest number of malcontents. It was impossible for such fortune not to excite the jealousy of other generals who believed that they possessed merit equal to that of the First Consul.[11]

Nor was Pasquier alone in this assessment of the situation. As the much-hated and utterly unscrupulous Minister of Police, Joseph Fouché, wrote:

I perceived, day by day, how much easier it was to get possession of the sources of opinion in the civil hierarchy than in the military order, where the opposition was often more serious from its being covered. The counter-police . . . was very active in this respect; the officers called malcontents were suspended, exiled or imprisoned. But the discontent soon degenerated into irritation among the generals and colonels, who, deeply imbued with Repub-lican ideas, saw clearly that Bonaparte only trampled on our institutions in order to advance more freely to absolute power . . . At a dinner at which some twenty discontented officers had met with some old republicans and violent patriots, the ambitious projects of the First Consul were brought upon the *tapis* without any restraint. When their spirits had once become elevated by the fumes of wine, some of the parties went so far as to say that it was indispensable to make the new Caesar share the fate of the former . . . So great was the excitement that a colonel . . . famous at that time . . . as a good shot, affirmed that he would pledge himself not to miss Bonaparte at fifty yards' distance.[12]

With two of the worst malcontents – Bernadotte, who headed the Army of the West, and Moreau, who headed the Army of the Rhine – in key positions, it could be argued that continuous warfare was essen-tial. In the early summer of 1802, indeed, the dangers of a state of peace had been made all too apparent by the discovery of the so-called 'conspiracy of Rennes'. One of a number of similar intrigues that was afoot at this time, this was led by Bernadotte's chief-of-staff and involved an attempt to whip up a revolt among the large number of troops that were being concentrated in Brittany prior to dispatch to almost certain death from yellow fever in the West Indies. Though the plot was uncovered before much more had been achieved than the distribution of two seditious handbills, it had still been frightening enough. Much alarmed, Napoleon initially threatened to have Bernadotte shot, but wisely backed away from this impulse in favour of offering 'Sergeant Belle-Jambe', as the Gascon general was known, the post of governor of Louisiana, and then ambassador to the United States (other generals who were sent off on convenient diplomatic missions at this point included Lannes, who was sent to Lisbon, and Brune, who was sent to Constantinople). Also interesting, meanwhile, is the suggestion that war was, if not imminent, then at the very least not far away. Let us take, for example, the following account of a review at the Tuileries in 1802:

After the infantry and dismounted cavalry had formed squares, [Bonaparte] went round . . . on foot to talk to the soldiers . . . To one he said, 'Have you seen active service?' 'No.' 'You're lucky.' To another, 'You will have good generals.' The moment he had done speaking to one particular square, the soldiers began smoking, talking and joking to one another, or repeating what *le petit bonhomme* had said to them. One heard Bonaparte say to a soldier, 'You are a jolly fellow. You will fight well.' 'Place yourself near me, *mon général*, and you'll see.' I felt the greatest eagerness to see Bonaparte, I own, and the moment he came up to where I was I only thought of him as a conqueror amid his troops.[13]

In addition there were serious worries about civilian society. Napoleon had come to power ostensibly offering France peace, but he also wished to offer her prosperity, and this too seemed to demand the continuation of a belligerent foreign policy that would give *la grande nation* resources and markets that she could not otherwise command. And only thus could Napoleon seek to counter the growing chorus of voices accusing him of overthrowing liberty and establishing himself as a despot. By the time of the peace of Amiens this opposition was starting to make itself felt. As early as February 1801 various members of the tribunate had sought to block the formation of the special tribunals that Napoleon deemed necessary to suppress the brigandage that affected much of

France on the grounds that they were a threat to the rule of law. At the end of 1801 there had been a serious tussle with the tribunate and the legislature over the appointment of three new members of the senate, while the two chambers concerned had then proceeded to reject a series of government proposals including the first clauses of the Civil Code. And finally, in April 1802, the introduction of the Legion of Honour was met with concerted opposition on the grounds that it would lead to the creation of a new aristocracy. By one means or another, this resistance was overcome and the powers of the assembly reduced still further, but the inference was all too clear: republican principle would clearly have to be undercut by a prosperity that in the end could not but depend on armed force. Nor did this just apply to the notables. It was this group that was most likely to be moved by the denunciations of leading oppositionists such as Daunou and Constant, but there was, too, the question of the *sans culottes*. For this group the Consulate was little more than a fraud. Representative democracy was dead. The working man was encumbered with an ever tougher and more intrusive police system and various hostile measures, including the much-hated *livret* or passbook. And in January 1801 the leaders of political radicalism were decimated by a savage purge unleashed on the pretext of the terrorist bomb that almost cost Napoleon and Josephine their lives in the Rue St Niçaise on 24 December 1800. In fact, the bomb was planted by royalists, but the First Consul had for some time been looking for a means of settling with Jacobinism. In the short term, peace was a helpful antidote to unrest, but peace without economic prosperity was not an attractive prospect. Although Napoleon had succeeded in defusing the situation by buying up cheap flour outside the country, at the very time that the Treaty of Amiens was being signed the price of bread was rising sharply, giving rise to fears of serious unrest. And, to reiterate, economic prosperity was impossible to attain except through war: in the long term France needed both markets and raw materials, while, as a mercantilist, Napoleon himself believed that these objectives could only be secured through force.

Setting aside the connection that could be made between continued military victory and the restoration of order, the effect of Napoleon's reorganization of France was in a number of ways simply to increase his ambition. The debates that surrounded the Civil Code and the rest are a case in point. At the very beginning, notes Chaptal, the First Consul had on occasion been prepared to defer to men of greater knowledge and experience. However, as time went on, so matters began to change:

From the moment that Bonaparte acquired ideas, whether true or false, concerning all the objects of administration, then he ... no longer consulted anyone ... with any intention of embracing their advice. He constantly followed his own ideas; his opinion was his only rule of conduct; and he tartly mocked all those who uttered ideas that were different from his own. Seeking ways to ridicule these last, he would often strike his head and say, 'This instrument is more use to me than the counsels of men of supposed instruction and experience.'[14]

After enduring a sharp learning-curve – one disconcerting habit of Napoleon's, for example, was initially to argue a course of action opposite to the one that he actually intended to follow to flush out his opponents and give the impression that he was yielding to argument – the First Consul's entourage discovered what was expected of them. Not, indeed, that much could be expected of them. As Gohier observes, his councillors of state mostly consisted of 'men who were committed to the pursuit of power for its own sake and had only marched in the ranks of the Republicans so as to avail themselves of the spoil of the republic'.[15] This, perhaps, is unfair. Not all the men who surrounded Napoleon were devoid of critical judgement and a spirit of independence. Self-serving and egotistic *par excellence*, Talleyrand had negotiated the twists and turns of the 1790s with consummate skill, went on to serve the Bourbons in 1814, and within a few years had effectively broken with his master over the issue of foreign policy. But the fact is that the welcome that Napoleon was prepared to extend to anyone who would rally to his rule, be they constitutional monarchists, Jacobin extremists, Thermidorian conservatives or royalist emigrés, was an open invitation to set aside all principle and play the role of echo to the First Consul.

The result, needless to say, was a reinforcement of both Napoleon's habit of command and of his sense of infallibility. In the absence of the First Consul, the Council of State was utterly ineffectual. 'I should say of the Council of State and the members of that assembly,' wrote Molé, 'what has been said with so much truth of our great armies and the generals that commanded them. When Napoleon was at their head they became irresistible and the generals under his orders all seemed great captains. When he was absent those armies had difficulty holding their own, and the lieutenants of Napoleon quarrelled, were jealous of each other and could do nothing . . . One might often compare them to the figure "o" which owes all its importance to the number preceding it.'[16] Napoleon, then, reigned supreme. To quote Molé again:

As soon as his thought took shape, he let it fall from his lips, indifferent to the form in which it was clothed. Little he cared for the matter in debate. Contemptuous of all set rules, placing himself above the conventions, he regarded as the privilege of his superiority over other men the right of thinking aloud and letting his brain conceive and his mouth utter, relying on the attention and respect with which his slightest word was received by his hearers, the most eminent of which felt themselves a long way inferior to him. He had no fear of finding himself contradicting himself. With his ingenuity in discovering subtle and plausible reasons in support of all opinions, he attached less importance to selecting them well than to proving that his mind revolved every aspect of every question, and that there was not a single idea they could suggest which had not already occurred to him.[17]

With every day that passed, Napoleon was being confirmed in his belief in his own infallibility. At the same time, the state that he was ruling was becoming ever more powerful as a vehicle of his ambition. To understand this we must return to the beginning of the Consulate in 1800. One of the most enduring elements of the Napoleonic legend is that Brumaire rescued France from irremediable chaos, that Napoleon, in fact, was the saviour not so much of the Revolution but of France herself. This is an exaggeration: up-to-date work on the Directory shows that it had not only arrested the slide to military disaster prior to the future First Consul's return from Egypt, but that it also introduced a number of important internal reforms that helped pave the way for Napoleon's success. Yet in the long term the military picture was very bleak. Given her population of 29 million, it might be thought that all that France had to do to acquire a mass army was to introduce universal military service. Needless to say, however, matters were not nearly so straightforward, an effective system of conscription being contingent upon an equally effective process of political and administrative reform.

France had in fact possessed a system of universal conscription since 1798, the so-called Loi Jourdan introduced in that year decreeing that all unmarried men other than sole breadwinners, government officials, priests and students, and the physically unfit, would become liable for military service at the age of twenty in accordance with a quota system filled by ballot. However, although it was to be the basis for conscription to the French army throughout the Napoleonic period, at the time of its introduction the Loi Jourdan was little more than a dead letter. From the time of the first appearance of compulsory service on an ad hoc basis in the emergency of 1793, this had been hated by the peasantry who constituted the bulk of the population: service in the army meant loss of home, family and the security of familiar surroundings, and brought with it privation, danger and death; soldiers were notoriously brutal and licentious; and finally conscription deprived peasant communities of much-needed labour, while being rightly perceived as socially unjust (for, in general, the towns and the bourgeoisie suffered less than the countryside and the peasantry). Nor did large sections of the peasantry think the Revolution was worth fighting for: in many parts of the country the financial burdens under which they had laboured had actually worsened since 1789; they had benefited little from the sale of the lands of the Church and the emigrés; and they had periodically been subject to ruthless requisitioning by the representatives of the hated *bourgs*. Added to this was the question of religion. We should not overgeneralize here as many peasants hated the Church. However, in Brittany, Normandy, Flanders, Poitou and many other areas, the Catholic Church was still a strong focus of rural life, and yet it had been subjected to the most virulent anti-clericalism. Across large parts of France, peasant unrest in consequence reached massive proportions, the problem of public order being worsened still further by the growing incidence of desertion, and by extension, brigandage. By 1798, so serious had the problem become that the Directory was quite incapable of enforcing its authority over local government and with it both taxation and conscription. With its difficulties augmented by the military disasters of 1799, the Directory turned in desperation to a revival of the Jacobinism of 1793, but in doing so it only deepened the crisis: much alarmed by what they saw as a further threat to property and order, and financially very badly hit by economic depression and the Directory's attempts to stabilize the financial situation by slashing payments on the national debt and reorganizing the fiscal system, the notables – the men of property, much of it obtained in the course of the Revolution, who formed the bedrock of French local government – withdrew their support from Paris. Sabotaged by popular resistance and propertied non-cooperation alike, the Loi Jourdan had therefore proved a complete failure, with only 131,000 of the first 400,000 men called up ever reaching their units.

When Napoleon came to power, then, France essentially had the makings of a large-scale war effort, but not the ability to capitalize upon them. Within a very short space of time, however, the First Consul had changed all that, initially by reinforcing the structures of government. A council of state was established to help draft legislation and provide Napoleon with expert advice. The ministries were reorganized and various measures introduced to coordinate their work; the bureaucracy, the fiscal system, the judiciary and the very law itself (through the promulgation of the famous Civil Code of 1804) were rationalized and reordered; and in February 1800 the whole system of local government was transformed. Whereas the ideal since the Revolution had been that the law should be implemented by elected local councils, authority was now placed in the hands of officials appointed by Paris, the administration of each department now being headed by an all-powerful prefect, who was also given many responsibilities that had hitherto been handled at the level of the town hall. In theory highly efficient, the system ensured that the men in charge of local affairs were now entirely dependent upon Paris for their survival. Highly paid and very often hailing from other parts of France than the areas in which they served, the prefects, in theory at least, were also immune to bribery and the pressures of local interests. And finally, as a further means of subordinating the administration to the regime, Napoleon systematically packed it with men who were in the end likely to be loyal to him, including his brothers, Lucien and Joseph; Generals Berthier, Masséna, Brune, Marmont, Lefebvre and Sérurier, all of whom had served under Napoleon in Italy or Egypt; and such representatives of the *savants* who had accompanied Napoleon to Egypt as Gaspard Monge and Claude Berthollet.

One appointment was particularly vital. Placed under Lucien Bonaparte, the Ministry of the Interior became the very heart of the Napoleonic regime. Armed with a purview that covered almost every aspect of French society, including agriculture, commerce and education, this gave Paris powers of intervention that were all but unprecedented, while at the same time providing Napoleon with a mass of information that was simply unavailable to previous regimes. If conscription could be imposed, for example, it was in part because the Ministry of the Interior conducted no fewer than three general censuses in the period

1803 to 1811. Nor was it just a matter of knowing what resources were available. From the endless reports submitted to Paris by the authorities, the regime was also able to respond to local conditions in a remarkably sophisticated manner. Also of interest here is the Ministry of Police, whose agents spied on the populace certainly, but not so much to lock them up – there were comparatively few political prisoners under Napoleon – as to keep Paris informed of what they were thinking. Far from being imposed in a universal manner, then, conscription was, so far as possible, tailored to what the population was likely to bear. If the eastern provinces that bordered on Germany (where there was a long tradition of military service) were therefore hit disproportionately hard, memories of the Vendée got Brittany off much more lightly, while the Pyrenees were eventually let off scot-free in exchange for the formation of special local militia known as the Chasseurs des Montagnes. Far from seeing a regime whose watchword was terror, we rather see one that in many respects sought to negotiate with its population and to impose pragmatic boundaries on the action of the state. 'I was far', wrote Fouché, 'from limiting my duties to espionage . . . As I was informed of all, it became my duty to . . . make known to the head of government the discomforts and sufferings of the state.'[18]

These measures undoubtedly instilled in the system a new degree of energy, but the mere remodelling of the state was not enough. Backing up the prefects were military resources that were both more powerful and more reliable: efforts were made to rotate National Guard battalions so that they served outside their own locality; the Gendarmerie Nationale was purged, rebuilt with reliable veteran soldiers, placed under an Inspector General, and greatly increased in size; and Paris and other large cities were permitted to form municipal guards. More immediately, the lull in hostilities following the battle of Marengo also allowed the dispatch of large numbers of troops into the interior to suppress brigands and round up deserters, their activities being strengthened by the introduction of special judicial measures that effectively authorized summary execution. This offensive did not solve the problem overnight – between December 1804 and July 1806 there were no fewer than 119 anti-conscription disturbances of various sorts in metropolitan France, while as late as 1805 desertion was running at a rate of around 800 men per month – but little by little the situation was visibly changing. In 1798 draft evasion had stood at 37 per cent; in 1806 it stood at 27 per cent;

in 1810 it stood at 13 per cent; and in 1811 it disappeared altogether. Nor was it simply men who refused to go along with conscription that felt the weight of repression. In Normandy and Brittany the *chouan* bands that had throughout the 1790s at one and the same time kept counter-revolution alive, given aid and sustenance to draft evasion and terrorized all those who stood by the state, were hunted down by the newly invigorated authorities. Equally brigandage was gradually closed off as a survival strategy for those who chose to live outside the law: in the department of Seine Inférieure, for example, the number of highway robberies (for which government mail coaches were a common target) declined steadily from 1800 onwards, until a final attack in April 1807 was followed by six years of absolute peace. We look some way into the future here, of course, but even so, by the time that relations began once again to break down with the British, the immediate problem had been resolved. 'The English ministers ... make a great mistake if they think they can dictate laws to a nation of forty millions,' boasted Napoleon. 'They think I am doubtful of my position and therefore afraid to go to war. Why, I can raise two million men if I want them.'[19]

Men, meanwhile, were matched by money. In the realm of taxation Napoleon was in no sense an innovator. If there was one area of government in which the Directory had had some success it was that of the development of the fiscal system. In the period 1797–9 the tax structure inherited from the Revolution had been completely reorganized by the Minister of Finance, Jacques Ramel de Nogaret. Direct taxation had been based on three property levies – on land, movable property and servants, and doors and windows – and a licence that was payable by the proprietors of all commercial and industrial businesses. Backing these up were an array of indirect taxes: abolished in the course of the Revolution, these now returned in the form of internal customs dues – the old *octroi* – stamp duties and a levy payable on tobacco. The Consulate let this be: from 1804 onwards there was a steady increase in the number of indirect taxes payable on consumer goods, but for the time being Napoleon let well alone other than to impose a moderate additional levy known as the *centimes additionnels* on the four direct taxes. What he was interested in was rather the state's ability to collect the revenue theoretically assigned to it. Despite genuine efforts by Ramel, who had transferred the task of tax assessment and collection from agents of local government to new officials responsible to the treasury and launched a major drive to collect the large number of outstanding arrears, returns were very low. With its foreign revenues in steep decline thanks to the military successes of the Second Coalition, in June 1799 the Directory had imposed a forced loan that echoed the most radical measures of the Convention and greatly shook the confidence of the notables. This situation was now put right. As early as 24 November 1799 a new law reorganized the machinery of tax collection so as to increase the control of the Ministry of Finance over the network of tax-farmers who operated the system at municipal and departmental level and tighten up the system of inspection and accounting. From 1802 onwards, immense labour was expended on a new survey of property whose aim was to ensure that nothing escaped the scrutiny of the state. Thanks also, of course, to the greater police powers now available, the net result was that the French state acquired a new measure of financial stability: in 1801, indeed, there was a small surplus of income over expenditure.

Thanks to the regime's greater ability to resort to repression, the inhabitants of Napoleonic France knew that open opposition would have unpleasant consequences. However, the political settlement that followed 18 Brumaire was characterized as much by the carrot as it was by the stick. While Napoleon was certainly concerned above all to boost the power of the state – whose interests, of course, he had come to identify with his own person – he was well aware that his rule could not be consolidated unless, as he put it, 'we can plant on the soil of France some masses of granite'.[20] In real terms, this meant that the new regime would have to conciliate key elements of society. The peasantry, for example, were bought off by the abandonment of revolutionary dechristianization, the Concordat of 1801 restoring freedom of worship to the Catholic Church, and the nobility by the welcome given to any emigré who chose to return to France. Also helpful was a reduction in conscription: between 1800 and 1805 the number of men taken by the army amounted to a mere 78,000 per annum. As for the urban poor, they got employment and cheap bread: faced with a real threat of famine, in 1802 the government introduced a series of special measures designed to ensure the flow of grain to Paris and prop up manufacturers affected by the current slump in trade. And humbler folk of all sorts were cheered by the restoration of the traditional calendar with its seven-day week and profusion of religious holidays. Most importantly, however, the propertied classes in general received especially favourable treatment. Thus the notables were guaranteed possession of the land they had obtained from the Church and the nobility since the Revolution, while both nobles and bourgeois were given a very high degree of representation in the political and administrative structures created by the regime (and with it generous salaries and other emoluments), a monopoly of higher education, protection from the worst rigours of conscription and de facto domination of the officer corps. They were also favoured by Napoleon's fiscal policy, which relied ever more heavily on indirect taxation, and they could rely on the regime to protect their economic interests through such measures as restrictive labour legislation and the Civil Code. Of particular note here was the First Consul's determination not to repeat the mistakes of the 1790s with respect to the printing of paper money. Thus, the thoroughly discredited *assignats* did not reappear while tight controls were imposed on government borrowing and financial speculation, and the currency stabilized by the creation of a Bank of France. And, finally, to repeat a key point just made in another context, brigandage was no longer the all-consuming nightmare it had threatened to become under the Directory. Under Napoleon, in short, property and person were secure.

So often has the Civil Code been cited as an example of the First Consul's beneficence that it needs to be discussed here in some detail. What is most striking to the modern observer is, first, its profound social injustice, and second, the extent to which this injustice was the work of Napoleon himself. What we see is not a universal charter of justice, but rather a device designed to propitiate the elites through whom France was now to be ruled. While there were certainly many clauses that benefited all classes of society, the code was directed above all at men of property, whose defence it enshrined. At the same time, alongside the clauses for which it is usually remembered, there was an insistence – and here we must thank Napoleon himself for taking a particular interest in this part of its provisions – on the dominant role of the *père de famille* that swept aside many of the changes that France had experienced in 1792. In particular, the position of women deteriorated dramatically. No longer did they have equal rights to divorce (for which the grounds were considerably restricted) while they could also be imprisoned for adultery. On top of this, they were made completely subordinate to the will of their husbands and denied the rights they had been granted to maintain control of their own property, to enjoy a share in family property, to inherit on the death of their husbands, to sign contracts and to stand witness in court. Along with their children, they could be thrown on the streets at any time while they were also denied the right to sue for divorce if they were abandoned. Just as grim was the position of children: fathers could have them imprisoned for periods up to six months, veto their marriages until they were well into adulthood, make use of their property as they saw fit while they were still minors, and discriminate between them in matters of inheritance. All this was primarily predicated on the desire to maintain the stability of the family as an economic unit, but there was also a political subtext: both women and youth had played a prominent role in many of the revolutionary *journées* and it was from the first recognized that the family was an important means whereby pressure could be placed upon recalcitrant conscripts. For Napoleon, clearly, fathers were one more arm of state repression and control.

At the time of the Consulate, however, it was still conciliation that was the order of the day. Alongside this went propaganda, Napoleon also making great efforts to persuade public opinion that his policies were in the national interest. For example, if the propertied classes were co-opted into the regime, it was in part so that, as leaders of local society, they could become ambassadors among the people. Equally, if an emasculated legislature continued to meet in Paris, it was in part because it acted as a forum in which Napoleon could justify his policies and extol his successes. And if plebiscites were repeatedly used to legitimize changes in government – in 1800 to approve the consular constitution and in 1802 to make Napoleon First Consul for life and usher in constitutional changes that increased his powers still further – it was to create an image of national unity and pay lip-service to the principle of the sovereignty of the people. In this respect, moreover, every aspect of cultural life was pressed into service as a mouthpiece of the government. With regard to the press, for example, Napoleon on the one hand imposed rigid censorship, and on the other ensured that his message reached the widest possible audience by having papers produced in cheap editions and read aloud in public places. Amongst the intelligentsia, writers who supported the regime were patronized and encouraged but those who did not were harassed, imprisoned or forced into exile. And in education, teachers fell increasingly under the control of the state and *lycée* students were made to wear uniform, do drill and study a national curriculum that combined utility with propaganda. Granted freedom of worship, the Church, too, found that the price was the use of religion to underpin the regime – a convenient St Napoleon was even discovered – and the conversion of the pulpit into an instrument of political indoctrination. Finally, the arts – painting, music and architecture – continued to be appropriated to glorify Napoleonic rule. Much of the resultant output was either stereotypically grandiose or wholly conventional in its glorification of war and conquest, but on occasion there were also signs of greater subtlety. Gros's famous 1804 painting of Napoleon's visit to the plague hospital at Jaffa is a good example. In this we see Napoleon as warlord, certainly, but alongside this are also other images – the compassionate leader ministering to his men without fear for his own safety, and even the medieval monarch warding off the disease known as the 'king's evil'. The message was unmistakable: the man on horseback was also a man of peace, and the man of blood a man of healing.

How far all these policies had an influence on French society it is hard to say. But there is no doubt that in the wake of the Treaty of Amiens the consular regime was extremely popular. Excellent harvests, rising wages and low levels of conscription all ensured that the populace were content, while the notables could feel a great deal of satisfaction at the regime's social and economic policies, not to mention the manner in which the gains of 1789 had seemingly been confirmed. Amongst the intellectual community Napoleon was still the supreme patron of the arts who had revealed the wonders of Ancient Egypt. For devout Catholics the First Consul was the man who had ended the persecution of the Church. And among Frenchmen of all conditions the return of peace was a welcome relief if only because taxation temporarily returned to the levels of 1791. Much the same was true of the gradual restoration of law and order and the reform of the judicial system, one of the results being to render justice much cheaper and more accessible. In July 1802 the plebiscite that made Napoleon First Consul for life therefore attracted 3,568,855 votes in favour to only 8,374 against. These figures, of course, cannot be taken at face value: voting was not only public but by signature, and in the army at least there was some intimidation. But even sceptics accept that the general message of the plebiscite cannot be gainsaid: in 1802 Napoleon had the general backing of France. The result, of course, was to increase his self-confidence and sense of mission still further. Appearing before the Senate on 3 August after victory had been declared, he stated:

The French people wills that the whole of my life should be consecrated to its welfare. I obey its will ... By my efforts ... the liberty, equality and prosperity of France shall be secured against the caprices of fate and the uncertainties of the future. The best and greatest of nations shall be the happiest, and its happiness will contribute to the well-being of Europe. I have been summoned by command of the people ... to restore universal justice, order and equality.[21]

For those with ears to hear, these words were profoundly ambiguous. Through a combination of factors, Napoleon had restored at least a measure of order to France, and thereby made it possible for her considerable resources to be converted into actual military power. Setting aside the issue of the *grande France* that Napoleon had created, meanwhile, there is also the issue of his personality. The field of psychobiography is at best controversial – it may, indeed, even be regarded as positively dubious – but a number of those close to Napoleon at this time have left us with a picture of a man fundamentally uncomfortable with a life of peace. One such observer was Claire de Rémusat, who arrived at the consular court as one of Josephine's ladies-in-waiting in the autumn of 1802:

Bonaparte lacked education and good manners: it was as if he had been irrevocably destined to live out all his life either in a tent, where anything goes, or on a throne, when anything is permitted. He did not know how to enter or to leave a room; he did not know how to greet people, how to get up, how to sit down. His gestures were rapid and abrupt, as was his manner of speaking ... It seems to me that the attire worn by the First Consul at that time is worth remarking on. On ordinary days he wore one of the uniforms affected by his guards, but it had been laid down that on ceremonial occasions he and his two colleagues should wear a red robe embroidered with gold ... This costume embarrassed Bonaparte and he tried to escape it as much as possible ... With his scarlet and gold, he ... generally wore the waistcoat from his uniform, his campaign sword, breeches ... and a pair of boots. What with his unkempt *toilette* and his small stature, this get-up looked very strange, but no one would have been well advised to laugh at him.[22]

Nor is Chaptal much more flattering. In his eyes Napoleon 'had the manners of a second lieutenant of no family', while he was horrified by the lack of courtesy and respect which he habitually accorded his ministers, generals, servants and guests at court: the First Consul frequently flew into violent rages at the slightest misdeed, failed to appear at his own levees, and wrecked formal banquets by bolting a few mouthfuls of food and then getting up before his fellow diners had so much as embarked on the soup. This last tendency was perhaps the fruit of a personal dynamism and energy that few could equal – Chaptal reports that Napoleon could travel back to Paris day and night from the depths of Poland and plunge straight from his carriage into a meeting of the council of state without displaying the slightest fatigue – but even in his eating habits there was something of the camp: as is notorious, his favourite dishes – mushrooms, fried onions, fried potatoes – were the stuff of any soldier's skillet. To return to Napoleon's manner, there is mention of traits that would today be put down to hyperactivity, some of them deeply unpleasant:

Napoleon was by nature habitually destructive. In the council chamber the midst of a discussion would find him, knife in hand, cutting at the arms of his chair and scoring deep grooves in its wood . . . For a bit of variety in this respect, he would seize hold of a pen and cover the papers in front of him with lines of ink, crumpling up each sheet into a ball after he had finished with it and throwing it on the floor. As for pieces of porcelain, they could hardly be put in his hand without getting smashed. I remember that one day he was presented with an equestrian statue of himself that had been executed with true perfection by the china factory at Sèvres. Placing it on a table, he first broke its stirrups and then a leg, and, when I remarked that the artist would die of hurt were he to see his work being thus mutilated, he coldly replied, 'All that can be fixed with a bit of paste.' Caressing a child, he would pinch it so hard that it cried. At Malmaison he had a fowling piece in his office and he was constantly firing this through the window at the rare birds that Josephine used to keep on the lakes in the grounds. This malign impulse to destroy was so great that he could not enter the hothouse at Malmaison without cutting down or pulling up one of the rare plants that were buried there.[23]

Coupled with this suppressed violence was an egotism that is even now quite chilling. His favourite topic of conversation was himself;

he despised women and treated them with contempt and, it seems, considerable sexual brutality; and he regarded other men with the utmost cynicism:

While some of his intellectual qualities were remarkable ... his soul was lacking. There was no generosity, no real greatness. I never knew him admire, I never knew him understand, an act of decency. He always denied the existence of sentiment; he put no store in sincerity; and he openly admitted that he judged a man's ability in accordance with the extent to which he could engage in deceit – on such occasions, indeed, he would take much pleasure in recalling that in his infancy one of his uncles had predicted that he would govern the world on account of the fact that he was always lying ... Every means of governing men that might debase them was made use of by Napoleon. He shunned the bonds of affection, he took pains to divide his followers from one another, he sold his favours with the aim of spreading disquiet, and he believed that the best way of attaching men to his cause was to compromise their integrity and sometimes even to blacken their reputation. As for virtue, he only pardoned it when he was able to subject it to ridicule. One cannot even say that he truly loved glory, the fact being that he himself would not have hesitated to say that what mattered was success.[24]

These words of Claire de Rémusat are closely mirrored by Chaptal. For example:

Napoleon never experienced a generous feeling. Hence the dryness of his company; hence the fact that he never had a single friend. He regarded all men as ... instruments that could be made use of to further his caprices and his ambition ... Walking across the field of Eylau, surrounded by 29,000 corpses, he prodded a body with his foot and said to the generals who surrounded him, 'This is so much small change.' On his return from the battle of Leipzig he came across Monsieur Laplace. 'It looks as if you've lost weight.' 'Sire, I have lost my daughter.' 'Well, that's no reason. You are a geometrician: measure what's happened with a ruler and you will find that it comes to precisely nothing.' It is to this insensibility that one must attribute many of the actions of his rule ... Napoleon had no attachment to his family. It was out of vanity alone that he raised it up rather than affection for any of its members or regard for their merits. He did not appear to care about the dissolution of his sisters ... and often spoke with scorn of his brothers.[25]

This very negative picture of the French ruler is clearly open to discussion. Chaptal's insistence that Napoleon felt no love for his family is particularly questionable, while it is also important to note that the First Consul was not a monster: political executions were extremely rare under his rule and even the number of political prisoners was not very great. Personally, too, he was capable of great charm and his generosity was notorious, although this naturally begs the question of whether these traits can be taken at face value. However, recent biographers of Napoleon have been inclined to agree that there were elements in his behaviour that suggest a man for whom a pacific foreign policy, with its corollaries of trust and self-restraint, would have been very difficult. One alarming feature was the personal violence of which the French ruler was capable: even in a good mood he was apt to pinch cheeks – a famous gesture – pull ears and tweak noses, while in a bad one he could become very wild indeed, kicking over tables and physically assaulting the object of his anger. Another characteristic was the febrile nature of his mind: as several observers have pointed out, he was constantly coming up with new plans, schemes and dreams, and these served as a spur to his ambition even if they were as often as not never taken up or set aside after a longer or shorter trial. To quote the painter Joseph Farington, 'I noticed that he . . . had a feverish look, which indicated a mind unsettled.'[26] Yet another is the evidence that even at this early stage Napoleon was under immense physical and mental strain: accustomed to a working routine that was frightening in its intensity, he did not just mutilate the furniture but also himself, constantly scratching at the patches of irritation that resulted from the unpleasant skin disorder – itself almost certainly the fruit of stress – that he had been suffering from as early as 1793. More positively, there was a dynamism that needed at all times to find an outlet. At times, indeed, he all but erupts from the page: 'I have seen Bonaparte near where I could examine his countenance and observe its changes and expression,' wrote Lady Elizabeth Foster. 'I am not disappointed. I never saw a face it would be more impossible to overlook. I never saw one which bore a stronger stamp of thought, penetration and a daring mind.'[27] And last but not least there were the linked traits of impatience and a refusal to brook failure: Napoleon grew bored quickly, wanted immediate results, would not recognize the word 'impossible', and was a poor loser to whom winning was always more important than playing the game (he could not, for example, play cards without cheating).

One aspect of his nature that invites discussion here is Napoleon's relationships with women. Attempting to analyse these relationships with any degree of credibility is clearly a difficult matter, but it is worth pointing out that other scholars have at least raised the matter as a factor in the First Consul's behaviour on the international stage. In brief, the argument runs as follows. In 1796 a rather gauche and inexperienced Napoleon had fallen head over heels in love with a well-connected and sophisticated older woman, who proceeded to become his wife. The idyll unfortunately did not last: always promiscuous, Josephine almost immediately betrayed Napoleon with the young army officer, Hypolyte Charles. Beyond all doubt Napoleon was deeply hurt when he was informed of this infidelity shortly after his arrival in Egypt, and it is probably this experience that accounts for the deep scorn for women that he evinced as ruler of France. As is well known, he stayed with Josephine – continued to love her even – but his sexual response was to take a string of mistresses while treating her with a curious mixture of tenderness, brutality and contempt. What, however, was the impact of all this on his conduct of international relations? One response might well be 'nothing at all'. Yet at the same time Napoleon's evident need for military victory, for dominance on the international stage, may still have had a sexual dimension. We shall never know if the prospect of battle aroused him physically, as has sometimes been argued, but it is not unreasonable to envisage a scenario in which triumph in the field filled a void in his personal life. Unable to inspire love, he could at least inspire fear.

Taking all this together, it is difficult to see how the Treaty of Amiens could have contained Napoleon. An unquiet soul, he needed military glory on personal and political grounds alike, while as ruler of France he controlled a state that was the richest and most populous in continental Europe and whose internal problems he was in the process of getting under control. Buoying him up, too, was immense confidence in his own abilities, an unblemished record of military success and contempt for the potential opposition. 'Conscription forms armies of citizens,' he remarked. 'Voluntary enlistment forms armies of vagabonds and crimi-nals.'[28] As for Britain, he was particularly scathing:

People talk of the wealth and good government of England. Well, I have just seen the English budget, and am going to publish it in the *Moniteur*. It shows a deficit of from five to six hundred million francs . . . Of course her resources are considerable, but her expenditure is out of all proportion. People are infatuated with England without knowing anything about her . . . There is nothing in England that France need envy. Its inhabitants desert it the first moment they can get away: there are more than 40,000 on the Continent at the present moment [i.e. February 1803].[29]

We have, then, a man who was at the very least ready and willing to risk a resumption of conflict, even if he was not actually bent on such a course per se. How, then, should we interpret Napoleon's occasional remarks to the effect that the continued war was inevitable on ideological grounds? For example:

If we are to hope for good faith or durability in our treaties, one of two things are necessary. Either the other governments of Europe must approximate more closely to mine or my government must be brought more nearly into harmony with them. Between these old monarchies and our new republic there is sure to be a constant danger of war. There lies the root of the European discord . . . In our position I look upon peace as a short respite only, and I believe that my ten years of office [he was speaking before being awarded the Consulate for Life] will be passed almost entirely in fighting.[30]

The answer, of course, is quite simple: by conjuring up the spectre of foreign counter-revolution, Napoleon was in effect giving himself carte blanche to take the initiative and strike as he chose. As he told Thibaudeau:

If our neighbours understand how to keep the peace, I will make peace secure, but, if they oblige me to take up arms again, it will be to our advantage to take them up ourselves before they have been allowed to rust by long disuse . . . Be quite sure that it is not I who will break the peace. No, I have no intention of being the aggressor, but I have too much at stake to leave the initiative to the foreign powers. I know them well. It is they who will either take up arms against us, or will supply me with just motives to declare war.[31]

Whatever Napoleon's motives may have been, it is difficult not to conclude that it was thanks to him that all chance of a lasting peace was lost. As Talleyrand admitted, 'Hardly was the peace of Amiens concluded when moderation began to abandon Bonaparte; this peace had not received its complete execution before he was sowing the seeds of new wars.'[32] While there were some French troop withdrawals – specifically from Naples and Switzerland – far from living quietly within the borders allotted to him at Lunéville and Amiens, Napoleon continued actively to intervene in the affairs of the areas bordering upon them. Let us begin with Holland, whose interests, it should be said, had repeatedly been trampled on in the negotiations that had led to the final peace settlement. French troops continued to occupy the Batavian Republic throughout, while considerable pressure was put on the Dutch to cease all trade with Britain. Then there was Switzerland. In 1798 this country had become a unitary state – the Helvetic Republic – but such was the strength of cantonal feeling that there had ever since been great pressure for the adoption of a federal constitution. With the situation worsened by the bitter personal rivalries that divided the revolutionary leadership, the result was chaos: between January 1800 and April 1802 there were no fewer than four *coups d'état* as the different factions vied with one another for power. For France, however, this situation did not matter as long as she was in de facto control of the area (which was as crucial as ever: without Switzerland's Alpine passes, the direct route to northern Italy was barred). Indeed, with the peace settlement at Amiens it could be turned to her advantage. If Switzerland, unlike Holland, was evacuated immediately, the reason was simple. In the summer of 1802 a compromise constitution had been imposed on the country by means of a rigged plebiscite, and so unpopular was the result that no sooner had the French pulled out – which they did with suspicious speed – than outright civil war broke out. Needless to say, this was exactly what Napoleon wanted: within a matter of weeks the First Consul had come forward as a mediator, sent 12,000 troops into the country, and summoned a conference of notables in Paris. From this there emerged in January 1803 Switzerland's fourth constitution in five years. In itself, the so-called Act of Mediation was by no means a bad solution to the political problems thrown up by the Helvetic Republic. Radicals were conciliated by the retention of equality before the law and conservatives by the restoration of the old cantonal system. In much modified form, indeed, it has remained the basis of the Helvetic Confederation to this day. But, as was all too clear, a neutral Switzerland was not on the First Consul's agenda. By backing the conservatives in the struggle over the form that the Swiss state should take, he had won over a powerful force that would otherwise have had no difficulties in aligning themselves with the ranks of France's perpetual opponents. There remained, of course, the radicals, but as 'Jacobins' they had nowhere else to go and in consequence no option but to be grateful for such sops as Napoleon chose to throw them. To sum up, Switzerland had been established as a stable French satellite, international knowledge of this being reinforced by the fact that in August 1802 the First Consul had stripped her of the important frontier district known as the Valais so as to make certain of French control of the vital Simplon pass.

The annexationist and interventionist drive visible in Switzerland was also on show in Italy. Enlarged by the considerable tracts of Piedmontese and Venetian territory, the Cisalpine Republic – now renamed the Italian Republic – was reordered along the lines of consular France, with Napoleon becoming its president. A Napoleonic nominee, Francesco Melzi d'Erill, was appointed to be its de facto ruler – his actual position was Vice-President – while the rest of the administration was selected from the ranks of a congress of 450 notables that was convened at Lyons. As did Melzi and his supporters, in August 1802 they dutifully proceeded to introduce conscription and in the following year negotiated a French-style concordat with the papacy. In September 1802, much against the will of Talleyrand, Piedmont was annexed to France, along with Elba and Piombino, and then in October of the same year Parma passed under French administration. If the Italian Republic did not swallow up the whole of Italy, it seemed that France would. As Talleyrand observed, 'In order to rule, and to rule hereditarily, as [Napoleon] aspired to do . . . he deemed it necessary to annex to France those countries which he alone had conquered . . . never understanding that he might be called to account for so monstrous a violation of what the law of nations considered to be most sacred.'[33]

But it was in Germany that Napoleonic intervention was at its most dramatic. Thus, within a matter of months the Holy Roman Empire was effectively dismantled. So important was this last development that it must needs be looked at in some detail. Essentially a heterogeneous collection of independent kingdoms, principalities, bishoprics, abbeys, free cities and feudal fiefs united only by the theoretical allegiance of their rulers to the house of Habsburg, the Empire was a major bastion of Austrian influence, and as such had become the object of Napoleon's ire. Yet it was also threatened with destabilization from within, for many of the rulers of the larger and middling states were increasingly determined to absorb the free cities, the territories of the Church and the host of petty principalities and baronial estates. Such a policy could not but prove disastrous for Austria, whose strongest supporters in the Empire had traditionally been the bishops, abbots and imperial knights, but the problem of finding some compensation for the evicted Italian Habsburgs was now attracting even Francis II to the process. Having occupied and annexed the left bank of the Rhine, the French had proposed that the German rulers affected should be compensated by the acquisition of fresh territory east of the river. This principle, indeed, had been formally agreed at Campo Formio, and an international conference was duly initiated at Rastatt to arrange matters. Thanks to the War of the Second Coalition, however, this meeting was cut short and no further progress was made until France revived the issue at Lunéville. In doing so, of course, she hoped to break Austria's hold on the Holy Roman Empire and complete the chain of satellite states that protected the 'natural frontiers' by the creation of a pro-French bloc in southern and central Germany. What this implied was maximizing the principle of 'compensation' so as to wipe out Austria's traditional supporters in the imperial Diet and strengthen middling states such as Bavaria that could be presumed to have a strong interest in ridding themselves of the Austrian yoke. But France was not the only player in the process. Austria and Prussia wanted to obtain more land; Russia to protect her German clients (see below); and the host of minor German princes to survive and if possible augment their dominions. It was a veritable maelstrom, and one that would clearly require careful management.

Despite apparent difficulties, achieving Napoleon's goals proved almost ridiculously simple. In the first instance, as France was a guarantor of the constitution of the Holy Roman Empire by virtue of the treaty of Westphalia of 1648, the First Consul had a legitimate right to intervene in German affairs. At the same time, the French ruler had long since correctly identified gaining the support of Alexander I as the key to the situation, and all the more so as the tsar was for a variety of reasons closely involved in the fate of Germany. Thus, by virtue of the treaty of Teschen of 1779, which had seen Catherine II mediate an Austro-Prussian peace settlement in the wake of the War of the Bavarian

Succession, he could claim to be the guarantor of the Holy Roman Empire's constitution, while he also had numerous connections among the rulers of the states of Germany: his mother was a princess of Hesse, his wife was a princess of Baden, his brother-in-law was Duke of Oldenburg and a cousin the ruler of Württemberg. No sooner had Alexander come to the throne, indeed, than a new envoy had been sent to St Petersburg in the person of General Duroc. Alexander had received him warmly enough. 'Tell the First Consul that I am attached to his glory,' he had said. 'I do not want anything for myself; I only wish to contribute to the tranquillity of Europe.'[34] In saying this, he was probably sincere enough. As Sophie Tisenhaus, a Polish countess who later published her memoirs as the Comtesse de Choiseul-Gouffier, remembered:

The philanthropic character of the emperor seemed to promise uninterrupted peace to his happy subjects. No idea of conquest or ambition had thus far entered the head of this young sovereign . . . That which was not less remarkable was the admiration which he involuntarily felt for the man whose character could in no way be in sympathy with his own. But it must be admitted that that prestige of glory and power which then surrounded Napoleon was well calculated to seduce the imagination with all the fascination of the marvellous. Alexander could not consider as a usurper the extraordinary man who, having rescued France from the abyss of revolution, continued still to direct her destiny under the modest title of consul.[35]

Friendly relations having been established, the wooing of Russia continued: it is, for example, significant that the troops sent to reconquer St Domingue (see below) included all the Polish volunteer forces that had been raised from Austrian prisoners of war in Italy. Yet, naïve and idealistic though Alexander was, he did not immediately rush into the arms of Napoleon. His first Foreign Minister, Nikita Panin, was violently opposed to the French Revolution and Napoleon alike, and was in consequence inclined to seek an alliance with Britain. Indeed, a peace settlement was signed with her in June 1801. Yet Alexander always had reservations. Deeply resentful of Britain's commercial pretensions, the tsar had insisted on Britain agreeing to respect the maritime rights not just of Russia but also of the Baltic states as the price of peace, while he also strongly suspected Britain of complicity in the murder of his father and greatly disliked Panin who was notoriously arrogant and overbearing. By the autumn of 1801, then, Russia was engaged in serious negotiations with France, and in early October the way was cleared for an agreement by the replacement of Panin by the more malleable Victor Kochubei. Within days there followed the treaty with France that formally put an end to Russia's participation in the Second Coalition. This agreement being accompanied by a secret codicil that effectively promised Napoleon Russian support for his German plans, the way was open for the First Consul to remake Germany, so long, that is, as he respected the interests of Alexander I.

In the circumstances, this was little hardship. Many of the states with which the tsar had family ties were ones which he would have wished to strengthen anyway, and, if Alexander had rather ostentatiously taken Prussia under his wing in a state visit to Memel in the summer of 1802 that had seen him strike up a warm relationship with Frederick William and his queen, Louise of Mecklenburg-Strelitz, this presented little problem, for giving land to Prussia could not but threaten Austria. But how was France actually to impose her views? Here, too, there was no difficulty. In theory, the reorganization of the Holy Roman Empire was a matter for its own institutions, and in February 1801 a meeting of the imperial Parliament, or Diet, had been summoned at Ratisbon to ratify the treaty of Lunéville and negotiate the programme of territorial adjustments to which it had necessarily given rise. The result, however, was deadlock, and, more particularly, a three-way split between those who wanted no secularization at all (the ecclesiastical rulers, the free cities and the imperial knights); those who wanted some secularization only (Austria and some of the minor states); and those who wanted complete secularization (Prussia, the other Protestant states of the north and centre, and the most greedy of the Catholic states of the south). After months of wrangling, it was finally agreed that there was only one way forward, namely the establishment of a deputation of the Empire's princes headed by the Archbishop of Mainz and imperial arch-chancellor – the president of the council of princes who nominally 'elected' the emperor – Karl von Dalberg, that could lay the matter before France and Russia, discuss any solution that they might come up with and then report back to the Diet.

To act in this fashion was completely to sell the pass to Napoleon. In readiness for this all-too-predictable moment, the French Foreign Ministry had long since been engaged in drawing up a plan of action. Seeing which way the wind was blowing, a number of states – among them Prussia and Bavaria – had already come to an agreement with France as to what their gains should be, and most of the others now rushed to follow their example. There followed scenes of the utmost indignity: a swarm of German princes and their representatives descended on Paris, where they engaged in a desperate battle for territory and, in the less fortunate instances, survival. Bribery, it appears, was common, and Talleyrand, in particular, is supposed to have made a fortune. How far these efforts changed anything is another matter, however: when the Franco-Russian terms were finally published in late 1802, they essentially read very much as Napoleon had always wanted, the one real difference being that the First Consul was unable to prevent Prussia from obtaining her compensation in north-central Germany rather than on the Baltic coast, as he had intended. As for the deputation appointed by the Diet, it was helpless to do anything other than ratify Napoleon's terms and present them to the full Diet in the so-called *Reichsdeputationhauptschluss*. As for the First Consul's proposals, they were all too predictable. At a stroke, 112 of the territories that made up the empire disappeared. Gone were all the fifty-two imperial cities other than Hamburg, Bremen, Lübeck, Frankfurt, Nuremberg and Augsburg; gone were all the ecclesiastical territories apart from one special unit that was created for Dalberg and the estates of the Teutonic Knights and the Order of St John. As for where the land involved went, for Napoleon's clients the proceeds were almost literally fabulous. To list all the territories that changed hands would be tedious in the extreme, but in brief, the compensation negotiated at Paris in almost every case far outweighed the land that had been lost on the left bank of the Rhine. Prussia, for example, lost 137,000 inhabitants and gained 600,000; Bavaria lost 580,000 and gained 854,000; Baden lost 25,000 and gained 237,000; and Hesse-Darmstädt lost 40,000 and gained 120,000. Gains in income, meanwhile, were even more marked as many of the new territories were more valuable than the ones that had been lost, while states that had consisted of a scattered patchwork of territories now emerged as compact geographical units with relatively sensible frontiers.

As to what all this meant, there could no doubt. Austria did not emerge from this 'scramble for Germany' empty-handed. On the contrary, she obtained several bishoprics in the South Tyrol, while that of Salzburg was given to the Duke of Tuscany. Nevertheless, what had occurred was a disaster. The Holy Roman Empire survived, but the virtual annihilation of the free cities and the princes of the Church had completely broken Austria's predominance, all the more so as many of the vacant electorates were given to Protestant rulers such as the Duke of Württemberg and the Landgrave of Hesse-Cassel. If this lost Austria control of the college of princes, in the Diet things were still worse: whereas there had once been thirty-four ecclesiastical votes, there were now only two. For the time being the imperial knights hung on, but their days, too, were clearly numbered, and several of the rulers in whose states their territories were situated proceeded to seize their domains willy-nilly. Even were they to manage to stave off this threat, they were in any case little substitute for the bastions that had been lost. And, if Austria had been eclipsed, France was in the ascendant: though much expanded in size, the southern states, in particular, remained terrified of Austria, and therefore looked to Napoleon for protection, in effect now joining the ranks of France's satellites. As Cobenzl lamented, 'What a lesson we here receive regarding the slight regard which we enjoy abroad.'[36]

In Germany as much as Italy, then, Napoleon continued to expand his influence. Needless to say, none of this activity was to Britain's taste, her unease being heightened by the actions of Napoleon in other areas. British trade continued to be discriminated against, both in France and her satellites, and French activity in the wider world showed no signs of abating. Having already dispatched an expedition to Australia, acquired Louisiana from Spain and restored slavery in the French colonies, the First Consul now extended French hegemony in the Mediterranean by agreements with the rulers of Tunis and Algiers, kept open the possibility of a fresh expedition to Egypt, attempted to restore French influence in India, dispatched a large force to reconquer St Domingue from the victorious slave revolt of Toussaint L'Ouverture, and commenced a large programme of naval construction. Hardly had peace been signed than the most gloomy views were being expressed in London, along with the expectation – in some cases, the hope – that a new war was inevitable. As Lord Minto, the erstwhile British ambassador to Vienna, wrote to his wife on 26 November 1802:

I am convinced that both our government and the French will avoid actual war if possible: our ministers because they cannot face the difficulties of it nor could be trusted to carry it on; the French because they wish to have

possession of all we have ceded first, and to carry on their plans of aggrandizement both in Europe and abroad without opposition till they are as strong
as they wish for the contest with us. But with these dispositions to postpone
the rupture on both sides it seems difficult to avoid it . . . Nothing seems
more improbable than concession on the part of France: accordingly she is
going on as rapidly as she can without regard to our representations. Switzerland is to be first disarmed, then garrisoned by a French army which they
must pay for that service. She has taken the Duke of Parma's dominions. It
is thought at Vienna that Tuscany will go the same way, and that the King
of Etruria will not be allowed to return from Spain. Everybody here is
dejected, and most people terrified, seeing the storm preparing to burst at
last upon ourselves.[37]

In the same vein we have a letter written by Lord Hobart to Lord
Wellesley on 14 November 1802:

We have received intelligence from an authority which we believe is to be
depended upon that Bonaparte is extremely anxious to obtain possession of
Goa, and that nothing is more probable than his endeavouring to intimidate
the court of Lisbon into a surrender of it to the French government. He has
already threatened the Portuguese with the full weight of his displeasure if
Monsieur d'Almeida [sic] is not dismissed from his situation of Minister for
Foreign Affairs . . . To the peremptory demand of D'Almeida's dismissal an
evasive answer has been given, and, as Bonaparte has declared his intention
not to transige upon the subject, I should not be surprised if a sacrifice in
territory was substituted for that of the Minister. In the event, however, of
Portugal being involved in hostilities, she will claim and probably receive
support from this country.[38]

Few of Napoleon's actions actually infringed the letter of either the
Preliminaries of London or the Treaty of Amiens but they certainly
infringed what the British regarded as its spirit, and gave them reason
to suspect that worse was to follow. The problems in the relationship,
meanwhile, were worsened by the protests which the French ruler began
to voice with regard to Britain's internal arrangements. In justice, it has
to be said here that Napoleon had a point: in December 1800 he and
Josephine had narrowly escaped assassination at the hands of royalist
agents funded by the British. To protest, then, at the continued presence
of such conspirators on British soil was not so very objectionable. Nor,

perhaps, was it out of the question to demand the expulsion of the Bourbon princes then in Britain. Napoleon being Napoleon, however, diplomatic representation was immediately elevated to the status of an ultimatum. And with the reasonable there was mixed the unreasonable. To object to emigrés appearing in public wearing their old Bourbon orders was simply petty, but of much greater import was the issue of the press. For years a variety of newspapers had in article and caricature been alternately lampooning and demonizing the First Consul. Some of the material was undoubtedly scurrilous in the extreme, but even so the French ruler might have been better advised to shrug such attacks off. Such was certainly the advice of his ambassador, Andréossy, but Napoleon was too conscious of his parvenu status to tolerate such abuse and in consequence demanded that all the papers concerned should be shut down immediately. As the erstwhile Jacobin, Bertrand Barère, told one British visitor to Paris, 'Your newspapers are a daily source of irritation to the passionate disposition of the First Consul, who is so . . . vain that he is capable of declaring war against you merely on account of the insulting attacks of the English journals.'[39]

Faced by this attitude, the Addington administration decided to take a stand. The ambassador sent to France when normal diplomatic relations were finally resumed in November 1802, Lord Whitworth, was an associate of the old war party, while Addington quietly ordered a delay in the evacuation of both Malta and Egypt. Then in January 1803 there appeared the Sebastiani report. A tough and dynamic infantry officer who had fought with Napoleon in Italy and collaborated with the coup of 18 Brumaire, Horace Sebastiani had in 1802 sailed from Toulon with orders, first, to secure the recognition of the rulers of the North African coast and then to reconnoitre the situation in Egypt and Palestine. Published in the official *Moniteur* on 30 January, the document suggested that Egypt would be easy meat for reconquest, the Mamelukes being in considerable disarray and the British garrison weak and poorly commanded. Finally, as if this was not enough, on 18 February 1803 Whitworth was treated to a spectacular tirade in Paris:

In this [a continued British presence in Malta] no consideration on earth can make me acquiesce. Of the two I would rather see you in the possession of the Faubourg St Antoine than Malta . . . My irritation against England is daily increased because every wind which blows from England brings

nothing but hatred and enmity against me. If I had felt the slightest inclination to take Egypt by force, I might have done it a month ago by sending
25,000 men to Aboukir . . . What have I to gain by going to war? A descent
upon your coasts is the only means of offence I possess . . . I am well aware
of the risks of such an enterprise but you impel me to incur them. I will
hazard my army, my life, in the attempt . . . There are a hundred chances to
one against me, but I am determined to make the attempt, and such is the
disposition of the troops that army after army will be found ready to engage
in the enterprise . . . If I had not felt the enmity of the British government
on every occasion since the peace of Amiens, there is nothing I would not
have done to prove my desire to conciliate – participation in indemnities . . .
treaties of commerce, in short, anything that would have testified confidence.
Nothing, however, has been able to overcome the hostility of the British
government, and thence we are now come to the point: shall we have peace
or war? Will you or will you not execute the Treaty of Amiens? For my part
I have performed its conditions with scrupulous fidelity . . . Peace or war
depends on Malta. It is in vain to talk of Piedmont and Switzerland. They
are mere trifles and must have been foreseen when the treaty was going
forward. You have no right to speak of them at this time of day . . . Malta
. . . is doubtless of great importance [from] a maritime point of view, but it
has a value far more important in my eyes: it touches the honour of France.
What would the world say if we were to submit to the violation of a solemn
treaty signed by ourselves? Would they not doubt our energy? For myself,
my part is taken: I would rather put you in possession . . . of Montmartre
than of Malta.[40]

   This bombast proved counter-productive, however. In London, it was
perceived as the 'trick of an Italian bully' and an attempt 'to frighten us
into submission, to blind us by fear'.[41] This alone was enough to suggest
that firmness was the only possibility, but, setting that aside, Britain was
no longer quite so isolated. Thus Alexander I had belatedly realized that
he had been bamboozled by Napoleon over the Holy Roman Empire in
that, rather than enhancing their status, and, by extension, Russian
influence, the territory lavished upon his German connections had clearly
made them so many French puppets. Also alarming in his eyes was
Napoleon's assumption of the Consulate for Life, the tsar commenting
that the French ruler had 'missed the glory . . . of proving that he had
worked without personal aims for the happiness and glory of his

country' and stood revealed as simply 'one of the most famous tyrants that history has produced'.[42] At the same time Alexander, disillusioned with the chances of achieving domestic reform, was becoming less inclined to side with those of his advisers who advocated a policy of disengagement from the rest of Europe. In September 1802, then, St Petersburg saw the appointment of a new Foreign Minister in the person of Alexander Vorontzov, an anglophile whose brother was Russian ambassador to London and who balanced generally pacific inclinations with a determination not to see Russia humiliated on the international stage. More specifically, there were also growing doubts about Napoleon's intentions in the Mediterranean and more particularly in the Ottoman Empire: not only were French agents known to be penetrating the Balkans, but Constantinople had come under pressure from Paris to allow French ships unrestricted access to the Black Sea. Also an issue in the tsar's mind were the rights of the smaller states in Europe: Alexander envisaged the defence of such polities as his responsibility, and was much concerned by the manner in which Napoleon was riding over them roughshod. None of this meant that Alexander was eager to challenge France – on the contrary, Russia backed away from providing the international guarantee of Maltese independence that had been agreed at Amiens as the price of British withdrawal – but by early 1803 the Russians were hinting that they would not be averse to the Union Jack continuing to fly from the walls of Valetta, and even that they might be persuaded to sign a defensive alliance.

Thus encouraged, the British not only stood firm over Malta, but called out the militia and ordered the expansion of the navy by some 10,000 men. The First Consul was more angry than ever and on 13 March a court levee was interrupted by a stormy scene in which Whitworth was again taken to task. Accounts of this confrontation differ, but there seems little doubt that it was violent in the extreme. Let us take, for example, the version of Claire de Rémusat:

A few days before the outbreak of war, the diplomatic corps assembled at the Tuileries as normal. While it was assembling, I went to the apartments of Madame Bonaparte. Going into the chamber where she made her *toilette*, I found the First Consul sitting on the floor, gaily playing with little Napoleon, the eldest son of his brother, Louis . . . He seemed in the best humour in the world, and I told him the letters sent home by the ambassadors after that audience would speak of nothing but peace and concord ... At this Bonaparte laughed and went on playing with the child. Shortly afterwards, a message came to the effect that everyone had assembled. At this, all the gaiety disappeared from his countenance and he jumped to his feet. Meanwhile, I was struck by the severe expression that he adopted: his skin paled ... his lips contracted, and all this in less time than it takes to tell. Saying in a low voice nothing more than 'Let us go, ladies', he marched precipitately from the room and went down to the *salon*. Entering the room without greeting anyone, he went straight up to the British ambassador and immediately began to complain of the proceedings of his government. His rage appeared to grow worse by the minute and soon reached a point which terrified the assembled company: the harshest words, the most violent threats tumbled one on top of the other from his trembling lips. Nobody dared move. Struck completely dumb, Madame Bonaparte and I looked at one another in astonishment ... Even English phlegm was not up to this, and the ambassador could hardly find the words to respond.[43]

As to what was said, the tenor of Napoleon's remarks appears to have been more or less as follows:

So you are determined to go to war. We have already fought for fifteen years: I suppose you want to fight for fifteen ... more. The English wish for war, but, if they are the first to draw the sword, I shall be the last to put it into the scabbard ... If you would live on terms of good understanding with us, you must respect treaties. Woe to those who violate them![44]

This outburst, however, was not the end of the story. All those around the First Consul were shocked by his behaviour, and in some cases at least proceeded to tell him so, while even Napoleon could see that he had placed himself in the wrong. Within hours considerable efforts, then, were being made to conciliate Whitworth, and they were so successful that the ambassador came to the conclusion that what had happened had simply been a flash of temper. But the Addington administration was not appeased. On the contrary, on 3 April fresh demands arrived from London: Britain was to receive Malta, and France to evacuate Holland and Switzerland, compensate the king of Piedmont (whose domains were now restricted to the island of Sardinia) for his losses in Italy and provide a satisfactory explanation of her intentions *vis-à-vis* Egypt. Free trade was not mentioned and there were even further con-

cessions on offer in the form of recognition of France's acquisition of
Elba, but this was clearly a toughening of London's position. Yet the
French ambassador firmly maintained that Addington and his Foreign
Minister, Lord Hawkesbury, still did not want war. In this he was quite
right: the British Prime Minister especially had committed his entire
reputation to the peace settlement and was genuinely horrified at the
prospect of fresh fighting. At the same time Britain was unprepared for
war. As Lord Minto wrote:

No one could have imagined the total want of preparation, and the total
impossibility of a very sudden preparation, in which this country has been
placed . . . We had till the last fortnight at most one ship of the line able to
go to sea. We cannot have five ready for a month to come . . . The press [i.e.
press gang] has done very little . . . and there is a want of seamen that one
does not at present know how to supply. The hasty and total reduction of
all our force, as if it were impossible to apprehend anything from France
again, seems a sad infatuation.[45]

But the prospect of fresh French aggression in the Mediterranean
loomed so large that Malta was simply no longer negotiable. On this,
indeed, depended the survival of the government. As we have seen,
many voices had been raised against the peace settlement in the British
establishment, while there was considerable hatred of the 'Jacobinism'
supposedly represented by the First Consul. 'The government of France,
while Bonaparte remains as First Consul,' wrote Lord Malmesbury, 'is
like that of Persia under Kauli-Khan: it knows no bounds, either moral or
civil [and] is ruled by no principles, and to pretend . . . that Bonaparte's
ambition is circumscribed, or that, with the means of doing everything,
he will do nothing, is talking criminal nonsense.'[46] Much the same view
was held by George III, who felt that he had been forced into making
peace because 'I was abandoned by everybody, allies and all', and,
further, that the idea that 'Jacobinism was at an end' was 'a most
erroneous and dangerous maxim', while a conversation between the
Duke of York and Lord Malmesbury saw the former speak 'with great
anxiety and alarm on the situation of affairs and [deplore] the deficiency
of ability and want of vigour in the present administration to oppose
. . . the insolence of France'.[47] In favour of peace in 1801, Pitt was also
now inclined to a more robust line, as was revealed by a long conversation he had with Malmesbury as early as 8 April 1802:

Rode with Mr Pitt in Hyde Park ... He owned that he had, when the preliminaries were signed, thought that Bonaparte had satisfied his insatiable ambition and would rest content with the power and reputation he had acquired; that for a moment, therefore, he was disposed to believe he was becoming more moderate [and] more reasonable, and that, having so completely attained every object of his wishes ... would remain quiet, and consider a restoration of peace ... as a wise and salutary measure, not only for France, but for the maintenance of his own high situation and ... popularity. However, all that had passed since went to convince him that he had been in error, and that ... [Bonaparte] was, and ever would remain, the same rapacious, insatiable plunderer with as little good faith and as little to be relied upon as he formally found him to be ... In consequence, he (Mr Pitt) was obliged to return to his former opinions, and to declare that no compact ... made with him could be secure ... Still, he did not regret having spoken in favour of the peace: it was become a necessary measure, and rest for England, however short, was desirable.[48]

It should be noted that Pitt was not counselling immediate war and remained opposed to intervention across the Channel or North Sea. As he remarked in the same conversation, 'The torpid and disgraceful state of public spirit in all the European courts puts it ... out of our means to prevent Bonaparte's attempts to ... aggrandize himself on the Continent, for, unassisted as we probably shall be by the courts he is trampling on, it will not ... be practicable for us to hinder him.'[49] What Pitt suggested, then, was rather the limited policy of standing firm on matters relating to Britain's own interests, arming for a new conflict, and going to war if absolutely pushed to it by some direct attack. But in view even of this line, inaction was impossible. Nor was it likely: within the Cabinet, too, there was much distrust of Napoleon. For Lord Hawkesbury, 'Bonaparte was himself a rank Jacobin with a Jacobin mind, Jacobin principles and Jacobin projects ... who has attained his point, got supreme power in his hands and is exercising this as all Jacobins would in the same situation.'[50] Equally, for the Home Secretary, the Earl of Chichester, 'Bonaparte is only a Jacobin chief who has attained his end ... The thief, while he is breaking into your house, employs very different means, and is a very different person from the thief who has ... got possession of it. Bonaparte pillages Italy, Flanders, Florence and all the palaces at Rome, but he adorns and decorates

St Cloud and the Tuileries with a luxury and expense surpassing those of Louis XIV.'[51]

Thus it was that a government whose every instinct was for peace was forced to embark on a course that was likely to have the very opposite result. And here it should be stated very firmly that, if there was indeed unreasoning hatred of Napoleon and the French Revolution amongst the Pittites and Grenvillites and their ilk, these forces were at every turn given credibility and oxygen by Paris and its policies. For an account of the manner in which Addington's mind was working, we can do no better than to turn once again to the diary of Lord Malmesbury. On 19 February 1803, Malmesbury was summoned to see the Prime Minister at Downing Street. Somewhat to his surprise, a weary and concerned Addington unburdened himself to him in embarrassing detail:

After many good-humoured expressions of regard and friendship, [Addington] said he had had it frequently in his wishes for some time past to . . . ask my opinion on points on which with him my sentiments would have great weight . . . After this preface he went on by stating in a very clear and distinct manner the system he had . . . acted on since His Majesty had first called him to take a share in his councils: that he at that period considered peace as an advisable and even necessary measure, from the state the continent was at the time of his taking office and from that of the Exchequer, not quite exhausted, indeed, but fatigued and so circumstanced as not to be able anywhere to hurt or make any impression on France; that, therefore, as soon as the expeditions to the Baltic and Egypt were over, peace became his immediate object. That peace certainly was then his favourite wish, and never could be but in his mind most desirable, but he never expected he would have lived even to have seen the day when he should stand accused of preferring peace when inglorious to the character or injurious to the interest of the country . . . Yet of this he did stand accused, and he had borne the accusation in silence . . . because he was conscious it was undeserved and because he felt within his own breast a complete vindication of his conduct . . . The time was now near when this justification would become manifest . . . His maxim, he declared, from the moment he took office was, first, to make peace, and then to preserve it, under certain reservations in his mind, if France chose and as long as France chose, but to resist and bear all clamour and invective at home till such time as France (and he ever saw it must happen) had filled the measure of her folly, and had put herself completely in the wrong, not only by repeated acts of unprovoked insolence and presumption, but till these acts were, from their expressions and inference, declaratory of sundry intentions the most hostile and adverse to our own particular interest, a violation of treaty and dangerous to the interest of Europe . . . Simple acts of insolence and impertinence, however grating, he had passed over, because he never would put on a par the sober and ancient dignity of Great Britain with the infatuated mushroom arrogance of Bonaparte. Acts of this kind lost their impression when we considered by what sort of a character they were committed . . . It was as if a sober man was to resent the impertinence of one drunk [or] for a gentleman to commit himself with a carman . . . It was for this [that], although he had treasured them up, he had advised no notice to be taken of various little foolish tricks, insults of omission and commission, which Bonaparte had practised towards this country, and . . . waited till insolence was coupled with hostility . . . This was done in the most unquestionable way by Sebastiani's report, and, if Bonaparte had studied how to fulfil his prediction, he could not have accomplished it better.[52]

There was also some reason to believe that the very nature of the French regime suggested that it might well fold if confronted by opposition. On this subject Malmesbury is once again very interesting:

Friday, 4 February [1803]: Lord Pembroke at Park Place. He had passed three months at Paris; seen people of all descriptions; heard everybody; and, as he is an excellent observer and patient listener, great faith is due to his report. He said he could not have believed any person to be so universally disliked as Bonaparte if he had not daily proofs of it: this [is] occasioned by his rapid rise, by his intemperate character, by his tyranny, and the evident use he makes of his power. This hatred, however, leads to nothing: his power remains the same and he is obeyed implicitly. England is manifestly the great object of his hatred and jealousy, and all his plans, all his thoughts, go to attain the means of lowering, if not also of subduing it, but, although there is a sufficient degree of national ill-will towards us prevailing generally, yet so vexed and tormented were the French by the war that it must be some much stronger motive than simply national dislike that can again make them relish war. This feeling also makes them endure Bonaparte's oppression and arrogance, which, bad as it is, is more tolerable than the system of violence in Robespierre's time or the capricious and wanton violence of the Directory. The army in part partake of these feelings, and, although they might be tempted by the prospect of plunder, yet the great majority of them would fight with reluctance. The generals, too, who were formerly his companions, are jealous of Bonaparte. He cannot trust them with a command, and he dares not trust himself from Paris for any length of time.[53]

If these musings are a little unclear, greater clarity is evident from a conversation which Malmesbury had a fortnight later with Addington's Foreign Secretary, Lord Hawkesbury: 'Lord Hawkesbury said he thought the First Consul very like Paul [the late tsar], really mad, that his temper grew quite outrageous, and that his unpopularity amounted to perfect hatred. "It must be madness," Lord Hawkesbury said.'[54] But even if Napoleon was mad, in practical terms this made little difference. To quote Lord Hobart:

All speculations upon what such a man as Bonaparte will do under any circumstances must be too liable to error for us to trust to common reasoning upon any subject in which he is concerned. His intentions are warlike, his interest, in the view most people take of it, pacific, but as he is notoriously influenced by the utmost rancour and hatred of England ... the only safe line for us to take is to be prepared for hostilities, and, indeed, I can see little expectation at present of their being avoided unless the prevailing sentiment in France, which unquestionably is for the maintenance of peace, should be declared in a way that may alarm him for the safety of his person and government.[55]

War, then, loomed. At this point, however, Napoleon was checked by gloomy reports from both the army and the navy. The former, it seemed, was in no state to go to war: the cavalry were short of horses and many units badly under-strength. As for the latter, things were even worse: as France's programme of naval construction was still in the earliest of stages, a resumption of hostilities threatened renewed colonial and commercial disaster, and all the more so as the bulk of such seaworthy vessels as Napoleon possessed were at this time for the most part deployed in small groups in the Caribbean. Realizing that he had badly overplayed his hand, Napoleon therefore attempted to draw back. The agreeable and pacific Joseph Bonaparte was put in charge of relations with Britain; promises were made of a guarantee of the integrity of the Ottoman Empire; and suggestions were made that Britain might have Corfu or Crete instead of Malta. But there was no longer even the limited basis for trust that had existed a year before, and Britain's only response was to offer either to limit her occupation of Malta to a period of ten years, in the course of which she would construct an alternative base on the nearby island of Lampedusa, or to grant the Knights of St John the right to govern the island under the aegis of a British garrison. Otherwise her terms must be agreed to, and that within the space of seven days. There followed more efforts at conciliation: Britain might have Malta for ten years, if France could occupy Naples's Adriatic coast for a similar period; alternatively, Britain might keep her garrison on the island until such time as an international guarantee of its neutrality had been negotiated and a fresh garrison provided for its fortifications. This most recent proposal was a real possibility: at the last moment Alexander had repented somewhat of his increasingly anti-French stance and not only offered his services as a mediator, but hinted that he might provide Russian troops. But it was too late: on 12 May 1803 Whitworth left Paris. As the painter Farington confided to his diary, 'Lord Whitworth is returning from Paris. War is therefore inevitable.'[56]

Hostilities began six days later when a British frigate opened fire on a French convoy in the Channel. In a sense the symbolism was very fitting: just as it had been the British who initiated the crisis, so it was the British who fired the first shots in the war. However, neither this, nor the incontestable fact that Britain's retention of Malta constituted a prima facie breach of the Treaty of Amiens, makes the collapse of the peace settlement her responsibility. On the contrary, in the last resort Napoleon in effect willed the fresh conflict. To have avoided hostilities, he would have had to make serious concessions, but to have backed down would have been to damage the prestige that was in the end the only basis of his power. Indeed, one has to question whether his last-minute efforts to avoid a rupture were ever anything more than mere shifts designed either to win time or to discredit the British. That this was the case – that Napoleon was determined on war, come what may – is certainly suggested by the memoirs of his old acquaintance, Laure Permon, who had since 1800 been the wife of his trusted aide, Jean Andoche Junot (who reputedly had dreams of an invasion of England that would make him Duc de Westminster):

Without any doubt Napoleon was set on the rupture with England. Who would think of denying it? He may have wanted to postpone it until an opportune moment, but that was where he wanted to go. He had too many scores to settle with haughty England to set them aside for very long.[57]

Also important here is a consideration of events in the western hemisphere. As we have seen, the lull in the fighting in Europe had been accompanied by a serious attempt on the part of Napoleon to regain control of the erstwhile jewel in the French Caribbean crown, St Domingue. This campaign was embarked on in a spirit of extreme bravado that says much for Napoleon's temperament at this time. Among those presented to him at the Tuileries was a returned emigré named the Comte de Vaublanc. An army officer who had been born in St Domingue and seen service there prior to the Revolution, Vaublanc was quizzed by the First Consul about his knowledge of the island, and was horrified to learn that such an expedition was in the offing. As he later recalled:

I made various objections and told [Bonaparte] that the problem of sickness meant that success could never be allowed to depend solely on the force of arms alone . . . He heard me out but answered me in jocular fashion. As far as this particular matter was concerned, he was possessed by the all-too-common defect of refusing to listen when it comes to matters of which we know nothing . . . This fault surprised me in a man as brilliant as the First Consul.[58]

Precisely as Vaublanc predicted, the campaign soon ran into serious trouble. Headed by Napoleon's brother-in-law, General Victor Emmanuel Leclerc, 35,000 French troops had invaded the rebellious colony in February 1802. An officer of little worth, Leclerc completely ignored local opinion and badly mismanaged the conduct of the war. After months of desperate fighting, Toussaint L'Ouverture was persuaded to sign a peace treaty with the French that would have given the blacks their freedom and amnestied all those who had fought against the French, but, under orders from Paris to restore slavery, Leclerc reneged on the deal and kidnapped L'Ouverture, who was promptly deported to France where he died in prison a year later (in circumstances, incidentally, that are less than creditable to Napoleon: the Haitian leader was kept in terrible conditions and left without proper food or medical attention). In response, the blacks rose in revolt again and the war resumed. Waged with the most revolting cruelty, it was still going on the following spring with no sign of French victory. Leclerc and thousands of his men had succumbed to the dreaded yellow fever, and reinforcements sent to the Caribbean were dying as fast as they arrived.

This frightful struggle Napoleon never abandoned per se. In April 1803, however, French policy in the western hemisphere was revolutionized. Throughout the winter of 1802–3 an expedition had been fitted out in the Dutch port of Helvoetsluys preparatory to sailing for Louisiana and establishing a French presence on the mainland of the Americas. There is no reason to believe that Napoleon was anything but serious in his determination to restore the western branch of French colonialism. However, almost literally overnight, French policy changed. Ever since Spain's retrocession of Louisiana to France, American diplomats had been working desperately to get Paris to sell the territory to the United States, but thus far they had been continually rebuffed. Yet all of a sudden it was announced that Louisiana was up for sale after all. Hardly able to believe their luck, the Americans snapped it up, and on 30 April the whole territory – an area over four times the size of France, stretching all the way from the Gulf of Mexico to the Canadian frontier, embracing modern-day Louisiana, Arkansas, Missouri, Iowa, Oklahoma, Kansas, Nebraska, Minnesota, North Dakota, South Dakota, Colorado, Wyoming and Nebraska – duly passed into the orbit of the Stars and Stripes at a price of $80 million. At a stroke Napoleon had cut his losses in the West while at the same time filling his war chest in Europe and hamstringing Britain. It was beyond doubt a major coup and one that makes it even harder to acquit Napoleon of blame for the events of May 1803. According to Madame Junot:

The sale was very painful to him, and those who are so carried away by passion that they continue to uphold erroneous ideas and attack him for what took place, should remember that, if he really had been the man bent on personal gain of their imagination, his interest would surely have been to hang on to a province whose possession would very shortly have become a major threat to the United States.[59]

In the end, the evidence is incontestable. Napoleon may not have been a driven man in psychological terms, but as a ruler he depended above all on glory. In political terms, military success was also necessary to him, while his reorganization of France stimulated his sense of superiority and created the conditions in which war might bring fresh rewards. This is not to say that Napoleon deliberately sought a rupture of the Treaty of Amiens. Indeed, though he may have believed that war with Britain and the other powers was inevitable in the end, he had no desire for the breathing space he had obtained in Europe to come to an end after only one year. Yet he never ceased to risk war. Far from respecting the very favourable balance that had been secured at Lunéville and Amiens, he continued to expand French influence in the most ruthless fashion. This in turn destabilized the Addington administration, which was then forced to breach the Treaty of Amiens and demand concessions that in the last resort the First Consul's pride would not allow him to accept. Finally, what it came down to was that Napoleon could not accept the notion that there should be curbs on his freedom of action. At the same time, however, Britain had no means of imposing those curbs except through war. With neither Britain nor France prepared to make fundamental concessions, there could in the end be but one outcome.

4

Towards the Third Coalition

In May 1803, the whale went to war with the elephant. Possessed of the most powerful navy in the world, Britain stood supreme at sea, but on land she was a comparative weakling capable of fielding only puny expeditionary forces of a few thousand men, drawn from an army that had in the 1790s been notorious for the poverty of its human and material resources. With France, however, the picture was completely reversed. Though by no means the invincible force of legend, the French army was an impressive military machine with many victories to its credit, whereas the French navy was in a truly pitiable condition and virtually incapable of putting to sea. How the two belligerents were to strike at one another was therefore most unclear. Particularly outside Europe, ways were naturally found of doing so, but in the end the resolution of the struggle would necessarily revolve around one issue and one issue alone. To overcome France, Britain had to put together a continental coalition that could overthrow Napoleon or, at the very least, bring him to the peace table, while to defeat Britain Napoleon had to frustrate these aims and mobilize a substantial part of Europe against London. Even then victory was not guaranteed for either side. As the events of 1805 would show, for example, such were France's advantages on land that even the most powerful coalition was not necessarily proof against her, but in the short term the international relations of the war could be said to boil down to a contest for the support of Austria, Russia and Prussia. Meanwhile, the fact that there was such a contest is significant. With hindsight, it is possible to argue that it was a struggle that the French were always likely to lose, but the key issue here was not some irreconcilable fracture in European diplomacy but rather the tensions encapsulated by the figure of Napoleon Bonaparte. In 1803 Europe was not divided *ipso facto* between the *ancien régime* and some new and deadly ideological rival. On the contrary, traditional foreign policy interests had survived unchanged, while overtly political consider-ations were very much in abeyance, and all the more so as Napoleon initially appeared as just one more player of the diplomatic game and, secondly, very much in retreat from the Revolution.

The general view of Napoleon in the capitals of Europe has already been examined. However, the absence of any real ideological hostility towards him was not the only reason why the French seemed to have some chance of winning the race to build an overwhelming coalition. Setting aside the fact that Spain, the Batavian Republic, the Cisalpine Republic, the Helvetic Confederation and the south German states were all highly vulnerable to French pressure, if not actually pro-French, the British were hampered in their search for allies by a whole range of factors. Not the least of these was the influence of French propaganda. Even before hostilities had resumed, it had been a standard line in France that the chief culprit for Europe's misfortunes was British greed and ambition, and this message now became one of the central rallying cries of the French war effort. Hardly had Napoleon marched against Austria in September 1805 than he was denouncing the Third Coalition as 'this new league woven by the hatred and gold of England', and threatening the destruction of 'the Russian army which the gold of England has transported from the extremities of the universe'.[1] As Madame de Staël recalled, 'The official gazettes were ordered to insult the English nation and its government. Every day absurd descriptions, such as "perfidious islanders" and "greedy merchants", were repeated in the papers without cease ... In some articles the authors went back to William the Con-queror and described the battle of Hastings as a revolt.'[2] In taking this line Napoleon was helped by the simple fact that there was no love lost for Britain on the Continent. One of the chief difficulties faced by London in 1803 was its distinctly unimpressive war record: on land the British army had hardly a victory to its credit, while at sea its ships had won only four major victories – victories, what is more, that seemed to have more to do with enshrining Britain's commercial monopoly than they did with defeating the French. As late as the Waterloo campaign of 1815, bitter distrust of Britain continued to be rampant, and this despite all Wellington's victories in Spain and Portugal. In 1803, how-ever, there was no Salamanca or Vittoria to draw upon. Indeed, the British army was at that point a force of little or no account in terms of continental warfare. There had been some minor successes in the campaign of 1793–5 in the Low Countries, and then again in the invasion of Holland in 1799, but the British had never put sufficient troops into the field to have a major impact, and in both 1793 and 1799 operations had concluded in retreat and evacuation. However, what stuck most in the craw of foreign observers was not so much that the British army had failed to distinguish itself in the European campaigns in which it had served, but rather that Britain's commitment to the fighting beyond the frontiers of Europe had the appearance of being of an entirely different order. In the fighting in Holland, Belgium and Flanders, there was nothing to equal, say, the triumphant battle of Alexandria, nor, still less, the energy and enterprise which was displayed in seizing colony after colony in the West Indies. Equally, British troops were always in short supply in Europe, but always seemed to be available in abundance when it came to dispatching expeditions to the colonies: in the whole of 1793 less than 4,000 redcoats appeared in the Low Countries, whereas in September 1795 alone 33,000 men set off for the Caribbean. If there was a general feeling that London was completely unreliable as an ally, that it was in fact quite willing to let everybody else do all the fighting, it was therefore hardly surprising.

Let us examine this problem in more detail. Barely a single one of the powers who had fought alongside Britain in the 1790s had much reason to applaud her conduct. As a case in point, we may first turn to Spain. At war with France between 1793 and 1795, in 1796 she had changed sides. In doing so she was in one sense only reverting to the anti-British stance that had characterized her foreign policy throughout the eighteenth century. Yet it was also connected with a more recent series of complaints. For example, the Jay Treaty with the United States of 19 September 1794 had seriously jeopardized Spain's interests in Louisiana, while the British had failed to send Spain financial help and could be accused of having abandoned the Spanish forces that had been sent to assist in the defence of Toulon in 1793. At the same time the British had seized goods bound for Spain in neutral ships – they did not even draw the line at naval stores paid for by the Spanish government – and plied a lively smuggling trade on the coasts of both Spain and her American colonies. In the words of the royal favourite, Manuel de Godoy, British policy was all too easy to interpret: 'Britain first, Britain second, Britain third and Britain always. As for everybody else, they could have the crumbs and the left-overs.'[3]

Austria, meanwhile, had even more to complain of. Throughout the Wars of the First and Second Coalition Britain had in effect expected Austria to fight for British interests in the Low Countries for nothing. No subsidies were ever forthcoming for Vienna, nor any guarantees respecting Prussian and Russian gains in the east, and Francis's attempts to rid himself of the troublesome Austrian Netherlands by means of the so-called Bavarian exchange were consistently blocked. Indeed, far from getting anything herself, Austria found herself constantly being badgered to put still more into the allied cause in an attempt to get unreliable partners to fight harder, while at the same time being forced to watch Prussia being given a free hand in Poland and being paid large sums of money in exchange for doing almost nothing. Not until May 1795 was Austria finally offered a formal deal. In exchange for a loan of £4.6 million, whose terms, incidentally, were extremely demanding, she was to keep 170,000 men deployed against France. A second loan of £1.62 million was forthcoming in 1797, but this was still less than generous when set beside the terms that had been offered Prussia, which amounted to a subsidy of £1.6 million a year, with an additional £2 million in results-based bonuses, in exchange for an army of a mere 62,000 men. In addition, Vienna still could not get London to recognize its interests in Eastern Europe where the British were now chiefly interested in a deal with Russia, while insult was added to injury when in 1796 Pitt opened peace overtures with France without even consulting the Austrians. Nor did matters improve with the coming of the Second Coalition: Austria once again received no subsidy. She was expected to commit all her forces to the war, abandon all say in the Allies' war aims and conduct of operations, and see both Russia and, still more annoyingly, Prussia offered the most generous of terms. At this, even observers connected to the British government expressed embarrassment. As William Windham confided to his diary on 8 November 1799, 'Messenger from Vienna. Long report of a conversation with Thugut in which Thugut presses against us some facts in our conduct . . . which it does not seem easy to answer. One sees . . . that much of their conduct arises from the suspicion, not very ill founded, of our attempting with the aid of Russia to *forcer la main à l'empereur.*'[4] To make matters worse, the British approach rested on a fundamental miscalculation of the assistance likely to be derived from the eastern powers. In the end, Prussian help could not be obtained at all nor Russian help retained, and in 1800 it finally looked as if Britain would have no option but to back Vienna to the hilt. The Austrian defeat at Marengo notwithstanding, on 23 June the British ambassador to Vienna, Lord Minto, signed a pact whereby Britain promised to pay Austria a subsidy of £2 million. Even then, however, only the first instalment – one third of the money – was authorized for payment immediately, the remainder being kept back for payment in two further tranches in September and December. No wonder, then, that Thugut responded to the news of the subsidy with 'the greatest possible coldness in language and manner'.[5]

Underlying all this is a point that is well worth making when one considers Britain's reputation in Europe in 1803. French propaganda, as we have seen, attributed all Europe's travails since 1792 to 'Pitt's gold'. In reality, British foreign policy in the 1790s had not revolved around subsidies. They had been paid, certainly: between 1793 and 1802 £9,200,989 had gone in subsidies to eleven different states. But this was as nothing to the sums that were later disbursed: in 1812 the total was £4,441,963; in 1813, £5,308,679; and in 1814, £10,016,597. The fact is that in the Revolutionary War the British only used subsidies relatively sparingly, if only because, until Pitt's reforms began to take effect from 1799 onwards, the British government simply could not afford to pay the massive bribes of legend. As the war was initially paid for in large part by increasing the national debt, there was a natural unwillingness to spend more money than was absolutely necessary, while the Bank of England was convinced that paper bills could not be issued unless their sum total was covered by the country's reserves of bullion. Indeed, even as it was, London sometimes experienced considerable difficulty in meeting its commitments, as in 1800 when a financial crisis in Germany caused a sudden fall in the value of British bills of exchange. Had several major powers ever needed paying at the same time, it is probable that the money would simply have run out. By the time that the Napoleonic Wars had broken out, of course, things were very different. The great increase in taxation overseen by Pitt and the abolition of the rule laying down that all paper money should be redeemable in gold had ended many of the constraints under which the governments of the 1790s had been operating. This allowed for a massive change in British policy that would see money offered to anyone who would fight the French. But in May 1803 this change had yet to be vouchsafed to Britain's potential partners, and such was the distrust of London that, as we shall see, even when the new largesse began to be revealed, continental attitudes were slow to change.

In financial as much as military terms, then, there was considerable reason to question British commitment to the war. Further strength was lent to France's propaganda claims by the impact of Britain's activities in the colonies and on the high seas. For statesmen such as Dundas, every sugar island that was filched, every merchantman that was seized and every port that was blockaded was a blow against France's power, and, in particular, her ability to finance her war effort. But for inhabitants of the Continent with interests in the colonial trade – and this numbered not just Frenchmen, but also Spaniards, Portuguese, Dutchmen, Germans, Danes and Swedes – there was a different side to the story. Overseas trade did not cease altogether: neutral ships continued to ply the waves and a degree of indirect contact with the colonies was maintained through a variety of shifts and subterfuges. Yet the French Revolutionary Wars had none the less wrought considerable havoc. The Batavian Republic offers a good example. Here distress was very great. Between 1785 and 1789 an average of 324 ships were entering the river Maas every year, whereas in 1799 only ninety-five vessels appeared. The ports, then, were very quiet, whilst a similar fate befell the many industries that in one way or another served maritime interests. For example, West Zaandam had seven shipyards and ninety sawmills in the 1780s, whereas in 1800 it had just one of the former and seven of the latter. Fishing, too, suffered terribly: between 1793 and 1795 the villages of Middelharnis, Vlaardingen and Maasluis lost two-thirds of their vessels. As a result poverty soared: by October 1800 one third of the population of Amsterdam were in receipt of poor relief while in Vlaardingen the proportion was one half. The problems of the Batavian Republic were particularly severe: the Dutch economy was disrupted not just by the decline in shipping, but also difficulties with the import of such items as Belgian coal and German pipe-clay. However, even neutral states were not immune to the difficulties that beset Europe's coasts. As the British envoy to Prussia reported to Lord Grenville, for example, 'The towns want maritime trade and manufacturers.'[6] All this was particularly unfortunate for Britain. It laid her wide open, of course, to France's charges that she was only fighting the war to beggar her commercial rivals, and all the more so as her own ports were clearly booming – between 1785 and 1800 the value of the West Indian trade rose by 150 per cent, whilst the war years had seen the number of British merchantmen rise from 15,000 to 18,000. And, despite the retreat at Amiens, the fact was that the British Empire had seen significant gains thanks to the wars of the 1790s, most notably Spanish Trinidad and Dutch Ceylon. If French propagandists who argued that all that interested the British was the enslavement of the rest of the world gained a certain audience in Europe, it was not to be wondered at.

In this struggle for public opinion, it has to be said that the British were in many respects their own worst enemies. Unlike most states in Europe, Britain – or, more specifically, England – had already developed a strong national consciousness with a vibrant popular content. Inherent to this national consciousness was a sense of superiority that can at best be described as being intolerably smug. Buttressed by Protestantism and a variety of historical events that had achieved a mythic status in the public consciousness – the Reformation, the defeat of the Spanish armada, the English Civil War, the Glorious Revolution and, most recently, the final overthrow of the Jacobite cause – the British felt that they were more prosperous, more advanced and more free than any other people in Europe. Mixed in with this was a racism that shines forth very clearly from, say, Gillray's cartoons depicting a bluff and hearty John Bull defying a weedy and pasty-faced Napoleon. Frenchmen, Germans and other continentals did not find Britain a comfortable environment, and the Englishman abroad was no more popular than he is today. Here are the words of Joseph Sherer, an officer who served in the Peninsular War under Wellington and was markedly more reflective than many of his comrades:

The English . . . cannot make themselves beloved. They are not content with being great; they must be thought so and told so. They will not bend with good humour to the customs of other nations, nor will they condescend to soothe (flatter they never do) the harmless self-love of friendly foreigners. No: wherever they march or travel, they bear with them a haughty air of conscious superiority, and expect that their customs, habits and opinions should supersede, or at least suspend, those of all the countries through which they pass.[7]

Sherer's remarks are reflected all too clearly in the primary sources. Memoir after memoir makes it quite clear that there was tremendous prejudice towards all foreigners and in particular Catholic foreigners. To cite an anonymous officer of the Guards' recollections of the Spaniards:

When roused to energy, they may be induced to act, but, with pompous promises and grandiloquent phrases, postponement and the fear of troubling, their lazy intellects predominated. It was always *mañana*, but never today with them. To put off everything seemed looked upon as the acme of all that was clever, and never to do that which another could do for them was the perfection of dexterity. Their whole mind, in short, seemed bent upon doing nothing and – they did it.[8]

The same theme surfaces again and again in other contexts. It is particularly prevalent in accounts of the campaign of Waterloo, one British soldier writing, 'Had the number of troops which Wellington commanded all been British, the contest would not have lasted so long, nor would the French have left the field with so large a fragment as did escape the army. But he had to trust to the Belgians and others in places where they very early in the day showed the seam of their stocking to the enemy.'[9] So marked was this sense of superiority, that there is a tendency almost towards messianism, a common belief that poor, benighted foreigners of one description or another would make excellent soldiers if only they were given British officers.

What impact did this mixture of jeers, smears and condescension have on inter-allied relations? It is difficult to believe that the scorn and contempt in which many British generals and diplomats held the rulers, statesmen and commanders whom they encountered was not perceived in at least some of the corridors of power. Here, for example, is the opinion to which Lord Minto gave voice on the subject of General Suvorov in a private letter to his wife written in Prague on 3 January 1800:

I am here to see Suvorov on business, and am not sorry for the opportunity of seeing one of whom one has heard so much and such extraordinary things. Indeed, it is impossible to say how extraordinary he is. There is but one word that can really express it. I must not on any account be quoted, but he is the most perfect Bedlamite that ever was allowed to be at large. I never saw anything so stark mad and, as it appears to me, so contemptible in every respect. To give you some little notion of his manners, I went by appointment to pay my first visit ... After waiting a good while in an ante-chamber with some *aides de camp*, a door opened and a little old shrivelled creature in a pair of red breeches and his shirt for all clothing, bustled up to me, took me in his arms, and ... made me a string of high-flown flummery compliments which he concluded by kissing me on both cheeks, and I am told that I was in luck that my mouth escaped. His shirt ... was made of materials, and of a fashion, and was about as clean and white, as you may have seen on some labourers at home.[10]

And, to cite a second instance, we have a private letter written on 16 November of the same year by William Windham:

The aspect of affairs is not good ... one emperor mad, another weak and pusillanimous; the King of Prussia governed by narrow, selfish and shortsighted counsels; no vigour, no energy, no greatness of plan but in the French, and they accordingly govern everything. Nothing is so clear to me as that a small portion of the soul of Mr Burke ... would have rescued the world from this fate long ago.[11]

Britain's representatives abroad were men of culture and breeding who were not generally in the habit of behaving with overt discourtesy (though if the admittedly hostile Lord Holland is to be believed, William Windham opened his career as British envoy to Tuscany 'by horse-whipping in the public drive ... M. Carletti, the chamberlain and favourite of the Grand Duke').[12] None the less it is clear that their prejudice towards the products of the 'decayed' absolutism of the eighteenth century could not be hidden. With the British throne currently in the hands of the increasingly erratic George III and all too soon set to pass into the hands of his drunken eldest son, however, such arrogance was hard to accept. As Charles James Fox remarked of the constant abuse of Bonaparte, 'They should not throw stones whose houses are made of glass. The "crazy king, old mad George" would be just as polite, and, as wicked persons would say, rather better founded.'[13] The British officer who wrote of 'the sovereigns of Russia, Austria, Prussia, Bavaria, Württemberg and a host of petty German powers' becoming 'wonderfully courageous and enthusiastically devoted to England a few hours after the battle of Waterloo' was exaggerating.[14] Yet it is clear that forging a great international coalition was always going to be an uphill struggle for the British. And if Britain frequently had as much to complain of in

the conduct of Austria and her other allies as they did in the actions of
the court of St James, it can only be observed that this misses the point:
as matters stood in 1803, it really seemed that Britain needed Austria,
Russia and Prussia far more than they needed her. In addition, when
war broke out again it is important to remember that it was the British
who had in the end provoked the crisis and Napoleon who could present
himself as the injured party. Reinforced by the immediate publication
by Paris of copious documentation which stressed the importance of
Malta as Britain's *casus belli* to the exclusion of everything else, there
was therefore a belief that the mainspring of everything was British
imperialism. Typical enough are the views of the Neapolitan
commander, Roger de Damas:

England's one desire . . . is to drag the whole continent into the fray. It is
her great hope that the French conquests may rouse all the chief powers,
and the temporary ruin of Naples is nothing to her if a general conflagration be the result of it. In war and politics, moreover, everything is a matter
of compensation. If the French invade the kingdom of Naples, the English
compensate themselves with Sicily, which their superior navy enables them
to occupy more easily. Consequently, though the English may prefer
Naples to be an independent monarchy when the war is over, it does not
matter to them at all whether it be more or less in disorder while the war
is going on, nor, at the end, whether one dynasty or another be reigning
over it.[15]

Nor had the events of 1800 been forgotten. As Lord Holland remarked
of the peace offensive that Napoleon had launched immediately after
Brumaire, 'That step made him popular in Europe; and if he was insincere in the offer, our haughty and offensive repulse gave him all the
advantage which he could expect to derive from his insincerity. It
removed from his government to that of England the reproach of continuing the war without necessity.'[16] Particularly unfortunate was the
fact that in 1803 Napoleon was ostensibly struggling to keep the peace
until the very last minute: his last proposals, indeed, arrived in London
on 16 May. Well, then, might Castlereagh lament, 'It will be difficult to
convince the world that we are not fighting for Malta alone.'[17]

How these difficulties were resolved in favour of the British is something that we can postpone for the time being, though it should be noted
that Pitt, at least, seems to have believed that a war between Britain and

France would inevitably tend to the creation of an alliance against the latter. As Malmesbury wrote in his diary in April 1802, the erstwhile prime minister hoped 'that some one of the great continental powers might awake to a due sense of its honour and interests, and that in a future contest we might derive . . . that aid and co-operation that it was out of the question to look for . . . at this moment.'[18] What cannot be postponed, by contrast, is a consideration of the balance of forces as they stood in May 1803, especially as this throws much light on Britain's overwhelming need for allies. Taking Napoleon and his allies first of all, France had emerged from the Revolution immensely strengthened. With over 29 million inhabitants, she was second only to Russia in terms of population, and by far the most advanced state in continental Europe. Though political paralysis and widespread unrest had done much to nullify these advantages under the Directory, Napoleon had put an end to these disorders and was now in an excellent position to capitalize upon the very considerable financial and demographic resources at his disposal. Making full use of the military advances of the *ancien régime* and Revolution, he was in the process of building an army that in size and quality had no equals, consisting of 265 infantry battalions, 322 cavalry squadrons and 202 batteries of artillery, the whole amounting to perhaps 300,000 men. At the same time – in contrast to the situation elsewhere – replacements and reinforcements were little problem, for the entire male population was theoretically eligible for military service. Even at sea, if France's immediate position was very weak – in 1803 Napoleon had only twenty-three ships-of-the-line ready for immediate service – her shipbuilding potential easily equalled that of Britain, while the design of her vessels was actually more advanced. In short, having already embarked upon a large-scale programme of naval construction, Napoleon could in the long term entertain serious hopes of naval supremacy.

Nor, of course, did France stand on her own. Holland, Genoa and the Italian Republic were all quickly forced to enter the war against Britain, and to place their armed forces at France's disposal. The most important element here was the Dutch fleet, which in 1801 had fifteen ships-of-the-line, but in all three states high levels of population meant that the introduction of conscription could offer major advantages to the French. As we have seen, this step had been taken in the Italian Republic in August 1802, and by 1803 that state could field sixteen infantry battalions, eight squadrons of cavalry and thirteen batteries of artillery. By contrast, conscription remained a taboo subject in Holland, but even so the Batavian Republic could field twenty-eight battalions of infantry, twelve squadrons of cavalry and an unknown number of artillery batteries. As for Genoa, her contribution was essentially naval: in addition to putting her small fleet at France's disposal, the Ligurian Republic had to guarantee the recruitment of 6,000 sailors. Nor was this an end to France's demands: Holland had to provide transports for 62,000 men and 4,000 horses; Genoa to find large quantities of naval stores; and the Italian Republic to pay an annual subvention of 20 million francs. Yet even this did not exhaust the list of support for France beyond her borders. Permitted to remain neutral, Switzerland was nevertheless in September 1803 forced to maintain the various Swiss units in the French army – some sixteen infantry battalions and four artillery batteries – at a strength of 16,000 men, for the duration of the war. Eager to stay out of the conflict, Spain secured this privilege at a cost of a monthly subsidy of 6 million francs. If she was forced to enter the war, however, Spain could in theory call upon an army of 130,000 men (153 infantry battalions, ninety-three cavalry squadrons, forty artillery batteries), a navy of thirty-two ships-of-the-line, and all the resources of her Latin American empire. And, last but not least, all of these states were forced to close their ports to British ships, Napoleon's grand design for a continental blockade already being well under way. As yet unaffected by the trade embargo, there were also the middling states of southern Germany. All these states were for the most part in the process of a programme of state-building which brought with it a major increase in their efficiency – a development which also affected France's formal satellites – and could be expected to lend France considerable military support in the event of a continental war. In 1805, for example, Bavaria could field twenty-eight infantry battalions, twenty-four cavalry squadrons and eleven artillery batteries, and Baden nine infantry battalions, seven squadrons of cavalry and two artillery batteries. And mention should also be made here of Denmark. Negligible as a land power – the Danish army had a mere thirty infantry battalions and thirty-six cavalry squadrons – even after the defeat of Copenhagen of 1801 Denmark retained a powerful fleet of twenty ships-of-the-line. Though she was currently neutral, her maritime interests remained such as to suggest that sooner or later she must come into conflict with the British, and so she too must, at least potentially, be placed in the French camp.

Of France's various auxiliaries, few were in any sense ready to go to war. Of the Dutch, for example, Lord Malmesbury wrote, 'Their fleet is left as it was at the peace: no new ships building or old ones fitting out.'[19] As for the Spaniards, their navy was in dire straits: with the government's finances in a state of collapse, all shipbuilding had come to an end in 1796, while a terrible epidemic of yellow fever that was currently assailing her Mediterranean coast was literally wiping out much of the manpower on which she relied to crew her fleet. Nor was the Spanish army in much better condition: run down in favour of the navy in the reign of Charles III (1759–88), it had since 1796 experienced a variety of attempts at reform, but these had come to nothing. 'The means of recruiting this army are in general very slender,' wrote the French diplomat, Bourgoing. Nor was the officer corps very impressive: 'The obscure and monotonous life they lead, without any manoeuvres on a grand scale, and without any reviews, at length deadens all activity or leads to unworthy objects.'[20] But notwithstanding all these deficiencies and supreme at sea though she was, Britain's chances of making headway against such an array on her own were very limited. In Germany, George III was Elector of Hanover, but such benefit as might have accrued from this was nullified by the latter's military weakness – it had only twenty-six infantry battalions, twelve cavalry squadrons and six artillery batteries – and strategic vulnerability. Though unrivalled in its training, seamanship and morale, the Royal Navy had been greatly reduced in size since 1801 (only thirty-four ships-of-the-line were actually in service, although a further seventy-seven were in reserve). As for the army, at some 130,000 men at full strength (115 battalions, 140 cavalry squadrons, forty batteries) it had, at the very least, plenty to occupy it. Needless to say, with her rapidly growing population and immense financial, commercial and industrial resources, Britain could in theory expect both to raise a much larger army and to expand the navy enormously. Also encouraging was a series of reforms currently being introduced to improve the army's tactical efficiency. Nevertheless, with most of the German states whose troops had traditionally been hired to augment her forces now aligned with France, conscription a political impossibility, home defence a major priority, and transporting large numbers of troops to the Continent a serious logistical problem, she could not but look to foreign allies.

Britain could reasonably expect to count on Portugal and Naples, but neither were powerful states in military terms. Portugal could in theory field twenty-eight battalions of infantry, forty-eight squadrons of cavalry and thirty-two batteries of artillery, but in 1803 these numbered only 30,000 men, instead of the 50,000 they should have amounted to at full strength. As for Naples, details of the organization of the Bourbon army have not been located, but of its 24,000 men, only 10,000 could actually be mustered for service, while nothing had been done to prepare for a resumption of hostilities. To quote Damas, 'Not a man was employed, not a redoubt was built, not a fortress was repaired.'[21] In military terms, the only possible counter to French preponderance were the large professional armies of Austria, Prussia and Russia. At full strength they were impressive indeed. Thus, assuming that all her formations were complete, Austria could supposedly field over 300,000 men – 255 infantry battalions, 322 cavalry squadrons, and 125 artillery batteries. For Russia the figures were even greater, amounting to perhaps 400,000 men, including her swarms of Cossacks – irregular horsemen recruited from the settler communities of the southern and eastern frontiers who paid for their land and personal freedom by means of military service. First-line regular units numbered 359 infantry battalions, 341 cavalry squadrons and 229 artillery batteries. Alone amongst the eastern powers, Russia was also a major naval power with fleets in the Baltic and the Black Sea that in 1805 amounted to forty-four ships-of-the-line, allowing her to overcome some of the limitations of her geographical isolation (needless to say, they also made a Russian alliance particularly attractive to Napoleon). As for Prussia, its 175 battalions, 156 squadrons and fifty batteries amounted to some 254,000 men. If Prussia came into the fray, moreover, there was a strong possibility that she would be assisted by the forces of a number of minor states such as Brunswick and Saxony whom geography placed in her sphere of influence rather than that of France. Of these, Brunswick had four battalions of infantry and four squadrons of cavalry, and Saxony thirty-two battalions of infantry, forty squadrons of cavalry and twelve batteries of artillery.

Of course, mere numbers were not everything: for a variety of reasons, the armies of the eastern powers were militarily inferior to the forces of Napoleon. In most textbooks, it is argued that this stemmed from the simple fact that France had gone through a political revolution that transformed her capacity to make war and, by extension, that in military terms the *ancien régime* remained just that – *ancien*. But this is an over-simplification. The tactical system used by the French army was certainly both flexible and highly effective, but the forces which had resisted the troops of the French Revolution had proved far more capable of dealing with it than they have generally been given credit for. Indeed, the Old Order was not at all the pushover of legend. To take the example of the reformed British army of 1803–15: in almost every respect – organization, tactics, recruitment – this was a classic army of the eighteenth century, and yet it never lost a battle against the French. Nor is it really possible to argue that revolutionary ideology was of much account in the equation: France's men may have been citizens, but that did not make them fight harder on the battlefield. What mattered was the introduction of universal conscription: French generals could risk battle more easily than their opponents and employ tactics that other armies would have found suicidal, and only on a few occasions did they fail to outnumber the enemy. On top of this, French armies were better articulated than their opponents in that their system of higher formations – brigades and divisions and, under Napoleon, corps – was more highly developed and could in consequence deliver a heavier punch on the battlefield.

Command, too, was important. The generals of the *ancien régime* were for the most part neither superannuated dodderers nor the products of gilded aristocratic youth, but rather tough professionals who often had substantial records of success. Many, indeed, were commanders of talent, and a few men of genius: one thinks here of Wellington, the Archduke Charles and, for all his oddities, Suvorov. But all too often they were operating with one hand tied behind their back thanks to the imposition of a variety of political controls. For example, in the summer of 1799 allied operations in Italy, Switzerland and southern Germany were disrupted disastrously by interference from both London and Vienna. Political control was often asserted from Paris, but generals were as often spurred on as they were held back, while they were more likely to defy their political masters. Nor should this last surprise us, for the French Revolution gave the French army access to new leadership cadres driven by a very different set of priorities than those that were the norm among their opponents. Few of the men concerned were the complete nobodies of legend: far from having sprung from poverty, they were for the most part the scions of solid professional or commercial families, or men who might well always have become officers in the French army but whose patents of nobility were not accompanied by the connections with the court that were necessary to achieve high rank. Many had already been soldiers in 1789: senior non-commissioned officers, junior officers from the provincial nobility (like Napoleon) and *officiers de fortune* who had come up from the ranks were all common. What all these men shared was the knowledge that under Louis XVI they would have been unlikely to make their name – that they would in the vast majority of cases have been condemned to a lifetime of obscurity, boredom and low pay. With the coming of the Revolution everything was transformed. All of a sudden anything was possible, and this bred a hunger for victory, an aggression and a vigour that was far less likely to be found in the ranks of their opponents. Thus, at Valmy the Duke of Brunswick chose not to fight in order to preserve his army, whereas for a Napoleon, a Hoche or a Moreau, there was far less need to worry about preserving the lives of soldiers who could always be replaced with fresh conscripts, and little sense in adopting a strategy whose goal was anything other than total victory (in the days of Robespierre and the Terror, indeed, their lives had literally depended on it). Equally, to the Duke of Brunswick, it mattered not a whit in personal terms whether he conquered northern France – come victory or defeat, he would still be the owner of great estates and a prominent position in society – whereas to Napoleon, his whole future lay in conquering northern Italy. And, of course, with Napoleon at the helm, all these advantages were multiplied a thousandfold: the same ruthlessness, the same ambition and the same drive headed not an army of 30,000 men, but a nation of 30 million.

Against Austria, Russia or Prussia alone then, France had a very good chance of victory. Indeed, even fighting together, any two of them were probably not up to defeating France. Thus Austria and Prussia had failed to worst the Republic in 1792 just as Austria and Russia had failed to do so in 1799. That said, there were scenarios that even France could not risk. In 1803 she was the most populous state in Europe, but the fact remained that France hardly dominated the Continent in demographic terms. Austria's population has been estimated at 27 million, Prussia's at 8.7 million and European Russia's at 37.5 million. If the diplomatic divisions that had so undermined the allied war effort were overcome – in other words, if Austria, Russia, Prussia all joined with Britain in making war on France – and if they agreed to subordinate everything else to the need to break the latter's power, not least embracing French methods of mobilization and introducing measures of military reform to emulate the efficiency of the French army on campaign and on the battlefield, then Napoleon faced a grim prospect, the avoidance of which had to lie at the very heart of his strategy.

In 1803, 'a grand coalition' seemed a most remote prospect. 'I do not venture,' wrote Lord Hobart, 'after all the disappointments that this country has met with, to hazard a speculation on foreign politics. The power and intrigue of France have so baffled all calculations that, although we must always look to a combination of the great powers . . . as calculated to be productive of the most salutary consequences, my mind is not sufficiently sanguine to reckon upon such an event until I see it absolutely accomplished.'[22] The detailed reasons for this we shall examine shortly, but one general issue that should be highlighted is that both Austria and Russia could easily be sidetracked into wars with other opponents. We come here to the Ottoman Empire: weak enough to present a tempting target, it was yet strong enough to put up a good fight if attacked. Under the reformist rule of Sultan Selim III (1789–1807), it had greatly improved its fighting power. In possession of a powerful and up-to-date Western-style battle fleet of twenty-two ships-of-the-line, with the aid of French experts Selim modernized his artillery and built up a new regular army. Organized and trained on Western lines, by 1806 this Nizam-i-Cedid had reached a strength of 24,000 men. However, effective though this force was, it was but a small component of an Ottoman array that was as enormous as it was ineffective. The heart of the regular army still consisted of the 196 2,000- to 3,000-strong regiments of janissaries, a force notoriously ill trained, undisciplined and unfit for war. Backing up these regular infantrymen were hordes of noble light cavalry, mercenary irregulars, and poorly trained peasant levies, but these troops were of even less use than the janissaries as well as being under the control of local satraps who might or might not be prepared to rally to Constantinople's call. Ottoman armies were therefore no match for Western-style forces in open battle. In the words of a Polish exile who had fled to Constantinople, 'The Turkish artillery received some improvement, but . . . nothing could be done with the cavalry.'[23] Nevertheless, the empire's amorphous political organization and sprawling nature made it a difficult foe to defeat and it remained an important factor in diplomatic calculations.

And it was not just the Ottomans who might distract Alexander I. At the other extreme of the Continent, there were Russia's traditional enemies, the Swedes. With between seventy and eighty infantry battalions, sixty-six cavalry squadrons and seventy artillery batteries, Gustav IV could put a significant force into the field. Sweden's geographical remoteness was countered by her powerful navy – twelve ships-of-the-line together with a large number of heavily armed galleys specially designed for amphibious operations in the shallow waters of the Baltic – and her possession of the important bridgehead of Swedish Pomerania. At best, of course, Sweden might be brought into a coalition against France: less of a maritime nation than Denmark, she was also relatively safe from French coercion. And, according to Addington, at least she was 'most anti-French and coming towards us'.[24] At the current moment, however, this seemed a forlorn hope, as Russia and Sweden had fallen out over a small island that stood in a river on the Finnish frontier and appeared to be on the brink of war. Alexander and a number of his senior advisers visited the site in person, while the language used by the Russians in particular was extremely severe, in part perhaps because the Russian government needed a foreign policy success in the wake of the German disaster of 1802. 'Not being able to overcome the strong,' wrote Czartoryski, 'the chancellor attacked the weak.'[25]

Even if Sweden could be persuaded to join the British, the latter's task was magnified by the fact that to strike at Napoleon and defend her own interests, London would have to adopt a series of measures that played straight into the First Consul's hands. In the long term, the goal was a continental coalition, but in the short term this seemed quite unattainable, so much so that it could almost be set aside altogether. As Lord Castlereagh stated, 'I think it unwise to risk what may continentally be called the last stake where there is neither vigour nor concert to oppose to the power of an enemy impregnable at home, and, in opinion, irresistible abroad.'[26] Indeed, Addington at least believed that, even if a coalition could be formed, pressing for such a goal would be counter-productive: with matters in the state they were, the only result would be to hand Napoleon easy victories and delay the moment when success might be attained. This is not to say that coalition diplomacy was neglected altogether. On the contrary, Denmark and Sweden were contacted with hints of commercial concessions in return for a defensive alliance, while in July 1803 a simultaneous approach was made to both Austria and

Russia, in which the former was wooed by concessions on the repayment of earlier British loans and the latter by the promise of a subsidy, not to mention a blatant attempt to appeal to Alexander's well-known vanity:

The Emperor of Russia is placed in a situation which may enable him to render the most important services to Europe. It is in consequence of his interposition that Europe can alone expect that the cabinets of Vienna and Berlin should suspend their ancient jealousies . . . His Majesty trusts that the Emperor of Russia . . . will perceive that the only hopes of tranquillity for Europe must be derived from a combination of the great powers of the continent with His Imperial Majesty at their head.[27]

But nothing came of any of this, and all Britain could do in Europe was to adopt a waiting game. Impelled by sheer frustration and his desire for military glory, Napoleon would inevitably embark on a cross-Channel invasion. Yet this was something that Addington believed Britain could repel. She would, of course, have to strengthen her defences, rebuild the navy and greatly expand her land forces, but, provided these steps were taken, there was no reason to believe that a French invasion would be successful. As the First Lord of the Admiralty, Lord St Vincent, put it in a speech to the House of Lords, 'I do not say, my Lords, that the French will not come. I only say that they will not come by sea,'[28] Were Napoleon to fail in the invasion, then his prestige would suffer such a blow that the powers of Europe might be encouraged to roll back the frontiers of French power. Of course, there was always the chance that Napoleon might baulk at the prospect of an invasion, but then his prestige would also be damaged, and he might even be overthrown. To quote Lord Hobart, 'I am inclined to credit the reports we receive from France of Bonaparte's situation being rather precarious . . . Symptoms of dissatisfaction have shown themselves in the only quarter where they can be of importance, the army. The invasion of England is not so popular as might have been expected from the hope of pillage and plunder . . . and it is said that . . . they do not anticipate the probability of being drowned without sensations that are not quite comfortable.'[29]

In the circumstances, Britain's strategy was not a bad one. But if a coalition was ruled out – and with it offensive operations on the Continent – the only targets available were economic, colonial or maritime ones, precisely the goals that had made Britain so unpopular in the Revolutionary War. France's ports were therefore blockaded – a move that was soon extended to foreign harbours that fell under French control – and the navy hastily put back on a war footing (so hastily, in fact, that many of the ships that were dispatched to the Mediterranean under Lord Nelson had to have their proper rigging fitted while they were already at sea). Within six months, seventy-five ships-of-the-line and 114 frigates were in commission. At the same time, there was also a renewed offensive in the wider world. By the end of the year Santa Lucia, Tobago, Berbice, Demerara and Essequibo had all been captured, the remnants of General Leclerc's army driven from St Domingue, and the Maratha Confederacy – France's last source of native allies in India – shattered beyond repair by an offensive in the Deccan that produced victories for the future Duke of Wellington at Assaye and Argaum as well as other successes at Delhi and Laswari. All this was perfectly understandable: the captured colonies had been useful bases for both French commerce raiders and attacks on British islands; the colonial trade continued to be central to the British economy; and the Marathas were potentially a serious danger to British influence in India. But the fact remains, there was nothing to suggest a direct commitment to Europe: to all intents and purposes, Britain still seemed to be fighting the wars of the eighteenth century.

Yet even in distant India Britain was fighting Napoleon. In 1803 the Maratha Confederacy was in theory the most powerful polity on the Indian subcontinent, occupying, as it did, a huge expanse of territory stretching from the Punjab to the frontiers of Britain's key ally, Hyderabad. But in practice the Confederacy was weaker than it appeared. The ruler of this empire was the hereditary prince of the state of Satar, but he had almost no authority, real power seemingly lying in the hands of a chief minister known as the Peshwa. Yet the Peshwa in turn was also all but impotent, for power was actually exercised by a large number of local rulers who paid lip service (and not much else) to his suzerainty. While some of these rulers were little more than petty robber-barons, others – Jeswunt Rao Holkar, Maharajah of Indore; Daulat Rao Scindia, Maharajah of Gwalior; the Rajah of Berah; the Gaikwar of Baroda – were immensely powerful. Holkar and Scindia, in particular, possessed not just the swarms of irregular cavalry that typified most Indian armies, but also large forces of modern artillery and European-trained infantry. Scindia, for example, could put into the field seventeen battalions of 'Western' infantry, nicknamed the 'Immortals of the Deccan'.

In consequence, the Maratha Confederacy was hardly a unified state. Great and small, all of the Maratha rajahs and maharajahs were engaged constantly in raiding and warfare between themselves, which meant that there was nothing that resembled a common foreign policy. Eager to advance their own interests, many of the minor rulers were actually signing so-called 'subsidiary treaties' with Britain (see below). Enthusiastically fostered by Wellesley, British penetration of the subcontinent seemed set to continue indefinitely.

In 1803, however, the picture was transformed as the Peshwa was deposed by Holkar and replaced by a puppet ruler. An imposing figure noted as a bold and courageous military commander, the new strong man threatened to bring all the Maratha Confederacy under his sway. To Britain's alarm, in the summer of 1803 three French agents were captured at Poona with documents calling on both Holkar and Scindia to rise against the British and granting Scindia's chief European adviser, a French mercenary named Perron, the rank of general in the French army. Meanwhile, having set out from Europe prior to the outbreak of hostilities with Britain, a small French fleet suddenly appeared off Pondicherry with a fresh garrison for this old French colonial possession. Finding the British in occupation of Pondicherry, the French withdrew to Mauritius, but there was clearly a need for action. To put an end to the growing threat, Wellesley immediately offered Holkar a subsidiary treaty, but the Maharajah was simply too powerful to be interested in surrendering his independence. Not surprisingly, then, Wellesley signed a treaty with the rightful Peshwa that in effect promised to restore him to power in exchange for the Maratha Confederacy becoming a satellite state. In acting in this fashion, Wellesley was not working as an agent of the British government. Though the Governor General was a political nominee – since the passage of the India Act of 1784, the East India Company had accepted that the decision as to who should hold the post should lie in the hands of the British government – Wellesley had not been sent out with an imperialist agenda. What is more, in going to war against Holkar and his allies, he was acting without the knowledge of London and against the wishes of the Board of Directors of the East India Company, who were only interested in commercial penetration rather than direct political control. After the fact, his successes were initially approved by the British government – 'Nothing can have made a greater sensation than what they have done', wrote his brother, Gerald

Wellesley[30] – but in large part this was simply because Wellesley was a Tory, because much of the fiercest denunciation of his policies came from the Whigs and, finally, because in 1803–4 the priority had to be preventing Napoleon from gaining a foothold in India. When the immediate crisis passed, the government abandoned its support for the Governor General, and made no attempt to sustain him against the revolt of the East India Company's directors that finally brought him down in 1805. If successive administrations continued to be uninterested in expansion in India thereafter, this can perhaps be put down to wartime conditions: thanks to the gradual modernization of India's armies, Wellesley's wars had far outstripped in cost and scale those of earlier eras. Thus, in the First Mysorean War, the British had employed 10,000 men and been able to triumph over odds of some seven to one, whereas in the fourth such conflict – the final struggle against Tippu Tib – victory over a markedly weaker enemy had taken 50,000 men. Still worse, meanwhile, the lion's share of the fighting now had to be undertaken by British regulars: at Assaye, Wellesley's 13,500 men included just two regiments of British infantry and one of cavalry – some 2,200 men – and yet they accounted for 650 out of his 1,600 casualties. Given the situation in Europe, gaining fresh territory in India was therefore simply not a British objective. When Wellesley returned from India in 1805 he was given only the most grudging of thanks by parliament, cold-shouldered by many of his erstwhile allies and barely escaped impeachment at the hands of an old enemy who had secured a seat in the Commons.

The 'making of British India' for which Wellesley stood was, then, the work of one powerful and vigorous enthusiast, albeit one who had many adherents (most notably, Lord William Bentinck, who became Governor of Madras in 1803). The India Act of 1784 had stated unequivocally that wars of conquest were 'measures repugnant to the wish, the honour and the policy of this nation' and expressly prohibited the Governor General from waging military campaigns without the sanction of parliament except in self-defence (a very flimsy justification in the case of the Marathas: setting aside their incipient state of civil war, Holkar had initially shown a strong desire to keep the peace). The basis of this opposition to wars of aggression was reasonable enough: it was believed that the constant Indian warfare of the mid-eighteenth century had been the fruit of foreign intervention, and that, now the French had been all but ejected from the subcontinent, all the British had to do was to sit back and let the profits of trade flow into their coffers. From the beginning, however, Wellesley rejected this maxim. Indian rulers, he argued, were a militaristic caste, bent on war, from which it followed, first, that foreign intervention did not in itself encourage conflict, and, second, that the stability envisaged by the India Act was a chimera that was unlikely ever to be realized. What was needed instead was British control, for only British control could genuinely deliver the riches of empire. To implement this policy he had a wonderful excuse in the residual French presence, while the relatively easy conquests of the Fourth Mysorean War of 1799 stimulated his ambition for glory, which was, in its way, nearly as great as that exhibited by Napoleon (notoriously vain and self-indulgent, Wellesley was furious when a distinctly unenthusiastic government rewarded him not with an English peerage but with an Irish one). Unlike Napoleon, war was not central to his policy: his favoured device, the so-called 'subsidiary treaty' whereby Indian rulers accepted British overlordship in return for a guarantee of British protection, was just as acceptable when achieved by diplomacy as it was when it was achieved by battle. But he would brook no opposition, and adopted a 'take it or leave it' approach that was very reminiscent of the First Consul. And he was all too clearly a genuine imperialist and, in consequence, a great embarrassment in Europe. With Wellesley at the helm in India, how could Addington deny that Britain was in an expansionist mode? Nor was Wellesley the only colonial administrator with a penchant for aggression. In Ceylon the Dutch had confined themselves to a chain of ports around the coasts of the island, and left the interior to its own devices under the rule of the Kingdom of Kandy. When the British took over, however, the Governor, Frederick North, took exception to the independent stance affected by the Kandians and in February 1803 embarked on the conquest of the interior.

If expansion in India is difficult to attribute to the Addington government, it does have to bear full responsibility for another aspect of the British war effort that was just as damaging. No sooner had war begun than a French invasion threatened. Such warships as the French had in their own ports were made ready for sea; the squadron that had been sent to assist in the reduction of Toussaint L'Ouverture was summoned home; the programme of naval construction was accelerated; 160,000 men were concentrated on the Channel coast; a start was made on amassing a flotilla of invasion craft; a programme of improvements was begun at Calais and Boulogne; and finally Napoleon himself set out on an ostentatious tour of inspection of the Channel coast. In consequence, home defence was obviously a high priority. Part of the way forward here lay in the construction of coastal fortifications – hence Kent's Royal Military Canal and the Martello towers that still dot Britain's southern coasts – but Britain also required large numbers of fresh troops. It is difficult to imagine any British politician ever committing himself to the obvious course of conscription to the regular army. Traditional hostility to standing armies, concern for civil liberty and the sheer unpopularity of military service all rendered anything other than a few meaningless gestures unthinkable, and in consequence the government revived the Volunteer movement of the 1790s. As before, the result was that large numbers of men rushed to enlist in extravagantly uniformed units of cavalry and infantry that for the most part would have been of little use had the French actually crossed the Channel and were in any case available for home defence only. Of rather more use was the decision to expand the county militia by an additional 76,000 men (a move that was politically acceptable despite the fact that it involved conscription as the militia only served at home and was often embodied only on a part-time basis). But none of this increased the regular army: it was hoped that men recruited to the militia would get a taste for life with the colours and volunteer for service with a line unit, but it was several years before this system began to produce significant results. In general, then, the army had to rely on civilian volunteers, and in this it was singularly unsuccessful: between June and December 1803 the 360 recruiting parties sent out into the country raised the grand total of 3,481 men, or fewer than ten apiece. This was unsurprising: while the army paid a bounty for all recruits, far more money was available to anyone who would take up arms in the navy or sell themselves as a substitute for men called up to the militia. Thus the regular army remained very small: indeed, so miserable was the trickle of recruits that it actually declined by 13,000 men during the first nine months of the war. Yet without a strong regular army that could dispatch substantial forces of troops to the Continent, there was little chance of persuading potential foreign allies that they should take up arms alongside Britain.

The British were in a quandary. No means of raising a powerful army existed, nor was there any chance of securing a change in public perception of the armed forces. With the Volunteers as ubiquitous as they were full of bombast and self-confidence, even the threat of invasion was not sufficient to persuade the populace that more men were needed for the regulars, while the inflated tone of the propaganda that swamped the country hardly lessened 'little Englander' convictions that John Bull could thrash the French without the assistance of a troop of benighted continentals. So necessary was foreign aid, however, that increasingly it was Britain that was benighted. It helped a little that on 7 May 1804 Addington was replaced as prime minister by William Pitt: not only was the latter known as a man of action, but Addington was an unimpressive figure who was regularly jeered at in the House of Commons as a coward and caricatured as a small boy playing at soldiers. But in the end the return of Pitt made no difference, for the reality was that, despite his immense qualities as a war leader, he had no more to offer than Addington. To quote William Cobbett, 'Mr Pitt's system . . . is worn out . . . as well as with regard to military glory as with regard to domestic liberty.'[31]

In the end what saved Britain was that she was fighting an opponent who could be all but guaranteed sooner or later to antagonize the powers of Europe. Once again, then, we come to the personal influence of the First Consul, for in 1803 none but a Napoleon could have driven them to war. Let us begin with Austria. Here the chances of an alliance were zero. As the Austrian ambassador, Starhemberg, had told Addington, 'We are a giant, but a giant exhausted, and we require time to regain our strength.'[32] In part, the trouble was financial. Thanks in particular to the inability of the Habsburgs to draw with any degree of adequacy on Hungary, Austria's resources were simply not sufficient to meet the demands of war against France. Meanwhile, Francis was unwilling to increase taxes for fear of internal unrest. The Turkish war of 1787–9 had already seen the introduction of paper currency in the form of bonds known as *bankozettel* – and in the course of the 1790s the total sum involved had steadily increased: indeed, between January 1799 and January 1801 the amount in circulation actually doubled. From 1795 onwards depreciation therefore set in while prices began to rise alarmingly. Also on the rise was the national debt, which soared from 390 million gulden to 613 million gulden between 1792 and 1801. And finally, thanks to Lunéville, the central government had lost a considerable amount of tax revenue. Money, then, was short – so short, indeed, that the Ministry of Finance wanted greatly to cut the military budget –

but this was not the only issue. In the campaigns of 1799–1800, the Austrian army had suffered heavy losses, but replacing the missing men would not be easy, especially as most of the Holy Roman Empire was now off limits to the Habsburg recruiting parties that had traditionally operated there (and in the process brought in large numbers of troops: prior to 1801 perhaps half the army's volunteers had come from its territories). There was a system of conscription in existence, but this did not affect all of Francis's domains – the Tyrol and Hungary, for example, were both exempt – and was by no means universal even where it was in operation. Yet increasing the number of men conscripted or broadening the basis on which they were taken would be likely to exacerbate social unrest: in the course of the War of the Second Coalition at least 27,000 men had fled their homes rather than face the draft, while desertion had reached epic proportions. Equally, extending conscription to Hungary and the Tyrol would only serve to cause a return of the troubles of 1789–90 (when both these provinces had almost risen in revolt).

Logically enough, this financial and military weakness was reflected in a change of atmosphere in Vienna. As we have seen, the Habsburg regime had never been the most enthusiastic of France's opponents. Neither Francis nor his leading military commander, the Archduke Charles, were at all enamoured of war, and both were inclined to gather round them figures who were not inclined to challenge their perceptions: the emperor's highly influential 'Cabinet secretary', Franz von Colloredo, for example, was notoriously timid and indecisive. At the same time there was much dislike of the British alliance, and especially of William Pitt, who was perceived as being unnecessarily forceful and abrasive. And, finally, Francis was also increasingly mistrustful of the Archduke Charles, who had in 1801 been appointed head of the new Ministry of War and Marine and was currently pushing through a major programme of military reform, the effect of this being to put the emperor in mind of the Thirty Years War when the power of the throne had temporarily been eclipsed by powerful commanders such as Wallenstein. Until now, Austria had been held to her course by the forceful Thugut, but he was now gone, and his replacement, Count Ludwig Cobenzl, was much more ambiguous in his attitude towards the struggle. 'I knew well', wrote Lord Malmesbury, 'that Cobenzl was in his heart French, that he had been brought up to admire and fear them, and that, whether a Bourbon or a Bonaparte, this sentiment in his mind would remain the same.'[33] This typical piece of British contempt for foreigners was far too sweeping: the Austrian chancellor was determined to restore the Habsburgs' fortunes by, first, addressing the state's internal problems, and, second, standing up to France. Indeed, by 1804 he had fallen out with the Archduke Charles on account of the latter's endless pessimism. But it is perfectly true that Cobenzl was much impressed both by France's military power and Napoleon's personal capacities – he had, after all, headed the Austrian delegation at both Campo Formio and Lunéville – and that he was unwilling to risk a war until Austria was ready for action, something that in his eyes would not be the case for another ten years. If he began to press for an alliance with Russia in 1803, it was not because he wanted to march on Paris but because he wanted to find a means of stopping Paris from marching on him. Here and there the odd fiery spirit could be found who favoured war, one such being the fanatically anti-French propagandist, Friedrich von Gentz, and another Baron Karl von Mack, a vain and incompetent officer who had suffered military humiliation in 1798 and was now thirsting for an opportunity to restore his reputation. But even had he wanted to, the chancellor could not have provided the leadership needed by a war party: 'Although he shone in the salon,' wrote Metternich, 'Cobenzl was not the man to lead a cabinet.'[34]

Even in the wake of the murder of the Duc d'Enghien (discussed below), Cobenzl would not move. As the British ambassador to Vienna, Arthur Paget, wrote of an unsuccessful attempt to get Cobenzl to agree to an alliance in April 1804:

The Vice-Chancellor contended that any such concert would be a direct violation of their system of neutrality from which the emperor would not easily be brought; that it was a wise system not to talk before the means of supporting your language were proved to exist; that this country was not in a situation to go to war; that, although their present situation was unques-tionably a bad one . . . it was not desperate, and that, by endeavouring to improve it a worse might, and probably would, succeed; that the French had 100,000 men in Italy; that their whole force now upon the coast might at a moment be equally turned on this country; that the Austrian army was at this moment upon the peace establishment, etc., etc. . . . These and similar arguments was I doomed to the pain of listening to . . . I never witnessed the display of so much ignorance, weakness and pusillanimity on the part of any individual calling himself a statesman.[35]

This was, needless to say, grossly unkind to Cobenzl. But in 1803 the fact remains that all the British could hope for from Vienna was that Austria might be prepared to enter another coalition with them when the circumstances were right – but this did not seem likely for a very long time. Francis II, the Archduke Charles, Cobenzl and Colloredo all agreed that war could only be considered after a long process of internal reform. The most obvious policy was simply to revive the bureaucratic absolutism of Joseph II to eradicate provincial and noble privilege, and mobilize the resources of all Francis's dominions. But this was something that the emperor simply would not do. Temperamentally averse to interfering with the rights of his subjects, he also dared not risk a repeat of the turmoil of 1789–90. Reform, then, was inclined to be both gradualist and piecemeal. Denied the empire-wide system of conscription he wanted, for example, Charles had to content himself with reducing the length of service owed by men who volunteered for the army in the hope that this would produce more recruits. In the same way, a variety of fiscal reforms were introduced – there was, for example, a considerable rise in import duties – but the perquisites of the nobility were left untouched. Far from provinces such as Hungary being stripped of their privileges, Francis was forced to turn to them cap in hand. By means of its largely noble triennial Diet, Hungary had the right to set its own levels of taxation and conscription. In 1796 (the last occasion on which it had met) the Diet had rallied to the Habsburg cause and voted a subsidy of 4.4 million gulden, the dispatch of large quantities of supplies and an increase of 5,000 in the number of soldiers sent by Hungary to the regular army. This last move brought her quota up to 52,000 men, but as all the recruits concerned were volunteers, in practice this total was never met. In 1802, the Diet was summoned again after a break in 1799. Asked for 2 million gulden, the deputies agreed to grant Vienna less than half this figure, and would only make limited concessions on the issue of recruits for the army. To say that no progress was made in these years towards a revived Austria was unfair – the Archduke Charles did achieve a significant degree of reform in the field of the empire's administration – but so slow was the rate of change that Britain was clearly going to have a long time to wait. Even as late as 6 August

1805, Minto was writing in his diary, 'I hear that Austria has declared positively she will take no part in any confederacy against France, and assigns her total want of means as the motive of this conduct. I am sorry for it, thinking a continental war the only chance of terminating our difficulties, though even that chance may not be good. But the longer it is delayed, the worse prospect of success there will be as Bonaparte will increase his strength every year, and resistance may come at last when it is too late.'[36]

So much, then, for Austria. What, though, of Prussia? Once again, not much could be expected. Still wedded to the principle of neutrality, Prussia was regarded with great scorn by the Addington government. As Malmesbury confided to his diary on 14 June 1803, 'Lord Hawkesbury with me by his own appointment at seven . . . Speaking of Prussia, he said nothing could be more feeble and pusillanimous than the king and his ministers.'[37] In a general sense, Hawkesbury was not far wrong: Prussian policy in respect of Napoleon at this point could not have been more pacific. However, it was not a question of cowardice. When absolutely pushed to it, Frederick William was not afraid to act: deeply convinced of his duty to protect Prussia's foreign trade, he had been anything but backward with regard to joining the League of Armed Neutrality in 1801. But all the arguments that had kept the king out of the War of the Second Coalition had greatly intensified since 1800: Prussia had done extremely well out of the reform of the Holy Roman Empire, while the debate on the need for military reform was now raging more loudly than ever. And to these points had been added new ones. In the first place, there was much admiration of Napoleon, who it was assumed was putting all to rights in France. And, in the second, though fearful of France in the long term – as he told the Swedish ambassador, 'We will be the last to be eaten: that is the limit of Prussia's advantage'[38] – Haugwitz was at the moment more concerned with Vienna than Paris. The Austrians having shown a strong desire to challenge certain aspects of the new territorial dispensation in Germany – in August 1802 Austrian troops had gone so far as temporarily to occupy the district of Passau in an attempt to deny it to Bavaria – his current goal was an alliance with France and Russia that would cow Francis and his advisers into complete submission and at the same time contain Napoleon. Nor was the army any more committed to a war against France. A few generals, including, not least, the future hero of Waterloo, Gebhard von

Blücher, were increasingly concerned at the growth in French power, while plenty of officers were spoiling for a fight. To quote the general staff officer, Carl von Muffling, 'There were at that time in the Prussian army from the generals to the ensigns, hotheads without number, and those who were not so by nature assumed a passionate, coarse manner, fancying that it belonged to the military profession.'[39] But, again, these 'hotheads without number' had other targets than Napoleon: while some looked to a war with Austria, others, like the founder of the newly formed general staff, Christian von Massenbach, wanted to expand Prussia's gains in Poland at the expense of Russia. And, precisely because they had other targets, no strong party emerged in favour of war with France, the result being that nothing stood in the way of continued Prussian neutrality. More than that, indeed, Frederick William was positively fawning in his attempts to ensure Napoleon's continued favour, and the only action that he took to protect Prussia's interests as hostilities approached was to beg the First Consul not to invade Hanover.

All this left just Russia as a possible ally for the British, but in reality she, too, was not much of a staff to lean upon. As Lord Malmesbury wrote, 'On Wednesday 27 April [1803], with Vorontzov [i.e. the Russian ambassador] for two hours; he communicated to me several dispatches . . . The result of them struck me that Russia was now what she has ever been since she had held . . . a place among the greater powers of Europe – cajoling them all and courting flattery from them all, but certainly never meaning to take an active part on behalf of any of them . . . I fear we here rely too much on Russia: she will give us advice, but not assistance.'[40] This seemed true enough at the time that it was written: although the new Foreign Minister, Count Alexander Vorontzov – the elder brother, it will be recalled, of the ambassador to London, who was Semyon Vorontzov – was friendlier to Britain than any of his predecessors, he was little inclined to become involved in the troubles of central Europe and anxious to avoid a breach between Britain and France. It did not help that as the winter of 1802–3 drew to a close Napoleon made a determined attempt to calm Russian feelings. His hints at a partition of the Ottoman Empire were dropped, for example, while for the first time mention was made of compensation for the King of Piedmont. Far from backing the British, on the very eve of war the Russian government suddenly announced that it would instead mediate between the combatants and provide a garrison for Malta. Meanwhile the desperate attempts of Addington and Hawkesbury to secure an alliance were met by the not very helpful response that Russia could not move unless Austria did so first, the fact being that there was otherwise no way that a Russian army could actually get to grips with the French. In any case, this was hardly an enticing appeal. The reign of Paul I had badly disrupted the military, which had been torn apart by a purge of the 'easterners' who had dominated it in the reign of Catherine II, and it would be some time before a happy medium was restored to its ranks. And, finally, setting aside the issue of what might happen if it came to a fight, there were plenty of Russians who hated Britain: in Paris, for example, the diehard republican Bertrand Barère, found that the new newspaper he had established to stir up popular feelings against Britain – it was called *The Anti-British Journal* – was eagerly snapped up by officials of the Russian embassy.

The end to Britain's isolation was therefore going to be some time coming. Come it did, but before we examine how this occurred, we must turn to an episode in the Mediterranean that is of some significance for the wider march of international relations. European affairs were suddenly invaded by a new player in the form of the United States. By 1800 Britain's old colonies ranked second only to Britain in terms of international trade, and their substantial merchant fleet operated from Norway to the Cape of Good Hope. In the Mediterranean, however, the Americans, like many other small powers, had a major problem in the shape of the so-called 'barbary corsairs'. Crewing fast galleys and operating with the sanction of the rulers of such cities as Algiers, Tunis and Tripoli (all of whom were theoretically vassals of the Ottoman Empire), these pirates were an ever-present danger in the sea lanes of the eastern Atlantic and the Mediterranean alike. The French Wars had made matters significantly worse, for the British, French and Spaniards, alike had more pressing things to do than chase the corsairs. Much affected by this, the Americans at first attempted to negotiate free passage for their ships by a series of bribes: in 1795, for example, it was agreed that Algiers should receive a lump sum of $642,500, a sloop and an annual tribute of $21,600. However, outrages of various sorts continued, and in February 1801 President Jefferson responded by declaring war on Tripoli and sending a small naval force to the Mediterranean. For over two years little happened: the American squadron was too small to achieve much and cutbacks in the naval budget meant that it could not easily be reinforced. Not until September 1803 did the fighting hot up, and even then it was a sporadic affair of raids and coastal bombardments that eventually petered out with a compromise peace that was signed on 4 June 1805. In most respects, then, the American war against Tripoli was little more than a sideshow. Yet for all that, it was not unimportant. Setting aside the inconvenience it caused to Britain – Tripoli was an important source of food and drinking water for British ships operating in the Mediterranean – the war put Europe on notice that the United States would not just adopt a policy of passive defence, but if necessary reach out across the Atlantic. For the time being the priority was defence, such naval construction that took place therefore revolving around the launch of a number of gunboats that could only be used with any safety in the bays and estuaries of the southern and eastern coast. But just as Britain could hope that Napoleon would sooner or later drive one or other of the powers into an alliance with London, so the French ruler could hope that Britain would sooner or later drive the United States into a fresh war in the defence of her commerce.

Keeping in mind these non-European factors, let us now return to events in Europe. From the very beginning Napoleon had followed a course of action that could not but destabilize the neutrality that reigned east of the Rhine. Thus, practically his first move in the conflict had been to defy convention by accompanying the outbreak of war with the seizure not just of all those British merchantmen and British cargoes caught in French ports, but also some 10,000 British nationals who found themselves on French soil. More importantly, determined to hit Britain wherever he could, within a matter of days Napoleon had sent his troops into Hanover (which capitulated without resistance, though much of its army escaped by sea to Britain where it became the nucleus of the so-called 'King's German Legion'). And, finally, in order to cut off British trade, and, in the latter case, to further his designs in the Mediterranean, the north German coast and the Neapolitan ports of Taranto, Otranto and Brindisi – all of them situated in the hugely sensitive region of Apulia – were also occupied by French soldiers. All this unsettled the powers of Europe. With French troops lining the North Sea from Holland to Denmark, Austria, Prussia and Russia alike had good reason to fear for their commercial interests, while Napoleon had contrived simultaneously to trample Prussian pretensions in northern Germany underfoot; revive the threat posed by the invasion of Egypt to Russia's interests in the eastern Mediterranean and the Balkans; and mount a head-on challenge to Alexander I's dynastic diplomacy in Germany. As even Napoleon's Minister of Police, Joseph Fouché, admitted, 'There had never been, till then, an example of such violence against the rights of nations.'[41]

Yet it was not just Napoleon who was inflaming the situation: another figure that is of particular interest here is Prince Adam Czartoryski. Born in 1770, Czartoryski was a Polish nobleman who stemmed from a family associated with the reform movement that had in the 1780s and early 1790s striven desperately to reconstitute the power of the Polish state. In 1795 he was sent to the Russian court by his parents as a pledge of their submission and good faith, and there he soon made the acquaintance of the future Alexander I. Fuelled by a common interest in many of the ideas of the Enlightenment and a shared sense of romantic benevolence, a warm friendship grew up between the two young men, and when Alexander came to the throne it was only natural that Czartoryski should have become a member of the so-called 'unofficial committee'. In this body the prince played a major role, but far more important here are his views on foreign affairs. Appointed Deputy Foreign Minister under Vorontzov in September 1802, he was for the next three years the dominant influence on Alexander. The cause closest to Czartoryski's heart was that of Polish independence: for him the eclipse of Poland was a disaster of the first order, and one made even worse by his having taken no part in the desperate and unavailing last stand of 1794–5. As he recalled of himself and his younger brother, 'Love of the fatherland, its glory, its institutions and its liberties, had been instilled in us by our studies, and by everything we had seen or heard around us. As can be imagined, that sentiment, to which we aspired with our whole being, was accompanied by an invincible aversion towards all those who had contributed to the ruin of our beloved country.'[42] Next to this he loathed Napoleon as a social upstart, a despot and a danger to peace and order. As he wrote in his memoirs:

All those who had let themselves be carried away by enthusiasm in the first moments of the French Revolution had seen Bonaparte as the hero of liberalism: he seemed to them to be destined by providence to secure the triumph of the cause of justice, and to overthrow by great actions and immense victories the obstacles without number that reality presented to the desires of the oppressed nations ... Any hope, any belief, that this would be the case was swept away as soon as Bonaparte was placed at the head of affairs in France. His every word, his every action, showed that he only understood the power of the bayonet ... He ceased to be the champion of justice and the hope of oppressed peoples. By abandoning these claims – the central pillar of the Republic, for all its vice and insanity – Bonaparte rejoined the ranks of the ambitious and of the ordinary sovereigns of Europe, showing himself to be a man of immense talent, but one who had no respect for the rights of the person and who wished only to subordinate everything to his caprice ... It was as if Hercules had quitted the path of duty in favour of using his strength to subjugate the world for his own profit ... Thus, with him in power, such was his ambition and his injustice that they over-shadowed all the other ambitions, all the other injustices, that assailed humanity: viewed in the light of the sinister and devouring flames that blazed around his head, they paled into insignificance.[43]

Yet Czartoryski was no mere *beau sabreur* committed to nothing more than some desperate Polish revolt, or, for that matter, some romantic counter-revolutionary crusade. If Poland was to be free, he realized, it would have to be with the sanction of Russia, and what better way was there for him to win this sanction than by playing on Alexander's naïve idealism and interest in political reform? Poland, then, would be restored as a sovereign kingdom and given a liberal constitution, but she would remain tied to Russia through the provision of a Russian monarch in the person of Alexander's brother, Constantine. But Czartoryski did not stop with Poland. Sincerely devoted to his version of the cause of free-dom, he also saw that Alexander would be more likely to back his ideas if they were broadened out from Poland alone (though he took care to represent a free Poland as a state that would out of gratitude and self-interest alike for ever after rally to the defence of Russia). In addition to restoring Poland, he believed that Russia should also press for the establishment of free states elsewhere. There should be a Greek state, a South Slav state, and a Danubian (i.e. Romanian) state – all of them, of course, under the protection of Russia – while Italy, Germany, the Low Countries and Switzerland were all to be organized as national federations. All this was linked in with a general plan for order and stability. According to Czartoryski's grand design, even under Napoleon France was not an irrevocable enemy, nor still less a country whose form of government was to be decided by the force of foreign arms. On the contrary, she was to enjoy her natural frontiers and be allowed to govern herself as she chose. That said, she was to be allowed to cause no more trouble: headed by Russia and Britain (whom Czartoryski saw as natural partners), the Polish prince's 'Europe of the peoples' would stand firm against French aggression. But it was not just France that would be stopped from going to war: as all the historic nationalities of Europe would be satisfied with their lot, none would wish to fight each other. By the same token, as all the peoples of Europe would be free, political strife, too, would disappear, leaving international Jacobinism with no scope for its machinations. So bizarre was this scheme that it is difficult to know what to say about it, not the least of its many problems being that it took no account whatsoever of the enormous difficulties presented by Austria (a kingdom of Hungary was no problem, but what of the rest of the empire?). At the same time, the Polish grandee's plans meant war with Prussia whom he wanted at all costs to drive from her acquisitions in Pomerania. Reduced to practicalities, in exchange for granting a semi-independent Poland, what Alexander was being offered was hegemony in Eastern Europe, the destruction of Russia's chief great-power rivals, control of the European elements of the Ottoman Empire (which Czartoryski clearly believed was doomed), and the chance to play the benevolent reformer which had proved so elusive in his own dominions. And for all this the war of 1803 provided the perfect opportunity: join with Britain against France, Czartoryski was saying, and Alexander would find the world at his feet.

However, Czartoryski or no Czartoryski, neither Russia nor anyone else responded to Napoleon's aggressive demeanour by taking up arms. On the contrary, though the Russian ambassador to Paris, Morkov, had, in Lady Holland's words, for months been 'scurvily treated by Bonaparte, who seems to make a point of saying offensive things to him',[44] Alexander responded to the conflict in a manner that was pacific in the extreme, the peace terms that he put forward in response to Napoleon's last-minute request for mediation actually representing a slight advance on Amiens. As for Austria and Prussia, the former kept quiet, and the latter did no more than dispatch a special envoy to Paris with a very polite request for an explanation of the occupation of

Hanover. The diplomat concerned, Johann von Lombard, was both an admirer of Napoleon and a long-term proponent of an alliance with France, so a sustained 'charm offensive' was more than sufficient to reassure him, while the pill was further sweetened by proposals for an alliance that seemed to offer the hope of guarantees against both Austria and Russia. However, though welcomed in Berlin, these friendly over-tures were not good enough for Frederick William. Good relations with France were all very well in themselves, but an alliance with Paris alone carried with it the risk that Prussia might be forced to take sides in a general European war, and this the Prussian king did not want at all. There then emerged a plan whereby Prussia would ally herself with both France and Russia, but this proved to be a non-starter: Alexander might not have wanted war with France at this stage, but he no longer saw her as a trustworthy partner either, while Napoleon was unwilling to come to terms with a state that had sufficient independence to have attempted to force a compromise peace upon him. At risk of standing alone, Prussia now did the only thing possible and turned back to France; the winter of 1803–4 was then taken up with intensive attempts to secure an agreement with Napoleon even though doing so implied the acceptance of French intervention in Prussia's hitherto sacrosanct sphere of influence in northern Germany.

Not even the most aggressive action on the part of Napoleon was enough to push the eastern powers into war with France, then: indeed, the potential crisis arising from the occupation of Hanover and Apulia had seemingly fizzled out. But this seems only to have encouraged Napoleon to push his luck still further. First of all, we have his reaction to the arrival of the Russian peace proposals in July 1803. Shortly after the outbreak of war, the French ruler had assured Morkov that he would respond favourably to Russian mediation: providing that Britain evacuated Malta and that Malta then received a Russian garrison, he would let the British have Lampedusa, evacuate the Batavian Republic, Switzerland and Naples, and give the King of Piedmont the territory Russia wanted him to have in Italy. These terms, in fact, were not very different from those which eventually arrived from St Petersburg, but by the time they came in, the situation had changed: Napoleon had defied the courts of Europe with impunity over Hanover and Apulia and now felt little need to be conciliatory. Nor, indeed, could he be conciliatory, for to do so would have been a blow to the image on which he was so dependent. The Russian peace terms were in consequence rejected out of hand as being even worse than those that had been proposed by Britain, while, to cover his tracks the First Consul fell upon Morkov at a state dinner at the Tuileries, and accused him in the most violent of language of both spying and being in league with emigré conspirators. Not surprisingly, there followed a sharp exchange of correspondence, and the end result was that the ambassador left Paris for home: he claimed, indeed, that he was in fear of being poisoned. Much angered, Alexander responded by trying to pressurize both Prussia and Austria into a defensive alliance and raising the possibility of an alliance with Britain. With rumours circulating of either an impending French invasion of the Greek mainland or a French-inspired revolt in the Peloponnese, the Russians also strengthened their position in the eastern Mediterranean by reinforcing the small Russian garrison that had been left in the Ionian islands and restoring friendly relations with the independent Christian principality of Montenegro, which had been disrupted for the past two years by intrigues in the court of its prince-bishop ruler, Peter Negos. As Czartoryski observed, 'For once the laughs were not on the side of the First Consul.'[45]

By the end of 1803, then, relations between Napoleon and the central figure in any future coalition had started to unravel. As yet, however, there was little sign that Russia was willing actively to take up arms: indeed, her approaches to Britain, Austria and Prussia had all essentially been designed to get them to do all the necessary fighting and keep the bulk of the Russian army out of harm's way. Opinion in St Petersburg was deeply divided. Czartoryski and Vorontzov favoured war, but Alexander opposed the anti-Prussian aspects of the former's policies and distrusted the British nearly as much as his father had done, while plenty of observers could be found who wanted Russia to have no truck at all with the affairs of the West. And if Czartoryski wanted war with France and Prussia, he did not want Britain to acquire a share in the future of the Ottoman Empire. To push Russia over the brink, something more was needed, and, Napoleon being Napoleon, this was soon forthcoming.

We come here to the so-called 'tragedy of Vincennes'. On 20 March 1804 the Duc d'Enghien, a distant connection of the French royal family, was kidnapped from his country retreat in neutral Baden and executed after a summary trial on suspicion of involvement in a royalist conspiracy. According to the Napoleonic legend, this was a necessary act of

1. Napoleon Bonaparte, c. 1803. Young and handsome, the then First Consul captivated figures as diverse as Alexander I of Russia and Ludwig van Beethoven, while his rise to power defused fears of 'Jacobinism'.

2. Surrounded by his staff, Napoleon gives orders to his troops during the battle of Austerlitz (2 December 1805). In what was to remain his greatest masterpiece, 26,000 Austrians and Russians were killed and wounded for the loss of less than 10,000 of the emperor's own troops.

3. A sardonic French comment on Austerlitz: Napoleon has only to place the tip of his sword in the scales for William Pitt, Francis II and Alexander I to be hoisted sky-high.

4. Horatio Nelson falls mortally wounded on the deck of his flagship, HMS *Victory*, at the battle of Trafalgar. The greatest naval commander of his age, Nelson did more than any other figure to cement Britain's control of the seas in the Napoleonic era.

5. The battle of Santo Domingo, 6 February 1806: the battle of Trafalgar did not end the naval war, this action seeing Admiral Sir John Duckworth smash a French squadron that had evaded the British blockade of Brest and sailed to the West Indies.

6. Napoleon's conquest of Prussia in 1806 allowed France to avenge herself for the catastrophic defeat of her forces by Frederick the Great at Rossbach in 1757: in this picture French troops pull down the monument that had been erected to celebrate the triumph of *der alte Fritz*.

7. The *grande armée* enters Berlin in the wake of the battles of Jena and Auerstädt. In an extraordinary blitzkrieg campaign, Napoleon destroyed Prussia as a military power in a mere three weeks.

8. The brothers Bonaparte bestride Europe in this cartoon of the era. With Napoleon emperor of France, Joseph King of Naples, Louis King of Holland and Jerome King of Westphalia, 1807 was the heyday of the 'family monarchies'. As Lucien Bonaparte had by this time fallen out of favour with the emperor, the fifth figure may represent Napoleon's brother-in-law, Joachim Murat, who had been made Grand Duke of Berg.

9. Napoleon, Alexander I of Russia and Frederick William III of Prussia meet at the peace conference at Tilsit in July 1807. Also featured in the painting are Frederick William's queen, Louise of Mecklenburg, whose nickname of 'the only man in Prussia' did not stop her from attempting to use her beauty to charm Napoleon into adopting a softer line, and the French Foreign Minister, Talleyrand.

10. Contemporary British cartoon highlighting the efforts of Talleyrand to restrain Napoleon from French conquests. At the conference of Erfurt in September 1808, the French Foreign Minister is reputed to have gone so far as to urge Alexander I to resist Napoleon.

11. Supported by a handful of Spanish troops under Captains Luis Daoiz and Pedro Velarde, armed civilians fight desperately to defend Madrid's artillery depot in the rising of 2 May 1808. Though more of a mass panic than a conscious uprising against the French, the Dos de Mayo set Spain ablaze.

12. An angry Napoleon tears his hair, kicks over the furniture and hurls curses in all directions in a Spanish cartoon typical of the torrent of propaganda unleashed by the uprising of May 1808.

13. 21 July 1808: Francisco Javier Castaños receives the surrender of the army of Pierre Dupont following the battle of Bailén in southern Spain. For an emperor used only to victory, it was a moment of unparalleled humiliation.

statecraft and by no means a step that the French ruler embarked on lightly. 'After the sentence had been executed,' wrote a young Belgian nobleman who was shortly to become a senior official at the Napoleonic court, 'as soon as the emperor heard of it at Malmaison, he was observed to be troubled, preoccupied, sunk in thought . . . walking up and down his apartment, his hands at his back, his head bent. And thus he remained a long time, absorbed in contemplation.'[46] Other observers were less convinced. Now unhappily married to Napoleon's brother Louis, Hortense de Beauharnais had a very different impression. 'I remain convinced, from the knowledge that I have of Napoleon's character . . . that he never felt the need to justify himself. As doubt was not something which he ever acknowledged, his view, I am sure, was "I did the thing; therefore I had the right to do it." '[47] At the same time, as she observed, the execution bestowed certain political advantages on Napoleon: 'From that moment all those who had rallied to the Revolution attached themselves to the First Consul. "He will not be a Monk," they said. "Herewith the proof. One can count on him." '[48] And that Napoleon was aware of this, there was no doubt. Indeed, according to Pasquier, it was precisely for this reason that he had the duke executed. As the future Prefect of Police wrote, 'Bonaparte . . . let it be known . . . that he wanted . . . to inspire all those who had attached themselves to his fortune with the confidence that all chance of a reconciliation between himself and the house of Bourbon had disappeared.'[49]

And it was not just statecraft. In fairness to Napoleon, as revealed by a series of arrests in the winter of 1803–4, there really was a plot to overthrow the First Consul in that the *chouan* leader, Georges Cadoudal, and the repentant radical, General Pichegru, who had been banished following the coup of 18 Fructidor in 1797, had been trying to persuade the victor of Hohenlinden, General Moreau, to mount a coup. The main figures in the plot were soon dealt with – Cadoudal and Pichegru were sentenced to death and Moreau banished – but their interrogation had produced rumours of some Bourbon prince coming to lead the revolt. With the unfortunate Enghien just over the frontier, the conclusion was obvious. As Napoleon himself remarked, 'The Duc d'Enghien was a conspirator just like any other, and it was necessary to treat him as any other might be treated.'[50] The observer is still, however, left with the feeling that what moved Napoleon was in the end little more than a desire to flex his muscles. With the war at a standstill, he was suddenly presented with an opportunity to lash out and deliver a mighty blow that would serve to remind Europe of his power. To turn around the words of Hortense de Beauharnais, the thing could be done, and so Napoleon did it. And there is, as ever, the question of the First Consul's ambition, both Bourrienne and Staël hinting very strongly that Enghien's death was engineered as a means of paving the way for his elevation to the throne. Thus, 'Napoleon would not confess the real cause of the death of the Duc d'Enghien, but inexorable history will relate that he was proclaimed emperor three months after his assassination.'[51] Still more damning was the blunt manner in which he summed up the affair for Josephine and Claire de Rémusat: 'From time to time it is no bad thing to show who is master.'[52]

Whatever the reasons for the execution, there can be no doubt as to its impact. In the famous words of Joseph Fouché, 'It was worse than a crime: it was an error.'[53] Though in receipt of a British pension, Enghien was not in arms when he was taken, but rather was living quietly in neutral territory, while he was never given anything even remotely approaching a fair trial. In Napoleon's household even, there was much grief: news of the execution produced a noisy scene between Josephine and her husband, whilst Eugène de Beauharnais later wrote, 'I was very upset on account of the respect and attachment in which I held the First Consul: it seemed to me that his glory had been sullied.'[54] What of the execution's impact outside France? Amongst the intellectual community, the First Consul's reputation as a hero of justice and reform took a serious blow – it was at this point that Beethoven famously scratched out the original dedication to the 'Eroica' symphony – and it is clear that there was widespread shock. In the words of one observer, 'The assassination of the unhappy Duc d'Enghien proved, even to the admirers of Napoleon, of what terrible excesses ambition could render him capable. All Europe shuddered with horror at that deed by which the most sacred rights were violated.'[55] Connected with the ruling house of Baden by marriage, Gustav IV of Sweden called for an immediate crusade against Napoleon, and was so upset by the affair that he became increasingly obsessed with the belief that the French ruler was the beast of the Apocalypse. Though effectively a French satellite, Duke Frederick of Württemberg accused Napoleon of violating international law. And as for Russia, in Czartoryski's words, 'This event produced the strongest impression on Alexander and the rest of the imperial family; far from hiding this, this was expressed without constraint.'[56] Acting in his role as guarantor of the constitution of the Holy Roman Empire, Alexander I protested at the violation of Baden's neutrality and demanded an explanation of Napoleon's actions, while he also enjoined the Diet of the Holy Roman Empire to register its own protest. The court went into mourning and the tsar openly snubbed the French ambassador, Hédouville, at a court levee that was held the day after the news arrived in St Petersburg. The First Consul, however, was unmoved: Sweden was ignored; the Diet of the Holy Roman Empire bullied into submission; and Alexander rebuffed with a stinging dispatch in which Napoleon pointedly inquired whether the tsar would not have seized the murderers of his father if he had discovered that they were in hiding in some town just outside his own frontiers. With the French ambassador withdrawn for good measure, there could be but one response: the Russian chargé d'affaires in Paris was instructed to ask for his passports, while troops began to be massed in Poland and Galicia. It was a key moment: though war was still not inevitable, from now on Alexander was committed to curbing Napoleon's power.

If Napoleon was serious in his desire to avoid a war with Russia, now was the moment to adopt a policy of moderation. On the contrary, on 18 May 1804 there came the declaration that France was henceforth a hereditary empire. For apologists for the French ruler, this step is easy enough to explain. Napoleon himself was anxious to ensure the permanency of his regime, while the French people were in favour of the change and even beginning to demand it. At the same time, the step was not so very great: after all, had not Rome continued to call itself a republic even when it had long been ruled by the caesars? But all this was so much casuistry: the growing clamour for the First Consul to become emperor was all too clearly manufactured by the administration – the plebiscite held to ratify the establishment of the empire in the autumn was little short of farce – while the mere fact of making the regime hereditary was not enough to scotch royalist conspiracy: aside from anything else, Napoleon and Josephine had yet to produce an heir. Once again what mattered was naked ambition: the First Consul wanted to be a ruler as other rulers, to enjoy the trappings of monarchy and, perhaps above all, to break down yet another of the barriers that hemmed him in. To quote Thibaudeau, 'Each time that the question of securing the power of the executive was mooted, the word heredity came

to the front, and for the last six months it had been openly talked about
in society. Every day people wondered when the First Consul was going
to complete the "stability" of his government. The discovery of the
conspiracy of [Cadoudal] and Pichegru furnished an excellent pretext
to carry out the execution of a plan which had been maturing for
the past three years.'[57] Also instructive, meanwhile, is Napoleon's own
comment on the change: 'The people and the army are for me: anyone
who did not know how to seize the throne in such a situation would be
a real fool.'[58]

With French power as unrivalled as it was, the impact of this pro-
nouncement should not be underestimated. That the Bourbons had been
replaced by a new dynasty was not in itself a problem: very few statesmen were so committed to the cause of legitimism that they wanted
Louis XVIII and nothing else. The issue was rather the imperial title,
which suggested that the erstwhile First Consul was laying claim to the
mantle of Charlemagne and, beyond him, the Roman Empire. Secure
in her northern bailiwick, an area that had never fallen under the suzerainty of either the Caesars or Charlemagne, Prussia could respond to
the change with equanimity and recognized Napoleon's new title without demur. But for Austria and Russia it was a different matter. For
both powers, the new dispensation threatened to exclude them from
Germany, while neither the Habsburgs nor the Romanovs were happy
about granting equal status to the Bonapartes. In consequence, Austria
dragged her feet over the issue of recognition and, despite threats of
war, did not give way until she had secured a promise that Francis would
be acknowledged as hereditary emperor of Austria and the Holy Roman
Empire granted precedence over France. As for Russia, she joined with
Sweden in refusing Napoleon her recognition while at the same time
putting pressure on Turkey to follow this example. With varying degrees
of enthusiasm, the tsar and his advisers began to work for a new coalition that would drive Napoleon back at least to the limits agreed at
Lunéville and Amiens, obtaining for this purpose the promise of substantial British subsidies. Meanwhile an ultimatum was sent to Napoleon
demanding that he evacuate Hanover and Naples, and the French ruler's
refusal to comply led Russia to break off diplomatic relations once and
for all in September 1804. And, last but not least, Czartoryski moder-
ated his hostility to Prussia: the territories of Thorn and Posen would
be restored to a Russian-controlled Poland, certainly, but Potsdam

would now be compensated with further lands in western Germany.

With a Franco-Russian rupture now a fact, it would appear that a wider conflict was inevitable. However, even now there were other complications. In October 1804, for example, Britain had shocked European opinion by launching a surprise attack on a defenceless Spanish treasure fleet on the grounds that she had been covertly aiding France and might as well be forced openly to enter the war. Prepared, seemingly gratuitously, to extend her problems by going to war against Spain, Britain further irritated the Russians by making difficulties over assisting them against the French in the Adriatic: a naval squadron, it seemed, would be no difficulty, but even so few as 10,000 men would take many months to assemble. Nor would Britain pay out the money that Russia wanted: 'Pitt's gold' would be in evidence, certainly, but only in limited quantities. With other problems occurring over the question of Malta, which Alexander was determined to claim for himself, having previously been ceded its sovereignty by the Knights of St John, the year 1804 drew to a close with an Anglo-Russian alliance seemingly out of reach, despite the fact that Alexander had dispatched a special envoy to London in the person of his friend and confidant, Nicolai Novosiltsev. As for the other partners who would be necessary – and it should be reiterated that Alexander was not prepared to send in his forces unless Austria moved as well – only Sweden was prepared to go to war. Despite clear evidence that Napoleon was planning the formation of a new German confederation that would finally overthrow the Holy Roman Empire, all that Austria would agree to was a defensive alliance that would come into play in the case of further French aggression in Egypt, the Balkans, Italy or Germany. As for Prussia, fears that Napoleon might launch a surprise attack were countered by suspicions of Russia and Sweden, the most that Frederick William was prepared to offer being an agreement to resist any French advance across the Prussian frontier provided that he was sent a Russian auxiliary force of at least 40,000 men.

Given Czartoryski's foreign policy, the growth of hostility to France in St Petersburg might appear a mere pretext for the annexation of fresh territory in Eastern Europe and the Balkans. In this respect Serbia offers a very useful test case. In February 1804 a major revolt broke out in the Ottoman *pashalik* of Belgrade under the leadership of a local chieftain named Djordje Petrovic (or to use the name by which he is invariably known, Karadjordje). Initially, this was no nationalist convulsion.

National feeling among the populace was very weak, if not non-existent, and many of the inhabitants had to be coerced into taking arms. The goal of the revolt was not independence, but rather autonomy on the lines granted to the Ionian islands (despite governing themselves, they in theory acknowledged the sovereignty of the Sultan in Constantinople). Indeed, the greatest loyalty was expressed with regard to the person of Selim III, the chief goal of the insurgents being rather to break the power of the oppressive Turkish landlord class – the *chiftliks* – and, still more so, the undisciplined bands of marauders known as *yamaks* into which the janissaries that garrisoned the region had deteriorated. Nor was a desire to support the rule, and even strengthen the authority, of Constantinople surprising: under Selim III, who had been on the throne since 1789, fears that the Balkans might otherwise revolt had led to a great push for reform that for ten years had made a real difference to the Serbian position. Recently, however, things had got much worse: following Napoleon's attack on Egypt, the Sultan's need for the support of every man he could raise had led him to abandon his attempts to protect the Serbs. Meanwhile, the *yamaks* had murdered Selim's governor, the sensible and moderate Hajji Mustafa, and replaced him with their own man, while at the same time venting years of suppressed frustration on the populace and its leaders, the clergy of the Serbian Orthodox Church and the tribal chieftains known as the *knezes*. Hence the revolt of 1804: desperate to save their heads, priests and chieftains banded together and established an assembly at the town of Orasac, while irregular levies attacked the *yamaks* and exacted a terrible vengeance.

We have, then, a revolt in the Balkans, but do we also have Russian imperialism? Evidently not. Prior to 1804 the Russians had almost no contact with the Serbs of the Ottoman Empire, and they returned a non-committal but on the whole rather discouraging answer to a delegation that had travelled to St Petersburg with the news that an insurrection was brewing. When revolt actually broke out, moreover, the Russian position was at first one of neutrality: the commander of the Russian forces on the Adriatic coast refused to supply the rebels with arms, while the Foreign Ministry declared the affair to be of no interest to Russia, characterizing it as merely one more of the incessant disturbances that plagued the Ottoman Empire. Still more interestingly, proposals emanating from the Serbian exiles who had a century before fled to the Habsburg-controlled Vojvodina for a South Slav union of the sort put forward by Czartoryski were simply ignored. Czartoryski aside, neither pan-slavism nor imperialism marked Russian policy in the Balkans: the aim was neither to conquer the area, nor to partition it with France, but rather to prop up the Ottoman Empire as a dependent state that would keep the southern approaches to Russia in friendly hands. Since 1799, indeed, St Petersburg had been allied to Constantinople, and, greatly alarmed by French designs on the Balkans, the Russians were at this time trying to strengthen their military ties with Selim III.

With matters in this state Napoleon played straight into the hands of his opponents. The coronation ceremony held in Paris on 2 December 1804 greatly reinforced the fears that his assumption of the imperial title had already summoned up. The crown was a laurel wreath in the style of those associated with the caesars, and the robe was not only the purple of imperial Rome but also emblazoned with the bee, a creature that had a thousand years before been the badge of Charlemagne. Presiding over the ceremony was Pope Pius VII, whose presence Napoleon at one and the same time required as a means of legitimizing his rule, expressing the supremacy of the temporal power and reinforcing his claim to the mantle of Charlemagne, who had himself been crowned by Pope Leo III over a millennium before. If Pius was treated with scant courtesy by Napoleon, this generated little concern: Pius had been elected at a conclave held in Venice in the very midst of the allied victories of 1799 and had spent the first few months of his papacy as a de facto prisoner of the Austrians, who coveted large parts of his domains and were no friends of ultramontanism. But few could miss the significance of the new emperor's actions, while still more grim was the symbolism of the new regimental standards awarded to the French army in a dramatic parade on the Champ de Mars: in place of a spearhead, the pole was now topped by a bronze eagle on the lines of that carried by the Roman legions. And all the time international law continued to be trampled upon: on 25 October the British minister in Hamburg, Sir George Rumbold, was arrested as a spy by a detachment of French troops, subjected to considerable ill treatment, transported to Paris and imprisoned in the Temple prison, where, as he later told the Earl of Malmesbury, his 'first idea . . . was that he was to perish by secret means, and that, in order to attribute to him suicide, they would forge papers . . . to demonstrate the state of despondency he was under'.[59]

'This fresh violation of the rights of nations,' wrote Fouché, 'roused the whole of Europe.'[60] Yet, despite all this, as 1805 dawned a new coalition was still far away. On 11 April Britain and Russia admittedly succeeded in concluding a treaty of alliance that committed Russia to war unless Napoleon agreed to conform to Amiens and Lunéville, and laid down the aim of excluding the French from Holland, Switzerland and northern Italy. This was the work of Novosiltsev, but when the terms reached St Petersburg there was great dissatisfaction. Hampered by contradictory instructions, the Russian envoy had been completely outmanoeuvred. The issue of Malta remained unresolved; the proposed subsidy – £1.25 million per annum for every 100,000 men deployed by the Russians – was nowhere near what Alexander expected; there was no mention of the freedom of the seas; and it was intimated that both Austria and Prussia would receive extensive territorial gains as part of the eventual European peace settlement. In consequence, the treaty for some time remained unratified. But Alexander's displeasure was not the only problem. The alliance, it was agreed, would only come into force in the event of Austria going to war; more than that, Russia would not have to take up arms until Vienna had been at war for at least four months. But this meant that the whole negotiation was null and void, for Austria had no intention of taking part in an offensive war, and still less so one in which she would clearly be expected to do the bulk of the fighting. For the time being, then, there was neither a treaty, nor an alliance nor even friendship: at few moments in the Napoleonic Wars, indeed, were Anglo-Russian relations to hit such a low point. And – not that it mattered very much without Russian involvement – Gustav IV's eagerness for a crusade against France had been greatly dissipated by fears for Swedish Pomerania, the last remnant of the once great Swedish empire on the southern and eastern shores of the Baltic. Thus Sweden would participate in a war, certainly, but she would neither act without Russia nor move her army beyond the Pomeranian frontier.

It is difficult to see where the Third Coalition would have been without Napoleon. At the start of the year there had been some sign that the French ruler was still at least prepared to pay lip-service to moderation. Rumbold was released within a matter of days thanks to the intercession of Frederick William III, and on 1 January the new emperor had sent a further letter to George III lamenting France's continued war with Britain and inviting him to make peace. Much in the style of the similar communication of December 1799, this missive – which offered nothing in the way of concessions – was primarily designed to embarrass Pitt, but the mere fact that it was written suggests some recognition of the need to play the peacemaker. Within a matter of months, however, the gauntlet was flung down once again. In May 1805 Napoleon descended on Milan and crowned himself King of Italy amidst yet more pomp and ceremony. As yet the only territories affected were those of the erstwhile Italian Republic, which now became the Kingdom of Italy, and Napoleon did not take up the reins of government in person, but instead installed his stepson, Eugène de Beauharnais, as viceroy. This was meagre reassurance, however, for the French ruler's new title clearly implied a claim to the whole of the Italian peninsula. And, if this was not enough, in early June Napoleon suddenly announced the annexation of Genoa – the Ligurian Republic – Parma and Piacenza, and appropriated Lucca as a principality for his younger sister, Elise. This was just too much. In response, Britain and Russia resolved their differences and ratified the treaty of 11 April. This, of course, left Austria, but she was not far behind and was now prepared to take the offensive. Even Francis II and the Archduke Charles could not tolerate French control of the whole of Italy, and the belief was growing in Vienna that Napoleon was contemplating a direct attack on the Habsburgs. At the same time, for once real support was on offer in the form of a one-off bonus of a further £1,666,000, an annual subsidy of £4 million and a Russian expeditionary force of 75,000 men (support, incidentally, that was not likely to be on offer indefinitely: the Russians, in particular, made it very clear that, unless the army they had massed on the frontiers of Galicia was set in motion very soon, it would have to be withdrawn). The choice was either to join a grand alliance now or fight alone later. Nor was Austria the only new recruit. Having blown hot and cold on the issue of war for the previous year, Gustav IV of Sweden now agreed to put 12,000 troops into the field in exchange for the enormous subsidy of £150,000 per year, plus further one-off payments amounting to £112,500.

Why had Napoleon acted as he did at this crucial moment? Setting aside his own explanation that as emperor he could hardly be president of a republic, one argument is that he always wanted to turn east, and was therefore eager to create a pretext for such a move by forcing the eastern powers into the open. A war in central Europe was certainly a possibility in Napoleon's mind as early as the summer of 1804, while it later suited him to claim that Austria was always the real target of his war effort. As Metternich wrote:

In one of my longer conversations with Napoleon in the journey to Cambrai, whither I accompanied the emperor in 1810, the conversation turned upon the great military preparations he had made in the years 1803–1805 at Boulogne. I frankly confessed to him that even at that time I could not regard these offensive measures as directed against England. 'You were very right,' replied the emperor, smiling. 'Never would I have been such a fool as to make a descent upon England, unless indeed a revolution had taken place within that country. The army assembled at Boulogne was always an army against Austria. I could not place it anywhere else without giving offence, and, being obliged to form it somewhere, I did so at Boulogne, where I could while collecting it also disquiet England. The very day of an insurrection in England, I should have sent over a detachment of my army to support the insurrection, [but] I should not the less have fallen on you.'[61]

But this is less than convincing: aside from anything else, the argument is simply too convenient for the emperor. Nor is it helpful to explain the imposition of French rule in the Italian Republic in rational terms relating to reform or political control: so slavish was the devotion of Melzi and his fellows to France that the emperor's assumption of the throne made little difference. Once again, then, one is reduced to the personal dimension: Napoleon wanted simply to augment his own glory and, in particular, reinforce his links with Charlemagne, who had himself worn the iron crown that was placed on Napoleon's head in Milan.

None of this means, however, that Napoleon was overly concerned at the prospect of war with Austria and Russia. Thus, by the summer of 1805, all was not well with the 'Army of England'. Getting across the Channel had always presented problems, and on 20 July 1804 a sudden squall that sprang up in the midst of a grand review of its barges, sloops and pontoons not only left 2,000 men dead, but convinced many observers that success was out of the question. But not Napoleon: he spent most of the year that followed devising ways and means of concentrating a vast naval force that could descend on the Channel and clear the way for invasion. At first these schemes all came to grief, but in March 1805 the Toulon fleet of Admiral Pierre Villeneuve managed to slip out of port and, after a long voyage, reach the West Indies.

However, a rendezvous with a small squadron that had escaped from Rochefort went wrong, while the Brest fleet of Admiral Honoré Ganteaume failed to break out at all. At the point that Napoleon made his great démarche in Italy, Villeneuve was still at large, and there was some faint hope that he might link up with the Spanish squadron in El Ferrol and raise the blockade of Brest. However, whether even the emperor believed such a scenario to be possible must be open to doubt: one of the reasons why Ganteaume never escaped from Brest was that he had received orders from Napoleon that he should on no account attempt directly to confront the British ships on patrol outside. And at the same time one can sense compulsion pure and simple: faced by the growing evidence that Napoleon intended to transform the Italian Republic into a monarchy, Austria had responded by indicating that she had no objections to such a course provided that France's Milanese satellite remained independent. But accepting such a limitation would have implied that other powers had a say in what Napoleon could and could not do. And to this there was but one answer: the Italian Republic would not just become a kingdom, but also a kingdom ruled by the emperor and all but surrounded by French territory.

Whatever the reason for Napoleon's actions, there is no doubt that by them he single-handedly created the Third Coalition. Yet, great though the sense of shock was, Europe was still not completely united against him. Opportunistic as ever, Prussia weighed up the advantages and disadvantages of empire and coalition, and in fact put out feelers to both camps. From Russia there came nothing more than the offer of a triple alliance with Austria and Russia that would guarantee Germany against any further French encroachment, whether political or military, but the French response was very different: to obtain a Prussian alliance, Napoleon was prepared not just to promise Frederick William that he would be given Hanover with the coming of peace, but also to hand that state over to Prussian occupation straight away, while at the same time guaranteeing the integrity of Germany and Switzerland. With Russia becoming ever more menacing – news arrived not only of Russian troops massing on the frontier, but also that a pro-Russian insurrection was being stirred up in Prussian Poland – Potsdam veered very much in the direction of Paris: if Napoleon engaged in any more serious acts of aggression in Germany or anywhere else, argued Frederick William's new chief minister, Karl August von Hardenberg, then Prussia should probably join Britain and Russia, but, unless and until that proved the case, she should seek to retain the emperor's friendship.

Another state playing a double game was Naples. At first sight this is somewhat surprising. Unlike Frederick William III, Ferdinand IV did not enjoy good relations with Napoleon. Setting aside the fact that he regarded him as an upstart and a 'Jacobin', he had recently been faced by a demand that the commander of the Neapolitan army, Roger de Damas, should immediately be dismissed as an enemy of France, or, in other words, an emigré. For good measure, Ferdinand and Maria Carolina were also accused of planning a new war. Now, as it happened, Damas was not an emigré – he had been in the service of first Russia and then Naples since 1786 – and the queen attempted to keep the peace by writing a personal letter to Napoleon in which she sought to calm his fears. The sequel, however, was all too predictable:

The style of the queen's letter was firm, dignified and friendly, and she had no doubt that, unless Bonaparte were seeking for a pretext to break the peace, he would adopt a more reasonable and cordial tone . . . But this hope was short-lived: Bonaparte's answer . . . was full of rancour and arrogance. He laid all the troubles of the past at her door, and made her responsible for all that was yet to come, and he ended with . . . some impertinent fatherly advice to the effect that she would do well to be careful lest she should fall victim to her own actions and be reduced to begging for assistance at the courts of her kinsfolk . . . These were his final and least harsh expressions. The queen shed torrents of tears as she was reading this fatal letter, and, if it had the effect of increasing her bitterness and hatred towards this man, who could wonder?[62]

To reinforce this message, Napoleon proceeded to rattle his sabre: in the midst of the carnival celebrations for 1805, an ultimatum was received from the commander of the French forces in Naples, Marshal Gouvion St Cyr, announcing that he would march on the capital unless both Damas and Elliot, the British ambassador, left the country within three days. In the end a compromise was negotiated – Elliot was allowed to stay and Damas was removed from command of the army and sent to Sicily – but it was clear that for Napoleon the affair constituted unfinished business: for example, a Neapolitan nobleman who attended the festivities surrounding the emperor's coronation as King of Italy was treated to a violent tirade 'that culminated in an unseemly and unbridled attack upon the queen'.[63]

All this was very alarming, but the way forward was less than clear. Ferdinand and Maria Carolina feared and hated Napoleon and longed for his defeat, but with the country partially occupied by French troops they could at best play a double game. On the one hand Napoleon was offered the promise of neutrality if only he would respect Naples's independence, while on the other secret approaches were made to Russia which on 10 September produced what looked like an agreement to go to war. In exchange for the immediate dispatch of an Anglo-Russian expeditionary force, Naples would resist both any increase in the French forces stationed on her territory and any expansion of the zone in which they were deployed. Yet the dissimulation continued: above all, it was not made clear what 'resistance' actually meant. In the event, the answer proved to be 'not very much'. Almost before the ink on the agreement with Russia had time to dry, Napoleon decided to reinforce St Cyr with an extra 6,000 troops; the Neapolitan response to this was not even to protest, let alone take up arms, but rather to sign a treaty of alliance with France that committed Naples to closing her ports to British ships and defending her territory against any foreign incursions.

Although the Neapolitan government had clearly not wanted to take this step – the king had to be bullied into signing the treaty by his ministers, and hastened to tell the Russian ambassador that he considered it null and void – there was a subtext. Ferdinand and Maria Carolina did not feel in danger just from France, but also from Britain. In the midst of the quarrels that beset Anglo-Russian relations in the easy summer of 1805, the Russian ambassador to Naples had informed the king that the British were planning to seize Sicily. Strictly speaking, this was true enough: in March 1805 Sir James Craig was given 8,000 men and directed to occupy Sicily should Naples join Napoleon or experience a complete French takeover. But this was only part of the story: Craig was informed that the very strong preference of the British government was that he should occupy Sicily with the permission of Ferdinand IV. And, beyond that, it was not ruled out that the British expeditionary force should engage in operations on the mainland in support of the Neapolitans in company with the Russian troops currently occupying the Ionian islands. But with plenty of observers in the

Neapolitan court only too ready to believe the worst of Britain, the damage could not be undone. Setting aside the unfortunate impact which the affair had on Anglo-Russian cooperation in the Mediterranean, the Neapolitan government excluded Elliot from the negotiations that led to the September pact and ever afterwards adopted an air of suspicion and hostility. The tangled story of Anglo-Sicilian relations is something to which we will return, but for the time being let us simply cite the recollections of one of Craig's staff officers, Sir Henry Bunbury. When the British eventually arrived at Messina, they were kept waiting in the harbour for four weeks before they were given permission to disembark, and the governor 'allowed us just what he could not refuse to allies [and] threw everything in our way that he could without giving open offence'; as for the queen, further incensed by the eventual abandonment of the mainland without a fight, she is described as 'boiling with rage against the . . . English, whom she seized every occasion of stigmatizing by the most insane abuse'.[64]

Prussia and Naples aside, however, by the middle of August 1805 the Third Coalition was taking shape. Britain, Austria, Russia and Sweden all stood together, and also hoped to win the support of Naples and, just possibly, although it now seemed most unlikely, Prussia. As summer drifted into autumn, so Alexander also pursued the possibility of bringing in both Denmark and Turkey. What, though, did the new league stand for? British observers have generally tended to seize upon a famous memoir written by William Pitt for the Russian government in January 1804. Billed as a plan for the reconstruction of Europe, this specified that ideally the French should evacuate the Low Countries, Italy and Germany and accept frontiers based on those of 1792 (there was never any suggestion that the erstwhile papal enclaves of Avignon and Orange should be taken away). The United Provinces, Switzerland, Tuscany, Modena and Piedmont were all to be restored as independent states, while the United Provinces, Piedmont, Austria and Prussia were all to receive substantial new territories. The United Provinces would be given all of Belgium north of a line stretching from Antwerp to Maastricht; Piedmont given Genoa and western Lombardy; Austria the so-called 'Legations' (i.e. the district centred on Bologna and Ferrara that constituted the northernmost province of the Papal States) and what was left of Lombardy; and Prussia the southern part of the Austrian Netherlands, Luxembourg and the left bank of the Rhine. As for the resultant settlement, it would be guaranteed by Britain and Russia, bolstered by a new code of international law, and further stiffened by German and Italian defence unions of which the respective kingpins would be Prussia and Austria. Albeit at the cost of the frontiers of 1789 – for many minor states would either be stripped of some of their land or erased altogether – France would be shut in by an expanded Piedmont backed up by Austria in the south and an expanded United Provinces backed up by Prussia in the north. Even better, meanwhile, Pitt's plan did away with the need for total victory. With a proper cordon sanitaire in place along her frontiers, the Allies could rest easy as to what should be done with France herself: while Pitt considered the restoration of the Bourbons to be desirable and believed, indeed, that this object should be promoted, he did not see it as necessarily a fundamental principle of allied policy and, by extension, was prepared to allow Napoleon to remain on the throne.

This scheme, it can be argued, was in essence a conversion of the vague, misty and ill-thought-out views that Alexander I brought to the coalition into a practical design for the future well-being of Europe. As expressed by the instructions issued to his special emissary, Novosiltsev, in the autumn of 1804, the tsar's plans were certainly open to question. While there was clearly much common ground – the restoration of the United Provinces, Piedmont and Switzerland, and the evacuation of Germany and Italy – Alexander wanted much else. Where Pitt envisaged the restoration of a modified form of the Holy Roman Empire, Alexander wanted the 'third Germany' to become a national federation; where Pitt had little interest in the details of the political settlement to pertain in each state, Alexander believed that it was essential to intervene in this respect; where Pitt looked on the whole to states that were historic units, Alexander harboured dreams of a Europe built on national units and natural frontiers; and, finally, while Pitt did not look beyond a treaty by which the new dispensation could be guaranteed, Alexander wanted a new system of collective security and a code of international law. Inherent to all this were certain ideas which the British were inclined to regard not just as harmlessly idealistic, but dangerous and even hostile. Thus in the new Europe it would not only be France that would be placed under constraint, but also Britain, for the tsar wanted her to agree to a general freedom of the seas and envisaged concessions on other fronts as well. Much of this Pitt dodged: his memorandum said nothing about maritime commerce, nothing about Britain's colonial gains, nothing about Malta (whose surrender had not been mentioned by Novosiltsev, but certainly tied in with the spirit of the tsar's ideas) and nothing about Alexander's 'brave new world'. With regard to the Low Countries, the British Prime Minister also failed to put forward the far more logical course of action represented by giving Prussia the United Provinces rather than the Austrian Netherlands, and making the latter a buffer state ruled, say, by the House of Orange: to have done so would have been to risk transforming Prussia into a dangerous naval rival. To cement the alliance, Pitt was therefore in the end forced to meet Alexander halfway: Britain would give up all her colonial conquests, open up the question of neutral rights to discussion after the war, and consider evacuating Malta in exchange for Menorca. But the Anglo-Russian treaty of 11 April 1805 – the central pillar of the Third Coalition – contained none of this; all that Pitt agreed to was that the peoples of Switzerland and the United Provinces should be allowed to determine their own mode of government, that the King of Piedmont should be encouraged to grant his subjects a constitution, and that the powers of Europe should consider the possibility of establishing some form of 'league of nations' when peace was restored.

Was this scheme really the framework of a new order? Hardly. There were, of course, many superficial resemblances to the Vienna settlement of 1815, and all the more so as the treaty of 11 April backed away from some of the odder features of Pitt's schemes (such as, for example, the idea that most of Belgium should be given to Prussia). But in practice Alexander's vision of a new Europe went by the board. If the West was to be ruled by a new model of territorial arrangement in which military and strategic considerations were allowed to outweigh the demands of legitimism, in the East all was much as before. Thus, even if this was cloaked in some instances by the desire to restore a Polish state, powerful elements within the Russian government wanted fresh territory in Poland, and this meant that Austria and Prussia must be compensated in their turn. And, if special interests operated in the case of Russia, so they did in the case of Britain, except that here the goal was not territorial gain but security from invasion and the right to rule the sea. Nor was this an end to the differences that marked the two settlements. As Paul Schroeder has pointed out, in essence what we have here is an attempt by Britain and Russia, first, simply to impose their own agenda on the

rest of Europe, and, second, to get more or less powerful auxiliaries –
the Austrians, the Prussians, the Neapolitans, the Swedes and the Danes
– to do the bulk of the fighting for them (of the 400,000 men who were
originally to be committed to the alliance, only 115,000 were Russian
and fewer than 20,000 British). Hence his belief that the treaty of
11 April 1805 was not progressive at all, but rather backward-looking
and thoroughly eighteenth-century.

So how did war actually break out? On 8 August 1805 Austria finally
acceded to the Third Coalition, and less than a month later sent a large
army under General Mack across the frontier into Bavaria. The 'War of
the Third Coalition' had begun. In just two years, Napoleon had converted an Anglo-French war into one involving the whole of Europe. In
May 1803 Britain had not only stood alone, but had been regarded by
the rest of Europe with hostility and suspicion. By 1805, of the great
powers only Prussia remained outside her embrace. Far from buying
foreign support with 'Pitt's gold', Britain had had little to do with this
result, the chief pressure for the formation of the Third Coalition having
come from Russia. Just as the events of 1802–3 revealed to Britain that
she had no option but to stand firm against Napoleon, so those of
1804–5 showed Alexander I that he too had to fight. And why was this
the case? The answer was simply 'Napoleon'. Warned by Fouché that
his conduct could not but provoke a wider war, the emperor's response
was: 'I must have battles and triumphs.'[65] The same observer recalled,
'One day, upon my objecting to him that he could not make war against
England and against all Europe, he replied, "I may fail by sea, but not
by land; besides, I shall be able to strike the blow before the old coalition
machines are ready. The people of the old school understand nothing
about it, and . . . have neither activity nor decision . . . I do not fear old
Europe." '[66] Beyond this there was yet another problem. To quote Claire
de Rémusat, an observer who was very close to him at this period,
'The greatest error of Bonaparte, an error that stemmed from his very
character, was that he did not measure his conduct by anything other
than success . . . His innate pride could not support the idea of a defeat
of any sort.'[67] The emperor could not accept that there were limits,
whether military, political, diplomatic or moral, to what he could do,
and over and over again rammed home this same message. Madame de
Rémusat, it will be objected, was a witness hostile to the emperor, and
therefore hardly someone to be trusted. But precisely the same idea may

be found in the words of men who remained loyal admirers of Napoleon to the death. Commenting on the campaigns of 1805–7, for example, Lavallette wrote, 'It was not those two years of triumphant battles that suggested to the emperor the idea of conquering Europe in order to become its master . . . This idea arose naturally out of his own genius and character, for these terrible world-conquerors all belong to the same family: the first everywhere, or death.'[68]

5

Austerlitz

The small Bavarian town of Wertingen had rarely figured very prominently in German history. A sleepy place south of the Danube about twenty-five miles north-west of Augsburg, it had for most of its life remained a quiet backwater. In the War of the Spanish Succession two mighty armies had clashed with one another a few miles away on the other side of the Danube at Blenheim, but few ripples of that conflict had reached the local peasants and townsfolk. Equally, in August 1796 French troops from Moreau's Army of the Rhine and Moselle had passed through the town en route for Augsburg, but there had been no fighting, and the town had also escaped seeing any action in the campaign of 1800. On 8 October 1805, however, Wertingen was suddenly pitchforked into the very heart of Europe's affairs. Late the previous night it had without warning been occupied by about 5,000 men of the Austrian Army of the Danube under Baron Franz Auffenberg. Sent to the area to investigate rumours that enemy troops had crossed the Danube east of the Austrian base of Ulm, the troops were cooking their midday meal when suddenly news arrived that a large French force was approaching from the north-west. A pot-pourri of units that was a perfect representative of the polyglot Austrian army – Germans from the infantry regiments of Chasteler, Spork, and Kaunitz rubbed shoulders with Czechs from those of Stuart and Württemberg, Poles from that of Reuss-Greitz and Hungarians from that of Jellacic – the white-coated Habsburg troops rushed to form up, but it was too late. With over 8,000 infantry and 4,000 cavalry, led by Marshals Murat and Lannes, the French fell upon the unfortunate Auffenberg without more ado. Fighting bravely, his men put up a fierce stand around Wertingen itself, but it was to no avail: by the end of the afternoon over 3,000 men had been killed, wounded or taken prisoner for the loss of perhaps 200 Frenchmen.

Unimportant though it was, this brief action set the scene for the next two years. In a series of outstanding campaigns, Napoleon was to overrun central Europe at the head of his *grande armée*, and inflict defeat after defeat on armies of the *ancien régime* that seemingly had no answer to his men, his methods and his genius. But the triumphs which for the rest of the Napoleonic age were to adorn the standards of so many French regiments were not just the result of superior tactics, organization or generalship. The French war-machine was anything but perfect in 1805, while Napoleon was quite capable of making serious errors. At the moment when Lannes and Murat collided with Auffenberg at Wertingen, for example, the emperor thought that the army of General Mack lay ahead of the *grande armée* to the south-east, rather than far to its right at Ulm. Equally, in 1805 much of the French cavalry was poorly mounted and cut a poor figure in the face of that of the Austrians and Russians. It is therefore important to remember that many other factors were crucial in the dramatic events of 1805–7. Thanks to Napoleon, the French state was far better able to sustain an offensive war than had ever been the case in the 1790s. But also important was the diplomatic context to Napoleon's wars. From the very beginning the Third Coalition was a mismanaged and ill-coordinated venture, while resistance to the emperor was constantly undermined by the continuing belief of many European statesmen that the 'great game' of conventional eighteenth-century power politics was still in operation. As they were about to learn, nothing could be further from the truth.

As we have seen, a number of British statesmen had been unenthusiastic about seeking continental allies for fear that to do so would simply be to hand Napoleon fresh victories. Although a coalition was in the end vital to Great Britain, in the short term they were proven entirely right. For Napoleon, the end of the impasse on the Channel coast in all probability came as a great relief. Until the very last minute invasion appears to have been his intention: not only did he fly into a violent rage when news arrived that Villeneuve had made for Cádiz rather than the Channel (see below), but the troops were plucked from the midst of incessant amphibious exercises. 'Twenty times', wrote an artillery officer, Baron Hulot, 'in the fifteen days that followed [the emperor's] return [to Boulogne on 3 August 1805] I went down to . . . Calais or Dunkirk to . . . supervise the embarkation of the artillery.'[1] Yet there remained enormous obstacles that Napoleon cannot have been blind to even if he would not admit to them in public. Despite prodigious expenditure, the ports around which the *grande armée* was encamped were still insufficient to get all the troops to sea in a single tide, while the disaster of 20 July 1804 was anything but reassuring. In short, the French were simply not ready to make the attempt even if they could obtain the necessary naval superiority. And Napoleon knew it: as he observed to one of his aides-de-camp on 4 August, 'This invasion is by no means a certainty.'[2] Yet nor could the 'camp of Boulogne' be maintained for very much longer. As the months dragged on, so the problem of boredom became ever more acute. As Raymond de Fezensac, a young *ci-devant* who had enlisted in the 59me Régiment d'Infanterie de Ligne as a gentleman volunteer in 1804 and went on to become an aide-de-camp to Marshal Ney, remembered of the soldiers, 'Sleeping . . . singing songs, telling stories, getting into arguments over nothing, reading the few bad books that they managed to procure; this was their life.'[3] Nor, meanwhile, did the waiting suit Napoleon himself. Organizing the invasion was a project that had taken years and, dreams of winning control of the Channel notwithstanding, could well take many years more. How much longer could a fresh injection of martial glory be delayed?

The emergence of the Third Coalition came as manna from heaven, particularly as France was in the grip of a serious financial crisis brought on by heavy government borrowing and the slow manner in which the regime had been paying the numerous contractors engaged in the construction of the invasion flotillas. And, if any further pretext was required, on 23 August news arrived at Boulogne that there would be a further lengthy delay before the invasion flotilla could sail. Its only hope of success had been that the French and Spanish squadrons scattered around the coast of Europe from Toulon to Brest might somehow slip through the British blockade and either unite in the West Indies, thereby forcing the Royal Navy to leave the Channel unguarded, or else join together for a desperate struggle off the British coast itself. By 1805 it was the former plan that was in the ascendant and at the end of March the Toulon squadron had succeeded in dodging the British blockade, escaping through the Straits of Gibraltar and reaching the island of Martinique. No other ships succeeded in joining them there, however, and, with Nelson bearing down upon him, the French commander, Admiral Villeneuve, eventually decided to sail back to Europe in the hope of uniting with France's other main battle squadrons, which were trapped in Brest and Rochefort. Encountering a British squadron off Finisterre, he was driven into port at El Ferrol. Here he might yet have accomplished much – there was a substantial Spanish squadron at Ferrol while the French ships at Rochefort had managed to get out of port in the confusion – but a mixture of disillusionment, misapprehension and muddle caused Villeneuve to flee for the safety of Cádiz, whither he was followed by the largest force the British could muster. Even more ominously, command of this force was given to the hero of Aboukir and Copenhagen, Horatio Nelson, a leader who radiated aggression and self-confidence, inspired absolute devotion amongst his subordinates, and united tactical genius with a savage hatred of the enemy.

All this left Napoleon both furious and disgusted. As Ségur recounts, even the relatively innocuous news that Villeneuve had taken shelter at El Ferrol provoked an explosion:

It was about four o'clock in the morning of August 13th that the news was brought to the emperor . . . Daru was summoned and on entering he gazed on his chief in utter astonishment. He told me afterwards that he looked perfectly wild, that his hat was thrust down to his eyes, and that his whole aspect was terrible. As soon as he saw Daru he rushed up and thus apostrophized him; 'Do you know where that fool of a Villeneuve is now? He is at Ferrol. Do you know what that means? At Ferrol? You do not know? He has been beaten; he has gone to hide himself . . . That is the end of it: he will be blocked up there. What a navy! What an admiral! What useless sacrifices!' And, becoming more and more excited, he walked up and down the room for about an hour giving vent to his justifiable anger in a torrent of bitter reproaches and sorrowful reflections.[4]

That Napoleon was aggrieved that two years had been lost there was no doubt. But he was soon happily making the best of a bad job: 'Well,' he said, 'if we must give that up, we will at any rate hear the Midnight Mass at Vienna.'[5] No sooner had he spent his rage at Villeneuve's retreat to Ferrol, indeed, than he is supposed to have sat Daru down and dictated the plan of campaign that, exactly as he had predicted, saw him reach Vienna by Christmas. Before telling that story, we must first wrap up matters naval, however.

With the invasion attempt definitively abandoned, Napoleon might have done best to leave Villeneuve's fleet in port. However, perturbed by Sir James Craig's expedition to the Mediterranean, the emperor ordered him to make for Naples so as to put ashore the 4,000 troops who had been attached to his squadron and assist St Cyr in the task of overawing Ferdinand IV. Despite the fact that neither his own ships nor the Spanish squadron stationed in Cádiz were remotely fit for battle, the French admiral realized that compliance was the only hope of saving his career – Napoleon had in fact dispatched Admiral Rosily to replace him – and on 20 October he put to sea. Alongside him sailed fifteen Spanish men-of-war, commanded by Admiral Federico Gravina. The presence of these forces provides a useful opportunity to discuss the relationship that had developed between France and Spain since the latter's forced re-entry into the conflict in November 1804. In brief, Franco-Spanish relations were extremely poor. Initially, the royal favourite and dominant figure in the regime, Manuel de Godoy, had affected enthusiasm for the war. In this, he may even have been genuine: once hostilities had become inevitable there was, after all, no barrier to dreams of retaking Gibraltar or seizing a slice of Portugal. But the fact is that Spain had little choice: Britain was clearly bent on making war on her, while Napoleon made it quite clear to the Spanish ambassador to Paris – none other than the same Admiral Gravina – that any other response than military action would incur great displeasure on his part.

On 9 January 1805, then, a convention had been signed whereby the Spaniards promised to arm naval squadrons at El Ferrol, Cádiz and Cartagena by the end of March. At first all went well enough: by a variety of means Napoleon encouraged Godoy to believe that Spain would indeed be permitted to move against Portugal and in response the favourite threw himself into the task of readying the Spanish navy for war. Much was achieved: six ships-of-the-line were able to join Villeneuve from Cádiz when he sailed through the Straits of Gibraltar into the Atlantic in April after escaping from Toulon, while strenuous efforts, not least on the financial front, had by the same date got another twelve ready in the other two naval bases mentioned in the convention. Naturally enough, these efforts, which had been made in the face of considerable opposition in the ministry and the naval establishment, persuaded Godoy that he was entitled to some reward and, in particular, to make use of Spain's forces to pursue military objectives of interest to Madrid. One obvious possibility was an attack on Gibraltar and another a descent on one or other of Britain's possessions in the Caribbean. To Napoleon, however, such designs were of no account, and the unfortunate Godoy found that he was expected to commit all Spain's forces to the invasion of Britain. Still worse, it appeared that what Spain had achieved thus far was not enough: Napoleon not only wanted more ships mobilized than the Spaniards had promised, but was in effect demanding the transfer of a number of additional vessels to the French navy.

In the event this particular spectre did not become a reality, but neither did Godoy's dreams of territorial acquisitions. On the contrary, these were pointedly ignored: no fewer than three attempts to interest Napoleon in a march on Lisbon received no response whatsoever. Only when it became clear that the Portuguese, for all their neutrality, remained loyal to their traditional friendship with Britain did Napoleon take an interest in the subject and even then Godoy's hopes were soon dashed. Given the emergence of the Third Coalition, Napoleon no longer had any troops to spare for Portugal and began to speak in terms of the Spaniards sending troops to Italy or even Germany. An angry Godoy therefore began to drag his feet in Madrid. He was deeply conscious of the faulty state of many of the ships, the tactical superiority of the British and Spain's chronic shortage of trained manpower. In recent years this had been exacerbated by successive epidemics of yellow fever that had killed many thousands of people in the coastal communities of Andalucía – in Málaga alone, there were 6,343 deaths between 22 August and 1 October 1804. Told that new orders had arrived, laying down that the combined squadron should sail for Naples and add the many soldiers embarked on Villeneuve's ships to St Cyr's army, in Cádiz Gravina and his officers fiercely opposed leaving port. Only through accusations of cowardice coupled with news that Nelson had detached a part of his squadron to replenish its supplies were they got to sea at all, and when they did so the results were much as both they (and, in fairness, Villeneuve) feared. Though somewhat outnumbered by his opponents, Nelson closed in immediately and attacked the French and Spaniards off Cape Trafalgar. Sailing in two parallel lines, the British fleet cut the straggling Franco-Spanish array into several different fragments, and then battered it to pieces. Nelson, of course, was killed, but the combined fleet was broken beyond repair – of its thirty-three men-of-war, eighteen were lost and most of the rest crippled.

Trafalgar's significance is a matter of some dispute. In the short term it mattered little: Britain had already escaped the threat of invasion, and it did nothing to affect events in central Europe. Nor did it permanently establish the fact of British naval predominance, for the French shipyards were over the years able to make up Villeneuve's losses and force the British to continue to commit immense resources to the naval struggle. All that can be said for certain is that, despite much bluster, Napoleon never again attempted to launch a frontal assault against Britain: henceforth victory would have to be attained by some form of economic warfare. In that sense, then, Trafalgar may be said to have changed the whole course of the war, for Napoleon was now set to embark on a course of action that carried with it at the very least the risk of pitching France against the whole of the rest of the Continent. And, for those with eyes to see, Trafalgar showed very clearly that there could be no partnership with Napoleon. Having been forced to enter the war against their will, the Spaniards found their strategic interests and their resources ruthlessly commandeered to serve France's interests. A substantial portion of their remaining naval strength – the central pillar of their colonial empire – had in effect been thrown away on a futile plan to send a few thousand extra soldiers to overawe a state that was not just friendly to Spain but situated in a secondary theatre of operations. Already under great pressure, Godoy's credit on the home front was squandered and with it a financial effort that had quite literally emptied Spain's coffers: among other measures, a loan of 10 million florins had had to be taken out in Holland to finance the fleet's mobilization.

To talk of Trafalgar in this fashion is possibly to speak with the benefit of hindsight. But for Napoleon, the news was still irritating enough: hearing of the battle he supposedly 'started up full of rage, exclaiming, "I cannot be everywhere!" '.[6] This is understandable enough, for Trafalgar constituted a considerable blow to his prestige. Yet marching through southern Germany, he was infinitely better off than he might have been. Let us here quote Pasquier:

What would have become of [Napoleon] if, having disembarked on the English coast with the élite of his forces, he had only kept control of the sea for a short time. What would have become of France had the great Austrian army commanded by the Archduke Charles marched across Bavaria and appeared on the banks of the Rhine? Given that there would not have been sufficient forces to put up an effective resistance, they would probably have got across and France would then have been invaded . . . In the face of that situation, the only answer would have been the one that he himself made to several people who dared to raise the possibility with him. 'If the invasion had succeeded, such would have been the enthusiasm in France that the women and children of Strasbourg could have thrown back the Austrians by themselves.' Is that answer not rather more clever than it is to the point?[7]

As it was, the French experienced not tragedy but triumph. The allied plans had initially seemed threatening indeed. In the first place, the array of enemies facing France had grown yet again. The Franco-Neapolitan treaty of alliance, or strictly speaking, of neutrality, had originated in strategic considerations relating to the military situation in Italy: Masséna was badly outnumbered in the north, whilst St Cyr's troops were scattered across the centre and south of the Italian peninsula in a number of small detachments and, in consequence, wide open to attack. Pulling them out in order to reinforce the French forces in Lombardy therefore made a great deal of sense, the only means of keeping Naples in line therefore being an agreement of some sort. No sooner had the resultant treaty of 9 October been signed than St Cyr got his men on the road. On this occasion, however, French policy failed. Freed from the threat of reprisals, the Neapolitans denounced their agreement with Paris, appealed for Anglo-Russian protection and mobilized their army. In the wake of this development a veritable war of encirclement threatened France. Linked by 53,000 troops in the Tyrol, 90,000 Austrians would invade northern Italy and 140,000 Bavaria, while 100,000 Russians marched to their aid. Joined by an Anglo-Russian army of 40,000 men which was being concentrated in the Mediterranean, the Neapolitans would threaten France's southern flank, whilst 50,000 seaborne British, Russians and Swedes liberated Hanover and went on to assault Holland. Last but not least, 50,000 further Russians were to be dispatched to galvanize the Prussians into action and join with them in a victorious march across Germany. In short, over 500,000 men would join together in a concentric advance against a French force that, even counting the forces of Napoleon's satellites, seemed unlikely to amount to much more than 350,000. Nor were operations neglected in the wider world, the end of August seeing a small British expedition taking ship to evict the Dutch from their strategically placed colony at the Cape of Good Hope.

Imposing as this array seemed, matters were by no means as one-sided as at first appeared. Sometimes described as the most proficient army the world has ever seen, the *grande armée* was not without its problems. For one thing, it was so short of horses that some of its cavalry had actually to fight as infantrymen. For another, it is certainly possible to question the received wisdom that its men had spent all their time at the 'camp of Boulogne' being drilled and trained without let-up. Some accounts do speak as if this was the case: 'The troops assembled there', wrote Emile de Saint-Hilaire, 'were occupied and disciplined in the style of the Romans; every hour had its own job and the soldiers were forever swapping their muskets for their pickaxes.'[8] Much the same sort of thing, meanwhile, is recorded by Hulot: 'Everywhere one saw nothing but parades, simulations of attack and defence, forced marches and changes of bivouac. This spectacle filled us all with the same impression: woe be to the foreigner who is set about by such an army!'[9] But other memories were less sanguine. To quote Fezensac, for example, 'The regiment was rarely assembled to manoeuvre in line. There were one or two excursions – simple route marches that approximated to the sort of distance one might cover in the course of an easy day in the field – a few rounds of target practice conducted without any method, and that was about it: no training for our skirmishers, no bayonet practice . . . no attempt to construct the simplest work of fortification.'[10] Whether the army was ever quite the disciplined machine that it has been made out to be is therefore a moot point. Nor were its logistical capacities up to the task of supplying the troops, who not only suffered all the rigours of campaigning, but all too often went hungry. To quote Fezensac's memories of the march into Germany:

This short campaign was a summary of all that was to follow. The excessive fatigue, the want of supplies, the rigours of the season, the disorders committed by marauders, nothing was wanting . . . The brigades and even the regiments were often dispersed and orders to get them to a certain place often arrived late as they had to pass through many different hands. The result was that my regiment often had to march day and night, and for the first time I saw men sleeping as they marched, which is something that I would never have believed possible. In this fashion, we would arrive at the position we were supposed to occupy but without having had anything to eat or drink. Marshal Berthier, the chief of staff, had written that in the war of invasion planned by the emperor, there would be no magazines with the result that generals would have to provide for their men from the countries through which they passed. However, the generals had neither the time nor the means . . . to feed so numerous an army. As the countryside found out in the most cruel fashion, what this amounted to was to authorize pillage, and yet for the whole length of that campaign we did not suffer any the less from hunger . . . The bad weather made our sufferings even worse. A cold rain fell, and sometimes wet snow in which we waded up to our knees, while such was the wind that we could never light a fire. The sixteenth of October in particular – the day when M. Phillippe de Ségur waited upon Mack with the first demand that he surrender – the weather was so awful that nobody stayed at their post. There were neither pickets nor sentries . . . [and] everyone sought such shelter as he could. At no other moment, except in the campaign in Russia, did I suffer so much or see the army in such disarray.[11]

For all their problems, the French did possess many advantages. From Napoleon downwards, the men at the head of the army represented the very cream of revolutionary generalship. Officers and men alike were on the whole veterans of some years' service; the army's tactical system was more adaptable than that of its continental opponents; and Napoleon had greatly improved upon the organizational model that he had inherited from the Republic through the establishment of army corps and the concentration of part of the artillery and cavalry into special reserves of great fighting power. Able as a result to move very fast, operate on a broad front that facilitated attempts at envelopment, display an extraordinary level of flexibility and hit very hard on the actual battlefield, the army also enjoyed high morale. Spirits were lifted by the simple fact that the men were on the move at last: Hulot described feeling 'sincere joy'; newly commissioned as an officer, Fezensac remembered, 'I was delighted to make war'; while Jean-Baptiste Barrès wrote, 'We left Paris quite content to go campaigning . . . War was the one thing I wanted.'[12]

This spirit of confidence and enthusiasm was the fruit of much cossetting. Ever since 1799 Napoleon had done all that he could to cultivate the army. Parades and reviews were a constant feature of public life; the new flags now carried by each regiment were inscribed with gold letters spelling out the personal relationship between the emperor and his soldiers; the extensive employment of generals as ambassadors was a clear statement of the intimate connection between Napoleon, French foreign policy and the military; and the vast majority of recipients of the

Legion of Honour – the new decoration instituted by Napoleon for services to the state – proved to be members of the armed forces. Nor was the Legion of Honour the only reward open to the emperor's followers. Few soldiers could aspire to rise so far – only twenty-six men ever received the title – but the glittering figures of Masséna, Murat, Ney, Lannes, Augereau and the other marshals of the empire served as living object lessons in what could be achieved by courage and devotion. Showered with estates, they became fabulously wealthy. As yet the greatest glory still lay in the future. But even so the result was a mood of real excitement. To quote Elzéar Blaze:

None but a soldier of that period can conceive what spell there was in the uniform. What lofty expectations inflamed all the young heads on which a plume of feathers waved for the first time! Every French soldier carries in his cartouche-box his truncheon of marshal of France; the only question is how to get it out.[13]

Nor was it just a case of promotion. In his field garb of plain grey overcoat and unadorned black tricorn, the emperor looked the very epitome of the common soldier of the Revolution – his nickname, after all, was 'the little corporal' – and he was always displaying the affability, simplicity and familiarity of manner that invoked such love amongst the troops. To cite just one of the stories told of him at this time, a private soldier suddenly stepped out in front of Napoleon's horse to present him with a petition. Badly startled, the mount shied, and Napoleon flew into a rage, striking the man with his whip. Almost immediately, though, he collected himself and made the soldier a sergeant on the spot.

Thus far we see only a force of the sort that the American scholar John Lynn referred to as 'an army of honour' – an army whose members sought to advance their own interests and were concerned only with their own status and prestige. Yet despite the eclipse of overtly Republican generals such as Moreau and Pichegru – who were either dead or in exile – and the cult of imperial glory in which the army was the centrepiece, many of the soldiers continued to persuade themselves that they were fighting, if not for the Republic, then at least for its ideals. In this they were encouraged by Napoleon. The very first bulletin of the campaign calls the army 'only the advance guard of the people'.[14] Inspired by such language, many soldiers could believe, along with Charles Parquin, that the army's goals remained 'the great ideals of the

French Revolution – the ideals of liberty, of unity and of the future – which, as everyone knows, the emperor Napoleon personified'.[15] As proof of the depth of feeling that underlay such comments one has only to point to the particular hatred with which many soldiers regarded the Catholic Church. Wherever popular resistance was encountered – in other words in Spain, Portugal, the Tyrol and southern Italy – it was the Church that got the blame, and the Church that paid the price. 'It was the monks who did most to make war against us,' wrote one soldier of the war in Spain. 'We cornered fifty of them in a church and massacred them all with the points of our bayonets.'[16] Underlying all this was a sense of cultural superiority that deepened with every mile that the army moved east and south. As one hussar officer in Spain put it: 'With regard to the knowledge and the progress of social habits, Spain was at least a century behind the other nations of the continent.'[17]

To return to Parquin, we see here not just the conviction that the army was fighting for the Revolution, but also faith in the person of Napoleon himself. Confidence in its leader was one of the French army's most potent weapons, and one that was, of course, sedulously cultivated by the French ruler, not least by the constant pretence that he made of sharing its privations. But if this was indeed pretence, Napoleon at least made a genuine point of moving amongst his troops: the scene that took place on the eve of Austerlitz is particularly famous:

His army was but half as strong as that of the enemy. His soldiers had hitherto always been victorious, but, with so small a force . . . it was of the utmost importance to him to know whether the confidence of the troops in their own superiority would . . . be sufficient to make up for their inferiority in numbers. It therefore occurred to him to go on foot, accompanied by Marshal Berthier only, throughout the camp and listen unnoticed to the chat of the soldiers round their fires. By eleven o'clock he had already traversed a great distance when he was recognized. The soldiers, surprised at finding him in the midst of them, and afraid that he might lose his way going back to his headquarters . . . hastened to break up the shelters they had made of branches and straw to use them as torches to light their emperor home. One bivouac after another took up the task, and in less than a quarter of an hour 60,000 torches lit up the camp, whilst passionate cries of 'Vive l'empereur!' resounded on every side.[18]

Mixed in with the aura of greatness were little touches of humanity. At Ulm it was observed that the French ruler's famous greatcoat got singed when he sat too close to the fire. Nor had Napoleon lost his common touch. Writing of the same battle, one soldier remembered, 'We were eating jam made from quinces . . . The emperor laughed. "Ah!", said he. "I see you are eating preserves; don't get up. You must put new flints in your guns: tomorrow morning you will need them. Be ready!" '[19] Not many soldiers actually received the favour of a personal word of enquiry or encouragement from their commander, of course, but that is not the point: the stories of such encounters doubtless grew in the telling, while the troops believed that they were cared about. As one François Avril wrote, 'We have observed with the greatest interest the tender care taken by His Majesty to improve the lot of [the] . . . warriors charged with the task of defending the integrity of French territory.'[20] Close proximity to the emperor, meanwhile, brought a genuine sense of well-being. Reviewed by Napoleon in the midst of some particularly inclement weather, a common soldier named André Dupont-Ferrier wrote, 'I don't think I have ever been as cold as I was that day, and I don't know how the emperor could bear it . . . but it seemed that his very presence warmed us, and repeated shouts of "Vive l'empereur!" must have convinced him how much he is cherished.'[21] Just as important was the sense that Napoleon was looking to each and every soldier for his survival. 'We saw the Emperor Napoleon pass . . . He was on horseback; the simplicity of his green uniform distinguished him amidst the richly clothed generals who surrounded him; he waved his hands to every individual officer as he passed, seeming to say, "I rely on you." '[22] The consequences were enormous. 'The presence of the emperor,' wrote one veteran of the Austerlitz campaign, 'produced a powerful effect on the army. Everyone had the most implicit confidence in him; everyone knew, from experience, that his plans led to victory, and therefore . . . our moral force was redoubled.'[23] Well might Wellington remark, 'His presence on the field made a difference of 40,000 men.'[24]

Yet war is not just a matter of battles, and the 40,000 extra soldiers that Wellington equated with Napoleon's presence were in 1805 very nearly countered by six times that many fresh enemies in the form of the Prussian army. As the *grande armée* swept across Germany en route for the Danube, its progress was marked by wholesale pillage. 'I am absolutely tired out, and cannot imagine how the body can support such constant fatigue,' wrote Thomas Bugeaud. 'Hunger is another tyrant. You can easily imagine whether ten thousand men coming into a village can easily find anything to eat. What distresses me more is the annoyance of stealing from the peasantry: their poultry, their bacon, their firewood [are] taken from them by grace or force. I do not do these things, but when I am very hungry I secretly tolerate them and eat my share of the stolen goods.'[25] In Baden, Württemberg and Bavaria, all of which had rallied to Napoleon, this was bad enough, but on 3 October 1805 Marshal Bernadotte's I Corps – a force that occupied the outermost flank of the great wheel in which the *grande armée* engaged as it headed from the Rhine to the Danube – violated the neutrality of the small Prussia territory of Ansbach. Undertaken for no better reason than the fact that avoiding Ansbach would have cost Bernadotte's men a few more days on the road, this action almost led to disaster. By the beginning of October war between Prussia and Russia had seemed all but certain, for on 19 September Potsdam had been informed that Russia had announced that she was going to march 100,000 troops across Prussian Poland and Silesia. As we have seen, the intention was to pressurize the Prussians into joining the Third Coalition, but instead they responded to this 'rough wooing' by mobilizing their army and announcing that they would resist any encroachment on their territory. In the event, however, the French reached Ansbach before the Russians reached Silesia. In the face of this provocation, even Frederick William could not remain inert. The French emissaries who had come to Berlin to win over the Prussians to the French cause were summarily dismissed, orders given for the army to take Hanover by force and the Russians told that they might cross Silesia. Moreover, on 3 November Prussia formally acceded to the Third Coalition by the treaty of Potsdam.

According to Paul Schroeder, none of this should be sufficient to persuade us that Prussia was genuinely bellicose in intent. The king remained indecisive and reluctant to go to war. As for his confidants and advisers, a clear majority still favoured peace: hence, perhaps, the fact that discussions regarding Prussia's accession to the Third Coalition did not begin until Alexander, who had come west to join his armies, met Frederick William III in person. All of this, he continues, was reflected in the treaty of Potsdam, which in the first instance offered only armed mediation and, in the second, by means of a secret clause, made Hanover the price of active intervention in the struggle. On top of this there was the manner in which Prussian pressure was brought to bear. The peace terms, which, it was agreed, should be presented to Napoleon in person by the former Prussian chancellor, Haugwitz, were certainly such as to give rise to the suspicion that he would reject them – they included independence for Holland, Switzerland, the German states and the *ci-devant* Italian Republic. But at the same time it is impossible not to notice that four weeks were allowed for the discussion of the subject, and that Haugwitz deliberately put off his departure for Napoleon's headquarters for eight precious days. With Napoleon and the *grande armée* now well and truly off the leash and winning dramatic successes in Germany, Schroeder's conclusion is that Potsdam represented less an advance towards joining the Coalition, than a retreat from it.

Even supposing the Prussians had finally gone to war, there is no guarantee that they would have intervened with any great enthusiasm in the campaign. For one thing, they were not ready for war in 1805. When the crisis broke, their army had just embarked upon a series of reforms designed to increase the number of native Prussians under arms – it should be remembered that a considerable proportion of the troops were foreign mercenaries at this time – and create a trained reserve, and this led to a preference for caution. Potsdam's lack of enthusiasm is confirmed by Clemens von Metternich, who was then Austria's ambassador to the Prussian court: 'From the first moment the emperor [i.e. Alexander] and I fell under the ill will of the Prussian negotiators. With ill-concealed anger, they resorted to every imaginable pretext to protract the arrangements which, in face of the calamitous circumstances of the war on the Danube, grew more and more urgent.'[26] And, last but not least, there remained the question of Hanover. Shortly after the signature of the treaty of Potsdam, a special envoy had arrived from London at the Prussian court in the person of Lord Harrowby. Authorized to offer the Prussians a subsidy of £2.5 million if they would accede to the Anglo-Russian alliance, go to war with an army of 200,000 men and promise not to make a separate peace and to guarantee the independence of Holland and the states of northern Germany, Harrowby was appalled by the clause in the treaty that gave Hanover to Prussia. Nor was Pitt better pleased when he was given the news by the special envoy dispatched to London by Alexander, Count d'Oubril. It was judged that losing Hanover would cause a recurrence of the infirm George III's 'madness', and thereby give rise to a regency under the Prince of Wales, who was very much a friend of the Whigs and therefore entirely capable of ejecting Pitt and bringing to power a government that might seek a compromise peace with Napoleon. It being a choice of standing firm or losing the war anyway, Pitt therefore threatened to cancel all the British subsidies that had been promised unless the independence of Hanover was respected.

To return to Prussia, Napoleon was still taking a major chance, for a sudden display of vigour on the part of Frederick William might have caused him serious problems, while there were certainly elements in Prussia that were itching for war, or, at least, convinced that Prussia had to act. As the emperor seems to have suspected, however, vigour was not something to be looked for from the Third Coalition. Setting aside the Prussians, the latter's actions were marked by a complete lack of coordination. No better prepared than the Prussians – under the aegis of General Mack they, too, had been engaged in a number of last-minute military reforms which had not yet settled in – the Austrians pushed their armies into Bavaria without waiting for the Russians, who in turn marched ten days later than they had agreed, while the Swedes would not move unless the Prussians did so too. Nor were matters any better in Italy. Deeply pessimistic at the renewal of war with France, the Archduke Charles allowed himself to be persuaded that he was out-numbered two to one by the French, and therefore secured orders from Vienna that he should remain on the defensive. Naples, meanwhile, did nothing, while the British and Russian forces sent to help her did not even disembark on her soil until 20 November, by which time catastrophe had struck elsewhere and made all hopes of an offensive impossible. Yet much of the leadership of the Coalition remained extraordinarily opti-mistic. So sure was Czartoryski of victory, for example, that he positively welcomed Prussia's intransigence as he believed that the war with Pots-dam that must follow would clear the way for Alexander to declare himself king of a reconstituted Poland as soon as the Russians had entered Warsaw. If so, it was dramatic testimony to the survival of interests that had nothing at all to do with the overthrow of Napoleon and for many years were greatly to impede the coalition-building that was the only means by which he could be resisted.

Needless to say, the result of all this was that the initiative passed to the French. Untrammelled by any significant threat to its northern flank, the *grande armée* swung smoothly across the Rhine and then headed south-eastwards with the aim of defeating the invaders of Bavaria. Convinced that no French forces could appear until late October, by which time he believed that Kutuzov's Russians would have come up in his support, Mack had advanced to the Danube, and moved as far west as Ulm. To his considerable surprise, Napoleon, who had believed that his adversary was much further east, therefore suddenly found himself in the rear of the Austrians, and hastily swung his army westwards to envelop them. In the confusion, some of the emperor's prey managed to get away, but on 20 October Mack laid down his arms with over 20,000 men. Other detachments of his forces (like those caught at Wertingen) had already been overwhelmed, while still others were routed or forced to surrender in the course of the next few days. In scarcely a fortnight, no fewer than 60,000 of the 75,000 men whom Mack had led into Bavaria had been killed, wounded or taken prisoner. It was, beyond doubt, a shattering blow. In England Pitt refused to credit the first reports, but Malmesbury 'clearly perceived he disbelieved it more from the dread of its being true than from any well-grounded cause' and 'observed but too clearly the effect [confirmation] had on [him]', remarking, 'his look and manner were not his own, and gave me . . . a foreboding of the loss with which we were threatened'.[27]

Elsewhere things had gone rather better for the Austrians – in Italy the Archduke Charles had repulsed a French attack at Caldiero – but the general situation was catastrophic. Although the first Russians had at last arrived on the frontiers of Bavaria, they were few in numbers and exhausted. Still worse, the French were heading straight for Vienna. By hard marching, the Russians and most of the Austrian troops still in the vicinity got away to Bohemia, but on 12 November the capital was occupied. The war, however, was not over. Thanks to the arrival of more Russians, there were now over 80,000 allied troops in Bohemia. Convinced that he could win a great victory, Alexander I, who had now arrived at headquarters, overruled the fugitive Francis II's preference for an armistice, and ordered an offensive. Napoleon was not quite ready for this – among other things his men were exhausted – and, both to win time and to encourage Alexander to walk into the trap that was being laid for him, he requested an interview with the tsar. In response, the Russian ruler dispatched one of his personal favourites, Prince Peter Dolgoruky, to enquire as to the nature of his terms. The offer, clearly, was not a serious one, but it served a useful purpose, for the prince, a leading member of the war party in the Russian court, chose to indulge in an ostentatious show of contempt, and, by seemingly spurning a chance for peace, allowed the emperor and his apologists to blame the Allies for the continuation of the war. At the very least, Napoleon was given the chance to play the injured innocent. As he is supposed to have said to Dolgoruky, 'How long have we to fight? What do you want from me? What does the Emperor Alexander desire? If he wants to enlarge his states, let him do it at the expense of his neighbours, Turkey especially, and then he will have no disputes with France.'[28]

Even supposing that the words were sincere, at this stage they could achieve nothing. On 1 December, then, the two armies deployed near the town of Austerlitz. Given that the *grande armée* was considerably outnumbered, what followed was possibly the most masterly battle of the emperor's career. Enticed to attack the French right in an effort to sever Napoleon's communications with Vienna, the Allies left their centre unguarded, and this allowed the emperor effectively to split them in two. Thrown into complete disorder, his enemies fought with great courage, but by the end of the day – the first anniversary of Napoleon's coronation – their left was all but surrounded and the rest of the army streaming off the field in varying states of disorder. All in all their casualties amounted to some 25,000 men, while the French had suffered losses of only 8,000. In the Allied camp, all was despair. Witness to the scene was Czartoryski:

The emperor was extremely cast down: the intense emotion that he had experienced made him ill ... In every village one heard nothing but the confused shouts of people who had sought to drown their misfortunes in drink ... If a few squadrons of French cavalry had been sent after us to complete our defeat, I have no idea what might have happened. Amongst the Coalition forces there were neither regiments nor *corps d'armée*: the only thing to be seen were armed gangs wandering aimlessly from place to place in a state of complete disorder and adding to the general desolation through their marauding.[29]

Austerlitz dealt a death-blow to the Third Coalition. Russia still had plenty of troops, and the Archduke Charles had evacuated Italy and concentrated a substantial force on the frontiers of Hungary. But news of the defeat finally removed all hope of Prussian assistance: arriving at

Napoleon's headquarters in the immediate wake of Austerlitz, Haugwitz proffered Prussia's friendship and committed her to an offensive-defensive alliance known as the treaty of Schönbrunn that promised her Hanover in exchange for a guarantee of France and her satellites and the cession of a number of territories in Germany (one of them, ironically enough, was Ansbach). At the same time, news of the defeat paralysed allied operations in northern Germany and persuaded Austria, whose equally shaken emperor had also been at Austerlitz, to seek an immediate peace settlement on the grounds that further resistance would be fatal (the Archduke Charles, indeed, was warning Francis that to continue the war would be to risk political revolution and the dissolution of the empire). As it was, peace was bad enough. By the treaty of Pressburg of 26 December 1805, Austria was forced to cede Venetia, Dalmatia and Istria to the Kingdom of Italy, Vorarlberg, Tyrol and Trentino to Bavaria, and the isolated pockets of territory still held by Austria in south-western Germany to Baden and Württemberg. Also ceded to the courts of Munich, Baden-Baden and Stuttgart were the territories of those imperial knights unfortunate enough to reside within their frontiers. In addition, Napoleon had to be accepted as King of Italy, and Bavaria, Württemberg, Baden and Hesse-Darmstädt recognized as independent states, while Austria also had to pay an indemnity of 40,000,000 francs. For all this, the only compensation was that Austria was allowed to regain Salzburg, whose Habsburg ruler, the erstwhile Duke of Tuscany, was shifted to the Grand Duchy of Würzburg. As for the Russians, they hastily evacuated their forces from Germany and Bohemia alike, and began to examine the possibility of a separate peace. In Britain news of the defeat literally finished William Pitt. Worn out by a variety of ailments and years of heavy drinking, the Prime Minister was already a sick man, and there is no doubt that Austerlitz came as a heavy blow. 'Roll up the map of Europe,' he is supposed to have said, 'it will not be wanted these ten years.'[30] With British policy in ruins, early in the morning of 23 January 1806 the Prime Minister – Napoleon's greatest and most consistent opponent in the whole of Europe – passed away. It was a fearful blow. To quote Lord Auckland, 'Our situation is desperate. There is nothing to look to.'[31] Nor was the mood any better in Austria. In the words of the propagandist Gentz, 'Everything is surely over now, for the little that remains can be so easily supplied in imagination that even the pleasure of surprise no longer remains to us.'[32]

This was a key moment in the history of the Napoleonic Empire. For the emperor, of course, it was a time of triumph. Present at imperial headquarters, Talleyrand later wrote:

Never has a military feat been more glorious. I still see Napoleon re-entering Austerlitz on the evening of the battle. He lodged at a house belonging to Prince von Kaunitz, and, there, in his chamber, yes, in the very chamber of Prince von Kaunitz, were brought at every moment Austrian flags, Russian flags, messages from the archdukes and from the emperor of Austria, and prisoners bearing all the names of all the great houses of the Austrian monarchy.[33]

In this situation, the temptation to inflict a heavy blow on Austria, build up the south German states as useful allies, and issue a dire warning to the rest of Europe was overwhelming. Equally, it is no coincidence that a few days after Austerlitz, an isolated Bavarian enclave on the right bank of the Rhine, centred on the city of Düsseldorf, was given to Napoleon's brother-in-law, Joachim Murat, as the Grand Duchy of Berg, nor that in February 1806 Joseph Bonaparte was proclaimed King of Naples – that we should see, in other words, the first steps in the creation of the so-called 'family monarchies'. On one level it is possible to defend all these actions on strategic grounds: Berg, for example, was a useful 'bridgehead' in northern Germany. Yet serious questions must be asked of Pressburg and the other treaties with which it is associated. 'The system that Napoleon then adopted ... was the first act to be reckoned among the causes of his fall,' wrote Talleyrand, who rightly went on to point out that there was something 'impolitic and destructive in this method of overthrowing governments in order to create others which he was not slow to pull down again, and that in all parts of Europe'.[34]

What makes this statement all the more prescient is that Napoleon had been offered a very clear alternative by Talleyrand. As the *grande armée* marched into Germany in October, the Foreign Minister had penned a long memorandum in which he argued that France's best interest lay in making Austria an ally. Serious territorial losses were pressed for, certainly, but it was at least realized that the pill had to be sweetened by a little sugar. In consequence, Austria was not just to be stripped of her western marches, but also given a place in Napoleonic Europe by means of an Austro-French alliance against Russia, and hints that Vienna might seek compensation in the Balkans. After Austerlitz, indeed, Talleyrand went still further: Austria, he held 'was indispensable to the future safety of the civilized world'.[35] There was a great deal of sense in this: given that there were certainly elements in the Habsburg court, including, not least, the Archduke Charles, who saw territorial acquisitions in the Balkans as the best way out for Vienna, it was not too much to hope that Francis might be persuaded to turn east. Without a powerful state centred in the southern part of east-central Europe, the region would remain a perennial bone of contention as France and Russia vied with one another for control. And, finally, it was well understood that lasting peace settlements needed a readiness to compromise and to give all parties a stake in the new arrangement. But Napoleon could see none of this. Campo Formio, Amiens and Lunéville had all been compromise peaces, and had, by extension, set limits on French power. Although Napoleon had undermined all three of them in the months after they had been signed, such was the military situation at the time when they were negotiated that he had had no option but to pay lip-service to the principle of reciprocity. In the aftermath of Austerlitz, however, things were very different. For the first time truly possessed of the whip hand, Napoleon shrugged off moderation in favour of the complete humiliation of his opponent, and in doing so ensured that Austerlitz had settled nothing.

For the time being, however, in central Europe the guns fell silent. Indeed, as the Swedes remained quietly within their enclave at Stralsund, it was only in the Mediterranean and the wider world that the fighting could continue. In the former theatre, as we have seen, Naples had been occupied by the Anglo-Russian expeditionary force, which, together with the Neapolitan army, was now manning her northern frontier, but the Allies were short of supplies and increasingly at odds with one another. Realizing that their position was hopeless, in January 1806 the British and Russians retired to the respective havens of Sicily and Corfu. Hard on their heels, nearly 40,000 French troops marched across the frontier, defeating the Neapolitan army at Campo Tenese and besieging Gaeta. Left with no option but to flee, the royal family took ship for Sicily, their place being taken by Joseph Bonaparte. Since it was at this time, too, that Holland was transformed into a kingdom under Louis Bonaparte, this constitutes a convenient moment to discuss the role played by notions of family in Napoleon's foreign policy. According to the many apologists for the emperor, the rise of the family courts is to be attributed either to his devotion to his family, or to the demands of the long struggle against Britain. Of these, the first argument, which is particularly associated with the *fin-de-siècle* French historian, Frédéric Masson, holds that it was Corsican clan loyalty that fuelled Napoleon's ambition, and Corsican clan loyalty that led Napoleon to shower kingdoms and principalities on his brothers and sisters. What we see is therefore not Napoleon the conqueror but Napoleon the family man, whilst the theory also provides admirers of the emperor with a useful apologium for the empire's ultimate collapse: it was not Napoleon who was to blame, but rather Joseph, Louis, Caroline and the rest, on all of whom Masson heaped contempt as ambitious ingrates who were as incompetent as they were self-serving. As for the second argument, of which a modern exponent is Vincent Cronin, this claims that the enthronement of Napoleon's siblings was essentially a defensive measure designed to protect France from a vengeful world and ensure that her satellites were in safe hands. This latter position was certainly that adopted by Napoleon himself in defence of his actions. If Joseph was placed on the throne of Naples, it was because Ferdinand IV and Maria Carolina had proved themselves to be unreliable, treacherous and utterly lacking in gratitude: the peace settlements of 1796 and 1801 had cost them almost nothing in the way of territory, and in 1803 they had been allowed to remain on the throne when the emperor had had but to raise his little finger to sweep them aside. As Napoleon said in the proclamation announcing their downfall:

Soldiers! For ten years I have done all that I can to save the King of Naples, whereas he has done all that he can to secure his downfall . . . Should we show mercy for a fourth time? Should we for a fourth time trust a court without faith, honour or reason? The dynasty of Naples has ceased to reign: its existence is incompatible with the peace of Europe and the honour of my crown.[36]

Much the same reasoning is visible in the decision to transform the Batavian Republic into a kingdom under Louis Bonaparte. Politically, the Dutch were as unreliable as the Neapolitans. As Napoleon told Talleyrand, 'If . . . French troops were to evacuate Holland, we would have an enemy government on our frontiers.'[37] In addition to all this, the Dutch had been giving little support to the war effort: given the command of an invasion camp set up at Zeist in 1804, Marmont complained that he met 'the greatest opposition from everybody' and that the Dutch government saw his plans as 'an object of expense'.[38] Initially, an attempt had been made to find a domestic solution by instituting a version of the French constitution of 1800, complete with the leading politician, Rutger Jan Schimmelpenninck, as 'Grand Pensionary'. But Schimmelpenninck achieved next to nothing, and the fact that he was rapidly losing his sight was inclined to undermine confidence in him as a substitute Napoleon. In March 1806 the Dutch government was given a stark choice between annexation and becoming a monarchy, and on 5 June Louis Bonaparte was duly declared King of Holland. Louis, of course, owed his new position to the fact that he was loyal to Napoleon, but it carried a heavy price: no sooner had he arrived in The Hague than Louis was receiving letters from Napoleon informing him that he could expect no money from the French treasury and should therefore aim to meet all his requirements himself: 'You must strip your council of all hope that I will send it money; unless you do this, it will not give you the means you need to get to grips with your affairs.'[39] The Bonapartes, in short, were not just satraps whom Napoleon could rely on to defend the French empire; they were also satraps who could extract men, money and other useful resources at a rate that men like Schimmelpenninck would be most unlikely to go along with. There were always other issues – the family courts were a useful means of both disseminating French tastes throughout the empire and winning over the old aristocracies, while they were also an indication that Napoleon was the head of a dynasty like any other – but the conclusion is inescapable: at the heart of the satellite monarchies was the issue of, first, exploitation in the service of an aggressive foreign policy, and, second, the continued glorification of the emperor.

Inherent in this construction of an imperial dynasty was also the adoption of traditional methods of royal foreign policy. Thus in the aftermath of Austerlitz Napoleon embarked on a series of marriage alliances with the states of southern Germany. In January 1806 Eugène de Beauharnais married Augusta-Amalia, the daughter of the newly enthroned Maximilian-Joseph of Bavaria (in a story that is frequently extremely depressing, it is pleasant to note that this particular arranged marriage turned into a genuine love-match that gave both parties much happiness). Stéphanie de Beauharnais, a second cousin of Eugène and

Hortense, was pressed into service as a suitable match for Prince Charles of Zahringen, heir to the Grand Duchy of Baden; and Jerome Bonaparte, who had married an American girl named Elizabeth Patterson whom he had met when his ship (he had become a naval officer) called at Baltimore, was stripped of his bride and in August 1808, having first become King of Westphalia (see below), forced to take Princess Catherine of Württemberg in her place. In addition, attempts were made to bully Lucien into divorcing his wife and taking another foreign bride, but Lucien refused point-blank to cooperate, thereby making final a breach that had been deepening ever since Napoleon had become First Consul for life. Lucien or no Lucien, however, in the short term Napoleon could count the policy a success, and it remained a feature of the emperor's foreign policy for years to come. Thanks to a variety of distant connections of Josephine, Joachim Murat and the husband of Elise Bonaparte, Felix Bacciochi, the Bonapartes also forged somewhat tenuous links with the princely houses of Hohenzollern-Sigmaringen, Arenberg and Salm-Salm.

Nor were the marriage alliances the only strand of the policy that he now pursued. For obvious reasons, the great block of territory that Napoleon dominated in central and southern Germany now stood at the centrepiece of his strategy and foreign policy. A gigantic *place d'armes*, it was also a convenient base for the *grande armée*. Able to live off the fat of a very prosperous land – a land, moreover, whose inhabitants were not French – Napoleon's forces could strike north-east, east or south-east as opportunity offered or the situation dictated. Occupying this central position, they were also well positioned to preserve France herself from vengeance at the hands of Austrians, Russians or Prussians. But south-central Germany was not only of great strategic value to the French ruler and his forces. Geographically speaking, it had become the very heartland of the Napoleonic imperium. What was required, now, was not just military occupation or a series of dynastic alliances. And so we come to the establishment of what was to become known as the Rheinbund or Confederation of the Rhine. Created in July 1806, this consisted of a permanent alliance of sixteen states in central and southern Germany – Bavaria, Württemberg, Baden, Berg, Hesse-Darmstädt, Nassau-Usingen, Arenberg, Nassau-Weilberg, Hohenzollern-Sigmaringen, Hohenzollern-Hechingen, Salm-Salm, Salm-Kyberg, Isemberg-Birstein, Liechtenstein, Ratisbon-Aschaffenberg (the artificial collection of territories that was given to Dalberg) and the imperial fiefdom of Leyen. This has been seen as one of Napoleon's greatest and most lasting achievements. While simultaneously taking steps to get control of the wreckage of the Holy Roman Empire – on 7 May Napoleon's uncle, Cardinal Fesch, was appointed Dalberg's deputy and successor – the emperor simultaneously had the French Foreign Ministry draw up a scheme for a new structure that would take its place. Various ideas were considered, but in the event, rather than trying to incorporate the whole of Germany, it was agreed that a deal should be offered only to the rulers of the states listed above, the latter constituting a solid block of territory that brought together most of Germany south of a line stretching from Düsseldorf to Bayreuth and also united all Napoleon's German allies. In short, French control was being established in that part of Germany that was most amenable to Napoleon himself and most necessary to his strategic concerns. Particularly interesting is the fact that the northern frontier of the new confederation broadly matched the sphere of influence Prussia had claimed in the period 1795–1803, the inference being that Napoleon was not seeking a direct confrontation with Frederick William III. Indeed, Prussia was treated to soft words and encouraged to consider forming its own North German Confederation; and Murat was slapped down in his attempts to round out his frontiers at the expense of Prussia:

You proceed in far too hare-brained a fashion . . . It is no part of my policy to upset the King of Prussia: my aims are directed elsewhere. It is essential that you avoid being such a difficult neighbour . . . I recommend prudence and tranquillity to you . . . This is the sort of thing you ought to think about before insulting great powers for the sake of rash plans and *démarches*.[40]

As to Napoleon's new creation, its internal arrangements were clear enough. Both collectively and individually, the members of the Rheinbund were bound in a perpetual alliance (both offensive and defensive) with France. They further agreed to give up all say in activating the alliance to Napoleon and to contribute a certain number of troops to the common cause (Bavaria, for example, had to find 30,000 men, Württemberg 12,000 and Berg 5,000). All the imperial knights and the surviving free towns were taken over by one or other of the member states, Nuremberg, for example, going to Bavaria. As for common institutions, the confederation got a diet composed of two 'colleges' – the house of kings and the house of princes – under the joint presidency of Dalberg and a 'protector', who was, of course, none other than Napoleon. To protector, meanwhile, was added the task of mentor, for Napoleon was given the sole right to nominate Dalberg's successor. As for the Holy Roman Empire, it was no more: the member states declared themselves to have seceded from their erstwhile parent body. To the north a considerable swathe of territory still belonged to the empire, but a dispirited Francis could no longer summon the energy to keep up even the pretence of dominion, and on 6 August declared himself to be no longer Francis II of the Holy Roman Empire, but simply Francis I of Austria (a title he had in fact used since September 1804).

What are we to make of this new Germany? For admirers of Napoleon, it was a great work of creation, even, indeed, an act of liberation. Specialists in the history of modern Germany have also been inclined to take a favourable view on the grounds that the states of the Confederation of the Rhine generally imposed a series of reforms whose general tenor was one of modernization (examples include Blackbourn, Hughes and Shanahan). Other scholars, however, have been more reflective. For Blanning the story of the 'third Germany' is one of unremitting exploitation, while Sheehan points out that the collective institutions that might have given it a degree of national meaning never came to be. This last judgement seems fair enough: the Confederation of the Rhine enshrined not unity but continued division. Setting aside the tiny contingents of the minor principalities, which were combined into special 'Rheinbund' regiments, the states all continued to field their own independent armies and were left free to develop their own traditions of government. Napoleon, then, did not unite Germany. But did he at least reform it? Even here progress was very patchy. In the territories placed under French rulers – Berg in 1806 and a year later, Westphalia – the cause of reform was certainly pushed forward with vigour, but here as everywhere else Napoleon saw reform as a means of establishing more efficient systems of conscription and taxation. Beyond this, he was also conscious of the value of reform as a propaganda weapon. For example, there is the famous letter sent by the emperor to Jerome Bonaparte when he became King of Westphalia in 1807: 'It is necessary that your people should enjoy a liberty . . . unheard of amongst the inhabitants of Germany . . . Such a style of government will be a stronger barrier against Prussia than . . . even the protection of France. What people would wish to return to the arbitrary administration of Prussia when it could enjoy the benefits of a wise and liberal government?'[41] In the states that remained German-ruled, too, matters of strategy were paramount. All the states of the so-called 'Third Germany' were conglomerations of territory put together from literally dozens of different sources. Given this situation, it was imperative that they were subjected to a programme of rigid political and administrative centralization and rationalization, for only in this fashion could they be transformed into viable concerns. Without efficient systems of conscription and taxation, they would also be unable to meet the demands of their treaty obligations with Napoleon, or for that matter to stave off Austria should Napoleon suffer some catastrophic reversal of fortune or, indeed, die on some battlefield. But social and political reform was a very different affair, and here the German states were inclined to pick and choose. A few – most notably Bavaria – plumped for the full French model in the most enthusiastic fashion, while the long-standing paternalist tradition known as 'cameralism' ensured that many states showed at least some concern for issues relating to religious freedom, education and public health. But the degree of change was highly variable and the whole system remained redolent of foreign domination and exploitation, as witness the fact that the congress of German rulers brought together to discuss confederation in July 1806 was given a mere twenty-four hours to accept the terms on offer on pain of permanent military occupation.

In Italy too there was little on view except the naked face of French imperialism. This was particularly true of Napoleon's dealings with the papacy. Relations with Pope Pius VII had been deteriorating ever since Napoleon's coronation in 1804. Occupied by first Austrian and then French troops since 1799, the northern provinces of the Papal States – the so-called Legations of Bologna, Ravenna and Ferrara – were not, as Pius had hoped, returned to Rome in exchange for his cooperation with the ceremony in Notre Dame, but incorporated into the Kingdom of Italy. No concessions were forthcoming on the Concordat with the Catholic Church in France, the provisions of which were proving increasingly onerous and inconvenient, and Napoleon did not even get round to sending to Rome all of the gifts that he had promised Pius in commemoration of the coronation. To a certain extent, Pius had been able to even the score by turning his return from Paris to the Holy See into a cross between a triumphal progress and a revivalist mission, but worse was to follow. In the summer of 1805 came not only a reorganization of the parish structure in northern Italy that was both wide-ranging and completely unilateral, but the announcement that the Civil Code – and, with it, of course, divorce – was to be imposed throughout Napoleon's Italian dominions. All this was deeply shocking to Pius, and he therefore fought back hard. Faced with demands that he annul Jerome Bonaparte's marriage to Elizabeth Patterson, he refused, while Lucien Bonaparte, who had fled to Rome, was treated with special favour. And, as for demands that he close his ports to British ships and expel British subjects resident in his dominions, he again refused: Britain might be Protestant – a point on which Napoleon continually harped – but the Papal States were neutral and Pius was a man of peace who hated the maelstrom to which Europe was being reduced and would have no part in any war. In response, Napoleon placed the papal city of Ancona, central Italy's chief Adriatic port, under French occupation and made the extraordinary claim that, as the successor of Charlemagne, he was the pope's feudal overlord (on the grounds that the Papal States were originally a fief granted to Pope Leo III by the Frankish ruler). On this, too, Pius stood firm, but suffered the consequences: the French army that brought Joseph Bonaparte to power in Naples had occupied the whole of the Marches – the Papal States' eastern seaboard – and Napoleon made it very clear to his ambassador in Rome that he wanted the head of Pius's Secretary of State, Cardinal Consalvi: 'I have been annoyed to learn that Rome's behaviour has not been what I could have expected. My wish is that you should live in amity with the Secretary of State and that, if you should have any reason to complain of him, you should inform me while still maintaining good relations with him: I will then find the means of getting rid of him.'[42]

If Napoleonic imperialism was well and truly on the march, it was not the only factor in European politics in early 1806. In the Balkans, events continued to follow an independent course. Here, as we have seen, the Serbs had risen in revolt in February 1804. Within a year Serbia was free, at least in the sense that the freelance bands of soldiers who had been terrorizing the *pashalik* of Belgrade for years had mostly been destroyed. Yet independence was still not part of the Serb agenda. What they wanted was rather political and military autonomy within the over-arching framework of the Ottoman Empire, and, in addition, the acceptance by Constantinople of a Russian guarantee of their privileged status (the Danubian provinces of Moldavia and Wallachia had secured a similar arrangement in 1802, as had the Ionian islands – the so-called 'Republic of the Seven Islands' – in 1800). But securing these moderate goals was not just left to Turkish generosity; in addition, a three-man delegation was sent to St Petersburg. In Constantinople matters did not go well. Well aware that in the Ionian islands the Russians had interpreted 'protection' to mean occupation, and, further, that the concessions made to Corfu and its fellows had excited the aspirations of the Greeks on the mainland, the Turks stood firm and simply promised good government. However, their credibility was undermined by the fact that the troops they sent to restore order simply ran amok in their turn. With matters in this state, encouraging news arrived from St Petersburg. The Russians still did not want to encourage Serbian separatism, still less to jeopardize relations with Constantinople, but they clearly saw that trouble in the Christian communities of the Ottoman Empire had its uses. If it was terrified of revolt in the Balkans, for example, the Ottoman government might be scared into improving its relations with Russia. In consequence, a limited amount of financial assistance was secretly extended to the Serbs, and the Russian ambassador in Constantinople was ordered to persuade the Turks to meet the Serbs' demands. Yet there was an issue here that the Serbs did not appreciate. What they had got was not the 'blank cheque' which they wanted. To obtain full-scale Russian support, it was not sufficient to be Christian or even Slav. Also important were matters of geopolitics. As their lands spanned the direct road to Constantinople and the Straits, the Romanians and the Bulgarians always mattered to the Russians, whereas the Serbs occupied only the most indirect of approaches to the Aegean. This did not mean that Serbia was of no importance whatsoever, but in the end Serbia mattered to Russia in proportion to the probability of French or Austrian aggression in the Balkans, and this was governed by events in the rest of the Continent. As those same events might well prove of far greater consequence to the Russians than developments in the Balkans, the Serbs faced what was at best a precarious future.

Designed to avoid the risk of the Serbs turning to France, to extend Russian influence in the Balkans and to preserve the integrity of the Ottoman Empire, the compromise arrived at by St Petersburg might have secured its objectives but for the fact that matters now got out of hand on the ground. Excited by the news from the *pashalik* of Belgrade, the Serbs of the next-door *pashalik* of Leskovac revolted in their turn. At the same time, the Turks learned of the Serbian mission to St Petersburg, which had hitherto remained unknown to them. Convinced that the whole of the Balkans was about to erupt and that Russia was acting in bad faith, they mobilized a large army at their stronghold of Niš and in mid-August marched on Belgrade. Met by the Serbs at Ivankovac, they were roundly defeated by them on 18–19 August 1805. It was the Serb Valmy. Immediately after the battle, an assembly of notables was convoked near Belgrade, and this proceeded to create a permanent twelve-man state council. Meeting for the first time at Smederevo two months later, the council voted to establish a western-style army, reach out to the Serbs of the *pashaliks* bordering on that of Belgrade and seek help from the Austrians and the Russians. In theory the objective remained autonomy within the Ottoman Empire: indeed, the Serbs continued to try to conciliate Constantinople. But to secure Russian help – in the end the only hope of victory – they also had to persuade St Petersburg that they were viable allies in the Balkans and also that a South Slav army might one day serve alongside the Russians against the French or Austrians. Needless to say, the resultant military posturing killed all hope of a peaceful settlement and plunged the western Balkans into all-out war. This situation was, of course, not entirely unconnected with Napoleon. If conditions had deteriorated to such an extent in the Serbian lands that the populace had been driven to revolt, it was in part because one of the subsidiary effects of the attack on Egypt had been to completely disrupt Selim III's attempts to end the tyranny of groups like the *yamaks*. Equally, if the Russians had encouraged the Serbs in their demands, it was partly because they were terrified of French designs in the Balkans. Finally, as implied above, Serbia's fate largely rested on developments in central Europe. But in the end this was a Balkan quarrel – quite literally, given the fact that the *yamaks* were frequently as much Slavic in their origins as their *hajduk* enemies. And, had Napoleon never existed, such was the extent of its misgovernment that Turkey-in-Europe would always have been a powder-keg.

As for the wars of Napoleon, meanwhile, at sea and in the colonies Britain continued to reign supreme: January 1806 saw the British occupy the vital Dutch colony of the Cape, and the following month witnessed the destruction of a small battle squadron that had managed to slip across the Atlantic in an attempt to assist the French garrisons who were still hanging on in the Caribbean. Similarly, the troops evacuated from the mainland of Italy by the Royal Navy secured Sicily for Ferdinand IV and Maria Carolina. And for Russia too, her navy allowed her to maintain a foothold in the Mediterranean, where it kept the Republic of the Seven Islands as a secure base for the army of General Anrep. Otherwise, however, the picture seemed bleak indeed. Prussia had reverted to her previous neutrality. Supported though she was by 6,000 British troops who had landed at the mouth of the river Weser under General Don, and 20,000 Russians who had been sent by sea to Stralsund, Sweden was helpless; and Austria was completely out of the game. In the southernmost provinces of Naples, brutal French requisitioning had sparked off a serious peasant insurrection, but this offered little hope. In the words of Sir John Moore, the insurgents were '*mafia* . . . lawless banditti, enemies to all governments whatever . . . fit to plunder and murder, but much too dastardly to face an enemy'.[43] In Britain there were added reasons for despair and self-doubt, the near simultaneous loss of both Nelson and Pitt having struck home very deeply, and in the circumstances, it is perhaps a wonder that resistance continued at all. Russia had been badly shaken. The vacillating Alexander had lost all faith in Czartoryski, on whose aggressive policy he blamed all his difficulties. To make matters still worse, in the aftermath of Austerlitz Alexander had been treated to a display of Napoleonic charm that was not unlike that received by his father, Paul I. Following a somewhat flowery exchange of courtesies, the remnants of the Russian army were allowed to withdraw unmolested, and many prisoners were sent back to Alexander. All this was sufficient to persuade Alexander to renounce all thought of offensive operations, the tsar calling home the troops that had been sent to Stralsund and announcing his intention 'to remain absolutely passive and not to budge in any way until the time we are attacked on our own soil'.[44] Yet the immediate way out that was clearly available to Alexander was not taken. Encouraged by the storm of protest that erupted in the war party in Berlin in response to Haugwitz's signature of the treaty of Schönbrunn, not to mention repeated assurances from Frederick William III that the deal with France was meaningless and Prussia anxious not to forsake her friendship with Russia, Alexander did not make peace and sought rather to shore up Russia's defences. By the end of January 1806 a new alliance was being offered to Potsdam: in exchange for remaining neutral should Napoleon attack Russia, and guaranteeing the integrity of the Ottoman Empire, Prussia would receive massive assistance from St Petersburg should she then be turned on by the French. Conducted with the utmost secrecy, these negotiations eventually bore fruit, and on 1 July 1806 a treaty was concluded that made Prussia at one and the same time the ally of both France and of Russia, even though these countries were at war with one another (technically, indeed, the treaty of Schönbrunn meant that Frederick William was actually at war with Alexander!).

The Russo-Prussian accord of July 1806 is not just of interest from the point of view of St Petersburg, however. The diplomacy engaged in by Potsdam also bears examination. At the heart of Prussia's conciliation of Napoleon was Christian von Haugwitz. Foreign Minister until 1804, when he had been replaced by his great rival, Karl August von Hardenberg, Haugwitz had been treated by the latter with some scorn: it was no coincidence, for example, that Hardenberg picked on him as the 'messenger boy' who was charged with the task of carrying Prussia's terms to Napoleon's headquarters. By this act of spite, however, Hardenberg had unwittingly pitchforked his predecessor into the very heart of the diplomatic scene and given him the opportunity to forge a new policy and impose it on Potsdam as a fait accompli. At the same time Haugwitz rehabilitated himself in the eyes of Frederick William III, who was delighted to have been rescued from the prospect of war with France. These tactics paid off – in March 1806 Hardenberg was dismissed as Foreign Minister and replaced by Haugwitz, but the former had seen this move coming and early in the New Year set himself up as the champion of a deal with Russia. Eager to keep all his options open, Frederick William had seen the value of such an arrangement and therefore placed Hardenberg in charge of the negotiations with Russia, which were conducted in the utmost secrecy. With the treaty signed, Hardenberg had good reason to expect that he would soon replace Haugwitz once more. Not for the first time, then, *ancien-régime* foreign policy was influenced by power struggles played out in cabinet and chancellory.

The Russo-Prussian deal was not the only evidence that Russia had no intention of giving Napoleon a free hand. In the Adriatic, too, Alexander still showed fighting spirit. Though Czartoryski's misty dreams of Greek and South Slav national states were out of favour, the Ottomans were threatened with the occupation of the Danubian principalities if they succumbed to the growing French pressure for an alliance (see below). A substantial Russian military force concentrated on the Moldavian frontier under General Ivan Mikhelson, and the Austrians were encouraged to send arms to the Serbs. To counter France's gains in the Adriatic, troops were sent to occupy Cattaro, the latter being the southernmost of the former Venetian enclaves that had dotted the coast of Dalmatia and had all been ceded to France. In response, a French force was dispatched to take over the ancient Republic of Ragusa, and on 26 May a small advanced guard seized the capital. A few days later the 1,000 men involved were attacked by Russian troops sent up the coast from Cattaro. Interestingly, in an echo of later Balkan conflicts the Russians were joined in their assault by considerable numbers of Serbian and Montenegrin irregulars. Despite heavy bombardment the outnumbered French garrison, which was commanded by General Lauriston, held out bravely, and on 5 July 1806 relief arrived in the shape of the main body of the French army of occupation under Molitor, whereupon the Russians withdrew (their hopes of plunder gone, the Serbs and Montenegrins had long since dispersed to their homes).

Russia, then, was not going to suffer France to penetrate areas that she regarded as her traditional sphere of interest. That did not mean, however, that Alexander was genuinely happy about fighting on (the treaty with Prussia, for example, was above all a defensive measure). In this respect, he was much influenced by events in Britain. Here, the death of Pitt had produced a complete change in the administration rather than simply a new prime minister. There was no Pittite who could form a government, still less keep one in power. All the men who were in later years to play prominent roles in the struggle against Napoleon – such figures as Lord Wellesley, Lord Hawkesbury, Lord Castlereagh, Spencer Perceval and George Canning – were either too junior, too discredited or too lacking in credibility. In this situation, there was nothing for it but to look elsewhere. Amongst the Tories there was still Addington, now Lord Sidmouth, who, though very much in favour of continuing the war and eminently acceptable to George III, would have nothing to do with the Pittites as the men he believed had brought about his downfall (a feeling which they heartily reciprocated). The king was most unhappy – he begged Hawkesbury, who had been serving as Home Secretary, to take over as premier – but in the end there was nothing for it but to form a coalition ministry that has gone down in history as that of 'all the talents'. Thus, Lord Grenville became Prime Minister and Charles James Fox Foreign Secretary, though George III hated him as a dangerous radical who was suspected of having passed information to, first, the Americans in the war of 1776–83, and, second, the French in the war of 1793–1801. Also part of the Cabinet were William Windham as Secretary of State for War and the Colonies and Sidmouth as Lord Privy Seal, the latter also insisting on the appointment of his loyal supporter, Lord Ellenborough. The Whigs would have preferred to do without Sidmouth, but his presence was necessary to reassure George III. As for Sidmouth, who in turn hated Grenville and Fox, he only accepted their invitation out of a desire to oblige George III and to keep watch on men whom he regarded with the utmost suspicion and mistrust.

The new government, then, was hardly a strong one, while it faced great hostility on the part of the now-excluded Pittites. Nor was there much enthusiasm in the press and among educated opinion in general. Yet sentiments about the war were just as pessimistic, and it has to be said that if any government could achieve peace it was one such as that now headed by Grenville. Thus, given that Grenville was an introvert entirely lacking in charisma, the dominant figure in the Cabinet was the warm, generous and ebullient Fox, a man fiercely against war with France. A leading supporter of parliamentary reform, Fox had welcomed the French Revolution as a latter-day 1688, and thereafter had continued to exude sympathy for it. When peace had come in 1802 he had been delighted and, naturally enough, had travelled to France to see Napoleon at first hand. Powerless to do anything to end the war of 1792–1802, he was not going to pass up the chance of a reconciliation with the French ruler now, and especially as he genuinely saw no hope of victory. 'If Bonaparte does not by an attempt at invasion or some other great impudence give us an advantage, I cannot but think this country inevitably and irretrievably ruined,' he told Grenville. 'To be Ministers at a moment when the country is falling and all Europe sinking is a dreadful situation.'[45]

Very soon, therefore, the French capital was playing host to a British peace mission headed by Lord Yarmouth, a wealthy peer of radical tendencies who had been interned in France since 1803. In fairness to Fox, these overtures were communicated to the Russians, who feared trickery, particularly as Fox treated the Russian ambassador to London with such coldness that he asked to be replaced. On top of this, meanwhile, came news that Russian merchant vessels were once more being stopped by the Royal Navy. Increasingly concerned that Napoleon might entangle him in a war with Austria and send help to Persia, which had been at war with Russia since 1804, Alexander responded by dispatching his own envoy to Paris in the person of Count d'Oubril. Commissioned both to keep watch on Yarmouth and, should occasion offer, to conclude a separate deal with France that would safeguard Russian interests, the Russian diplomat eventually allowed himself to be persuaded to sign a treaty that recognized Napoleon's acquisitions in Dalmatia (including Cattaro, which was to be evacuated) and accepted that Joseph should remain as King of Naples and gain Sicily in exchange for a French evacuation of Germany and recognition of the independence of both Ragusa and the Ionian islands (concessions, incidentally, which clearly Napoleon did not intend to honour). To compensate Ferdinand and Maria Carolina, Spain was to be forced to give up the Balearic islands (a point which says much about the way France treated her allies). Why D'Oubril signed this treaty is unclear, for it did not meet Russia's basic aims (he had been told to get for the Neapolitan monarchy not the Balearic islands, but rather the possessions of which Austria had just been deprived in Dalmatia, the aim, of course, being to exclude the French from the Balkans), while at the same time being certain to face rejection in London. All that can be said in defence of D'Oubril is that the French adopted a very hard line in the talks they held with him, and left him with the impression that Russia could otherwise expect a full-scale attack in the Balkans. What made the treaty particularly unacceptable was the fact that no sooner had D'Oubril signed on 20 July than Napoleon awarded himself permanent control of Germany by means of the establishment of the Confederation of the Rhine. Returning to Moscow, its hapless progenitor found himself banished to his country estates and on 14 August the new Russian Foreign Minister, Andrei Budberg – a mediocre and rather colourless figure who had replaced the discredited Czartoryski in late June – declared the treaty to be null and void. France might still have peace, but only at the price of abandoning all claim to Sicily, finding territorial compensations for the King of Piedmont, restoring Austria's Dalmatian territories and guaranteeing the territory of the Ottoman Empire.

Of none of this was there any chance. Indeed, a letter from Napoleon to Joseph written on 21 July makes this quite clear: 'I hope that the vigour you will display in keeping up a strong army and fleet will be of powerful assistance to me in becoming master of the Mediterranean, the principal and constant goal of my policy . . . You must mobilize six men o'war, nine frigates and a number of barques, and in addition maintain a force of 40,000 men . . . I would rather sustain ten years of war than leave your kingdom incomplete and the possession of Sicily in contestation.'[46] All this made Fox's hopes of peace increasingly forlorn. Although there was growing friction between Britain and Russia – St Petersburg's apparent willingness to let Prussia keep Hanover was a particular source of trouble – Sicily was not somewhere that Britain could sacrifice easily. Thanks to Napoleon offering to force Prussia to disgorge Hanover (albeit in exchange for concessions elsewhere), talks had carried on through the summer. It had also helped that Yarmouth was easily flattered and very much inclined to take a pro-French line. But growing fears over Sicily led to the dispatch of a second envoy in the person of the tougher Lord Lauderdale, whereupon the atmosphere changed enormously. Talleyrand, for example, claims that the new envoy 'spoiled' the peace talks, and Malmesbury that he 'acted well and with spirit, and proved what I had ascertained at Paris and Lisle in 1796 and 1797 – that, though revolutionary France was ever ready to listen to pacific negotiation, it never meant, and probably never will mean, to conclude a just and equitable peace'.[47] But in plain English, this meant that, unlike Yarmouth, Lauderdale was not prepared to elide the issue of Sicily. At first there had been hints that France might not press the claims of Joseph Bonaparte, but it soon became clear that there was no shifting Napoleon on the issue, leading Fox to suspect that the emperor had never been acting in good faith.

As British heels dug in, so Napoleon responded with threats. Such bullying, however, was most ill timed, for the British had just received some good news. In the dark days of January, it is just possible that a diplomatic *coup de main* on the part of the French ruler might have secured a peace deal. At that point the situation in Sicily – the keystone at this time of Britain's war – looked very bleak. Ferdinand IV was at best a figure of fun and the island's military resources were almost non-existent. Let us here quote Henry Bunbury, a British staff officer serving with the expeditionary force that had been landed there:

If Ferdinand had been a mere noble of Naples with plenty of game to shoot, plenty of good things to eat and drink and a few toadeaters and buffoons on whom he could have played off his jokes, he would have passed through life with the credit of being a good-humoured comical fellow and a capital sportsman ... but, placed upon a throne, and tried by difficult times, his ignorance, narrow-mindedness, cowardice and treacherous deceit arose in dark relief ... It appeared evident [too] that the government possessed ... no magazines, no ammunition, no artillery; that even the important fortresses of Syracuse and Agosta were almost without garrisons and entirely destitute of ordnance and stores. Of troops there were nominally 8,000, really about 6,000, rank and file of all sorts (each bad of its sort). And here were we, 7,000 English and foreigners in our pay, undertaking to defend the great island of Sicily against Napoleon.[48]

However, by the summer things were different. No serious attempt had been made to assault Sicily. In Calabria the French were distracted by the popular revolt that had broken out following their arrival. And, finally, a sudden raid on the mainland coast that was launched by the British commander in Sicily (now not the original Sir James Craig, but rather Sir John Stuart) secured a surprise victory at Maida on 4 July. This was not much of a battle, but it did at least suggest that even if the French managed somehow to reach Sicily the British army could put up a good fight. Reassured by the news of Russia's rejection of a separate peace, by September Fox was insisting that peace should not be bought at the expense of Britain's security, Russia's friendship or the interests of the Sicilian Bourbons. As he told his nephew and devoted admirer, Lord Holland:

Bad as the queen and court of Naples are, we can in honour do nothing without their full ... consent, but even exclusive of that consideration and of the great importance of Sicily ... It is not so much the value of the point in dispute as the manner in which the French fly from their word which disheartens me ... The shuffling insincere way in which they act ... shows me that they are playing a false game, and in that case it would be very imprudent to make any concessions.[49]

The fact is that Fox had become utterly disillusioned with Napoleon. Wherever one looked in the first eight months of 1806, one saw nothing but bullying, aggression and bad faith, and it was quite clear that even

friendship with France did not bring immunity: if Austria and the Papal
States were treated badly, so were Spain, Holland and the Kingdom of
Italy. It is important to note that there was both moderation and flexibility in the British position: there was, for example, no suggestion
that France should give up Belgium, while even Sicily might have been
surrendered if Napoleon had permitted Ferdinand and Maria Carolina
to take over in Dalmatia. Nor were France's terms rejected outright. But
for the time being further negotiations seemed pointless, Yarmouth and
Lauderdale therefore being called back to London. Just at this point,
however, Fox fell sick and died. On St Helena, Napoleon was to make
much of this event: 'Assuredly . . . the death of Fox is one of the great
fatalities of my career . . . Had he gone on living, affairs would have
taken a different course: the cause of the people would have been
advanced, and we would have established a new order of things in
Europe.'[50] On another occasion the opinions expressed were still more
grandiose: 'Under the school of Fox, we would have understood one
another . . . We would have accomplished a good deal [and] maintained
the emancipation of the peoples and the reign of the princes alike. In
Europe there would have been a single fleet, a single army. We would
have governed the world, and, whether by the force of persuasion or the
force of arms, established peace and prosperity for all.'[51] This, however,
is nonsense from start to finish. For all Napoleon's claims, it is quite
clear, like Addington before him, Fox had been pushed into a corner,
and further, that even had some sort of deal been done it would have
depended on more than the Talents to bring peace to Europe.

If the struggle continued, then, it was not the fault of Britain and
Russia, both of whom had made a genuine attempt to make peace. Peace
did not come because Napoleon refused to abandon his ambitions in
the Balkans and had reverted to his eastern dreams of 1798. Ever
since peace had been signed with the Ottoman Empire in 1802, French
diplomacy had been seeking to re-establish the strong links that Paris
had traditionally enjoyed with the Ottoman government. By 1804 this
policy had had some success – it had helped enormously that Britain
had proved extremely slow to evacuate Egypt – but not to the extent
that was hoped. Constantinople, for example, refused to repudiate its
treaties with London and St Petersburg. With tension growing with
Russia, Napoleon therefore stepped up his diplomatic offensive, shower-
ing Selim III with protestations of friendship and promises of French

support. Yet this still did not produce the desired effect, for the Ottomans refused to recognize Napoleon as emperor, let alone *padishah* (a title that literally meant 'great king' and was traditionally given to the ruler – in 1804, as for most of the previous century, the Tsar of Russia – that the Turks viewed as the most powerful figure in the Christian world). Nor would they close the Bosporus and the Dardanelles to the warships and convoys of troops that the Russians were currently sending to the Ionian islands. By the beginning of 1805, then, relations between Paris and Constantinople were very poor: indeed, the French ambassador, Marshal Brune, had come home in disgust, having left the conduct of Franco-Turkish affairs in the hands of a subordinate. As for the Turks, they appeared to have gravitated wholly towards Russia, for in September 1805 they renewed the eight-year alliance they had signed with St Petersburg in 1798.

Austerlitz changed all this, however. The Ottoman Empire could be partner, but at the same time it could also be prey, and there was no longer anything to stop Napoleon from striking out from his Adriatic bridgeheads. Whether it was the Mamelukes in Egypt or the Wahhabites in Arabia, subject groups were being stirred up against Constantinople in order to add to the pressure on Selim III to turn to France. The French had also been instrumental in the establishment of the Republic of the Seven Islands, while their acquisition of Dalmatia had given them direct access to the Turkish frontier. Among the tiny handful of writers and intellectuals that had emerged in Greek circles – examples here include Christos Perraivos and Adamanthios Koraes – there was much enthusiasm for the emperor. And, finally, it was not so very long since a French army had invaded Egypt. At the current moment, Napoleon did not want war with Constantinople, and still less to partition the Ottoman Empire. But Selim III did not know this, while Napoleon was all too clearly on the move in the Balkans. In reality, his target was pro-Russian Montenegro, but there was a growing fear that plans were afoot to secure Bosnia, Serbia, Moldavia and Wallachia for Austria as compensation for her losses in the west: after all, such a move would not only embroil Vienna with St Petersburg and check any further Russian expansion in the Balkans, but give Napoleon an ideal pretext to seize, say, the Peloponnese. With Selim already very worried by Russian activities in the Mediterranean – not only had a large part of the Baltic fleet been sent to the Ionian islands, but the Russian presence there was provoking unrest in mainland Greece – no sooner had news of Austerlitz arrived than Constantinople gave in to all Napoleon's demands: the Bosporus and Dardanelles were closed to Russian shipping and the French ruler recognized as *padishah*.

With Turkish intransigence at an end, Napoleon's real interests in the Balkans were now revealed. Turkey was not just to be a helpful neutral, but an active partner in France's war with Russia. To achieve this result, the efforts of French diplomacy were redoubled. Far from supporting the Serbian revolt, then, the French denounced it and accused the Russians of both stirring it up and fomenting further revolts in Greece. In addition General Sebastiani, one of France's leading experts on eastern affairs, was appointed to Constantinople in place of Brune, and the Turks encouraged to think that full sovereignty might be recovered in the Danubian principalities and even that the Crimea – lost to Russia in 1783 – would be returned to them. The Russians, Constantinople was told, were in no state to put up much of a fight, while every effort was made to calm the understandable fears caused by France's advances in the Adriatic. Indeed, Napoleon promised to leave well alone: 'I have no desire whatsoever to partition the empire of Constantinople: if someone was to offer me three quarters of it, I still would not take anything. I want to reaffirm and consolidate this great empire, and make use of it as a counterpoint to Russia.'[52]

Despite serious Russian fears to the contrary, Napoleon was not aiming at fresh conquests in the Balkans in 1806, but rather a fresh sphere of influence that would exclude Russia from the region and distract her from fighting France in central Europe and the Adriatic. In pursuing this policy the French ruler was encouraged by developments which had taken place with regard to distant Persia. In 1801, as we have seen, she had become embroiled in a war with Russia over Georgia. Even in the face of fierce Persian resistance – in April 1804 a Russian army was defeated at Yerevan with the loss of 4,000 men – more and more of Georgia fell into Russian hands. Also lost were large parts of what is today Azerbaijan. Left without help by his chief allies, the British – with fears growing in respect of Russian intentions towards India a British mission had negotiated a military alliance with Persia in 1801 – Fath Ali sent an envoy to France asking for support. Receiving this communication early in 1805, Napoleon dispatched a mission to Persia. The business of establishing diplomatic relations was not without its problems – one of the diplomats concerned died within days of reaching Tehran, while another was seized in the wilds of Turkish Armenia by a local *pasha* who probably hoped to hold him for ransom. However, by the middle of 1806 the French had secured their objective. Fath Ali's heir, Abbas Mirza, a fiercesome warrior who was given to making pyramids of the skulls of the men killed by his forces in battle, professed himself to be a warm admirer of Napoleon, and an ambassador, Mirza Muhamed Riza Qazvini, was soon on his way to Paris. It was not until May 1807 that a military alliance was finally concluded, but in the circumstances this was just a formality, as the Persians were already attacking the Russians in Georgia, Azerbaijan and Daghestan.

Eager to prove good allies, the Turks were also being very helpful. In a move that had been under consideration for some time, on 24 August the Porte deposed the rulers of Moldavia and Wallachia. Known as *hospodars*, these men were the successors of a line of princes who had ruled the Romanian people since the Middle Ages. Forced to submit to the Turks in the mid-sixteenth century, the principalities of Moldavia and Wallachia had proved more fortunate than the Christian states further south. In exchange for a heavy tribute, they were granted autonomy under the rule of nominees of the Ottoman government, these last invariably being drawn from a small number of wealthy Greek families resident in Constantinople. Under pressure from Russia, who from the peace treaty of Kuchuk Kainardji of 1774 onwards had claimed the right to intervene in Turkish affairs in defence of the Ottoman Empire's many Christians, this system was modified in 1802 after parts of the Danube valley were devastated by marauding janissaries belonging to the command of the *pasha* of Vidin, Pasvanoglou. Henceforth the rulers were to be appointed for a maximum of seven years only and could neither be chosen nor dismissed without Russian approval; the Russian consuls in Bucharest and Jassy also being given a say in matters of government. Needless to say, the men appointed – Constantine Ypsilanti of Wallachia and Simon Muruzi of Moldavia – held markedly pro-Russian views, and so their removal constituted a major foreign policy statement. Promptly threatened with war by St Petersburg, where powerful elements in the Foreign Ministry were always in favour of a forward policy in the Balkans, the Turks requested foreign mediation, but the Russians correctly interpreted this as a mere stratagem and sent their troops across the frontier anyway. In doing so, however, they had miscalculated: much encouraged by the fact that the *grande armée* was currently pushing into Poland (see below), on 18 December 1806 Constantinople declared war.

The struggle that followed is all but unknown to anglophone readers. Yet it is doubtful whether the rest of the Napoleonic Wars can match it in terms of savagery. Emblematic of the style in which it was waged is the fate of the Danubian provinces' large community of Muslim Tartars. The emigré Duc de Rochechouart had in 1806 enlisted in the Russian army as a volunteer:

The Russian army of invasion was not big enough to ... defend the great extent of territory which it quickly occupied ... Only being able to count on the Christian population of the two provinces of Moldavia and Wallachia, the general in chief for this reason could not but fear the Muslim population: indeed, he believed that in the case of defeat ... the mass of horsemen of which it could dispose ... would augment his troubles. In consequence, it seemed to him to be prudent to treat ... the whole of this inoffensive populace as so many prisoners of war, and all of them, old and young, man and beast, were pitilessly dragged away from their homes and occupations ... and sent over 800 leagues away to the province of Kursk in the depths of winter ... To escort the multitude, whose aspect recalled on a small scale that of the Jewish people when they were sent into slavery in Babylon, he chose three regiments of Cossack irregulars. Something like 15,000 souls ... were marched away to the north-west ... Afterwards we heard that only two fifths managed to reach their place of exile, all the rest dying en route.[53]

To this early example of ethnic cleansing, there was added an unremitting diet of pillage and massacre. All the parties to the conflict made much use of irregular troops among whom pillage was both a natural instinct and, in many instances, their only means of subsistence, while the traditional rivalry between different ethnic and religious groups served to inflame the situation still further. Mixed in with all this was the further problem that among the Turks and the Serbs in particular there flourished semi-independent warlords whose loyalty to their nominal masters was tenuous in the extreme. In 1810, for example, the Serbian leader Karadjordje was almost overthrown by a rival chieftain named Milenko Stojkovic. Already a way of life, banditry was swelled by the thousands of desperate refugees who fled to the forests and mountains. If we consider, too, the appalling record of Turks and Russians alike, it can be all too easily understood that the result was a conflict of near indescribable horror. Entire communities were put to the sword in a manner not seen even in the worst moments of the Peninsular War; thousands of women and children were sold into slavery; and death was frequently accompanied by torture and the most extreme cruelty. When Belgrade fell to the Turks in October 1813, for example, the city's fate was truly terrible: 'Men were roasted alive, hanged by their feet over smoking straw until they were asphyxiated, castrated, crushed with stones, and bastinadoed. Their women and children were raped and sometimes taken by force to harems . . . Outside the Stambul gate . . . there were always on view the corpses of impaled Serbs being gnawed by packs of dogs.'[54] In response to such atrocities, the Serbs gave way to a fury that was just as terrible. This is what happened following an insurgent victory at Cucuga on 3 April 1806:

In their flight the Turks threw away their arms and clothing in order to run the better, but to no purpose. The Serbs caught up with them and killed them, some with swords, some with knives and some with daggers, while others had their brains beaten out with cudgels and staves . . . They say that over 2,800 Turks perished and only those got away who had good horses . . . When our army mustered again at the camp at Ub, I saw that many of our soldiers had bloodstained swords . . . and that their gun-butts also were smashed and broken; they were laden with every sort of spoil.[55]

Nor were the Russians much better. Sent with an amphibious force to raid the Circassian coast, no sooner had the first town been entered than Rochechouart again witnessed terrible scenes:

The Cossacks went off in all directions and set light to all the houses . . . In a few moments everything around us was in flames, and the result was a veritable theatre of desolation in which the cries of the dying were joined by the screams of women and the bellowing of beasts caught by the flames.[56]

If the conflict was one of unrivalled savagery, it was also anything but a minor affair. In Dalmatia, things were never very serious: setting aside an unsuccessful Russian attack on Cattaro in October 1806, which led to a fierce action at Castelnuovo, the French forces in Ragusa for some time had little more to contend with than sporadic skirmishes with bands of Montenegrin frontiersmen. But elsewhere it was a different story. In Serbia, furious fighting had already been raging for the past two years. On 18 August 1804, for example, 15,000 Turks had been put to flight at Ivankovac, while 22 August 1806 saw the insurgents defeat a Turkish force of 60,000 men at Deligrad, the final seal seemingly being set on Serbian victory when Karadjordje stormed Belgrade at the head of some 25,000 men on 12 December. Thus encouraged, the Serbs rejected conciliatory Ottoman peace terms – the result, it seems, of French pressure aimed at avoiding the complete dismemberment of Turkey-in-Europe – and threw in their lot with Russia, while at the same time negotiating an alliance with Montenegro and – on 31 March 1807 – formally declaring their independence. Meanwhile, with the outbreak of the Russo-Turkish War, fierce fighting also erupted in Wallachia, where the Russians had concentrated a force of nearly 40,000 men under General Mickhelson and now attacked Ottoman forces entrenched in the fortresses of Ismail, Giurgiu and Braila. This Russian thrust was thrown back, but in recompense on 22 May and then again on 1 July attempts on the part of the Turkish fleet to sally out of the Dardanelles were defeated by the Russian squadron of Admiral Senyavin, which had established a forward base on the island of Tenedos. In addition, a Turkish attempt to attack Bucharest with 40,000 men was heavily defeated at Obilesti on 14 June. Thereafter, the guns fell silent for some months, but only while both sides were rushing up fresh troops: by the end of 1807, indeed, the Russians could call on 80,000 men and were talking of deploying as many as 150,000.

In effect the Turkish declaration of war on Russia may be regarded as the consummation of the foreign policy that Napoleon had embarked on in the wake of the battle of Austerlitz. As such, it stands in direct contradiction to one of the central tenets of the Napoleonic legend – that the treaty of Pressburg marks one of the points at which Napoleon would have liked to stop – that it was the moment, indeed, when he gained the central objectives of his foreign policy in the shape of the Rhine frontier and control of Holland, Switzerland, western Germany and northern Italy. According to Napoleon's admirers, if the emperor went to war again it was to extract fresh 'securities' from a concert of powers unwilling to accept his triumph. This, however, is simply not true. In 1806 both Russia and Britain had been positively eager to make peace, and they might well have agreed to terms that would have left the Napoleonic imperium almost completely intact. As for Austria and Prussia, they simply wanted to be left alone. To have secured a compromise peace, then, would have been comparatively easy. But in the service of this goal Napoleon was prepared to make no concessions, or, at least, to give up no part of his booty, as witness, for example, the rejection of Russia's demands for Ferdinard IV of Naples to be given Dalmatia. Indeed, Russia was to be humbled not just in Dalmatia, but also in the Danubian provinces, to which end Napoleon pursued an alliance with the Ottoman Empire. Still less would Napoleon pay the price of peace with Britain in the shape of giving up Joseph Bonaparte's claim to Sicily. At all times, then, the picture was the same. Dominant on every front, Napoleon was not necessarily bent on fresh aggression per se, but he would give nothing up, saw coercion as the only route to agreement and insisted on occupying a geographic position that gave him the greatest possible freedom of action and, above all, opened the way for future offensives. All this was accompanied by a diplomatic style that was brutal in the extreme and favoured bilateral negotiations in which he might overawe his opponents rather than general congresses in which he himself might be overborne. Where does this leave us? Certainly not, of course, with a Europe that was united against Napoleon and looking only for an opportunity to expel him from the Low Countries, Germany, Italy and the Balkans and, still less, put an end to his rule in France. But if the events of 1805–6 had proved anything, it was that the emperor could defeat even the strongest constellation of enemies if it was not bound together by absolute commitment and absolute unity. To reach that point there was still a long and difficult road to travel, but in his extremism the French ruler was propelling potential opponents along it ever faster. 'When I entered the imperial government in the month of June 1806,' wrote Pasquier, 'Napoleon had reached the summit of his power and glory. Founded in the first instance on the ascendancy of his personal genius and the moral impact of his early victories, his authority had been reinforced still further by his recent triumphs, but there was nothing to shield it from the dangers that were necessarily brought by his excessive confidence in his star.'[57]

6

Zenith of Empire

In the summer of 1806 Europe was temporarily more or less at peace, or, at least, experiencing a period of 'phoney war'. Technically speaking, both Britain and Russia remained at war with France, and there was some fighting in both Italy and the Balkans. At sea and in the wider world, too, operations went on unabated: the Royal Navy kept watch on Europe's coasts; a British expeditionary force seized Buenos Aires; and French commerce raiders based in ports as widely spaced as Brest and Mauritius raided the sea lanes and on occasion achieved considerable success. Serious peace negotiations, however, were in place, and, although these soon broke down, it is difficult to see how anything comparable to the campaign of 1805 could have been revived. Neither the Talents nor any other British administration could possibly have committed themselves to major land operations on the Continent without the support of at least one of the great powers, and in the wake of Austerlitz this seemed a long way away. Austria was out of the fight; Prussia in the French camp; and Russia at best resolved on a defensive policy. Yet, in a development that was expected by nobody, and, least of all it seems, Napoleon, the autumn saw the Continent once more plunged into full-scale military operations and a resumption of coalition warfare. Pushed to the limit by the emperor, Prussia went to war against France and, like Austria before her, secured the active support of Russia. But the results were no better than in 1805. In a series of operations that took the *grande armée* to the very frontiers of Russia, the emperor broke one enemy army after another and truly made himself master of Europe. At no moment, indeed, was the power of the French imperium greater, and Napoleon's sense of exaltation knew no bounds. As he proclaimed to his army on 22 June 1807:

Frenchmen! You have been worthy of yourselves and of me. You will return to France covered with laurels after having obtained a glorious peace which carries with it the guarantee of its duration. It is time our country should live at rest, secure from the malignant influence of England.[1]

As we shall see, these were hollow words. Even before the fresh round of fighting broke out, it could be argued that Napoleon had committed a cardinal error in reorganizing Germany in a manner hostile to the interests of Austria or Prussia. But far more damaging were the events that followed in the course of the next twelve months. Not content with the challenge he was already mounting to Russia in the Balkans, Napoleon established a Polish state and thereby struck at the very heart of Russia's pretensions to be a great European power. And in the Continent as a whole the emperor conscripted each and every one of its inhabitants into a great self-denying ordinance that sought to close its ports to British trade and in the end bankrupt London into surrender. As Fouché observes, this was a man who was giddy with triumph: 'The delirium caused by the wonderful results of the Prussian campaign completed the intoxication of France . . . Napoleon believed himself the son of destiny, called to break every sceptre. Peace . . . was no longer thought of . . . The idea of destroying the power of England, the sole obstacle to universal monarchy, became his fixed resolve.'[2]

The long-term consequences of these developments – in essence, a guarantee of further conflict and, more particularly, direct police action on the part of France – will be looked at in due course. What is of concern here is why Prussia should suddenly have opened hostilities on her own when a year earlier she could have done so in the company of a powerful coalition. In brief, Frederick William suddenly discovered the limits of Napoleon's friendship. Trouble began with the very agreement that Haugwitz had signed with Napoleon after Austerlitz at Schönbrunn. In the first place, there was the issue of Prussia's international obligations, for under the terms of the treaty of Basel of 1795 Prussia was actually a guarantor of Hanoverian independence. In the second there was Prussia's neutrality, the latter's restoration clearly being of the utmost importance. And in the third instance there was that of the future: if Hanover was to be taken over by Prussia, the British subsidies that might one day become necessary to Prussia would clearly not be forthcoming. Amidst much anger, then, Haugwitz was sent back to

Napoleon to suggest a number of amendments to the treaty, one suggestion being that Hanover was not to be annexed but rather simply occupied and held as a bargaining counter that might be returned to its ruler in exchange for a variety of other territories at the end of the war. This, however, did no good at all. On the contrary, Haugwitz was confronted with terms that were even worse than before. Hanover would not only be Prussian, but Potsdam would now have to close her ports to Britain's trade. Failure to accept these terms, it was hinted, would lead to war and, with Prussia in no condition to fight – for reasons of cost, the army had immediately been demobilized – on 9 March Frederick William ratified the new agreement and thereby, to all intents and purposes, declared war on Britain.

The consequences of this act were very serious. Hardly a shot was exchanged between the British and Prussians, but such was the loss of customs revenue that the state's income fell by 25 per cent. As if this was not bad enough, Prussia also experienced a period of unparalleled humiliation. Thus, in July 1806 Napoleon organized his new Confederation of the Rhine without any reference to Prussia. To add insult to injury, the emperor suggested that Frederick William should form a confederation or even an empire of his own in northern Germany, while at the same time either inciting states that might have been involved in this scheme to reject the whole idea (Saxony and Hesse-Kassel) or making it clear that he would not evacuate them (Hamburg and Lübeck). Still worse, it then transpired that the abortive negotiations with the Talents had seen Napoleon offer to return Hanover to Britain. To the dismayed Frederick William, it really seemed that the end of Prussia was at hand, especially as there were persistent rumours of French troop movements to the south and west. As he wrote to Alexander I, '[Napoleon] intends to destroy me.'[3] On 9 August, then, the Prussian army was mobilized, and on 1 October this step was followed by an ultimatum calling for France to agree to withdraw all her forces from Germany by 8 October or face war. Even then some question remained whether Frederick William was really in earnest, however. There were certainly voices in Prussia calling for war, but the king himself was almost certainly bluffing. Such at least was the opinion of Ferdinand von Funck, a cavalry officer who became a close adviser of the King of Saxony in the wake of the battle of Jena:

All circumstances point clearly to the fact that Frederick William III . . . always cherished the secret hope that Napoleon would shirk a struggle with the erstwhile military prestige of Prussia, and, as soon as he saw things looking serious, negotiate for the repurchase of Prussian friendship either by the restoration of the Franconian provinces ceded in exchange for Hanover, or perhaps of the territories of Westphalia sold at the peace of Lunéville, or by the free-will offering of part of Saxony. By this means Frederick William would have silenced the malcontents in his own country by the prestige of fresh and cheap aggrandizement.[4]

Also interesting here are the memoirs of General Muffling. Sent to join the staff of the Duke of Brunswick, Muffling discovered that the newly appointed Prussian commander-in-chief was anything but enthusiastic: 'I found the duke, as generalissimo, uncertain about the political relations of Prussia with France and England, uncertain about the strength and position of the French *corps d'armée* in Germany, and without any fixed plan as to what should be done . . . He had accepted the command in order to prevent war.'[5]

At this point it might be asked what intentions Napoleon had with regard to Prussia. Such was the manner in which Potsdam was goaded that it would be logical to assume that the emperor wanted war and was intent on its instigation. A new land campaign was by far the easiest means of winning fresh laurels and such a venture was all the more tempting in view of the presence of the *grande armée* in southern Germany (following the Austerlitz campaign, it had gone into cantonments along the river Main). At the same time there was also the issue of Potsdam's flirtation with the Third Coalition, and the two issues together have certainly led some historians to argue that there was a blueprint for a march on Prussia. This, however, is almost certainly not the case. Intent on establishing the Confederation of the Rhine, the French ruler – at least in the short term – had no desire to destabilize the situation in Germany. According to Talleyrand, he was, as Frederick William hoped, afraid of Prussia. 'It was not without secret uneasiness that the emperor went for the first time to measure his strength against [Prussia's],' wrote Talleyrand. 'The ancient glory of the Prussian army imposed upon him.'[6] But this is most implausible. Much more to the point is the fact that he had other schemes on his mind – the conquest of Sicily; the dispatch of an army to Portugal to end British access to the vital port of Lisbon;

and conceivably even a new attempt to invade England. As for Prussia, the reality seems rather to be that he regarded her not at all. There being no evidence whatsoever that Prussia would ever go to war, the emperor in consequence had no compunction about riding roughshod over her interests. To quote a letter the emperor wrote to Talleyrand on 12 September 1806, 'The idea that Prussia could take me on single-handed is too absurd to merit discussion . . . She will go on acting as she has acted – arming today, disarming tomorrow, standing by, sword in hand, while the battle is fought, and then making terms with the victor.'[7] What we see, then, is a typical mixture of contempt and over-confidence. Napoleon did not want a fresh war in 1806, but at the same time he simply did not know what was required to keep the peace. Truly it was a most revealing moment.

Whatever Napoleon's motives, the result is not in dispute: at the end of the first week of September Prussia's forces entered Saxony en route for the river Main. For Frederick William, this was an act of desperation that was embarked on in a spirit of the utmost fatalism. As his confidant, Lombard, wrote:

The king . . . was unfortunately not a born general. He had long known as well as anyone that he would have to draw his sword whether he liked it or no, but always he . . . had flattered himself that some catastrophe independent of his own decisions would solve the difficulty. At last . . . he yielded, but quite against his will, of that I can assure you.[8]

That said, there were many voices in Prussia clamouring for war. Eager to supplant Haugwitz, Hardenberg was in the forefront, as was Frederick William's queen, Louise, a fiery young woman who had increasingly come to hate Napoleon. Bizarrely, a shaken Haugwitz had also privately joined the war party, although he hoped to postpone the breach long enough to get the army fully ready for action and secure assistance from Britain and Russia. And there were, too, many bellicose army officers. 'France', wrote General Blücher, 'means honestly by no power, least of all by your Royal Majesty . . . Whoever represents France's conduct to Your Royal Majesty in any other light, whoever advises Your Royal Majesty to continue making concessions and remain at peace with this nation is either very indolent [or] very shortsighted, or else has been bought with French gold . . . Each day gained in declaring war against France is of the greatest advantage to Your Royal

Majesty ... One successful battle and allies, money and supplies are ours from every corner of Europe.'[9] So great was the pressure in the officer corps that the king, who had before him the example of the murdered Paul I of Russia, may genuinely have feared for his position. Some officers – Blücher is a good example – genuinely believed that the prestige of the Prussian army and state alike were at stake; others looked to war as an opportunity to justify arguments for reform; and still others were simply anxious for glory after eleven years of peace in an age of general warfare. Something of their frustration comes over from a letter written by the future military theorist, Carl von Clausewitz: 'War is necessary for my country. Moreover, when all is said and done, it is war alone that can make me attain happiness.'[10]

Thanks to Napoleon, such vainglory could be dressed up in the garb of German patriotism: on 25 August a considerable stir was caused in Prussia and elsewhere by the execution of a Nuremberg bookseller named Palm who had made the mistake of printing and distributing an anonymous pamphlet lamenting Germany's prostration. As for victory, it was assured. 'When I draw a conclusion from all the observations that I have occasion to make,' opined Clausewitz, 'I always arrive at the probability that it is we who are going to win the next great battle.'[11] 'Unconscious of danger,' wrote the Countess of Schwerin, 'the army, in all the glory and order of a grand parade, went to meet its destruction. Unconscious, too, did the leaders seem, for the enemy circled us round about and no one had any news of him. In Naumberg, when already outflanked by the French, the court continued to live the careless life of Charlottenburg and Potsdam.'[12] Another witness of the army's over-confidence was the Baron de Marbot, a young cavalry officer sent to Berlin bearing dispatches for the French embassy: 'The officers whom I knew ventured no longer to speak to me or salute me; many Frenchmen were insulted by the populace; the men-at-arms of the Noble Guard pushed their swagger to the point of whetting their sword blades on the stone steps of the French ambassador's house.'[13]

To return to the Countess of Schwerin, her remarks are redolent of the hindsight that has often surrounded discussion of the Prussian decision to go to war in 1806. At the time the outcome did not seem so clear-cut on either side of the battle lines. What is true, though, is that Potsdam was in no way ready to take up arms against Napoleon. Prussia stood entirely alone. Despite her secret pact with Russia, no arrangements had been made for military cooperation, and the Russians were sceptical as to whether Prussia would actually do anything. With Britain there had been no contact whatsoever, and the emissary that Haugwitz dispatched to negotiate a treaty of subsidy as soon as war seemed likely could have hoped to achieve very little even had he been granted more time. Grenville mistrusted Prussia at the best of times and was convinced that in the current circumstances all she was out to do was to secure further 'compensations' in Germany, while he was disposed to do nothing at all for her unless he received a guarantee that Hanover's independence would be restored, and saw clear proof that Prussia had exerted herself as far as her own resources would permit. According to Lady Holland, Grenville was none the less 'very warlike' – she implies, indeed, that he welcomed the Prussian declaration of war – but in general hostility to Prussia was rife in Britain.[14] The Earl of Malmesbury, for example, wrote:

The six months I was with the Prussian army in 1794 . . . fixed in my mind the opinion . . . that the military defence of Prussia was, like its geographical position, a rope of sand, which would fall to pieces when brought into action, or vigorously opposed. The two succeeding kings to Frederick [the Great] hastened the dissolution of this baseless fabric. Féderique Guillaume [i.e. Frederick William II] . . . was enervated by debauchery and . . . without any of those substantive virtues necessary to govern so helpless a kingdom such as that over which he reigned. He exhausted the public treasure, and . . . every act or measure of his went to . . . weaken the monarchy. His son, also Féderique Guillaume, began by shedding tears, not for the loss of his father, but from the labour and trouble a crown brings with it, and this, not from philosophy, but from an indolent, sleepy, selfish, torpid mind. He is wilful and obstinate, yet without a system or opinion.[15]

Nor were the states that might have supported Prussia in northern Germany any more forthcoming. It did not help that the Prussians opened the campaign by pouring into Saxony. Brunswick, Hesse-Kassel, Oldenburg, Mecklenburg-Schwerin and Mecklenburg-Strelitz all declared their neutrality, while the court of Dresden only joined Prussia because it was that or go to war with her (not that Saxony was especially impressive as an ally, her army numbering a mere 20,000 men). As for the Swedes, Gustav IV rightly suspected that Potsdam had designs on the territorial enclave that Stockholm still held on the coast of northern Germany and therefore remained aloof.

Everything, then, rested on the shoulders of Prussia's own soldiers, but this was to ask too much of them. So precipitately did Prussia go to war that there was not time to call up all the reserves – in contrast to most of the armies of Europe, the bulk of Potsdam's soldiers were reservists who were only mobilized in time of war – and Frederick William therefore took the field at the head of a field army of only 150,000 men, when the number might have been at least 200,000. By the same token there were neither magazines for the field army, nor adequate stocks of food in any of the country's fortresses. As for the quality of the army, the ordinary soldiers were well drilled enough, but their efficacy was undermined – as with Austria in 1805 – by a piecemeal series of military reforms that, though well meant, had made things worse rather than better. Thus the army had for the first time been organized into divisions in the French style, but they were, on the one hand, too big and, on the other, very poorly put together. The cavalry were mixed in with the infantry, as had been the case in the French army in the 1790s, and each division was also given too much artillery, the result being, first, formations that were difficult to manage and, second, a considerable dilution in the striking power of horsemen and cannon alike. Finally, in face-to-face conflict with the French, the infantry would certainly be at a disadvantage. There were a number of specialist light-infantry battalions – a few of them riflemen and the rest soldiers known as fusiliers armed with a lighter version of the standard musket – trained in skirmishing tactics, but there were never enough of these units and attempts to make good the want by using the third rank of each line battalion as skirmishers were no substitute as the men had no proper organizational structure. Though the basic tactical system remained sound – the linear formations in which the Prussian army was to fight in 1806 were exactly the same as those in which the British army triumphed at Waterloo – the army therefore went to war at a considerable disadvantage.

As if all this was not enough, Prussia moved on Napoleon at a moment of maximum British distraction. In September 1806 London's attention rested not on Eastern Europe but on the Spanish empire in America. In 1805 Britain had dispatched an expeditionary force to the Dutch colony

of the Cape. The local militia having been quickly worsted at Blauewberg, on 18 January 1806 the governor surrendered. At this point,
however, matters took an unexpected turn. Thrusting, ambitious and
greedy for prize-money, the commander of the squadron that had transported the British forces to the Cape, Sir Home Popham, suddenly sailed
off to attack Buenos Aires, which at this time was the capital of the
Virreinato de la Plata, an enormous territory incorporating present-day
Argentina, Chile, Uruguay, Paraguay and Bolivia. Though Popham had
with him only a very few troops – no more than 1,600 – on 25 June
1806 the ill-defended city duly fell. Exultant at this success, the victor
now set his sights on even greater spoils. Eager to see himself established
as pro-consul of a new colonial empire, he sent a grandiloquent report
of the possibilities on offer in South America to London together with
a consignment of something over £1 million that had been looted from
the treasury of the Spanish administration. Although the government
had known of what was afoot since July, it was not until Popham's
victory dispatch arrived on 13 September that news reached the public.
Coming 'out of the blue' as it did, the result was immense excitement,
especially as Popham's supporters staged a victory parade in which his
loot was ceremonially dragged to the Bank of England in a train of
wagons. Typical of the talk being bandied about in educated society,
perhaps, was the remark heard one evening at a soirée held at the home
of the artist, Joseph Farington: '[Crauford] Bruce thought the capture
of Buenos Aires . . . a great acquisition to commerce. He said it would
be attended with the good effect of disseminating our cultures into every
corner of South America. That country, it was agreed, can never again
be held by Spain.'[16]

With cheering crowds flooding the streets, the Talents would have
been hard put not to respond in a positive fashion, all the more so as
many manufacturers had been pressing for measures to give them more
open access to the South American market. At the same time various
factors made intervention an attractive prospect at the current moment.
A substantial force of troops was available in the 10,000 men gathered
for dispatch to Lisbon should the French invade Portugal. A well-known
Venezuelan malcontent named Francisco de Miranda, who had been
lobbying the British government for support ever since 1783 and was
currently trying to stir up a revolt in his homeland, chose this moment
to announce that the whole of South America was on the brink of

flinging off its chains. And at least one member of the Cabinet – the egregious William Windham – had always been in favour of getting up a revolution in Spain's dominions anyway. Intervention, then, was always likely, and on 9 October 3,000 men put to sea bound for Buenos Aires under General Auchmuty. Some way ahead of them, meanwhile, were another 2,000 soldiers who had been dispatched from the Cape of Good Hope by its conqueror, Sir David Baird.

In one sense, the British decision was understandable enough. Popham's action had been that of a piratical adventurer, but Spain was still France's chief ally and the Latin American market an important target for British trade; indeed, the Continental Blockade made it absolutely vital. Equally, access to South American bullion would have been most welcome. Turning to wider issues, meanwhile, ever since 1793 British strategy had revolved around a policy of exerting pressure on France in the West Indies and elsewhere whenever there was no chance of effecting anything in Europe. Even the idea of raising South America against the Spaniards, or at least striking at such cities as Buenos Aires, was not new. On the contrary, Miranda's schemes had been given serious consideration by William Pitt, and the latter had actually gone so far as to ask Sir Arthur Wellesley to prepare a plan for an expedition to the river Orinoco. Equally, Popham ever afterwards argued that he had been given tacit permission to attack Buenos Aires before leaving London. Had a British army been sent to Stralsund or Danzig in February 1807 much might have been achieved, but the whole argument reeks of hindsight: in September 1806 Buenos Aires did not just seem a reasonable place at which to hit the enemy, but was one of the few places at which the enemy could be hit.

To a certain extent, then, it is possible to sympathize with the Talents, while Auchmuty's little force was so small that its presence in England would have made little difference. What happened next, however, throws doubts on the credibility of the Grenville administration. There were serious questions over the financial probity of both Popham and Miranda. That they not only knew one another but had since October 1804 been working closely together to secure British intervention in South America should also have given the Cabinet pause for thought. More than that, it should have been obvious to all concerned that the two men were mere adventurers whose only object was the pursuit of wealth and self-aggrandizement. Initiating major plans of conquest in

South America was hardly in Britain's interest at this point, for it laid her wide open to the charge that she was interested solely in the expansion of British naval, economic and commercial dominance in the wider world. Yet caution was thrown to the winds. Working quite separately from one another, Windham and Grenville came up with two different plans for fresh operations in the Spanish empire. Windham had no hesitation in wanting General Robert Craufurd to take a force of 5,000 men, sail halfway round the world, establish a de facto protectorate over what is now Chile, and link hands with Popham in Buenos Aires. As for Grenville, what he wanted was to have present-day Mexico invaded by one force coming from Britain and another coming from India (in part composed of native sepoys, this last was also supposed to conquer the Philippines). Bewilderingly enough, the British commanders sent to South America were also told that they were on no account to stir up open revolt amongst the inhabitants. As Lord Holland shows, this contradiction was all too revealing:

Mr Windham, though he plumed himself on his disdain of all popular clamour, had greatly heated his imagination with the prospect of indemnifying ourselves in the New World for the disappointments which we had sustained in the Old. Lord Sidmouth, Lord Moira and others, not excepting entirely Lord Grenville himself, were anxious to court the commercial interest by opening new sources for their adventures, and they were not insensible to the censures lavished already on our defensive system of warfare which they foresaw would be much augmented and aggravated if Sir Home Popham's expedition were to fail for want of further support from home. Yet the same persons, and Lord Grenville more especially, were averse to any measure which should pledge Great Britain to separate the colonies of Spain from the mother country. Such an undertaking would, they apprehended, be an insurmountable obstacle to peace, and, by involving us in an extensive project, would call for exertions that would yet further exhaust our diminished resources ... No division ... among us ensued, but the policy adopted did partake of the irresolute and discordant opinions of the council. We should either have abandoned all projects on Spanish America, or made the liberation of these colonies a main object of our war. We did neither. We sent succours to our army at Buenos Aires ... The force was quite inadequate to a contest, and our language was not sufficiently explicit to induce the inhabitants to throw off the yoke of Spain. It is not surprising that such ill-concerted and irresolute policy met with no success.[17]

So absurd was the tone of what was planned that it is difficult to write of the South American scheme with patience. Setting aside the enormous distances and logistical difficulties involved, the dangers of attempting to make use of Indian troops outside the subcontinent were shown that same year by a serious mutiny at Vellore, while the Talents' general lack of realism was underlined by that fact that on 12 August the first troops who had landed at Buenos Aires had been forced to surrender by a resurgent local militia. At least this had the effect of persuading the British to concentrate all their efforts on the vicinity of the Río de la Plata itself, to which end a fast ship was dispatched to stop Craufurd from heading off to Chile (Grenville's plan for a pincer attack on Mexico had not yet come to fruition, and was now abandoned). Arriving off the Río de la Plata, the first 5,000 men who had been sent to help Popham seized Montevideo, where they were joined first by the 4,800 men actually brought from Britain by Craufurd and then another 1,600 men who had been dispatched direct from London. Alongside this last contingent came a new commander in Lieutenant-General John Whitelocke, an officer who had served creditably enough in the West Indies in the 1790s, but seems to have acquired his new position for no better reason than the excellent family connections he enjoyed in Whitehall.

In all then, by June 1807 almost 11,500 men had been concentrated in the Banda Oriental, as modern-day Uruguay was then called. What, however, was this force expected to achieve? Whitelocke's orders called for him to capture Buenos Aires, and this ought in theory to have been within his powers: though possessed of an imposing citadel, the city lacked outer walls and was garrisoned only by local militiamen. Beyond this, the general's aim was presumably simply to hold on to Buenos Aires and Montevideo as gateways for British trade with South America and bargaining counters at some future peace conference. But this was at best a difficult task. In the first place the militias the Spaniards could draw on were both very numerous and well trained. At the same time the overthrow of the first troops to land at Buenos Aires had done much to stimulate colonial self-confidence, and it was by no means clear that the British would be able to obtain the loyalty of the inhabitants.

Merchants of the coastal littoral could hope to make great profits from the new links with London, Bristol and Liverpool, but considerable parts of the interior had economic systems that looked north and west to other parts of the Spanish empire as well as local elites that deeply distrusted the commercial oligarchy that dominated Buenos Aires and Montevideo. Inherent in the whole strategy, then, were serious problems, but in the event Whitelocke and his men proved unable to carry out even the first part of the plan. Having disembarked a substantial force of troops on the right bank of the Río de la Plata, on 5 July 1807 the British general marched his men into Buenos Aires from several different directions. At first there was no resistance and soon the redcoats were well inside the city. But they had walked into a trap. Hiding on the flat roofs typical of the city, the defenders opened fire and very soon the attackers were falling on all sides. Unable to fight back effectively, Whitelocke's men were cornered and by the end of the day almost 3,000 men – half the total force involved in the attack – had been killed or wounded. Unable to extricate the survivors, the following day the British commander surrendered. The terms he negotiated were by no means harsh – in exchange for surrendering Montevideo and evacuating Buenos Aires, the British were simply allowed to sail away unmolested – but it had been a strategic failure of the first order and one that might well have brought down the Talents had they not already been brought down by the perennial issue of Catholic emancipation three months earlier. And the blow to Britain's prestige and morale was substantial. As Lord Auckland wrote to the Speaker of the House of Commons, Lord Colchester:

The Buenos Aires catastrophe is most vexatious, and the more so as an old friend in the confidence and conduct of the government writes to me that nothing but the senseless absurdity of Whitelocke could have produced what has happened; that it is the more mortifying because at Montevideo our garrison was living on the best possible terms with Spaniards; that our trade was increasing rapidly; and [that], if we had chosen to play the game of independence, we could have placed all the Spanish provinces on their legs without bloodshed or revolutionary convulsions. My correspondent adds, 'Many important and feasible projects which we were indulging are gone forever.'[18]

The impact of this prolonged escapade on the situation in Europe is obviously the next issue that needs to be taken into account, but, before we do so, we must first consider the effect that Whitelocke's defeat had in Spain's American empire. Prior to Britain's intervention, the Virreinato de la Plata and its fellow colonies had hardly been a hotbed of revolt: Miranda's every attempt to raise the standard of independence had collapsed in ignominious failure. That said, there were certainly many tensions in colonial society. The native-born population of European descent, the so-called *criollos*, were given few opportunities for advancement by the Spanish government, and yet considerable elements of it had long since become wealthy and powerful as planters, merchants and ranchers. Until the mid-eighteenth century, indeed, they had been the dominant forces in colonial life, but under King Charles III (1759–88) the so-called 'second reconquest' had imposed much tighter control on Spain's American possessions. Control of the military and local government had passed to bureaucrats dispatched from Spain, while a determination to ensure that the empire did more to support the metropolis in financial and economic terms ensured that the *criollos* found themselves under great pressure on a number of different fronts. A further bone of contention was constituted by the Church: bishops were now Spaniards rather than *criollos*; the expulsion of the Jesuits from the domains of Charles III came as a heavy blow as the order had recruited very well in the American colonies; and, most recently, moves in the direction of disamortization (see below) had caused considerable economic disruption. Nor were they alone in this: a series of changes in the laws that governed trade between the empire, Spain and the rest of the world left local industries completely unprotected, undermined the position of many local merchant oligarchies and failed to satisfy the desire of planters and ranchers for wider access to the European market. Indeed, local manufactures were positively discouraged: on 17 June 1804 Lady Holland, who was at this point living in Madrid, confided to her diary that 'a *cédula* had lately been issued ordering all the cotton machines in Spanish America to be burned or destroyed'.[19] Finally, all this was buttressed by racial prejudice: European Spaniards looked down on the *criollos* as a community that had been irremediably tainted by its environment and become genetically, sexually and morally corrupt.

By the early 1800s, then, there was much discontent with Spanish rule, fed by a degree of intellectual and ideological stimulation from the writings of the Enlightenment and the example of the American Revolution (the French example, by contrast, had little impact: from Buenos Aires to Mexico City it seems to have evoked universal horror). But discontent was one thing and revolution quite another. The *criollos* might have increasingly been conscious of themselves as Americans, but on neither a continental nor a proto-national level was there any semblance of political organization. For the most part, the modern states of Latin America existed in neither map nor imagination, while the native elites were divided by distance and economic interest. Though strained by the pitiful depths to which Spain had slid under the tutelage of Charles IV and Godoy, emotional ties with the metropolis often remained very strong. But, above all, there was the issue of race. The *criollos* might have outnumbered the *peninsulares* (i.e. European-born Spaniards) by almost ten to one, but they were themselves outnumbered by the Negroes, Indians and people of mixed race who constituted the vast majority of the population by at least five to one. And they were terrified of them. If Madrid persisted with the sort of policy that had enabled many *pardos* and *mestizos* to buy the status of pure whites, what would become of their social predominance? Yet social and economic superiority came at a terrible price: in 1781 a large part of the central Andes had been ravaged by the great Indian revolt of Tupac Amaru, while the fate of the European inhabitants of St Domingue at the hands of the followers of Toussaint L'Ouverture was an object-lesson in the consequences of political disunity. Discontented they might be, but at the moment when Sir Home Popham appeared off Buenos Aires revolt was unthinkable.

By the time of Whitelocke's surrender, however, all this had changed. Britain's intervention in the South Atlantic had completely upset the premises on which continued Spanish rule had been based: the *criollo* oligarchy had discovered that they could assume responsibility for their own fate without at the same time precipitating the end of the world as they knew it. If the British had been resisted, it had been no thanks to the Spanish viceroy: a model of procrastination, indecision and coward-ice, he had been arrested and replaced by a substitute chosen from the ranks of such military talent as was available at Buenos Aires. Nor had resistance led to chaos: improvising an army on the basis of the cadres provided by the militias which had been the sole garrison of the Virrein-ato de la Plata, the *criollos* not only marched to victory, but found that *pardos*, *mestizos* and Negroes alike had all responded to their call. The masses, then, did not necessarily have to be fought, but could rather be co-opted, and the *criollos* further discovered that building an army was a wonderful means of cementing their social superiority: who else were the officers of the regiments that defeated the British if not the sons of the local elite? Even now revolt was not inevitable, but an important corner had been turned.

What of events in Europe? Here the campaign that followed Prussia's decision to join the war was dramatic indeed. Left all but unsuccoured, the Prussians would have done best to mass their army behind the river Elbe, but, exactly like the Austrians a year earlier, they elected to move forward and marched south-westwards into Thuringia. Invading Saxony in his turn, Napoleon got around their eastern flank and threatened their communications with Berlin. Desperate to escape the trap, the Prussians fled north-eastwards, only to collide with the *grande armée* along the river Saale. While Napoleon himself surprised a Prussian flank-guard that had been detached to watch the Saale at Jena, the corps of Marshal Davout, which was far out on the French right, suddenly found itself confronted with the main Prussian column under the Duke of Brunswick near Auerstädt. Faced by overwhelming odds, Davout pulled off one of the most extraordinary feats of the Napoleonic Wars. Feeding his three tired divisions – they had been marching all night – into line as they arrived, the marshal first checked the Prussian advance, and then launched a ferocious counter-attack that caused the increasingly demoralized enemy to disintegrate altogether. At Jena, meanwhile, Napoleon had been having a much easier time of it. Increasingly out-numbering the Prussians as the day went on, he first pressed the enemy back and then crushed them altogether by means of a great turning movement that overran their left flank and laid them open to a massed cavalry charge. A last-ditch counter-attack by a fresh corps that had just come up from the west made little difference and by dusk on 14 October the entire Prussian army had been beaten. 'The struggle was keen, the resistance desperate, above all in the villages and copses,' wrote one officer, 'but once all our cavalry had arrived at the front and was able to manoeuvre, there was nothing but disaster; the retreat became a flight, and the rout was general.'[20] As at Austerlitz, the emperor seized the moment to endear himself to his troops and refurbish the legend that he was but one more soldier. During the night before the battle he spent much time personally supervising the construction of a rough track that would allow the French to get artillery up onto the summit of the plateau on which the battle was fought before grabbing a little sleep in the midst of the imperial guard. All this is recalled by a then private of the imperial guard named Jean-Roche Coignet: 'The emperor was there, directing the engineers; he did not leave till the road was finished, and the first piece of cannon . . . had passed in front of him . . . The emperor placed himself in the middle of his square, and allowed [the soldiers] to kindle two or three fires for each company . . . Twenty from each company were sere sent off in search of provisions . . . We found everything we needed . . . Seeing us all so happy put the emperor in a good mood. He mounted his horse before day and went the rounds.'[21]

In view of the great debate that was precipitated by these events, it is worth pointing out that the Prussians were not defeated by either lack of enthusiasm among their soldiers or the supposed inferiority of their tactics. The defective system of military organization described above did not help as it ensured that no Prussian troops could compete with the French on equal terms. But what really lost Frederick William the Jena campaign was the chaotic situation that reigned in the high command. At best a mediocre leader, the commander-in-chief, the Duke of Brunswick, was hampered by the presence of Frederick William III on the one hand, and the hostility and resentment with which he was regarded by many of his fellow generals on the other. On top of this, though the army had recently been given a general staff, this body had been divided into three parallel sections, whose heads – Gerhard von Scharnhorst, Karl von Phull and Christian von Massenbach – all hated one another. Nor had the general staff been permitted completely to supersede the army's *Oberkriegskollegium* – the body responsible for the military's internal administration – in the elaboration of plans of campaign. As a result the unfortunate Brunswick was deluged with an endless variety of different schemes. A weak individual, he then proceeded to compound his problems by eschewing personal responsibility in favour of a series of councils of war that brought together his leading generals and advisers. In some respects the decision to advance was understandable: it meant that the troops could be fed by someone other than Prussia and it was the best way of proving to Britain and Russia that Prussia was in earnest. But the best chance of success was a swift and smashing blow into the heart of the French positions on the river

Main, designed to take advantage of the fact that Napoleon was not expecting Prussia to go to war, whereas Prussia's movements were in reality slow and indecisive. Plans were only adopted after vitriolic meetings lasting many hours, such as the one that was held at Erfurt on 5 October, and these hardly boosted the high command's cohesion. 'Scharnhorst,' recalled the staff officer, von Muffling, 'thanked heaven when, about midnight, the conference came to an end, as no result could be expected from such a meeting. No one who was present at it could deceive himself as to the issue of the war.'[22] And even then decisions were on a number of occasions modified or ignored, or communicated to the army in language so vague as to allow recalcitrant commanders to interpret them more or less as they thought fit.

The result could not have been more catastrophic: Brunswick's forces did not reach a position from which they could strike at the *grande armée* until the first days of October, although they could have hit the French a full month earlier. By October it was too late, for Napoleon's forces were now fully mobilized and on the move. Once the campaign had properly begun, moreover, the articulation of the Prussian forces broke down altogether. In the chaos, supplies dried up: 'For three whole days before the battle of Jena the troops had . . . no bread,' wrote Funck. 'They had to fight on empty stomachs.'[23] As for the battles, they broke every principle of the military art. At Jena Napoleon, who began the day with 46,000 men and ended it with some 50,000 more, was initially faced by a mere 38,000 men, and it was not until they had been shattered beyond repair that the 15,000-strong corps of General Rüchel – a force that had begun the day only a few miles to the west at Weimar, but had taken many hours to march to the sound of the guns – flung itself on the French. And at Auerstädt, the Prussians did not bring up all their overwhelmingly superior forces – Brunswick had 50,000 men to Davout's single corps of 26,000 – but rather launched a series of piecemeal assaults, the timid Frederick William proceeding to make matters far worse by insisting on keeping back a large reserve whose use might just have turned the balance in favour of the beleaguered Brunswick. Compare all this with the French camp. Napoleon resolved on war around 9 September, and had his men on the move on 8 October. From the start there was but one plan of operations – an offensive from the headwaters of the river Main north-eastwards towards the Saxon city of Leipzig and, ultimately, the key fortress of Magdeburg, that was designed to cut the Prussians off from Berlin – and within six days the *grande armée* had advanced a hundred miles or more. At this point Napoleon, it is true, completely misjudged the situation and came to the conclusion that the Prussians lay somewhere to the north of him when they were in fact on his left flank, but when the enemy's situation was revealed by cavalry reconnaissance such was the disposition of the *grande armée* that a flurry of orders was sufficient for its corps to change face on the march and start moving west across the river Saale. Nor was diplomacy forgotten, the emperor dispatching a letter to Frederick William whose honeyed words served to deepen the confusion in the king's tortured mind: 'Why shed so much blood? To what end? I have been your friend these six years ... Why let our subjects be slaughtered?'[24]

To return to the issue of Prussia, if Jena and Auerstädt were by no means a total disgrace, what followed was by any standards a catastrophe. No sooner had the guns fallen silent than the victorious French armies launched an invasion of Prussia that carried all before it. Broken into several fragments and reduced to a state of semi-starvation, most of what remained of the Prussian army was rounded up with hardly a fight, while many fortresses capitulated at the first summons (in fairness, it should be remarked that few of them were provided for a siege). Berlin fell without resistance on 24 October, and everywhere the populace remained quiet. As the governor proclaimed, 'The king has lost a battle. The first duty of the citizens is to keep quiet.'[25] Prussia was not yet out of the war – Frederick William had escaped to the east – while a little honour was salvaged by the gallant General Blücher, a fiery officer who had had a horse killed under him at Auerstädt and escaped capture only by dint of some desperate swordplay. Ordered to take command of another division and make for East Prussia, Blücher found the way blocked, yet unlike most of Prussia's generals, he did not lose hope. Shelter might yet be found in the coastal regions north of the river Elbe and with it the possibility of linking up with the Swedish forces in Stralsund or even a British expeditionary force. Meanwhile, a force based in this area might at least win time for the king to reach East Prussia, rally such forces as he could and join up with Russians. But such hopes proved short-lived. Harried all the way by French cavalry and desperately short of food and ammunition, Blücher got his ever-diminishing band of fugitives to Lübeck. Here, however, he was finally cornered on 6 November by Marshal Bernadotte, and after a desperate battle forced to surrender. As even the French recognized, it had been a good effort, but it did nothing to alter the awe-inspiring nature of Napoleon's triumph. For all that, Napoleon might have done well to note the reservations that were later expressed by one of the members of his council of state:

In France enthusiasm was at a peak: nothing could have appeared so incredible. However, in the middle of this most understandable atmosphere, one noted that a sentiment was gaining strength that thereafter never ceased to grow, a sentiment that the conqueror was far too much inclined to ignore and which yet would later do much to explain the misfortunes of the last days of his reign. France, beyond doubt, was proud of his victories, but she wanted to enjoy their fruits, and of these in her eyes the first ought to have been peace. Only moderation in victory could have achieved this result, and, generous as it is, the French character ensured that there was a general disposition to believe that that moderation existed. On all sides was to be found the belief that someone who had risen so high would not be found lacking in the only quality that could assure his conquests: with every battle that was won, with every town that was taken, the first assumption was that this new success offered the pledge of a peace that could not but be very close. Was that calculation reasonable? Above all, could it be accommodated with the character that might have been imputed to a man who for ten years had never ceased to risk the most redoubtable dangers, and had been followed by such rare good fortune? One might well have doubted it, but it must be said that the hope was understandable enough ... It is so natural to believe in that which we desire![26]

This desire for peace was not unknown to Napoleon, for it was hinted at by a delegation of the senate that travelled to Berlin to congratulate him upon his victories. Then, too, there was the Foreign Minister. As an acute German observer who had frequent dealings with French headquarters noted:

Talleyrand ... desired some political *rapprochement*. He regarded it as a possibility for the first time after the collapse of Prussia. The new English ministry still seemed undecided in its policy; the nation wanted peace ... It was only with reluctance, therefore, that Talleyrand had drafted the decree ... that was designed to bar every coast to the English [see below] ...

Talleyrand continued to buoy himself up with . . . hopes of convincing the English Cabinet, or of inducing it to recognize by pressure of public opinion, that many of the advantages arising out of the war might, on conclusion of peace, be shared by England. But it was essential that Napoleon should cease going on giving the English Cabinet a pretext, by his speeches no less than his measures, for reconciling the nation to their policy by the bugbear of his name. The objective on which Talleyrand staked all his efforts and all his influence was to persuade the emperor, even against his own inclination, to adopt an attitude of moderation.[27]

This, to put it mildly, was the vainest of hopes. Ensconced in Berlin amid the adulation of his generals, he had, after all, vanquished the ghost of Frederick the Great, whose great victory at Rossbach was now avenged. With the *grande armée* at the very peak of its performance, all this was reflected in his disposition: 'Having arrived in Berlin, Napoleon did not just speak and act as a victor moved by self-righteous anger, but affected the language and attitude of a sovereign who commands his subjects. Loyalty to the prince who had fled before him was treated as rebellion, and, angered by the defiance of certain nobles who had stayed in communication with that unfortunate monarch, in the palace of Frederick the Great himself he cried out, "I will bring these petty courtiers so low that they will be reduced to begging for their bread." His proclamations and bulletins constantly mixed insult with menace, whilst misfortune . . . was not even respected when it came to the person of the Queen of Prussia.'[28] Even before the fall of the Prussian capital, Napoleon had taken a hard line: a personal appeal for an armistice on the part of Frederick William was rejected out of hand, while the dispatch of a special envoy to the emperor's headquarters in the person of the erstwhile ambassador to Paris, Lucchesini, succeeded only in eliciting peace terms that were grim in the extreme. These terms were more or less those that the Prussians were forced to accept the following year but with the added demand that they should go to war with Russia if the latter should attack the Ottoman Empire, something that was by now almost certain. After much agonizing, Frederick William and his advisers screwed themselves up to accept these terms, only to discover immediately that no terms at all were on offer any more. Once again the Prussians were just too late.

In the wake of Jena and Auerstädt, the emperor seems to have envisaged Prussia in the role of a satellite state that could seal his eastern frontier against Russia, whose attitude to a continuation of the war could not yet be predicted with any certainty. On 1 November, however, a large Russian army crossed the frontier into Prussian Poland. Moved by the plight of Frederick William and Louise, for both of whom he had conceived a warm affection, and determined that Prussia should not make a separate peace with the French, Alexander had decided to re-enter the war. Beyond the issue of Prussia, meanwhile, was that of Germany: the abortive D'Oubril treaty had made the cost of peace without victory very clear to the tsar, and he was in consequence deter-mined to put an end to the Confederation of the Rhine. Napoleon could have peace, but the terms would in essence be those of Lunéville and Amiens. The Russian advance, of course, in turn raised the issue of Poland. Hitherto Napoleon had had little interest in the Polish question – indeed, it is clear that, had Russia recognized the gains that he had made since 1803, she could have had peace, for the emperor had no desire to wage a winter campaign in the depths of Poland. Continued war with Russia, however, transformed matters, for now Napoleon was free to lay claim to the mantle of hero and liberator. In the absence of any fear of provoking Russia, a Polish state could be restored and Poland's manpower made available to the *grande armée*. As yet no concrete assurances were given, for there were serious worries that going too far might provoke Austria into re-entering the war, but even so Napoleon summoned a number of Polish exiles to his presence and hinted that a serious military effort against Russia might well buy Poland her freedom. So far as Prussia was concerned, this meant that the terms that had been on offer were now obsolete, for she could no longer be guaranteed her lands east of the Elbe. Instead of a treaty, then, all that Frederick William's emissaries could obtain was a truce and even then one whose price would be the evacuation of Silesia and of Prussia's gains from the second and third partitions of Poland. To accept this, however, meant the certainty of peace being made over the heads of the Hohenzol-lerns, and this even the badly shaken Frederick William III could not accept. On 21 November Napoleon's terms were rejected, leaving Prussia's agony to drag on. As for the emperor, he had no hesitation in picking up the gauntlet thrown down by Alexander: on 5 November the first French troops entered Poland (it is noticeable that a special mission was simultaneously dispatched to Vienna to secure a declaration of

Austrian neutrality). For the *grande armée* the move was scarcely welcome. While cantoned in and around Berlin, the troops had lived a life of relative ease and plenty – many memoirs, indeed, comment on the seeming generosity with which they were treated by the local populace – but now things were very different:

It was . . . the beginning of a most terrible winter in a deserted country covered with woods and with roads heavy with sand. We found no inhabitants in the deserted villages . . . The weather was terrible: snow, rain and thaw. The sand gave way under our feet, and the water splashed up over the sinking sand. We sank down up to our knees. We were obliged to tie our shoes round our ankles with cord, and when we pulled our legs out of the soft sand, our shoes would stick in the wet mud. Sometimes we had to take hold of one leg, pull it out like a carrot, lift it forwards, and then go back for the other, take hold of it with both our hands, and make it take a step forwards also . . . The older men began to lose heart; some of them committed suicide rather than face such privations any longer.[29]

Once again, we see a hint of imperial overstretch. But to such problems Napoleon was blind. Convinced, as he put it, that 'impossible' was not a French word, his reaction was essentially one of irritation: 'The emperor showed some ill-temper . . . At Posen I saw him . . . mount his horse in such a rage that he vaulted right over it, and give his groom a cut with his whip.'[30] As for checking his course, in the autumn of 1806 there seemed no limit to Napoleon's capacity for extending the scope of his operations. We come here to the issue of the Continental Blockade. Despite Austerlitz and Jena, Britain remained unbowed. Hence the famous 'decree of Berlin' of 21 November 1806. Supreme at sea, Britain was to be defeated by the power of the land: throughout the territories ruled by or allied to France, all commerce with Britain was to be ended and all British ships and their cargoes seized. Such would be the financial and economic chaos that would then ensue, it was argued, that Britain would sooner or later be forced to surrender. There was, however, one problem with this scenario. No state could hope for peace with France unless it followed the Blockade's stipulations. Yet this was very hard. Many states might be prepared to accede to the decree for a time: the British had for years been interfering with the commercial freedoms of the Continent and their industry was advancing by such leaps and bounds that a measure of protectionism was welcome to many governments. But in the end there was no doubt that French soldiers would have to police the embargo, or at least force recalcitrants to accept its dictates. Not only had many goods supplied by Britain become staples of daily life – particularly colonial products such as sugar and tobacco – but the customs duties they brought were an important source of revenue. For many parts of Europe, too, Britain was an important market: from Spain and Portugal there came sherry, port and brandy, from Prussia wheat, and from Russia and Sweden naval supplies of all sorts. Yet the very concept of recalcitrance was an impossibility, for the policy's only hope of success was the closure of the whole of Europe to Britain's trade. Napoleon had committed himself to a course which had neither an end nor a point of return. Even worse was the fact that the blockade contained within it the seeds of a grand design of the most exploitative sort. British exports and re-exports were to be excluded from the Continent, certainly, but no attempt was ever made to exploit the situation for the benefit of the whole of Europe. On the contrary, the blockade was from the start an integral part of an economic policy designed to harness the rest of Europe to France's economic needs. In particular, French industry was to be protected and the rest of the Continent literally transformed into a captive market. In short, what the decree of Berlin presaged was nothing less than a Europe cast as a vast 'uncommon market' – a colonial empire – and a Napoleon bent on universal mastery.

Before the full implications of the Continental Blockade could be revealed, however, Napoleon still had a war to win. Protected by the onset of winter, Frederick William had retired to Memel, gathered around him the 20,000-strong garrison of East Prussia, and sanctioned a series of desperate efforts to remedy the defects of the Prussian army; meanwhile, in Pomerania and Silesia the dislocation brought by the passage of the *grande armée* and the desertion of many Prussian soldiers had given rise to a problem of public order so serious that it had almost become an extension of the Prussian war effort. As Funck remembers:

Prowling marauders infested the country from Breslau to Kolberg. The latter, it is true, as they were waging war on their own account, confined themselves to highway robbery, intercepting couriers and raiding moneys that small villages had collected to meet the French imposts . . . The inhabitants dreaded them more than the French themselves. But they might, if the Prussian government had given them a leader, have proved quite serviceable.[31]

In Stralsund 9,000 Swedish troops were ready to defend themselves against French attack, while Gustav IV himself remained defiant. As Lady Holland noted approvingly, 'The King of Sweden, though very wrong-headed and ill-gifted with . . . common sense, has some notion of honour . . . Bernadotte, either at Altona or Hamburg, made some overtures to the Swedish minister . . . [He] talked of the old alliance between France and Sweden and threw out hints of Bonaparte's willingness to give him Norway. The only notice the king . . . bestowed upon this was . . . to have the whole proceeding laid before the Danish government.'[32] And, last but not least, large numbers of Russians, perhaps 120,000 men, were in the process of marching to join the Prussians. With them was the British officer, Sir Robert Wilson, and according to him, officers and men alike were eager to avenge the defeat of Austerlitz. Referring to the subsequent decision of the Russian advance guard to fall back before Napoleon, he wrote, 'When Bennigsen retired from Yankova on the approach of Bonaparte and sought to evade the enemy by forced marches . . . the Russian murmur at retreat was so imposingly audacious, the clamour for battle so loud and reiterated . . . that Bennigsen was obliged to . . . soothe their discontents by an assurance that he was marching to reach an appropriate theatre of combat.'[33] Aided though he was by fresh German allies, most notably Saxony, which had changed sides, and Hesse-Kassel, which had hastily abandoned its initial neutrality, the emperor was none the less in a difficult position, particularly as it was by no means clear that Austria would not attack him in the rear. Nor could it be guaranteed that Britain would not send a force of troops to the Baltic. When the weary *grande armée* trudged into Warsaw on 28 November, its troops therefore had little hope of going quietly into winter quarters.

On one count at least, Napoleon need not have worried. If there was one direction from which no aid was to be expected, it was that of Great Britain. News of Jena and Auerstädt had caused little stir in political circles, there being a strong opinion that it was only to be expected. As Joseph Farington confided to his diary, '[James] Boaden I met while walking before dinner. We talked of the defeat of the Prussians. "What else", said he, "could be expected? The weaker are overpowered by the stronger." '[34] And amongst the Foxites, in particular, there reigned a mixture of glee and indifference. 'Let these devils punish one another,' wrote Sir Phillip Francis. 'I have no pity for any of them. Bonaparte is an avenging demon sent on purpose to scourge these nations for submitting to be the slaves and instruments of mean, barbarous tyrants who differ from him in nothing, but that, with equal malignity, they have none of his magnanimity and not the smallest portion of his abilities.'[35] Nor were such views confined to the radical wing of politics: himself a north German ruler, George III always had good reason to fear Prussia, and had been outraged by the loss of Hanover, while there was a general feeling among men like Grenville that Prussia simply could not be trusted. To these deep-seated prejudices there were now added reports of the most depressing kind. The first British envoy sent to Prussia, Lord Morpeth, had fled back to Britain in the wake of Jena and Auerstädt, and it was some time before a replacement reached Frederick William's refuge in Memel in the person of Lord Hutchinson. What he found there did not make for much in the way of confidence. There were few troops and the regime was bankrupt and the court in great disarray: one German eyewitness speaks of seeing 'the young and unfortunate Queen Louise, eyes reddened by tears, wandering through the muddy and badly paved streets of that little town with her children'.[36] All that was forthcoming was some £200,000 in treasury bills. This is understandable enough: confined to the poorest and most remote corner of his dominions, Frederick William would not have been able to do very much even with the most substantial bankroll. Yet amazingly, Grenville being determined to keep down government expenditure, the British applied the same thinking to Russia. Desperate for assistance, Alexander appealed for 60,000 muskets; the guarantee of a £6 million loan on the London market, of which £1 million was to be advanced straightaway in coin; and the dispatch of an expeditionary force to Western Europe. All he got was the muskets and £500,000 in silver, and £80,000 of that was confiscated by Sweden when the ship carrying it reached the agreed handover point of Göteborg, on the grounds that it was owed her for previous services. It was also made clear that this help was the product not of some new subsidy agreement but rather of the settlement of debts that were still outstanding from the deal of 1805. As for an expeditionary force, the dispatch of troops to South America had squandered Britain's only serious disposable reserve. Some more men might have been found, but this would have entailed major reductions in the garrison of the home islands and this in turn was a risk that the Talents were not prepared to take; meanwhile, there was in any case a serious shortage of transports. But if troops were out of the question, more money should have been dispatched, especially as February 1807 saw the last batch of reinforcements being sent to Buenos Aires. Nor is it easy to understand why no assistance was promised to Austria should she enter the war (as Russia was, in fact, pressing her to do). With Britain's credit badly damaged in Stockholm, Memel and St Petersburg alike, the episode was not one in which London could take much pride.

But this may be too sweeping a judgement. On the surface, coalition warfare had indeed revived in Eastern Europe, but observers in Britain had good reason to mistrust the Prussians and, quite possibly, the Russians as well. Napoleon had left one chink of light in his dealings with Frederick William III: if Prussia could prevail upon Britain and Russia to enter negotiations with Napoleon, then it was intimated that she might expect not only an armistice but favourable peace terms. Whether Napoleon was genuine in creating this impression is not relevant: implicit in the idea was the probability of a general international conference of the sort he so disliked, and it is probable that he just intended to sow confusion amongst his enemies and win time for French power to establish itself in Poland. Nor were the terms Napoleon intended to offer very promising, extending as they did to a recognition of the new order in Germany and Italy, the restoration of all the colonies taken by Britain to their original owners, freedom of the seas for all, the restoration of the *status quo ante* in Wallachia and Moldavia and a guarantee of the Ottoman Empire's independence and territorial integrity. That said, however, the fugitive Prussian court was quite ready to seize on whatever it was offered. Desperate to escape the war and restore what he nostalgically viewed as his partnership with Napoleon, Frederick William therefore dispatched an emissary to St Petersburg in the faint hope that Alexander would agree to fresh peace talks and get Britain to do the same. With this envoy – an aide-de-camp of the king's named Krüsemarck – went an impassioned appeal for Russia to see reason that painted Prussia's position in the starkest terms and expressed great hopes for the planned congress. The initial response was disappointing, but finally, much disillusioned with the British, Alexander did agree to a meeting provided, first, that Napoleon clearly laid out his terms and, second, that it took place in some neutral location. But in the end all this came to nothing: by the time Alexander's response reached Napoleon, January was already far advanced. With the *grande armée* now fully assembled in Poland, there was no need for further dissemblance. As Talleyrand wrote to Napoleon: 'The dispositions of the Russians depend upon events, and events depend on Your Majesty.'[37]

Still, the gesture had been a useful one, for gaining an extra month or so had mattered to Napoleon. In marching east, he had had strong hopes of further reinforcement. Although he seems privately to have been contemptuous of such aspirations, there were many Poles who not only were desperate to restore Polish independence, but also regarded France as a potential saviour. By liberating Poland, then, the emperor might secure a further source of manpower. The *grande armée* having been stretched increasingly thin, no sooner had Napoleon entered Warsaw than a junta of notables was established to administer the territories occupied by the French. No specific promises were given about the future, but at first it seemed that there was little need to do so: 'At Posen ... the grandees of Poland came to do homage to the emperor in their oriental costumes.'[38] Still smarting from the events of 1794, when a Russian army under Suvorov had stormed the eastern suburb of Praga and massacred a large part of the inhabitants, the Poles 'received us with enthusiasm as brothers and liberators'.[39] Chief among the collaborators was Prince Josef Poniatowski, a leading aristocrat who had been a hero of the war of 1794 but had latterly been courted by Frederick William III and appointed governor of Prussian-ruled Warsaw. But beyond that, Napoleon was disappointed: much of the aristocracy remained hostile and many Polish revolutionaries were convinced 'Jacobins'. Indeed, the leader of the insurrection of 1794, Tadeusz Kosciuszko, refused every blandishment to become involved, for, as the nationalist nobleman Oginski remarks, 'Whilst he respected Napoleon's military talents, he saw in him a conqueror consumed by ambition and a despot.'[40] Indeed, few of the elites were anything other than sceptical:

The friends of liberty asked themselves if one could expect the restoration of the republic of Poland from the hands of a man who had destroyed the liberty of his own country, and the wisest feared that Napoleon only saw the exaltation of the Poles as a means of obtaining men and subsidies for the execution of his ulterior projects.[41]

As for the common people, they were simply indifferent to the nationalist appeal (in this respect the famous legions that had fought for the French in the 1790s were but a flash in the pan, only about one fifth of the men involved actually being genuine Poles). As Marbot complained, 'The emperor . . . had hoped that the whole population of the country would now rise as one man at the approach of the French armies. But no one stirred.'[42] According to Marbot, this was because the French ruler would not openly declare the re-establishment of a Polish state, but the simple fact was that amongst the bulk of the population of Eastern Europe nationalism was nothing like a major force. Nor could Napoleon risk attempting to broaden the appeal of his regime by immediately decreeing, say, the abolition of feudalism, for to do so would have been to alienate the local nobility: if Poniatowski, for example, had rallied to the French, it was only because he wished to ensure that the control of affairs did not fall into the hands of radicals such as the commander of the Polish legions of the 1790s, General Dabrowski. In the event, sufficient men were found to raise three legions of 9,000 men apiece, but the whole affair has been much mythologized. Such recruitment as took place was in large part the fruit of poverty and despair, the fact being that the Polish 'war of liberation' of 1807 was to be no more a national war than its later German counterpart.

To return to the war with Russia, Napoleon did not follow up the occupation of Warsaw as rapidly as might have been expected, much time being needed to rest and re-equip the *grande armée* and gather the magazines needed for a winter campaign in an area of Europe that was particularly poor. Despite the fact that the Russian army was now concentrated only fifty miles to the north of Warsaw, it was not until 22 December that the French moved forward again, the plan being to envelop the Russian army in its positions between the rivers Ukra and Narew. However, the advance was slowed by atrocious weather, while the Russians bought time with a number of fierce delaying actions. Within a few days, indeed, it was clear that the Russians had got clean away and a frustrated emperor had no option but to order his exhausted and hungry troops to break off the pursuit and return to Warsaw. Sadly for the exhausted *grande armée*, the respite proved short-lived. Following the so-called 'manoeuvre on the Narew', the Russian army had acquired a new and much more aggressive commander in General Levin August von Bennigsen, and after less than a month he launched a sudden counter-offensive against the French left. Frantically concentrating his scattered forces, the emperor responded by striking northwards into East Prussia. Once again, however, the Russians escaped, and by early February the *grande armée* had been reduced simply to following up their retreat as they fell back northwards towards Königsberg. Initially, Bennigsen had hoped to get away without a fight, but on 7 February Napoleon caught up with him at Eylau, the result being perhaps the most dreadful battle of the entire French Wars. Always ferocious fighters who made lavish use of artillery, the Russians were not only ensconced in a strong defensive position, but could also expect help from a Prussian force that was marching to their aid, the total numbers of those engaged on each side probably being about equal. Attacking amidst howling blizzards, the French therefore ran into serious trouble. 'Several times during the day snow fell for an hour at a time in such quantities that we could not see two paces before us, and bodies of troops in movement lost their bearings ... Marshal Augereau was wounded and his corps, left without a leader, suffered horribly: his infantry, drawn up in squares, was positively annihilated where it stood.'[43] With their initial assaults thrown back, it was not until late afternoon that the French could make any progress, and even then their advance was checked by the timely arrival of the Prussians, who on this occasion fought very well. Had he held on through the night, it is possible that Bennigsen might have scored a notable defensive victory, but in the last resort his nerve failed him and he fell back on Königsberg. On the field of battle, meanwhile, there lay some 40,000 casualties, of whom 25,000 were French. It was a terrible scene. In the words of a French infantryman:

The countryside was covered with a dense layer of snow, pierced here and there by the dead, the wounded and debris of every kind; in all directions the snow was soiled by wide stains of blood, turned yellow by the trampling of men and horses. The spots where cavalry charges had taken place, and the bayonet attacks, and the battery emplacements [had stood] were covered with dead men and dead horses. The wounded of both nations were being removed with the aid of Russian prisoners, which lent a little life to this scene of carnage. Long lines of weapons, of corpses, of wounded men, showed the emplacement of each battalion. In short, no matter where one looked one saw nothing but corpses and ... men dragging themselves over the ground; one heard nothing but heartrending cries. I came away horror-struck.[44]

For Napoleon, Eylau was beyond doubt a sobering experience. Unusually, he was visibly shocked at the carnage, and made no attempt to pursue Bennigsen. Imperial propaganda did its best to call the struggle a victory, but even this claim was not beyond doubt. Ever since, indeed, there have been those who have argued that the battle of 7–8 February was in fact a defeat; after all, perhaps one third of the French troops who were engaged had fallen. And, but for certain errors on the part of Bennigsen, who at a number of crucial moments failed to exploit the tactical opportunities that he was offered, it certainly would have been a defeat. It is true that the myth of the emperor's invincibility was not quite shattered: the failure to secure outright victory could with some justice be blamed on the weather, the want of good roads and the mistakes and failures that marred the performance of some of his marshals. But the *grande armée* had clearly been shown to have its limits. Still worse, the troops were desperately short of food, while beneath the surface grumbling had risen to unheard-of heights. The war in Poland had never been popular – one song going the rounds had it that the *grande armée* had only crossed the Vistula to secure a throne for Jerome Bonaparte – and to make matters worse the emperor appeared to have lost his common touch. The sort of anecdotes that litter accounts of Austerlitz and Jena are largely absent from the story of Eylau. Therefore the morning after the battle resounded to cries of 'Long live peace!' and 'Peace and bread!', while the army remained in a sullen mood for months afterwards:

'His Majesty is coming', said our colonel at the moment of a review. 'I hope he will not be received as he was last time, and that the soldiers will cry "Vive l'empereur!". Look to it gentlemen: I shall hold you responsible if every man does not shout lustily.' We returned to our companies, paraphrasing the colonel's harangue, and the following were among the murmurs that we heard in the ranks. 'Let him give me my discharge and I'll shout as loud as they please . . . We have no bread: I can't shout on an empty stomach . . . We are owed six months' pay: why don't we get it?' The emperor arrived: the colonel and some of the officers shouted as though they would split their throats; the rest were silent.[45]

In private Napoleon was well aware of the desperate straits to which the *grande armée* had been reduced. As he wrote to Joseph Bonaparte:

Staff officers, regimental commanders, subalterns, nobody has had the clothes off their backs for the past two months, and some of them for the past four (I myself went for fifteen days without taking off my boots), and all this in the midst of snow and mud. There has been no bread, no wine and no brandy, and we have lived off potatoes and meat alone. Making long marches and countermarches without the slightest luxury, we have frequently had to fight at the point of a bayonet under a hail of canister, while the wounded have had to be evacuated in open carts over distances of up to fifty leagues . . . We have had to wage war with all its force and all its vigour.[46]

After spending some days making ostentatious efforts to succour the wounded, Napoleon pulled his men back and allowed them to take shelter in the towns and villages of a swathe of territory stretching as far back as the river Vistula, his own headquarters being established at the town of Finkenstein. Not surprisingly, there also followed talk of peace. Even before Eylau, the rigours of winter campaigning in the wastes of East Prussia and Poland had shaken the emperor's self-confidence sufficiently to attempt to isolate Russia to persuade her to make peace. On 29 January Frederick William had been offered peace in exchange for an alliance and, in particular, a Prussian guarantee of the Ottoman Empire. However, this overture was ignored – Frederick William could stomach the fresh war against Russia that it implied even less than the continued struggle with France – and in the wake of Eylau General Bertrand was therefore dispatched to the Prussian court with the offer of an immediate peace settlement. To secure this goal, Napoleon was prepared to drop the idea of a Franco-Prussian alliance, but, convinced by Hardenberg and others that the peace offer was almost certain to prove a trap, Frederick William stood firm, and the most that Bertrand could obtain was a promise to inform the Russians of Napoleon's desire for peace. Behind the scenes Frederick William did his utmost to persuade Alexander to take the French ruler at his word, while he also sent an emissary to Finkenstein in the person of General von Kleist on the pretext of arranging an exchange of prisoners. Such was Napoleon's despondency and state of nervous exhaustion – in his discussions with von Kleist he displayed considerable agitation and constant mood swings

– that he even resurrected the notion of a general peace conference. The price of such a conference, however, would be an armistice, and this alone was sufficient for Alexander to veto the idea when the plan reached him, for it was quite clear this would benefit the French more than the Russians. Beyond this, however, there was still no sign of any moderation on the part of Napoleon: Prussia, it seemed, was only to be restored in exchange for the surrender of Britain's colonial conquests. With the Russian forces still strong, it seemed preferable to fight on, leaving the wretched Frederick William no option but to tag along. As for Napoleon, another Eylau was not a pleasant prospect, but as in 1803 he could at least adopt a cloak of outraged innocence. In the words of the seventy-eighth bulletin of the Polish campaign: 'There is no pacific overture to which the emperor would not have listened; there is no proposition to which he would not have responded.'[47]

Eylau beyond doubt constitutes an interesting moment in Napoleon's development. A distinct shock to his system, it was countered by a vigorous propaganda offensive and even more vigorous search for a scapegoat. For various reasons, this turned out to be Marshal Bernadotte, who supposedly failed to act on orders that would have added his detached corps to the French battleline and given Napoleon the edge that he was so desperately lacking. There was nothing very new about this except in one particular: in a letter directed to Fouché in the aftermath of the conflict, the emperor told him to spread a series of false reports to the effect that the Russians had been beaten to their knees, and then in the very same breath informed the Minister of Police that they were 'true'. Even though Bernadotte and other generals might have made mistakes, to make that the excuse for Eylau was to beg the question of whether manoeuvres such as those of Ulm and Jena could ever really be replicated outside the very favourable logistical circumstances afforded by such areas as western and central Germany. To this incipient tendency for Napoleon to believe his own propaganda was added a growing want of balance. Whether it was in his interviews with foreign emissaries or his relations with the beautiful Polish countess, Maria Walewska, who was 'planted' on the emperor by a clique of noblemen eager to advance the cause of Polish independence, there were frequent outbreaks of rage and frustration. And, with all this, of course, went a commitment to wiping away the memory of failure: when Fouché wrote to him from Paris begging him to make peace at the earliest possible opportunity, his response was that he needed 'one more victory'.[48]

As the weeks passed, the *grande armée* began to recover its strength, and active operations began once more. Stralsund had been under siege since the end of January, and it was now joined by the Prussian strongholds of Danzig and Kolberg. And there was still no help to be had from Britain, whose leaders were now not only hamstrung by the pernicious effect of the expedition to Buenos Aires but also in receipt of the gloomiest possible account of the campaign from their representatives in the field. Thus, the British ambassador to Prussia, Lord Hutchinson, kept up a consistent tale of woe even when it was clear that Napoleon was in considerable difficulties, while his counterpart in St Petersburg, Lord Douglas, was a Foxite convinced that resistance to France was futile. To make matters worse, both men lacked personal charm and offended or otherwise alienated many of those with whom they came into contact. Not favoured with much in the way of news or confidences, they slipped ever deeper into diplomatic paranoia and saw treason on all sides. Some effort was made to persuade Austria to fight, but even then subsidies were only offered in the event of Vienna actually entering the war. As Lord Holland rather disingenuously put it, 'We studiously disclaimed ... all disposition to induce the latter power to declare war by subsidies. Our policy was to succour those states who would voluntarily resist the power of France, but not to bribe them to engage in the contest ... The quarrel, we said, must be her own, the cause must be her own, and, if she were not, from a sense of her own wrongs and dangers, prepared to make a national war against France, it was neither our interest nor our wish to engage her in hostilities.'[49] With nothing on offer from Britain, the result was a foregone conclusion: the substantial party in the Austrian court that was opposed to any resumption of hostilities was easily able to maintain the upper hand. This is not to say that Vienna remained completely aloof. On the contrary, Austria clearly had a strong vested interest in clipping the wings of the Napoleonic eagle. Mobilizing an army of 80,000 men in Bohemia to give weight to her stance, her new chancellor, Philipp von Stadion, pressed Napoleon to accept Austrian mediation and even elicited a hint to the effect that an international peace congress would not be opposed by him. Yet this meant nothing: all that the emperor wanted to do was to keep Austria quiet while there was little prospect of him accepting any peace proposals that did not translate into complete victory for France.

In the main theatre of operations, then, Britain's influence was negligible. Only in the Mediterranean were things any different. Here there were both ships and troops aplenty and the opportunity to make use of them in a manner that was both safe and effective. What is more, the Talents even had a strategy. By means of the application of British seapower, they would compel the Turks to make peace with Russia and thereby free General Ivan Mikhelson's army for operations in Poland. As early as November 1806 a British squadron had been dispatched to the Bosporus under Admiral Duckworth. But fighting was not deemed a likely possibility: British men o'war, it was cheerfully assumed, would simply have to appear in the Sea of Marmara for the Turks to cave in. Yet nothing of the sort occurred. An advanced guard of three ships-of-the-line, a frigate and a sloop penetrated the Dardanelles without resistance and anchored off Constantinople, but the Porte showed no signs of giving way: on the contrary, they massed large numbers of guns to fire on Duckworth's ships. In an attempt to exert greater pressure and to rescue the first group of ships, on 19 February 1807 Duckworth entered the Sea of Marmara. There was some resistance but nothing of any importance, and talks were soon under way. Almost immediately, however, it became clear that the Turks were merely playing for time. There being nothing for it but to cut and run, on 28 February Duckworth set sail for the Dardanelles. Much reinforced, the Turkish gunners stationed there cannonaded his ships as they passed through and inflicted a certain amount of damage as well as some 300 casualties. If Duckworth's retreat was embarrassing, what followed was even worse. To put further pressure on the Turks, the garrison of Sicily had been ordered to send an expedition to Egypt. Very soon, then, 6,000 men had been disembarked near Alexandria, where they were soon joined by Duckworth and his ships. Again there had been a strong belief that there would be no resistance, but this proved a false hope. With large Turkish forces gathering on all sides, an attempt was made to secure the vital agricultural resources of the Nile delta, but two attempts to take the coastal port of Rosetta were beaten off with heavy losses. For some months the British clung on to Alexandria, but by late August they were under siege, the city eventually being evacuated on 14 September. In fairness, it has to be said that the absence of the troops involved made little practical difference to the course of the war, for another Maida-style descent on Italy would not have done much to affect the situation in Poland, other than perhaps deprive Napoleon of a few reinforcements. But the diplomatic consequences were bad enough. Allowed to land on the mainland unsuccoured, a Neapolitan attempt to invade Calabria was crushed at Mileto on 28 May and the French were enabled to claim that the British had once again placed selfish imperial objects above the interest of their allies.

Yet sending troops to mainland Europe did present many problems. So long as they remained fairly close to the coast, relatively small forces of British troops could operate with relative ease, although in northern Europe, at least, they could only hope to survive if they were acting in conjunction with field armies belonging to one or more of the great powers. For a substantial field army, however, the situation was very different. What it required, like any similar force, was a secure strategic base – an area in which it could establish permanent hospitals and magazines and rely on supplies of all sorts, not to mention baggage animals and transport (unlike the French army, the British did not maintain a permanent baggage or artillery train, and instead relied on hiring the necessary animals and wagons locally). If such a base could be established on enemy territory, all well and good, but in 1807, except perhaps in the extreme south of Italy, this was simply unthinkable. All that was left, then, was the territory of friendly states – Sicily or, just possibly, Portugal – but this required a considerable sacrifice of sovereignty on the part of the state involved, and an equally considerable degree of harmony between the two powers. In Sicily this was not forthcoming. The king and queen and their leading courtiers uniformly blamed the British for the loss of the mainland in 1806, and had only to look to Gibraltar, Menorca, Corsica and, most recently, Malta to see examples of the way in which British presences in the Mediterranean had a way of becoming permanent. Particular fury, meanwhile, had been caused by Sir John Stuart's refusal to march on Naples after the battle of Maida. To quote the commander of the Neapolitan army, Roger de Damas:

The political and military character of the English ... makes them unique as a nation ... It was in their power to conquer Naples – it is so still. They overcame all the obstacles that might have made it impossible, and deliberately retraced their steps as soon as those obstacles were safely passed. Their inexplicable conduct cannot fail to give them a reputation for being very dangerous allies. Not one of their calculations is ever influenced by higher considerations. Their whole policy is a rule of mercantile algebra, and we have not yet seen an English general whom self-respect or honour or enthusiasm can move to go beyond his orders . . . General Stuart, it seems, came to Calabria with the sole object of erecting scaffolds and preparing tortures, to which from that fatal moment the unfortunate and too credulous Calabrians were abandoned . . . Sicily occupied by the English is merely a kind of maintenance-allowance granted to a Nabob . . . The English are . . . shameless in their exactions . . . and every moment some fresh bitterness is added to the discomfort of the unfortunate sovereigns.[50]

British complaints of Neapolitan hostility were legion, and relations were not helped by the perception that the Sicilian administration was not just obstructive, but also incompetent and corrupt. Here Lord Holland is typical: 'In Sicily the misgovernment of the court was daily endangering our interests. The queen, as she advanced in years, grew more ungovernable in her revenge and not more moderate in the indulgence of other passions.'[51] Then there are the views of Sir John Moore, for whom the queen was 'violent, led by her passions, and seldom influenced by reason'; King Ferdinand, 'an indolent man, hating business'; and the chief minister, Circello, 'quite an old goose'.[52] This is not to say that the British did not have a point. The attitude of the court towards its Sicilian domains was disdainful in the extreme; Maria Carolina was wildly extravagant and inclined to favour a variety of dubious favourites; the court and administration were dominated by emigrés from the mainland; recruitment to the army was at a complete standstill; and, to cap it all, the queen was suspected of maintaining secret contacts with the French. All this was an unacceptable threat to the garrison's security and the response of the Talents was to tighten the screw: the British ambassador was authorized to stop the subsidy received by the regime of Ferdinand and Maria Carolina as well as to demand the removal of certain figures from the court or even the exile of the queen herself. Thus the scene was set for a long conflict that was to last for most of the war.

How this dilemma was resolved is something that must be left for another chapter. For the time being, what matters is simply that no

British army landed on the Continent. Battered and bleeding though he was, Napoleon was allowed to recover the initiative. Despite an attempt to relieve Danzig from the sea, by the end of May 1807 it had fallen to the French, while at Stralsund a truce negotiated in April effectively put an end to fighting there as well. In consequence, all that was left to the Allies on the Baltic coast anywhere west of Königsberg was Kolberg, where, in a desperate stand that was later much mythologized, Gneisenau continued to hold out until the end of hostilities in July. From the beginning of the year onwards depressing news had also been coming in from Silesia, where a series of Prussian garrisons, of which the most notable was Breslau, had been blockaded by the French since the beginning of the year and were gradually being mopped up. At the same time, the arrival of substantial French reinforcements meant that the Allies were heavily outnumbered: in comparison with 220,000 imperial troops, the Russians had only some 115,000 men in the field, while almost no Prussian forces remained other than a few garrison and second-line units. Yet Bennigsen would still not give up and the beginning of June brought a fresh Russian offensive. Before we examine this, however, we must first spare a few words for the peace negotiations that marked the relative lull in operations that had followed Eylau. Yet again there was a disposition to come to some arrangement with Napoleon that ill accords with the idea of a general crusade against his rule. On 21 April, Frederick William wrote a letter to Napoleon on behalf of Prussia, Russia and Britain, proposing that a congress should be held in neutral Copenhagen to negotiate a peace settlement that would be not only stable but also honourable to all parties. No specific terms were laid down for this settlement, but evidence of the Allies' moderation may be found in a specific promise to respect the integrity of the Ottoman Empire and a hint that Britain might be made to surrender her colonial gains. To this Napoleon replied that the Ottomans, who had deliberately been excluded from the proposed conference, must also be admitted. This demand was accepted by the Allies, but the fact that Napoleon had made it kindled deep-rooted concerns about his good faith. Let us here quote Frederick William:

It cannot be disguised that . . . it will only be by the most vigorous pursuit of the war . . . that we can succeed. The consequences which Napoleon will perhaps draw from the proposed basis may be such as, far from facilitating the general peace, only make it more and more distant, especially if he regards himself as master of the part of ... Europe he now occupies and thinks to establish a system of compensation upon this state of occupation ... But to refuse the opening of the congress would be to play into the hands of Napoleon ... We must therefore ... hasten it as much as possible ... But ... this determination of the powers at war with France ought not to excuse any of them from vigorously pursuing operations against the common enemy.[53]

If a lasting peace was to be achieved, it could only be obtained on the battlefield – hence the advance of Bennigsen's army. There followed nearly two weeks of complicated manoeuvring. Caught off balance, Napoleon redeemed the situation by spreading false intelligence implying that a large force of French troops had outflanked the Russians and was about to fall on their rear. Having initially plunged many miles southwards from his starting point south of Königsberg, Bennigsen obligingly lost his nerve and hastily retraced his steps, thereby giving the emperor time to pull his forces together and send them into action. Spooked though he may have been, the Russian commander was still full of fight and inflicted a bloody nose on the French at Heilsberg on 10 June. Thus encouraged, he then launched a major counter-attack at the town of Friedland. Thus far he had conducted quite a skilful campaign, but this move proved a serious mistake. Bennigsen believed that the French troops facing him constituted little more than a division, but he soon found himself embroiled with the entire *grande armée*, and the battle that followed shattered the Fourth Coalition beyond repair. To attack the French, Bennigsen had had to move his entire army across the river Alle, of which the only crossings available were the single bridge at Friedland, three pontoon bridges and a minor ford. Still worse, his positions were overlooked by higher ground, and divided by a sizeable stream that ran down to the river just north of the town, while his army was badly outnumbered. No sooner had the French attacked, then, than the Russians were forced steadily back. As might have been expected after Eylau and Heilsberg, the action was no walkover. Lejeune paid tribute to the defenders' 'superhuman efforts'; Coignet wrote, 'The Russians fought like lions: they preferred to be drowned rather than surrender'; while, for Sir Robert Wilson, 'Never was resolution more heroic or patience more exemplary than that now displayed by the

Russians.'⁵⁴ But by nightfall it was all over: having suffered at least 20,000 casualties and been reduced to a state of the utmost confusion, Bennigsen's army was in no fit state to fight on, while Alexander was driven to abandon Königsberg and forced to ask for an armistice. As for Napoleon, he was exultant. 'Friedland,' he proclaimed to an aide-de-camp, 'is worth Austerlitz, Jena and Marengo, the anniversary of which I celebrate today!'⁵⁵

If Friedland had been a shattering blow to Alexander, it was not the only reason why he decided to make peace. He suspected that the British had designs on Egypt, resented their failure to force the Dardanelles, and could not but feel that they had set far more store on Britain's interests in the wider world than they had on the struggle in Europe. Such suspicions were not helped by the fact that in the spring of 1807 London was besieging Alexander with demands that Russia should renew an exceedingly favourable commercial agreement that had been negotiated between the two powers some years before and was now about to expire. On 26 March, true, the more vigorous Portland admin-istration (headed, as its name suggests, by Lord Portland) had supplanted the Talents amidst much talk of both a substantial increase in subsidies and a British expeditionary force, but this was a question of too little, too late while there was in any case no way that troops could be got to the Baltic in the short term. Less important but just as irritating, mean-while, were the actions of the Swedes, who, as well as seizing the £80,000 referred to above, had failed to provide Kolberg and Danzig with all the naval support that might have been expected. Sent to Alexander's headquarters with assurances of aid, the British envoy, Leveson-Gower, was subjected to a veritable tirade:

I was interrupted by the emperor, who . . . said he was persuaded of the good intentions of the English government . . . but that he had to complain of the whole burden of the war having fallen upon his armies . . . that hopes had been held out that a British force would be sent to . . . Germany – month after month, however, had passed, and no troops were even embarked – that the Russian army had by its bravery hitherto maintained the contest and in every battle which had been fought had gained an advantage . . . but that it ought not to be forgotten that the chances of war were uncertain, and that this was the last act of the great drama which had occupied the attention of the world for the last fifteen years.⁵⁶

If Alexander was thoroughly disillusioned by the summer of 1807, irritation was not the only motive for his conduct. Much of the Russian court and nobility were pressing for peace – an ominous development given the fate of Paul I. In addition, the mobilization of large numbers of men both for the regular army and for a new militia known as the *opolcheniye* had given rise to a shortage of manpower in the countryside. Tramping across Russia en route for a depot at Kaluga, one prisoner of war noted, 'All the soldiers were away with the army after vast levies had been raised in this enormous empire for the campaign of 1807. Often because of the lack of soldiers, we had women as our escorts and these were usually as old as possible ... At this time of year every ... man, woman and child old enough to work was busy in the fields.'[57] And in the Balkans the spring of 1807 had produced, if not a series of Russian reversals, then at least a period of fierce fighting that suggested a long and difficult war. Narrowly defined in terms of immediate dynastic interest, Russia's foreign-policy aims did not even in themselves require a war with France. The establishment of a Russian sphere of influence in Eastern Europe presupposed the partition of Poland and the Ottoman Empire, but did not stand in the way of French control of Belgium, the Rhineland, Germany or northern Italy, or, for that matter, a French presence in the Balkans. Given that France and Russia had a common interest in combating Britain's pretensions on the high seas, peace with France might even be turned to profit. As for the alternative policy – that of building a coalition against Napoleon and striving for some general settlement – this had, it was felt, been given a fair trial and proved wanting. In a convention signed with Prussia at Bartenstein on 26 April in which the signatories had pledged not to make a separate peace, Alexander had set forth peace terms which he regarded as a model of moderation and forbearance. Russia herself would obtain no territory from the war; Prussia would be restored minus Hanover but with frontiers that were more secure in other respects; Germany would be confederated in a new body headed conjointly by Austria and Prussia; Austria would get back the Tyrol and her gains in Venetia; and the Ottoman Empire would receive a guarantee of her frontiers and the restoration of her authority in Moldavia and Wallachia. The Bonapartes, by contrast, would keep Naples, Piedmont and Holland, but only if compensation was found for their erstwhile rulers. But neither Austria, whom it was hoped might thereby have been attracted to join the Fourth

Coalition, nor Britain showed the slightest interest in these terms: both of them saw the new Germany envisaged by the convention of 26 April as little more than a cloak for Prussian aggrandizement (and rightly so, this part of the agreement having very much been the work of the Prussian chancellor, Hardenberg). The consequence was profound disillusionment in the mind of the tsar (who seems to have been completely blind to the manner in which he had been manipulated by the Prussians) and with it a conviction that he should concern himself with Russia and Russia alone.

Curiously enough, developments in the French camp were at this very moment paving the way for such a move. Now that Friedland had wiped away the memory of Eylau, Napoleon was anxious to make peace: not only did the morale of his forces continue to show evidence of strain, but East Prussia was no place to subsist the *grande armée*, as well as being a long way from the heartlands of the empire should, say, Austria decide to go to war. Beyond this, meanwhile, there is the question of his attitude towards Russia. According to the nineteenth-century French historian Albert Vandal, 1807 saw the French emperor come to the conclusion that the only means of securing peace in Europe – by which both he and Vandal meant overthrowing Britain and securing the French imperium on the Continent – was to secure a lasting alliance with Russia. The only one of the continental powers with whom France had no real quarrels, Russia was also the only one of them that she could not beat outright. As experience had shown that neither Prussia nor Austria could be trusted in such a role, the only possibility was a deal with Alexander I. Indeed, it seems that Napoleon had been thinking of this for some months. As he had written to Talleyrand on 14 March, 'I am of the opinion that an alliance with Russia would be very advantageous.'[58]

At the time that he penned these remarks, Napoleon had deemed such an alliance unlikely, and he had therefore continued to spin his web against Russia: one of the actions he took at his headquarters of Finkenstein was to sign a treaty of alliance with the emissary that had been sent to him from Persia, Mirza Muhamed Riza Qazvini. But in the wake of Friedland everything changed. The events that followed are well known. On 25 June Napoleon and Alexander met on a specially constructed raft moored in the centre of the river Niemen at Tilsit. As remembered by one Russian participant, it was a splendid scene and yet at the same time a very tense one:

Almost everyone was in parade uniform. [Alexander] was wearing the Preo-brazhensky regiment's uniform . . . He had on white pantaloons and short boots. His . . . hair was powdered white. He wore a high hat with cockade and a black plume. A sword at his side, a sash tied around his waist and the blue ribbon of the Order of Saint Andrew completed Alexander's dress . . . My eyes did not leave [him]. I felt that he was concealing, with an artificial calm and a relaxed attitude, the true feelings that lay beneath the surface of his open and benevolent features. He was about to greet the greatest man of the time – military leader, politician, lawgiver and administrator – a man with a dazzling aura as a result of his astounding, almost legendary career. This was also the man who had conquered the whole of Europe in the last two years and defeated our army twice, and who now stood on the very borders of Russia. He was coming face to face with a man renowned for captivating people, endowed with an extraordinary ability to size up and take measure of his opponents. It was more than just an interview; through this meeting Alexander had to charm the charmer, seduce the seducer and outwit an acknowledged genius . . . Barely half an hour had elapsed when someone came into the room and announced, 'He is coming, Your Majesty.' An electric spark of curiosity coursed through us all. The emperor rose nonchalantly and . . . went outside with a calm face and measured step. We burst pell-mell from the room and dashed down to the shore to see Napoleon galloping at full speed between two ranks of his Old Guard. His escort and suite consisted of at least 400 men on horseback. The roar of enthusiastic greetings . . . was deafening even on the opposite bank of the Niemen.[59]

Though the French ruler stole a psychological march on Alexander by ensuring that he got to the raft first and in consequence assumed the role of host, friendly relations were soon established: Napoleon, in particular, appears to have made the greatest possible effort to charm the impressionable Alexander. Aided perhaps by the intimacy of their first meeting, which took the form of a private conversation in a pavilion that had been pitched on the raft, there seems to have developed a genuine personal empathy based in the case of Alexander on hero worship, and in the case of Napoleon on something that seems to have come close to physical attraction. Alexander was beyond doubt flattered outrageously by Napoleon, not least in being allowed to adopt the role of saviour of Prussia (Frederick William and Louise, by contrast, were openly cold-shouldered by him even when the latter turned on the full force of her considerable charm and beauty).

For all the courtly gestures, however, the realities of power were very clear. Whether it was in the glittering array that rode down to the Niemen with Napoleon, the soldiers of the Guard – a force that had hardly fired a shot in the campaign and was in consequence in the most beautiful order – that lined the road to the river, or the constant parades, field days and reviews, Alexander was left in no doubt of the power of the French war machine. Yet in a sense the show of force was unnecessary. The tsar knew he had no option but to take what terms he could get, and found that on the surface at least they were not too unfavourable. Unlike most of Napoleon's victims, Russia was required to surrender neither money nor territory – indeed, she actually obtained a sizeable slice of Prussian Poland – but she did grant Napoleon a free hand in Europe, recognize the Napoleonic settlement in Italy, Germany, the Low Countries and Poland, agree to French occupation of the Ionian islands and Cattaro and effectively commit herself not only to joining the Continental Blockade and going to war with Britain, but also forcing Sweden, Denmark and Austria to do the same. Concealed here was French acquiescence in a descent on Swedish Finland, while Russian hegemonism was also flattered by an agreement to dispatch a large army against Persia as a first step in a march on India. As for the Russo-Turkish War, Napoleon would mediate a settlement, and then go to war with Constantinople should it prove obdurate (to get around the problem of France's alliance with Turkey, it was claimed that this had been the fruit of a personal accord between Napoleon and Selim III, the point here being that the latter had been toppled in a palace coup on 27 May). Beyond this there is no record of what was decided, but it is generally assumed that there was a common understanding that France's intervention would be followed by the partition of the whole of the Balkans. Whether Russia would get out of all this the peace and security that Alexander hoped for was a moot point, but for Britain it was a bitter blow. To quote a private letter penned by the new British Foreign Secretary, George Canning, to the British ambassador to Constantinople, 'The peace with France is as little so as we could wish ... If after all France is peremptory, and Bonaparte retains at [St] Petersburg ... all the influence which he acquired over the emperor's mind at Tilsit, we must be prepared for the worst . . . Make our peace with Turkey as soon as you can.'[60]

Setting Britain's difficulties aside, on the surface at least, Russia did quite well out of Tilsit and Alexander came away believing that Napoleon was both friend and partner. In the first place, it was not just Turkey that had been betrayed but also distant Persia. As we have seen, contacts had been steadily improving between Napoleon and the Shah, and on 4 May 1807 a treaty signed at Finkenstein had duly committed France to guaranteeing the integrity of the Persian empire, recognizing Georgia as a possession of Persia and forcing the Russians to withdraw to their original frontiers. All this, however, had been ignored at Tilsit, and the French mission to Tehran was thereafter in effect abandoned to its own devices. Though instructed to maintain friendly relations with the Persians in the hope of keeping the way open for a future invasion of India, its head, General Gardanne, was given no support other than a tardy letter to the Shah full of empty promises. In February 1808 he was authorized to mediate between the Persian government and its Russian assailants, and in April an armistice was signed that temporarily brought hostilities to an end. Realizing the fragility of their position, the Persians made the most of the few cards they had and explicitly warned the French that the consequence of abandoning them would be a growth in British influence. This, however, availed them nothing at all: at Erfurt (see below) the subject of Persia was again avoided, while the Russians were allowed to resume hostilities. As for the Gardanne mission, in February 1809 it left Persia for home, an angry Shah being left to sign a treaty of friendship with Britain whereby he committed himself to resist any attempt to send troops across his territory towards India in exchange for British support against Russia (consisting of nothing very substantial, this could not change the fact of Russian military superiority, though it was not until 1813 that the Persians finally gave up the struggle and surrendered all claim to Georgia). Much of this lay in the future, but even so Alexander had good reason to hope that Persia would be left to him to settle as he wished. Nor was this an end to the advantages offered him by Tilsit. The negotiations with Napoleon also promised victory in the Balkans. At Tilsit the Russians had agreed to sign an armistice with the Turks, and on 24 August such an agreement had duly been negotiated at Slobosia. Apparently misled by the account of the Tilsit agreement given him by the Turkish plenipotentiary, Galib Efendi, into believing that the Danubian provinces were to be given back to the Porte, General Mikhelson had initially accepted that Wallachia and Moldavia should be evacuated, but when news reached Alexander he had refused to ratify the peace terms and ordered his troops to remain put until such time as a formal treaty had been negotiated. The Turkish forces having all withdrawn in accordance with what had been agreed at Slobosia, the Russians could therefore look on Moldavia and Wallachia as safely in their sphere of influence.

No such satisfaction could be felt in Prussia. She was forced to pay a heavy indemnity, maintain a large French garrison, recognize the Confederation of the Rhine, now expanded to include the whole of Germany apart from herself and Austria, accede to the Continental Blockade, and accept the loss of half her territory. Her western territories (except, in the first instance, Hanover) were used to create Westphalia, a new state centred on Kassel that went to Napoleon's brother, Jerome, and to augment Berg and Holland, both of which got small frontier districts. As for the bulk of Prussian Poland, this was used to create a reborn Polish state known as the Grand Duchy of Warsaw, that was placed under the rule of the King of Saxony (as noted above, a district in the east centred on Bialystok went to Russia). Until the indemnity was paid, the rump of Prussia – a territory that was all but entirely indefensible and for the most part very poor – was to be occupied by French troops. The actual size of the indemnity was not stipulated, however, and thus it was that Napoleon was left free to set it at so high a price that Frederick William would never be able to rid himself of the *grande armée*. As for Prussian influence in Germany, it was reduced to nothing. This was rammed home in the treatment meted out to the few states that had to the end remained under Potsdam's sway. Oldenburg, the two Mecklenburgs and Saxony were given their independence, but only at the price of joining the Confederation of the Rhine, while Hesse-Kassel and Brunswick were swallowed up by Westphalia. In short, the entire edifice of Hohenzollern power was at an end. Well might a shattered Blücher write, 'My heart sobs over the disaster which has fallen on the state and upon my master.'[61] As for Frederick William, he could only fume impotently, describing Napoleon as 'that monster choked out of hell, formed by Beelzebub to be the scourge of the earth'.[62]

Tilsit, then, found the Napoleonic empire at what proved to be its zenith. Napoleon himself was the unchallenged ruler of a much enlarged

France; French potentates had been placed on the thrones of Holland, Berg, Westphalia, Naples and the Kingdom of Italy; Germany and Switzerland were entirely under French control; and Spain had become a humble ally, albeit a somewhat fractious one. Britain could still count on Sweden, but her supremacy at sea had availed her very little. Not only had she failed to make any impact at all in the campaigns of October 1806 to June 1807, but her various expeditionary forces had come to a bad end. As for her vigorous response to the Continental Blockade, the Orders in Council which resulted would plunge Britain into fresh complications over the tight controls they imposed on neutral shipping. With Napoleon in control of much of the European coastline, the future was distinctly uncertain. What would occur next was, of course, impossible to say. But such was Britain's predicament it is entirely possible that she would have been forced to give in. Fortunately for the Portland administration, however, their opponent was not a rational European statesman, but Napoleon. If he had only allowed Russia to believe that she was a French partner rather than a French vassal, the emperor might have won the war, but, exactly as had been the case in 1803, he could not let matters be. If England stood all but alone, it was therefore fairly clear that she would not do so for very long. As the British ambassador to Vienna remarked most prophetically to Stadion, 'these fresh successes [will] lead probably to fresh pretensions on the part of France', and persuade Napoleon, 'to whom no project [seems] preposterous or impossible', to 'adopt that of carrying his army into the heart of Russia and attempt to dictate the law even at Saint Petersburg'.[63]

7

Across the Pyrenees

There are few historians who would deny the significance of the period immediately after Tilsit in the history of Napoleon Bonaparte. It was at this point that the emperor was drawn to intervene in the affairs of the Iberian Peninsula, and thereby to spark off a chain of events that are traditionally held to have had a major role, if not *the* major role, in the downfall of the French imperium. Why, then, did Napoleon reach out across the Pyrenees? The reasons which led him to intervene in Spain and Portugal are not entirely clear. Many authors have assumed it was always the intention of the emperor to move south, while others have suggested that the idea first entered his mind at the time of the battle of Jena. It is possible to mount a case for both positions. The former has at its heart the undeniable fact that by 1807 Charles IV had become the last representative of the Bourbon family to retain his dominions intact. As such, he was a constant reminder to the parvenu Bonapartes of their want of legitimacy and, still worse, a potential encouragement to royalist subversion. Beyond that, it might also be argued that, as product of and heir to the French Revolution, Napoleon could not but be committed to smashing the symbols of the system that it had overthrown. At least this was the opinion of Talleyrand: 'Napoleon, seated on one of the thrones of the house of Bourbon, considered the princes who occupied the other two as his natural enemies, whom it was his interest to overthrow.'[1] Another confidant of the emperor to hold this view was the commander of the Imperial Guard, Marshal Bessières. As he told one of his aides-de-camp, 'So long as Napoleon remains in power, no European throne can be filled by a Bourbon.'[2] Yet another variant on the theme came from the Conde de Toreno, a veteran of the *cortes* of Cádiz who wrote the standard Spanish history of the contest. According to him, the key was historical precedent and example: the

French 'had never forgotten the foreign policy of Louis XIV, and, in particular, his attempts to harness the Spanish nation to the wagon of his fortune'.[3] There is some sense in this: if the policy of Napoleon remained faithful to that of Louis XIV in the Low Countries and Germany, as it did, why should this not have been the case for the Iberian Peninsula, and all the more so as Charlemagne – a figure who was a far greater influence on Napoleon than the 'sun king' – had also looked beyond the Pyrenees? To all this there can be added the fact that in the France of 1807, the notion of an attack on Spain was certain to enjoy wide popularity. Spain, it was said, was not just a natural zone of French influence, but a fruit ripe for the picking.

This can be described as the structuralist argument. But what of the alternative position, which might in turn be deemed the functionalist view? There is the equally undeniable fact that in the autumn of 1806 Spain had come very close to betraying her alliance with France. To explain this something must be said about Spain's experiences in the period 1796–1807. For the whole of this time, Madrid had been in alliance with Paris and, by the same token, usually at war with Britain. From this, however, she had gained nothing: not only had her diplomatic interests been repeatedly flouted, but her entire position as a world power had been thrown into jeopardy. The loss of much of her fleet at Trafalgar left her with few means of physically remaining in touch with her far-flung dominions, let alone keeping them under her control. Indeed, to keep any share of the colonial trade at all from 1796 onwards Madrid had been forced to abandon the traditional policy that had kept all trade with the Americas in Spanish hulls and to authorize the involvement of neutral vessels. At home the impact of the war against Britain had been catastrophic. Thanks to the widespread issue of paper money in the form of credits to the national debt, the inflation that had already held the country in its grip had been greatly intensified. In many parts of the country economic activity was at a standstill: whether we are talking of industries that depended on external markets, such as the brandy and cotton production that took place in Catalonia, or industries such as ship-building and rope-making that were kept going by the sinews of empire, the activities of the Royal Navy ensured that demand for their products was at best uncertain. With revenue from the colonies in free fall, the state could neither afford to engage in the sort of programmes of public works that had regularly given employment to thousands of labourers, nor even to pay its soldiers and officials. Desperate to raise more money, the regime launched a sustained attack on the lands of the Church that had by 1808 seen the expropriation and sale of one sixth of its territory and the destruction of much of the machinery of charity that had traditionally sustained the populace in times of want.

On top of all this came an extraordinary succession of catastrophes and natural disasters. Unseasonal weather led to a series of harvest failures that reduced large parts of the country to famine conditions. As we have seen, yellow fever killed thousands of people in Andalucía and the Levante, while a massive outbreak of malaria ravaged New Castile. On 30 April 1802 a newly completed dam designed to create a reservoir in the upper reaches of the river Segura burst and let loose a tidal wave that killed as many as 10,000 people in Lorca and Murcia; and on 13 January 1804 Granada, Málaga and Cartagena were hit by an earthquake so severe that it brought down roof tiles and set chandeliers trembling as far away as Madrid. Just to complete this tale of woe Segovia suffered a plague of locusts. For something of the atmosphere that prevailed in the *salons* of the capital, we can do no better than turn to the diary of Lady Holland, who together with her husband, the future British Foreign Secretary, travelled extensively in Spain in the brief period between 1802 and 1804 when that country was not at war with Britain:

Great failures [occur] throughout the Peninsula in corn crops, especially about Seville and in Portugal. Yesterday there were only 4,000 *fanegas* of wheat in Madrid, and, but for a fortunate supply this morning, a ferment would have taken place in the town. Bread is exorbitantly dear; many bakers' shops have been assaulted. Within these ten days the streets are infested by robbers, who . . . insult and even strip those they fall upon. In consequence of this, numerous patrols on horseback go about the streets soon after the Angelus . . . We have not been without alarm at the possibility of the yellow fever reaching Madrid: it was brought to Málaga by a French vessel from Sainte Domingue and from thence was spread to Antequera . . . The number of deaths at Málaga amount to sixty a day . . . A cordon of troops [has been] placed around the district . . . A considerable alarm [has] prevailed in consequence of the report of a violent contagious fever having broken out in the prisons . . . The fever was brought . . . by some criminals newly apprehended . . . Some fear the prisoners . . . came from La Mancha, where 48,000 persons are sick of putrid disorders in consequence of the scarcity of provisions and want of fuel. Luzuriaga affirms that the famine is so dreadful and universal that the population of Spain will be materially diminished. At Burgos the people die like flies, [and] the villages are deserted as the miserable peasants crowd into the towns to obtain relief from the rich and pious.[4]

As if all this was not enough to encourage popular discontent with the regime, trouble was brewing for its *éminence grise*, Manuel de Godoy, in a variety of other ways. Not the least of these stemmed from the military policy he had followed in the wake of the war of 1793–5. In 1795 Spain had made peace with France and in 1796 she had joined with her in an alliance against Britain. Godoy knew that this arrangement could only ever be temporary: so arrogant and aggressive was the government of the Directory that sooner or later Spain would be compelled to go to war once more. And, France was in his eyes no ally: 'In so far as France is concerned,' he told Queen Maria Luisa, 'the only thing that can be counted on is that the French will never be friends of anything other than their own interests.'[5] At best, the treaty of San Ildefonso was a device that might buy Spain a little time while at the same time staving off the depredations of the British. From as early as 1796, then, the favourite was preparing for war. Special reports were commissioned on the fortifications that guarded the Pyrenean frontier, while a committee of senior generals was set the task of proposing a programme of military reform. This last measure proved abortive, the determination of a variety of vested interests to resist any change ensuring that no progress was made. But Godoy pressed ahead anyway and instituted a number of measures of his own. Not the least of these, particularly in terms of its impact on the course of events in 1808, was the decision to cut the size of the enormous royal guard by half, but even more important was the favourite's determined efforts to extend the army's limited conscription to the whole of the country, large parts of which had hitherto been free of the burdens which it imposed. In every province in which moves were made in this direction, there was furious resistance, and in Valencia and Vizcaya the result was outbreaks of open revolt. As Lady Holland wrote:

About a fortnight ago the peasants in a district near Bilbao assembled tumultuously, went to the *señoria* (or house where the magistrates meet) and demanded the decree which had been passed for enrolling men to serve between the ages of fifteen and fifty. When they obtained it, they read it aloud and to show their contempt for it, tore the paper, trampling it with their feet. They seized the *corregidor*, and compelled him to give up to 200 muskets which had been deposited since the French War in the *señoria*. They insisted on the decree being annulled, which could not be done, but the *corregidor* promised that a general meeting should be convened to take it into consideration. By the last accounts it appears that the decree has been rescinded, and the *corregidor*, who is a *gallego* and abhorred by the Vizcayans, nearly murdered.[6]

However, popular resistance was not just fuelled by the issue of military reform. Very much a man of the Enlightenment, Godoy was much exercised by the issue of bull-fighting. Convinced that this sport was at one and the same time economically wasteful, a humiliating mark of Spain's backwardness and a threat to public order (on account of the simple fact that it caused the populace to assemble in huge crowds), the favourite took the unprecedented and never-to-be-repeated step of banning the *corrida*. Nor was this the only measure that grated upon a populace wedded to what the court and its advisers saw as 'superstition'. There was, for example, the epic battle waged by the regime to force through its insistence that on public health grounds dead bodies should no longer be interred in churches, but rather in municipal cemeteries established in open country beyond the limits of each town and village, and the attempt made to prohibit the wearing of the cloaks traditionally worn by men in many parts of Spain because they made it too easy for malefactors to hide weapons and mask their features from detection. With young men of any aspiration aping French fashions and mannerisms and even peppering their speech with snatches of French, the result for the rest of the population was a genuine fear that an attempt was afoot to strip Spain of her soul.

Popular distrust of the regime was fuelled by court politics. One problem that Godoy was never able to escape was that of his origins. A scion of the provincial nobility who had first come to the court in 1788 as a trooper in the royal bodyguard, he had owed his meteoric rise – by the end of 1793, he was not only chief minister but also a Captain General (field marshal) and a grandee of the first rank – entirely to royal patronage. Seeing so lowly a figure reach so exalted a position was hardly likely to please titled aristocrats whose pedigree went back for hundreds of years and who were already much upset by the grant of titles to a large number of bureaucrats of quite modest origins. Godoy therefore became identified with the Bourbon monarchy's hostility to the privileges of the nobility, and this in turn meant that it was not long before a clique of aristocrats was conspiring to bring down the favourite or, at the very least, frustrate his plans. With this group, meanwhile, there lined up the more traditionalist elements of the clergy, and between the two of them there emerged a devastating campaign of black propaganda. Nobles such as the Duque del Infantado and the Conde de Montijo sent servants out into the streets and taverns to spread stories of Godoy's lasciviousness and venality, while conservative churchmen blamed the ills that were afflicting Spain on the judgement of Heaven. There was, perhaps, little that the favourite could do about this, but he certainly did himself no favours. The constant claim that he was the lover of the Spanish queen – a staple of the stories spread by his opponents – is almost certainly untrue, but he did take endless bribes, exploit his position to secure a constant supply of sexual favours, and enjoy a lifestyle that was opulent in the extreme. As such, he repelled the one party in the state – the outright supporters of Enlightenment – that might have been expected to back him unreservedly. Setting aside his assumption of the role of grand voluptuary, this group soon found that his ability to advance their aims and offer them protection was extremely limited. The crucial moment here came in 1801 when Charles IV, a timid monarch who lacked the courage and energy necessary to stay loyal to the enlightened absolutism of his predecessor, Charles III, dismissed the highly reformist ministry headed by Mariano Luis de Urquijo. As Godoy was himself temporarily out of favour at the time, this was not his fault, but the assault on progressive thinking continued even after he was brought back a few months later. The result, of course, was that the favourite was stripped of all credibility. 'Not only is he without a party or an adherent,' wrote Lady Holland, 'but he has no friend on whom he can rely.'[7]

Provided that he had been guaranteed the support of the king and queen, Godoy's isolation might not have mattered so much. But, as events repeatedly showed, even at the best of times this could very easily be withdrawn. In 1798 French suspicions of Godoy's reformism had led to such pressure on the king and queen that he had in effect been removed from the position of chief minister. Far worse, Charles IV was now an elderly man subject to bouts of serious illness: on several occasions, indeed, he had seemed on the point of death. And not only was this the case, but the heir to the throne, Prince Ferdinand, hated the favourite for the manner in which he had, in his eyes at least, usurped the affections of his parents. Around the prince there gathered a coterie of conspirators who all in one way or another felt that they had been particularly slighted or ill used by Godoy, amongst the most important being the prince's erstwhile tutor, Canon Juan de Escoíquiz, and the senior guards officers, the Duque del Infantado and the Conde de Montijo. Nor did it help that the king's first wife, Maria Antonia of Naples, was a ferocious critic of the French alliance and when she died after only a short period of marriage, it was therefore easy for Escoíquiz and his allies to convince the prince – a surly and suspicious individual – that she had been murdered. Even more absurdly he was persuaded that Godoy intended to seize the throne when his father died, and this in turn gave fresh material to the conspirators, who could now spread it abroad that Ferdinand, who they naturally painted in the most glowing terms, was to be deprived of his birthright. By the same token, of course, Spain was to be deprived of her salvation: already Ferdinand was being portrayed as *el rey deseado*, the handsome young prince who would put all to rights by chasing out the hated Godoy and his cronies.

All this lent a certain urgency to Godoy's diplomacy. First, he made a series of attempts to escape the alliance with France, which was self-evidently not only undermining him but failing to deliver the only positive goals that had ever been hoped for from it. As will be recalled, the favourite had struggled frantically to avoid being sucked back into open war with Britain after 1803, by, for example, attempting to form a league of neutrals that could band together to resist any attempt at coercion. Then, once the fighting had been resumed, he had done all that he could to keep Spain from having to engage in real fighting. In the period before Trafalgar, Spain's admirals were for months hampered by a complete want of support from Madrid. Streams of orders had been issued for the arming and provisioning of Spain's navy, but these had been accompanied by little in the way of money and, after a series of measures that appear as little less than sabotage, on 14 October the Spanish commander at Cádiz, Federico Gravina, was in effect informed that there was none left. 'Our expenses,' wrote the favourite, 'have for some time been exorbitant ... Such is our state, and the result is that we must not only avoid any outlay that can be avoided, but make such payments as are absolutely indispensable with all the delay that can be managed.'⁸ Already unhappy, Godoy was shaken still further by the fact that in May 1805 a United States deputation headed by James Monroe not only demanded that Spain pay compensation for all the American ships she had taken in the period of her alliance with France, but also hinted at a determination to seize Florida, which was at this point still a Spanish possession. Though doubt and indecision had stayed Godoy's hand in 1805 in the face of Russian attempts to get Spain to join the Third Coalition, the overwhelming catastrophe of Trafalgar made him move swiftly in the direction of a separate peace with Britain and, ultimately, an outright attack on France.

This prospect, it has to be said, was very much to Godoy's taste. Given command of the Spanish forces sent to invade Portugal in 1801, he had been entranced by visions of military glory and come to fancy himself a great general. Surrounded now by little more than a crowd of flatterers, Godoy acquired an overly favourable view of his attempts to reform the army. As far back as the War of the Oranges, in fact, he had written in the following vein to Maria Luisa:

To the devil with files of papers when I am on the point of making the enemy listen to reason at the cannon's mouth. Never shall I be able to live without soldiers in future; the sight of them thrills me and I was born never to leave them. I cannot express to Your Majesty the pleasure that swells my heart ... Let me never hear talk of political intrigues again, and be sent with my soldiers to the ends of the earth! I want never to leave the colours. May Your Majesty deign to let me serve her with the sword for no shorter time than I have served her with the pen!⁹

The only problem, of course, was that Spain could not hope to take on France alone. In these circumstances, Napoleon's unexpected war with Prussia therefore seemed an ideal opportunity: the Prussian army, after all, had for many years been the model for Spain's own troops, and it was generally expected that it would prevail over the French. The result was one of the least well-timed calls to arms in the history of armed conflict. Issued on 5 October, the peroration of this document read: 'Come forward ... beloved countrymen; come forward and swear your oaths beneath the banners of the most beneficent of sovereigns; come forward, and, should the God of victories give us the happy and lasting peace for which we pray, I shall cover you with the mantle of gratitude.'[10]

Spain and France, then, were at the very brink of war, but just a week later Napoleon smashed the Prussians at Jena and Auerstädt. To say that this news came as a shock to Godoy is a considerable understatement, but he reacted with some aplomb: all he had been trying to do, he announced, had been to galvanize the populace into greater support for the war against England. With this explanation, Napoleon claimed to be satisfied, but he knew very well what Godoy had been planning. Spain's efficacy as an ally of France also remained a severe problem. The difficulties that had been encountered in putting together a viable battle fleet; the absence of any activity in the ship-building yards (construction for the Spanish navy had effectively ceased in 1796); the failure to make any impression on the Royal Navy; the want of funds to pay the monthly tribute that had prior to the end of 1804 kept Madrid out of the war; and the hunger and lack of pay that stalked the army – all conspired to create the impression that Spain was ruled by a regime that could not give Napoleon the support he required. And yet for centuries Spain had been overflowing with bullion and could still lay claim to the greatest empire in the world. This was not something Napoleon was likely to tolerate, while Godoy's discomfiture was further increased by Britain's remaining deaf to his attempts to secure a separate peace. Indeed, from this point on, the views of structuralists and functionalists coincide. Whether or not the emperor had always intended to bring down the Spanish Bourbons, there now began a programme whose every action was designed to erode Spain's independence and freedom of action, and ultimately to lay her open to the sort of manoeuvre that was to bring down the Bourbon monarchy in 1808.

For this view, there is some circumstantial evidence. Nothing, for example, could be more suggestive than the fact that at the end of 1806 Napoleon suddenly demanded amongst other things – most notably Spain's accession to the Continental Blockade – that Madrid provide him with a corps of 14,000 infantry and cavalry for service in northern Europe. Some 6,000 of these men, it is true, came from the Spanish forces sent to garrison the Kingdom of Etruria for its Spanish princess, but even so, the corps concerned amounted to roughly one tenth of the number of soldiers Spain had under arms. There is no reason to believe that the men sent were deliberately selected as the country's best troops, but the blow was made worse by the need to mount the five cavalry regiments involved, which was only made possible by many of the army's other riders giving up their own horses. And then, of course, there is Napoleon's decision to intervene in Portugal in September 1807, discussed in more detail below, which allowed him to send large numbers of troops across the Pyrenees. Certainly both Fouché and Talleyrand claimed later that the emperor explained the move to them in terms of the overthrow of the Bourbons. Indeed, Talleyrand implied that it was this revelation that led to his resignation from the post of Foreign Minister in August 1807, Napoleon having shown beyond all possible doubt that he had no intention of respecting Talleyrand's post-Austerlitz policy.

Yet none of this is proof of anything. Napoleon and Talleyrand certainly fell out in the aftermath of Tilsit – an observer who was present at Napoleon's headquarters in Poland talks of 'a vague rumour floating about Warsaw that there had been a violent altercation between [Talleyrand] and the emperor'[11] – but whether the subject was the need for peace is another matter. Apart from anything else, the Franco-Russian accord had been arranged behind the Foreign Minister's back at a moment when Napoleon had given him cause to believe that he would accept the Austrian mediation to which Talleyrand so aspired. And whether there was really any plot to overthrow the Spanish Bourbons will always be unclear. Passing through Dresden in the aftermath of Tilsit, Napoleon observed, 'They do me too much honour if they believe that everything that I have done was premeditated. I have seen myself forced into actions I should never have dreamed of. It is a general human weakness to assume definite plans everywhere ... whereas more often chance and necessity were, in fact, the main factors. I can conceive nothing more inept than commendation for prudent calculations which were never made.'[12] This, of course, does not prove anything either, but a careful consideration of the history of French intervention in Spain and Portugal suggests that there was in fact no fixed scheme in the emperor's mind; indeed, that in the short term it grew out of nothing more than frustration at the situation that emerged in the wake of the treaty of Tilsit. This being the case, it is worth taking a moment to look at the state of Europe in more detail. In brief, this was somewhat curious. On the one hand, Napoleon stood supreme on land. By common consent, the army he led at this point was the very best and most effective that France ever fielded in the whole period from 1792 till 1815. The European powers had one by one been humbled and forced either to beg for mercy or to curry friendship. By means of the Continental Blockade, the emperor could hope at the very least to inflict substantial damage on Britain and even to force her to make peace. And yet on the other, London remained absolutely unbowed. Not only had the ineffectual 'Ministry of all the Talents' been replaced by the Portland administration, but by June 1807 the latter was showing signs of putting up a real fight. In an important but unsung step, the Cabinet raised the rates payable to the owners of vessels hired as military transports, and in this fashion raised the tonnage available to the government in this area from 115,000 tons to 168,000 in a mere four months. The regular army was swelled by the recruitment of 25,000 volunteers from the militia, whose ranks were then made up by the authorization of fresh ballots. The first division of what was intended to be an army of 34,000 men was dispatched to the Swedish enclave of Stralsund; and Prussia and Sweden were all promised substantial financial support. On 27 June the new Foreign Secretary, George Canning, and the Prussian ambassador to London signed an agreement which promised the latter's government £1 million in payments spread over a period of one year if it would in exchange put every man that it could into the field against the French; equally, Sweden got a promise of £50,000 per annum. Already in receipt of a British subsidy that had been agreed in 1805, Russia got considerable quantities of arms as an extra as well as an ambassador who was a popular figure in the Russian capital and had much experience there. And finally, a new envoy was also dispatched to Vienna with a clear promise that a declaration of war would lead to substantial British support.

If any further proof of the Portland administration's commitment to the struggle is needed, it may be found in the Danish affair of July–September 1807. It was learned in London that a large French army was massing on the borders of Holstein with a view to marching on Copenhagen and forcing the Danes either to join Napoleon or to surrender their fleet. Whichever turned out to be the case, the end result was the same in that French seapower would be swelled by the addition of twenty or more warships. Also likely to suffer were Britain's communications with the Baltic and with them her chief source of naval supplies. This being something that London could hardly view with equanimity, it was therefore immediately resolved that a British fleet should sail to Denmark. With them went 18,000 men while orders were sent to the 12,000 men that had already gone to Stralsund to join them immediately. On 30 July the first British ships anchored off Copenhagen, and a British envoy went ashore with promises of an alliance if the Danes would only surrender their ships to Britain's protection. An alliance, however, was meaningless, and the Danes knew it: even 30,000 British troops were hardly likely to be able to save Denmark from invasion and conquest, while just a day after the British had arrived a message had been received from Napoleon that left the Danish government in no doubt that they must join him or face war. With the frontier only a few days' march away, the future Frederick VI – he was at this point only Prince Regent – decided to try to make a fight of it until such time as the French sent help, and therefore defied the British.

Given this answer, there was nothing for it but to open hostilities. Invading Zealand, the British blockaded Copenhagen and on 29 August routed a relief column at Kioge, an action notable chiefly for being Sir Arthur Wellesley's first taste of action since his return from India. But time was pressing, and the defenders of the Danish capital showed no signs of cracking. Determined to secure the Danish fleet, the British therefore resolved to bombard them into surrender. There followed a grim affair that showed Britain at her most ruthless. Copenhagen was largely built of wood and the combination of red-hot shot and the use of the newly invented Congreve rocket soon turned the city into an inferno. Firing began on the evening of 2 September, and five days later the exhausted Danes surrendered. At least 2,000 civilians were dead, but the British had secured their immediate objective: for the loss of a mere 250 men, the entire Danish fleet had been neutralized – fifteen battleships and a number of smaller vessels were got away to England, while several other ships were torched in their docks. Also taken was a considerable quantity of naval stores. This, of course, meant the end of Danish naval power: in theory, the ships concerned were supposed to be returned to Copenhagen with the coming of peace, but few survived the war and the money and resources that might have formed the basis for the construction of a new fleet were lacking. As for the Baltic, it was now brought firmly under British control in naval terms: after this second Danish *tour de force* on the part of the Royal Navy, there was no appetite to take it on in the messrooms of its Russian counterpart, and no way that Napoleon could mount a direct challenge to its ships himself.

But Copenhagen also came at a terrible price. In the first place, the ruthless treatment of the Danes did not sit very comfortably alongside some of the loftier flights of British rhetoric and, in fairness, prompted much disquiet at home, while at the same time handing Napoleon a wonderful propaganda weapon. 'We shall,' as General Paget wrote, 'henceforth be dubbed the nation of Saracens instead of the nation of shopkeepers.'[13] Given that in the end Britain could only hope to defeat Napoleon through the formation of a powerful continental coalition, this was most unfortunate, and all the more so as unfavourable contrasts could always be drawn between the alacrity with which Britain had suddenly found plenty of men and ships to intervene in Denmark and the way in which she had dragged her feet on other occasions. And, finally, even in the short term the expedition had not achieved all its goals. The Danish fleet was safe, certainly, but Copenhagen had also been Canning's response to the Franco-Russian accord that had been agreed at Tilsit. We should remember that at this point it was not known for certain in London whether this was a simple peace settlement or an alliance. In the first place, then, we see a veiled threat: what could be done at Copenhagen could also be done – the Russians might infer – at St Petersburg. But it was accepted that Alexander might simply have been coerced into surrender by Napoleon. By establishing a base in Zealand – as the British troops did not sail away with the Danish navy – Canning therefore hoped to persuade the tsar to rejoin the fight and even send troops to Denmark himself. But in all this, Canning had badly misjudged the situation. Alexander had always seen himself as the champion of the smaller states of central Europe, and in any case had no desire to risk another Friedland. Meanwhile, he had also just acquired a new foreign minister in the person of Count Nicolai Rumiantsev, who was the son of one of the greatest heroes of Catherine the Great's wars against the Turks and as such convinced that Russia should not be fighting Napoleon but rather marching on Constantinople. Bitterly anti-British, indeed, he had been a fierce opponent of the Third Coalition. In short, all Canning had achieved had been to drive Russia even deeper into Napoleon's arms.

The impression of belligerence generated by the Portland administration was reinforced by the fruitless efforts of the continental powers to get Britain to make peace. Head of the queue was the diplomatic activity engaged in by Russia in the late summer and early autumn of 1807. At Tilsit Alexander I had agreed to go to war against Britain if the latter did not make peace by 1 November, but in the first instance all he was called upon to do was to offer Russian mediation. In this goal he genuinely hoped he might be successful, while the fact that Russia would in effect not be called upon actively to take up arms until, say, May 1808, on account of the long northern winter and the icing-over of the Baltic, was also reassuring. The delay would, after all, give more time for the Continental Blockade to take effect and allow Alexander to share in victory without necessarily having to fire a shot. As early as the beginning of August, then, the new Russian ambassador to London, Maximilian Alopeus, presented the British government with the offer of Russia's good offices. Although this had in fact been settled at Tilsit – essentially Britain could have Hanover in exchange for surrendering all her conquests in the wider world – the form a settlement might take was not revealed, and Canning therefore responded that Britain would not open peace talks until she had heard the terms on offer – terms, more-over, that she expected to favour Britain. When a supplementary message arrived to the effect that Alexander had only done a deal with Napoleon in order to check any further French progress in Poland and the Baltic, the answer returned was scarcely less conciliatory: this time Canning demanded not only the conditions of the proposed Russian mediation, but a detailed explanation both of the treaty of Tilsit and the general trend of Russian policy.

In a situation in which Russia could make no progress, it was unlikely that anything more could be expected from Austria or Prussia. Both powers had a strong interest in peace – the Prussians, especially, were deeply aware of the likely impact of the Continental Blockade – while both had good reason to curry favour with Napoleon. Terrified at their isolation, the Austrians were currently trying to secure an alliance with France. The governments of both Francis and Frederick William there-fore instructed their ambassadors in London to raise the possibility of a general peace. In this they acted in very different fashions. Fearing that they were about to be attacked themselves and seeing no other means of propitiating Napoleon, the Austrians adopted a hectoring tone, whereas the Prussians, who saw a general negotiation as the only means of getting a better deal than the one they had got at Tilsit, were flattering and conciliatory. Yet neither approach had any effect. The Prussians were told that there was no hope of peace negotiations being opened for the foreseeable future, and the Austrians, who had, like the Russians, offered themselves as mediators, that nothing could be agreed until it was learned on what basis the peace should be negotiated. As Napoleon would not consent to do any specifics, Vienna was no more successful than St Petersburg. The process took some time – the Austrian ambassador in London, Count Starhemberg, was much more pro-British than his government and in consequence was desperately anxious to avoid a breakdown in relations – but by early January 1808 the end had come and Starhemberg requested his passports.

The British stood firm, which is hardly surprising. Though they were very different from one another and, in the end, bitter rivals, the chief figures in the Portland administration, Canning and the Secretary of State for War and the Colonies, Lord Castlereagh, were absolutely committed both to the struggle against Napoleon, and to a Eurocentric strategy based on the aid of strong continental allies. There were differences between them in terms of approach and personality: whereas Canning was fiery, emotional, enthusiastic and a brilliant orator, Castlereagh was a poor public speaker and in general much more cautious. But in their perception of the war they were as one. Importantly, the issue was not the restoration of the Bourbon monarchy; indeed, it did not matter that much whether France was a republic, a monarchy or an empire. This is not to say that ideological considerations did not matter: Canning and Castlereagh were opponents of political reform at home, and acted throughout under the assumption that Napoleon was a 'crowned Jacobin'. But in their eyes the danger lay not in French ideas, but in French bayonets. What mattered was that France should respect international law. As no treaty, frontier or regime was safe under Napoleon, Britain must fight France to the end, or at least until such a time as a peace settlement could be imposed on her that would strip even the emperor of his ability to disturb the peace. Mixed in with this, of course, were views that mirrored traditional British interests – to both Canning and Castlereagh, it was axiomatic that Belgium and Holland should be kept out of French hands and, by the same token, that Britain should rule the waves. More than that, the coming of the Continental Blockade had in their eyes elevated the war into something new: one of national survival. Yet there was, too, a genuine sense of a wider commitment to the Continent as a whole that imbued the conduct of the war with a strong sense of mission that was reinforced by a sincere horror of the suffering that was being inflicted on the peoples of Europe.

Canning and Castlereagh – and beyond them their colleagues and political allies – were determined to fight Napoleon. In practical terms, however, the odds were very much stacked against them. In the first place, their only allies were Sweden and Sicily, neither of whom possessed the capacity to conduct the large-scale military campaigns that Britain needed from coalition partners. On the contrary, both needed defending. Yet troops were exactly what the British were short of. Although the number of men they had under arms had soared, far too many of them were serving in forces that could not be required to serve abroad. Still worse, neither Britain nor her colonies could be entirely stripped of regular troops. Strive though the British did to employ local auxiliaries and foreign manpower, the result was that they did not have sufficient men to do very much themselves. Nor was raising a respectable field army the only problem: setting aside the dangers of storm and shipwreck, transporting even the most modest expeditionary force required large numbers of specialized ships, while simply getting the forces on and off ship was a most complex undertaking. These difficulties were doubly unfortunate for they forced Britain back on methods of war – above all, blockade and colonial aggrandizement – that both antagonized potential partners on the Continent and confirmed suspicions that the British were avoiding the sort of commitment they themselves required of their allies. Nor were the methods of warfare on which they relied particularly cost-effective. Colonial offensives were notoriously wasteful in terms of lives, while blockading Europe's coasts inflicted immense wear and tear on the Royal Navy. Some amelioration in the demands on Britain's resources was at hand as by July 1807 the South American and Egyptian imbroglios were coming to an end. But even so the sinews of war were clearly at a premium. On coming into office in March 1807 the Portland administration had found that it had at best 20,000 troops available for service overseas, and that even this meagre force could not all be used at the same time for want of transports, this being a situation that was only to improve very slowly.

The political foundations of the British war effort were no more solid. The Portland administration may have been more committed to the struggle than its predecessor, but it was also very vulnerable. Amongst

Whigs like Richard Sheridan, Lord Grey and Lord Holland, it was felt even now that Napoleon personified the cause of progress. In the course of the 1790s, a number of Whigs – most famously Edmund Burke, but also the current Prime Minister, Lord Portland – had become supporters of the war, but this gain had been offset by the defection of a number of disillusioned Tories to the peace party. Meanwhile, if the failure of the talks of 1806 had temporarily silenced most of those who opposed the war, the Portland administration was also hampered by other factors, not least the personality of George Canning. While there was no doubting his talents, his energy or his hatred of Napoleon, the Foreign Secretary was a man of questionable judgement whose determination to defeat the French blinded him to political realities, and made him impatient with more circumspect colleagues. Highly mercurial in temperament, he was also very vain and deeply ambitious, and it was only too predictable that sooner or later this would produce serious tension in the Cabinet. To make matters worse, being aged and unwell, Lord Portland was unable to provide much in the way of leadership or keep the dynamic Canning in line. At risk of internal strife, the Cabinet also had to run the risk of losing the support of the throne. In ordinary circumstances, this would not have been an issue. King George III both loathed Napoleon and shared his ministers' antipathy to the Catholic emancipation that was the foremost domestic issue of the day. But the king was prone to bouts of porphyria that periodically left him completely incapacitated and threatened to have him replaced with the pro-Whig Prince of Wales, there being no guarantee that the latter would not oust Portland the moment he assumed the regency.

However, Britain's stability cannot just be measured in terms of Westminster. Just as important was the Continental Blockade. Almost a year into its existence this measure was still being tightened up. The response of the British had been to introduce a series of 'orders-in-council' whose general trend was to declare all ships originating from the ports of France and her allies and satellites to be legal prize, and to impose severe limitations on the movement of neutral vessels: they might put to sea, but only with the proviso that they visited a British port and paid a heavy duty on their cargoes. To Napoleon this was unacceptable, and in the course of a visit that he paid to the Kingdom of Italy in November and December 1807 he issued two fresh decrees – the so-called Decrees of Milan – that declared that any vessel that complied with Britain's regulations was liable both to confiscation on its return to port and to capture on the high seas by French privateers. This put the Portland administration under greater pressure than ever. Over the course of time and through changing circumstances, Britain circumvented the Blockade by developing new markets and undercover links with the Continent, but in 1807 it was by no means clear that things would work out so well. To make matters worse, the United States, not only the chief neutral state but also a commercial operator of great importance, was so exercised by the situation that on 22 December 1807 President Jefferson passed into law a total embargo on all trade with Britain and France alike. Hit by both a squeeze on exports and a general increase in the price of raw materials, many British industries were soon in the grip of a severe slump, the situation being worsened still further by the actions of French commerce raiders and a poor harvest. The handloom weavers of Lancashire, in consequence, mounted an impressive campaign to petition parliament for a minimum wage and many northern merchants and manufacturers began to organize petitions for peace. Hand in hand with the demands of such men, meanwhile, went others for political change: in the general elections of 1807, for example, Westminster, then the most representative seat in the country, returned the popular demagogues, Sir Francis Burdett and Lord Cochrane, on a platform of electoral reform. Nor could such displays be disconnected from opposition to the war: Burdett was a leading light in the peace movement, while the massive strike that falling wages and ever increasing lay-offs eventually produced among the handloom weavers of Lancashire in May 1808 was accompanied by loud demands for an end to hostilities. For the time being there was no repetition of the rumours of a secret insurrectionary movement of the sort that had been heard in 1802 at the time of the so-called 'black lump' conspiracy in Yorkshire, but for all that the country was far from wholly united behind the war effort. Between 1803 and 1805 there had been a genuine danger of invasion, and this had encouraged a strong degree of 'Church and King' loyalism. But by 1807 things were very different, and there were many observers who could not understand why Britain should fight on for, as they saw it, the interests of Austria, Russia and Prussia.

For victory to come, then, Napoleon probably had only to wait. Waiting, though, was not in his nature and he remained obsessed by the constant need to secure fresh triumphs and thereby, as he put it, ensure that he continued to be feared. Worth citing, too, is the fact that the departure of Talleyrand had removed at least a possible restraining influence. Talleyrand may not have been quite the force for good that he always claimed, but his successor as Foreign Secretary, Champagny, was not nearly so independent a figure. At all events, no sooner were the discussions at Tilsit over than Napoleon was looking around for a new target. The obvious choice was Portugal, and all the more so as an attack on that state had been aborted by the campaign of Jena and Auerstädt. Pretexts for an attack were plentiful: Portugal was not part of the Continental Blockade, had been defaulting on the indemnity she had been paying France since the 'War of the Oranges' of 1801, and had frequently allowed British warships to revictual from her shores. And there was much to gain: Portugal possessed wealthy colonies and a fleet that, if no great size, was not to be despised, while Lisbon was a vital base that offered major advantages to whichever side could incorporate it into their war effort. And finally she ought to present few problems. Her army was minimal and her ruler, the Prince Regent John, notoriously dull-witted, while the agreement of the Russians to evacuate the Ionian islands and in effect join the French meant that it might even be possible to attack Lisbon from the sea, as the Russian commander in the Adriatic, Admiral Senyavin, would have to pass that way as he brought his forces home to St Petersburg.

Behind all this the issue of genuine strategic requirements is discernible. Should any defender of Napoleon wish to do so, it is possible to argue that what mattered in the end was always the war against Britain. Thus, successive British Cabinets had refused to give in, and so the emperor needed all the ships and all the coasts that he could obtain. To quote a letter written by Napoleon to Charles IV to justify the attack on Portugal, 'We can only obtain peace by isolating England from the Continent and closing the latter's ports to her commerce. I count on Your Majesty's energy in securing this objective: if tranquillity is to be restored in the world, England must be forced to make peace.'[14] Nor should it be forgotten that Britain had attacked Copenhagen because Napoleon was on the brink of sending troops to seize the Danish fleet himself. Moving away from the issue of grand strategy, there is also the argument that what mattered above all was Napoleon's loyalty to his own family – that what he really wanted was to seize the throne of Portugal for some sibling. Yet somehow these arguments remain unconvincing. The

Portuguese fleet may have been substantial, but it was by no means big enough to make much of a difference, while most of its ships-of-the-line were mere 'Fourth Rates' and therefore incapable of standing up to the much bigger and well-armed vessels favoured by the Royal Navy. With Portugal taking only 4 per cent of British exports, forcing her to join the Continental Blockade was hardly a matter of the greatest importance. And, finally, by 1807 Napoleon's family was well provided for, not that there is any evidence that they were a consideration in respect of Portugal. Joseph was King of Naples; Louis, King of Holland; Jerome, King of Westphalia; Murat and Caroline, Duke and Duchess of Berg; Elise, Duchess of Lucca and Princess of Piombino; and Eugène de Beauharnais, Viceroy of Italy.

There remains the issue of the control of Lisbon itself, but, important though this port was, the game hardly seems worth the candle. In consequence, the honest observer is forced back on the atmosphere that reigned in the Tuileries at this point. The return of Napoleon to Paris on 27 July 1807 was marked by the celebration of a 'Te Deum' in Notre Dame, immense demonstrations of loyalty and much pomp and ceremony, and the same sort of scenes were repeated a little over a month later when Napoleon's brother, Jerome, was married to the daughter of the newfound King of Württemberg. As one of the guests remembered:

The ceremony took place in the Diana gallery at the Tuileries ... All the magnificence of the most sumptuous court were deployed on this occasion. The quantity of pearls, diamonds and precious stones of all sorts which added their brilliance to the costumes of the women was truly prodigious, and the effect was all the more striking when one recalled the miseries of the end of the previous century: a few brief years had sufficed to bring back the most excessive behaviour.[15]

Still more impressive, and at the same time more militaristic, were the celebrations that accompanied the return of those few troops – primarily the Imperial Guard – who were brought back to France from Poland. Among them was the Chasseur officer, Jean-Baptiste Barrès:

The city of Paris had erected ... a triumphal arch of the largest size. This arch had only a single arcade, but twenty men could pass through it marching abreast. At the spring of the vault ... one saw great figures of Renown offering wreaths of laurel ... From the morning onwards the arch was surrounded by an immense crowd ... At noon, all the corps having arrived, the eagles were united at the head of the column and ... 10,000 men in parade uniform moved forward to march past under the triumphal arch to the sound of the drums and the bands of the corps, numerous salvos of artillery, and the acclamations of the immense mass of people who had assembled on the spot. From the barrier to the palace of the Tuileries the same acclamations accompanied us ... All the roofs and windows ... were packed with sightseers. Poems in which we were compared to the 10,000 Immortals and warlike songs were sung and distributed as we went by ... In short, the enthusiasm was absolute, and the festival worthy of the great days of Greece and Rome.[16]

Given Napoleon's character, such scenes could not but spur him onward, and all the more so as the Napoleon of this period was very far from being the romantic hero of Brumaire and the Consulate. Amongst those who have left us a personal description was the young nobleman, the Duc de Broglie:

I had a glimpse of the emperor as he went by on his road to Bayonne. He stopped for breakfast, like any ordinary traveller, at the inn ... He was no longer that young First Consul, slim, unconcerned, with his slightly olive complexion and his stern scowl, whom I had met for the first time striding through the Tuileries ... Even outwardly everything had altered, He had grown very burly in waist and shoulders, his little legs were thick and fleshy, his complexion sallow, his forehead quite bald, and his features strongly put one in mind of a Roman emperor as we see them on their coins. I will not say, like the servant at the inn, that in all he did he seemed to have the crown on his head and the sceptre in his hand, but, standing there like other lookers-on, crowding round to watch him go in and out, it struck me that everything in him had the air of an emperor, but of an emperor of the worst period.[17]

Whatever the reason, Lisbon's fate was already settled. On 19 July 1807 the emperor sent orders to Talleyrand to instruct Portugal to close her ports to Britain's shipping, arrest all British subjects, confiscate all British merchandise, and declare war. Within a few days, meanwhile, word had also gone out to concentrate a large force at Bayonne preparatory to a march on Lisbon. Such a march, of course, could only be made across Spain, but this presented few difficulties. Having, as we shall see, for years been trying to get Napoleon to intervene in Portugal, the Spanish royal favourite, Manuel de Godoy, was delighted with the news. Unsettled by rumours that Ferdinand IV of Naples was to be persuaded to surrender Sicily to Joseph Bonaparte in exchange for the Balearic islands, he may also have seen cooperation as a means of propitiating Napoleon. Occupation forces were therefore soon being mobilized in Galicia, León and Extremadura, the Spanish ambassador in Lisbon also being ordered at all times to second his French counterpart. As for the unfortunate Prince Regent of Portugal, the choice facing him was made very clear. In the words of Napoleon himself:

I conceive the peace that reigns on the Continent, in respect of which I have received with great pleasure the congratulations of Your Royal Highness, as but a step towards the peace that should reign on the sea. All the measures that I have taken have been directed at this goal, and they have been adopted by every power that, like Portugal, has a direct interest in making England respect its independence and its rights. No half-measure can have the same success or demonstrate the same attachment to the common cause.[18]

Threatened by France and Spain alike, Portugal now found herself in a terrible situation. Often wrongly stigmatized as a decayed despotism in which obscurantism vied with inefficiency, Portugal had under the leadership of the Marquês de Pombal, the chief minister of José I (1750–77), in fact become the very model of enlightened absolutism. Key reforms included the complete reorganization of the government of empire and metropolis, a great reduction in the power of the Church and nobility, the establishment of a modern army, and the creation of a modern system of education. The arts and sciences had been encouraged, and everything possible done to stimulate economic development. Pombal had long since vanished from the scene – indeed, he had ended his life in disgrace – but his influence had survived and allowed textiles and the wine trade to thrive. Nor had the Revolutionary and Napoleonic Wars been much of a setback. There had been war with France from 1793 to 1797 and a brief Spanish invasion in 1801, but hostilities had been nominal and trade buoyant, while the definitive treaty of peace had cost Portugal no more than the cession of a small part of the Alentejo and the payment of indemnities to Madrid and Paris. Napoleon's sudden ultimatum spelled disaster, however. As the eighteenth century had progressed, the Brazilian gold, sugar and tobacco that had hitherto been the bedrock of Portugal's well-being had begun either to run out or fall in value. Some relief was obtained by the discovery of diamonds and an increase in the cultivation of cotton, but even so the emphasis had increasingly begun to shift to the metropolis's own products and manufactures. As Britain took a large part of the wine that was Portugal's chief export, joining the Continental Blockade was unthinkable, and yet fighting France and Spain was not much of an option either. Some attempt had been made to reorganize the army since the peace of 1801, but no more than 20,000 men were under arms out of a theoretical total of some 48,000. In the circumstances, then, the only hope was to play for time in the belief that Britain would send troops or ships to defend their old ally (something that was not so improbable: British expeditionary forces had repeatedly been sent to Portugal in the eighteenth century, while in 1806 even the lacklustre Talents had dispatched a squadron to Lisbon the moment that invasion threatened). Thus, while Napoleon was told that Portugal was prepared to declare war on Britain and close her ports to her ships, the chief minister, Antonio de Araujo, appealed to the Portland administration for help and in general made it very clear that he was still loyal. 'The French [are] insisting on all British subjects being turned out of the country and their property [being] confiscated,' wrote one British resident. 'The Prince Regent's reply to this is that he will sooner risk the loss of his kingdom than act so treacherous a part against such a friend and ally as England has ever been to Portugal.'[19]

Napoleon was unready for war: the troops had to be scraped together from depots all over France and their Spanish counterparts faced enormous logistical difficulties. Lisbon was therefore told it need only detain British subjects on a provisional basis and sequester rather than confiscate their goods, the original deadline of 2 September also being extended for a further month. Yet this meant nothing. Indeed, in the wake of Copenhagen the emperor was more inclined to severity than ever. 'About this time', wrote Fouché, 'was known the success of the attack upon Copenhagen by the English, which was the first blow given to the secret stipulations of Tilsit, in virtue of which the navy of Denmark was to be placed at the disposal of France. Since the catastrophe of Paul I, I never saw Napoleon abandon himself to more violent transports. What most struck him in this vigorous enterprise was the promptness of the resolution of the English ministry.'[20] Typical of these 'transports'

was the outburst witnessed by Metternich at Fontainebleau on
16 October: 'I will no longer tolerate an English ambassador in Europe;
I will declare war against any power who receives one at his court after
two months from this time. I have 300,000 Russians at my disposal and
with that powerful ally I can do everything. The English declare they
will no longer respect neutrals on the sea; I will no longer recognize
them on the land.'[21]

In Portugal, meanwhile, it had been decided that heroics had better
be set aside in favour of other methods. Although news had now been
received that no aid would be forthcoming from the British, reports
from Paris suggested that Napoleon's entourage could be bribed into
dissuading him from taking action. Napoleon was once again told that
the government would not give way, but as a mark of good faith, the
batteries that protected Lisbon from the sea were placed in a state of
defence and 6,000 troops thrown into the coastal fortress of Peniche.
Meanwhile, large amounts of gold and jewels were placed at the disposal
of certain confidential agents in Paris. Whether a more positive answer
would have made any difference is unclear, but Napoleon now had all
the pretext he needed while his 25,000-strong intervention force – the
so-called First Corps of Observation of the Gironde – was ready for
action. No sooner had he received the Portuguese answer, then, than
Napoleon ordered its commander, General Junot, to cross the Spanish
frontier and make all haste for the Portuguese capital: 'You will tell . . .
Junot,' the emperor told his Minister of War, General Clarke, 'that my
ambassador has left Lisbon, and that there is therefore not a moment to
lose if the English are to be forestalled.'[22]

While this had been going on, the Spanish government had been
making little trouble. Aside from anything else, on 29 August French
troops had suddenly invaded the so-called Kingdom of Etruria. Originally the Duchy of Tuscany, Etruria had been ceded to the Bourbons in
1801 in the person of Charles IV's eldest daughter and her Italian
consort. However, Etruria having become a centre of smuggling and
espionage, Napoleon had resolved on its annexation. With Spain's only
hope of compensation lying in Portugal, cooperation with the emperor
therefore became all the more important. Nevertheless, deeply mistrustful of Godoy, the emperor decided to bind the Spaniards to his plans
even more closely. On 25 September he made contact with Godoy's
personal representative in Paris, Eugenio Izquierdo, and agreed the treaty

of Fontainebleau. Under its terms, Portugal was split into three with the north handed over to the King and Queen of Etruria, the centre kept under military occupation until the end of the war and then disposed of according to circumstance, and the south given to Godoy. In the meantime Napoleon agreed to guarantee the existing domains of the Spanish Bourbons and to allow Charles IV to style himself 'Emperor of the Two Americas'. Also settled was the question of how Portugal would actually be occupied, the basic plan being that 28,000 French and 13,000 Spanish troops would march on Lisbon from León, while another 16,000 Spaniards moved across the frontier from Galicia and Extremadura. A further 40,000 French soldiers would be assembled at Bayonne to ward off British raids, although it was agreed that these troops would not enter Spain without the prior agreement of Madrid. And with all this Godoy and his advisers professed themselves to be well satisfied. According to the erstwhile chairman of the Committee of Public Safety, Bertrand de Barère, who had become a close friend of Izquierdo:

At the time of the journey to Fontainebleau, M. Izquierdo . . . called on me and said, 'I have just concluded the Spanish affair, and I hold a treaty signed by the emperor, but the most remarkable circumstance in connection with the matter was the meeting which preceded the signature. I was present with the imperial court at the court theatre. General Duroc sent for me during the performance and ushered me into a cabinet where he left me alone, requesting me on behalf of his master, to read the draft of a treaty which lay on the table and to insert in it, without leaving the Cabinet and without communicating with anyone, any alterations, additions or modifications which I might consider suitable, and at the same time to state my reasons for such changes. I did not refuse the proposal, and during the play I was engaged in writing on the margin of the treaty my corrections and variations. At the end of the performance General Duroc returned, took possession of my notes, and said that he would immediately submit them to the emperor. At midnight I was conducted into his presence, and after a few unimportant remarks the treaty was drafted afresh. This was soon accomplished and the treaty was then signed. We thereby avoid war and cement our union with France. If you peruse the treaty, you will see whether I have really promoted the interests of Spain.'[23]

With this analysis Barère begged to differ: according to his own account he saw clearly that Fontainebleau at the very least jeopardized

Spain's freedom of action – but the die had long since been cast. Last-minute efforts at negotiation by the Portuguese had been quashed by threats that, unless they surrendered forthwith, the house of Bragança would be deposed, and on 18 October the first French forces started crossing the frontier. By the time that Fontainebleau was formally ratified on 29 October 1807, French troops were already deep inside Spain. At their head marched the notoriously fiery and ambitious General Jean Andoche Junot, a close associate of Napoleon, who had first met him at the siege of Toulon in 1793 and had since distinguished himself in Italy, Egypt and Palestine, as well as serving as French ambassador to Lisbon. Nicknamed 'The Tempest', Junot had his sights set on glory. He had never had an independent field command, had missed the dramatic campaigns of 1805–7, and had been denied the marshal's baton that had fallen to so many of his colleagues. Apart from a few battalions composed of Swiss mercenaries or the scrapings of the old Hanoverian and Piedmontese armies, the 25,000 men that he commanded were all veteran units of the French line. Another European capital, then, seemed doomed to occupation at the hands of the French.

Nor was Lisbon alone in this, for in Italy the tempo of events had continued to speed up and thereby to reinforce the impression of a Napoleon in a state of perpetual motion, not to mention a Napoleon who could not resist the opportunity to engage in ostentatious displays of armed force. With the Kingdom of Etruria now once again in French hands, Italy's last independent ruler was Pope Pius VII. Relations between emperor and pontiff had been deteriorating ever since the latter's return from Napoleon's coronation. Pius and his Secretary of State, Cardinal Consalvi, were outraged by the regalist measures which the emperor had imposed on the Church in France and his Italian dependencies. And likewise they could not accept his insinuations that the pope was a vassal of Napoleon. With the rift further deepened by the occupation of the Adriatic city of Ancona for strategic reasons by French troops in the autumn of 1805, Pius therefore defied the French ruler. A new catechism introduced in France to reinforce loyalty to Napoleon was not approved, for example, while doubts were cast upon the sudden discovery of a 'St Napoleon', whose feast day coincided not just with Napoleon's birthday but the feast of the Assumption. Equally, obtaining a decree of nullity to get rid of Jerome Bonaparte's American wife met with such difficulties that Napoleon was left with no option but to give up on Rome and bully the French hierarchy into exceeding their powers and doing as he wanted. As for Ancona, Napoleon was sharply informed that he could either surrender the city forthwith or face a breach in diplomatic relations. The emperor, however, did not back down and Pius was put under more and more pressure to accede to the Continental Blockade and turn the Papal States into a French ally. But this he would not do. The papacy, he argued, was neutral and, indeed, had no option but to remain so. At the same time, he would not hand to Napoleon or anyone else the role of the Church's temporal protector, and this meant in turn that he must *ipso facto* continue as the ruler of a sovereign state. As a conciliatory measure, he did accede to French pressure to divest himself of the services of Cardinal Consalvi, who resigned in June 1806, but that was all. Indeed, by the summer of that year the French ruler was facing excommunication. This was no empty threat, and Napoleon knew it: as a human being he had no belief in redemption, nor still less care for his immortal soul, but to have incurred such a penalty would have inevitably been to undermine the sanction that he had received at his successive coronations as emperor of France and king of Italy. For a little while, then, the emperor held off – it helped in this respect that Pius made a number of minor concessions that suggested he could be swung over to Napoleon's view – but in November 1807 time ran out for the papacy: French troops occupied the Adriatic provinces of the Papal States and four months later a large garrison installed itself in the fortress of Sant' Angelo in the centre of Rome itself. The Pope was still on his throne, but he was now staring Napoleonic power full in the face.

Back in the Peninsula tension was increasing by the day. With the signature of the treaty of Fontainebleau, it appeared that salvation was at hand for Godoy, but in fact the appearance of the French armies coincided with a dramatic deterioration in his situation. In addition to blackening the favourite's reputation and ensuring that the machinery of power could be immediately taken over by them should Charles IV die, the *fernandino* conspirators had early in 1807 decided to guarantee the succession of their figurehead by marrying Ferdinand into the Bonaparte family (the fact that the only possible candidates were very junior did not deter them). Secret negotiations were therefore opened with the French ambassador, in the process of which Ferdinand was persuaded to write a letter openly begging for Napoleon's protection. However, tipped off about the plot, in a dramatic confrontation at the royal palace of El Escorial on 27 October, Charles and Maria Luisa confined the prince to his quarters and ordered an investigation into his affairs. Ferdinand's papers revealed little more than that he hated Godoy, wanted him imprisoned, and had been in some sort of contact with Napoleon. Rather more suggestive, perhaps, were a series of orders appointing supporters of Ferdinand to key positions in the state, but it is apparent that there was no suggestion that Charles IV should be overthrown – all that Ferdinand wanted to do being to ensure that Godoy did not block his accession to the throne in the event of the king's death. None the less the king and queen decided that the prince had been plotting their downfall. Bullied into admitting that this had been his aim, Ferdinand was eventually pardoned, but those he named as his collaborators – Escoíquiz, Infantado, Montijo and various others – were arrested and, despite the collapse of an attempt at a show trial, sent into internal exile.

For Godoy all this was a catastrophe. The general (and wholly incorrect) view of the plot was that the whole affair had been an audacious attempt to eliminate Ferdinand, and the banishment of Escoíquiz *et al.* a monstrous abuse of justice. Perversely, therefore, Ferdinand's prestige had been boosted still further. As one pamphlet put it:

Neither a mad and unnatural mother such as Maria Luisa, nor a cowardly and talentless adventurer such as Godoy could possibly call into question the estimation which the people felt for Ferdinand. On the contrary, his first appearance in public following his release from detention was a real triumph: all the inhabitants of the towns and villages round about descended on El Escorial and massed to greet him: while many cheered him from a distance, others pressed in close to salute him in person, kiss his hands or his clothes, and assure him that they had never believed the accusation.[24]

Even more disastrously, the affair convinced Napoleon of either the need for, or the possibility of, intervention over the Spanish throne. The emperor knew that Godoy could not be trusted and was dissatisfied with Spain's performance as an ally, but had hitherto expressed no intention of taking any hand in her affairs. Yet the idea that she might be transformed into another family monarchy can hardly have been alien to his mind: there had been talk of such a move since at least 1804; meanwhile, anxious for a throne, the dashing Murat was actively promoting the idea. Whatever the truth of the matter, things now started to happen. Charged by Charles IV with complicity in Ferdinand's plotting, the emperor announced that the prince was under his protection and forbade any mention of France in connection with Ferdinand and his accomplices, and on 13 November ordered the 25,000 men he had been holding in reserve at Bayonne – the Second Corps of Observation of the Gironde – to cross the frontier into northern Spain. Meanwhile, fresh troops – the Corps of Observation of the Ocean Coasts and Division of Observation of the Western Pyrenees – were concentrated at Bordeaux and Saint-Jean-Pied-du-Port under Marshals Moncey and Bessières, and magazines established at Bayonne and Perpignan, strenuous attempts also being made to acquire as much intelligence as possible about Spain's armed forces, fortresses, roads and political situation. And, for the first time, there appeared a hint of menace in the correspondence of Napoleon with Charles IV:

It is in the interests of the peoples both of Your Majesty and of myself that we should wage war against Portugal with vigour ... An expedition to Portugal failed some years ago because, at the very moment that I believed that this great gateway was going to be closed to the English, Your Majesty judged it time to make peace. I have too much confidence in his loyalty and political principles to believe that the same thing would happen today. Whilst they are no doubt painful for the sensitive heart of a father, a few arguments in the palace should have no influence on the march of affairs.[25]

El Escorial, then, led directly to French intervention, but whether Napoleon intended to overthrow the Bourbons is another matter. However, the Spanish state had not done much to rehabilitate itself in his eyes: as usual, mobilization had gone very slowly, while news was soon reaching the emperor that Junot's forces, which by now were massing on the Portuguese frontier, were going hungry. That this was not the fault of the Spaniards, but rather of a sudden change in Junot's orders, is neither here nor there. As for the march of the Spanish troops into Portugal, it was hardly an auspicious affair. According to Thiébault, 'General Caraffa's Spanish division lost 1,700 or 1,800 men from hunger or fatigue, drowning in torrents or falling down precipices.'[26] This may be an exaggeration, but even so it is clear that there was considerable confusion. As a Spanish infantry officer remembered, 'It seemed impossible that that short and easy march could have been directed by soldiers.

Units got lost, the soldiers dispersed, and in a word the disorder and confusion reached such a point that I can affirm that I have never seen its equal in the wake of the most complete defeats.'[27] Once again it was a poor advertisement for Spain as an ally, and one that Napoleon was unlikely to forget, particularly as Spain was now acquiring greater prominence in his strategic plans. With the emperor currently pressing for the conquest of Sicily, Spanish naval support would be very valuable, and yet the Spanish navy was in a pitiable condition. Reduced to perhaps fifteen serviceable men-of-war, even these were in need of many repairs, while crew, spares and supplies were all extremely scanty. Only with the greatest difficulty were six ships from Cartagena got to sea with the aim of joining the French squadron at Toulon. With all this, of course, Napoleon was much displeased, especially as nothing would dissuade him from the belief that, thanks to her empire in America, Spain was awash with money. If this potential was not realized, the reason was simple: the Spaniards were corrupt, the Spaniards were inefficient, the Spaniards were incompetent. What was needed, therefore, was the strong hand of France. Yet despite all this there is still no evidence that Napoleon was planning a change of dynasty prior to the end of 1807. In January 1808, indeed, the emperor was still thinking of a marriage alliance: meeting his estranged brother Lucien in Mantua, he sought very hard to persuade him to send his daughter, Charlotte – the only Bonaparte girl available – to Paris as a bride for Ferdinand. And in a conversation that he had in Venice with Joseph Bonaparte, he specifically claimed: 'I have enough hard labour lined up for me: trouble in Spain will only help the English . . . and waste the resources that I get from that country.'[28]

If Napoleon was undecided, he was certainly keeping his options open, while his preparations were accelerated still further by the news that 7,000 British troops had arrived at Gibraltar from Sicily. Commanded by General Pierre Dupont, the 25,000-strong Second Corps of Observation of the Gironde was therefore moved from Vitoria to Valladolid, where it was well placed to march on Madrid, the Corps of Observation of the Ocean Coasts and Division of Observation of the Western Pyrenees being sent to replace it in Navarre and the Basque provinces, and yet another new formation – the Division of Observation of the Eastern Pyrenees – mobilized at Perpignan. Not counting the forces of Junot, over 50,000 French troops were now in Spain, and still others massing on the frontiers. Small wonder, then, that Godoy was starting to feel distinctly alarmed, not least as Izquierdo was now reporting rumours that the emperor was about to carry out some great stroke in Spain. Yet, beyond engaging in conciliatory gestures such as awarding Napoleon the Order of the Golden Fleece, there was nothing he could do.

Before looking at the events that followed, however, we must first return to Portugal, where by early November John and Araujo had agreed to implement all Napoleon's demands immediately, and were asking only for a guarantee of the Bragança dynasty. Their efforts were to no avail. Concerned that the British might send an army to Lisbon, Napoleon ordered Junot to hasten his march. However, the road he was directed to take was the worst possible alternative. What followed was a terrible ordeal – by the time that Junot reached Lisbon on 30 November he had no more than 1,500 men still with the colours. Already, though, the strong hand of France had failed in Portugal. John may have attempted to propitiate Paris, but he had also been careful to keep open his links with the British, who had promised to help the royal family escape to Brazil. Preparations for flight were therefore soon underway, and on 29 November a convoy of eight men-of-war, four frigates and twenty-four merchantmen put to sea and headed for the Atlantic, where it was met by the British naval squadron that had been sent to blockade the Tagus some weeks before. With them went not just the whole of the royal family, but the entire contents of the treasury and the national archives, many works of art, and large numbers of the nobility, the bureaucracy, and the wealthier inhabitants of Lisbon, attended by perhaps half the coin in circulation in the country. Also safely aboard ship was the British merchant community and much of its trading stock. Like Copenhagen, it was another demonstration of the versatility brought by British control of the sea (and another red rag to the Napoleonic bull). And, of course, there were many direct benefits to Britain: in exchange for the loss of the minuscule market represented by Portugal, she obtained access to the whole of Brazil.

The events that ensued in Portugal followed a familiar pattern: most of her army was marched off to France to serve in the *grande armée*, and the country subjected to the beginnings of a typical programme of Napoleonic reform. As for Spain, Napoleon remained set on her regeneration, but was by no means decided as to how to proceed. At this point he was still free to depose Charles IV and replace him with Ferdinand, whom he knew to be not only extremely compliant, but also much loved by the people. Why, then, did he fail to embark upon so obvious a course? The answer is simple. Spain appeared to be in a state of utter disintegration; her army was ill prepared for war; and he was being told by the various agents he had sent across the Pyrenees that there was a general disposition to accept any solution he cared to impose. The Spanish Bourbons could not be trusted, and there was no reason to believe that a regime headed by Ferdinand VII would be any more efficient than one headed by Charles IV. Lucien, it transpired, was unwilling to permit the match between Charlotte and Ferdinand. And finally, with ever larger numbers of troops in Spain, there simply seemed no reason why he should not take drastic action – which would reinforce his prestige, ensure that Spain was transformed and create another throne for his family. Who, after all, could frustrate such a course? The Spanish army was decrepit, and popular revolt in his experience at best a minor threat to be accepted and crushed. Warned by Fouché that Spain might not be an easy target, he therefore exploded: 'What are you talking about? Every reflecting person in Spain despises the government; the Prince of the Peace . . . is a scoundrel who will himself open the gates of Spain for me. As to the rabble . . . a few cannon shots will quickly disperse them.'[29] To the very end Napoleon kept his options open. 'Murat assured me in 1814,' reminisced Lord Holland, 'that he had no instructions . . . Not a syllable had been communicated to him of the object of his expedition.'[30] Indeed, even at the famous conference that was soon to be held at Bayonne, there was a possibility of another outcome. According to Escoíquiz, who had come to Bayonne with Ferdinand and was the first person in the rival Spanish delegations to be told of Napoleon's plans, the emperor told him 'that he was not entirely resolved on the execution of his project'.[31] That said, however, the end of the Bourbon dynasty was now looming: in late March Napoleon wrote to his brother, Louis, who was then King of Holland, and offered him the throne. 'The King of Spain has abdicated . . . Since that moment the people have called out to me with loud voices. Being certain that I will not be able to achieve a solid peace with England without giving a great impulse to the Continent, I have resolved to place a French prince on the throne . . . The climate of Holland does not suit you, while Holland will never emerge from the ruin in which she finds herself . . .

Given all of this, I thought of you . . . You will be the ruler of a generous nation which possesses 11,000,000 inhabitants and has important colonies. With economy and activity, Spain could have 60,000 men under arms along with fifty men o'war in her ports.'[32]

The mention of a battle fleet fifty vessels strong brings us to the issue of strategy. This was obviously of considerable importance in the decision to install a Bonaparte king in Spain, but not just because of the war against Britain. A regenerated Spain would obviously be of great assistance in the struggle against Britain, but in the winter of 1807-8 a more pressing issue had arisen. At this point we come to the question of Franco-Russian relations and, more particularly, the Ottoman Empire, whose pro-French foreign policy had been unaffected by the palace coup that had replaced the reformist Selim III with his younger and more malleable cousin, Mustafa IV. For the Porte, Tilsit had come as a blow as heavy as it was unexpected. Great things had been hoped for from a French victory over Russia – the French ambassador Sebastiani, indeed, had promised the restoration of the Crimea, the recognition of full Turkish sovereignty in the Danubian provinces and a guarantee of all the empire's territories – and all these now evaporated. Still worse, now that France and Russia were allies, the Ottomans were in danger of a joint attack.

Yet as the months went by the threat failed to materialize. Having secured Alexander's acquiescence at Tilsit by giving him to understand that substantial territorial gains were on offer in the Balkans, Napoleon started to backtrack. An attack on the Ottoman Empire might well lead to the conquest of the Balkans, but the sultan would be so weakened by such a blow that it was impossible to see how he could then keep control of the rest of the empire. But without good relations with Constantinople, how could Napoleon hope to seal off the coasts of Anatolia, Syria, Palestine and Arabia from British trade? And how, too, could the British be stopped from moving in and seizing whatever territories they might be interested in? As 1807 moved to its close, however, Alexander became more and more irritated. No difficulty was found, for example, in getting French troops to Cattaro and those of the Ionian islands that had been held by Russia. Still worse, Napoleon was now demanding Silesia as compensation for Russia keeping Moldavia and Wallachia, despite his promise at Tilsit to evacuate the region. With Alexander desperate to achieve a foreign policy success that would counterbalance the disastrous effects of his accession to the Continental Blockade (see below), the result was renewed Russian pressure in the Balkans. As we have seen, Alexander refused to ratify the armistice with Turkey, while at the same time ordering his troops in Moldavia, Wallachia and the island of Tenedos (where the Russians had established a major naval base) to stay put, and in effect trying to entice Napoleon into an attack on the Ottomans with promises of Albania and Greece. Partitioning the Ottoman Empire was still not to Napoleon's taste, but at this point he seems to have decided that partition was inevitable, and that his goal should be to turn it to his advantage. In so far as this was concerned, there were two obvious objectives, the first being to embroil Austria with Russia and the second to challenge Russian foot-dragging in respect of opening hostilities against Britain. In consequence, the emperor brought in the Austrians and secretly offered them a broad swathe of territory stretching right across the Balkans from Bosnia to Bulgaria (a move that would also have the happy effect of limiting Russia's territorial gains to Moldavia and Wallachia and allowing Napoleon to claim Silesia as compensation), while at the same time proposing to Alexander that 50,000 French, Austrian and Russian troops should advance on Constantinople from their respective bases in Dalmatia, Croatia and the Danubian provinces with a view to partitioning the Ottoman Empire and then marching on India. Whether this last idea was intended as a serious suggestion is a moot point – what Napoleon was really thinking of was almost certainly a scenario that would see him regain Egypt with the aid of Russian naval power – but in the end this mattered very little: Russia would be at war with Britain, and Alexander left not only with almost nothing, but also very much dancing to Napoleon's tune.

It is in this context, then, that the decision to overthrow the Bourbons must be seen. With a major war brewing in the eastern Mediterranean, Spain had suddenly become not just more important as a naval partner, but also a vital strategic base: if Napoleon was to seize the North African littoral, for example, it was Spain's ports that were best placed to launch such a campaign. That the Ottoman Empire had become the centre of the emperor's attention is further suggested by events in Italy. At the beginning of 1808 elaborate preparations were in train for an invasion of Sicily, but these were now suddenly cancelled in favour of a naval expedition to reinforce the garrison that had held out in Corfu throughout the years of hostility with Russia. If the Ottoman Empire was to be partitioned, Corfu was an obvious forward base from which to make a dash at Egypt and forestall any moves that Britain might make; important though it was, Sicily could wait. Then in March came the decision to strengthen the empire's grip on central Italy by annexing Tuscany – the erstwhile Kingdom of Etruria – Parma, Lucca, Guastalla, Piacenza and Piombino to France (as ruler of Lucca and Piombino, Elise Bonaparte was compensated with what amounted to the vice-royalty of the four new departments made up from the new annexations), the aim being to give the emperor complete control of the roads leading to the vital ports of Taranto and Brindisi. As to what all this was for, from 12 April a series of orders directed Napoleon's Minister of Marine, Admiral Decrès, to concentrate the Toulon fleet at Taranto with the aim of transporting 30,000 men to a destination that was first Tunis or Algiers and later Egypt.

To be still more explicit, the city that mattered most in the deliberations of the powers in 1808 was not Madrid but Constantinople. No sooner had Napoleon's letter of 2 February arrived in St Petersburg than a vigorous debate began as to exactly how the Ottoman Empire in Europe was to be partitioned. With Alexander, Rumiantsev and the French ambassador Caulaincourt as the main protagonists in the drama, a series of secret meetings saw France and Russia battle it out in a determined effort to secure victory for their different solutions. To complicate matters, Russia was already engaged in a campaign that it could at least argue was being waged on Napoleon's behalf. This affair was the Russo-Swedish War of 1808–9. Given that it reveals the difficulties the Portland administration was labouring under in the wake of Tilsit, this conflict is worth some consideration. At Tilsit Russia had agreed to put pressure on Sweden to join the Continental Blockade. But Sweden was also an old enemy whose territories in Finland had long been an object of Russian desire, and whose fleet, being specially designed for the shallow waters of the Baltic, was a serious threat to the Russian coast. It was soon clear, then, that a Russian attack was coming. In these straits Sweden had the full support of Britain: Canning was eager to keep her in the war and to do so was prepared to bribe her with the promise of both the captured Dutch colony of Surinam and the prospect of annexing Norway (a particular goal of Gustav IV). To obtain this latter goal it was suggested the Swedish army should occupy Zealand

and with it Copenhagen, the intention being that the island could then be swapped for Norway come the peace settlement. And on offer, too, were 10,000 of the British troops who had been sent against the Danes. All this Gustav IV would have been glad to accept, but all chances of a deal were wrecked by elements in the regime who distrusted Britain in the wake of Copenhagen and the loss of Swedish Pomerania, and wanted to revive Sweden's traditional alliance with France. Yet, hating Napoleon as he did, Gustav would not take the concomitant step of joining the Franco-Russian entente, the consequence being that his country soon found herself under attack: on 22 February 1808 a Russian army invaded Finland, while the end of the month saw Denmark declare war as well.

To return to the question of the Ottoman Empire, there was no particular reason for Alexander and Rumiantsev to make an issue of the conflict in their discussions with Caulaincourt: in the first instance, in fact, the Russians swept all before them. But the mere fact that they were currently fighting the Swedes strengthened their hand with Napoleon, and Caulaincourt therefore found that the bargaining was very fierce. The Russians demanded the Danubian provinces, Bulgaria, European Turkey and Constantinople, whereas the French wanted to restrict them to the first two alone, and to claim the whole of Albania, Greece and the islands of the eastern Mediterranean for themselves. About the only matter on which there was general agreement was that Austria should get little more than Bosnia (given the stiffening attitude in St Petersburg, Caulaincourt seems to have given up the earlier plan to give Vienna Bulgaria). There was, then, a complete impasse, the central issue being who should control Constantinople and the Dardanelles. To secure this area Alexander was on paper prepared to offer France almost anything. One plan had France getting not just Albania, the Aegean islands, Crete, Cyprus and most of Greece, but also Asia Minor, Syria and Egypt. But, taking his cue from the instructions he had received from Paris, Caulaincourt would not budge on the Dardanelles, although he was prepared in the end to surrender Constantinople. And so finally all that could be agreed was that the two emperors should hold another Tilsit-style conference in the hope of coming to a mutually acceptable solution.

If Alexander stood firm over Constantinople, it was in part because he was under pressure from England. At the last minute, when diplomatic relations between Britain and Russia were on the point of formally being broken off, the Russian ambassador in London, Alopeus, was suddenly told by Canning that Britain would enter peace talks with Napoleon without prior conditions. In acting thus, Canning was almost certainly convinced that the emperor would not accept the offer, generous though it was. Although Napoleon could not have prevented Britain from hanging on to her colonial conquests, there would have been nothing to stop him from retaining the Low Countries and Hanover, not to mention all France's acquisitions in Italy. In effect, then, Canning was warning Alexander that Britain would disengage from Europe, withdraw into her maritime empire and leave Russia to enjoy her friendship with France and see how well she liked the experience. As Alexander was now rather less charmed by Napoleon than he had been at Tilsit, the effect on St Petersburg of Canning's proposal was dramatic: at worst, Russia might actually find herself facing Napoleon alone, and as a result securing the Dardanelles assumed more importance in Russian eyes than ever.

It was a key moment – possibly *the* key moment. Agreement with St Petersburg offered the only real hope of defeating Britain, so why did Napoleon not give Alexander what he wanted? On one level, the answer was primarily economic and strategic. With Russia in control of the Dardanelles, the tsar would be able to challenge France's commercial presence in the Orient; restrict or even cut off the supply of Egyptian cotton; build up an unassailable naval and military presence in the Levant; and completely block the overland route to India (not that this was of any real value: the French mission that had been dispatched to Persia had been sending back a stream of reports that suggested that it would at best have been a road paved with bones). But it was not just that. Also important was the issue of psychology. To give the tsar the principal objective sought by all of his predecessors was simply a concession too far for Napoleon, while there was much pleasure simply in denying Alexander the object of his desire. In the event, the whole issue came to naught, for 2,000 miles to the west events were unfolding which shattered the eastern mirage once and for all, but pride and vainglory had none the less clearly triumphed over the dictates of strategy.

There was, then, a strong hint of nemesis in the air. What, though, was happening in the Iberian Peninsula? Backed up by sufficient reinforcements to make them fully fledged army corps, between 9 and 12 February the Divisions of the Eastern and Western Pyrenees crossed the border into Navarre and Catalonia, occupied Pamplona and Barcelona, and seized control of the citadels that dominated the two cities. Thoroughly alarmed, the Spanish government had for some time been pressing for an explanation of France's conduct, while simultaneously requesting the implementation of the promised partition of Portugal and the nomination of a Bonaparte bride for Ferdinand. To all these communications the emperor had replied with a mixture of disdain and obfuscation, while at the same time continuing to proclaim his friendly intentions. Faced by increasing evidence of French duplicity, Godoy responded by ordering the Spanish troops in Portugal to return to Spain (most got away apart from those in Lisbon of whom the majority were disarmed and interned). Then came another shock. In a long memorandum dated 24 February, Napoleon denounced the anarchy in the royal household, accused Spain of bad faith and announced that he no longer considered himself bound by Fontainebleau. Spain was now promised the whole of Portugal, true, but in exchange she would have to surrender all the territory between the river Ebro and the Pyrenees and sign a permanent and unlimited alliance with France. In acting thus, Napoleon hoped both to justify his conduct hitherto and to provoke the Spaniards into a resistance that would provide the pretext he needed to overthrow the monarchy. If this was his intention, then he was certainly successful: Charles IV agreed with Godoy and his other advisers that he should flee to America by way of Seville. The court had already moved to the palace of Aranjuez on the river Tagus south of Madrid, so it was well placed for such a move, while to gain time, Godoy ordered the royal guard to move there from its barracks in the capital, and directed a variety of troops to hold the line of the Tagus. Garrisons stationed in the French zone of occupation were ordered to put up no resistance and a conciliatory response was made to Napoleon's demands, but nothing could disguise the fact that war was imminent. As a miserable Godoy lamented, 'I am in such a state . . . that I should like to put on . . . a sack and go and hide in a corner.'[33]

The French, meanwhile, were on the move again. On 20 February, Joachim Murat had been appointed to the command of the 60,000 French troops who were now in Spain, and on 2 March he was ordered to establish his headquarters in Vitoria, where he soon received the support of a 6,000-strong detachment of the Imperial Guard. On 6 March the French occupied the fortress of San Sebastián, with Murat receiving instructions the next day to launch the forces of Dupont and Moncey southwards towards Madrid, whose occupation, the emperor's lieutenant was told, was to be followed by the dispatch of Godoy and the Spanish royal family to a meeting with Napoleon at either Burgos or Bayonne. Meanwhile, though half-hearted efforts were still made to convince the Spaniards that all was well – the march on Madrid was explained by talk of securing Cádiz against the British, besieging Gibraltar, or even sending troops to Africa – the French were increasingly reckoning on armed conflict. As Napoleon wrote to Murat, 'I hope with all my heart that there will be no war, and am only taking so many precautions because it is my habit to leave nothing to chance. But if there is a war, your position will be a very good one.'[34]

The trap, then, was about to shut, but events were now disrupted by fresh developments. For Ferdinand and his supporters, the so-called *fernandinos*, war with France was unthinkable. First of all, they remained convinced that the emperor intended to place Ferdinand on the throne or, at least, get rid of Godoy, and second, they believed – quite rightly – that war would lead to defeat and the overthrow of the entire dynasty. Terrified of what might occur, Ferdinand summoned his henchman, Montijo, and ordered him to organize a rising that could present the emperor with a fait accompli in the form of a new monarch who would be only too eager to throw himself on Napoleon's mercy and do his will in every particular. In stirring up revolt, there was little difficulty. Across the Peninsula there was a widespread conviction that the French were out to do no more than rescue Ferdinand from the clutches of Godoy. 'Our troops', wrote Lejeune, 'had been welcomed in Spain . . . and the loyal populace, who . . . received us as if we were their brothers, impatiently awaited the day when the emperor . . . would remove the hated minister.'[35] Acting from ignorance as much as intent, the French had done nothing to dampen such hopes: 'The French . . . knew not what was the work which they were destined to perform, but, hearing nothing from their hosts but curses upon the authors of the misfortunes of the country, they associated themselves with the public indignation, and . . . repeated that the army was come into Spain only to execute justice upon a villain.'[36] At this point, too, Napoleon had assumed none of the demon-like qualities he would soon acquire in the eyes of most Spaniards. Among the educated classes, he was widely admired – the emperor himself later remarked that the regime was 'never afraid of him' and 'looked on him as a defender of royalism'.[37] Influenced by vague ideas that the emperor had saved the Church from the revolutionaries, the crowd were content to follow the lead of the elites. As a French officer, Foy, wrote, 'It was obvious that the reign of Napoleon had entirely effaced the antipathy of Catholic Spain to [the] new France.'[38] Yet beneath the surface trouble was brewing. 'The soldiers', wrote a young seminarian named Robert Brindle whom the arrival of the French had caught at the English seminary in Valladolid, 'were quartered in private houses and brought distress and misery into every family. Their right to anything which they chose to covet few had the hardihood to call in question. If complaint were made, it must be proffered to a French officer, and insult or an additional grievance were the result.'[39]

At this stage virtually the only troops actually at Aranjuez were the royal guard, whose aristocratic officer corps had never forgiven Godoy either his lowly origins or the fact that in one of the few military reforms he had succeeded in pushing through he had cut the guard's size by half. Meanwhile, the population of Aranjuez was wholly dependent on the court for its prosperity, and was currently much swelled by the hordes of courtiers and retainers who travelled with the royal family on their migrations from one royal palace to the next. At the same time, many of the villages around Madrid happened to be fiefs of the leading *fernandinos* and could thus be galvanized into action by economic means. Yet bribery was probably barely needed. For all their discontent, the populace retained a touching faith in the protection supposedly afforded them by the monarch. The news that the king intended to leave them to their fate therefore caused as much fear as the possibility that Godoy might evade his doom caused fury. Disguised as one 'Uncle Joe', Montijo had within a very few days succeeded in massing a large crowd around the palace at Aranjuez and whipping the Guard's hatred of Godoy to fever pitch. Initially it seems that the plan was for the revolt to be sparked off by the departure of the royal family, but, thanks to Charles's vacillation, this did not happen. In the event, however, no catalyst was needed. As the Secretary of State, Pedro Cevallos, informed the Secretary of the Council of Castile: 'About one o'clock in the morning [of 18 March] there occurred a clash between some hussars and Guardias de Corps, and this was followed by the assembly of many soldiers and civilians who had taken fright at rumours that the king and queen and royal family were leaving.'[40]

What followed was a frightening affair. The hussars referred to were members of Godoy's recently formed personal bodyguard – 'a troop of brilliantly uniformed soldiers who were regarded by their fellows with envy and hated by the people'[41] – and the violence with which they were assaulted set the scene for three days of mayhem. Nor was the trouble confined to Aranjuez. In Madrid, for example:

Hardly had night fallen than a furious crowd invaded the house of Don Diego, the younger brother of the favourite. Having smashed in the doors and discovered that the building was empty, they began to throw all its rich furniture out of the windows . . . until they had made an enormous pile of tables, beds, wardrobes and pianos, to which they set fire . . . When the *plebe* had finished enjoying this . . . costly bonfire, they . . . headed for the house of the Príncipe de Branciforte, Godoy's brother-in-law. However, a notice had been put on the door . . . announcing that the property of the favourite and his close relatives had been confiscated . . . This was enough to calm down the rioters, and they spent the rest of the night processing through the streets . . . and drinking at the cost of the taverners . . . [The next day] the whole garrison . . . were called out of their barracks by bands of women bearing pitchers of wine in their hands, and . . . the soldiers, mixing with the people, bore in their firelocks the palm branches which, as a precaution against lightning, are commonly hung at the windows.[42]

In Toledo a bust of Godoy was hung from a gibbet; in San Lucar de Barrameda a botanical garden he had established was wrecked, and in Zaragoza, radicalized by recent regulations that had extended the academic year by three months, the students of the university forced their lecturers to barricade themselves into the building's cloister and seized the portrait of the favourite that hung in the main lecture hall. Placed on a makeshift hurdle, it was then dragged through the streets to the city centre. There, wrote one of the leaders, 'We made a bonfire whose flames leapt higher than the roofs, whereupon, having been well kicked and spat upon, His Excellency . . . was thrown upon the fire.'[43]

Back in Aranjuez, the king and queen were terrified. With the bulk of the guard in a state of rebellion and the favourite himself hiding in the attic of his palace, whence he had fled as the mob poured through the main door, Charles IV quickly agreed to have Godoy arrested, but, under Montijo's orchestration, the disturbances continued unabated. Told by one regimental commander that only Ferdinand would enjoy the loyalty of the troops, Charles and Maria Luisa caved in, and on the morning of 19 March they abdicated the crown into the hands of their son. Driven from his hiding place by thirst, Godoy narrowly escaped a lynching, and was placed under close arrest. Sent to rescue him by Murat, a French officer discovered a pitiful figure: 'Two leagues from the suburbs I came upon Godoy. Although this unhappy man was terribly wounded and covered with blood, the guards who escorted him had been cruel enough to put irons on his hands and feet, and to tie him to a rough open cart where he was exposed to the scorching rays of the sun, and to thousands of flies attracted by his wounds, which were scarcely covered with coarse linen rags. I was indignant at the sight.'[44]

For all its popular aspect, there is no doubt as to what the so-called *motín de Aranjuez* represented. Inspired by elements from outside its ranks though it may have been, a section of the army – in this case the royal guard – had sought to impose its views by 'pronouncing' against the regime. Challenged by this call to arms, Godoy and his royal patrons found that they had few defenders. The officer corps as a whole was disgruntled and rebellious; much of the upper nobility and the Church was hostile; reformist circles had long since lost all faith in Godoy's political credentials; and the common people were in a state of open revolt. As for Ferdinand, he was seen as a saviour, the reception that he received when he rode into Madrid on 24 March being captured by Alcalá Galiano:

In truth, in all the different scenes of popular enthusiasm that I have witnessed, nothing . . . has ever equalled those which I now describe. The cheers were loud, repeated and delivered with . . . eyes full of tears of pleasure, kerchiefs were waved . . . from balconies with hands trembling with pleasure . . . and not for a moment did the passion . . . or the thunderous noise of the joyful crowd diminish.[45]

Popular though the new king was, his security was far from assured. Murat had occupied the city only the day before and, despite increasingly abject attempts to win France's favour, refused to recognize Ferdinand; still worse, indeed, Charles IV was persuaded to protest against his abdication and appeal to Napoleon for assistance. With the two rivals openly craving his mediation, the emperor was ideally placed to recast the kingdom as he wanted. Charles, Maria Luisa and Ferdinand were all summoned to meet him for a conference at Bayonne while, as a sop to the former king and queen, Godoy was rescued from captivity and whisked to safety in France. With all the protagonists in the drama united in his presence, Napoleon announced that the rival kings were both to renounce the throne and hand it to the emperor. To this demand Charles made no resistance, and on 5 May, after some days of unedifying squabbles, such feeble defiance as Ferdinand was willing to offer was also overcome in exchange for guarantees of Spain's territorial and religious integrity.

In the eyes of Napoleon, the 'heaviest part of the work' had now been done.[46] But even as the Bourbons departed to a decorous exile – Charles, Maria Luisa and Godoy to Italy, and Ferdinand to Talleyrand's chateau at Valençay – the Peninsula was astir. Indeed, more than that, the flames of rebellion were spreading on all sides. Why had the emperor acted as he had? For answer we might begin by turning to Napoleon himself:

The old king and queen . . . had become the object of the hatred and scorn of their subjects. The Prince of Asturias was conspiring against them . . . and had become . . . the hope of the nation. At the same time [Spain] was ready for great changes . . . whilst I myself was very popular there. With matters in this state . . . I resolved to make use of this unique opportunity to rid myself of a branch of the Bourbons, continue the family system of Louis XIV in my own dynasty, and chain Spain to the destinies of France.[47]

The preoccupation with *raison d'état* is repeated in other sources. As he told his close ally in the Council of State, Pierre-Louis Roederer, for example:

Spain . . . must be French. It is for France that I have conquered Spain; it is with her blood, her arms, her gold. I am French in all my affections . . . I do not do anything except for . . . love of France. I dethroned the Bourbons for no other reason than that it was in the interest of France to assure my dynasty. I had nothing else in view except French strength and glory . . . I have the rights of conquest: call whoever governs Spain king . . . viceroy or governor general, Spain must be French.[48]

While there is a kernel of truth in these claims, it would be foolish to take them too far. At bottom opportunism was the key. Napoleon had been motivated neither by an altruistic desire to spread the benefits of freedom and enlightenment, nor by a gigantic strategic combination, nor by an overwhelming clan loyalty that made the creation of family courts the centrepiece of French foreign policy. Strategic, ideological and historical factors were present in his thinking, and the final factor in the decision to overthrow the Spanish Bourbons was almost certainly the changing situation in the Balkans and the eastern Mediterranean. Yet would the emperor in the end have acted otherwise in a situation in which nothing seemed to stand between him and a stroke that was more audacious than anything he had yet attempted? To this there can obviously be no certain answer, but what can be said is that the decision to invade Portugal – the bridge that led to intervention in Spain – was the product not of rational consideration but of the emperor's constant need to demonstrate his prowess, impose his stamp upon affairs, and emphasize his contempt for diplomacy. In the end no strategic pretext was necessary for his assault on the Spanish monarchy. To quote a pamphlet that was published in insurgent Seville in 1808, 'Napoleon . . . may be compared to the vine, a plant that if it is not pruned, throws out its branches in all directions and ends up by taking over everything. He wants peace, but at the same time wishes to dethrone kings . . . create new monarchies and destroy old republics . . . to undo the very globe, and remake it in accordance with nothing other than his own will.'[49]

With the emperor already casting around for new schemes of conquest – in May 1808 there emerged a truly visionary plan for an invasion of India by way of the Cape of Good Hope – war was set to continue ad infinitum. However, it did so under new circumstances for Napoleon. The details of the Bayonne affair were such as seriously to tarnish the emperor's image. For him to have dethroned the Spanish Bourbons was unsettling enough, but for him to have done so by what appeared to be nothing more than one long process of deceit and chicanery was a shattering blow to his reputation. Even men who in other respects remained loyal admirers of the emperor to their graves later professed themselves shocked by what had happened. 'Thus was consummated', wrote one of Murat's aides-de-camp, 'the most iniquitous spoliation which modern history records . . . The conduct of Napoleon in this scandalous affair was unworthy of a great man. To offer himself as mediator between a father and son in order to draw them into a trap and then plunder them both – this was an odious atrocity.'[50] Indeed, even Napoleon was a little shamefaced at what he had done: 'However it may have been, I disdained ways that were tortuous and banal: I felt myself to be that powerful! I struck from too great a height. I wanted to act both in the fashion of that Providence which remedies the ills of mortals by means that are their equal, however violent, and in a manner unfettered by judgement. At all events I confess that I embarked on the affair in a very bad way: the immorality was too patent, the injustice too cynical, and, because I had fallen, the whole thing became utterly villainous, and presented itself to the world in a state of the most hideous nudity, stripped of all grandeur and all the numerous benefits that had filled my intentions.'[51] There was, to be sure, a certain self-pity here: in retrospect Napoleon could see all too well the damage that Bayonne had done him: '[England] was lost: the affair of Copenhagen had revolted every spirit and destroyed her reputation on the Continent. As for me, I was basking . . . in advantages that were the very opposite of this situation. And then this unfortunate Spanish affair came along and suddenly turned public opinion against me while at the same time rehabilitating England.'[52] But even at the time Napoleon's tone was defensive. As he wrote to Alexander I:

Disorder in this country had reached a degree difficult to imagine. Compelled to intervene in its affairs, I have been led by the irresistible force of events to a system which guarantees both the happiness of Spain and the tranquillity of my own states. In her new situation Spain will really be less dependent on me than she was before, but I shall derive the advantage that, when she finds herself normally situated, and with nothing to fear on the land, she will use all her resources to rebuild her navy . . . I am well aware that my action in Spain will open a vast ground for discussion. People will . . . allege the whole thing was a premeditated plot. But in fact, if I had thought of nothing but the interests of France, it would have been quite simple to extend my southern frontiers at the expense of Spanish territory, for everyone knows that ties of blood go for little in calculations of policy, and are null and void at the end of twenty years.[53]

Whether this is blatant cynicism or self-delusion, it was enough to fool Alexander. Nor was the tsar alone: in Vienna and Berlin, too, there were still those who believed that it was possible to live in a state of peace and friendship with Napoleon. But Bayonne was not forgotten, and, fittingly enough, was very soon to present Napoleon with the worst crisis of his career to date.

8

From Madrid to Vienna

In May 1808 Napoleon Bonaparte was truly at the pinnacle of his power. From September 1805 until June 1807 his forces had fanned out across the Continent driving all before them. But in the early months of 1808 the tempo of French aggression was raised to fresh levels. Two dynasties – the Bourbons of Naples and the Braganças – had already been driven from their thrones and a third had now been physically sequestered and forced to give up its rights. Not for nothing, then, did the Ottomans accord Napoleon the title of *padishah* – 'King of kings'. Inherent in this situation, however, was an obvious danger. At Tilsit Napoleon had, or so it seemed on the surface, for a brief moment come to terms with reality. Driven by the dictates of the war against Britain, he had established a partnership with Russia. Part and parcel of this was an agreement in effect to share the domination of continental Europe between two 'superpowers', and this in turn offered France her only way forward. Allied with Russia, she could genuinely hope for a successful end to the war against Britain, while Russian cooperation also set clear limits to her war effort and removed the very real danger that she would end up having to force the blockade single-handed on the whole of an unwilling Continent. At the same time, caught between the millstones of France and Russia, Austria and Prussia would of necessity have to choose the path of submission. But in reality Tilsit was not all it seemed. Far from being an act of policy, it had simply been a useful shift that put an end to a campaign Napoleon had found very difficult to sustain and which had involved some of the worst fighting of his career. What it did not amount to was a recognition that there were limits beyond which the French ruler could not go. In the first place, the concept of sharing power was not one which the emperor accepted. As a master of manipulation, Napoleon had gulled Alexander by adopting the guise of friend and ally, but as a human being he was completely incapable of translating this play-acting into reality in the way that the settlement required. There was little prospect that the mixture of adulation and flattery that had brought emperor and tsar together at Tilsit would lead to a genuine partnership. Whether it was the treaty of Amiens or the treaty of Lunéville, settlements with France had always sooner or later foundered on the rock of Napoleon's ambition, and now that ambition had been inflated to fresh heights. Tilsit was doomed, the only question being how long it would take for the breach with Russia to become manifest.

According to traditional British accounts of the Napoleonic Wars, if the French hegemony that had been established at Tilsit was eventually challenged, it was in large part because of the events that the overthrow of Charles IV and Ferdinand VII unleashed in Spain and Portugal. If Napoleon had believed that the Bourbons could be removed quietly, then he was sorely mistaken. On the contrary, sporadic disturbances in Spain, most notably a serious rising in Madrid on 2 May, forever after remembered as the Dos de Mayo, had by the beginning of June become a full-scale national uprising that was quickly seconded by a further revolt in Portugal. Of all the events of the French Wars, there is probably none that has been more misunderstood. Generally the revolts have been portrayed as the product of outraged patriotism, but this view is difficult to sustain. In both Spain and Portugal the risings were actually very murky affairs that reflected many of the tensions besetting the body politic. The various provincial risings – for there was no concerted national uprising as such – were engineered by a variety of dissident groups for their own purposes. In Spain, in particular, the insurrection's leaders included disgruntled office-seekers, radicals eager to make a political revolution, prominent civilians resentful of the privileges of the military estate, discontented subaltern officers eager for promotion, conservative clerics horrified by Bourbon anti-clericalism, and members of the aristocracy opposed to the creeping advance of royal authority. As for the crowd, its motivation was as much material as it was ideological. There was intense loyalty to Ferdinand VII, but this stemmed not so much from who he was as from what he represented. As Godoy's enemies had deliberately represented Ferdinand as a ruler who would as if by magic right all Spain's ills, the populace believed he would rescue them from the terrible conditions that they were enduring. With the vast majority of those in political and military authority men who owed their prominence to Godoy, this persuaded the populace that Napoleon's intervention was somehow the work of the favourite. Added to this was a general belief that the French were bent on killing the entire population: the Dos de Mayo, for example, was commonly believed to have been an unprovoked attack on the people of Madrid. From here it was but a short step to a great social convulsion. Those in authority were seen as traitors: it hardly assisted their cause that in most cases they had been urging the people to remain quiet and accept whatever Napoleon might decree. But they were also men of property and privilege, and this made the rising as much a *jacquerie* as a movement against the French.

The social and political background to the Peninsular War is a subject that the current author has pursued in depth elsewhere, so here we will confine ourselves to the military history of the conflict. The forces sent to Portugal were expelled by a British army under Sir Arthur Wellesley after a battle at Vimeiro (21 August 1808) and another contingent of almost 20,000 men commanded by General Dupont were forced to surrender at Bailén by a Spanish regular army commanded by Francisco Javier Castaños. Forced to draw back beyond the river Ebro, the invaders then received major reinforcements and Napoleon came to Spain to take charge of operations. The emperor, indeed, was furious: Bailén was an unparalleled blow to his prestige. What made the humiliation still greater was, first, that Dupont was a highly experienced commander who had won much acclaim in the campaign of 1805, and, second, that it came in the wake of a serious Spanish defeat at Medina de Río Seco in Old Castile that had encouraged hopes of an early end to the war. The very day Bailén was fought Napoleon was writing to Joseph, 'There is nothing so extraordinary in you having to conquer your kingdom. Phillip V and Henry IV were obliged to conquer theirs, too. Be gay; do not let anything get you down; and do not doubt for an instant that things will work out better and be concluded more promptly than you think.'[1] A few days later, we find that the tone of his correspondence is very different: 'Dupont has sullied our banners. What ineptitude! What baseness!'[2] Needless to say, such a defeat could not go unavenged, and by the beginning of November a much reinforced Armée d'Espagne was poised to deal out brutal retribution under the leadership of Napoleon himself. There followed a whirlwind campaign which saw the Spaniards suffer major defeats at Espinosa de los Monteros, Gamonal, Tudela and Somosierra. With the Spanish armies in tatters, and the provisional government known as the Junta Central, that had been formed in the wake of the battle of Bailén, in flight for Seville, on 4 December the emperor recaptured Madrid. Meanwhile, the position had also been restored in Catalonia, where the French army of occupation had for the last few months been bottled up in Barcelona.

With matters in this situation, it seemed entirely possible that the French would go on to overrun the entire Peninsula and end the war. All possibility of this, however, was precluded by a last-minute intervention in the campaign on the part of the British. Having cleared the French from Portugal, the British expeditionary force had advanced into Spain under the command of Sir John Moore (Wellesley had returned to England following a furious controversy over the surrender terms agreed in the wake of Vimeiro). For various reasons it had taken a long time for it to get ready for action, and for a while it looked as if Moore would have no option but to withdraw into Portugal. Eventually, however, Moore resolved on an offensive against the French forces guarding Napoleon's communications in Old Castile under the command of Marshal Soult. As this brought the full weight of the French armies in northern Spain against his 20,000 men, he was soon forced to retreat to the coast of Galicia in search of rescue by the Royal Navy. But so many troops were pulled after him that the French had effectively to abandon their plans for the immediate conquest of southern Spain. As for Moore and his army, almost all the troops were rescued after a rearguard action at La Coruña on 16 January 1809, but their commander was mortally wounded by a cannon ball at the moment of victory. Though his conduct of the campaign is open to much criticism, his sacrifice was not in vain. As an early French chronicler of the conflict admitted, 'The movement against Soult . . . forced Bonaparte to delay the execution of his designs against Andalucía and Portugal. There was not a soldier to defend the passes of the Sierra Morena, and there were but few English left in Portugal.'[3]

For the student of Napoleon, there is much to ponder in these events. The fact that many of the French troops sent to Spain in the course of the winter of 1807 were second-line units of the poorest quality speaks volumes for the extraordinary overconfidence with which the emperor embarked on the overthrow of the Spanish Bourbons. At the same time his decision to throw almost every man he had into the pursuit of Sir

John Moore suggests a want of judgement of another sort: the British forces were so far from Madrid that to have caught them was almost impossible, particularly in the depths of an icy Castilian winter. Typical enough were the experiences of the aide-de-camp, Lejeune:

I found the whole of the Imperial Guard at San Rafael . . . The storm had been so terrible on the mountain that many men and horses had been swept over precipices, where they had perished. The grenadiers, exhausted with fatigue, were sleeping on the frozen ground covered with masses of snow and ice beside their fires, which were all but extinguished by the rain and hail which were still falling . . . There was not a square foot of shelter . . . not already invaded by sleepers piled one on top of the other.[4]

Whatever the implications of Napoleon's conduct, the campaign of November 1808 to January 1809 set the pattern of operations for the whole of the next year. The French controlled most of central and northern Spain, together with a separate area around Barcelona, while Spanish armies held southern Catalonia, the Levante, Andalucía and Extremadura. As for Portugal, she too was in allied hands with a British garrison in Lisbon and such few troops as the Portuguese could muster deployed to protect Elvas, Almeida and Oporto. Called away from Spain by the growing fears of the new war with Austria, Napoleon had left instructions for his commanders – most notably, Soult, Ney and Victor – to crush allied resistance by a series of powerful offensives, but this plan quickly foundered. The Spanish armies defending Andalucía proved unexpectedly aggressive; the British reinforced their presence in Portugal and, once again commanded by a rehabilitated Sir Arthur Wellesley, repelled a French invasion; the province of Galicia rose in revolt; and the cities of Zaragoza and Gerona both put up desperate resistance when they were attacked. By the summer the initiative had passed to the Allies, and the rest of the year was dominated by two major attempts to recover Madrid. Of these, the first – an Anglo-Spanish offensive from the west and south – led merely to stalemate, a major triumph at Talavera on 28 July being deprived of all effect by serious divisions in the allied command and the fortuitous arrival of massive French reinforcements. The second offensive, however, led to disaster. In the wake of Talavera, Wellesley – now Lord Wellington – refused to engage in any further operations in Spain, and pulled his men back to the Portuguese frontier. In consequence, the offensive was the work of the Spaniards alone.

Operating on exterior lines from the north-west, the west and the south in terrain that greatly favoured the vastly superior French cavalry, they had no chance, and were routed at the battles of Ocaña and Alba de Tormes with terrible losses. For the French it was a moment of triumph. In the words of an order of the day issued by Joseph Bonaparte on the field of Ocaña:

His Majesty hastens to inform the army that the imperial forces . . . have secured a signal victory at Ocaña. The Army of La Mancha . . . has been destroyed. All of its baggage, all of its artillery and thirty standards have fallen into our hands . . . [and] the number of prisoners, amongst whom are numbered three generals, six colonels and 700 other officers, amounts to 25,000. The terrain is strewn with dead, and 40,000 muskets lie abandoned on the battlefield . . . It really appears as if not one battalion of the [enemy] army remains in a state fit to fight.[5]

The defeat of the main Spanish field armies and the British decision to concentrate on the defence of Portugal opened a new phase in the conflict. So serious had been the Spanish losses in the campaigns of 1809 that there was little left to put into the line. Nor could these losses be made up: though generous, British supplies of arms and uniforms were insufficient to the task of equipping whole new armies from scratch while resistance to conscription among the populace had reached enormous heights, the war never having been the popular crusade of legend. Meanwhile, with the new Austrian war fought and won (see below), Napoleon was pouring large numbers of fresh troops into Spain, and so the initiative passed back to the French. With the Spaniards further emasculated by the outbreak of revolution in Latin America – by now their chief source of revenue – the next two years saw constant French advances. City after city fell into the invaders' hands while the Spaniards lost more and more of such troops and resources as remained to them. By late 1811 all that was left of Patriot Spain was Galicia, the Levante and the blockaded island city of Cádiz, which had in 1810 become the new capital.[6] Penned up inside Portugal, the British, meanwhile, could do nothing to arrest the march of French conquest. In the end, indeed, it is clear that Napoleon's commanders could have completely crushed resistance in Spain and then marched against Portugal in such overwhelming force that even Wellington could not have overcome them, despite the masterly defensive strategy whose details we shall examine shortly. All that was needed was for the French armies in the Peninsula to receive a constant stream of replacements and reinforcements. Thanks to the impending invasion of Russia, however, the supply of men dried up in 1812, the Armée d'Espagne even being stripped of a number of troops. As could be expected, the French forces suddenly found themselves badly over-extended, and all the more so as Napoleon insisted that they continue with the offensive against Valencia launched in the autumn of 1811. As General Suchet, the commander of the French forces in Aragón and Catalonia, put it, 'The emperor was all impatience at Paris.'[7]

The events of the autumn of 1811 are worth a moment of extra consideration in the context of a discussion of the international relations of Napoleonic Europe. At this point it is clear the French were winning the war in Spain and Portugal. As fortress after fortress was taken and army after army shattered, it became ever more clear that sooner or later Spanish resistance was likely to collapse altogether. In large parts of the country, the famous guerrillas – in reality a mixture of bandit gangs; bands of levies, volunteers, deserters and liberated prisoners of war organized into semi-regular fighting forces by a variety of army officers and charismatic civilian adventurers; and flying columns of regular troops – continued to plague the French, but it is by no means clear that they could have survived indefinitely. In 1811 and 1812 successive British thrusts across the Portuguese frontier forced the French to concentrate their forces and allowed the guerrillas to run amok, but for the whole of 1811 Wellington was never able to advance very far into Spain. With the battered Spanish armies also incapable of any great feat of arms, the invaders put considerable resources into the war in the interior, while the experience of southern Italy suggested that they were entirely capable of dealing with popular insurrection. As we have already seen, in the wake of the French invasion of Naples in 1806 a serious revolt had broken out in the province of Calabria. Under the leadership of a variety of local chieftains, bands of irregulars had taken to the hills. What followed was a bloody and savage war, but the Calabrian insurgents were even less engaged by issues of ideology or nationalism than the Spaniards, while they also did not enjoy the same degree of regular assistance: occasional descents on the coast *à la* Maida were no substitute for the support afforded by the presence in Spain of substantial allied field armies. It is, then, no surprise that by 1810 the war in

Calabria had been put down, thereby establishing beyond doubt the French army's ability to develop effective anti-guerrilla strategies.

Victory in the Iberian Peninsula, then, was by no means an impossibility for Napoleon. The last Spanish forces could be subdued; the last Spanish fortresses beaten; and the last Spanish guerrillas hunted down. After that, there would remain Portugal, but it was doubtful whether Wellington would be able to hold out alone, and even if he could there was always the issue of support for the war in Britain. It was perhaps inevitable that the retreat of Sir John Moore, the inability to translate victory at Talavera into further advances and the withdrawal into Portugal produced outbreaks of what Wellington referred to as 'croaking' among the Whigs. For a long time figures such as Grey and Grenville refused point-blank to accept there was any chance of victory in the Peninsula and condemned it as a futile struggle. In addition, the more radical of the so-called 'friends of peace' were furious at what they perceived as Spain's continued domination by the Church and the aristocracy. To them, indeed, the war was not only futile but indefensible: to resist Napoleon when he was seeking to invade Britain was one thing, but Copenhagen and the British expeditions to Latin America suggested that the struggle had become one of aggression and even expansion. So long as things went relatively well, the opposition leaders had little hope of winning the support of the independent MPs who were the key to gaining victory in the House of Commons. In the first half of 1810, in fact, repeated attempts to defeat the government were all firmly quashed. Nor is this surprising, for the Whigs had nothing credible to offer in their criticism of the war. In 1808 the Whigs had temporarily rallied to the cause of resistance as Britain was seemingly no longer fighting as the ally of despotism, but rather of a people united in its determination to defend its independence abroad and secure its liberty at home. Yet in Spain even British commanders who were favourable to the Whigs like Sir John Moore discovered that the crusade in which observers like Sheridan or Lord Holland took such a delight was a chimera, while every attempt to criticize Wellington foundered on the unpalatable fact that the Spaniards could not be relied upon. But unable in practice to come up with any alternative scheme for the prosecution of the war, in almost every Commons debate on the subject the Whigs ended up humiliated and discredited.

Yet the collapse of the Spanish cause would almost certainly have changed matters in this respect. Not only would it have spurred the opponents of the war to fresh efforts, but there were limits even to what the government, now headed by Spencer Perceval, could accept. By the end of 1810 Britain's ability to bear the cost of the war was clearly faltering, and it was only with some difficulty that Wellington had persuaded the Cabinet to give him the resources he required to take the offensive in the spring of 1811. Indeed, such were London's financial worries that there were serious proposals for his forces to be reduced. With the hope of victory gone – the Anglo-Portuguese army could not have fought the war single-handed – the Perceval administration would have quite probably given up even its commitment to the defence of Portugal.

Setting aside the government's deficiencies – on the surface it was hardly an impressive body – what makes this even more likely is the economic context. After two years of renewed confidence and growth in part brought about by the greatly improved access Britain now enjoyed to the Latin American market, in 1811 there was a serious economic slump. The causes were complex, but essentially a poor harvest coincided with a change in Napoleon's operation of the Continental Blockade: that in effect legalized the importation of British goods and badly hit the many speculators who had been profiting from the wholesale smuggling trade that had grown up since 1806. With this, in turn, came a great wave of bankruptcies and a significant upturn in unemployment. It may also be significant that 1811 saw the peak of the enclosure movement in the countryside and, by extension, an increase in migration to the towns, just at a moment when house-building – one of the trades most suited to absorb large numbers of unskilled labourers – was at a low ebb through the cumulative effect of years of high taxation. Distress was acute, and its expression assumed forms that were much more frightening than the 'peace petitioning' of 1807. General unrest and rioting spread across key industrial areas of the country, and this was underpinned by much criticism of the war, and, in particular, the Orders-in-Council, which were, entirely wrongly, held responsible for the slump in trade. Nor were these measures just hated by the handloom weavers and framework knitters who were at the heart of the unrest. On the contrary, by 1811 the Orders-in-Council were the subject of an extremely vociferous campaign on the part of the many commercial interests who also felt that they stood in their way. So great was the pressure that in June 1812 the government, which had the previous month been taken over by Lord Liverpool, was forced to capitulate, while 1813 saw a further move towards free trade with the publication of revisions to the East India Company's charter. And, finally, there was the issue of political reform. Stimulated first by the major scandal that broke in 1809 concerning allegations that the Duke of York's mistress had intervened in army promotions in return for bribes and then by the government's foolish attempt to quash discussion of the abortive expedition sent to Holland in 1809, several motions were introduced in the House of Commons calling for the reform of parliament, and, while these were defeated, the number of votes they received was by no means inconsiderable. Even put together, all this did not amount to a revolutionary crisis, but the collapse of resistance in Spain would have provoked a storm that neither Perceval nor Liverpool would have found it easy to ride out. Would they, indeed, have been willing even to make the attempt? The chief enthusiast for the continuation of the Peninsular War at all costs was Wellington's brother, the Foreign Secretary, Lord Wellesley, but he was both notoriously lazy and extremely arrogant and could therefore hardly be said to have had the confidence of his colleagues.

British commitment to the Peninsula was not a given, therefore, but for the time being Wellington's army fought on. Indeed, its achievements were considerable. Particular attention should be paid here to Wellington's defence of Portugal in 1810–11. In accordance with France's resumption of the offensive in the Peninsula in 1810, the summer of that year saw some 65,000 men under Marshal Masséna move across the Portuguese frontier and besiege the fortress of Almeida. This fell very rapidly thanks to the chance explosion of its main powder magazine, and the French moved on towards Lisbon. Wellington had anticipated such a move and put together a comprehensive plan of defence. From the beginning the countryside in the path of the invaders would be devastated and the French forces harassed by the irregular home guard known as the *ordenança*. If possible, the French would then be brought to battle and forced to retreat, to which end the Portuguese army had been completely rebuilt under the direction of Sir William Beresford and the main routes towards Lisbon blocked by field works at a number of obvious defensive positions. Failing that, the countryside would continue to be devastated, while the Anglo-Portuguese army fell back on Lisbon, along with the bulk of the civilian population. Waiting for them would be probably the greatest single engineering feat in the entire Napoleonic era in the form of the so-called Lines of Torres Vedras, an impenetrable belt of fortifications stretching from one side of the peninsula on which Lisbon was built to the other. Whether this plan would have sufficed to hold off the French had they ever unleashed the sort of massive offensive that would have followed the final conquest of Spain is unclear – Wellington certainly had his doubts – but against the 65,000 men brought by Masséna, it was more than adequate. Despite the defenders achieving complete success on the battlefield itself, an attempt to turn the French back at Buçaco failed due to the marshal's discovery of an unguarded track around Wellington's northern front. But when the French reached the Lines of Torres Vedras they found that they could go no further. In this situation Masséna did his best, but through Wellington's scorched earth policy his supplies collapsed and in March 1811 he abandoned his headquarters at Santarem and fell back on the Spanish frontier. Behind him he left scenes that were among the very worst the Napoleonic Wars had to offer. To quote one British officer:

The Light Division ... entered Santarem, where we remained about an hour. How different this town now appeared ... The houses are torn and dilapidated, and the few miserable inhabitants moving skeletons; the streets strewn with every description of household furniture, half-burnt and destroyed, and many ... quite impassable with filth and rubbish, with an occasional man, mule or donkey rotting and corrupting and filling the air with pestilential vapours ... Two young ladies had been brutally violated in a house that I entered, and were unable to rise from a mattress of straw ... Kincaid and I went into a house where an old man was seated: he had been lame in the legs for many years. A French soldier ... had given him two deep sabre wounds on the head and another on the arm ... It is beyond everything horrid the way these European savages have treated the unfortunate Portuguese. Almost every man they get hold of they murder. The women they use too brutally for me to describe. They even cut the throats of infants. The towns are mostly on fire – in short, they are guilty of every species of cruelty. I have seen such sights as have made me shudder with horror, and which I really could not have believed unless an eye-witness of them.[8]

However, clearing Masséna from Portugal was one thing, and invading Spain quite another. For the whole of 1811, indeed, the situation on the Portuguese frontier was a stalemate. Authorized by the British government to enter Spain once more, Wellington soon found that this was easier said than done. The crucial border fortresses of Ciudad Rodrigo and Badajoz had been greatly strengthened by the French and every attempt to besiege them was met by massive French counter-offensives, as at Albuera and Fuentes de Oñoro. Repelled though these were, they cost Wellington heavy losses and dissuaded him from marching too far into Spain, while progress was in any case rendered still more difficult by a lack of adequate siege cannon. Of course, the French were in no better state. Twice, indeed, they refused battle rather than attack Wellington in powerful defensive positions inside Portugal, while an attempt on Elvas or Almeida (now back in allied hands again) would have been out of the question. Yet until the end of 1811 the British remained able to exert only the most marginal influence on the situation in Spain, the only thing that changed this situation being Napoleon's insistence on continual attacks in the Peninsula at the same time as he was massing his armies for the invasion of Russia. By stripping its defenders of troops, this completely destabilized the position on the Portuguese frontier. Seeing his chance, Wellington struck across the border and was quickly able to capture the fortresses of Ciudad Rodrigo and Badajoz, win a major victory at Salamanca and liberate Madrid. Thanks to a variety of problems, of which by far the greatest was the de facto collapse of government and society in Spain, in November 1812 Wellington was again forced to retreat to Portugal. But the French were never fully able to recover and were further weakened by the withdrawal of still more troops in the early months of 1813. Aided by the continued attempts of the French to hold more territory than they could garrison, in May 1813 Wellington was therefore able to launch a fresh offensive that led to the defeat of King Joseph's main field forces at Vitoria on 21 June. Bitter fighting continued in the Pyrenees, with the French vainly trying to relieve the besieged fortresses of San Sebastián and Pamplona, but they were repelled at Sorauren and San Marcial, while in October 1813 Wellington invaded France and, after several fierce battles, established himself in an unassailable position south of Bayonne. Though French troops stayed in part of Catalonia until the end of hostilities in April of the following year, to all intents and purposes the Peninsular War was over.

The British triumph in Spain and Portugal was, then, at least as much the work of Napoleon as it was that of Wellington and the Anglo-Portuguese army. To return to the crucial moment in the autumn of 1811 when the march of French conquest was derailed by the emperor, the whole episode is redolent of the attitudes that were now sapping the French imperium, and had in fact threatened its survival from the very beginning. In brief, Napoleon for a long time refused point-blank to pay sufficient attention to the threat represented by Wellington's forces, and consistently put other issues first. In the spring of 1810, for example, rather than returning to the Peninsula, as was generally expected, he remained in France to pursue his increasingly desperate search for an heir. In part, the problem was psychological: the very fact that the British could maintain an army on the soil of mainland Europe was a constant source of irritation to him, and his instinct was to play the matter down. As Madame de Rémusat noted:

The emperor did not like the Spanish affair; in fact, it bored him. Recognizing that he had commenced it badly, conducted it in a most feeble manner, and greatly underestimated its difficulty and importance, he affected to set little store by it so as not to let it humiliate him . . . Always an improviser, it was more to his taste to draw a veil over all that displeased him, and renew his fortune and reputation from scratch.[9]

But in the last resort Napoleon despised 'the sepoy general' and his men. Wellington, the emperor was convinced, was a cautious general who was unwilling to take the offensive and unlikely to win offensive battles. To the end he underestimated the number of men available to Wellington and refused to regard the Portuguese forces that made up an important part of his field army as anything other than a disorderly rabble, when in fact Beresford had made them, as even the normally austere Wellington put it, the 'fighting cocks of the army'.[10] Never having had to face a British army in battle, Napoleon knew nothing of the superiority of British infantry tactics, or the effects of Britain's deadly Baker rifles and shrapnel shells. The news of Salamanca, which he received in the depths of Russia on the very eve of the battle of Borodino, therefore came as a severe shock, but still he made light of the situation. 'The English have their hands full there: they cannot leave Spain to go and make trouble for me in France or Germany,' he told General Caulaincourt. 'That is all that matters.'[11]

All this is most instructive of the way in which the French ruler's mind had been developing, but there are other hints that all was not well. Time and again he sent orders to the Peninsula that were either completely out of date or incapable of being realized in the first place. Take, for example, his plan to seize Lisbon in 1809. Between the middle of January and 10 February 1809, Marshal Soult, whose troops were still absolutely exhausted from their pursuit of Sir John Moore, was expected to occupy the whole of Galicia, fight his way past not one but two border fortresses, capture the major city of Oporto and present himself before the walls of Lisbon. Even if there had been no resistance whatsoever, the programme would have been hard to achieve – Galicia and northern Portugal were poor regions characterized by few roads, little in the way of food and transport and, in winter, constant rain and snow. In the circumstances Soult did quite well to take Oporto on 29 March. 'Napoleon was . . . living in a non-existent world, created by his own imagination,' complained Marshal Marmont. 'He built structures in the air; he took his desires for realities; and he gave orders as if he was ignorant of the true state of affairs.'[12] Unwilling to travel to Spain himself, he also refused to appoint an effective commander-in-chief to act in his stead until it was far too late, and then selected the distinctly inappropriate figure of Joseph Bonaparte, despite the fact that he not only possessed no experience as a field commander but also, largely thanks to Napoleon, was regarded with complete contempt by the marshals and other generals he was supposed to direct. In part this was the fruit of the same over-confidence of which we have just spoken, but also there was something else: obsessed with keeping power in his own hands, the emperor was loath to see too much slip into those of even his closest and most devoted subordinates.

The Peninsular War reveals much about the character of Napoleon. At the same time, however, it also highlights the difficulties Britain had in building and maintaining the sort of continental coalition which was her only chance of bringing the war to a successful conclusion. This problem was bad enough with powers such as Austria and Russia, but in respect of smaller or weaker states who found themselves totally dependent on Britain for their survival it was even worse. This had already been demonstrated in Sicily in the months preceding the outbreak of the Peninsular War. Since the first months of 1806 Ferdinand IV of Naples and his wife, Maria Carolina, had been living in Palermo under protection of a British garrison. Yet relations between the king and queen and their protectors were far from good. Earlier tensions in the relationship were revived by the peace negotiations of 1806, which had given rise to the suspicion that Sicily – indeed, the entire Kingdom of the Two Sicilies – might be bargained away in the pursuit of wider objectives. Ham-fisted British diplomacy – in this case the suggestion that a permanent garrison might be maintained on the island even in peacetime – also gave rise to suspicions that there might be plans to seize the island or at the very least secure some coastal city as a new Gibraltar. And, as ever, there was strong commercial pressure. Britain wanted her produce and re-exports to be given free access to all Sicily's ports and suggested that British merchants resident on the island should be given special privileges. With some difficulty a treaty of alliance was eventually negotiated – but bitter disputes arose over exactly how much money had been paid to the Sicilian regime by London. There were also constant clashes over strategy: Maria Carolina, especially, was all for sending expeditionary forces to the mainland and encouraging the cause of popular revolt, whereas most British observers believed that there was no hope of reconquering Naples by force and that the Calabrian insurgents were in reality mere brigands who could achieve nothing other than to draw down the wrath of the French on their unfortunate fellow citizens.

Added to all this was a political dimension. In the first instance, Sicily was desperately poor, and the misery of the common people made for considerable social tension: by 1807, indeed, there was a real possibility of famine. In the second, the local nobility were extremely jealous of their feudal privileges, and looked on the arrival of the court at Palermo with considerable concern, for ever since the 1780s the monarchy had been trying to erode their power. And, in the third, there was a strong feeling among educated opinion that Sicily was being both neglected and exploited. For example, the king and queen insisted on giving the chief positions at court, and in such armed forces as they were able to maintain, to nobles who had escaped with them from the mainland. That a number of these noblemen were French in origin did not help: although they were all either emigrés or men who had been in Neapolitan service for many years, it began to be said that some of them were French agents. Keen to ensure stability, the British were inclined to press a reformist agenda on Ferdinand and Maria Carolina, especially given Sicily's inability to sustain much of a war effort. The entrenched privileges of the nobility, encapsulated by the survival of the island's medieval parliament, ensured that tax revenues were low; the defences of such towns and cities as possessed them were mostly in a state of complete disrepair; and there was little in the way of an army or militia, nor much hope of recruiting fresh soldiers. Demands that something be done to remedy this situation, however, only produced charges that the British were being unreasonable, while Maria Carolina compounded the resultant anger by periodic attempts to find some alternative to the British alliance. As one possibility was a deal with Napoleon that would have given Ferdinand back his old throne in return for getting the British to withdraw from Sicily, the wildest rumours were soon gaining ground. The queen, it was said, wanted to block reform so as to provoke a pro-French revolt. Equally, if she was constantly urging the British to invade the mainland, it was to engineer their destruction and thereby rescue the Bourbons from their control. Small wonder, then, that by 1808 there were those in Britain who believed the only way forward in Sicily was to take the island under direct rule, sideline the king and queen and force through a programme of reform from the outside.

Nor were matters much better with regard to Sweden. As we have seen, back in February 1808 Russia had invaded Finland. Only weakly garrisoned, much of the south had soon been occupied, along with Gotland and the Åland archipelago. Meanwhile, Sweden was also threatened with invasion from Denmark, which had joined the war and immediately received the assistance of a considerable detachment of the *grande armée*, including the Spanish division commanded by La Romana. In consequence, in April a substantial British expeditionary force was sent to Göteborg under Sir John Moore. The dispatch of this force had been dictated by the need to cement Britain's credibility as an ally, but by the time it arrived the need for its presence had been supplanted by military necessity. In brief, thanks in large part to the loathing provoked by Gustav IV among the nobility on account of his continued support for the policies of enlightened absolutism associated with his father, Gustav III, many officers opposed the war with Russia or saw it as a chance to discredit Gustav. Resistance had therefore been sporadic at best, and on 7 May the supposedly impregnable fortress of Sveaborg – an imposing citadel situated on an island just off the coast from modern-day Helsinki (then called Helsingfors) – surrendered without firing a shot. Moore's arrival, then, came as something of a godsend for the embattled king, but in the event relations between the British and Gustav IV proved turbulent. Part of the problem was the result of a simple muddle: Moore had been given to understand that his forces were to be commanded by himself alone, while the Swedes believed that control of the expeditionary force was to belong to Gustav. At the same time, Gustav IV was anxious to fight an offensive war, whereas Moore wanted rather to fight a defensive one. Indeed, the king insisted that Moore's division had been sent for the express purpose of launching attacks on the enemy positions ringing the Baltic, and refused to let them disembark from their ships. To all this, of course, Moore objected very strongly:

The King . . . is a man of honourable, upright mind, but without ability and every now and then proposes measures which prove either derangement or the greatest weakness of mind. He has no minister, but governs himself, and, as he has neither the habits nor the talents requisite, Sweden is . . . a country without a government, or . . . one that is only governed by fits and starts. The King is perfectly despotic: whatever he orders must be done, and, unfortunately, when he gives orders he depends entirely . . . on his own impressions as facts. He does not see the perilous position he is in, and nobody dares represent it to him. He is speculating on conquests when he has already lost one province, and has not the means to defend the rest. In short, his situation is such that it is next to impossible that he can sustain himself . . . Our troops . . . might check his enemies so far as to . . . give the King time to rouse his people . . . but it is not a prince such as he that could rouse a people or direct their efforts with ability. The natural consequence . . . is that his people become indifferent, and many adverse . . . In such a state of things we can do him no permanent good: he will not follow our counsels, and our force alone is not sufficient.[13]

Setting aside the distraction offered by the Spanish insurrection – Gustav IV appears to have suspected that Moore was looking for a pretext to withdraw his troops so as to get a share of the glory in the Peninsula – at issue were two fundamental problems. In the first place, behind the Swedes' intransigence was fear of Britain's underlying intentions. Were a British garrison to be installed in Göteborg, what guarantee was there against that city becoming a Baltic Gibraltar? And, in the second, Gustav had expectations of Britain which she simply could not satisfy. To the embattled Swedish monarch, Britain's resources seemed infinite – in 1807 he had, after all, been offered one of the most generous subsidy deals of the entire Napoleonic period – but Moore was deeply conscious that the 12,000 men that he commanded represented a substantial part of Britain's disposable resources. In consequence, they had to be carefully husbanded, but the British commander's insistence that this was the case produced a total breakdown of relations that ended with Moore being placed under house arrest in Stockholm. Escaping from custody in disguise, Moore fled to Göteborg, and within a matter of hours his troops were under sail for England. Assisted by a British squadron that had also been sent to the Baltic, the Swedes fought on, but the relationship between the two allies never recovered. Indeed, the winter of 1808–9 was to see a fresh crisis. Faced by the need to renew his subsidy treaty with Britain, Gustav IV resorted to very aggressive tactics. The unfortunate British ambassador was suddenly confronted with the announcement that unless the subsidy for 1809 was raised to £2 million from its current level of £1.2 million, and £300,000 found for him immediately, Gustav would cut off all trade with Britain. Somewhat shaken, the ambassador caved in, and made over the £300,000 while at the same time referring the subsidy issue to his superiors. London, however, was made of sterner stuff, and a furious Canning vetoed the increase. Desperate for money to carry on the war, the king gave way in his turn, but he only did so with the worst possible grace. In this, it is at least arguable that Gustav had a point. Given British support, it is possible that an invasion of Danish-ruled Norway might have succeeded, the defenders being in such disarray that they had been forced to negotiate an armistice, while the generous aid sent to Spain and Portugal left Gustav feeling that he had been abandoned. And so, in a sense, he had. The Baltic entanglement had become a nightmare for Britain, and all the more so as Canning was convinced that without it Russia would long since have been reconciled with Britain. Few tears, then, were shed when Gustav was overthrown by a military coup a mere twelve days after he had accepted the new subsidy deal, even though the regime that replaced him under Gustav's uncle, the aged and childless Charles XIII, made peace, accepting the terms of the Continental Blockade and surrendering Finland and the Åland islands to Russia.

To return to Iberia, from the very beginning the Spanish alliance in particular posed immense problems. In part, the cause lay with the overheated atmosphere in which the alliance had emerged in June 1808.

Despite claims that William Pitt and others predicted such a development, the news of the Spanish insurrection arrived in England as a bolt
from the blue. Nothing was known about it until two messengers that
had been dispatched from Asturias arrived in London on 8 June 1808
(as a matter of fact, the British governor at Gibraltar, Sir Hew Dalrymple,
had been contacted about a potential uprising a few days after the Dos
de Mayo, but only his first reports on what was going on had turned up
in London by the time the deputation arrived from Asturias). With the
French cause clearly in the ascendant, the result was the most wild
excitement. For the Whigs, the Peninsula afforded a cause with which
they could identity – a people rising to free itself from despotism – and
a means of fighting the war which not only promised certain victory in
their eyes, but also freed Britain from association with the autocracies
of Eastern Europe. And for the Tories it offered the equally noble sight
of a populace fighting just as heroically not to make a revolution, but
to defend the traditional social order and the religious and political
institutions which sustained it. What no one doubted, meanwhile, was
that the Spanish people *were* fighting heroically, and that this was a
cause to which Britain must rally.

Within a very few days, then, the basic principle had been resolved:
Britain would support the Spanish revolt to the full extent of her abilities.
But what this meant to the Portland administration was one thing, and
what it meant to the Spaniards quite another. Much as Gustav IV had
done, the Spaniards assumed that Britain's resources were far greater
than was actually the case. Troops were not at first seen as being that
important – when he made his first landfall in Spain, indeed, Sir Arthur
Wellesley was advised to sail on to Portugal and land his men there
instead – but there was almost no limit to the arms, equipment and
money that were asked for. To this was added a further complication in
that Britain embarked on the Peninsular War with the sense that she
was rushing to the rescue of 'gallant little Spain', whereas the Spaniards
believed that it was rather Spain who was rescuing Britain. Needless to
say, the general concord of the summer of 1808 did not survive for very
long. As we have seen, the Spanish revolt was an extremely complex
phenomenon which had little in common with the great popular crusade
of Britain's imagination: enthusiasm for the struggle was at best limited,
and the provisional government that was formed at Aranjuez in September 1808 was an unwieldy affair that had difficulty imposing its

authority. Conscription, then, did not go well while there were very few volunteers. At the same time, it proved very difficult even to get the Spanish armies to the front, let alone coordinate their activities or suppress the feuding that characterized the high command. Slow to get his army into Spain at all, let alone to the front line on the river Ebro, Moore was incensed by what he found, and concluded, along with many of his men, that the Spanish war was a mere sham – that both he and the British government had been deceived. A terrible affair, the retreat to La Coruña was therefore blamed on the Spaniards, while many stories spread of their supposed cruelty, ingratitude, cowardice and incompetence. Yet there is also the Spanish point of view to be considered here. Moore's army was slow to arrive in Spain; the behaviour of many of the British troops was nearly as bad as that of the French soldiers they were supposed to be opposing; and the British had failed to make a stand even when they reached the shelter offered by the eminently defensible frontiers of Galicia.

The campaign of Sir John Moore set the tone for what proved to be a most acrimonious partnership. As the years of conflict continued, fresh recriminations kept surfacing with regard to the conduct of operations. The battle of Talavera saw the British complaining that the Spaniards had failed to supply them with adequate food, and the Spaniards complaining that Wellington had deliberately sabotaged their operations. The battle of Ocaña saw the Spaniards maintaining that defeat had come because the British commander had refused to support their offensive. After the first siege of Ciudad Rodrigo the captured Spanish governor accused Wellington of deliberately abandoning him to his fate when his forces were a mere day's march away to the west. The battle of Barosa saw the British, this time commanded by Sir Thomas Graham, arguing that they had been betrayed by the Spaniards. The battle of Albuera saw complaints that the excessive Anglo-Portuguese casualties had been the product of the Spaniards' inability to manoeuvre, and that it was invariably necessary for the British to do all the fighting. And the siege of Burgos and the miserable winter retreat that followed found Wellington blaming the setback on the Spaniards and suggesting that their battered regular armies had failed to do enough to tie down his various French opponents. For these disappointments both sides had their own explanations. Time and again all the Spaniards saw of the British was their disappearing backs as they fled for the safety of their refuge of the moment, while loudly protesting the need to defend Portugal. This suggested that their allies did not have their hearts in the struggle, or, at least, that they were quite content for Spain to do the bulk of the fighting, in which respect it should be remembered that there were long periods – from August 1809 to July 1810, for example – when Wellington's forces hardly fired a single shot. Spanish disappointment was also fuelled by the influence of an ever-optimistic, not to mention wildly irresponsible, press, which consistently overestimated the number of British troops available for action. Encountering a group of Spanish soldiers on the Portuguese frontier in 1810, one British officer wrote:

They knew little of . . . the regular practice of war; they knew only that we had not fired a shot by their side since the battle of Talavera, that our companions in arms under Sir John Moore had fled through the strong country of Galicia without fighting two years before, and their angry and contemptuous looks told us plainly that they expected that we should retire through Portugal . . . with similar precipitation.[14]

As for the British, the Spaniards were, or so it seemed, incompetent, cowardly and unreliable, a judgement that was backed by their armies being beaten on almost every occasion that they took the field. The British viewed all this through the lens of the 'black legend': thanks to centuries of obscurantist Catholicism, Spain was backward, her leaders corrupt and her people cowed and apathetic. Irritation and disappointment therefore reaffirmed the already strong British sense of cultural superiority, and this expressed itself at best as haughtiness and arrogance, and at worst as outbursts of savagery that saw several liberated towns – most notably Ciudad Rodrigo, Badajoz and San Sebastián – brutally put to the sack. Even Wellington was by no means immune to the general sense of cultural superiority. 'The Spaniard,' he wrote to his aide-de-camp, Lord Burghersh, 'is an undisciplined savage who obeys no law, despises all authority, feels no gratitude for benefits conferred or favours received, and is always ready with his knife or firelock to commit murder.'[15] In the wake of the retreat from Burgos, in particular, his anger knew no bounds:

I have never yet known the Spanish army do anything, much less do anything well . . . A few rascals called guerrillas attack one quarter of their number and sometimes succeed and sometimes not, but as for any regular operation,

I have not heard of such a thing and successful [*sic*] in the whole course of the war.[16]

Such attitudes engendered a greater degree of suspicion and resentment among the Spaniards, increasing the likelihood that honest cooperation with the British would not be forthcoming. At the same time, by a variety of means, of which the greatest and most devious was appointing Wellington to be commander-in-chief of the Spanish armies in September 1812 (see below), the Spaniards sought to secure control of the operations of the Anglo-Portuguese army and keep it linked to operations in Spain. Yet these manoeuvres caused further outrage in Wellington's headquarters, and led to angry accusations of political interference. It was a vicious circle, and the mutual incomprehension which marked the relationship between the rival armed forces continued to fester until the end of the war.

To disappointment on the battlefield was added a variety of political and diplomatic problems. Chief amongst these was the burgeoning controversy that surrounded the linked issues of British subsidies, political reform, free trade and the Latin American revolutions. When Spain went to war with Napoleon, the Patriot authorities had bombarded the Portland government with petitions for help that took no account of Great Britain's abilities actually to meet their expectations. In April 1809, for example, the Spanish representatives in London asked for a loan of at least £10 million, and this at a time when Britain was simultaneously attempting to furnish assistance to the Austrians (who were, as we shall see, once more at war with France). Still more extreme was a draft treaty presented to the British government in August, of which the main terms were that Britain should provide Spain with an auxiliary force of 30,000 men for use in either Britain or America, sufficient muskets for 500,000 men, and a loan of 40 million reales (approximately £450,000) per month. Needless to say, Canning was outraged, remarking that the proposal was 'so utterly extravagant that it was useless to begin negotiating upon'.[17] At the same time no subsidy treaty was offered the Spaniards, the Portland administration preferring to use what money they could send to Spain as a weapon of diplomacy, and even then warning the Spaniards that the financial help Britain could offer would necessarily be very limited.

Canning's anger is understandable. In the course of 1808 Britain had dispatched £1.1 million to Spain as a free gift, along with perhaps 200,000 muskets and large quantities of other military supplies. Additional aid had, of course, gone to Portugal and when Canning's old friend and ally, John Hookham Frere, had been appointed as ambassador to Patriot Spain he had been given a further £650,000, supplemented in June 1809 by another £214,000 in treasury bills. And finally there came the costs of the British army itself, which for the year 1810 were calculated as at least £1.7 million. For all this, the return had hardly been brilliant. The Spaniards had effectively shown neither the political or military capacity to benefit from Britain's generosity nor the will to act on her suggestions. Despite British pressure, a single commander-in-chief had never been appointed for the Spanish armies. Portugal, meanwhile, stood in striking contrast. Here the British had succeeded in obtaining an influence never equalled the other side of the frontier. In part the reasons for this were fortuitous. By the time that news arrived in London of the Portuguese insurrection, which took place somewhat later than its Spanish counterpart, so much money had been committed to Spain that there was only £60,000 left for Portugal. From the beginning, then, the British had greater leverage in Portugal than they did in Spain, while a variety of other factors helped, including the absence of much of the political elite in Brazil and the country's long-standing ties with Britain (of whom, by contrast, Spain was a historic enemy). From the beginning, then, many concessions were forthcoming. Already in January 1808 a gift of £100,000 in a mixture of specie and credits had produced a declaration by the government-in-exile in Brazil that henceforward there would be no restrictions on foreign trade with Brazil. Although this did not fully meet Canning's expectations – what he wanted was a deal that would give Britain 'most-favoured nation' status by means of a preferential tariff – it was a good start. And there was more to come. In exchange for an agreement to meet the wages of that part of the Portuguese army attached to the British forces in Portugal and the guarantee of a £600,000 loan on the London market, Prince John placed his army under the command of Wellington, appointed Beresford to the command-in-chief of the Portuguese army itself, and agreed that British officers – a vital tool, it was felt, in the construction of the much-needed new army – could be given commissions in the Portuguese service. Supplies in kind had continued to flood in and the promise of regular payments from Wellington's military chest ultimately secured a place for the British ambassador to Lisbon in the council of regency established to govern the country in John's absence.

This is not to say that the relationship with Portugal was trouble-free. On the contrary, Wellington bombarded its administration with demands for such measures as a forced loan, an increase in the property tax, the introduction of a graduated income tax, the reinforcement of local government and a purge of the commissariat, only to find that his demands were simply ignored. Nor was British control especially popular: the powerful Sousa family set itself up as the voice of protest, and at various times caused much trouble. Yet, although it grew in inverse proportion to the reduction in the threat of French invasion, such discord was limited and the situation much better than it was in Spain. By the middle of 1809 there were simply not the reserves of hard cash necessary to meet the Spaniards' demands. Encouraged by the Portuguese example, Canning began to turn the screw on the Patriot camp. As early as the summer of 1808, it had been intimated that no more financial aid would be forthcoming unless some form of central government was brought into being, while attempts had also been made to press for the appointment of a commander-in-chief. Angered by the failure of the Talavera campaign of 1809, which he put down entirely to Spanish mismanagement, Lord Wellesley, now ambassador to the then Patriot capital of Seville, went still further and openly advocated the need for political, administrative and social reform:

It is evident that the independence of a nation must rest on the basis of her own internal force and public spirit, and that no country can attain or preserve happiness or glory by implicit reliance on foreign aid. For these great objects I should view with the most lively satisfaction any regular, deliberate and systematic attention to the increase and management of the military resources of Spain, and to the augmentation, composition, discipline and efficiency of the Spanish armies . . . But the source of every improvement must be the efficiency of the executive power, which can never possess sufficient force or activity without the direct assistance of the collective wisdom of the nation, and without the aid of that spirit which must arise from the immediate support of a people animated by equal sentiments of loyalty and freedom.[18]

The ideas contained in this note were developed further in a series of private conversations with the general secretary of the Junta Central,

Martín de Garay. What Wellesley required, it transpired, was the replacement of the Junta Central, which numbered more than thirty members at full strength, by a council of regency, the election of a national assembly or *cortes*, a general redress of grievances with respect to the governance and taxation of both metropolitan Spain and her foreign dominions, and the incorporation into the new Spain of the American colonies through a fair system of political representation. But the expression of such views was extremely indelicate. It was all very well to suggest that Spanish America was on the verge of revolution, but in 1809 there were few signs that a general convulsion was nigh in Spain's American possessions. Although a small rebellion broke out in Upper Peru (today Bolivia) in the summer of 1809, this was easily suppressed and appears to have been as much directed against rule from Buenos Aires as it was against rule from Spain. Less than two years before, British troops had invaded present-day Uruguay and Argentina, and it should not be forgotten that a British force had been available for service in the Peninsula within weeks of the rising breaking out because the Portland administration had returned to the idea of an American adventure. Faced by the French takeover in Spain, its initial response had been to resolve that a division should be sent to what is now Venezuela to support the adventurer, Francisco de Miranda, and stir up an insurrection that, if it spread, would put the riches of the Indies beyond the reach of Napoleon once and for all. Concentrated for this purpose at Cork, the troops concerned had been given to Sir Arthur Wellesley who in consequence became the archetypal example of the right man in the right place at the right time. And finally, the fact that Britain had been fighting on the side of Spain in the war of 1793–5 had not prevented her from engaging in a variety of actions that had damaged Spanish interests. With Britain continuing to seize French and Dutch possessions around the world – the period 1809–11 saw the capture of Martinique, Guadeloupe, Réunion, Mauritius, Dakar and Batavia – it is not to be wondered at that senior figures in the local junta were putting it about 'that the greatest circumspection was necessary with regard to England, that her views were dangerous, and, notwithstanding her apparent exertions for Spain, that her policy was to be dreaded'.[19]

Wellesley's references to Spanish America notwithstanding, the chief focus of Spanish suspicions prior to 1810 was the port city of Cádiz. British interest in Cádiz was so strong as almost to be an obsession. In

June 1808 and again in February 1809 there had been offers to give the city the protection of a British garrison, and in the wake of Talavera the issue was raised yet again. Canning proposed that the Junta Central should be informed that the admission of British forces to Cádiz would be integral to any further British advance into Spain. The pretext for this, of course, was that Spanish political and military unreliability was such that no British army could be risked in the interior of Spain unless it was assured of a safe refuge on the coast. But the military logic underlying the proposal was questionable, and the role of Cádiz as the centre of the colonial trade raised further suspicions in the Patriot camp, especially given Britain's continued presence in Gibraltar and her control of Menorca (which was in British hands from 1708 to 1756, 1763 to 1782, and 1798 to 1802).

For the first two years of the war Cádiz remained the chief territorial point of friction between the British and the Spaniards. Gradually, however, the issue of Spanish America began to supplant it. Initially, there were two basic problems: specie and free trade. From the very beginning of the war, indeed, Canning had maintained that, because of the shortage of specie that affected Great Britain, her ability to aid the Spaniards would be contingent on gaining access to American silver. His response to Spanish demands for help was therefore to request the Junta Central for permission to export specie directly from the Spanish colonies, or at least for Britain to be given a share of the vast quantities of bullion that were arriving at Cádiz. The empire was seen by the British government as a means of breaking the Continental Blockade and securing the revenues it needed to continue the war, while it was also conscious that exploitation of the market represented by the Spanish colonies would be a good way of assuaging the concerns of the commercial community in respect of the Orders-in-Council. It was not long, then, before the Foreign Secretary was ordering his representatives in Spain to discuss access to the hitherto exclusive colonial trade and, still more importantly, the produce of the empire's silver mines. Only limited progress was made, however. The Spaniards did sanction a few purchases of specie, but to demands for trade concessions Seville had but one answer. Recognizing that to relinquish Spain's commercial monopoly on the empire would equate to severing one of the most important links that bound it together, the Junta Central refused to make any commercial concessions except in return for a guaranteed subsidy (it might also be noted here that the British were already conducting a substantial contraband trade with the Spanish colonies through such entrepôts as Jamaica). Nor was their anxiety wholly selfish, for the shipments of bullion that were arriving at Cádiz were becoming ever more important as the tide of French conquest spread across Spain. Yet the British refused to take account of this concern, and continued to push the Spaniards, claiming that Spain's inability to supply its colonies with goods was provoking a revolutionary situation.

And there for a while matters might have rested. But in the first months of 1810 the situation was transformed. The French conquest of Andalucía early in the year led to the Junta Central's deposition, and the capital of Patriot Spain was hastily transferred from Seville to Cádiz. On one level this was helpful as the Regency that was now formed seemed less hostile to Britain: not only did the election of a new National Assembly at last go ahead, but British garrisons were admitted both to Cádiz and to the Moroccan enclave of Ceuta. But on another level the development was less welcome, as the move put the Patriot regime firmly in the pocket of Cádiz's powerful merchant community, just as the loss of Andalucía – in financial terms the central bastion of Spanish resistance – increased the Spaniards' dependence on America. And, finally, in April 1810 revolt broke out in Venezuela, an example soon copied in Buenos Aires, Chile and Mexico. In each case the catalyst was the fall of the Junta Central, an event that seemed to presage the complete collapse of Spain and with it the need for the local elites to take responsibility for their own destiny. In many areas of the empire there had of course been simmering discontent with Spanish rule, but in few instances would this have been enough to produce outright rebellion; indeed, in 1808 the colonies had on the whole rushed to support the cause of the metropolis. By the end of the year, the only areas of the Americas to remain loyal – chiefly Peru and Cuba – were the ones in which racial tension was so serious that the local elites did not dare jeopardize their position by stirring up a war. This was but the beginning of a long story: in Mexico and Venezuela social unrest led to the wholesale defection of the *criollos* and the restoration of the status quo; in Bolivia, Ecuador and Chile, Peruvian expeditionary forces were able to crush the rebels; in Uruguay, Brazilian troops moved in and established a Portuguese protectorate; and in Colombia, serious splits in the insurgent camp enabled loyalism to maintain a foothold. However, Argentina and Paraguay remained independent, while such was the disruption caused by the fighting that financial support for Spain fell dramatically. Thus, the 860 million reales received from across the Atlantic in 1809 fell to a mere 225.5 million reales the next year. As total domestic receipts in 1810 were only 182.2 million reales, the Regency was presented with a serious problem. As the commander of the British expeditionary force that was sent to Cádiz, Sir Thomas Graham, noted in April 1811, 'The government is quite bankrupt.'[20]

All this complicated matters tremendously. In Spain, and especially in Cádiz, the American revolts were greeted with extreme hostility. No matter what their political views were – and there were deep divisions between them – the Spanish deputies who attended the new Assembly that opened in Cádiz in September 1810 united in condemning the insurrection (there were a number of American deputies, but the colonies had deliberately been assigned a less generous level of representation than the metropolis, and they were therefore overwhelmed). At best the insurgents were regarded as self-seeking degenerates – there was a common perception that the American climate had encouraged sexual profligacy and sapped the moral and intellectual fibre of the *criollos* – who had gulled the savage and uncivilized masses into following their lead. As well as having to fight the French, successive regencies therefore found themselves committed to a highly expensive second front, which by 1814 had absorbed some 20,000 troops. Yet the *cortes* set its face against any moves in the direction of reform, even the political equality that was granted to the colonies in October 1810 being hedged about with so many qualifications that it was almost meaningless.

Needless to say, all this posed enormous problems in London. The Perceval administration could not openly support a revolt against its most important ally, but it feared the rebels might be driven into the arms of the French, wished to forge good relations with them, and had a strong interest in seeing them attain their independence. The administration was at the same time encumbered by a public opinion that was strongly pro-American. The result was a most unhappy compromise. British representatives in the Caribbean and elsewhere were forbidden to give direct assistance to the rebels, but insurgent emissaries were received in London. Rather than agreeing to Spanish demands that it should help put down the rebels by force, the British government offered to mediate between the belligerents in the hope of securing terms –

amongst them, needless to say, a liberalization of trade – that would restore the Americans to their allegiance. To the Spaniards this was totally unacceptable, for inherent in the very concept of mediation was the idea that they should make substantial concessions. Meanwhile, they knew perfectly well that the rebels were receiving a considerable amount of covert British help and, unofficial though this was, they could not be convinced the government was not behind this. Equally the Spanish could not be convinced that the Brazilian invasion force sent into what is today Uruguay was acting on the say-so of the Portuguese Prince Regent and his Spanish wife, María Carlota de Borbón. In their eyes, it was self-evident that the arrival of Brazilian troops at Montevideo amounted to nothing less than a covert British attempt to reverse the result of the campaigns of 1806–7. As a result, the Regency would only agree to mediation if the British promised to assist in repression should the negotiations fail. This meant of course that the British were regarded with more hostility than ever. Writing from La Coruña, Sir Howard Douglas noted a worrying tendency 'to attribute all our measures to selfish policy', while Henry Wellesley, who had taken over from his brother, Lord Wellesley, went so far as to claim that the American revolts 'have been the principal cause of all the trouble and vexation I have met with in my different communications with the government'.[21] Indeed, even Wellington was inclined to admit that the Spaniards had a point:

I hope that the regency will have firmness to resist the demand of free trade with the colonies; as a boon of the colonies, it might answer in some degree and might be connected with measures of finance which would probably give them a very large revenue. But we have no right and it is the greatest impolicy in us to demand it. Great Britain has ruined Portugal by her free trade with the Brazils: not only the customs [duties] of Portugal are lost, but the fortunes of numerous individuals who lived by their trade are ruined, and Cádiz will suffer in a similar manner if this demand is agreed to. Portugal would now be in a very different situation as an ally if our trade with the Brazils was still carried on through Lisbon, and I would only ask is it liberal or just to destroy the power and resources [of], and absolutely to ruin, our allies in order to put into the pockets of our merchants the money which before went into their treasuries and would now be employed in the maintenance of military establishments against the common enemy.[22]

By 1812, then, relations between London and Cádiz were very bad, but matters now deteriorated still further. Hitherto the Spaniards had, much to the irritation of many British observers, refused to accept the idea of any of their troops being placed under British control. On 22 September 1812, however, the *cortes* suddenly voted to offer Wellington nothing less than the command-in-chief of the Spanish army. This concession was made in the wake of Wellington's great victory at Salamanca (22 July 1812) and it was supposed by Henry Wellesley that the *cortes*' move came in recognition of the British commander's military prowess. In fact it was the product of nothing of the sort. A small number of deputies may have been acting in good faith, but at the root of the offer was the fact that two rival factions had emerged in Spanish politics. On the one hand there were the *liberales*, a progressive group who were strongly committed to a programme of radical political reform that encompassed such principles as equality before the law, freedom of speech, freedom of occupation, the sovereignty of the people and a constitutional monarchy. And on the other, there were the *serviles*, a rather larger group who were in their own way equally reformist but hoped rather to return Spain to a mythical medieval golden age in which the nobility and the Church would stand supreme and the monarchy be relegated to a mere figurehead. Infighting between the two had become more and more ferocious, and in the summer of 1812 the situation had suddenly tilted away from the *liberales*. Since 1810 the governance of Spain had been in the hands of a Council of Regency, and for two years this had been dominated by figures who were either more or less favourable to the *liberales* or too weak to stand in their way. In January 1812 a much more conservative body took office, and by August fresh changes had eliminated the only figure in its ranks who was believed to be progressive in his views. In this situation the *liberales* not unnaturally believed that their programme would be blocked for good, and decided to attempt to get yet another regency into office. To do this, however, they needed British support, and in this situation the command-in-chief offered itself as a most convenient bribe. But, committed as they were to the principle of the sovereignty of the people, the *liberales* had no intention of surrendering any real power to Wellington, while they also saw the offer as a potential 'Trojan horse' that would secure the Spaniards control of the Anglo-Portuguese army. Everything revolved around what was meant by the phrase 'command-in-chief'. Wellington would be given command of the Spanish field armies, certainly, but what the British did not realize was that that did not mean that they had been placed under his control. On the contrary, political responsibility for the army, and with it control of its organization and structure, continued, as laid down by the constitution, to lie with the Regency and *cortes*. In future, in short, Wellington would have to do exactly what he was told.

At first this reality was hidden from the British by elaborating the decree offering the command to Wellington in language of great complexity. Indeed, it is probable that neither he nor Henry Wellesley nor anyone in the new British government of Lord Liverpool (in May 1812 Perceval had been murdered by a lunatic) ever really understood the Spanish manoeuvre. But this hardly mattered. To the horror of the *liberales*, Wellington insisted on a number of conditions that made it clear that he would have the power to purge the officer corps of undesirable elements and exercise control of the military budget. None of this, of course, had been anticipated by the decree's supporters, while both the military and the political situation had now changed dramatically: in November 1812, as we have seen, Wellington had again been forced to retreat to the Portuguese frontier, while the danger posed by the conservative Regency that had been established in January had in large part evaporated. For the whole of 1813, the *liberales* and their supporters strove by every means in their power to undermine the new commander-in-chief's authority, sabotage his orders and rescue at least a part of the army from his control. Wellington, meanwhile, found himself battling against conditions that were near impossible. So chaotic was the situation in Spain it was all but impossible to gather the resources of men, food, transport and money that would have been needed to make the army an effective fighting force. Something of the sense of frustration that prevailed at his headquarters is communicated by the diary of the Judge Advocate General, Francis Larpent:

The Spanish government and Lord Wellington have not got on well together in spite of outward appearances. The moment any general acts cordially with us ... some reason is found for his removal. This ridiculous Spanish jealousy would be bearable if they supported it by exertion of their own so as to enable us to leave them to themselves, but we are now feeding and clothing their half-starved men in the front and they are doing very little in the rear to supply those they have or to increase their numbers. In short, five years' misery has not scourged them into reasonable beings, and turned romance heroes into common-sense soldiers and practical politicians.[23]

Only in the autumn did significant numbers of Spanish troops reach the line, and then their discipline proved so lax that most of them were sent to the rear almost immediately. Deeply frustrated, Wellington was driven to tender his resignation (though this was eventually rejected by the *cortes*), while there were moments when he seriously considered overthrowing the government. So weary was he of Spain, indeed, that in November 1813 he even proposed making the continued employment of British forces in Spain conditional upon the admission of a British garrison to the recently captured border fortress of San Sebastián. This, he claimed, would cut the Gordian knot: 'You may rely upon this, that if you take a firm, decided line, and show your determination to go through with it, you will have the Spanish nation with you, you will bring the government to their senses, and you will put an end at once to all the petty cabals and counter action existing at the moment.'[24] At all events, it is not a happy story, but in the end the commitment of the Patriot regime and the Liverpool administration to the war effort and Wellington's own dedication and common sense saved the Anglo-Spanish alliance from collapse.

All things considered, the survival of the Anglo-Spanish alliance can be considered as something of a minor miracle. It is important to note, however, that these sorts of troubles were not just restricted to Spain. At the same time that Wellington was experiencing such difficulties in the Peninsula, Britain also found itself coming under pressure in Sicily. In the course of 1809 skirmishing had continued between the court and the commander of the British garrison – the same Sir John Stuart who had won the battle of Maida in 1806 – over the direction that military operations should take. As before, the queen in particular favoured an invasion of the Italian mainland, but it was only with some difficulty that Stuart could be persuaded to launch even the most minor operation. Eventually Austrian requests for help in 1809 led him to sanction a two-pronged descent on Calabria and the city of Naples, but news of the Austrian defeat at Wagram caused its cancellation. As a result, Maria Carolina and her supporters were left even more disgruntled than before, especially as Stuart had agreed to a request from the commander of the Mediterranean Fleet, Lord Collingwood, to send a force to take the

Ionian islands from the French, a task that was quickly achieved in respect of all of them except Corfu. This dissatisfaction was in part justified, for Stuart was not an impressive figure and may well have wasted genuine opportunities at this time. But the British still had reason to complain of the utter inability of the Sicilian regime to muster a credible fighting force, while their allies would not give them the authority that might have allowed them, as in Portugal, to have made something of the situation. As the British were convinced that much of their subsidy to Sicily was being used to fund the expenses of the court, and were increasingly anxious to send some of the troops they had in Sicily to Spain, there was much discontent and a growing conviction that the only way forward was a change of regime. In this they were encouraged by their contacts with the island's nobles and merchants: eager to throw off the control of the court, the local elites saw the British as their salvation and sought to secure their patronage by affecting much admiration for the British model of constitutionalism.

A coincidence of political and military crises in 1810 precipitated dramatic change. Short of money as ever, in January of that year Ferdinand demanded a much larger subsidy from the estates than was customary, only for the barons to respond by persuading their fellow chambers to join with them in halving the sum required and proposing a radical reform of the tax system – henceforward there was to be a single levy of 5 per cent payable on the value of all landed property, irrespective of ownership. As the right of the nobility to determine the level at which it was taxed was central to Sicilian feudalism, this threatened the whole edifice of noble privilege, and some comment is required on the barons' motives. There was some recognition that the war effort had to be financed adequately, but the move was also motivated by shrewd economic calculation. Sicilian feudalism was fast becoming an embarrassment to many of its beneficiaries. Thanks in large part to the British presence, Sicily was experiencing a great economic boom. Perennially in debt, the barons were eager to benefit from this but were prevented from doing so by the feudal system. Being entailed, for example, estates could not be sold or rationalized; mining rights were often shared with the Crown or restricted; there was no free market in corn; and the peasantry enjoyed a variety of irritating rights with regard to pasturage and water courses. Finally, economics aside, feudalism also brought serious disadvantages to the barons' relationship with the Crown, for, as fiefs, all estates reverted to the Crown in the event of a noble house failing to produce an heir. In making their proposal, then, the baronial opposition was both asserting its economic interests and identifying itself with the cause of the nation. Faced by this rebellion, the king at first appeared to back down, making some judicious changes in the personnel of the government and promising to forgo the increased levies he had demanded. These changes paid off when the opposition was defeated in a second session of parliament in August 1810. But this was not an end to the matter. Still desperate for money, in February 1811 Ferdinand quite unconstitutionally established a national lottery, imposed a 1 per cent tax on all commercial transactions, and expropriated and put up for sale considerable quantities of Church and municipal land. The result was uproar and the new measures encountered extensive resistance. But this time the regime stood firm, pressurizing the deputation charged with the defence of the constitution when the assembly was not in session into declaring Ferdinand to be within his rights, and imprisoning five of the opposition's most important leaders. The royal triumph was to prove short-lived, however. At the very time it was outraging the barons, the court had also alienated the British.

In September 1810 Murat had attempted an assault on Sicily across the Straits of Messina. This had proved a fiasco, but the Sicilian response at every level had been one of apathy. It also became clear that Maria Carolina was in contact with both Napoleon and Murat. Enraged, and fearing that the court was now so unpopular that it might provoke a pro-French revolt, the British determined on intervention. The British government's aims were threefold. First of all, Maria Carolina was to be eliminated as a threat to the alliance; secondly, peace was to be restored to relations between Crown and country through a programme of domestic reform; and thirdly, mainland Italy was to be encouraged to revolt against the French through the example of a new and progressive administration in Sicily. London then selected a vigorous soldier and administrator of liberal views, Lord William Bentinck, as the instrument for this policy, whose obvious corollary was a change of government in Palermo. Arriving in Sicily as both ambassador and military commander in July 1811, Bentinck at first tried persuasion, only to be faced by a flat refusal to cooperate. Given fresh backing from London, Bentinck now applied considerable pressure, threatening to withdraw the British subsidy unless the administration was remodelled to include a respectable proportion of prominent Sicilians, the exiled barons freed, the court and government purged of treacherous elements, and the British ambassador appointed commander-in-chief of the Sicilian army. Faced with these demands, the court resisted, only to cave in when Bentinck ordered the military occupation of Palermo. Ferdinand agreed to withdraw from the government in favour of his son Francis, who now acted as Prince Regent. As for Maria Carolina, she was defiant to the last. 'This is a repetition of Bayonne!' she shouted at the British general sent to secure her person. 'Bonaparte did not treat the Spanish royal family worse than Bentinck has treated us! Was it for this that I escaped the axes, conspiracies and betrayals of the Neapolitan Jacobins? Was it for this that I helped Nelson to win the Battle of the Nile? For this that I brought your army to Sicily? General, is this your English honour?'[25]

As Francis quickly released the exiled barons and rescinded the unconstitutional measures taken by his father, the way now seemed clear for reform, but Ferdinand and Maria Carolina had no intention of letting their son have a free hand, and strove by every means to block any advance. Their relations with Bentinck were therefore in a state of permanent crisis: eventually he had to virtually deport the queen, who went into exile in first Constantinople and then Vienna, where she died in 1814. Yet, step by step, progress was made. In March 1812 a new ministry was formed which included the reformist leaders, Belmonte and Castelnuovo. In May new elections were called; and on 20 July the basis of a new constitution was agreed by the assembly. This document purported to be an exact copy of British political organization. There was to be a House of Lords and a House of Commons; parliament was to meet on an annual basis and to have the power of legislation; ministers were to be appointed by the king but be responsible to parliament; all taxation had to originate in the Commons; the monarchy lost its estates in return for a civil list; and Sicily was to enjoy the principle of the rule of law and trial by jury. Feudalism was now specifically abolished: baronial jurisdiction vanished, the old fees were in theory swept away, and the estates of the nobility converted into freeholdings. And last but not least, Sicily was given complete autonomy from Naples. All this was happily sanctioned by Bentinck, a somewhat vainglorious figure much influenced by concepts of liberal imperialism he had picked up in the course of several years' service in India under Lord Wellesley.

Despite being hailed by Bentinck as a great victory for Sicilian patriotism, the affair appears rather as a coup on the part of a faction of the nobility who were eager to break the power of the monarchy and advance their own economic interests. The abolition of feudalism in Sicily, as elsewhere, meant almost nothing in social terms. The peasants were effectively dispossessed of numerous and vital customary rights, deprived of access to the commons, and encumbered with greater burdens than ever (though all feudal dues were supposedly abolished, the decision as to what was and what was not a feudal due was left to litigation). By contrast the nobility, as well as gaining immensely from the unrestricted control they now possessed of their estates, had also to be paid compensation for what they were deemed by the courts to have lost. Furthermore, although a free market in land was created, entails per se were never abolished, the estates of the nobility therefore being guaranteed. Yet the predominance of the barons proved disastrous for the cause of constitutionalism, the political crisis of 1810–12 having exposed deep divisions in Sicilian society. Economically, the nobility had since the late eighteenth century been challenged by a non-noble oligarchy that had derived considerable income from usury, leasing land from the barons, or estate management, and this threat had been sharpened by new fortunes made during the war. Alongside this basic economic rivalry there also existed tension between greater and lesser nobles, between different regions of the country, and even between individual cities. In protest at the obvious sectionalism of the constitutionalists, there therefore emerged a radical movement which took as its inspiration the French Revolution and the *cortes* of Cádiz. A rapid process of disintegration now affected the baronial party because of personal differences between Belmonte and Castelnuovo and second thoughts about the wisdom of abolishing feudalism. As a result the radicals were able to seize control of the assembly. Demanding universal suffrage, a single chamber and the abolition of entails, they proceeded to block all supply, the result being that parliamentary government had soon broken down completely. Social disorder was meanwhile on the increase, with bread riots in Palermo and serious anti-seigneurial disturbances in the countryside, and by October 1813 Bentinck was left with no alternative but to dissolve parliament and impose martial law.

What makes the Sicilian example particularly interesting is that it clearly exhibits the limits of Britain's power in relation to her weaker allies. Sweden, Portugal, Spain and Sicily all displayed similar problems:

they were all relatively poor and underdeveloped; they were states in which the march of enlightened absolutism had only achieved a limited degree of success in its battle with the privileged orders; they were possessed of rulers, or at least executive authorities, whose competence was open to question; they were all under intense military pressure; and they were in no case able to mount the sort of war effort which the British desired. This generated different responses, however. In Sweden, the British threw up their hands in disgust, while in Portugal and Spain compromises were worked out that gave the British enough of what they required for them to refrain from taking matters any further. But in Sicily a combination of circumstances led Bentinck to extreme solutions. In this, however, he proved just as overconfident as Napoleon had been in Spain. Not only was little progress made in getting Sicily into a position in which she could stand on her own two feet, but the 'nation' to which Bentinck had sought to appeal proved to be no nation at all, but rather a collection of deeply antagonistic groups who were quite incapable of cooperating with one another in the common cause. In 1812 a large part of the British garrison was withdrawn for service in eastern Spain, where it formed the basis of an expeditionary force based at Alicante, while in 1813 Bentinck was able to join it for a few months in a series of operations that took him to the gates of Barcelona. But this was not so much the reflection of a sound state of defence as of the growing unwillingness of Marshal Murat, who had replaced Joseph Bonaparte as King of Naples, to take an active part in the war. Meanwhile, Britain found herself playing in effect the same role that France had played at Bayonne, and in the process to have justified some of the very arguments that were used against her to such effect in Spain. By 1813 it really looked as if she had come to Sicily with no other object than to annex it. Strategically, the British presence in Sicily had fulfilled its objectives – so long as Sicily and Malta were in British hands Britain could hope both to forestall another French invasion of Egypt and to intervene in the Ottoman Empire should this prove necessary – but politically it was a serious embarrassment.

States such as Spain and Sicily were to a very large extent dependent on Britain for their survival, and yet in each case substantial elements in the body politic proved deeply unwilling to accept British tutelage. As often as not, Britain's wishes were ignored and her representatives openly snubbed. Some of the reasons, such as opposition to reforms desired by the British and fear of British imperialism, we have already examined. However, also at issue was Britain's ability to sustain her allies. Over and over again expectations were confounded by developments elsewhere: in 1807 Sicily found that troops stationed there were sent to Egypt; in 1808 Sweden found that Britain's attention was distracted by the outbreak of insurrection in Portugal; in 1809 Spain and Portugal saw large numbers of troops that might otherwise have fought in the Peninsula sent to Walcheren (see below); and from 1810 onwards troops from Sicily fought in Spain. Added to this was a further issue. With British troops very thin on the ground, Moore and Wellington alike were well aware that defeat had to be avoided at all costs and were therefore inclined to adopt a cautious line that again did not sit well with the expectations of their allies. In the absence of supporting forces, however, Spaniards especially died by the thousand and this could not but fan the flames of anglophobia. But if anglophobia was strong even in states that received large amounts of British aid, it was still stronger in states like Austria, Prussia and Russia, which all had good reason to complain of tardy, inadequate or downright niggardly British support in the past and saw the Peninsular War as, at best, a sideshow. In short, Britain's turbulent relations with her Mediterranean and Baltic allies are suggestive of a deeper reality: that neither the Portland, nor the Perceval, nor the Liverpool administrations could possibly hope to orchestrate a general coalition against Napoleon. Whether it was jealousy of British prosperity, suspicion of British war aims, anger at British actions or resentment of British chauvinism, there were simply too many obstacles in the way.

As so often, then, we must once again turn to the figure of Napoleon Bonaparte. Engaged in an increasingly bitter struggle in Spain and Portugal which had already proved its capacity to deal the heaviest blows to his prestige, it would clearly have been sensible for the emperor to maintain peaceful relationships with the rest of the Continent, and in particular to retain the friendship and cooperation of Russia. But the emperor was hardly in a conciliatory mood. Let us first look at Prussia. At Tilsit the unfortunate Frederick William III had been forced to accept peace terms that were bad enough, but a year on the screw was being turned still further. In theory, by means of a separate convention signed at Königsberg on 12 July 1807, France had agreed to evacuate Prussia by 1 October 1807 provided that the latter paid off whatever sum it was agreed that she should pay in reparations. On the surface, this looked reasonable enough, but when the bill came in it proved to be almost 155 million francs, to which was added the 30 million francs calculated as being owed by the Prussian state to creditors of different sorts in the lands ceded to France. At least 100 million francs were to be found within a year for even this agreement to hold good, but this was impossible: the army by which Prussia was occupied amounted to 150,000 men; the plunder seized during the war was specifically excluded from the indemnity; and large parts of the east, in particular, were in a state of the utmost ruin and misery: 'In the villages . . . there was not an animal to be seen that did not belong to the army. The houses were all unroofed and most of the woodwork burned. Many of the inhabitants [had] absolutely starved to death or [been] obliged to remove and seek their livelihood in other places.'[26]

With Prussia facing complete ruin, her new chief minister, Baron Heinrich vom Stein, reacted with great vigour. Swingeing cuts were imposed in the budget through a series of reductions in pensions, salaries and the expenses of the court, and the first steps taken in the implementation of a major programme of reform designed to revivify the Prussian state. On the international front, meanwhile, attempts were made to enlist the good offices of Russia and convince the French that full payment was impossible: so desperate was Frederick William that Napoleon was even offered an offensive and defensive alliance and a guarantee of up to 40,000 men if he would only offer better terms. But the emperor remained deaf to all argument, and the increasingly desperate Stein concluded that the only way out was a new war in conjunction with Austria. With this in mind, he therefore sent a special envoy to Vienna while looking into the possibility of stirring up some sort of popular insurrection in Germany. Unfortunately for him the French intercepted some of his correspondence, and promptly imposed new terms that made matters even worse: Prussia would be freed of all French troops other than garrisons in Magdeburg, Glogau, Küstrin and Stettin and need now pay only 140 million francs in terms of actual reparations, but in exchange for this she found herself stripped of much revenue, confined to an army of 42,000 men, committed to a military alliance against Austria, and deprived of Stein, whom Frederick William was obliged to banish and send into exile. Even by the standards of Napoleonic peace settlements, it was a massive blow. Deprived not just of much of her territory and population, but also unable even to levy tolls on the entire length of such frontiers as remained to her, Prussia was economically ruined. Still worse, she was seemingly forever in Napoleon's pocket: with her main fortresses in the hands of the French, her army a mere shadow of its former self and Frederick William resolutely opposed to any move that might incur the emperor's ire, there was no chance of the national uprising of which a few diehard officers dreamed, and, indeed, no guarantee of Prussia's continued existence other than Napoleon's will.

In adopting a hard line, Napoleon was acting against the advice of many of his advisers, not least his ambassador to Russia, Armand de Caulaincourt, who told the emperor to his face that his conduct was creating a climate of fear in Europe, and urged him to withdraw all his troops from Prussia other than a token garrison in one single fortress. This, he claimed, 'would be of greater use to him than an army of 100,000 men and ten strongholds on the Oder, and . . . leave all his forces at his disposal to cover Spain and put an honourable end to the complications in that country'.[27] But Napoleon would not hear of such a move. Fears of a universal monarchy he just laughed off: 'France is large enough! What can I want? Have I not enough with my Spanish affairs, with the war against England?'[28] And Caulaincourt's plans for an evacuation of Germany, he scorned as 'a system of weakness'. As the ambassador continued, 'He objected that they would lose the fruit of all the sacrifices already made in order to make England bow, and that it was essential to close every port to the commerce of that power so as to compel her recognition of the independence of other flags . . . The emperor often listened to me with a genial air, but sometimes also with impatience. More than once he told me, though in a joking tone, that I understood nothing of affairs.'[29]

To return to Russia, it had been agreed that emperor and tsar should meet to settle the differences that had arisen over the Ottoman Empire. On 28 September 1808 the two rulers duly met at the small Saxon city of Erfurt, a spot chosen as it was roughly midway between the frontiers of France and Russia. Outwardly, all was well. The tsar was greeted not just by Napoleon but a large number of German princes, and the emperor conducted him in person to the sumptuous lodgings – furnished, incidentally, with fittings brought from Paris for the purpose – that had been selected for him to the sound of cannonades and church bells. To flattery, meanwhile, was added bedazzlement: as at Tilsit, the Imperial Guard put on an impressive display of military pomp; the German princes had been encouraged to attend so as to reinforce the notion of Napoleon as *padishah*; and Alexander was reminded of the superiority of French culture by the specially invited actors of the Comédie Française. As Napoleon told Talleyrand prior to the conference, 'I wish my journey to be brilliant . . . I wish to astonish Germany by my splendour . . . I wish the emperor of Russia to be dazzled by my power.'[30] As this suggests, Alexander was not the only monarch who was to be impressed and overawed. Erfurt was intended to be a restatement of Napoleon's control of the Confederation of the Rhine and a reminder to its rulers of his overwhelming power. 'I doubt whether the princes who came to pay court left satisfied,' wrote Caulaincourt. 'Their presence was doubtless flattering, but . . . these sovereigns found themselves treated rather as Austria had formerly treated her electors, and they may well have discovered that, although their new title had freed them from their former functions, it had no way altered their position with regard to their protector.'[31] Nevertheless, the chief object of attention was always Russia. Curiously, however, Napoleon did not display quite the same charm and consideration that had been on show in July 1807. In command of the Old Guard was Marshal Oudinot, who relates a minor but none the less telling anecdote:

One day we were riding into the country, the two emperors riding side by side. At a given moment ours, carried away by his thoughts, took the lead, whistling and seeming to forget those he was leaving behind. I shall always remember Alexander turning stiffly towards his neighbour and asking, 'Are we to follow?'[32]

Nor was this the only such incident. In general, indeed, 'The emperor Napoleon took command of the ceremonial of the congress like a sovereign in his capital.'[33]

Underlying the smiles, compliments and embraces, then, there was always something of an edge to the meeting at Erfurt. It was not long, for example, before Talleyrand, who had been invited to the meeting by Napoleon specifically to cultivate Alexander, was noticing that he seemed 'preoccupied'.[34] At all events, the meeting was a failure. The Russian ruler had come to Erfurt bent on securing French support for a partition of the Ottoman Empire, and believing he already had Napoleon's agreement to such a policy. All that was left was to arrange the precise details of the territorial settlement. Alexander felt he had every right to Napoleon's support: by joining the Continental Blockade and going to war against Sweden, Russia had more than fulfilled the obligations she had accepted at Tilsit. Nor had the tsar come to Erfurt in any spirit of suspicion or hostility. Prussia, it is true, was a problem, as Alexander believed Napoleon should renounce his aspirations to annex Silesia, evacuate what was left of Prussia and reduce the financial burden that had been placed upon her. He had no quarrel, though, with the basic principles by which Prussia had been treated. A number of figures at court had expressed fears that Napoleon might somehow spring a second Bayonne and kidnap him, but Alexander laughed at such alarmism. He also refused to listen to the denunciations of French policy emanating from Russia's envoys in Paris and Madrid, both of whom were convinced that the French ruler was bent on nothing short of universal dominion. Napoleon was his friend and what had happened in Spain was of little consequence. 'Russia,' wrote Caulaincourt, 'was silent concerning affairs in Spain, which the tsar expounded in his discussions with good will rather than irritation as regards his ally ... Nor was he displeased that the emperor's warlike ardour should find vent in the Peninsula ... The interest which England had in wresting that country from our influence and in saving Portugal was in his eyes a powerful instrument for inducing her to make peace. From this point of view the course of events was therefore serving the interests of Russia as well as our own.'[35]

Spain, then, was of no concern to Alexander, but in the summer of 1808, and, more especially, at the battle of Bailén, it was of huge concern to Napoleon. And now there was a further threat to be dealt with. Heavily defeated in 1805 and subjected to a diet of constant humiliation thereafter, Austria had until 1808 maintained a low profile. Under the leadership of the Archduke Charles, the army was strengthened through military reforms, but Charles himself believed that Vienna should cut its losses in Germany and Italy, abandon all notion of fighting Napoleon, and seek compensation in the Balkans. As for Emperor Francis – since 6 August 1806 Francis I of Austria rather than Francis II of the now defunct Holy Roman Empire – he remained as cautious as ever, all the more so as Russia now appeared as a potential enemy. For a time, a consensus even emerged that Austria should seek an alliance with

Napoleon. But it soon became clear that the emperor was simply not interested in such a deal. Still worse, his overthrow of the Spanish Bourbons provoked fears that he might treat the Habsburgs in the same fashion. A number of figures in the Austrian court had always been in favour of a new war. Francis's third wife, Maria-Ludovica of Habsburg-Este, had bitter personal memories of French aggression in northern Italy; the chancellor, Phillip von Stadion, possessed a deep nostalgia for the Holy Roman Empire (in which he had enjoyed the status of a so-called imperial knight); and the youngest of the emperor's brothers, the Archduke John, was a Romantic obsessed with the idea that the Tyrol – lost to Bavaria in 1805 – was the very cradle of the German nation and, as such, could only belong to Austria. In the wake of Bayonne, such figures had a credibility they had previously lacked, and they were now joined by others such as Metternich. In his eyes, at least, there was no longer any option: 'Austria was in a position in which she could not possibly maintain herself . . . Not only, then, was the renewal [of hostilities] in the nature of things, but it was for our empire an absolute condition of its existence.'[36] Though still hopeful war might be avoided, Francis allowed Charles to accelerate reform of the army, which he also ordered should be brought up to full strength, and rather reluctantly permitted Stadion to organize a propaganda campaign designed to stir up German nationalism and provoke an insurrection.

If the object was to secure better treatment from Napoleon, however, the effort was a futile one. On the contrary, on 25 July Napoleon dispatched a series of letters to the rulers of the Confederation of the Rhine warning them that Austria was bent on a war of revenge – a matter of particular sensitivity for states such as Baden, Württemberg and Bavaria – and that they should therefore get ready for war themselves: 'If Austria arms, then we must arm too . . . If there is one way of avoiding war, it is showing Austria that we have picked up the gauntlet and are ready for her.'[37] And, on 15 August, Metternich received a most clear and public warning of the likely French response at a formal reception at the palace of St Cloud:

Napoleon advanced towards me with great solemnity. He stopped two feet in front of me, and addressed me in a loud voice and pompous tone: 'Well, Monsieur Ambassador, what does the emperor, your master, want? Does he intend to call me back to Vienna?[38]

With Austria restless, not to mention the many thousands of French troops tied down in Spain, a French attack on the Ottoman Empire had to be postponed. Alexander, then, got something of a shock at Erfurt. Rather than discussing arrangements for a joint attack on Turkey, the tsar found himself facing demands that he should threaten the use of military force against Austria. Thus Napoleon's instructions to Talleyrand, whom he summoned from retirement to act as his chief negotiator, were as precise as they were cynical:

Now I shall go to Erfurt. I wish, in returning, to be free to do what I wish in Spain. I wish to be assured that Austria will be afraid and hold back, and I do not wish to engage in too precise a manner with Russia concerning the affairs of the east . . . You will insist greatly upon that, for Count Rumiantsev is sanguine about the eastern question. You will say that nothing can be done without public opinion, and that it is necessary that, without being scared by our combined power, Europe should see with pleasure the achievement of the great undertaking we contemplate. The security of the neighbouring powers, the legitimate interest of the continent, seven millions of Greeks restored to independence: all this constitutes a fine field for philanthropy. I will give you *carte blanche* for that. I wish only that it be distant philanthropy.[39]

More and more, in fact, it seemed the chief goal of French policy was to keep Vienna quiet. This was vital to Napoleon at this time. After twelve years of marriage, he was still childless and yet in every battle that he fought he risked death or serious injury. In consequence, he was desperate for an heir and that in turn meant a period of peace in which he could replace Josephine with a new bride – something that was already under discussion in the French court – and spend some time with whichever princess was chosen for the task. But Alexander was not happy about his interests being relegated to the realms of 'distant philanthropy'. As for the deal on offer, it was simply unacceptable. If the possibility of a marriage to the tsar's youngest sister, Anna, was raised at Erfurt, then it seems likely that this was only to test out the idea's reception.

Peace talks were to be offered to Britain – something that the tsar was increasingly anxious for – but only on terms that seemed unlikely to bear fruit, in that London would be required to recognize the new territorial arrangements in Europe and to force Patriot Spain and Spanish America to acknowledge Joseph Bonaparte as their legitimate monarch. And, in exchange for pressurizing Austria, Russia was offered little or nothing. In theory, she could have Finland and the Danubian provinces, but there was no mention of armed assistance from France and some suggestion that these annexations would not be recognized unless peace was forthcoming with Britain. As for the rest of the Ottoman Empire, she would be expected to guarantee its independence and integrity. Against all this, vague hints that in the future things might be very different counted for very little, while the tsar may have been encouraged by a Talleyrand who, according to his own account, was increasingly convinced that the emperor had to be stopped. Alexander's duty, he is supposed to have told him, was to resist Napoleon, who had now become a threat not just to the peace of Europe but also to its very stability.

Such was Alexander's discomfiture at discovering Napoleon's change of position over the Ottoman Empire that Talleyrand's intervention was hardly necessary. At all events discussions between the two emperors did not go smoothly. 'The tsar was unshakeable,' wrote Caulaincourt. 'Nothing could alter his resolve. He refused to see in the arguments and insistence of his ally anything but a proof of the hostile intentions and schemes of revenge of which he suspected him ... Alexander showed great character ... On one occasion, for instance, Napoleon ... tried the experiment of working himself up into a rage, and, losing control of himself, threw his hat ... upon the ground and stamped on it ... Alexander stood still ... and, looking at him with a smile, said, when he had calmed down a little. "When you become violent, I just become stubborn. With me anger is of no avail. Let us discuss and be reasonable, or I will go." '[40] In the end all that Napoleon could obtain was the promise that Russia would support him against Vienna should Austria attack him. Beyond that it was agreed that a joint peace offer should be made to Britain, and that France should keep Spain and Portugal and remain in occupation of Silesia, and Russia retain the Danubian provinces and Finland. As for the Ottoman Empire, it was guaranteed by both sides, though Russia was permitted to abandon her current armistice with the Turks and resume active military operations if negotiations with the Turks had made no progress by 1 January 1809. All this was agreed in a document signed on 12 October 1808, and the monarchs then parted amidst further protestations of friendship. These, however, meant nothing. What counted was that Alexander rode home with the firm conviction that Napoleon could not be trusted and, in particular, that he could not be allowed any extension of his power in Eastern Europe. War between France and Russia was neither inevitable, nor close – for one thing the current Foreign Minister, Rumiantsev, was a firm proponent of the French alliance – but it had suddenly become possible again.

No peace came from Erfurt. The talks offered to Britain were rejected out of hand and Austria was not dissuaded from the course on which she had embarked. Indeed, given Napoleon's belligerent attitude, the latter was driven even further down the road towards a fresh conflict. Among significant parts of the establishment there was still no enthusiasm for renewing the struggle, but on 23 December a resigned and despondent Francis resolved on war. Needless to say, the Austrians endeavoured to secure help from Russia, Prussia and Britain alike, but the first was unwilling to break with Napoleon when she was still embroiled in both Sweden and the Balkans; the second was cowed and under military occupation; and the third distinctly lukewarm. Given the constant French refrain that continental coalitions were the fruit of British gold, this last point is worth considering. With war looming, in October 1808 Vienna had contacted London with a request for money, but at £7.5 million the sum was far beyond Britain's means – it far outstripped any other payment that had previously been made – and it was made clear that, while help would be given, it would only appear after Austria had shown herself to be in earnest. A second and somewhat more moderate request met a slightly more encouraging answer, but only in April 1809 was it eventually agreed that £250,000 would be sent to Austria in silver and a further £1 million deposited in Malta for Vienna to draw upon at will. Nor is any of this surprising. Not only was there little faith in the Austrian army, but right up to the last moment it was feared that Vienna was not bluffing. As for reports that preparations for a great popular insurrection were underway in Germany, these were accorded little credence. In brief, far from 'Pitt's gold' buying an attack on Napoleon, it was rather the other way about.

When the Austrian armies crossed the frontier into Bavaria and the kingdom of Italy on 9 April 1809, they did so all but unsuccoured. Only in the Tyrol was any assistance on offer. Here the local inhabitants had become increasingly resentful of Bavarian rule, which was both destructive of provincial privilege and strongly anti-clerical, while there were also long traditions of irregular military service, with the result that, under the leadership of the innkeeper Andreas Hofer, talk of insurrection had assumed concrete form. Initially, however, Austrian success was considerable. With much of the old *grande armée* serving in Spain, Napoleon had only 80,000 troops available for service in Germany as opposed to the 180,000 who had marched to meet the Prussians in 1806. Nor did it help that politics dictated that the Austrians should be seen to be the aggressors: the French forces in Germany were kept well back from the border, while Napoleon himself remained in Paris and gave Marshal Berthier – normally his chief of staff – command of the deliberately misnamed 'Army of the Rhine'. Also, the spring thaw meant that the rivers of Bavaria were in full spate, with the result that the *grande armée* could not concentrate with any great speed. Hampered by the floods though he was too, the Archduke Charles therefore overran much of eastern Bavaria. Nor were matters much better for Napoleon elsewhere. The army of the Grand Duchy of Warsaw could put less than 20,000 men into the field; the Kingdom of Italy was largely defended by raw recruits; and the Tyrol was held by a mere 3,000 Bavarians. While Charles went forward in Bavaria, then, other Austrian armies captured Warsaw and scored successes in Italy and the Tyrol, where the local insurgents had soon eliminated the inadequate Bavarian garrison. And, finally, the Kingdom of Italy was swept by a wave of agrarian unrest. For a brief moment, indeed, the atmosphere was one of panic, as witness this account of the aftermath of the defeat of Eugène de Beauharnais at Sacile:

At length I reached Verona. All was in confusion. The wounded were coming in in large numbers, [and] fugitives, riderless horses, carts, baggage wagons [and] carriages [were] crossing each other . . . blocking the streets and filling the squares; in short, all the horrors of a rout . . . The authorities were without news and crowded round me to ask for some . . . The Viceroy . . . sent several *aides de camp* to . . . desire me to come straight to him . . . He was even more taken up with what the emperor would say and write than with the affair itself. 'I have been beaten,' he said, 'at my first attempt at commanding, and in a bad place too. The emperor will be furious; he knows his Italy so well.'[41]

Austria's success proved short-lived, however. Despite gallant attempts by two Prussian officers named Schill and Dornberg to whip up revolts in Westphalia and Prussia, Germany remained quiet, and so

Napoleon was able to fall on Charles with every man he had available. Thoroughly overawed, the Austrian commander was soon falling back on Vienna, which he proceeded to abandon to the French. Threatened with being trapped, the Austrian forces in the Tyrol and northern Italy fell back in their turn, while in the east the Poles countered the fall of Warsaw with an invasion of Galicia. On 21–22 May an attempt by Napoleon to cross the Danube just east of Vienna was thrown back by Charles at Aspern-Essling with heavy losses, but in Italy the Austrians were beaten at the river Piave and forced to retreat to Hungary where they were defeated for a second time at Raab. Meanwhile, in response to Napoleon's demands for support, a Russian army invaded Galicia and occupied Cracow. The *coup de grâce*, however, came at the battle of Wagram. Fought just outside Vienna on 5–6 July, this was a titanic struggle that saw Napoleon secure a narrow victory. Now badly outnumbered, Charles knew that his forces would not be able to endure another battle and was much alarmed by a proclamation that Napoleon had issued on 15 May in which he called on the Magyars to revolt and promised them an independent state. In practice, the results turned out to be non-existent, but when the French caught Charles up at Znaim, the Archduke promptly asked for an armistice. Yet Wagram had been a respectable performance on the part of the whitecoats. There had been little pursuit, and it was clear enough to veterans of Napoleon's campaigns that something was wrong. To quote the infantry officer, Elzéar Blaze:

Wagram had no great material results. That is to say there was no great haul of the net as at Ulm, Jena and Ratisbon. Scarcely any prisoners were made; we took from the Austrians nine pieces of cannon, and we lost fourteen . . . In general, after a battle an order of the day acquainted us with what we had done . . . In his proclamations to his army, which Napoleon drew up himself, he told us . . . that he was satisfied with himself, that we had surpassed his expectations, that we had flown with the rapidity of an eagle; he then detailed our exploits, the number of soldiers, cannon and carriages that we had taken. It was exaggerated, but it was high-sounding and had an excellent effect. After Wagram we had not the least proclamation, not the least order of the day . . . For upwards of three weeks we knew not the name it was to have in history.[42]

The Austrian collapse was not quite the end of the story, even if what remained made depressing reading for Napoleon's opponents. By the time of the battle of Wagram, Sweden was effectively out of the war: following a series of reverses, on 13 March Gustav IV had been over- thrown by an aristocratic faction sickened by what they saw as the king's mismanagement of the war effort and determined to put an end to enlightened absolutism and restore Sweden's traditional alliance with France. As for the British, 1809 was marked by an episode that was virtually epic in its futility. Driven not so much by a desire to aid Austria as one to strike a further blow against French naval power and undo the damage to its prestige incurred by what appeared to have been its failure in Spain, the Portland administration decided to land a large army at the mouth of the Scheldt and seize Antwerp. After much delay an army was duly assembled, and by 30 July the first British troops were going ashore. Vlissingen was besieged and captured, but the British advance was so slow that the defenders had time to reinforce Antwerp to such an extent that all thought of taking it had to be abandoned. An attempt was then made to retain control of the island of Walcheren, but its climate provoked an epidemic of malaria so terrible it had eventually to be evacuated. Only in Germany (where a flying column known as the Brunswick Black Corps had chosen to fight on despite Wagram), Tyrol and Calabria did active hostilities continue, but here too the French and their allies had the upper hand. The Brunswickers were forced to take ship for Britain, the Tyroleans gradually hunted down, and the Calab- rian *banditti*, as we have seen, subjected to ever greater pressure. Against this, the British occupation of most of the Ionian islands amounted to very little. Almost everywhere French arms ruled supreme.

All that remains to be said of the campaigns of 1809 is the territorial adjustments to which they gave rise. Needless to say, the chief casualty was Austria. On the battlefield of Wagram Francis I had responded to the news of defeat with the laconic remark, 'We shall have much to retrieve.'[43] Rarely could he have spoken a truer word. Already badly hit in 1805, the Habsburgs were now punished still further. Carinthia, Carniola and that part of Croatia south of the river Sava were annexed and joined with the territories lost in Istria and Dalmatia in 1805, and the city-state of Ragusa, which had been occupied by the French in 1807, to form the French-ruled Illyrian Provinces. Western Galicia, the portion of central Poland seized by Austria in 1795, was divided between Russia and the Grand Duchy of Warsaw; and Salzburg and some other border districts were ceded to Bavaria, which also got back the Tyrol (minus the largely Italian-speaking Trentino which was passed over to the Kingdom of Italy). Austria had to pay an indemnity of 85 million francs, reduce her army to 150,000 men, and agree to join the Continental Blockade. In addition, Joseph Bonaparte was recognized as King of Spain and Joachim Murat as King of Naples. There was still the issue of Hungary: although nothing had come of the proclamation of 15 May, Napoleon pointedly failed to guarantee Francis I's remaining possessions and continued to encourage his representatives to stir up Magyar separatism. With Austria all but bankrupt, further resistance was out of the question, and salvation was now sought in détente with France. The chief symbol of this was the marriage of the Archduchess Marie-Louise to Napoleon, the empress Josephine having previously been divorced on account of her failure to produce an heir. Stadion having resigned the post of chief minister in the wake of the battle of Wagram, Austrian foreign policy was now in the hands of Metternich, who had absolutely no illusions as to Austria's situation. As he wrote to Francis on 10 August 1809:

Whatever the conditions of the peace may be . . . we shall find our safety only by accommodating ourselves to the triumphant system of France. That this system . . . is most unsuitable for us, I need not repeat to Your Majesty. My principles are unchangeable, but to necessity we must yield. If the present war, with extraordinary means, is unsuccessful, to repeat the attempt with reduced strength against a stronger adversary would be an act of insanity. From the day when peace is signed we must confine our system to tacking and turning and flattering. Thus alone may we possibly preserve our existence till the day of general deliverance . . . For us there remains but one expedient: to increase our strength for better days, to work out our preservation by gentle means, without looking back upon our former course.[44]

Nor was Austrian withdrawal from the scene the only damage done to the cause of resistance to Napoleon. In Germany there were plenty of patriots who were ready to attribute the miserable failure of their hopes to want of British assistance. To quote the words of an officer fighting in the British army as part of the so-called King's German Legion:

From these heroic and loyal efforts of Schill and Dornberg, and from insurrections like that organized in the name of the Duke of Brunswick . . . it may clearly be seen that, if an English force of only 4,000 men had been landed on the banks of the Elbe, and about 10,000 in East Friesland, all Westphalia and Hanover and East Friesland would directly have taken up arms to protect their country, and to regain their liberty. One Hanoverian general, with a sufficient supply of money and arms, would certainly have collected in a short space of time 80,000 men, and the bad success of all the insurrections is to be attributed to the want of the authority and sanction of England.[45]

Just as bad, perhaps, was the manner in which Napoleon had posed as the defender of the states of southern Germany against Austrian aggression. Prior to one battle, for example, the French ruler assembled the commanders of the Bavarian troops attached to his forces and delivered a stirring harangue:

Bavarian soldiers! I stand before you not as emperor of France, but as the protector of your country and of the Rheinbund. Bavarians! Today you fight alone against the Austrians. Not a single Frenchman is in the first line . . . I have complete faith in your bravery. I have already expanded the borders of your land: I see now that I have not gone far enough. I will make you so great that you will not need my protection in any future war with Austria . . . We will march to Vienna, where we will punish Austria for all the evil it has caused your fatherland![46]

In one respect only was there any reason to take heart. The Austrian army of 1809 was very clearly not the Austrian army of 1805, and had meted out severe punishment to the French. At Aspern-Essling and Wagram imperial losses had amounted to over 50,000 men. The reason this was so was not because the soldiers of the Habsburg empire had been inspired by the appeal to German nationalism which had accompanied the campaign, but rather that the Archduke Charles had given the Austrian army the corps system. Hitherto used only by the French, this had been a key part in their ability to win decisive victories. Armies thus organized could operate on a broad front and thereby envelop their opponents, while on the battlefield they were infinitely more flexible in terms of their capacity to mass overwhelming numbers against one section of the enemy line or respond to attacks on their own. Broken down into the self-sufficient (and extremely substantial) sections represented by the *corps d'armée*, they were also much harder to smash:

one corps or another might be broken but the rest of the army could go on fighting unimpaired. In consequence, battles between two such armies were likely to be long struggles of attrition from which neither side would emerge triumphant unless they could manoeuvre themselves into a position from which they could attack the enemy from all sides – something which was now likely to become much harder. Significantly, in 1806 Prussia did not have the corps system at all, while in 1807 Russia was only groping towards it. When he next faced them, however, Napoleon was to find that both armies, like that of the Austrians, had moved on: hence the fact that the war of 1809 was the last conflict in which he would triumph.

The scales of conflict, then, were tilting against Napoleon, but this was also true in another sense. Four years of incessant campaigning had cost the French and their allies hundreds of thousands of casualties. The dead and wounded of Austerlitz, Jena, Auerstädt, Eylau, Friedland, Aspern-Essling and Wagram alone came to a minimum of 120,000 men, and to these must be added the losses suffered in many other actions, together with countless other men who had been lost to sickness. Casualties had in other words easily equalled the 210,000 men who had made up the original *grande armée* of 1805. The officer corps had been particularly hard hit – forty generals, including the brilliant cavalry leader, Lasalle, had fallen at Wagram, along with 1,822 men of the rank of colonel or below – while Aspern-Essling had seen the death of Marshal Lannes, who has often been rated as one of the very best of Napoleon's subordinate commanders. Making up these losses was not easy. Though by no means always a reliable observer, on this point the aide-de-camp Marbot is sharp enough:

On the evening of the battle the emperor rewarded the services of Macdonald, Oudinot and Marmont by giving them his marshal's baton. It was not, however, in his power to give them the talents required to command an army: brave and good divisional generals as they were when in the emperor's hands, they showed themselves clumsy when they were away from him, either in devising a plan of campaign, or in executing it, or in modifying it according to circumstances. It was held in the army that the emperor, not being able to replace Lannes, wanted to get the small change for him.[47]

But it was not just the officers. Also dead or maimed were thousands of the veteran sergeants, corporals and common soldiers who might have made good subalterns or provided the cadres around which the ever larger numbers of conscripts being called forth from France and her allies could have been mustered. Henceforth, then; French armies were far less sophisticated than before. Instead of the highly flexible system of infantry tactics with which Napoleon's troops had gone to war in 1803, from 1809 onwards battles were marked by the use of formations that were little more than bludgeons and, still worse, likely to incur terrible casualties. Also a feature after 1809 were small cannon attached in pairs to infantry regiments for close support, which in practice were more of a hindrance than a help. And as a result of these changes, the chances of achieving decisive victories on the battlefield receded still further, especially as the campaign of 1809 had also revealed the first signs of physical and mental weakness in Napoleon himself: many of his orders had been oddly imprecise, and after both Aspern-Essling and Wagram he had suffered genuine exhaustion.

There were domestic implications here as well. All across the Napoleonic imperium, the years 1808 and 1809 had seen a massive acceleration in the demands of the state for manpower. Where systems of conscription already existed, the pressures grew heavier. In France, 1808 saw the mobilization of three separate levies of 80,000 men, including many from the year groups of 1809 and 1810. In the Kingdom of Italy, the 12,000 men taken each year from 1806 onwards had to be supplemented by an additional levy of 9,000 men in 1809. In Baden the 8,000-strong army was at this same moment directed to find an additional 6,000 men in preparation for the war against Austria. And where no French-style system of conscription existed, it was now introduced: in Naples, for example, the ballot began in the summer of 1809. The extent of this 'blood-tax' can be exaggerated: even in the Kingdom of Italy, where conscription has generally been regarded as having been very severe, no more than 7 per cent of the available manpower was ever taken in any given levy, while the expansion of the state's frontiers meant there was actually a small decline in the proportion of the male population that had to be taken. Yet the impact was none the less severe enough, and in most parts of the empire there was considerable low-level resistance in the form of desertion and draft evasion. All this produced much brigandage, periodic riots and occasional outbreaks of wholesale insurrection. In France, at least, improved policing and ever-increasing legal penalties managed greatly to reduce the problem. But beneath the

14. As his armies marched across Europe, Napoleon continued to build up his navy in an attempt to take on the British at sea. Here we see the launch of the ship-of-the-line *Friedland*.

15. After Trafalgar, much of the action at sea consisted of small-scale skirmishes between British frigates and French privateers. In this print a British boarding party of sailors and marines is seen attacking an enemy vessel. Though they never received the attention accorded Aboukir or Trafalgar, such actions kept the seas safe for British commerce.

16. The wars of the Napoleonic epoch reached every corner of Europe. Here we see a Swedish column being pounced on by Norwegian ski troops in an action of the Baltic conflict of 1808–9.

17. Between 1804 and 1813 the Balkans were the scene of bitter fighting. Under Jordje Petrovic, or Karajordje as he was more commonly known, Serbia briefly achieved her independence from the Ottoman Empire, only to be overwhelmed in the wake of Napoleon's invasion of Russia.

18. Known as the Porte, the government of the Ottoman Empire played a major role in the diplomacy of the Napoleonic age, as witness this diplomatic reception at the court of Selim III.

19. Fought on 21–22 May 1809, the battle of Aspern-Essling was Napoleon's first defeat on the battlefield. Here we see the Austrian commander, the Archduke Charles, in the thick of the fighting. A somewhat histrionic individual who suffered from epilepsy and fits of depression, Charles was not devoid of courage, at one point in the fighting seizing a regimental standard and personally leading a counter-attack against the enemy.

20. For most of the period between 1809 and 1812 the chief theatre
of war was the Iberian peninsula, where the British Lord Wellington
led a small Anglo-Portuguese army in the defence of Portugal.
Amongst his victories was Fuentes de Oñoro (3–5 May 1811).

21. Wellington was not alone in his war in Spain. For much of the
time, indeed, the bulk of the fighting was done by the Spaniards.
Badly equipped and trained, however, they frequently fell prey to the
French armies, as in this action at Castalla on 21 July 1812.

22. The Russian general Uvarov at the battle of Borodino. Fought on 7 September 1812 in the course of the march on Moscow, this was one of the most terrible of Napoleon's battles.

23. A bloody affair that cost the French 10,000 casualties, the battle of Smolensk proved an empty victory for Napoleon and encouraged him to march ever deeper into Moscow.

24. Beneath a lowering sky, the retreating French army struggles to get across the River Berezina in the depths of the Russian winter. Only the most desperate heroism saved the *grande armée* from complete disaster.

25. A gleeful British comment on the events of 1812: Napoleon flees Russia pursued by a host of Cossacks.

26. Shattered at Leipzig in October 1813, the French army retreated across Germany. But its fighting spirit was not broken, and a Bavarian attempt to trap Napoleon at Hanau was heavily defeated.

27. This graphic view of the field of Waterloo is a fitting comment on a struggle that was more destructive and cost more lives than any conflict in European history prior to the First World War. Moved to tears by what he saw as he rode across the battlefield, the Duke of Wellington famously remarked, 'I hope to God I have fought my last battle ... Next to a battle lost, the greatest misery is a battle gained.'

surface the limits of popular acceptance were being placed under ever greater strain, and all the more so given the fact that in part the war had changed its character. If the Austrian campaign had been, like the struggles of 1805–7, a relatively civilized affair fought out within the so-called 'rules of war', the fighting in Spain and Portugal had, in popular legend at least, assumed a very different character. Men sent to the Peninsula did not just die in battle: just as often they were murdered or subjected to the most appalling tortures. In short, confidence in the empire was undermined even in France, while in Germany and Italy it was in effect smothered before it had any chance to take off. There was as yet no revolution, nor anything remotely resembling one, but from 1809 onwards it is hard to see the French imperium as anything other than a house of cards.

To conclude then, in the autumn of 1809 Napoleon was seemingly as unassailable as ever. Austria and Sweden were so cowed that they had both effectively changed sides; Prussia was helpless; Britain was securing only limited benefits from her few allies and seemingly unable to forge stable relations with junior partners; the cause of insurrection in Germany had been stripped of all credibility; and Russia was still an ally of France. Meanwhile, if the Peninsular War continued to rage unabated, it seemed likely that the French would eventually crush Spanish resistance and then turn on Portugal in irresistible force, while internal pacification was also making some progress in Italy. Nor, in the end, was the campaign of 1809 anything to be ashamed of: French control of Europe had been reasserted; a moment of great danger overcome; and Napoleon's Polish, German and Italian auxiliaries shown to be soldiers who were potentially very good. Yet it is hard not to have a sense that the wind had changed. Victory at Wagram had come at the cost of efforts that far outstripped anything that had yet been demanded of the French empire and had only been achieved with considerable difficulty. French armies, it appeared, could be beaten after all. And Napoleon himself had been shown to be fallible. All this brings us back to Tilsit. In the end what had brought Alexander into the French camp had been not so much the French ruler's personal charisma but the sense of awe that he generated. This aura, however, was now shattered, while at Erfurt the tsar had learned that Napoleon was not to be trusted. Russia's interests, it was now clear, would only be backed by France so long as they did not conflict with her own, whereas French interests were to be backed by Russia no matter what the costs to her own aspirations. The moment when Tilsit broke down had not yet come, but it could now be foreseen.

9

The Alliance that Failed

'The great proof of madness,' Napoleon is once supposed to have said, 'is the disproportion of one's designs to one's means.' If so, then the emperor stands condemned from his own mouth. Between 1809 and 1812 the demands of the Continental Blockade, coupled with his own impatience, *folie de grandeur* and scorn for lesser men, drove the French ruler into a policy that was too demanding even for the resources of *la grande nation*. Hitherto content to rule most of his dominions through satellite rulers, Napoleon came more and more to look for solutions to his problems through the imposition of direct rule from Paris. Yet this did nothing to make the Blockade – a weapon he was in any case now backing away from – any more impermeable, for Napoleon simply did not have the administrative and military resources to supplant the local officials and gendarmes on whom he had previously relied. At the same time, in doing so he also destabilized his domination of Europe. Already angered by Napoleon's betrayal of his interests in the Balkans, Alexander I began to recall his earlier championing of the rights of the smaller states of Europe. All thoughts of partnership with France disappeared and fears grew that Russia might herself be the victim of French attack. With the Blockade biting in Russia as much as anywhere, the tsar therefore broke with Napoleon, and even considered marching into Germany and precipitating the war he feared must come anyway. In the event this pre-emptive strike never came, but the ruler of France could not endure so blatant a challenge to his supremacy, particularly given the prolonged struggle in Spain and Portugal which was so sapping his prestige. Alexander had to be taught a lesson, and thus it was that the first months of 1812 saw immense forces of imperial troops massing on the frontiers of East Prussia in preparation for an invasion of Russia. The consequences of this decision will be looked at in the next chapter,

but for the time being, suffice it to say that Napoleon had again misjudged the capacity of the resources available to him, and once more
placed personal aggrandizement ahead of strategic calculation. It was to
prove a fatal error, and one which would have dramatic effects.

At the heart of the period from 1809 to 1812 lies Napoleon's precipitation of a breach in his relationship with St Petersburg. As late as the
outbreak of war with Austria in May 1809, Alexander was prepared
to cooperate with the emperor. Erfurt may have come as a terrible
disappointment, but the tsar nevertheless promised to give Napoleon
his support against Francis I should the latter go to war; and Rumiantsev
continued to believe that the alliance with France remained very much
in Russia's best interests. In preparation for war, 60,000 men were
readied for action on the frontiers of the Austrian portion of Galicia
under Prince Dmitri Golitsyn. That said, there was little enthusiasm
in St Petersburg. Caught in an unfavourable position, Napoleon was
desperate for Russian support and in the course of March sent no fewer
than eight messages to Alexander begging him to intervene. Typically
enough, however, the emperor was seemingly heedless of his partner's
interests. It was not enough for the Russians to threaten Austria's eastern
borders. On the contrary, troops were to be sent as far west as Dresden,
a city not only hundreds of miles from the Russian frontier, but wide
open to attack from Austria and Prussia alike, while some of the army
that had been sent to the Danubian provinces was to be turned around
and sent northwards into Transylvania. Awkward in terms of the military situation in the Balkans, this last request was also a blow to Russia's
diplomatic aspirations, for it reduced her ability to send aid to Serbia
which was increasingly envisaged as a protectorate in the style of Poland
prior to 1791. And on top of all this, everything was claimed to be
the fault of Russia: 'Monsieur Champagny: a courier must be sent to
St Petersburg. You will inform M. Rumiantsev ... that I remain convinced that, had a threatening tone been adopted at Erfurt, Austria
would have disarmed, and an end been put to this question.'[1]

Mention of the Balkan front was particularly tactless. Although there
had been sporadic outbreaks of fighting on the borders of Serbia, ever
since the autumn of 1807 conflict there had been at a relatively low ebb
(there had, however, been some campaigning in the east where the spring
of 1808 saw a Russian force defeat 30,000 Ottoman troops near Kars).
The armistice agreed at Slobosia had long since expired, but the Russians

had achieved their initial objectives and were not prepared to advance
any further south without first obtaining French support, while the Serbs
were fully taken up with the task of building a new regular army and,
under the influence of the Russian envoy, Rodofinikin, elaborating a
new system of government. As for the Turks, they had become totally
engrossed in their internal affairs. The coup that had brought down
Selim III in July 1807 led to a prolonged period of political turmoil. The
deposed sultan had been replaced by a cousin, who became Mustafa IV,
but the revolt had dealt a body blow to the empire in that it had
arisen out of the hatred of the traditional janissaries for the new-model
Western-style army Selim had been building up and had been accompanied by the massacre of many of its members. Horrified by the implications of this disaster, a group of prominent officials and military leaders
had come together to organize a counter-coup that would bring Selim
back to the throne and set the empire on the path of reform. In July
1808 the crisis broke: the leading Ottoman general on the Danube,
Bayrakdar Mustafa Pasha, marched on Constantinople with most of his
troops. The result was further chaos. It had been hoped to rescue Selim,
but bungling by conspirators ensured Mustafa IV was given sufficient
time to have him murdered. This, however, did not save Mustafa. The
conspirators had another candidate for the throne and immediately
installed him as Mehmet II. But the janissaries were not finished, and
fought back in a series of pitched battles which rocked Constantinople.
Among the dead was Bayrakdar: trapped inside an armoury by a horde
of janissaries, he blew himself up rather than let his enemies take him
alive. Not until the winter did the situation finally quieten down, and
even then the Ottomans did not resume active operations, preferring to
try and secure a negotiated settlement with Russia, who they thought
might be persuaded to give up Moldavia and Wallachia in return for
political concessions. But there was no hope of this. On the contrary,
Alexander was bent on both military victory and complete annexation of
the Danubian provinces. Along the Danube the Russians were planning a
series of offensives designed to take the long line of Turkish fortresses,
while in Serbia Karadjordje was hoping to push back the Turks from
his eastern and southern frontiers and liberate such towns as Niš. To be
asked, then, literally to turn his back on the Balkans came as yet another
proof that Alexander was never going to be treated by Napoleon as an
equal partner.

This is not the place to give a detailed history of the military operations in the Balkans that now followed, but it is fair to say that they remained a running sore for Franco-Russian relations. Dreams of the partition of Turkey-in-Europe that might have resulted from the active support once promised by France were now replaced by the reality of a savage war in which casualties were high and progress limited. The offensive launched in April 1809 did not produce victory. The Russians allowed themselves to get bogged down in the investment of the Turkish fortresses that guarded the line of the Danube – most importantly Nicopolis, Giurgiu, Rustchuk, Silistria, Galatz, Braila and Izmail. Not until July was significant progress made with the capture of Braila, and by then the Serbs were in serious trouble, having been badly beaten at Niš. Over the course of the summer they suffered further losses, particularly at Deligrad, while matters were made still worse by the fact that the Russians could do little to help them. So incensed was Karadjordje, indeed, that he appealed to both Napoleon and Francis I for help. In the event the crisis passed: the Serbs checked the Ottoman offensive at the river Morava; the vigorous Prince Bagration broke out of the Russian bridgehead across the Danube at Braila and conquered the whole of the Dobrudja in a campaign that pulled many enemy troops away from Serbia; and the Serbs rejected an Austrian attempt at mediation that might not only have taken Serbia out of the war but ultimately led to her incorporation in the Habsburg Empire. Alexander, then, was spared serious embarrassment, but even so 1809 had not gone well. If the Russians had occupied the Dobrudja, the close of the year saw them forced to abandon an attempt to advance across the Danube on the central front. Nor was 1810 much better. There were now 100,000 Russian troops on the Danube, but hopes to bring the war to a close came to nothing. Aided by a small Russian expeditionary force, the Serbs were able to win back much of the ground they had lost the previous year, but it took the entire year just to capture the last Turkish fortress along the Danube. Not only were the Turks still in the fight, but along the way the Russians experienced a number of humiliating setbacks. A Russian column under Sabaniev lost half its strength at Razgrad, for example, while premature assaults on both Shumla and Rustchuk were beaten off with terrible losses. And to cap it all, with Karadjordje restive still more troops had to be committed to Serbia.

As yet, of course, much of this lay in the future, but the impact of the

Balkan imbroglio can still be seen in the campaign of 1809. No troops were pulled back from the Danube, the Austrians were secretly informed that hostilities would be restricted to form alone, and it was not until 3 June that any troops entered Galicia. Nor did the Russians do very much even then, and the Poles got no help from the new arrivals who at first moved sluggishly and with great caution. At Sandomir, for example, on 15 June, two Russian divisions ignored all pleas for aid and stood idle a few miles from the city while the badly outnumbered Polish garrison fended off the assaults of 10,000 Austrians. In the end, what amounted to a non-aggression pact was negotiated with the Austrian forces in the region and Golitsyn agreed he would move no further forward than the line of the Vistula and its tributary, the Visloka. In the end this promise was broken, for, as we have seen, on 14 July a Russian force seized Cracow, but this was not the result of some sudden rush of blood to the head on the part of Golitsyn, but rather a defensive move designed to deal with the growing threat posed by Polish nationalism. In brief, no sooner had war begun than the Austrians had invaded the Grand Duchy of Warsaw in the hope of neutralizing the Poles and increasing Vienna's diplomatic leverage vis-à-vis the Prussians by seizing some of Potsdam's old territories in Pomerania. At first all had gone well: the Austrians had defeated the Poles at Raszyn and taken Warsaw. However, reaching Thorn, the invaders were repulsed. Still more embarrassingly, rather than retreating after the loss of their capital, the Poles had gone on the offensive and invaded Galicia where they proceeded to whip up an insurrection against Austrian rule. In this their commander, General Poniatowski, had much success. 'The zeal that animates the Galicians . . . has in no way diminished,' wrote Poniatowski. 'There are at this moment four infantry and four cavalry regiments forming, all uniformed and equipped at the expense of citizens who offered to form them . . . Several battalions are in a state to act in five days, and the total lack of weapons, which paralyses the efforts of the Galicians, is the only limit of the eagerness that they demonstrate for taking up the defence of the common cause.'[2] With the major cities of Lemberg and Lublin soon in Polish hands, the only option seemed to be to establish a Russian presence much further forward than had been intended: hence the decision to seize Cracow, this being the only means the Russians could see of preventing things from getting completely out of hand. It was for this reason, too, that in those areas they occupied the authority of the

Austrian administration was upheld and, where necessary, the representatives of the Grand Duchy of Warsaw chased out. Yet confrontation was no option either as it could only inflame Polish national sentiment, and it was therefore with great relief that the Russians greeted the armistice of Znaim, as this at least meant that Poniatowski would have no more opportunity to play the liberator.

Given what had occurred in the campaign of 1809, the territorial outcome is hardly surprising. Whereas the Russians had scarcely fired a shot, the Poles had established themselves as dependable allies of France. With the exception of its easternmost extremity – the district of Tarnopol – the Grand Duchy of Warsaw therefore obtained the prize of Western Galicia. But in so ruling Napoleon could not but offend Alexander. He had repeatedly told the tsar that he had no intention either of demanding any more land for the Poles in the future or of reviving the word 'Poland'. And yet the territory of his Polish satellite had been raised from 35,000 square miles to around 50,000 and its population more than doubled: approximately 2 million strong in 1807, the number of inhabitants was now over 4.3 million. This was not yet the old Kingdom of Poland, but it was still very much a Polish state. The army flaunted the traditional Polish four-cornered cap and white-eagle badge, and on its banners proclaimed itself to be the 'Wojsko Polskie' (lit. 'Polish army'); the Grand Duchy's constitution made use of many terms drawn from Polish history and tradition; the administration conducted its business in Polish; and the capital was Warsaw. As for Poniatowski's move to raise Galicia in revolt, it was quite clear that this had been sanctioned by Napoleon from the start. In the words of an order of the day issued by Poniatowski on 2 July 1809:

The commanding prince-in-chief has received orders provisionally to occupy Galicia in the name of His Majesty the Emperor and King, to replace the Austrian eagles with the French eagles, to give the order to all the tribunals to render justice in the name of the French emperor and to receive the oath of all authorities to this sovereign ... In addition, he informs the army that His Majesty the Emperor has ordered that a Galician army should be organized on the same basis as the French troops.[3]

What had been objectionable enough in 1807 was now an intolerable sticking point. Seeing which way Napoleon's decision in respect of Galicia was likely to go, Alexander had cleverly thrown all responsibility for the issue on him by opting out of the peace negotiations that followed the armistice of Znaim, and had thereby ensured that the French ruler was at least trapped into a move overtly hostile to Russia. However, that small success was little consolation, and so Alexander pressed the issue: France was to join with Austria, Prussia and Russia in guaranteeing the frontiers of the Grand Duchy of Warsaw by treaty (which would mean, of course, that there could be no further annexations), and further, agreeing that it should never be allowed to call itself a kingdom. Over the course of the winter such a convention was duly negotiated at St Petersburg by Caulaincourt, who was eager to keep the peace with Russia, but no sooner had it been referred to the French ruler than it was rejected out of hand. Some other state might one day restore a Kingdom of Poland, argued Napoleon, and in that case he might find himself committed to a war in which he had no part. This was true enough in itself, but the contingency that Napoleon envisaged was an unlikely one. The real reason was that the emperor objected to a potential option for further aggression in Eastern Europe being closed off to him (and that this was a real possibility was all too clear: in the course of 1810 the emperor commanded that large quantities of arms should be sent to the Grand Duchy of Warsaw in case its already substantial army should suddenly need to be expanded).

Once again we return to the question of personal prestige: a Napoleon circumscribed was a Napoleon frustrated, indeed, a Napoleon diminished. What he was incapable of doing, however, was to appreciate that a Napoleon who knew no limits was a threat to the interests of every other state in Europe. In this respect the mere existence of the Grand Duchy of Warsaw was a constant source of worry to Alexander. Just over the frontier were hundreds of thousands of Poles and Lithuanians. Many of them, of course, were ignorant peasants who lacked any concept of national feeling, but many of the gentry had been bitterly disappointed at Napoleon's failure to liberate them in 1807 and were seething with discontent at the imposition of Russian rule. As a conversation that he had with the Polish nobleman Michal Oginski in June 1810 demonstrates, the whole subject was a matter of great sensitivity to Alexander:

As I was leaving the emperor's office, he stopped me to show me a Paris newspaper which contained an article written by Prince Adam Czartoryski senior, about which he was very angry. In it he believed he had discovered Napoleon's real intentions. Thus, by flattering the Poles with the hope of the re-establishment of their entire kingdom, he was seeking to deepen the divisions between them and Russia. Speaking with complete sincerity and much emotion, the emperor complained bitterly of the foolishness of his Polish subjects. They hated the Russians and were less than attached to him, but he had had no part in the partition of Poland, and in his heart he had always condemned it; as for the Russians of the current day, they were guiltless of the evils the Poles had experienced in those times. Taking advantage of his candour, I observed to him that he was forgetting that I was myself Polish [and] that I had fought for my fatherland in the insurrection of 1794 ... 'I have not forgotten,' he answered. 'I know what you have done and I esteem you all the more for it ... Napoleon needs to win over the Poles, and is therefore flattering them with bright hopes, whereas I, by contrast, have always respected your nation, and hope one day to prove it to you.'[4]

If Poland and the Balkans were Alexander's immediate concerns, a number of other issues inclined to estrange him from Napoleon. One was the issue of the emperor's second marriage. At Erfurt the idea had been very tentatively raised that he should marry Alexander's second sister, the sixteen-year-old Grand Duchess Anna. The emperor had discovered that he had fathered a child by his Polish mistress, Maria Walewska (in other words, that his lack of an heir was the fault not of himself but of Josephine) and so on 22 November 1809 Caulaincourt was formally instructed to press the emperor's suit at the Russian court. This, however, did not produce the desired result. Though Napoleon made a variety of gestures that were intended to smooth the way for his proposal – the most famous was a verbal promise to obliterate the very word 'Poland' from history – the response in St Petersburg was to prevaricate. Setting aside the tsar himself, who was not keen on the marriage, the dowager empress was clearly opposed to it, as were the many great magnates who felt that closer links with France had to be resisted at all costs. Faced with a demand for a definite answer in February 1810, Alexander asked Napoleon to postpone the matter for two years on the grounds that Anna was still too young for marriage. This infuriated Napoleon: given the urgency of the case, Alexander's action amounted to outright rejection.

But it was not long before Russia also had cause for anger. The Grand Duchess Anna was not the only eligible princess in Europe, and Austria possessed an alternative bride in the Archduchess Marie-Louise, who was eighteen and the eldest daughter of Francis I. Desperate to forge links with France, Metternich had suggested this possibility as early as August 1809 and the matter had been unofficially discussed with Vienna in the course of the winter. No sooner had Alexander's definitive 'no' arrived in Paris, then, than Napoleon pounced. The very same post that carried the emperor's letter to Alexander acknowledging the rejection of Anna therefore also carried another announcing his betrothal to Marie-Louise. For once there had been no duplicity on Napoleon's part: to the very end it had been the Russian grand duchess who had been his favoured candidate. To save face, it was made out that the choice had been open and equal, and that ultimately it was Marie-Louise who suited France best. In St Petersburg, however, the betrothal was interpreted in a very different fashion. Napoleon, it was concluded, had been playing a double game designed to humiliate Russia. And even in Vienna, which had effectively been presented with a fait accompli, there was much dissatisfaction at the emperor's failure to obey the rules of protocol, let alone display a modicum of courtesy. In his correspondence with Metternich, Francis was sullen and resentful:

My consent to the marriage would secure to the empire some years of political peace, which I can devote to the healing of its wounds. All my powers being devoted to the welfare of my people, I cannot, therefore, hesitate in my decision. Send a courier to Paris, and say that I accept the offer for the hand of my daughter, but with the express reservation that on neither side shall any condition be attached to it: there are sacrifices which must not be contaminated with anything approaching a bargain.[5]

There is little need to discuss the issue of the Austrian marriage any further. After hastily being married by proxy to Napoleon in Vienna on 11 March, Marie-Louise was brought to France amidst great splendour and celebration. Reaching the chateau specially prepared for her reception at Compiègne, she was welcomed quite literally with open arms by Napoleon, and formally married to him in Paris in a series of lavish ceremonies held on 1 April. On a personal level, the marriage was a success: the couple quickly became completely infatuated with one another and it was not long before they had a healthy son who was christened Napoleon François Charles Joseph and immediately named King of Rome. Politically and diplomatically, however, the issue is of almost no significance. Inside France the decision to wed an Austrian archduchess is supposed to have damaged Napoleon's prestige by breaking some of the last links that bound him to the Revolution. At the same time, Josephine, who was gifted with a public manner far more winning than that of her replacement, remained extremely popular in the army. There may, then, have been some grumbling – even real anger – but radicalism was scarcely a major force within the empire, and there is little reason to believe that the eventual downfall of the empire had much of an ideological explanation: what mattered far more was war-weariness and opposition to conscription, and in this context the marriage to Marie-Louise was of little account beside, say, the war in Spain.

Nor was the wedding of any real account on the international stage. Napoleon clearly hoped it would buy him acceptance amongst the monarchies of Europe, while the fact that many details of events in France mimicked the reception of Marie-Antoinette – Marie-Louise's great-aunt – by Louis XVI in 1770 is yet one more example of Napoleon's desire to assume the mantle of the Bourbons. And, needless to say, the marriage ceremony itself was one more opportunity to parade the power and grandeur of the Napoleonic empire: the new empress was accompanied to the altar by four queens, a vicereine and three grand duchesses, all of them drawn from the extended Bonaparte family. But whether any of this had the slightest impact in the courts and foreign ministries of Europe is doubtful. To take the more particular cases of Austria and Russia, meanwhile, all that the new marriage alliance did was to confirm existing trends: Russia's relations with Napoleon were deteriorating well before February 1810, just as Austria had already embarked on the path of collaboration. Yet if Marie-Louise did not come as the harbinger of change, but rather, at best, its accelerant, it might be noted, though, that the precedents were not encouraging. Prior to the French Revolution, Austria had been France's chief foreign partner, but she had given her little support and had ultimately proved a broken reed. Moreover, the power to which Napoleon had linked himself was not even the relatively proud Austria of 1789, but rather the defeated, bankrupt and much reduced Austria of 1810. Compared to the partnership that might have been obtained from Russia, Vienna could offer little, even if it was true, as Talleyrand claimed, that the advent of Marie-Louise guaranteed that

Vienna wished 'to associate itself with the fortunes of the imperial dynasty that rules today in France, and that it has recognized the folly and iniquity of the contrary system which it has upheld for the last ten years, and that, having taken this resolution, Vienna would persist in it, leaving the Emperor Napoleon . . . to bequeath to his descendants all the advantages of the union that has today been agreed upon'.[6]

There were, however, a number of hidden problems here. Would the presence of Marie-Louise in France really be sufficient to deter Austria from going to war in all circumstances? Equally, what would occur should Napoleon not treat the Austrians with the courtesy and generosity with which Talleyrand, a long-term proponent of an alliance with Vienna, hoped he would respond? To these questions Talleyrand had no answers, but he did have an ingenious theory as to why Austria could be trusted more than Russia. In Vienna, foreign policy was the product of a system rather than an individual: when Francis died, his successors would in reality have little option but to carry on the affairs of the empire much as they had before. In St Petersburg, however, things were very different: 'In Russia everything revolves around the will of one man: there is no policy but his own. In consequence, the length of a reign is the length of everything else: no sooner does a new ruler come to the throne, than everything takes on a new aspect. Let us suppose, then, that the Emperor Napoleon has married the Grand-Duchess [Anna], and that in a year's time . . . the door should open and a courier be announced bearing the news that the Emperor Alexander has died. With his death, everything would be different: there would be no guarantee of an alliance with St Petersburg . . . and all the advantages of the marriage would disappear.'[7] Yet there are many assumptions here too: in the end it could no more be assumed that Vienna was wedded to continuity than it could that St Petersburg was wedded to caprice. As yet nothing could be certain, but there was definite feeling that French policy had miscarried. As Marshal Murat stated:

A family alliance has never failed to have grievous consequences for France. She will be compelled to endure all the mistakes of that government, and to share its heaviest and most dangerous burdens. The position in which Austria finds herself can be the only reason for her decision to conclude an alliance which, with her proud outlook, she must secretly detest. Austria, more than any other nation, has made a political maxim of the idea that 'sovereigns have no relatives'. France will be compelled at great cost to support her in her various policies, so often clumsy and treacherous, and in her campaigns, so poorly conducted, and when we need her as an ally we shall not find in her either energy or loyalty. An alliance with Russia is attended with none of these dangers.[8]

In short, Napoleon's efforts to pretend he had been free to choose between Anna and Marie-Louise had in the end served only to spread doubt and dismay amongst his own followers. As the former Second Consul, Jean-Jacques de Cambacérès, remarked to Pasquier, 'At heart, I am certain that within two years we will be at war with whichever of the two powers whose princess Napoleon does not wed. Well, a war with Austria does not cause me any worry, while I tremble at the idea of a war with Russia: the consequences are incalculable.'[9]

Before moving on to the many other issues that produced the war that Cambacérès so greatly feared, there are a few other matters that we ought to examine. We come here to the issue of Napoleon's health and attitude to business. One problem that is frequently highlighted is the emperor's failure to return to Spain in 1810, it being claimed that the arrival of Marie-Louise for a time drove all thoughts of campaigning from his head. However, this is a blind alley: there was no sense that Napoleon was needed in the Peninsula at this time, while the idea of a Napoleon living out a romantic idyll and neglecting all public business is wildly adrift. The French ruler remained firmly in touch with the march of affairs and, to prove the point, had hardly emerged from his wedding before he set off on a month-long tour of inspection of Belgium, Holland and northern France. This was scarcely a honeymoon – Marie-Louise, indeed, bitterly resented the experience – and something of the atmosphere that prevailed can be obtained from the memoirs of the Marquise de la Tour du Pin, who, as the wife of the Prefect of the Department of Dyle, entertained the royal couple when they arrived in .Brussels. At dinner the Marquise was seated at the left of the emperor: 'He talked to me all the time regarding the manufactures, the laces, the daily wages, the life of the lace-makers; then of the monuments, the antiquities, the establishments of charity, the manners of the people, the *béguines*. Fortunately, I was well posted regarding all these subjects.'[10] Nor was this so much idle table-talk. At the time, as we shall see, the empire was experiencing severe economic depression. With lace very much the staple of the local textile industry, Marie-Louise in consequence soon found herself 'visiting manufacturing facilities ... and purchasing a considerable amount of lace, which the emperor had suggested in order to bring new business to those factories that were encountering bad times'.[11]

That said, however, there does seem to have been a change in the emperor's demeanour and habits of work. Hunts, balls, dinners, soirées and receptions began to take up much more time than before and on a number of occasions the emperor arrived late for meetings of the Councils of State. Once Marie-Louise's child arrived on 20 March 1811, he also took time out to play the devoted family man. These developments should not be exaggerated – what one sees is a small degree of relaxation at a time when there was no great military crisis to engage the attentions of the emperor – but what of the vexed question of the emperor's health? The Napoleon who greeted Marie-Louise in 1809 was, if not the slight young man who had conquered Italy, at worst a little plump, and on the whole perfectly healthy and notorious for the simplicity of his tastes. To quote his secretary, Baron Fain:

To describe Napoleon's person, I go back to the period of his second marriage ... His height was five feet two inches. He was small but well-made; however, his neck was a little short and he had perhaps already too much belly. His tissue was soft and the lymph thick ... I never saw him take to his bed with illness ... The only indisposition I knew him to have was a bladder problem that sometimes made him uncomfortable ... He was temperate, he lived frugally and ate quickly ... Moreover, nature had gifted him with an unusual benefit, that of not being able to overeat, even when he would have liked to. 'If I go even slightly beyond my capacity,' he would say, 'my stomach renders up the excess.'[12]

This soon changed. A fleshy young woman who loved her food – some observers complained that she talked of little else – the new empress encouraged a similar liking in her husband. For the first time, Napoleon began to spend time at the table, to indulge in rich dishes of a sort that he had hitherto been inclined to shun, and, inevitably, to run to fat. The French writer Charles-Paul de Kock, who saw him in 1811, wrote, for example, that he appeared 'yellow, obese [and] bloated, with his head too far down on his shoulders'.[13] By the time the French ruler went back to war in 1812 he was a changed man. 'I follow the emperor when he goes out riding,' wrote one of his aides. 'We go the whole way at a walk. His Majesty rides much less quickly these days: he has put on a good deal of weight, and rides a horse with more difficulty than before. The Grand Equerry has to give him a hand in mounting. When the emperor travels, he does most of the journey by carriage.'[14]

And it was not just that Napoleon was fat. The day after Borodino, Philippe de Ségur had a disturbing conversation with Marshal Murat:

Murat . . . recalled having seen the emperor the day before . . . halt several times, dismount and, with his head resting upon a cannon, remain there some time in an attitude of suffering. He knew what a restless night he had passed and that a violent and incessant cough had shaken his weakened frame and at that current moment the action of his genius was in a sense chained down by his body, which had sunk under the triple load of fatigue, fever and a malady which, probably more than any other, drains the moral and physical strength of its victims.[15]

These words have a slightly sinister overtone, and it has certainly been suggested that the sudden onset of obesity was a symptom of a disorder known as Froehlich's Syndrome, which is linked to problems with a particular gland in the brain. Some form of venereal disease, too, has been hinted at, and such ideas may explain certain oddities that began to be noted in the emperor's behaviour, such as the apparent trance he slipped into during a court reception in 1811. Yet most Napoleonists appear to agree that, other than the bladder complaint mentioned by Fain (a problem known as dysuria, this was a type of cystitis) and a skin disorder that may have been psoriasis, the emperor as yet had no serious problems. What the period 1810–12 brought, then, was not so much a change in his medical condition, but rather a taste for soft living and the first advance of middle age. The punishing schedule of Napoleon's earlier campaigns was now less easy to withstand, so that at key moments such as Borodino illness struck and left the one-time superman in the dire condition recorded by Ségur. And, in moments of candour, Napoleon himself noted the change:

Even as he was walking and talking, the emperor showed signs of fatigue: he stopped, and, leaning against the billiard table, pushed the balls about with his hand, and seemed to drop off to sleep. He saw that I noticed. 'It's curious', he said, 'how one's constitution changes as one gets older without any decline in strength or deterioration of health. Our capacities change and our plans are bound to feel the effect. In other days I used to say to Montesquieu several times a day, " 'Montesquieu, bring me a glass of lemonade." Now it's a cup of coffee or a glass of Madeira I need and ask for. Believe me, M. Molé, after thirty one begins to be less fitted for campaigning. Alexander died before noticing any decline.'[16]

But if the first intimations of mortality were showing themselves, there is no evidence that they had any impact on Napoleon's statecraft or diplomacy at this stage. If *folie* there was aplenty, it was simply *folie de grandeur* rather than a symptom of some medical condition. In the period 1809–11, Napoleon engaged in a series of actions within the boundaries of his imperium that could only suggest an aspiration to universal monarchy. Before looking at this, however, we must first examine the strange affair of Marshal Bernadotte. A sergeant-major in the Bourbon army who had distinguished himself in the Revolutionary wars and risen to the rank of general, Jean-Baptiste Bernadotte was also the brother-in-law of Joseph Bonaparte. This family connection, however, did not prevent him from hating Napoleon, of whose fame and elevation to the Consulate he had been bitterly jealous. The Jacobinism that Bernadotte affected may be discounted here, all the evidence suggesting that it was never more than a convenient posture that suited his interest in the France of 1798–9. Appointed to the marshalate when it was created in 1804 out of a mixture of family loyalty and realpolitik, Bernadotte had fought in the campaigns of Austerlitz, Jena, Eylau and Wagram, but had not performed well. It is possible, indeed, that he had set out to engineer the humiliation of various rivals and even to secure the downfall of Napoleon in the hope that he could then seize the throne himself. At all events, by the winter of 1809 he was completely out of favour with Napoleon and associating with some of the empire's harshest critics. It is, then, ironic that circumstances turned him into what Alexander I perceived as a chosen agent of the emperor. In brief, the overthrow of Gustav IV had led to great confusion in Sweden. As a temporary measure the throne had been given to an aged uncle of the deposed monarch, but the new ruler – Charles XIII – was childless, and a search therefore began for a crown prince. Initially, the choice fell on Christian August of Augustenburg, who was connected to the Danish royal family. Within months, however, the new crown prince was dead of a heart attack and the search was on once again. Within the regime there had always been substantial elements who favoured a resumption of Sweden's traditional diplomatic ties with France, and a variety of factors ensured that this time the French party triumphed. Napoleon's growing differences with Russia prompted the hope that these might be exploited to regain Finland, which, along with the Åland Islands and a strip of territory in the far north, had been ceded to Russia in the treaty signed at Frederikshamn on 17 September 1809. Progressives hoped that a French ruler would favour the amendment of the highly aristocratic constitution that Sweden had acquired following the overthrow of Gustav IV. And, finally, many army officers were simply infatuated with the glories of French arms. First choice for the position was Eugène de Beauharnais, but he proved uninterested, whereupon attention switched to the highly improbable Bernadotte for no better reason than the decent treatment he had accorded some Swedish prisoners he had taken in the course of the campaign of 1806–7. With a delighted Bernadotte only too happy to accept the invitation, all was soon resolved, and in October 1810 he duly arrived in Stockholm as the future King Charles John.

It is not clear whether Napoleon acted for strategic reasons in sanctioning the departure of Bernadotte for Sweden. He knew well enough that the marshal was not to be trusted and, as we shall see, was becoming increasingly dissatisfied with the notion of satellite monarchy. But as far as Alexander was concerned, Bernadotte had been sent to the Baltic as a powerful agent of France. Certainly there was plenty of evidence that Sweden was preparing for war and sliding ever deeper into the French orbit. Immediate steps were taken to reform the Swedish army and introduce the French system of conscription, and Sweden also finally acceded to the Continental Blockade and in November 1810 formally declared war on Britain. To Napoleon, however, Russia's concerns were of no account. From Erfurt onwards in fact, there was hardly an action that the emperor took that did not in some way or other offend St Petersburg. At the heart of the matter, as usual, was Napoleon's belief that he should be allowed to do whatever he liked without regard to the feelings, interest or self-esteem of other rulers. To take matters in chronological order, the tsar had always fancied himself as the protector of the smaller states of Europe and had established a particularly warm relationship with Frederick William III of Prussia. At Erfurt, indeed, Alexander had spoken up for Prussia and obtained a verbal promise that most of France's troops would be withdrawn from her territory. Hardly had he returned home, however, than these misty notions of paternalism were challenged head-on by the overthrow of the Prussian chief minister, Stein. That the emperor should have desired to get rid of Stein is wholly understandable – he was, after all, an inveterate opponent of French domination – but even so the message was quite clear: Russian patronage notwithstanding, Frederick William III was not to be master even in what little was left of his own house. Angry and frustrated, all that Alexander could do was to make a very public statement of his disapproval by receiving Frederick William and Louise in great splendour at St Petersburg when they visited the city in January 1809. 'On this occasion,' wrote Sophie Tisenhaus, 'he displayed a grandeur, magnificence and generous hospitality like that shown by Louis XIV in receiving the unfortunate James II and his family when banished from England. Sumptuous equipages and furs of great price were prepared for their Majesties . . . and awaited them on the frontier of the country. The king and queen made their entry into St Petersburg in a state carriage. Notwithstanding the intense cold the troops were under arms before five o'clock in the morning. All the most illustrious and distinguished personages of St Petersburg awaited the royal travellers at court.'[17]

If Alexander was affronted by Napoleon's treatment of Prussia, he was also worried about Italy. At Tilsit Alexander believed that, in exchange for recognizing Joseph Bonaparte as King of Naples and quietly jettisoning his earlier demands for compensation for the King of Piedmont, he had secured an end to French expansion and, by extension, an unstated promise that the Pope was to be left unmolested as ruler of the Papal States. In 1808 Napoleon had put some strain on this by occupying Rome, but Pius VII remained on the throne of St Peter and as such a figment of propriety was maintained. However, the reality was that the papal administration had been left with little power: many leading officials were arrested or driven from their positions; the military was disarmed; the government press taken over; the curia purged of most of its members; and Consalvi's successors as Secretary of State repeatedly dismissed. Ensconced in the Quirinal palace, however, the Pope remained defiant. Every demand that he should accede to the Continental Blockade and in effect become an ally of France was rejected, while the French governor, General Miollis, found himself harassed at every turn by a variety of more or less subtle acts of passive resistance. With tension increasing by the day, a crisis could not long be avoided and on 6 September 1808 it finally came: when officers were sent to arrest the current Secretary of State, Cardinal Pacca, Pius ordered Miollis's emissaries to depart and in effect dared the governor to take him as well. The response was brutal: May 1808 had already seen the Papal States' Adriatic provinces go the way of the so-called 'legations' – Bologna and Ferrara – by being annexed to the Kingdom of Italy, and on 17 May 1809 Napoleon announced the annexation of the last surviving fragment of papal territory – including the city of Rome itself – to France. Faced by the complete loss of his territorial power, Pius responded by immediately excommunicating Napoleon, and at the same time ordering people and clergy alike to refuse to obey the orders of the new administration. The result was the final indignity: on the night of 5/6 July, a party of troops broke into the Quirinal palace and arrested both Pius and Pacca. Whether Napoleon meant this to happen is not quite clear (the commander of the raid had orders to take only Pacca) but, whatever the truth, the emperor did not back down. After a considerable odyssey, Pius was imprisoned in the episcopal palace at Savona. In this exile he was treated with respect and courtesy, but nothing could change the facts of the situation, especially as Pius made it doubly obvious by refusing to cooperate with his jailers' attempts to press upon him the trappings of a court.

There is no need to chart the long struggle between pope and emperor that followed (in brief, Pius was eventually stripped of his powers and transported to Fontainebleau where he remained a prisoner until January 1814). Romantic and sentimental as he was, Alexander was in all probability moved by the steadfast dignity and courage exhibited by Pius VII, but this was not the first time that popes had been ill-used by temporal rulers. More to the point was the violence to international agreements to which the tsar had been a party. Indeed, between 1808 and 1810 much of the territorial and political structure to which Alexander had agreed at Tilsit was in one way or another cast aside. First was the influence of the Continental Blockade. Despite the emergence in a few areas of new centres of industry, in most of Europe the effect of the Blockade was disastrous. Whereas wholesale smuggling and the alliance with Spain and Portugal had allowed the British to escape its worst consequences, for everyone else there was no escape. As state after state was forced to join the Blockade, so the depression that had characterized the coasts of France ever since the outbreak of war with Britain in 1793 gradually spread along the shores of the North Sea, the Mediterranean and the Baltic. Not surprisingly, one state hit particularly badly was maritime-leaning Holland, but economic decline was not the only result of incorporation in the French imperium. As was the case with all his satellites, Napoleon expected Holland to provide him with substantial armed forces. In one letter, he spoke of 50,000 men and twenty ships-of-the-line. The men concerned were not, as we shall see, raised by conscription, but their recruitment and equipment cost vast sums of money – 5 million florins in the second half of 1806 alone out of a national budget for the same period of only 14 million. Appearances being almost as important as armed strength, Louis Bonaparte's court was another burden: in 1806 its costs were estimated at 1.5 million florins. Further money was drained away by the relief of poverty, by the constant battle to keep Holland's dykes proof against the sea, the need to service Holland's spiralling national debt, the very real interest of Louis Bonaparte and his chief advisers in social reform, and, finally, accidents and natural disasters: on 12 January 1807 a powder barge caught fire in the centre of Leiden and blew up with the loss of at least 500 houses, and in January 1808 and then again in January 1809 there were serious floods on the coast and along the river Rhine. Under Louis Bonaparte, then, although a series of reforms ensured that the burden was spread far more fairly than before, the Dutch experience was one of steadily rising taxation. Small wonder that, with the economy in tatters, the Dutch responded in the only way they could: aided by Holland's proximity to England and numerous estuaries, rivers and other waterways, smuggling became widespread.

As king of Holland Louis Bonaparte was being expected to produce concrete results in an extremely unfavourable situation. But produce results he had to, come what may. Further, Louis was also expected to remould Holland in the approved Napoleonic fashion and introduce French systems of law and administration. As Napoleon wrote, 'The Romans gave their laws to their allies: why cannot France have hers adopted in Holland? It is also necessary that you adopt the French monetary system . . . Having the same civil laws and coinage tightens the bonds of nations.'[18] At this point, however, we come to a serious flaw in Napoleon's calculations. The French ruler had installed his brothers and sisters on their thrones primarily as agents of imperial policy and control. As he had told Louis to his face, 'Don't forget that you are first and foremost a French prince. I put you on the throne of Holland solely to serve the interests of France and help me in all I am doing for her.'[19] But from the very moment Louis and the rest entered their new palaces, they acquired an interest that was in many instances distinct from that of their master. The Bonapartes' fondness for wealth and power being quite insatiable, beyond all else they wanted to survive, and this meant that the need to obey Napoleon became balanced by an equally strong need to come to some form of modus vivendi with their new subjects. Add to this the fact that many of them were bitterly jealous of the emperor, and it becomes apparent that their relationship with Paris was never likely to be a happy one.

So much for the general picture, but in Louis's case it was augmented by other issues. Never the most cheerful or outgoing member of the Bonaparte clan, in 1802 he had been married against his will to Josephine's daughter, Hortense de Beauharnais. It was a disastrous match, and Louis therefore went to Holland with a considerable animus against Napoleon. According to his unhappy queen, the only reason he accepted the post was that he could thereby bully her more freely and put an end to the tyranny of living under the emperor's thumb: 'He was clearly revelling in the pleasure of becoming his own master ... No longer would a concern for appearances stand in the way of the enforce-ment of his rights in my respect. Once independent of his brother, meanwhile, he need no longer have any fear for his own position.'[20] Desperate to gain acceptance by his new subjects and weighed down by personal misfortune – in addition to his unhappy marriage, he also suffered from syphilis and acute rheumatoid arthritis – he also had more of a conscience than most of the Bonaparte clan. And finally, had not the Batavian Republic's representatives in Paris begged for him to be made king? As far as he was concerned, then, he was a Dutch ruler who should genuinely try to do the best for his people. Quick to learn Dutch, he filled his court with prominent local notables, created two new orders of nobility and took the constitution seriously. The Dutch national assembly met regularly and was allowed a considerable degree of inde-pendence, and Louis showed great zeal in informing himself of the state of the kingdom. Not surprisingly, he was soon attempting to shield

Holland from Napoleon's insatiable demands for men, money and the imposition of the Civil Code. If Holland was to be kept in line, he reasoned, a real effort must be made to respect its traditions and sense of identity.

If anything gives the lie to the image of a Napoleon concerned for the welfare of the peoples of Europe, it is his response to Louis Bonaparte. If Louis needed money, for example, it was Holland that should provide it, though Napoleon's only positive suggestion here – other than to increase taxation – was that Louis take the politically impossible step of repudiating the ever-rising national debt. As for the Dutch, they should be treated with exactly the same iron fist as everyone else. By 1807 Napoleon was demanding the imposition of conscription even though Holland was guaranteed exemption from this burden by the treaty that had brought Louis to power. As the emperor told Louis, 'You attach too high a price to popularity in Holland. Before being kind you must be master.'[21] Similar thinking applied to the Civil Code. What mattered here was absolute uniformity: 'If you amend the Code Napoléon, it will no longer be the Code Napoléon.'[22] The harder Napoleon pressed on these issues, the more Louis dragged his feet. Conscription was never imposed and the national debt left unrepudiated, while it was not until the spring of 1809 that the Civil Code was introduced, and even then it appeared in a form that was much amended. Had trouble been restricted to matters of this sort, Louis would probably have survived on the throne: Napoleon still had sufficient trust in him to make him his first choice as king of Spain. But Holland was not performing efficiently as an ally: the navy remained moribund; the army distinguished itself neither in 1806 nor 1809; and finally, Holland was one of the weakest links in the Continental Blockade. As Napoleon made very clear, this was completely unacceptable to him:

All my hopes have been deceived. The moment Your Majesty ascended the throne of Holland, you forgot that you were a Frenchman; ever since, you have . . . stretched your reason to breaking point in the endeavour to persuade yourself that you are a Dutchman . . . You have broken all the treaties you made with me. You have disarmed your fleets, dismissed your sailors, and disorganized your armies, so that Holland finds herself without armed forces on land or sea . . . Your Majesty will find in me a brother, if I find in you a Frenchman. But, if you forget the feelings that attach us both to our fatherland, you must not take it ill of me if I also forget those by which nature has attached us to one another.[23]

Confronted with Napoleon's anger, Louis had no alternative but to take action, but there were limits to what he could do, and by the end of 1809 the emperor was determined to take matters into his own hands. Thus, Walcheren and a number of neighbouring islands were annexed to France, and the French troops sent to Holland to help repel the British were reinforced and ordered to occupy a number of towns in the south of the country. As for Louis, he was told the complete annexation of Holland would follow unless he agreed to obey Paris's orders to the letter, and in general treated in a fashion that was as intimidating as it was humiliating. Realizing the only way out was to offer massive concessions, the king sought frantically to save at least something from the wreck, and on 16 March 1810 signed a convention that handed all of the country south of the river Waal to France and agreed that French troops should now be responsible for policing the Blockade. Yet even this was not enough, for by now Napoleon had almost certainly determined on the overthrow of his brother. A little time was bought by Louis offering to broker a peace with Britain: in brief, a Dutch banker with family connections in London was sent to warn the Perceval administration that Holland was on the brink of annexation in the hope that this would elicit an offer of negotiations. Yet Dutch independence was now such a meaningless concept that Perceval and his colleagues remained unmoved and, with their rejection of the Dutch mission, Napoleon finally fell on Louis with a vengeance. Hitherto Amsterdam had remained unoccupied, but after a minor affray in which the coachman of the French ambassador was set upon in the street, on 29 June French troops appeared outside the city demanding entry. Pushed to the limit, Louis wanted to fight, but his generals and ministers were more realistic: the capital, they argued, could not be defended even if the Dutch army had been in a better condition than was actually the case. There being only one other way out, on 2 July Louis abdicated and fled into exile in Bohemia, leaving his adoptive country to be annexed in its entirety.

The story of 'Lodewijk the Good', as he became known, reveals the futility of hoping that Napoleon would ever be anything other than a warlord or conqueror. Louis had made genuine efforts to get Holland to accept her place in the French imperium by persuading her that she *had* a place in the French imperium – that French control did not mean the complete loss of her independence or the complete neglect of her interests. The emperor, however, responded with a mixture of incomprehension and hostility, and, by the end, was openly accusing Louis of treason: according to Napoleon, Holland had become nothing more than an English colony. The fact was that Louis had been naïve and foolish in proceeding as he did. Nobody was more aware of this than his unfortunate queen, Hortense:

I could never understand . . . how the king could figure that he could rule as an independent sovereign and act in accordance with what he understood to be the good of the people he had been called to govern . . . It was assuredly a noble sentiment . . . but how could he set himself apart when all the sovereigns of Europe . . . had been forced to adopt the system of the conqueror? I said one day to one of his ministers who had come to me to complain of the severity of the emperor that . . . I was persuaded that my husband was ill-advised. Had he possessed a force that was capable of resisting the emperor, he could perhaps have separated the interests of Holland from those of France if he thought that was the right thing to do, but otherwise there was no option but to march shoulder to shoulder with her. In this fashion Holland, albeit at the price of a few more sacrifices, would one day find herself enjoying the benefits brought by territorial aggrandizement and the constant support of a powerful ally, whereas the contrary policy would simply irritate the emperor and lead him to annex a country that had not been following his orders.[24]

This sums up the dilemma of Napoleon's siblings and the other satellite rulers to perfection. They could either choose the path of resistance or acquiesce in the emperor's authority and surrender all pretence of representing the interests of their subjects. To put it another way, the emperor's power recognized no limits.

That this was the case continued to be demonstrated as 1810 wore on. In part, this was the result of a growing crisis in not just the Continental Blockade, but the entire European economy. Prior to the imposition of the Blockade, large areas of central and Eastern Europe had been heavily dependent on the export of raw materials and agricultural products to Britain. This trade, however, was now cut off. Meanwhile France was at the same time unable to import bulk goods easily and self-sufficient in many of the products involved, so that agricultural prices, and with them purchasing power, began to fall, the latter also having been hit very hard by soaring taxation (in France alone indirect taxation rose fourfold between 1806 and 1812). However, thanks to the technical deficiencies of French industry and France's enforced reliance on land transport, French imports were disproportionately expensive. As French production rose (as it naturally did), so a crisis of over-production came ever closer. This was finally sparked off by new developments in the imposition of the Blockade. By 1810 it was clear to Napoleon that he could not close the coasts to British goods, and further, that the expansion of French industry was constantly dogged by the high price of colonial raw materials. Just as clearly the commerce raiding by which the French had since 1803 been attempting to cut Britain's trade routes was increasingly ineffective as the British had by now captured most of France's foreign bases. In response, the emperor decided the only solution was to open up direct links with Britain, issuing a series of decrees – those of the Trianon and Fontainebleau – that on the one hand authorized the import of colonial goods and on the other restricted this trade to France alone. This was coupled with a severe clamp-down on the huge stocks of contraband that existed in many German, Dutch and Italian cities.

In promulgating the decrees of 1810, Napoleon had, of course, disregarded the interests of Europe as a whole, but even in France his actions had a negative effect. Speculation in colonial imports having become rife, the result was general ruin, with French merchants undercut by the new imports, and foreign ones stripped of their stocks. Inside and outside France there was a wave of bankruptcies and a squeeze on credit, the latter spreading the crisis to industry and inducing a severe economic depression. As if all this was not enough, the period 1809–11 was marked by abnormally severe weather and as a result the price of food and industrial crops soared by as much as 100 per cent. In terms of international relations the results were most severe. Even before the decrees of Fontainebleau, the Continental Blockade had been hard enough to enforce beyond the borders of France. As we have just seen, this factor played a major role in the demise of Louis Bonaparte, but it had also been visible in the destruction of the Kingdom of Etruria and the Papal States. With the new terms of the Blockade, the pressure for fresh advances was redoubled. Prior to October 1810 the situation had been bad enough, but at least the money made from getting around the

Blockade had gone into the pockets of enterprising local merchants and entrepreneurs. Now, however, those profits were to be siphoned off to France and, still worse, to a France protected by extortionate tariff barriers that seemed designed to de-industrialize the whole of the rest of Europe. In these circumstances the Blockade was likely to become even more porous than before, and thus it was that very shortly afterwards there was yet another extension in the frontiers of *la grande nation*. On 10 December 1810 the annexation was declared of the free cities of Hamburg, Bremen and Lübeck – all of them important ports or centres of trade – and the independent Duchy of Oldenburg, giving France control of the whole coast of the North Sea from Holland to Denmark (indeed, with Lübeck in French hands, Napoleon's frontiers reached almost to the shores of the Baltic).

As gaps still remained in the Blockade, the emperor at various times threatened to go even further, with both Swedish Pomerania and Naples being at one time or another mentioned as possibilities for annexation. But it was not just the Continental Blockade that was fuelling French expansionism. Also on view was a growing sense on the part of Napoleon that, even where they did not absolutely turn renegade, the Bonapartes were at best poor agents of the Napoleonic empire. Nowhere was this more true than in Spain and Westphalia, both of which witnessed major territorial changes at this time. To begin with Spain, since 1808 Joseph Bonaparte had, of course, been waging a long war to impose his authority and defeat the forces of resistance. In this he had made some progress, but victory was still far away and by 1810 Napoleon was increasingly sceptical about his competence. The problem was not so much Joseph's military abilities, limited though these were. The conduct of the war itself hardly involved Joseph and was entirely in the hands of the various army commanders. Rather at issue was Joseph's perceived weakness. Like Louis in Holland, *el rey intruso* was filled with vague notions of doing good, while he also believed his best hope of winning the war was to convince the Spanish people of the benevolent character of his rule and that a similar policy had worked when he was king of Naples. Great energy, then, was invested in a policy of conciliation and clemency. The court and administration were filled with grandees who had previously served the Bourbon regime, and Spanish prisoners were recruited en masse into Joseph's own armed forces. All too clearly this policy failed to deliver. On the contrary, resistance continued. In Joseph's eyes this was the fault of the immense brutality and heavy requisitioning that characterized the French occupation. According to the emperor, however, the fault was Joseph's. Already distrustful of his older brother – he had, in fact, been bitterly critical of his handling of affairs in Naples – the French ruler was encouraged in his dissatisfaction by the complaints that were reaching him from Spain. Typical were the views of Pierre de Lagarde, a senior official in the General Ministry of Police who was sent to Spain in 1809: 'Almost everything is hidden from the king . . . The most unbridled licence is never punished. To every rigorous measure, there is opposed the constitution, as if we were living in a time of profound peace. Your Majesty will perceive from the official gazette . . . this system of base conciliation, of impolitic concessions made to men who only become more insolent.'[25] Nor was Lagarde reassured when Joseph invaded Andalucía in January 1810:

The spirit of the expedition, it appears, is less military than conciliatory. Despite all the errors that have been made in this respect . . . the king's entourage has persuaded him that he has only to show himself for everyone to fall at his feet, and that the people, in spite of the fury of their leaders, are ready to repent . . . Yet it is this very mania . . . that has ever since your departure . . . led to every efficacious measure being discarded, and made it so hard to suppress the ferocious habits of disobedience, brigandage and murder favoured by . . . [Spain's] mountains and poor communications . . . It seems to me that, instead of continuing with concessions and sweet words that only serve to embolden the rebels, it would be better to accompany our resumption of offensive operations with the sort of code of conquest that would show every town and village what they had to expect . . . I dare to affirm, even . . . that any other system than that of military government and just severity will perpetuate Spain's troubles instead of curing them. In so far as this is concerned, there is no way forward other than Your Majesty . . . proclaiming it yourself: around the king there is no one, Frenchman or Spaniard, who will give him energetic counsel.[26]

Napoleon, of course, did not need informers to poison him against his brother. From the very beginning he had insisted Joseph should take a harsh line: 'It is necessary to be severe with the Spaniards. I arrested fifteen of the most turbulent here [i.e. Valladolid] and had them shot. Have thirty or so arrested in Madrid . . . When one treats rabble of this sort with kindness, they think they are invulnerable, but when some of them are hanged, they tire of the game and become properly submissive and humble.'[27] Equally: 'Above all, do not let yourself go short of money. If necessary demand some loans from the towns, corporations and provinces. There is plenty of money in Spain: it was found soon enough when she wanted to revolt!'[28] In December 1808, indeed, having reconquered Madrid on behalf of his brother, Napoleon had literally taken the law into his own hands and, without even informing Joseph, issued a series of decrees that abolished feudalism, dissolved the Inquisition and made way for the dissolution of many religious orders. Now he went even further. On 8 February 1810, Catalonia, Aragón, the Basque provinces and Navarre were taken out of Joseph's hands and placed under the authority of military governors answerable only to Paris. Two months later two more such units were created out of Burgos and Valladolid. And then on 14 July Napoleon gave the whole of Andalucía to Marshal Soult as a viceroyalty; 'King Nicholas', as he was known, was also handed the command of almost all the troops that had taken part in its conquest. In effect Spain had been dismembered. Joseph, of course, was horrified. Even before news of the decree arrived he had been protesting that the emperor could not genuinely wish to see him 'humiliated every instant by the orders that come to him from generals who impose contributions, issue proclamations, promulgate laws and make me ridiculous in the eyes of my new subjects'.[29] As he clearly saw, however, the creation of the military governments made his position impossible. To quote a letter he wrote to his wife, who had remained in Paris:

It matters a great deal to me that I know what the true intentions of the emperor are towards me . . . What does he want of me and of Spain? If only he would announce his will: then I would not be caught between what I have the appearance of being and what I really am: king of a country where conquered provinces are given over to the discretion of generals who impose whatever taxes they feel like and have orders not to pay any attention to me.[30]

Trapped in an impossible situation, Joseph considered abdicating, but, avaricious and easy-going, el rey intruso was no Louis. Instead of making good his repeated threats, he sought rather to negotiate with Napoleon, sending special emissaries to Paris and eventually travelling to the capital himself. Thinking that he had secured a few concessions, he stayed on the throne, only to be humiliated yet again when Napoleon announced that Catalonia would be added to France at the end of the war. But for all that, Joseph would not go and so he was still on the throne when Wellington finally caught the French at Vitoria in June 1813, his last service to his brother as king of Spain therefore being to provide him with a convenient scapegoat for defeat.

In Spain the problem was one of political, military and financial failure. This was also the case with Westphalia, but at least Joseph Bonaparte was conscientious and devoid of neither talent nor good intentions. In Jerome Bonaparte, by contrast, Westphalia had a king who lacked even these qualifications. Jerome was a singularly feckless figure; the youngest of the Bonaparte brothers – when he became king of Westphalia in 1807 he was only twenty-three – he had consistently been shown much kindness by Napoleon who had indulged his every whim. Extravagant, spendthrift and showy, he did not cut an impressive figure. 'Monsieur Coussens . . . dined with us,' wrote Lady Holland, for example. 'He is lately arrived from Philadelphia . . . At Philadelphia he saw Jerome Bonaparte, who was amusing himself with the luxury, state and profusion of a young prince; he describes him as rather clever with a decided dislike to the profession his brother has chosen for him, and only fond of horses, equipages, etc.'[31] Another observer was the German officer, Ferdinand von Funck:

As Napoleon's youngest brother he had had no share in his early fortunes beyond his sudden promotion from the status of a private individual to the rank of an imperial prince. He was good-natured, but frivolous and irresponsible . . . [and] had neither the firm fair-dealing of his brother Louis nor Joseph's scholarship, least of all the gifts of Lucien and Napoleon. His rapid rise in rank had fostered all the self-confidence of one born in the purple with the hotheadedness of an undisciplined, wealthy youngster. Because he had grown up to be the brother of the most powerful monarch in the world, he regarded nothing as impossible: everything had, in his opinion, to give way to his mere wishes . . . and even every naughtiness whereby he meant no harm had to be permitted him. He was therefore capable of committing acts of great harshness and injustice, not of any evil intent, but from sheer irresponsibility. Human beings did not count at all in his eyes. They were only there to submit to every whim of the Bonaparte family, called by destiny to rule over them.[32]

This, then, was the ruler that Napoleon placed in charge of the populous, strategically important and potentially quite wealthy state of Westphalia, a state, moreover, the emperor intended as a showcase for the benefits of incorporation within the French imperium. As he wrote to Jerome: 'It is necessary that your people should enjoy a liberty ... unheard of amongst the inhabitants of Germany ... Such a style of government will be a stronger barrier against Prussia than ... even the protection of France. What people would wish to return to the arbitrary administration of Prussia when it could enjoy the benefits of a wise and liberal government?'[33] As might have been expected, it did not turn out to be a happy arrangement. From the beginning the Westphalian court was vulgar even by the standards of the Bonapartes. Setting aside the immense sums of money lavished on the royal residences of Napoleon-shöhe and Catharinenthal and the extravagantly uniformed royal guard, typical enough was the opening of the Westphalian legislature on 2 July 1808, Jerome appearing at this event in a suit of white silk, a purple cloak and a plumed turban decorated with diamonds. Meanwhile, the life of the court was a constant round of entertainment on the grandest of scales in which Jerome took a vigorous part while at the same indulging his considerable libido with a parade of mistresses. This, of course, was not an atmosphere likely to attract men of the highest calibre, and while Jerome did obtain a number of loyal and effective servants, several of the leading figures in the court were disreputable adventurers. To quote the Dutch ambassador:

The Countess of Truchsee, who was born a princess of Hohenzollern, became the pre-eminent figure in the court, and acquired a considerable ascendancy over [Jerome] ... Factious, self-centred and full of ambitions, she managed to captivate the young monarch and pass herself off in his eyes as a person of honesty and good will ... General Morio, the first Minister of War, was a man of few talents who understood neither administration nor organization ... A dispute between the young Count of Westphalia and equerry of the king ... deprived the kingdom of the services of one of the most well-born and richest of its inhabitants, but the fact that he had once been Prussia's Secretary of State did not stop Count Schulenburg from ... dishonouring himself by coming to pay homage to Jerome and intrigue his way into employment.[34]

Perhaps this is to go too far. Strenuous efforts have been made to defend Jerome, and there is plenty of evidence to suggest that his administration struggled hard to meet the demands that Napoleon made of it. Nor was Jerome himself entirely without merit: though never much of a general, he did at least show courage and energy when faced by internal revolt in 1809. Unlike Louis, he also made strenuous attempts to enforce the Blockade in his dominions, which, landlocked though they were, controlled several of the main routes through which British goods were smuggled into the interior of the Continent. And even if Jerome did create a distinctly overblown royal guard, the Westphalian army was by no means a disaster. Conscription was enforced without too much difficulty, and by 1812 it had evolved as a reasonably effective fighting force. However, there is no doubt that the excesses of the court greatly increased the financial burden faced by Westphalia, which was required by treaty to maintain an army of 12,500 men, pay for the upkeep of 12,500 French troops, assume responsibility for both the debts of the old rulers of the region and the costs of French occupation in 1806–7, pay over a 'war contribution' of 26 million francs, and surrender half the estates of the Elector of Hesse and his fellows to Napoleon as donations. Despite considerable increases in taxation, by the end of 1809 the state was therefore all but bankrupt – the 47-million-franc national debt of 1808 had risen in a single year to 93 million francs – and it was with considerable relief that Jerome learned that Napoleon had decided to incorporate Hanover, which since 1807 had been under French occupation, into Westphalia. As a further boon, the emperor also slashed the 26 million francs owed by Westphalia to a mere 16 million. Nevertheless the outlook for Jerome was bleak. Over the past two years, Napoleon had become increasingly irritated with the reports he was receiving from Kassel, and by the summer of 1808 his tone was distinctly frosty.

You owe the sinking fund 2 million, and have let your various notes go unpaid: this is not the action of a man of honour. I will not suffer anyone to let me down in any respect. Sell your diamonds . . . and give up the foolish waste that is making you the laughing stock of Europe and will end up by exciting the indignation of your people. Sell your furniture, your horses, and your jewels, and pay your debts: honour comes before all. Not to do so demonstrates the worst possible grace when it is contrasted with the presents

that you give out and the unheard of luxury that characterizes your court
. . . I recommend three things to you: respect for, recognition of and attachment to both myself and the French people, to whom you owe everything;
the most severe economy . . . and finally the employment of your time in
learning the things that you do not understand.[35]

Even more striking is the furious letter written to Jerome in the wake
of the battle of Wagram, after Napoleon learned that his brother had
bungled the task of expelling the minor Austrian force that had invaded
Saxony at the start of the campaign of 1809:

I have seen an order of the day of yours that will make you the laughing
stock of Germany, Austria and France alike. Have you not got some friend
in your entourage who is capable of telling you a few home truths? You
are a king and a brother of the emperor, but these facts count for nothing in war. One must be a soldier, a soldier and nothing but a soldier; do
without cabinet ministers, diplomatic corps and court; bivouac with the
advanced guard every night; be on horseback day and night . . . You make
war like a satrap . . . You have a lot of ambition, but such spirit and good
qualities as you have are undermined by your fatuous behaviour and extreme presumption, not to mention the fact that you have no knowledge of
affairs.[36]

In view of these comments, it is hard to see why Napoleon should
have decided to hand over Hanover to Westphalia in 1809. Setting aside
Jerome's own misdeeds, the Westphalian army had not distinguished
itself in any way on its first real outing in the field: many of the soldiers
had deserted or given themselves over to plundering the countryside,
while the court favourites who had been given command had proved to
have little talent. At all events attempts were almost immediately being
made to claw back the gift. Hidden in the terms of the preliminary
agreement signed on 14 January 1810 were a series of clauses that served
substantially to reduce the financial value of the new territory, while it
was a further three months before the final terms of the transfer of
power were negotiated, and even then Napoleon refused to ratify the
so-called 'Act of Cession' that resulted. Sent into Hanover anyway,
Jerome's officials found their every action undermined by the French
civil and military authorities and the electorate's revenues seized from
under their noses. Before the end of the year the situation had grown

still worse. Oldenburg and the Hanseatic states did not in themselves constitute a contiguous block of territory, so when Napoleon seized them in December 1810 he rounded them out by taking the northern half of Hanover too. For Jerome it was a catastrophic blow – the territory involved included some of the richest in the entire kingdom – and one that could not but suggest that the whole of Westphalia might go the way of Holland. Nor was this the end of it: irritated by Bavaria's inability to suppress the Tyrolean revolt of 1809, Napoleon handed the Trentino over to the Kingdom of Italy, while the Swiss frontier district of the Valais (since the emperor's settlement of Switzerland an independent republic) was annexed by France on strategic grounds.

To return to Alexander I, angered though he may have been by Napoleon's constant flexing of his muscles, the travails of the various Bonaparte brothers were in the end of little account (it might, though, be observed that the annexation of Holland could not but raise eyebrows in St Petersburg: in his eyes, Tilsit had been meant to bring Britain to the negotiating table, whereas by annexing Holland Napoleon was in effect provoking her into greater intransigence). This was not the case, however, with those of the Grand Duke Peter of Oldenburg. Small and hitherto insignificant, Oldenburg was situated on the coast of the North Sea west of Hamburg. As such, it was a prime target for French annexation, but by treating it in this fashion Napoleon was again behaving as if he were ruling in a vacuum. For reasons that are of little consequence here, the ruling Holstein-Eutens had had connections with the Romanov dynasty for many years – Grand Duke Peter, in fact, was Alexander's uncle – and in 1809 the tsar's favourite sister, the Grand Duchess Catherine, had married the current Grand Duke's heir. For Alexander therefore, Oldenburg was very much a Russian dependency. As he had negotiated a specific guarantee of the grand duchy's independence at Tilsit, it was therefore with great anger that he received Napoleon's decision to snap it up. With the tsar already upset by the sudden death in July 1810 of Queen Louise of Prussia – which he attributed to the strain imposed on her by a fresh crisis in Franco-Prussian relations that saw the emperor demand the immediate payment of all Prussia's debts to France and suggest that this should be financed either by reducing the army to a brigade-sized royal guard or surrendering Silesia – his response was predictably violent. Though diplomatic relations were not absolutely broken off, a sharp protest was dispatched to Paris. All this achieved, however, was to add insult to injury, as the only compensation that was offered Grand Duke Peter was a minuscule territory centred on Erfurt that bore no comparison even with tiny Oldenburg.

More important even than Oldenburg was the state of feeling in the Russian court. As Alexander could never forget, Paul I and his grandfather, Peter III, had pushed the bounds of absolute rule too far and been murdered in palace revolutions. This fate now seemingly threatened him too: from 1807 onwards, indeed, there had been stories of plots against his rule, while there were certainly plenty of pretexts for conspiracy. In the Balkans, Russia's claims to be the protector of the region's Christians were losing credibility. As the senior Russian commander, Admiral Chichagov, wrote:

The inhabitants of the right bank [of the Danube] – all of them Christians – experienced all the horrors imaginable . . . Wherever the army passed, all their towns and villages were reduced to ashes. Meanwhile, whether by force or by persuasion, thousands of the inhabitants were made to cross over to the left bank; although they were promised food and shelter, the majority died of want and misery. In this fashion the hope of a people that had before looked to our armies for liberation from the evils stemming from the intestinal strife . . . that had assailed Rumelia for over twenty years was dissipated. As for the administration of the country that we occupied, it had fallen into such a state of disorder that famine broke out in Wallachia, which is surely the most fertile province in the whole of Europe. There followed the onset of contagious disease, and very soon the rate of mortality had become extreme. According to official figures which I was able to consult, between 1 May 1809 and 1 May 1810 more than 100,000 people were admitted to our hospitals . . . In the course of my journey through Moldavia and Wallachia to Bucharest, I noted that many houses had been abandoned, and I later learned that the householders had fled the country to avoid the endless requisitioning of the authorities and the perpetual vexations of the soldiery, and . . . were living a vagabond existence in the forests. In fact, discipline had declined to such an extent that pillage had become the order of the day.[37]

Setting the sufferings of the Balkan Christians aside, with victory still far away, Russia could not count on compensation on the Danube, still less a victorious march on Constantinople. Her only solid territorial gains to date were Georgia, Bialystok, Finland and Tarnopol, and this

433

seemed less than impressive compared with the conquests made under Catherine the Great.

Abroad, then, Russia's prestige was slipping. Nor were things much better at home. In the first place, the tsar's employment of the low-born Mikhail Speransky as chief minister caused unrest in the administration and the nobility. Some of Speransky's plans – most notably, the introduction of a constitution – were quite attractive in the wake of the caprice of Paul I, but in other respects they were very threatening. For example, Speransky was known to favour the emancipation of the serfs, among whom vague ideas that Napoleon was the anti-Christ had sparked a mood of millennial excitement. Equally, with his emphasis on quasi-Napoleonic models, the chief minister was self-evidently a 'westernizer' and therefore very much open to charges that he was betraying the soul of Mother Russia and in the process turning his back on her greatest strengths. And it was not just Speransky that raised hackles. In the army there was the tsar's insistence on employing the hated Alexei Arakcheev in a series of important positions, for Arakcheev had been one of Paul I's chief collaborators and in his pursuit of efficiency was inclined to use methods that were a throwback to the worst days of that monarch, while in the Orthodox Church there was great dislike of the idea of Russia allying herself with a ruler that it saw as an enemy of all religion.

But most troubling of all was the impact of the Continental Blockade. Between 1806 and 1812 exports dropped by approximately two fifths; customs revenue fell from 9 million roubles in 1805 to less than 3 million in 1808; the value of the paper currency that had become increasingly standard fell by a factor of about one half between 1808 and 1811; and the price of such colonial goods as sugar and coffee may have as much as quintupled between 1802 and 1811. As for trade with France, by 1811 the ratio of exports to imports had in terms of value arrived at the extraordinary figure of 1:170; to make matters even worse, meanwhile, the raw cotton that was what Russia most needed was being squeezed by items of high value and low bulk such as perfume. Here and there a few brighter notes were to be encountered – between 1804 and 1811 the number of Russians employed in factories and workshops rose from 95,000 to nearly 138,000, for example – yet the overall situation was terrible, particularly as Alexander had always put great value on increasing Russia's trading links with the outside world. At the same time he was also beginning to doubt the Blockade's chances of success. 'It was

... impossible for Alexander to close his eyes any longer to the sad condition to which the absolute cessation of commerce had reduced the empire,' wrote the Lithuanian countess, Sophie Tisenhaus. 'What limit, moreover, could anyone assign to this system, even more oppressive for those who had undertaken it than for those against whom it was directed. Had not England her colonies, her ships, all her seas at her disposition?'[38] As Alexander's problems mounted up, so opposition to his rule became ever more open, those involved including such members of his own family as the dowager empress and the Grand Duchess Catherine; prominent members of the armed forces like Admiral Alexei Shishkov and Paul I's sometime Foreign Minister, Nicolai Rostopchin; the leading writer Basil Karamzin; and the Minister of Justice, Georgi Derzhavin. In December 1810, then, Alexander decided to act. As a first step, the ban on neutral vessels had already been relaxed, but by imperial decree it was announced that tariffs on imports that arrived in Russia by land would be massively increased in relation to those payable on goods that came in by sea. Neither Britain nor France were mentioned directly, but in the circumstances nothing could be clearer: the former's colonial goods were to be allowed in while the latter's wines and manufactures were to be kept out. As such, Russia did not withdraw from the Continental Blockade – British ships continued to be seized in considerable numbers up until 1812 – but it was all too obvious that Alexander could no longer be counted upon to enforce it, and still more so that Napoleon's attempt to transform the whole of continental Europe into a captive market was not to be allowed to extend any further east than Warsaw.

As a shot across Napoleon's bows, the *ukase* of December 1810 was very pointed, and he would therefore have been well advised to take it very seriously. Yet the emperor's attitude towards the growing crisis is revealed only too well by the interview he accorded his ambassador Caulaincourt when the latter was recalled to France in the early summer of 1811. Arriving in Paris on 5 June, Caulaincourt immediately presented himself at court:

His Majesty received me coldly, and at once began heatedly to enumerate his ... grievances against the Tsar Alexander ... He spoke of the *ukase* prohibiting foreign imports, and of the admission of neutral ... ships into Russian ports, which, he said, was an infringement of the Continental

System. He went on to say that the tsar was treacherous, that he was arming to make war on France, that troops from Moldavia were on their way to the Dvina.[39]

Faced by this tirade, Caulaincourt stood his ground. The Russians, he said, had legitimate economic grievances, and Napoleon could not be surprised if they in effect followed the precedent established by the decrees of Trianon and Fontainebleau: that Alexander had never acted in anything other than good faith; that the reported troop movements were defensive measures that were entirely understandable in the circumstances; and that almost every action taken by Napoleon since the summer of 1809 had in some respect been detrimental to Russia's interests. Alexander, Caulaincourt insisted, did not want war, and all would be resolved if only Napoleon would give him the assurances he sought over the Grand Duchy of Warsaw and pull all his troops out of Prussia. 'Finally, I told the emperor frankly that, if he wanted a war, his government was doing everything it could to bring one about; it was even crying its purpose from the house-tops, and if he regarded the Russian alliance as worth maintaining, I was unable to understand what purpose all these pin-pricks could possibly serve.'[40]

As might have been expected, Napoleon's response was frosty. 'The emperor was extremely annoyed with me, and told me that I had been duped by . . . the Russians, that I did not understand what was going on.'[41] This angry outburst was followed by a series of specious attempts to paint the emperor as the injured innocent. His conduct towards Russia had been fair and moderate; he did not want war with Alexander; he wanted only for Russia to fulfil her treaty obligations and to behave as a friend and ally; he could not pull his garrison out of Prussia without enduring public humiliation. Yet still Caulaincourt would not give up. Going to war with Russia, he contended, would be difficult and dangerous: what would happen, for example, if the Russians evaded battle and retired into the interior? Napoleon, however, was no less stubborn. The Russians would be thrashed – 'one good battle', he said, 'would knock the bottom out of . . . Alexander's fine resolutions'[42] – and, with that subject dealt with, he returned to insisting that Russia wanted war, denouncing any attempt to make him compromise, and alleging that the Lithuanians were deluging him with appeals for their liberation. After five hours' argument, the interview concluded, leaving a weary Caulaincourt with no other hope of maintaining the peace than that the war in Spain would keep Napoleon from turning east.

Before leaving Russia, Caulaincourt had repeatedly been told by Alexander that he did not want war. But this was disingenuous. In the first half of 1811 the tsar was certainly considering a very different policy. Following the peace treaty signed with Sweden in 1809, Finland, it will be recalled, had been annexed by Russia. However, she was not simply absorbed into the Russian empire, but rather given the status of a Grand Duchy, even though its Grand Duke would forever be the tsar of Russia. Not only this, but Finland was also granted a constitution, albeit one that reflected the patterns of an earlier age: the Finnish assembly, for example, sat not as a single chamber but as four different estates. In this way, a figment of self-government was maintained without threatening Russian control: always virtually powerless, the assembly met for a single session in 1809 and thereafter did not come together again until 1863. The importance of these events here is that they offered a solution to the Polish problem, and, in particular, restoring the control of Poland which Russia had enjoyed in the eighteenth century. Much favoured by Czartoryski, this was hardly a new idea, but the new Grand Duchy of Finland gave it a credibility it might previously have lacked. And, convinced that Russian domination was the best means of protecting their privileges, many Polish nobles were very interested in such a scheme. In the course of the campaign of 1809, indeed, a deputation of Polish nobles had visited Golitsyn's headquarters and promised him the support of all Poles if only Alexander would reconstitute the old Polish state with himself as its ruler. Why not, then, turn the situation around by offering the Poles a Finnish-style settlement of their own that would bring together both the Grand Duchy of Warsaw and the vast swathes of Polish territory already possessed by the Russians?

Further encouraged by the way such a policy would enable him to live out his dream of playing the liberator, in January 1811 Alexander therefore committed himself to restoring the Kingdom of Poland on the basis of the frontiers she had enjoyed prior to the first partition in 1772 (included in these, of course, were not just the territories taken by Russia and the Grand Duchy of Warsaw, but Austrian Galicia and Prussian Pomerania). As for the political basis of the new state, this would be the radical constitution of 1791 which had greatly reduced the power of the nobility and created a strong central government. In all probability

Alexander would have preferred the much weaker constitution that had governed Poland earlier in the eighteenth century, but in the end he was persuaded by Czartoryski – still his chief agent in respect of Poland – that there was no other option if the new state was to be a credible entity. In proof of Alexander's good intentions, meanwhile, there was also much discussion of a constitution for Lithuania – in effect the northern half of the territories seized from Poland in the partitions of 1772.

Implicit in the idea of a Russian Poland was, of course, a war against Napoleon. Nor was this surprising. As challenge succeeded challenge, and slight succeeded slight, so Alexander became increasingly certain that the emperor was planning an attack upon him. 'Napoleon will never turn fool,' he told Czartoryski. 'It is something which is inconceivable, and those who believe it do not know him at all. He is someone who in the midst of the greatest turmoil always has a cool head. All his outbursts of anger are but put on for those around him ... He does nothing without having first thought everything through and worked everything out. The most violent and audacious of his actions are coldly calculated.'[43] And if Napoleon was bent on war, the only thing to do was to choose the moment at which Russia should fight and to do so in the best conditions possible. So far as Alexander was concerned, moreover, the moment for action had come. Napoleon was still deeply embroiled in the Peninsula, but such were the successes being won by his armies that this distraction could not be guaranteed to last for very much longer. The Poles, in fact, were not only being offered their historic kingdom, but also being summoned to rise in revolt. Nor were they to be Alexander's only allies. On 13 February 1811 Alexander wrote to Francis I asking for Austrian support and promising Moldavia and Wallachia if he would in turn cede Galicia to a restored Kingdom of Poland, while the idea of a war was also floated with Prussia and Sweden. All this was backed up by Russian troop movements and other preparations for war: the production of arms was stepped up, and a force of 200,000 men, including, significantly, five divisions taken from the Balkan front, was built up in White Russia, along with a network of magazines and entrenched camps.

Yet within a matter of weeks the whole enterprise had collapsed, not the least of Alexander's problems being that the Poles would not cooperate. In the first place war was likely to bring total devastation as the main fighting could not but take place on Polish soil. And, in the second, if there were some nobles who feared the social reforms initiated by the Grand Duchy of Warsaw, there were plenty of others who were prepared to set such fears aside, and simply saw Napoleon as a better bet. To quote Oginski:

Almost everything that happened at that time encouraged our hopes. Napoleon freely acknowledged the valour of the Poles, and seemed to take pleasure in securing their allegiance. He had increased the strength of the old [Polish] legions, as well as forming others that had distinguished themselves in the campaign of 1809. He had organized a unit of Polish lancers for which he evinced particular affection, and made it a part of his guard. And, if he had only given the title of the Grand Duchy of Warsaw to that part of Poland which he had seized from the King of Prussia, the new state had an army . . . a fiscal system, a senate, ministries for every branch of the administration and a legislature that resembled that of the old kingdom. As all this was on a scale that far outstripped the limits of its population and borders, one was led to suppose that the emperor . . . was hiding in his bosom projects that were still vaster and even more advantageous to the interests of the Poles.[44]

Czartoryski, then, was not only unable to deliver the support for which Alexander hoped but turned his back on the idea of war altogether, calling instead for the tsar to settle both the issue of Poland and his quarrels with Napoleon by negotiation.

While very useful, Polish support was not the most essential factor in the situation, however: with Austria, Prussia and Sweden on his side, Alexander might well have gone to war anyway. Yet there was no hope to be had here either. In Austria the Russian attempt to secure a rapprochement, let alone a military alliance, was shattered by Metternich, who abandoned his self-appointed mission in Paris and hastened back to Vienna to keep Francis on the path of peace and friendship with France:

Everything seems to indicate that the Emperor Napoleon is at present still far from desiring war with Russia. But it is not less true that the Emperor Alexander has given himself over, *nolens volens*, to the war party, and that he will bring about war because the time is fast approaching when he will no longer be able to resist the reaction of the party in the internal affairs of his empire or the temper of his army . . . Russia attempted long ago to engage us to take an active part on her side . . . It appeared to me necessary that, to answer these demands of Russia, sometimes apparent, sometimes concealed, a verbal declaration should be made . . . that Your Majesty is ready to exert yourself to the utmost for the maintenance of peace; that, in the event of war actually breaking out, Your Majesty would assume a neutral and independent position . . . [and] that, as Russia itself must see, any active cooperation on our part in her favour is quite impossible at a time when friendly relations subsist between Your Majesty and the French government, there being no grounds for any complaint against that power.[45]

In Prussia things were a little more encouraging in that much of the reform party in the army were avid for war. Led by Gneisenau, they argued vociferously for a mass revolt against the French. This move, they claimed, was the only way of restoring Prussia's honour and soul alike, but few except the most bloodthirsty of the officers concerned would move without Russia, and Frederick William remained as evasive as ever. In the end scared, perhaps, that even absolute submission to the French would not save his remaining dominions, the king gave way and in the summer the chief of the newly formed general staff, General Scharnhorst, was sent to St Petersburg to negotiate a deal. A military convention was duly concluded, but by then it was much too late: at the time that it had mattered, the Prussians would not march. And in Sweden, Bernadotte would only go to war in exchange for a promise of Danish-ruled Norway, but in 1810 Alexander had not yet reached the point when he might have been happy to sacrifice Denmark to please Sweden, and so here too there was no deal to be had.

All this being most discouraging, Alexander backed away from con-flict. Indeed, the idea of a pre-emptive strike was abandoned altogether, the fact being that Caulaincourt was speaking no more than the truth when he reported in June that Russia would not fire the first shot in a war against France. Everything, then, came back to Napoleon. What happened next can be discussed on two levels. First there are the facts. In brief, the emperor resolved on a policy of confrontation. Of this there is plenty of evidence. Caulaincourt was replaced by the more pliable Lauriston, a general who had a long history as one of Napoleon's more reliable lackeys, and the lacklustre Foreign Minister Champagny by the thoroughly dependable editor of Le Moniteur, Hugues Maret. Prussia, Sweden, Turkey and Austria were all contacted in respect of an alliance.

Albeit for purposes that were ostensibly 'defensive', troops began to be concentrated in Poland. And, as usual when hostilities were impending, a formal court reception was used to telegraph the imperial intent. At the levee held to celebrate Napoleon's birthday on 15 August 1811, the Russian ambassador Kurakin was subjected to a half-hour public tirade in which Alexander was accused of bad faith and warmongering. 'I am not so stupid as to think that it is Oldenburg that troubles you,' raged the emperor. 'I see that Poland is the real question. You believe I have designs on Poland. However, I begin to think you wish to seize it for yourselves. No! If your army were encamped in the very heights of Montmartre itself, I would not cede an inch of Warsaw, not a village, not a windmill. You're counting on allies? Where are they? You look to me like hares who are shot in the head and gape all around, not knowing where to scurry!'[46] To emphasize the point still further, Warsaw's ambassador, Count Dzialynski, was then treated to an equally public interview in which Napoleon plied him with questions, 'talking in a loud voice so that everyone would know how much importance he placed upon the interests of . . . the Grand Duchy'.[47]

As yet no rupture came: Kurakin remained in Paris, and he was even joined by two special envoys, Chernichev and the future Foreign Minister, Karl von Nesselrode. Equally, Napoleon neither issued an ultimatum to Alexander nor announced the object of the great mobilization that began to grip the empire. But the emperor was bent on breaking Russia once and for all. At all events every attempt to avert Napoleon's anger was rebuffed. The Dutch general, Dedem de Gelder, for example, was taken aside by Nesselrode, and told that Alexander genuinely wanted to live in peace with Napoleon, and that his only quarrel was with the Continental System. 'Neither we nor you need a new war,' said Nesselrode. 'If you have your cancer in Spain, we have ours in Turkey: the war that we are waging there is just as impolitic and disastrous as the one that you are waging in the Peninsula.'[48] This conversation Dedem felt duty bound to report to Maret, but the latter's response was crushing: 'Russia has but one choice: she must follow our system in its entirety, and for us to make certain, allow us to place French customs officials even in Reval and Kronstädt.'[49]

Among soldiers, statesmen and civilians alike, there was now but one assumption: war with Russia was coming. The prospect, however, was not popular: 'Napoleon's popularity now began to wane,' wrote one medical student. 'Troops were being raised without interruption for the Russian campaign although already every family was mourning a husband or son; further bloodshed was dreaded by all. The emperor superintended every detail of the preparations in person. Most of the regiments which were to take part were concentrated in Paris and reviewed minutely by him. The troops were full of eagerness. The very sight of Napoleon electrified them. But, alas, smooth chins were more numerous among them than beards. The war in Spain . . . had robbed us of the majority of our seasoned soldiers . . . The pressing need for men had lowered the standard age from twenty to nineteen and again to eighteen. They were mere children, and many of them were totally incapable of bearing up under the hardships of a campaign.'[50] To all this, however, Napoleon had but one answer. In the words of Hortense de Beauharnais, 'Unable to understand why it was necessary, the whole of France complained of a war that it did not want. The emperor persisted in regarding it as the last effort that would put an end to her labours. He believed that anything was possible to French valour, and would let nothing stop him.'[51]

To establish the facts is one thing, but to establish a motive for Napoleon's actions is quite another. In the face of every argument to the contrary – and to the bitter end Caulaincourt sought desperately to persuade him that Alexander still wanted peace, and that war with Russia would lead to disaster – he insisted that he himself wanted only peace, that Alexander was bent on war and that he was therefore conducting a defensive campaign. Mixed in with this was the claim that he was fighting a war for the liberation of Poland, and even that his aim was the defence of Western civilization from the menace of the east. As he told Caulaincourt (who was forced to accompany the emperor's headquarters as a most unwilling diplomatic adviser) when the *grande armée* reached Vilna:

I have come to finish off, once and for all, the colossus of the barbarians of the north. The sword is drawn. They must be thrust back into their snow and ice so that for a quarter of a century at least they will not be able to interfere with civilized Europe. Even in the days of Catherine the Russians counted for little or nothing in the politics of Europe. It was the partition of Poland which gave them contact with civilization. The time has come when Poland, in her turn, must force them back . . . We must seize this chance and teach the Russians an unpleasant lesson about their say in what happens in Germany . . . Since Erfurt Alexander has become too haughty. The acquisition of Poland has turned his head. If he must have victories, let him defeat the Persians, but don't let him meddle in the affairs of Europe.[52]

But too much should not be made of these claims. The idea of a crusade in favour of Western civilization had hitherto been notably absent from Napoleon's discourse, while Poland's real place in his thoughts is suggested by a conversation recorded by Oginski, who was told by the Grand Master of the Palace, General Duroc – always a close confidant of the emperor – that 'the re-establishment of an independent Poland could not be regarded as anything other than a chimerical project and was a dream that would never come true; that Poland had never truly been independent in any case; that she had existed in a state of anarchy for many years; that the freedom of which so much was made consisted of no more than the vehement speeches that the nobles had the right to pronounce in the meetings of the diet; that the servitude of the peasants had always been an obstacle to the establishment of good government; and, finally, that the Poles were too disunited in their opinions, and the nobility too jealous of its rights, for Poland ever to rejoin the ranks of the powers of Europe.'[53] Inside the regime, then, there were few illusions. 'The idea has been lodged in his head for more than a year,' one member of the council of state told an old friend who had come to Paris on official business in the autumn of 1811. 'The affairs of the Peninsula torment him from morning till night: the conflict is like a maggot gnawing away at him. He wants to deliver a great blow that will put the North [i.e. Russia] on its knees, and has persuaded himself that this will by extension settle the fate of Britain, and allow him to finish not only with her, but also with Spain and Portugal. Such at least I have gleaned . . . from the measures that he has one after another implemented . . . On top of this I will tell you what my reason alone has suggested to me. I could be mistaken, but is it not the case that we are again seeing the mania of heaping conquest upon conquest, and as much in times of peace as times of war? Is it not the case that, even though she now stretches all the way from Rome to Hamburg, France still seems too small to him?'[54]

If this was the opinion of men who were still loyal to Napoleon, it was pointless to look for anything better from those who had come to oppose him. One such was the former Minister of Police, Joseph Fouché, who blamed everything on 'the extravagant ambition of the chief of state'. Anxious to press the case for peace, Fouché waited on the emperor armed with a long report in which he warned of the dangers of war, only to come up against the same sort of stonewalling encountered by Caulaincourt:

There is no crisis: the present is a war purely political. You cannot judge of my position, nor of the general aspect of Europe. Since my marriage the lion has been thought to sleep: we shall see whether he does or not. Spain will fall as soon as I have annihilated the English influence at St Petersburg. I wanted 800,000 men and I have them. All Europe follows in my train, and Europe is a rotten old whore with whom I may do as I please . . . Did you not formerly tell me that you thought genius consisted in finding nothing impossible? Well, in six or eight months you shall see what things upon a vast scale can effect when united to a power that can execute them. I am guided by the opinion of the army and the people, rather than by yours, gentlemen who are too rich and who only tremble for me because you apprehend a fall. Make yourselves easy: regard the Russian war as dictated by good sense, and by a just view of the interests, the repose and the tranquillity of all. Besides, how can I help it if an excess of power leads me to assume the dictatorship of the world? Have not you contributed to it, you and so many others who blame me now, and would make a king *débonnaire* of me. My destiny is not yet accomplished: I must finish that which is but as yet sketched. We must have a European code, a European court of appeal, the same coins, the same weights and measures, the same laws: I must amalgamate all the people of Europe into one, and Paris must be the capital of the world. Such . . . is the only termination which suits my ideas.[55]

Fouché is hardly the most reliable of sources, but there seems no doubt that, even if these boasts of universal monarchy are an invention, Napoleon was in an exultant mood in the months leading up to war. Not only was the whirl of court life particularly brilliant at this time – 'Never were the entertainments of the court, the receptions, the banquets and the balls more numerous than they were in that winter of 1811–1812'[56] – but the emperor himself was in the finest of fettles. 'The . . . anxious looks of the courtiers appeared to me to form a strong contrast with the confidence of the emperor. He had never enjoyed such perfect health. Never had I seen his features . . . lighted up with a greater glow of mental vigour, of greater confidence in himself, founded on a deep conviction of his prodigious power.'[57] The fact was that, encouraged by placemen such as Maret, Napoleon was certain that he could win a great victory in Russia, and therefore saw no reason to draw back from confrontation with Alexander. The Russian army, he was sure, would be caught and beaten, leaving him free to impose his will on his opponent. As for the difficulties of a war in the depths of Russia, at this stage he was not even thinking of taking the offensive. 'Napoleon was convinced that the Russian army would open the campaign by crossing the boundaries of their own country,' wrote Metternich. 'The conviction expressed by me that the Emperor Alexander would await the attack of the French army and baffle it by a retreat, Napoleon opposed both on strategical grounds, and from Alexander's manner of thought and action, with which he imagined himself to be perfectly acquainted.'[58]

The campaign of 1812, then, was not quite as ill-judged as might be suggested by hindsight. Yet precisely what imposing the emperor's will on Russia meant seems not to have been considered. There would, doubtless, have been a greater Poland, while Russia would have been forced to accede once more to the Continental System and pay a heavy indemnity. But that still left the issue of how a wounded and embittered St Petersburg would be integrated within the Napoleonic imperium, let alone persuaded to accept the French customs officers talked of by Maret. Was Russia, like Prussia, to be forced to accept a permanent French garrison? To ask such questions is, of course, to assume that Napoleon was a rational being. According to some of his biographers, so irrational was the decision to go to war that it can only be explained by a 'mid-life crisis' in which an emperor beset by the coming of middle age responded to the disappointments of the war in Spain by indulging in a desperate bid for supreme glory and mastery. Such claims are naturally impossible to substantiate, but the somewhat less daring argument that Napoleon needed a fresh war to burnish his prestige does not seem unreasonable. And, even if this is not so, the charge that the emperor was simply gripped by overconfidence and vainglory remains. As Molé wrote:

It is a curious thing that Napoleon . . . never discovered the point at which the impossible begins. The more I saw of him, the greater was my conviction that he . . . thought only of satisfying his own desires and adding incessantly to his own glory and greatness. The slightest obstacle enraged him: he would sacrifice everything to overcome it, and, in his satisfaction at discovering that, whenever a collision occurred, nothing could withstand his power or his will, when it came to choosing between the present and the future he preferred the present as the more certain and subject to his will. In a word, he thought less of leaving . . . a dynasty behind him than a name which should have no rival and a glory which could never be excelled. Even more extravagant than fantastic in his ideas, his treatment of Spain and the head of the Catholic world had shown that unmoral action or abuse of power was nothing to him so long as he attained his object. But more than all it was his expedition to Russia and scheme for a continental blockade which made it plain to everyone . . . that death alone could set a limit to his plans and put a curb on his ambition.[59]

What makes the 'glory' thesis still more credible is that at this very time there resurfaced the so-called 'oriental mirage', the idea that Napoleon could establish an eastern empire on the lines of that of Alexander the Great while at the same time dealing the British a smashing blow by expelling them from India. This project was such a subject of palace gossip that it was soon being assumed it lay at the heart of the coming war. As one general asked Anna Potocka, a Polish noblewoman who had travelled to Paris in the suite of Marie-Louise, 'What do you want me to bring you back from India?'[60] Setting aside such exchanges, another factor that we must consider here is the place of Persia in the emperor's plans. The collapse of the Gardanne mission had not quite seen an end to Napoleon's ambitions in respect of that state, repeated attempts having been made to restore a French presence in Tehran. Are we, then, to take the remarks that Napoleon is supposed to have made to his aide-de-camp, Narbonne, at face value?

This long road is the road to India. Alexander left from as far away as Moscow to reach the Ganges. But for the English pirate and the French emigré who together directed the fire of the Turks, and, together with the plague, forced me to abandon the siege, after St Jean d'Acre I would have conquered half Asia and taken Europe in the rear in my bid to secure the thrones of France and Italy. Well, today I shall be marching from the extremities of Europe to take Asia in the rear so as to attack Britain. You know about . . . the missions of Gardanne and Jaubert to Persia. Nothing much has come of them, but I know enough of the geography and the condition of the population to get to . . . India by way of Erivan and Tiflis . . . Imagine Moscow taken, Russia overthrown, [and] the tsar reconciled or murdered by a palace plot . . . and tell me that it is impossible for a large army of Frenchmen and auxiliaries starting from Tiflis to reach the Ganges, where the mere touch of a French sword would be sufficient to bring down the framework of [Britain's] mercantile grandeur throughout India.[61]

Here one returns to the idea of the Russian war as a necessary step in the war with England, but to use this idea to justify Napoleon's actions at this point seems counter-productive. Given that the breach Russia represented in the Continental Blockade was insignificant, would closing it achieve the ends that were supposed? Was a march on India, even with the cooperation of the Russians, ever really a practical possibility? And would even conquering India be sufficient to knock Britain out of the war? As Narbonne said afterwards, 'What a man! What ideas! What dreams! Where is the keeper of this genius? It is hardly credible. One doesn't know whether one is in Bedlam or the Pantheon.'[62]

Whatever the reasons for Napoleon's actions, Europe was plunged into frenzied diplomatic activity. Realizing the convention Scharnhorst had signed with Russia offered little hope – rather than the Russians sending troops into Prussia, the Prussians were expected to abandon their homeland and march to join the Russians in Poland – in November Frederick William III buckled to French pressure and agreed to an alliance. Signed the following February, the resultant treaty not only provided Napoleon with an auxiliary force of 20,000 men, but also guaranteed the *grande armée* all the food it required. In Vienna the following month Metternich followed suit: Austria, it was agreed, would send 30,000 troops to join Napoleon and in addition surrender her remaining territories in Galicia to the Grand Duchy of Warsaw, the hope being that this would produce the restoration of the Illyrian provinces, the Tyrol and possibly even Silesia (until the 1740s an Austrian possession) and a French guarantee of the frontiers of the Ottoman Empire. In both Prussia and Austria secret efforts were made to reassure Alexander that the alliances with France had been signed for form's sake alone, but this was so much window-dressing: unless Napoleon suffered a catastrophic defeat, both powers were firmly in the French camp. Superficially, France could also claim the moral high ground. In April

1812 fresh peace proposals were dispatched to London. Spain would be restored to her 1808 frontiers and, along with Portugal, guaranteed by France and Britain alike; Naples would be left to Murat and Sicily to Ferdinand IV and Maria Carolina. As a further concession, Napoleon would permit the return of the Braganças to Lisbon, but Joseph was to remain as King of Spain, although he was to accept the constitution that had just been promulgated by the national assembly convened in Cádiz in 1810, while Britain was also to withdraw all her forces from the Continent. This approach, however, was rejected out of hand: as in 1803, Napoleon could claim that responsibility for conflict lay with London.

Yet the diplomatic war was by no means one-sided. In both the Balkans and the Baltic the emperor was taken unawares and deprived of alliances he had taken for granted. In the Balkans the Russians had once again started to win battles. The year 1811 had begun with them on the defensive and searching for a peace settlement, but Constantinople had rejected every advance, and in the summer began a major counter-offensive on the central sector of the Danube front. The chief target was the Russian outpost of Rustchuk. After withstanding a major assault on 4 July, the town was evacuated and in September the Turks set to work on the laborious task of getting their army across the Danube. Progress was slow and the beginning of October found them with their forces still split in two by the river. Commanding the Russians now was the immensely able and experienced General Kutuzov. Aided by the recall of some of the troops who had earlier in the year been marched off towards Poland, on 13 October he launched a daring manoeuvre that took a large part of his army across the river well to the west of the Turkish bridgehead. The next day the Turks found themselves attacked on both banks of the river simultaneously. Too strong to be routed and protected by massive defence works, the 36,000 men on the north bank managed to hold out, but across the river their comrades were soon driven off. Completely surrounded, lacking in food, shelter and firewood, deprived of all hope of relief and subjected to heavy bombardment, the troops in the bridgehead refused to surrender and, with great courage, held out until 8 December, by which time only 12,000 were left.

In a war thus far characterized chiefly by frustration, it was a great success. On the eastern front the Russian position was further improved by the capture of the fortress of Akhalkali in southern Georgia. Bolstered by hopes that the coming war between Russia and France would save them, the Turks stood firm in peace talks that Kutuzov opened in Bucharest – the Russians were at this point still demanding the surrender of Moldavia and Wallachia. In the face of this the Russians gave serious consideration to an amphibious landing in Bulgaria, followed by an assault on Constantinople. In the event, however, wiser counsels prevailed. Governed by the need to reach an immediate settlement, it was instead decided to offer the Turks generous terms. The Russians would keep the frontier province of Bessarabia, but otherwise restore to Constantinople all the territory they had occupied in exchange for a guarantee of autonomy for the Danubian provinces. Eager to gain an alliance with Turkey, the French ambassador, Latour-Maubourg, was full of cheap promises of the restoration of the Black Sea coast and the Crimea. In this instance, however, Napoleon paid the price for earlier faithlessness. In 1807 the Turks had been betrayed by Napoleon at Tilsit, and they now decided to settle with the Russians while they had the chance. On 28 May 1812 peace was finally signed, leaving an astonished Napoleon completely outflanked. As for the 50,000 Russians still on the Danube, now commanded by Admiral Chichagov, they were soon marching with all speed for White Russia. Indeed, had things gone as Chichagov planned, Russia would have gained still more from the situation. Why not, he argued, get the Turks to ally themselves with Russia and invade the Illyrian provinces while at the same time attacking the Austrians in the rear? Or, alternatively, in the absence of Turkish agreement to this plan, why not send Russian troops into Bosnia so as to whip up a great national insurrection amongst the Serbs, Croats and Slovenes of the Austrian empire and the Illyrian provinces? Though both schemes were very attractive to Alexander, nothing came of any of this: the Turks were not interested in fighting an offensive war, while the South Slav war of liberation was abandoned after a worried Metternich in effect promised to keep Austrian participation in the campaign to a minimum. There was, then, to be no Balkan front in the coming war, but even so the end of Russia's Turkish imbroglio was a major blow to Napoleon, as witness the fury with which he reacted to the news of peace.

In the Baltic, Napoleon also met with disappointment. As far as Sweden was concerned, he seems simply to have assumed that Bernadotte would join forces with him. Yet why he should have done so is unclear. The Continental Blockade had wrought much the same havoc in Sweden as it had done in Russia, and, like Alexander, Bernadotte knew that there were forces in the court and army that might very easily have him deposed or even murdered should he not satisfy their wishes. Meanwhile, the new crown prince still hated Napoleon, and had been much irritated by the fact that a scornful emperor showed no interest in giving Sweden Norway and had made it quite clear that if she wanted territorial gains she would have to fight for them in Finland, a region that Bernadotte was convinced had become untenable. Britain, by contrast, had proven much more proactive: in October 1811 the former British ambassador had paid a secret visit to Stockholm and promised Bernadotte he would be well rewarded should he ever go to war with Napoleon. Sweden was thus very much in the balance when the emperor committed an act of amazing folly. Moved by the purely military consideration that Swedish Pomerania might be the scene of a British amphibious landing, he ordered its occupation by French troops. The risk was in itself real enough, but since 1799 Britain's record in such operations had been mixed, and it is hard to see why the capture of Stralsund should have cost Napoleon much concern. However, in January 1812 French troops entered the Swedish enclave. There was no resistance, but Bernadotte was furious and immediately approached both London and St Petersburg in search of assistance. From the former came offers of arms, supplies (though not yet money) and an island in the West Indies, while from the latter came the promise of military and diplomatic support over the annexation of Norway. At the last moment Napoleon realized his error and hastily proffered Bernadotte some bribes of his own, but it was too late: on 5 April 1812 the Swedish government signed a treaty of alliance with Russia. About the only consolation was that Sweden's agreement with Russia was not much of a threat: desperate to win over Bernadotte, an increasingly worried Alexander accepted that no Swedish troops need land in Germany until Norway had been occupied, and even promised Bernadotte the help of 15,000 troops to secure this objective.

As both sides scrambled for allies and sought to free themselves from embarrassments elsewhere, they also prepared for war. On the French side, a stream of orders directed the creation of immense magazines of supplies in various eastern cities – one letter speaks of amassing sufficient biscuit, rice and forage at Danzig to sustain an army of 400,000 men and 50,000 horses for fifty days – the requisition of thousands of carts, wagons, horses and draught animals; the collection of up-to-date maps and topographical information; the establishment of new army corps; and the settlement of a thousand petty details of military organization. Also needed, of course, were fresh supplies of men: on 20 December 1811 a levy of 120,000 fresh conscripts was decreed in France, and the rulers of the surviving satellite states, the princes of the Confederation of the Rhine and France's assorted governors and viceroys were instructed to complete the recruitment of their forces and mobilize them for action. Typical was the letter dispatched to Marshal Davout, who was serving as Governor-General of the Grand Duchy of Warsaw: 'I see . . . that the Fifth, Tenth and Eleventh Regiments of Infantry, which should all muster 3,500 men, have all got only 2,500 or 2,600 . . . I see that the Ninth Regiment of Cavalry is only 400-strong: what is stopping it from fielding 1,000 riders? Make certain that all the units are up to strength. Men should not be lacking as the Duchy has 4 million inhabitants, which means that it should be able to provide 70,000 men . . . The Poles are only maintaining 42,000 men – only 10,000 men for every million inhabitants . . . Write to Prince Poniatowski and let him know how ridiculous this is.'[63]

There was still no open statement of intent – indeed, much of the correspondence is couched in terms of defending the Grand Duchy of Warsaw and the Confederation of the Rhine from attack – but there was no denying the urgency of Napoleon's language. On 27 January 1812, for example, Jerome Bonaparte received the following communication: 'The contingent of Your Majesty will be assembled and ready to march by 15 February. I request that you will let me have its strength in terms of generals, staff officers, infantry, cavalry and artillery, together with an account of its caissons and transport.'[64] And, last but not least, 27,000 men – two divisions of the Young Guard, some Guard cavalry and artillery and a Polish volunteer force known as the Legion of the Vistula – were withdrawn from Spain where several regions of the country were left dangerously undermanned. All this force was, in February 1812, set in motion for the east. In March the new *grande armée* began to stream into Prussia, and on 9 May Napoleon himself left Paris amidst much public display. But before he went to war one more task remained. First stop, though, was not the headquarters of the *grande armée*, but rather a great conference of all the German princes at Dresden. A dramatic act of political theatre, this was designed to emphasize the certainty of success and overawe any ruler foolish enough to think there might be any alternative to full cooperation. If one is to believe Napoleon's apologists, there was also the hope that in the face of this very public statement of support Alexander would even now back down. At all events the gathering, which was marked by balls, parades, receptions, banquets, reviews and firework displays, was a splendid affair. To quote Dominique Dufour de Pradt, a member of the Catholic hierarchy who had been appointed as 'ambassador extraordinary' to the Grand Duchy of Warsaw:

Anyone who wishes to give themselves a true idea of the commanding power which Napoleon exercised in Europe ... should transport themselves in imagination to Dresden so as to behold him at the period of his greatest glory ... His levee was, as usual, at nine o'clock, and only by being there could one possibly imagine the cringing submission with which a crowd of princes, confounded with the courtiers, who for the most part paid them but the slightest heed, awaited the moment of his appearance ... In effect, Napoleon was the God of Dresden, the ruler of all those rulers who appeared before him, the king of kings. It was on him that all eyes were turned; it was ... around him that the august hosts that filled the palace of the King of Saxony gathered. The sheer numbers of foreigners, military men and courtiers alike; the way in which couriers were constantly coming and going in all directions; the manner in which a crowd rushed to the palace on the least movement of the emperor, dogging his footsteps and gazing at him in a style that suggested a mixture of admiration and wonder; the expectation painted on every face ... offered the ... most imposing monument that was ever raised to the power of Napoleon. It was, without doubt, the highest point of his glory: while he might sustain it, to surpass it seemed impossible.[65]

Well might Napoleon celebrate his power. Assembling in Poland and East Prussia was the largest army ever seen in recorded history. In the front line were massed 490,000 men, while another 121,000 were following on behind them. Only 200,000 of these troops were ethnically French, however, the remainder – not counting the Prussian and Austrian contingents – being Germans, Poles, Italians, Belgians, Dutch, Croats, Swiss, Spaniards and Portuguese. Whether these men would fight effectively was unclear, while too many of them were mere boys of eighteen. Nor was morale high: there was much pessimism about the coming campaign. Yet when the full panoply of Napoleon's armed strength was finally revealed on the Russian frontier, it was a dazzling spectacle. Present with the emperor's headquarters was the painter Lejeune:

All the handsomest men of the day, in their most gorgeous martial costumes, mounted on the finest horses to be obtained in Europe, all alike richly caparisoned, were gathered about the central group of which we formed part. The sunbeams gleamed upon the bronze cannon ready to belch forth an all-destroying fire, and glinted back from the ... gilded, silvered and burnished steel helmets, breastplates, weapons and decorations of the soldiers and officers. The glittering bayonets of the masses of battalions covering the plain resembled from a distance the quivering scintillations in the sunshine of the waters of some lake ... when ruffled by a passing breeze. The crash of thousands of trumpets and drums mingled with the enthusiastic shouts of the vast multitude as the emperor came in sight, and the spectacle of all this devotion ... impressed us all with a sense of the invincibility of a force of elements so mixed, united in obedience to a single chief. Our confidence in that chief became yet more assured than ever ... and, when we looked round upon all the forces his mighty will had gathered together, our hearts beat high with joy and with exultant pride.[66]

In Russia too, of course, preparations for war had been going on for months. Under the direction of the extremely capable Minister of War, Mikhail Barclay de Tolly, a series of reforms had been enacted in the army in the hope of increasing its administrative efficiency, augmenting its operational flexibility and improving its training, while the Russian embassy in Paris had been exploited for all it was worth as a source of intelligence. Police surveillance of anyone suspected of political unreliability was intensified and since 1810 the populace had been subjected to three successive levies of conscripts that should in theory have produced 350,000 new recruits (in 1805, by contrast, the number of fresh troops raised to fight in the War of the Third Coalition had amounted to only 110,000 men). In all, the army now amounted to 490,000 men, and this total was augmented by a militia that had been organized in 1807, made up of serfs who in peacetime lived on the estates of their owners (whether this last force was of any value is another matter, however, one observer describing them as 'crowds of men ... collected regardless of age, poorly clothed and virtually unarmed').[67] During the course of 1811 and the first months of 1812, 220,000 men were sent to Lithuania and White Russia, where they were deployed in three separate armies, commanded by Barclay de Tolly, Bagration and Tormasov, of whom the first two were probably the very best of all Russia's generals. And on 21 April 1812 Alexander set out for Vilna to place himself at the head of his troops and secure the loyalty of the local gentry. There he found a region that could already bear witness to the rigour that was to characterize the Russian war effort. To quote one inhabitant of Vilna, 'I was struck with the misery of the country people, whom privation of the absolute necessities of life by the interruption of trade, the bad harvest of the preceding year, and the continual passage of troops and transports had entirely ruined ... The evil, as is always the case, weighed most heavily on the poor. The peasants lost their horses and even their cattle.'[68] History does not record how the populace felt about their sufferings. But among the soldiers, or at least their officers, there was much resolution. As one nobleman of Estonian stock, named Boris von Uxkull, wrote in his diary, 'What a sight, as novel as it is impressive, to see so many soldiers assembled, carrying out the decision of one person, governed by discipline, and inspired by the same unanimous courage and by the same feeling. The bearing of ... the infantry, especially, is magnificent. Very soon, perhaps, a battle will decide our destinies ... May the Almighty grant us the victory, for the right is on our side!'[69]

That Alexander was in earnest there is no doubt. But good intentions were not enough; also needed was a workable plan of campaign and a degree of unity at headquarters – and there was not much evidence of either. Though physically brave enough, Alexander himself was no general, and he also had a strong propensity to distrust native Russians in favour of men who were the products of Western civilization. Among the many foreigners who had fled to the Russian court was the Prussian staff officer Ernst von Pfuhl, a man who had singularly failed to distinguish himself in the Jena campaign but had succeeded in cultivating the air of a great military genius. Much impressed, Alexander allowed himself to be persuaded that Pfuhl had the secret of defeating Napoleon. As the German officer correctly divined, Alexander's instinct was to fight a defensive campaign that would exploit the difficulties that the *grande armée* would encounter in Russia to the full. 'If the Emperor Napoleon makes war on me,' Alexander told Caulaincourt, 'it is possible, even probable, that we shall be defeated, assuming that we fight. But that will not mean that he can dictate a peace . . . We shall take no risks. We have plenty of room . . . Our climate, our winter, will fight on our side.'[70] Sensing that these were the tsar's views, Pfuhl came up with a scheme that was neatly tailored to appeal not just to these ideas but to his vanity. In brief, a great fortified camp was to be constructed at Drissa on the river Dvina. Deep inside Russian territory – Drissa lies some 200 miles from the frontier – this was intended to fulfil the function that the Lines of Torres Vedras had played in Portugal and was to be garrisoned by the forces of Barclay de Tolly. While Cossacks devastated the country-side and deprived the French of food and shelter, Bagration would manoeuvre against their lines of communication and cut them off from the frontier.

Yet, as many of Alexander's Russian generals pointed out, this plan was little better than rank madness: Drissa was no Torres Vedras, while to have Barclay de Tolly and Bagration fight independently of one another was to hand Napoleon all the advantages of occupying the central position and risk defeat in detail, especially as everyone knew that the two commanders hated one another. Nor did it help that the ramparts and redoubts that had been thrown up on the Dvina proved to have been badly planned and constructed. 'Having observed the camp,' wrote General Yermolev, 'the commander-in-chief found it had been built for larger forces than those now deployed there . . . and noted that many fortifications had unsatisfactory communications between each other which weakened their common defence, while the enemy had favourable approaches to some of them . . . Even these flaws could not describe all the errors of this camp, deficiencies that were obvious to anyone proficient in military matters.'[71] Pfuhl, then, was scorned, but many of his Russian rivals were no better, fondly imagining that Alexander's forces could invade Poland and defeat Napoleon, when this was not only most unlikely, but also certain to play straight into the emperor's hands. Yet Alexander was not strong enough to hold his course and till the last moment wavered in his resolution. While retreating made sense, he could not forget the fate of his father and was unwilling to abandon the western frontier without a fight. Refuge was found in procrastination: no general council of war was held, while life in Vilna was characterized by endless balls and receptions. In the end, indeed, only once the French had actually crossed the frontier were orders given to implement the Drissa plan, and even then this was, in the words of Sir Robert Wilson, who was present at the tsar's headquarters, 'an announcement of great mortification to Alexander'.[72]

To return to the diplomatic situation, even now there had been no formal breach in Franco-Russian relations: both emperors gave out that they were merely embarking on extended tours of inspection. But the tension was extreme and matters soon came to a head. Prior to Napoleon's departure for the east, Kurakin presented him with Russia's definitive terms: Napoleon must withdraw completely from Prussia, evacuate Swedish Pomerania and accept Russia's right to establish the same system of trade licences Napoleon had permitted in metropolitan France, the quid pro quo being that Alexander promised to uphold the remaining provisions of the Continental Blockade. Needless to say, this note was ignored, and Kurakin announced that he was returning to Russia. This, however, did not suit Napoleon at all – to have let the Russians have the last say in the diplomatic exchanges that preceded the outbreak of hostilities would have been to risk being portrayed as the aggressor. Kurakin was therefore detained in Paris on the pretext that the emperor wished to make one last attempt to contact Alexander and the claim was assiduously spread that Napoleon wanted a peaceful settlement. To carry the fiction still further, one of Napoleon's aides-de-camp, the Comte de Narbonne, was dispatched to Vilna to seek an audience with the tsar. There was, however, no budging Alexander:

I shall not be the first to draw the sword. I have no wish to be saddled in the eyes of Europe with the responsibility of the blood that will be shed in this war. For eighteen months I have been threatened. The French army is 300 leagues from its own country and actually on my frontiers, whereas I am on my own territory ... The Emperor Napoleon ... is raising Austria, Germany, Prussia, all Europe, in arms against Russia ... I am under no illusions. I render too much justice to his military talents not to have calculated all the risks that an appeal to arms may involve for us, but, having done all that I could to ... uphold a political system which might lead to universal peace, I will do nothing to besmirch the honour of the nation over which I rule ... All the bayonets ... waiting at my frontiers will not make me speak otherwise ... Can the Emperor Napoleon, in all good faith, demand explanations when, in a time of total peace, he invades the north of

Germany, when he fails to observe the engagements of the alliance and carry out the principles of his Continental System? Is it not he who should explain his motives?[73]

From this moment the die was cast. On 16 June Kurakin was finally allowed to leave Paris, and eight days later the first French troops crossed the river Niemen. At the prompting of Rumiantsev, who had to the end opposed war, some days into the campaign Alexander sent a special emissary to Napoleon asking him to withdraw immediately in exchange for a promise of negotiations on the basis of the conditions Kurakin had communicated to him in April. Encountering Napoleon at Vilna, the envoy was treated in the most scornful fashion, however – 'Alexander is laughing at me. Does he imagine that I have come to Vilna to negotiate trade treaties?'[74] – and thus it was that the wars of Napoleon entered their last and most momentous phase.

In the east, all was set for a fresh conflict. As yet, however, it was limited to Eastern Europe. Other than the informal promises she had made to Bernadotte, Britain had played no part in events, and still had almost no contact with St Petersburg. Indeed, right up until the outbreak of hostilities she was still formally at war with both Russia and Sweden. Keen to emphasize his liberationist credentials, meanwhile, Napoleon even called the struggle 'the second Polish war' (the first one was the campaign of 1807), and in this he was supported by the enthusiastic response of nationalistic elements in the Grand Duchy of Warsaw. An officer of the Legion of the Vistula has left us this picture of the reception that Napoleon received when he passed through Posen, for example:

[The emperor] arrived at nine in the evening, escorted by a detachment of French and Polish Guards. He was met by a welcome as enthusiastic as the one in 1806. There were triumphal arches, illuminations and fireworks everywhere, marking the hopes of a people confident in the future ... A huge crowd choked the streets, which were as light as in any daylight. The population of the surrounding countryside had gathered to take part in the celebrations and were camping in all of the town's squares.[75]

Though Napoleon's attempts to place a favourable gloss upon his actions should be viewed sceptically, the specifically eastern aspect of the conflict should not be forgotten. If Poland was ever to be restored, if the Ottoman Empire was ever to regain the territory she had lost to

Russia in the course of the eighteenth century, if Sweden was to be restored to a position of predominance in the Baltic, if the steady expansion of Russian rule towards the west and south was ever to be checked, this was the moment at which it had to be achieved. Embedded in the war of 1812, in short, were several important themes in the history of European international relations that both predated and transcended the history of Napoleon Bonaparte.

Attempts to find a structural explanation for the war of 1812 should not be pushed too far, however. If the issues of Poland, Turkish control of the Ukraine and Swedish control of the Baltic had all been reopened, it was solely because of the influence of Napoleon, while the attack on Russia was intimately bound up with the war with Britain. To accept this, however, is not the same as accepting that Napoleon was somehow forced into war on account of Britain's continued resistance. Alexander and his advisers remained deeply anti-British and even in 1812 were willing seconds of the French on that front. As for the idea of a march on India, if Napoleon ever took this seriously – and there is little real evidence that he did – then questions really must be asked about his sanity. Nor is self-defence any use as an explanation: whatever the emperor may have claimed, there was no evidence that Alexander was still planning an offensive war. One is left, then, with one explanation, and one explanation alone: frustrated by the long war in Spain and Portugal, and the failure of the Continental Blockade to bring the British to heel, Napoleon was simply bent on flexing his military muscle and winning fresh glory. Here is the verdict of one of the many soldiers about to experience the horrors of the Russian campaign:

The treaty of [Schönbrunn] . . . crowned the prosperity of the fortunate Napoleon . . . since it secured forever the dynasty of a man, who [had] risen from the humblest rank of society . . . That period ought to have been esteemed the happiest of Napoleon's life. What more could the wildest ambition desire? From a private individual he saw himself raised to the first throne of the world; his reign had been one continued series of victories; and to complete his happiness, a son, the object of his most ardent wishes, was born to succeed him. The people, though oppressed under his government, became accustomed to it, and seemed desirous to secure the crown to his family. All the foreign princes who were subjected to his power were his vassals . . . Nothing was wanting to make him happy! Nothing – if he could be happy who possessed not a love of justice. To that sentiment Napoleon had ever been a stranger and consequently knew not enjoyment or repose. Agitated by a reckless spirit and tormented by ungovernable ambition, the very excess of his fortune was his ruin . . . Continually tormented by spleen and melancholy, the least contradiction irritated him . . . and poisoned the happiest moments of his glory . . . Despot over his people . . . and a slave to his ungovernable passions, he . . . adopted a false line of politics, and converted . . . the most useful and powerful of his allies into a dangerous enemy.[76]

10

Downfall

The first rule of warfare, Field-Marshal Montgomery once said, is *not* to march on Moscow. When the *grande armée* poured across the river Niemen on 24 June 1812, however, there was no thought of marching so far into the depths of Russia: what was intended was a very different campaign that would have given Napoleon fresh allies in Eastern Europe and in effect blackmailed Alexander into submission. To the surprise of most observers, this scheme went wrong, and in the process an essentially eastern conflict was subsumed into the broader history of the Napoleonic Wars and ended up becoming a general onslaught on France of a sort not seen even in the great crisis of 1793. In this development, the terrible human catastrophe that resulted from the march on Moscow was to play its part, but it should be remembered that in the end even defeat in Russia was not enough to bring about the general uprising against the Napoleonic imperium that was finally to bring it down. The retreat from Moscow did not shake the emperor's hold on France, Italy or Germany, and even in the dark days of 1813 he could have escaped with much of his power intact. That Napoleon did not do so is related not so much to the intransigence of the *ancien régime* as to his own lack of realism and failure of perception, not to mention his tacit acceptance that he was either a successful warlord or he was nothing. As he said, 'Death is nothing, but to live defeated and inglorious is to die daily.' The result being a refusal to compromise even in the face of the most desperate odds, the ranks of his foes grew so numerous that even Napoleon could not hold his own against them and, in trying to do so, strained the loyalties of France to such an extent that she turned her back on him.

Once again, then, the personal dimension was crucial. To the end Napoleon claimed he was fighting for France and that he could not accept a peace that was dishonourable for France. But if he truly believed this argument, the wholesale identification of his own interests with those of France is but one more example of the way in which the emperor deceived himself, if not those around him. Just as unhelpful was the way in which he constantly stressed, even after defeat in Russia, that there was no challenge that he and his armies could not surmount. The litany was a constant one: 'Victory belongs to the most persevering'; 'The moral is to the physical as three is to one'; 'How many things apparently impossible have nevertheless been performed by resolute men who had no alternative but death?'; 'Impossible is a word to be found only in the dictionary of fools', 'Great men seldom fail in their most perilous enterprises'; 'The word impossible is not in my dictionary.' In short, just as Napoleon had not understood the realities of strength in victory, in defeat he did not understand the realities of weakness, all his bravura coming down to little more than a willingness to stake France's all on a series of ever more improbable throws of the dice. In this, however, there lay but one hope – that somehow the coalition facing him would fall apart and thereby restore him to the position that he had been able to exploit so well prior to 1812. With every day that passed, however, Napoleon's conduct made this prospect ever less likely, the end result being ultimately a coalition the like of which the revolutionary and Napoleonic Wars had never seen.

In 1812, however, all this was far away. Indeed, as he explained to Metternich at Dresden, his plan of campaign was relatively rational:

My enterprise is one of those of which the solution is to be found in patience . . . I shall open the campaign by crossing the Niemen. It will be concluded at Smolensk or Minsk. There I shall stop. I shall fortify these two points, and occupy myself at Vilna, where the chief headquarters will be during the next winter, with the organization of Lithuania, which burns with impatience to be delivered from the yoke of Russia. I shall wait and see which of us tires first: I of feeding my army at the expense of Russia, or Alexander at the expense of sustaining my army at the expense of his country.[1]

With Napoleon the great exponent of the concept of the decisive battle, it is a little odd to find him discussing the campaign in terms of the occupation of territory. But battle remained at the heart of the emperor's intentions. If the Russians advanced, as he hoped, he would envelop them from the north and west somewhere in the region of the river

Narew: 'If the enemy takes the offensive on the right bank of the river Narew . . . he will present his flank to the Viceroy [i.e. Prince Eugène], who will fall upon his right. If he does so between the Narew and the Bug, V Corps and VIII Corps will be able to move via Ostrolenka and Pultusk and achieve the same effect.'² Supposing they did not move, however, the day of reckoning would simply come elsewhere. While Napoleon crossed the Niemen at Kovno with the majority of his forces, and marched directly on Vilna, supported to his right rear by two corps under Eugène de Beauharnais, the four corps forming his right wing, which had been placed under the somewhat unlikely figure of Jerome Bonaparte, were to fix in place the Second West Army of General Bagration. Striking south towards the impassable Pripet marshes, Napoleon would then cut Bagration's communications and smash his forces, together, it was hoped, with Barclay's centre and left.

What all this assumed was that the Russians would fight for Vilna. As Napoleon acknowledged, even a limited advance into Russia posed many problems. That he clearly recognized this is suggested by a conversation he had with Pasquier on the eve of his departure from Paris, in which he referred to the forthcoming campaign as 'the greatest and most difficult enterprise that I have ever attempted'.³ In consequence, everything possible had been done to ease the passage of the *grande armée*. In addition to the establishment of immense supply depots at Königsberg and other towns, the number of transport battalions was raised from fourteen to twenty-three, of which fifteen served in Russia, and the size of the individual units was greatly increased. Between the thousands of wagons in these battalions and the packs of the troops themselves, there were sufficient rations for twenty-four days, a far more generous allowance than in many previous campaigns. And more supplies could be brought up from the rear. If Kovno and Vilna were selected as the main point of penetration into Russia, it was in part because the river Niemen was navigable as far as the latter city. Yet within a very short time it became clear that even in the vicinity of the frontier the French faced immense problems. Even before the invasion began there were reports of trouble. On 20 June, for example, Poniatowski reported from Novogrodek that his men were going short: 'Thanks to the country's want of resources . . . the question of supply is becoming more difficult by the day, and it is only with the greatest efforts that it has been possible to issue the proper rations. Indeed, I have just been forced to order them to be reduced by half until such time as we have got in more in the way of subsistence.'[4]

Once the frontier had been crossed, things grew even worse. The forces led by Napoleon himself were immediately struck by violent thunderstorms and even freak blizzards, which caused havoc. Present with the Imperial Guard was Captain Coignet. 'I was half-dead with the cold: not being able to stand it any longer, I opened one of my wagons and crept inside. Next morning a heart-rending sight met our gaze: in the cavalry camp nearby, the ground was covered with horses frozen to death.'[5] Given the quagmires which the appalling roads quickly became, the wagon trains could not keep up with the troops. Yet the troops only had sufficient biscuit for four days. Present with the Würt-temberg contingent was a twenty-four-year-old infantryman named Jakob Walter:

We . . . believed that, once in Russia, we need do nothing but forage – which, however, proved to be an illusion. The town of Poniemon was already stripped before we could enter and so were all the villages. Here and there a hog ran around and then was beaten with clubs, chopped with sabres, and, often still living, it would be cut and torn to pieces. Several times I succeeded in cutting off something, but I had to chew it and eat it uncooked, since my hunger could not wait for a chance to boil the meat . . . Meanwhile, it rained ceaselessly for several days, and the rain was cold. It was all the more disagreeable because nothing could be dried . . . During the third night a halt was made in a field which was trampled into a swamp . . . You can imagine in what a half-numbed condition everyone stood here . . . There was nothing that we could do but stack the [muskets] in pyramids and keep moving in order not to freeze.[6]

Things were not much better in any other unit, and the roads, such as they were, were soon littered with the corpses of men and horses. Dysentery struck many units, and huge numbers of horses – 10,000 in the main army alone, according to Caulaincourt – literally dropped dead from overwork and undernourishment. Desperate to make progress, French commanders made extreme demands of their men all along the line. The vanguard of the main army, for example, covered the seventy miles from Kovno to Vilna in just two days. But this only made things worse, and by the time the Lithuanian capital was taken the number of dead and missing may already have amounted to 25,000 men. And, finally, for all the *grande armée*'s forced marches, both Barclay de Tolly and Bagration had successfully evaded the French spearheads and got away into the interior: indeed, hardly a shot had yet been fired.

It might be thought that such difficulties would have been sufficient to persuade Napoleon that a political settlement was essential, particularly as it was at Vilna that news reached him of Russia's peace settlement with Turkey. Yet Alexander's last-minute peace proposals were, as we have seen, simply scorned, and that despite the fact that a major pillar of Napoleon's strategy was falling apart around the very doors of his headquarters. We come here to the question of the invaders' relationship with the local populace. The war had been billed as one of liberation, and it was Napoleon's intention at the very least to set up some form of political base for his operations in Lithuania. Winning over the populace was not very high on the agenda of the *grande armée*, however. Major Faber du Faur, an artillery officer, like Walter a member of the Württemberg division, wrote:

There has never been a campaign in which the troops have relied so much on living off the land, but it was the way in which it was done in Russia that caused such universal suffering – for the soldiers of the army as well as the inhabitants. Because of its rapid marches and its enormous size, the army faced a dearth of everything and it was impossible to procure the barest necessity. It was around the time that we reached Ewe that one can date the start of this fatal requisitioning and the destruction of the surrounding countryside, which, naturally, had devastating consequences. Everyday as we broke camp, we could see clouds of marauders ... make off in all directions ... to find the barest of all essentials. They would return to the camp in the evening laden with their booty. Inevitably, this kind of behaviour made an unfortunate impression on Lithuania, which had so long been under the yoke of Russia and, instead of any benefit from its new alliance, saw only the oppression wrought by its new allies.[7]

The impact of all this on the local populace was most severe. Among those who awaited the coming of the emperor was the young Sophie Tisenhaus, whose father was one of Vilna's most ardent supporters of the restoration of Poland:

The French army, as they entered Vilna, had not taken bread for three days. All the bakers in the town were immediately employed in the service of the troops, and . . . want was cruelly felt by the inhabitants of Vilna . . . The country through which the Grand Army had passed had been ravaged and pillaged, and its corn had been cut green for the cavalry; it could not, therefore, supply the needs of the capital, and the people dared not expose their convoys on the roads, which were infested by marauders. Besides, the disorderly behaviour of the army was a consequence of the sentiments of its chief, for, having crossed the Niemen, Napoleon . . . declared to his troops that they were about to set foot on Russian territory . . . In consequence of this proclamation, Lithuania was treated as a hostile country, while its inhabitants, animated by patriotic enthusiasm, flew to welcome the French. They were soon to be despoiled and outraged by those whom they regarded as the instrument of the deliverance of their country, and compelled to abandon their homes and their property to pillage. Many took refuge in the depths of the forests . . . Each day brought the recital of new excesses committed by the French soldiers in the country . . . In the meantime, French arrogance . . . expected all obstacles to be removed, all difficulties to disappear . . . 'There is no patriotism among you,' said the French, 'no energy, no vigour!'[8]

Nor was pillage the only public relations disaster suffered by the invaders. Thus, Napoleon not only made no announcement of Lithuania's incorporation into the Grand Duchy of Warsaw but publicly made slighting remarks about the local nobility and bluntly informed a delegation that reached him from the Polish capital that he would do nothing to disturb his relations with the emperor of Austria – that Poland, in short, would never be restored to the totality of 1772. A provisional administration was established in Vilna, but enthusiasm was notably absent. 'The inhabitants seemed little disposed to respond to the appeals made to their patriotism,' wrote Caulaincourt. 'The pillage and disorders of all kinds in which the army had indulged had put the whole countryside to flight. In the towns the more respectable people kept within doors. Whatever the zeal of those Poles who had come with the army, the emperor had to send for any of the responsible persons of Vilna whom he might require, for not a soul presented himself or offered his services.'[9] With great effort, a Lithuanian army was eventually formed, but it never amounted to more than 10,000 men, was the product of hunger rather than enthusiasm and hardly saw action before disintegrating in the horrors of the retreat from Moscow. Indeed, even the nobility were slow to come forward: in June 1812 the whole district of Vilna 'could not furnish more than twenty men for Napoleon's guard of honour'.[10]

If Napoleon's policy was bedevilled by contradictions in Vilna, the same was also true in Warsaw. Great hopes had been fostered among Polish nationalists in the run-up to war, and there was much excitement. 'As soon as the news spread that war had broken out,' wrote the Countess Potocka, 'on all sides the young sprang to arms, and that before anyone had asked them to do so. Neither the menaces of Russia, nor the prudence . . . of their parents, could check their patriotic spirit . . . Children listened with feverish curiosity to the stories of their elders, and burned with ardour . . . Anyone without a uniform did not dare to show themselves in the streets for fear of being mocked by urchins.'[11] But Napoleon, less enamoured of the Poles than his public position suggests, realized that pushing the Polish question too far was folly, for his attack on Russia needed the active cooperation of Prussia and Austria. To act upon his rhetoric of liberation was therefore impossible. As his aide-de-camp, Lejeune, wrote:

Deputations of Polish noblemen arrived in rapid succession, eager to persuade him to decree the restoration of the Kingdom of Poland, and promising him . . . the loyal cooperation of the whole Polish nation . . . There is little doubt that Napoleon would gladly have met their wishes immediately, for an independent Poland would have been a steadfast ally to France, and have protected us from an invasion from the north . . . It must, however, be remembered that the emperor was terribly hampered in any decision as to Poland by the fact that he would not only have to dispose of that portion of the dismembered kingdom still in the grasp of Russia, but also of the provinces . . . assigned by treaty to Prussia and Austria respectively. Now Prussian and Austrian battalions were marching in line with ours . . . but there was no doubt that at the slightest hint of the emperor's intentions to take from their princes their [remaining] portion of the spoils of the old Kingdom of Poland, every Austrian and Prussian would have left our ranks to join those of the Russians. Napoleon . . . therefore . . . needed all his diplomatic skill . . . to evade destroying the hopes of the Poles or making any definite promise to them.[12]

To deal with the problem, a special diet of the Polish nobility was assembled at Warsaw under the presidency of no less a person than the father of Prince Adam Czartoryski, and allowed to proclaim itself to be a 'general confederation of the Polish nation'. Opening the deliberations of this body, meanwhile, Napoleon's 'ambassador-extraordinary', Dufour de Pradt, made vague promises of freedom, only to discover that the deputies voiced demands beyond anything his master was prepared to contemplate. After just three days, then, the Diet was dissolved and replaced by a small council of administration. Yet this was not the most politic of moves. At Tilsit the Poles had seen the emperor surrender the interests of Poland to his need for an alliance with Russia, and now, with 75,000 men under arms in the *grande armée* and her economy ruined by the Continental Blockade, the Grand Duchy of Warsaw was in a state of complete bankruptcy. On top of this, Poland, like East Prussia, had now been devastated by the concentration of the *grande armée*. 'The depredations of the army, and its agents,' wrote Pradt, 'had not ceased for an instant. I remember a little Jew whom I passed on the road to Warsaw and asked for news. "News?" he wryly replied. "There is not a thing to eat." '[13] But, it now transpired, all this was for nothing, all that had changed being that the emperor was sacrificing Poland's interests in favour of Austria and Prussia rather than Russia. The result, needless to say, was disillusionment in the army – so far as Napoleon was concerned, one cavalry officer concluded, 'the Poles have never been anything but an instrument of convenience'[14] – and apathy on the home front. 'The grandees, some elements of the lesser nobility and the so-called liberal professions remained in a state of excitement . . . but the mass of the nation turned their backs on the movement . . . The Poles may have wanted the restoration of their fatherland, but they did not want to achieve this at the cost of devastation and absolute ruin.'[15] And if Poland was apathetic, Prussia was downright hostile. Reduced to penury by the passage of the *grande armée*, its inhabitants were sullen and resentful. In charge of a depot of replacement horses for the artillery, Jean Noël complained, 'All of them, especially those in authority, did everything they could to harm our army. Our dealings with them were most unpleasant.'[16]

As the campaign unfolded, for a short while it looked as though a reduced version of Napoleon's master-plan might still be realizable. Barclay's army had got away to the east and north-east, but the forces of Bagration, though themselves in retreat, were still within reach. From Vilna, Marshal Davout's I Corps was hastily flung southwards and orders were dispatched to Jerome to abandon the defensive posture originally envisaged for him and press north-eastwards with all speed. Famously, however, the scheme went wrong: Jerome's forces did not arrive in time, and Bagration escaped. For this failure the King of Westphalia has been widely blamed, an opinion shared by Napoleon, who sharply reproved his brother and placed him under the control of Davout (as Davout and Jerome were old enemies, the latter took umbrage and promptly went home to Kassel). However, the balance of opinion is now that Jerome was hard done by. As a commander he was undoubtedly mediocre, but the situation facing him was quite imposs-ible. His men were deployed much further to the rear than the rest of the *grande armée*: at the onset of the campaign, indeed, they were anything up to 200 miles from the frontier. The fruit of Napoleon's desire to keep back his right so as to lure the Russian centre and left into a trap, this could not easily be undone when the orders came for Jerome to move forward. To get to their first objective – the town of Grodno – the troops had to follow a track barely wide enough to take a single wagon that wound for mile after mile through impenetrable forests, while the rain came down in sheets. Not until 30 June did they reach Grodno, and by then the troops were so exhausted that Jerome gave them two day's rest. Having already lost one sixth of his men, on 4 July he pushed on again in baking heat, but it was too late: he still had 100 miles to cover, and by the time he had reached his destination Bagration had long since gone.

Within a very few days, then, several factors had become clear. The physical problems of operating inside Russia were likely to be very great, if not insurmountable. The support of the local populace, non-Russian though it was, could not be counted upon. Horses and men alike were at serious risk of death by starvation and disease. The *grande armée* was so cumbersome and Russian distances so great it was going to prove almost impossible to set up the sort of battle of encirclement dreamed of by Napoleon. And, finally, the emperor could no longer exercise the sort of personal control that had been so important in earlier campaigns. At this point, in military terms, the best thing for Napoleon to have done would have been to abandon offensive operations, thin out his troops, consolidate the loyalty of the Poles and Lithuanians and wait for Alexander either to negotiate or to launch a counter-offensive. But this the emperor refused to do even though it fitted in perfectly with the general scheme of operations he had outlined to Metternich at Dresden. Such was the image he had created of himself that he was now its prisoner. 'Napoleon did not hesitate,' wrote Ségur. 'He had not been able to stop at Paris; should he then retreat at Vilna? What would Europe think of him? What result could he offer to the French and Allied armies as a motive for so many fatigues, such vast movements, such enormous individual and national expenditure? It would be at once confessing himself beaten.'[17] To quote another observer of the scene in Vilna, 'The fatal genius of Napoleon pushed him forward, and it was thus that, from illusion to illusion, he rushed to his ruin, rejecting the truth as an apparition whose presence he could not endure.'[18]

On 9 July, Napoleon left Vilna in search of the victory that every day made more pressing. But, of course, it was not to be found. Evading another French envelopment at Vitebsk, the Russians succeeded in concentrating their forces at Smolensk, leaving the invaders to lumber slowly along in their wake. And as Napoleon advanced so his forces disintegrated. In the first place the soldiers had to trudge along in the most overpowering heat. In the second, the already chaotic logistical situation collapsed altogether, the troops outstripping their now much diminished supply trains and discovering that the poor and thinly populated borderlands were unable to meet their requirements, matters being made still worse by the fact that the countryside in their path had also, of course, been devastated by the retreating Russians. Food was extremely scarce and in places even water was almost unobtainable. As Walter wrote, 'The men were growing weaker and weaker every day and the companies smaller and smaller ... One man after another stretched himself half-dead upon the ground; most of them died a few hours later ... The chief cause of this was thirst, for in most districts there was no water fit for drinking, so that the men had to drink out of ditches in which were lying dead horses and dead men. I often marched away from the columns for several hours in search of water, but seldom could I return with any ... All the towns not only were completely stripped, but also half-burned.'[19] As Caulaincourt admitted, the situation was catastrophic:

It had been hoped to obtain some supplies at Vitebsk, but the place was practically deserted. Moreover, the capital cities of these great Russian provinces were of less use than the smallest towns in Germany. Too much accustomed to relying upon the resources of the country, we had reckoned on being able to do the same in Russia . . . The lack of order, the indiscipline of the troops and even of the Guard, robbed us of the few means that remained at our disposal. Never was there a situation more deplorable . . . for those who could think and who had not been dazzled by the false glamour of glory and ambition . . . The innumerable wagons, the enormous quantity of supplies of all sorts that had been collected at such expense during the course of two years, had vanished through theft or loss, or through lack of means to bring them up. The rapidity of the forced marches, the shortage of harness and spare parts, the dearth of provisions, the want of care, had all helped to kill the horses . . . Disorder reigned everywhere: in the town as in the country around, everyone was in want.[20]

With tens of thousands of men and horses gone, much of what remained of his forces scattered all over the country in search of food, large numbers of troops detached to protect his line of communications, and the heat unendurable, even Napoleon seems to have considered giving up. 'I have,' he privately confessed, 'marched too far.'[21] Contributing to this dark mood was yet another missed battle: believing that Bagration was on the verge of joining him, on 26 July Barclay de Tolly turned at bay before Vitebsk and made ready to fight. Had Napoleon been able to attack immediately, he might well have struck the blow he so wanted, but his troops were not able to come up quickly enough and, hearing that Bagration had been delayed, Barclay was able to slip away again. On 28 July the French entered Vitebsk and with it took the easternmost city of pre-1772 Poland. All Lithuania, therefore, had been conquered. Also the rivers Dvina and Dnieper afforded the French a viable defensive line, especially as hopes were high that a flanking column that Marshal Macdonald had been leading towards the Baltic would soon take the fortress of Riga and thereby secure the *grande armée*'s left flank. 'Here I stop!' Napoleon exclaimed. 'Here I must look around me, rally, refresh my army and organize Poland. The campaign of 1812 is finished.'[22]

But this resolution did not last for very long. After a few days the army's stragglers started to come in and the troops became more rested and a little better fed. Meanwhile, Napoleon had been hoping the Russians would launch a counter-attack and afford him the chance of a knock-out blow that would force Alexander to make peace. No such offensive materialized, however, and very soon the emperor's resolve began to waver:

When he found himself somewhat refreshed by repose, when no envoy from Alexander made his appearance and his first dispositions were completed, he was seized with impatience. He was observed to grow restless. Perhaps it was that inactivity annoyed him ... and that he preferred danger to the weariness of expectation, or that he was agitated by that desire of acquisition which, with the majority of mankind, has greater influence than the pleasure of preserving or the fear of losing ... He was seen to pace his apartments as if pursued by some dangerous temptation. Nothing could fix his attention. Every moment he began, quitted and resumed his occupation. He walked about without any purpose, enquired the hour and remarked the weather. Completely absorbed, he stopped, then hummed a tune with an absent air and again began pacing. In the midst of his perplexity he occasionally addressed the people he met with such phrases as 'Well, what are we to do? Shall we stay where we are or advance? How is it possible to stop short in the midst of so glorious a career?' He did not wait for their reply, but still kept wandering about as if he was looking for someone or something to end his indecision.[23]

Military logic dictated only one decision, and Napoleon's head-quarters was not short of those desperate for the emperor to recognize the realities of his situation. Caulaincourt, Marshal Berthier, who was, as usual, serving as Napoleon's chief-of-staff, the emperor's aides-de-camp, Narbonne, Lebrun and Mouton, and the intendant-general, Daru, all sought to persuade their master to remain on the defensive. But they were countered by Joachim Murat who, though glad enough of a tem-porary halt to rest his troops, was urging a fresh advance. At the same time, such a course was a tempting prospect. Among the French troops especially, morale had far from broken down: many were spoiling for a fight and, convinced Napoleon was the only man who could save them, cheered him whenever he appeared; To the east of Vitebsk the country-side was more fertile and densely cultivated than it was in the marshes and forests of the western borderlands; and, as the forces of Bagration and Barclay de Tolly had at last managed to concentrate at Smolensk, the main weight of Russia's military power was little more than a hundred miles to the east. Though the Russian armies had succeeded in coming together, they still numbered no more than 120,000 men. In short, a heavy blow might still have been decisive, for with the bulk of the Russian field army gone, Alexander would at the very least have had to consider his options.

We come now to the question of popular Russian responses to the struggle. This is too complicated to be dealt with here at any length, but there is considerable evidence to suggest that the peasants remained hostile to serfdom and conscription alike. The famous 'scorched earth' policy that bedevilled the French was the work not of the people themselves, but of the forces of the state. If the region of Vitebsk was anything to go by, in fact, the serfs were on the brink of revolt. 'The neighbouring peasants,' wrote Berthier's aide-de-camp, the Duc de Fézensac, 'hearing of nothing but liberty and independence, conceived themselves justified in rising against their masters, and conducted themselves with the most unrestrained licence.'[24] This feeling had not been deliberately whipped up by Napoleon – he had refused to countenance such a course and had the disturbances suppressed. But clearly, peasant unrest would make it much harder for Alexander to call up fresh troops, and the emperor was, by extension, given grounds for hope. This proved fatal: 'The sight of his soldiers' enthusiasm at the sight of him, the reviews and parades, and, above all, the frequently coloured reports of the King of Naples and other generals, went to his head ... He was obsessed once more by his illusions and returned to his gigantic projects.'[25] To justify his thinking, Napoleon used all sorts of specious arguments – one example was his claim that the French military machine was an instrument more suited to attack than defence – but those around him were not fooled. As Ségur wrote, 'What would be thought if it were known that a third of his army ... were no longer in the ranks? It was indispensable, therefore, to dazzle the world quickly with the brilliance of a great victory and hide so many sacrifices under a heap of laurels.'[26]

Closely connected with these thoughts was the idea that the *grande armée* might dictate peace to Alexander from Moscow. Napoleon had vaguely mentioned such a prospect at various times but it was only at Vitebsk that the idea of reaching that city became prominent in his conversation. The emperor was clearly excited by the idea but there was no clear decision to march on Moscow. When the 182,000 men who remained available to Napoleon in the vicinity of Vitebsk set off on 12 August, the objective of the *grande armée* remained the defeat of the Russian army. Striking south to the river Dnieper, Napoleon got his men across the river, and then turned east towards Smolensk. Once again, the aim was to trap Bagration and Barclay, whose troops were mostly scattered to the west and north-west of the city, but a gallant fight on the part of an isolated Russian division caught at Krasnoye held up the encirclement while Napoleon also wasted some time on a grand review held in honour of his birthday on 15 August. Not until 17 August did the *grande armée* mount a full-scale attack, and by then the two Russian generals had managed to concentrate all their troops around the city. Moreover, still more fumbling on the part of the French – and especially, Napoleon himself – allowed the Russians to escape yet again after two days' fighting. With them there probably went the emperor's last chance of victory. At all events, he was visibly angered: 'At around five in the evening [of 19 August] we caught sight of the emperor riding along the Moscow road. He seemed much displeased and galloped past the soldiers without seeming to notice their acclamations.'[27]

Smolensk, it will be recalled, had been the furthest point Napoleon had considered advancing to at the start of the campaign, and even now the way was open to him to revert to the defensive strategy that had been considered at Vitebsk: so far as this was concerned, indeed, the capture of the fortified bastion Smolensk represented could be considered an important gain. The march on Smolensk, meanwhile, had been accompanied by the same difficulties as before. 'At this time,' wrote an officer, François, 'the army was much diminished ... by dysentery, by which many of the soldiers were attacked. This disease was caused by the scarcity of bread, which obliged the soldiers to live chiefly on meat ... The stagnant marsh water we drank also contributed to spread the disease. Few of the men, or even of the generals were exempt from it. The hospitals were full of sick, who had but little medical aid, for the ambulances and medicines remained in the rear.'[28] After a brief let-up in the wake of the departure from Vitebsk, the heat was again, as Napoleon himself put it, 'frightful'.[29] As for Smolensk, it had been a terrible fight, and the sights and sounds of the battlefield seem for a moment to have given even Napoleon pause. Nor did it help that the *grande armée*'s communications and foraging parties were beginning to be plagued by bands of desperate peasants who, if they were in fact motivated by nothing more than hunger and a visceral desire for revenge, none the less were a source of considerable concern. As Yermolev remembered, 'We had previously passed through Lithuania where the nobility, keeping the hopes of restoring Poland alive, agitated the feeble minds of the peasants against us. In Byelorussia, too, the oppressive authority of the landlords forced the peasants to desire change. However, here, around Smolensk, people were ready to see us as their saviours. It was impossible to express more hatred towards the enemy, or a more fervent desire to assist us . . . The peasants came to me with a question; could they take up arms against the enemy themselves and not be held responsible for it by the state?'[30] Faced by the uncertainty of catching the Russians, Napoleon therefore talked to Caulaincourt of halting the advance and even sent off a Russian officer who had been taken prisoner with an offer of peace terms. At the same time a crazy demand on the part of Poniatowski to be allowed to lead the bulk of the Polish forces in a march on Poland's erstwhile territories in the Ukraine was quashed.

In the end, however, caution came to nothing. Excited by false reports that the Russians were making a stand on the river Ouja, Napoleon urged his men on again. It was from the start a desperate gamble, though, and it was soon clear the emperor's luck had run out:

The army marched in three columns . . . It was impossible to come up with the enemy's infantry. Our advanced guard had only to contend with their light cavalry, which defended themselves no longer than was necessary to allow time for the main body to pursue its retreat unmolested . . . The emperor, expecting each day that the Russians would stop their rearward movement and give battle, allowed himself to be thus drawn on towards Moscow without bestowing a thought on the fatigue which his troops underwent, and without considering that he was no longer in communication with the rest of his army.[31]

The march, in fact, was a nightmare:

The further we advanced the more desolate became the country. Every village had been burned, and there was no longer even the thatch from the cottages for the horses to eat: everything that could be destroyed was reduced to ashes. The men suffered no less than the animals: the heat was intense, and the sand rose in masses of white dust as our columns advanced, choking us and completing our exhaustion. Our misery was intensified by the want of water in these never-ending plains.[32]

But still there came no request for an armistice, no suggestion of peace talks. All that the *grande armée* could do, then, was stumble on for mile after mile. Yet every step reduced the striking power that was its only hope of victory. Twenty thousand men had been lost at Smolensk and 16,000 more detached to act as its garrison, and the road east was littered with thousands of corpses. Marching in the rear of the main spearheads was the Württemberg division: 'From Dorogobuzh onward we met many, sometimes very many, soldiers who had dropped by the roadside from sheer exhaustion and had died where they lay for lack of help . . . The horses were in no better shape than the men . . . We found them lying by the roadside in droves.'[33] By early September Napoleon had with him no more than 130,000 men, but then suddenly news arrived that the enemy really had turned at bay. With the *grande armée* less than eighty miles west of Moscow, at last the fortunes of war seemed to have changed. 'On 5 September,' wrote Chlapowski, 'we . . . arrived before a . . . position fortified by entrenchments: the Russians were accepting battle.'[34]

What had happened? In brief, Alexander was facing a palace coup. Just as it is often assumed Napoleon was always bent on marching on Moscow, so it is taken for granted that Alexander was bent on drawing Napoleon into the depths of Russia and letting climate, geography and the Cossacks wreak havoc on him. Yet this is simply not true. Alexander had never intended to retreat further than Drissa, and the Russians had only retired as far as they had because the French had come on in such overwhelming numbers. Indeed, for weeks the only concrete objective had been to avoid disaster. But for Alexander as much as Napoleon, his credibility was at stake. To surrender all of Russia's gains in Poland was bad enough, but to be driven from Smolensk – one of the Orthodox Church's holiest sites – was to place at risk the estates of some of the greatest families of the Russian nobility. To complicate matters still further, frustrated and humiliated, the officer corps was rebellious and dissatisfied. 'If we persist in the pattern of retreat chosen by Barclay de Tolly . . . Moscow will fall, peace will be signed there, and we shall all march off to India to fight for the French . . . If I have to die, let it rather be here!' raged one cavalry officer.[35] Just as irritated was Boris von Uxkull:

We are running away like hares. Panic has seized everyone. Our courage is crushed; our march looks like a funeral procession. My heart is heavy. We are abandoning all our rich and fruitful land to the fury of an enemy who spares nothing in his cruelty, it is said ... One hears that they are burning and desecrating the churches, that the weaker sex ... are sacrificed to their brutality and the satisfaction of their infernal lusts. Children, greybeards – it is all the same to them – all perish beneath their blows.[36]

And, finally, having just triumphed over Speransky, whom the tsar had been persuaded to send into internal exile as a dangerous radical in May 1812, the 'easterners' in the Russian court and administration had since the start of the campaign been looking for a way to get rid of Barclay, who, though extremely competent, was seen as a foreigner. Aiding this were the conscious efforts of the regime to whip up a mood of militant 'Great Russian' nationalism. For weeks there were insinuations of cowardice and treason, and in the wake of the fall of Smolensk Alexander finally cracked. Having recently travelled to Moscow and promised, amidst scenes of great patriotic enthusiasm, that the city would never be taken by the French, he was faced with an increasingly dangerous situation:

The spirit of the army was affected by a sense of mortification, and all ranks loudly and boldly complained: discontent was general and discipline relaxing. The nobles, the merchants and the population at large were indignant at seeing city after city, government [i.e. province] after government, abandoned, till the enemy's guns were almost heard at Moscow.[37]

On 20 July, the tsar took the only step possible and appointed the most prominent soldier in the Russian army of Russian ethnic stock as commander-in-chief, in the person of the hero of Rustchuk, Mikhail Kutuzov, Alexander also hinting that he would adopt a more aggressive posture.

Oddly enough, Kutuzov, whom Alexander had never forgiven for Austerlitz, was never given any formal order to fight the French. But in the circumstances he had little option, and therefore deployed his army across the Moscow highroad at Borodino in a solid defensive position. By the time the French reached him, Napoleon's army amounted to no more than 130,000 men. Yet the Russians, who had 121,000 men, were still outnumbered, and for a moment a crushing victory seemed to be in the emperor's grasp: Kutuzov had not only deployed his army in such a position that it was in grave danger of being outflanked and trapped, but also arranged its command in a manner that can only be described as bizarre. Fortunately for him, when the main battle began on 7 September, Napoleon's generalship was even worse. For no very good reason the emperor rejected the idea of envelopment, and instead settled upon a series of massive frontal assaults that could not but lead to heavy casualties. With such a battle plan, the only hope of victory was that the Russian army would break in panic, but in fact the French were confronted with the most obstinate resistance. Gradually, however, the Russians were overborne, and by late afternoon it was clear that Napoleon had only to throw in the 18,000 men of the Imperial Guard, who constituted his last reserve, to win the day. But the emperor was tired and ill, and perhaps because of this failed to act. All the fighting achieved, therefore, was to prostrate both sides more or less equally, and allow the Russians to slip away yet again. It had been a terrible day. As Caulaincourt remembered:

Never had a battle cost so many generals and officers . . . There were very few prisoners. The Russians showed the utmost tenacity: their fieldworks and the ground they were forced to yield were given up without disorder. Their ranks did not break; pounded by the artillery, sabred by the cavalry, forced back at bayonet-point by our infantry, their somewhat immobile masses met death bravely, and only gave way slowly before the fury of our attacks. Never had ground been attacked with more fury and skill or more stubbornly defended.[38]

In all, casualties of the battle of 7 September 1812 amounted to 30,000 French and 44,000 Russians. Gone, too, was the last chance of French victory. Though the French now entered Moscow without a fight, Napoleon could do no more. 'Peace lies in Moscow,' the emperor had claimed after Borodino. 'When the great nobles of Russia see us masters of the capital, they will think twice about fighting on. If I liberated the serfs it would smash all those great fortunes. The battle will open the eyes of my brother, Alexander, and the capture of Moscow will open the eyes of his nobles . . . Swords have been crossed, honour is satisfied in the eyes of the world, and the Russians have suffered so much harm that there is no other satisfaction I can ask of them. They will be no more anxious for me to pay them a second visit than I shall be to return to Borodino.'[39] But from St Petersburg there was silence. Though physically ill and under great stress, Alexander would not respond to Napoleon's increasingly desperate communications. Borodino, after all, had been reported as a Russian victory and the tsar had come under such criticism from his sister the Grand Duchess Catherine – an influential figure in the court, and one much associated with Russian traditionalism – for losing Moscow that it was not hard to imagine his fate should he compound the disgrace by surrender. Yet with less than 100,000 troops, the emperor could not compel obedience to his will. With Moscow set alight by Russian agents, partisan activity increasing, supplies desperately short, Kutuzov's army a mere seventy-five miles to the south, large numbers of fresh conscripts pouring into Russia's recruiting depots, substantial regular forces closing in on his thinly protected lines of communication and the discipline and morale of the *grande armée* at breaking point, the position was clearly desperate. Once it became clear that Alexander would not make peace, retreat therefore became inevitable. For Napoleon it was beyond doubt one of the hardest decisions of his career:

Overcome in this struggle of obstinacy, [Napoleon] deferred from day to day the declaration of his defeat. Amid the dreadful storm of men and elements which was gathering around him, his ministers and aides saw him pass whole days in discussing the merits of some new verses he had received ... He would then pass whole hours, half reclined, as if lifeless ... On beholding this obstinate and inflexible character struggling with impossibility, his officers would then observe to one another that, having arrived at the summit of his glory, he no doubt foresaw that from his first retrograde step would date its downfall, [and] that for this reason he continued immovable, clinging to and lingering a few moments longer on this peak.[40]

Beginning on 19 October 1812, there followed the retreat from Moscow. Much time having been wasted by a pointless battle at Maloyaroslavets, the *grande armée* was soon assailed by heavy snow and bitter cold. Meanwhile, Kutuzov repeatedly cut the French column in two, thereby involving it in a series of desperate battles that delayed its march still further. With the army encumbered by immense caravans of baggage and non-combatants, food, clothing and footwear in short supply, and the soldiers exhausted by the endless retreat, formation after formation lost all cohesion as their men died by the hundreds or fell away to join the ever-growing crowd of stragglers. Barely escaping complete destruction when they were attacked from all sides at the river Berezina, the survivors staggered on under the command of Marshal Ney (Napoleon himself fled by sleigh on 5 December), but they were forced to leave behind almost all the remaining guns and baggage and were eventually reduced to barely 20,000 men. Behind them the road was strewn with sights that moved even the oncoming Russians to pity. 'I cannot leave out a description of the scene on the Berezina ... The bridges had collapsed in places and guns and various heavy transports had fallen into the river. Crowds of people, many of them women with infants and children, had come down to the ice-covered banks. Nobody had escaped the severity of the frost ... Fate, our avenger, presented us with scenes of all kinds of desperation and death. The river was covered with ice transparent as glass: there were numerous corpses visible underneath it for its entire width.'[41] It was an experience that imprinted itself indelibly upon the memories of all those involved. One such was Franz Roeder, an officer in the Lifeguard of the Grand Duke of Hesse, who made it all the way from Moscow to Vilna before finally being taken prisoner by the Russians:

There is confusion in my brain as though everything were tumbled together ... I am at present in a state which I find incomprehensible, inexplicable ... God! What appalling misery ... What a multitude have perished in this retreat ... My temples throb to bursting, my head swims and the tears pour from my eyes when I try to recall the scenes through which I have passed ... Dull and unfeeling, caring for myself alone, I [have] walked over living men, over brothers, who perhaps might have been saved with a little help, with one mouthful of food, with a hand to help them from the slippery ground where they had fallen ... How I myself must have suffered to be reduced to that! Am I also destined to endure as they did before I leave this earth?[42]

French losses amounted to perhaps half a million men. Nor were the disasters of 1812 limited to the horrors that had occurred in the east. In Spain, as we have seen, the Russian war had also led to catastrophe: having captured Ciudad Rodrigo and Badajoz, shattered the French at Salamanca and forced them to evacuate Andalucía, Wellington enjoyed the strategic initiative on the Portuguese frontier, while, particularly in Navarre and Aragón, much of the territory that was theoretically under

French control had been overrun by the guerrillas. While the allied triumph was marred by disputes between the British and the Spaniards, it was clear that the days of French success were over. In diplomatic terms, too, the situation was now very different. A conference between Alexander and Bernadotte at Åbo in Finland in August had not persuaded Sweden to join the fighting: with his country almost bankrupt, the Crown Prince was still insisting on remaining neutral until Russia had sent troops to help him conquer Norway. However, heavy hints from Alexander that Bernadotte might be given the throne of France should Napoleon be overthrown had made the prospect much more likely. Moreover, the eastern and western struggles against Napoleon had in July 1812 been linked. No sooner had the French invaded Russia, than first Sweden and then Russia signed peace treaties with Britain. As yet there were no formal alliances between the three – the only power actually to make a pact with Russia was Spain – nor still less any agreement on subsidies, but the Royal Navy provided such assistance in the Baltic as it could, while 100,000 muskets were sent to Russia and 20,000 more to Sweden, the latter also receiving £200,000 as an advance on what she might get in the future.

In all this, the French had only one piece of good news. At precisely the moment when it would have been most useful to have a substantial expeditionary force for service on the shores of the Baltic or the North Sea, Britain's attention was once again distracted by events on the far side of the Atlantic. The clash between Britain and the United States, known as the 'War of 1812', had been in the offing for some time. By 1800 the United States had emerged as a major trading power, and she had been caused considerable inconvenience by both the Continental Blockade and the British response to it. Between 1808 and 1812 American exports fell by some 40 per cent and with them the prices fetched by cotton and tobacco (and, by extension, land). In 1798 French privateering had caused such outrage in Washington it had produced a state of undeclared war with France, and under Napoleon's rule similar tensions had re-emerged. It was with Britain, however, that trouble was worst. Unlike their opponents, the British had the ability to impose their will on the high seas. The French could impound the relatively small numbers of American ships that reached their ports and were found to be in breach of the treaties of Berlin and Milan. Equally, they could seize a few American prizes in the Atlantic or the Caribbean. But as the Royal

Navy had de facto control of all the major sea lanes, American ships were far more likely to be stopped by the British than they were by the French. There was also the added problem of impressment. Constantly in need of men for the Royal Navy, the British argued they had the right to take them wherever they could find them, and American ships were a prime target. Not only did they provide an obvious haven for men who had fled the Royal Navy, but at this time the British government refused to recognize the nationality of anyone born in the United Kingdom as anything other than British. Even men who had been taken to the United States as young boys theoretically remained British subjects and, if sailors, liable to the so-called maritime press. Various estimates have been given of the number of men taken in this fashion over the years, but it may have reached 9,000. In the short term, there was little the American government could do other than protest, but there was no doubt that the issue was of considerable concern to public opinion (a force of genuine weight in the United States). Indeed, in June 1807 an ill-advised decision on the part of HMS *Leopard* to stop the American frigate *Chesapeake* in order to search for British nationals led to widespread anger and even demands for war. This the administration of Thomas Jefferson was not prepared to contemplate, but the issue of the restrictions that had been placed on American shipping was another matter. In an attempt to place pressure on both sides (but especially the British), in April 1806 a law was introduced banning the importation of a number of specified goods and articles which the government considered the United States could either do without or produce for herself, and on 17 December 1807 this measure was supplemented by a much more radical measure that prohibited the export of any goods from American ports.

The trade embargo, however, did not succeed. At this very moment, the British were acquiring new markets and sources of raw material in Latin America. With the economy sliding into ever deeper trouble, pressure began to mount for the use of force. Taking on the British at sea was impossible as the tiny American navy included nothing bigger than a frigate. An obvious target, though, was Canada, whose immense territory was garrisoned by less than 5,000 men. Such a course was doubly attractive. Ever since the War of Independence, settlers had been pushing westwards into the territory that today comprises Ohio, Indiana and Michigan, and these men and women inevitably impinged on the ancestral lands of a variety of Indian tribes. Well aware of the value of an alliance with the Indians, British agents had for years been encouraging them to resist the American advance. And at just this time they found a powerful ally in the great Indian leader, Tecumseh. Of mixed Shawnee and Creek backgrounds, Tecumseh hated white America and believed the Indians faced a choice of either fighting or being overwhelmed: in 1795 a variety of chiefs had been forced to sign away most of the state of Ohio after their defeat in the Miami War, and in 1809 another group were manipulated into giving up yet more land in Indiana. From the 1780s Tecumseh had been arguing that the only way forward was to form a great native confederacy and, aided by his brother, the shaman Tenskwatawa – better known as The Prophet – he now began to travel the frontier, preaching confederation. In this he was almost entirely unsuccessful, but in his home territory (present-day Indiana and Ohio) his message of rejecting the ways of the white man, cleaving to native traditions and living a life of self-purification won many converts. Less pressing, meanwhile, but in its way just as serious, was the issue of Spanish-ruled Florida, which at this time took in not just its current territory but also what was then known as 'West Florida', the southern half of present-day Alabama and Mississippi. Not averse to causing trouble, the Spaniards had, like the British, been giving help and succour to the local Indians, and many escaped slaves had found refuge in their lands. Well aware of the area's importance, the government had been trying to gain control of at the very least West Florida, but diplomacy had proved unsuccessful and, as with Canada, it seemed likely that only a war could solve the problem. With Spain currently an ally of Britain, the opportunity seemed too good to miss. In the south as much as the north-west, then, pressure began to grow for a war of aggression, the appetite of the so-called 'war-hawks' being whetted still further when in 1810 American settlers who had penetrated West Florida revolted against Spain and requested annexation (a development that led to Spain conceding all land west of the Pearl river).

It should not be assumed that the United States as a whole was bent on war with Britain. Jefferson may have been an ardent proponent of clearing away the Indians and of westward expansion, but he knew all too well that his army, thanks to cuts he had imposed in 1802, had just 3,000 men in 1807. To the end of his term of office, then, he hoped that economic means would be sufficient to force the British to give way.

Equally, while the shipowners and merchants of New England hated British control of the seas, they preferred to take their chances of making a profit under the Orders-in-Council rather than lose their income completely under the embargo. Yet the pressure for action remained constant. Indeed, if anything it increased. Under great pressure from commercial interests, in March 1809 Jefferson replaced the embargo with a new Non-Intercourse Act that in effect permitted trade with Britain and France through third parties. With Britain continuing to act high-handedly, as such hawks as Henry Clay of Kentucky were delighted to point out, it looked as if the United States had been beaten. When a new Congress met in 1811 it therefore contained a strong party of men eager for war, the general excitement being heightened both by the suppression of a further American rebellion in Florida and a major clash with Tecumseh's followers at Tippecanoe, where a militia column marching to destroy his headquarters was subjected to a surprise attack by Indians armed with British muskets.

From this moment onwards, war with Britain was very likely. Men like Clay kept trumpeting the evils of British control of the seas and boasting of the ease with which the Americans could conquer Canada. The new president, James Madison, added to the flames by authorizing a three-fold increase in the size of the army and claiming that British agents had been conspiring to secure the secession of New England. The distraction afforded by the United States having serious issues not just with Britain but also with France was resolved in a deal engineered by Madison whereby Napoleon promised that all American ships could come and go as they pleased in exchange for the United States reimposing the embargo on Britain. In practice, the situation remained much less rosy than Napoleon claimed it would be – American ships continued to be harassed – but the concession was enough to remove the French from the agenda, and speed up preparations for war with Britain. On 11 January 1812 the formation of thirteen new regiments was sanctioned together with the construction of twelve ships-of-the-line and twenty-four frigates. The next month the individual states were authorized to raise 50,000 volunteers and finally in April they were also directed to call out 100,000 militia. Finance was provided by a variety of increases in taxation (though it was agreed these should not be implemented until the actual outbreak of war), plans were drawn up for the invasion of Canada, and all shipping was confined to port. And, finally, despite the fact that the United States was far from ready for conflict – there were still, for example, only 7,000 men in the regular army – on 1 June Madison approached Congress with a declaration of war.

The struggle that followed has often been portrayed as the result of British foolishness and intransigence. This, however, is unfair. It is true that until 1811 Britain had been unbending in her response to American protests over maritime policies, and further that, although serious protest at home had led to a concerted parliamentary campaign against the Orders-in-Council that led to their abolition on 23 June 1812, the move came too late to placate Washington. But all the evidence suggests that many Americans were bent on war come what may – that the war, in fact, was rooted not in the Atlantic but the Great Lakes. In the successive votes that got the war through Congress, the representatives of New England – the region with most reason to object to British control of the seas – either abstained or voted against, while those of the South – the region next most affected – were divided, and those of Kentucky, Ohio and Tennessee unanimously in favour. The War of 1812 was, then, above all a war of American expansion, and it is no coincidence either that volunteering for the war was at its most enthusiastic on the western frontier, or that the first American attacks came in the vicinity not of Quebec and Montreal, but Niagara and Detroit.

The story that follows need not detain us here, except to say that, despite efforts to bring it to an end – backed up by the disappearance of the Orders-in-Council, the British offered peace talks as early as July 1812, while in September Russia put herself forward as a mediator – the war was still dragging on when Napoleon abdicated in April 1814: indeed, the very last shots were not fired until the embarrassing British defeat at New Orleans on 8 January 1815. What matters is that, whoever's fault it was, many British troops and, above all, much British shipping, were tied up in a difficult war the other side of the Atlantic. Thanks to the employment of local auxiliaries, not many troops were sent prior to 1814 – the total, apart from drafts of new recruits for units already in theatre, seems to have come to eleven infantry battalions, a battery of artillery and a regiment of cavalry. Yet the impact was still quite substantial: without the war with the United States, it might have been possible to send a much stronger expeditionary force to Germany in 1813 and thereby considerably enhance Britain's diplomatic standing. The war was hardly a triumph for the United States: her forces won few battles against the British, Washington had been occupied and the White House burned, and the navy had been unable to prevent a close British blockade. Yet it was a major landmark in her history. In the course of the fighting the chief bastions of Indian resistance east of the Mississippi had been broken: Tecumseh had been killed at the battle of the Thames on 5 October 1813 and on 27 March 1814 Andrew Jackson smashed the powerful Creek confederation at Horseshoe Bend. And at the very end of the war the tide also turned in the fighting against the British. Even before New Orleans, an invasion of New York State from Canada and an attack on Baltimore had both been frustrated, and the British in consequence offered the Americans generous peace terms. To all intents and purposes, the British abandoned any attempt to penetrate south and west of the Great Lakes. No more, then, could Indian leaders such as Tecumseh look for outside help. With the confidence of the United States greatly boosted, all America from Indiana to the Pacific was Washington's for the taking.

Before concluding this section it is worth saying something about the effect of the War of 1812 on Canada. For the time being her independence was safe enough, but she also emerged from the conflict as at least an embryonic nation. In 1812, well over half the population of Canada were of French origin, and Napoleon had dispatched a number of agents to whip up discontent at British rule. Yet, despite obvious sources of tension – the parliamentary institutions created in Canada in 1791, for example, did not accord the *québécois* the weight that their numbers suggested – these efforts at subversion came to nothing. The local Catholic hierarchy had been fierce in its denunciation of the French Revolution, and this, together with the policy of conciliation pursued by the British governor, ensured that the French population stayed loyal. Even among the population of Upper Canada, which was in large part drawn from American settlers, there was little trouble, and once war broke out the militia that constituted the bulk of the defence forces reported for duty with little resistance. Threatened from outside, in short, all sections of the populace came together, even if in doing so they were still defining themselves more as what they were not than as what they were.

What, though, of Europe? Here the chief effect of the outbreak of war between Britain and the United States had been to give Napoleon renewed hope. This was much needed. By the end of 1812 the emperor's military prestige had taken a terrible battering. Setting aside the destruction of the *grande armée* and Wellington's successes in Spain, in France the ability of the regime to maintain its authority had been called into question by the extraordinary Malet affair, which had seen an unknown officer of Jacobin sympathies, named Claude-François Malet, almost bring down the emperor by announcing that Napoleon had been killed in Russia. Not surprisingly, the result was stirrings of a sort that a few months before would have been quite unthinkable. Even less surprisingly, meanwhile, the rot began in Prussia. Of all the states that Napoleon had overcome, Prussia was the one that had come off worst. Stripped of much of her army, territory and population, and subjected not only to a heavy indemnity but also to the Continental Blockade and semi-permanent French occupation, Prussia had had to pay a heavy price for her earlier opportunism, while she had, as we have seen, played host since 1807 to a reform movement that many of its progenitors saw as a launch pad for a war of revenge and even a great pan-German uprising. And, finally, the concentration of the *grande armée* in East Prussia in the first six months of 1812 had been an experience that was even more traumatic than the campaigns of 1806–7. In the latter, the Prussian experience of fighting had been relatively brief: the campaign of Jena and Auerstädt had been over in a matter of weeks and then the bulk of the French forces had moved on into territory that had until 1795 been Polish. Both Eylau and Friedland had taken place in East Prussia, but again the incursions involved had been relatively short-lived. In 1812, however, it had been very different. With the countryside completely swamped, we are told that, even before it had crossed the frontier, the *grande armée* 'left a swathe of pillage and destruction in its wake'.[43] Now a divisional commander, Dedem de Gelder later wrote with great candour of what had occurred: 'We had crossed Prussia, not as an allied country, but rather as a conquered one. Ninety thousand horses had been seized from our last billets on the illusory condition that they would later be sent back. As for the order of the day laying down that we should gather in ten days' worth of supplies, this had not been anything other than an authorization of pillage and violence.'[44]

When the survivors of the *grande armée* staggered back across the Niemen into East Prussia, they were therefore confronted by general antagonism. 'The attitude of the inhabitants left me in no doubt as to their hostility to us,' wrote Lieutenant Colonel Noël of the artillery. 'I was certain we should have been attacked if they had known that we were not being followed by more troops. On our arrival in a village where we were to shelter, I sent for the burgomaster and told him that . . . at the slightest threat . . . the village would be burned down . . . To defy us, the inhabitants sang rude songs about us. The refrain of one of them was explained to us, "Five French to pay for one Prussian: it's not too much." '[45] None of this was enough to trigger a popular insurrection in the winter of 1812–13. But, particularly in the army, many officers remained genuinely concerned at the extent to which Prussia had been humiliated, and a number had resigned their commands, defected to the Russians and tried to organize a 'Russo-German legion' from German deserters and prisoners of war. In the wake of the French retreat this feeling boiled over. Frederick William had no intention of reneging on his alliance with Napoleon, but on 30 December 1812 General Yorck von Wartenburg, the commander of the Prussian forces sent into Russia, signed a separate convention with the Russians at Tauroggen and led his troops back into East Prussia. What would have happened next had the Russians remained on the frontier is unclear, but in the event they kept coming and the remnants of the *grande armée* were left with no option but to flee for the safety of first the Vistula and then the Oder (garrisons, however, were left in Danzig and a number of other places). There were plenty of fresh troops and ample magazines in the Grand Duchy of Warsaw and East Prussia, but the titular commander of the French forces, Marshal Murat, was exhausted and demoralized and he knew his forces were not to be relied on. 'The Cossack hurrah,' he later said, 'was ringing in every ear, and . . . half would have deserted the first night at the thought of bivouacs where no fires could be lighted from fear of their serving as conductors to that horrid screech.'[46]

The Russian decision to advance was beyond doubt one of the key moments in the international history of the Napoleonic Wars, and yet in many respects it was a very surprising development. The invasion of Russia had not expunged years of Russian anti-British sentiment. Peace had been signed with Britain in July but it was not until September that the prohibition on trade between the two states was lifted, and even then British imports continued to have to pay heavy tariffs. Nor was any formal treaty of alliance signed between the two powers. Many Russians, including Alexander, Rumiantsev and Kutuzov, remained suspicious of the British and there was a strong feeling among the 'easterners' that Russia had no need to involve herself in the travails of central and Western Europe, but should concentrate on her traditional foreign policy objectives. Russia could, for example, take a further piece of Poland as the price of peace – the Vistula was mentioned as a possible new frontier – but her troops should march no further. In taking such a line, the 'easterners' were reinforced by a variety of practical considerations: the very heavy levies occasioned by the war had imposed great strain in the countryside and in some places had given rise to worrying disturbances, Russia was in serious financial difficulties; and in the summer of 1812 the Ukraine had been struck by a severe outbreak of plague, this 'not only ruining the commerce of [Odessa], but reducing all the members of its numerous labouring and manufacturing population to a state of despair'.[47] Himself an easterner, Kutuzov was also able to put forward cogent military arguments. The army under his command had suffered very badly in the course of its pursuit of the French. Some 110,000 strong when it left its camp at Tarutino in October, it was now down to less than 28,000 men, and caution alone dictated that it should be given a little time to be rested, brought up to strength and resupplied.

Why, then, did the war continue? For answer, we must turn to the figure of Alexander I, who had again come west to Vilna. The invasion had had an impact upon him that can only be described as tremendous. Under great pressure, he had turned for comfort to the Bible and discovered in its pages both help and inspiration. The Lord would sustain him and send him his justice and by the same token deliver Russia. As for Alexander, the servant of the Lord, he would strike down the Napoleonic anti-Christ, and bring peace and freedom to the whole of Europe. To stop at the frontier, then, was to frustrate God's plan, but, even if this had not been the case, to Alexander it simply seemed folly not to go on. As he told his personal entourage, 'After so disastrous a campaign in Russia, and the great reverses which France has just met with in Spain, she must be entirely drained of men and of money . . . We have had the precaution . . . to have printed intelligence thrown in on all sides of France, and in all the ports, to deliver that country from the blindness in which she is plunged, and in which every effort is made to keep her. We know, moreover, that Malet's conspiracy is far from being suppressed, and that there are many malcontents in France. We must hope that all these events will unite in promoting the result desired – a solid peace in Europe.'[48] With plenty of fresh troops coming up, it was therefore very unlikely that the tsar would have held back, and all the more so as his entourage included a number of figures who were just as belligerent. One such was the erstwhile Prussian chief minister, Heinrich vom Stein, who had been invited to Russia to act as an unofficial adviser to Alexander and had since the day of his arrival been pressing for the liberation of Germany. Another was Rumiantsev's de facto deputy at the Foreign Ministry, Karl von Nesselrode. An experienced diplomat with close ties with the courts of both Prussia and Austria, by 1812 Nesselrode had in effect taken the aged Rumiantsev's place, for all that the latter continued to be the titular head of department. A thoroughly Western statesman – his father was German and his mother English – he had no time for either Russian traditionalism or Russian isolationism, and believed that it was in Russia's interest to be a European power rather than an Asiatic one. More immediately, it was also very much in her interest to help restore order to Europe by defeating Napoleon and working towards a general peace settlement, something which in his mind was tied up very closely with the principle of legitimacy. But in the end what mattered was not Stein or Nesselrode but the tsar, and, what is more, a tsar possessed by over-confidence, ambition and vain-glory, not to mention a determination to avenge himself on Napoleon and take his place as the greatest hero of the age.

Alexander's view of himself as servant of God and liberator of Europe should not, of course, be taken wholly at face value. As far as Germany was concerned, for example, he wanted to ensure that freedom did not interfere with the interests of his numerous princely relatives, as witness the way in which he infuriated Stein by insisting that the Duke of Oldenburg and his two sons be included in the so-called 'German com-mittee' – the body set up in St Petersburg in June 1812 to oversee German affairs and, so Stein hoped, organize a rising against Napoleon. More immediately of interest, however, was the issue of Poland. Thanks to Czartoryski, this had once more come to the fore. For Czartoryski, the involvement of the Grand Duchy of Warsaw in a war against Alexander I was a personal tragedy, and he had sat out the fighting in unhappy exile in Austrian Galicia. But with the Russians on the offensive, a way out of his dilemma offered itself, and in December he therefore wrote to the tsar begging him to adopt his old scheme of a restored Poland ruled by a Russian monarch (though no longer Alexander: Czartoryski now wanted the throne to go to the tsar's younger brother, the Grand Duke Michael. Nor was Czartoryski the only Pole to indulge in such dreams. The government of the Grand Duchy of Warsaw, for example, had been deeply alienated by the incessant demands of war, and the complete ruin faced by the nobles. 'Of the 600,000 livres in rents that I had in Lithuania,' complained one countess, 'nothing is left but the earth and the sky: all the rest has perished. For the next twenty years I can expect nothing from my erstwhile fortune.'[49] In Warsaw, then, Alexander knew that he would find plenty of more or less willing collaborators, and this again drew him on, especially as the acquisition of the whole of the old kingdom of Poland did not clash with his liberationist rhetoric. But if the Russians were coming, they were doing so on their own terms. As Alexander wrote to Czartoryski on 13 January 1813:

The successes with which Providence has decided to bless my efforts and my perseverance have in no way changed either my sentiments or my intentions in respect of Poland. Your compatriots, then, need have no fear: vengeance is a sentiment that is unknown to me and my greatest pleasure is to pay back bad with good ... Let me speak with complete frankness: in order to realize my favourite ideas on the subject of Poland, I am first going to have to overcome certain difficulties ... First of all, there is the question of opinion in Russia, the manner in which the Polish army conducted itself, the sack of Smolensk and Moscow, and the devastation of the entire country having reawakened old hatreds. Secondly, at the present moment to publicize my intentions in respect of Poland would be to throw Austria straight into the arms of France ... With sagacity and prudence, these difficulties will be overcome. However, it is necessary that you yourselves must help me accustom the Russian people to my plans and justify the predilection that everyone knows that I have for the Poles ... I must advise you, however, that the idea of my brother Michael [becoming king] cannot be entertained. Do not forget that Lithuania, Podolia and Volhynia are all regarded here as Russian provinces and that no logic in the world will ever be able to persuade Russia to allow them to be ruled by any monarch other than the one that sits on her own throne.[50]

This message was hardly reassuring for the Poles, but their fate was now sealed. On 12 January 1813 the Russian forces crossed the Niemen and marched into Prussia and the Grand Duchy of Warsaw. And what of Napoleon? Far from putting out the peace feelers that the circumstances suggested, he responded with defiance. Passing through Warsaw en route for Paris in the wake of his abandonment of the *grande armée*, he treated Dufour de Pradt to a tirade that is all too suggestive of his state of mind:

Raise 10,000 Polish Cossacks – all that is needed is a lance and a horse per man – and the Russians will be stopped . . . The army is superb: I have 120,000 men. And I have always beaten the Russians. They will not dare to do anything. They are no longer the soldiers of Friedland and Eylau. They will hang around at Vilna, while I go off and raise 300,000 men. Then success will render them audacious, but I will defeat them in two or three battles on the Oder, and in six months I will once again be on the Niemen . . . All that has taken place is nothing: it is a mere setback, the result of the climate. The enemy is nothing: I beat them everywhere. They tried to cut me off at the Berezina, but I made that imbecile admiral [i.e. Chichagov] look a fool . . . I had good troops and good cannon, while my position, which was protected by a river and a marsh 1,500 fathoms across, was superb . . . At Marengo I was beaten at six o'clock in the evening, but the next morning I was master of Italy . . . As for Russia, I could not help that it froze . . . Our Norman horses are weaker than the Russian ones: they cannot withstand nine degrees of frost. The same goes for our men. Look at the Bavarians: there is not a single one left![51]

Almost equally self-deluding are the remarks he made to Caulaincourt in the midst of the retreat. 'The war against Russia,' he said, 'is a war which is wholly in the interests . . . of the older Europe and of civilization. The Austrian emperor and M. de Metternich realize this so well that they often said as much to me at Dresden . . . The Viennese government understands perfectly that, apart from her contact with Austria over a long frontier, and all the divergent interests arising from such a situation, the designs of Russia upon Turkey make her doubly dangerous. The reverses France has just suffered will put an end to all jealousies and quiet all the anxieties that may have sprung from her power and influence. Europe should think only of one enemy. And that enemy is the colossus of Russia.'[52] Confined with Napoleon in first sleigh and then carriage for hour after hour as the emperor sped homewards, Caulaincourt was subjected to a constant torrent of words that painted a wholly imaginary picture of events. The Poles' lack of enthusiasm had been the result of Dufour de Pradt's incompetence. The *grande armée* had collapsed after his departure on account of the incompetence of Marshal

Murat. The rulers and peoples of Europe would see that he was fighting not just against the Russian menace but also the selfishness and commercial domination of Great Britain, and rally to his stand. Wellington would be driven into the sea in the Peninsula and an end made of Spanish resistance. The Spanish guerrillas were mere bandits. The British were on the verge of bankruptcy and unlikely to be able to fund a further coalition against his empire; tied up in the Peninsula, meanwhile, their army would not be able to intervene elsewhere on the Continent. The United States would triumph in her war with Britain and emerge not only much stronger but as a firm French ally. Public confidence in his rule had not been shaken. France had never been more prosperous or well governed, still needed him, and would rally to his support as soon as he had returned to Paris. The French navy was acquiring many new ships and would soon be able to challenge the British at sea once more. The commander of the Austrian army corps, Schwarzenberg, was a man of honour and would not betray him. Alexander was hopelessly irresolute and too democratic in his tastes to be able to govern Russia effectively or even last long on the throne. The war, then, would continue and Napoleon would win – indeed, must win. 'God has given me the strength and the zest to undertake great things,' he said. 'I must not leave them imperfectly accomplished.'[53]

How far Napoleon's optimism was convincing in the wake of the retreat from Moscow can legitimately be questioned. Announced in the famous 'Twenty-Ninth Bulletin', which appeared on the morning of the very day that Napoleon reached Paris, the news from Russia spread sorrow and despair on all sides. 'The whole of France had been in Russia,' wrote Hortense de Beauharnais. 'Our desires, our fears, our hopes, everything had been there ... And now that empire ... was sending her back nothing but the débris of her shipwreck ... Nothing equalled our disasters except our sorrow in bewailing them. Everything was shrouded in mourning.'[54] Yet the emperor was not to be discouraged. As Molé remembered of this time, he displayed 'a furious activity which perhaps surpassed everything he had revealed hitherto'.[55] By a variety of means a new *grande armée* was created. In September 1812, 150,000 men had been called up from the class of 1813, and many of these men were now ready to go into action. To supplement them, meanwhile, January 1813 saw the conscription of 150,000 men of the class of 1814 and 100,000 men who had previously been passed over from the classes of 1809, 1810, 1811 and 1812, as well as the mobiliz-ation of 100,000 men of the National Guard (though these men were initially promised that they would only have to fight in France). From Spain there came 15,000 men; from Italy, three French divisions and one drawn from the Army of Eugène de Beauharnais; and from the navy and the *gendarmerie* improvized gunners and cavalrymen. All this was backed by a massive propaganda effort:

Seconded by his intimate councillors, Napoleon employed every artifice calculated to palliate our disasters and conceal from us their inevitable consequences. He assembled the whole phalanx of his flatterers, now become the organs of his will . . . and all, with one voice, attributed the loss of our army . . . solely to the rigour of the elements. By the aid of deception of every kind, they succeeded in making it be believed that all might be repaired if the nation did but show itself great and generous, that fresh sacrifices could not cost her anything when weighed against the preservation of its independence and glory.[56]

With the administration of conscription still intact, the men came in well enough, while France's arsenals and workshops were able to supply plenty of muskets and cannon, as well as at least a semblance of uniform. Still loyal at this stage, the Confederation of the Rhine also produced considerable numbers of fresh troops. By these means, then, within four months of Napoleon's arrival in Paris, 170,000 men had been assembled on the river Main in south-central Germany. With his new *grande armée*, the emperor was confirmed in his determination not to bow down before Russia. The sheer mass of men he commanded, however, blinded him to serious problems. Far too many of his soldiers were raw recruits who lacked experience and were not physically strong enough to cope with the rigours of campaign life. Experienced officers and non-commissioned officers were lacking, and the cavalry could not easily be re-equipped with decent horses. And back in France the call-up of 250,000 men on top of the 150,000 men taken in September 1812 and the 120,000 men taken in December 1811 had placed a huge strain on the willingness of the population to cooperate. To push this further would invite disaster. Among the poorer classes, wrote Marbot, 'there was some grumbling, especially in the south and west, but so great was the habit of obedience that nearly all the contingent went on duty'. The real trouble, however, came from groups with more resources:

After having made men serve whom the ballot had exempted, they compelled those who had quite lawfully obtained substitutes to shoulder their muskets all the same. Many families had embarrassed and even ruined themselves to keep their sons at home, for a substitute cost from 12,000 to 20,000 francs at that time, and this had to be paid down. There were some young men who had obtained substitutes three times over, and were none the less compelled to go; cases even occurred in which they had to serve in the same company with the man whom they had paid to take their place.[57]

Commitment, then, was limited. As Fouché says, 'the reason why France willingly made the greatest sacrifices to support a man whose only success had been to tread the ashes of Moscow' was that the populace thought that 'their chief, chastened by misfortune, was ready to seize the first favourable opportunity of bringing back peace'.[58]

The stakes were therefore very high: whether any further levy on the lines of that of January 1813 could be made to take effect was open to serious doubt, especially as the security forces that had been the real mainstay of the whole system had themselves been stripped to reinforce the new *grande armée*. The fact was that the whole campaign was a desperate gamble and, still worse, one in which the odds against Napoleon were worsened by his own pride and over-confidence. Even as his forces evacuated East Prussia and the Grand Duchy of Warsaw, they were directed to drop off garrisons in all the region's fortresses. In the end, some 50,000 men were tied up in such places, and, occupy though they did plenty of enemy troops, they could perhaps have been put to better use fighting on the battlefields of Lützen, Bautzen, Dresden and Leipzig. To have evacuated Danzig, Thorn and the rest, however, would have been to acknowledge a shrinkage of the empire, and this the emperor would not do. Rather he would beat the enemy in Saxony or Silesia, and then claim back the eastern territories. The garrisons would then have come into their own, creating problems for any attempt to check the French counter-offensive. But, with its attenuated cavalry, could the *grande armée* really secure the sort of decisive victory that Napoleon's strategy required? To this question the emperor had but one answer: 'He enumerated with complaisance all the means that he would have at his disposal in three months' time, calculating that he would be able to reckon on 800,000 under arms . . . The rest being left to his genius, he was really convinced that he would recapture the empire of the world.'[59]

When it came to judging the situation, it did not help, perhaps, that Napoleon was in Paris. In France there was, despite everything, still a degree of support and even enthusiasm for the emperor. But it was not just France that had to be taken into consideration. In 1812 Napoleon had invaded Russia at the head of a force of which only half came from territories that were even notionally French. If the empire was to survive, what happened in Milan and Kassel was therefore just as important as what happened in Marseilles and Clermont Ferrand. And here all the evidence was that Napoleon was in severe trouble. All the satellite and allied states had suffered catastrophic losses in Russia, and they too now had to make strenuous efforts to gather in fresh troops. In the Kingdom of Italy, although Napoleon had sent back the two divisions from that state serving in Spain, the regular annual contingent of 15,000 men had to be supplemented by an additional levy of 9,000. Conscription had never achieved the same degree of acceptance in the domains of Eugène de Beauharnais as it had in France, and there was much resistance right from the start: draft-dodging grew more common; many villages saw the ballot disrupted by riots; and hundreds of men deserted and turned to brigandage. Nor was it just a matter of numbers. There was the same shortage of officers and non-commissioned officers as in France; there were only 1,500 horses for the artillery and cavalry; and there were insufficient muskets, uniforms, shakos and other necessaries. Else-where the situation was even worse. In the Kingdom of Italy, money was not lacking, the treasury having been exceptionally well managed by the Finance Minister Giuseppe Prina (although the efficiency of his fiscal machinery was hardly calculated to stimulate public enthusiasm). In Westphalia, however, by early 1813 the regime of Jerome Bonaparte was in a state of collapse. Of the 16,000 men who had fought in Russia only 2,000 had come back; the national debt now stood at some 200 million francs; the economy was in ruins; and the land tax was now pitched so high that in large parts of the country smallholdings and great estates alike were being taken out of cultivation. Active resistance was still rare – Westphalia was devoid of the mountain ranges that ringed the Kingdom of Italy – and a new army was somehow scraped together, but it was clear that popular support for the regime was almost non-existent. Indeed, Jerome lived in daily fear of insurrection, the story being that he constantly kept a coach and four ready to whisk him to safety at the first sign of trouble.

Of all this, Napoleon would take no account, while he also made little attempt to forestall the coming clash by diplomatic means. It was again hinted that he would accept a Bragança-ruled Portugal and a Bourbon-ruled Sicily, while a fresh Concordat, which on the surface included many concessions, was negotiated with the Pope in the hope that this would satisfy Catholic opinion at home and abroad. Yet the far more important question presented by Austria elicited far less flexibility. Despite growing evidence that Vienna was restive, such as the fact that the corps of General Schwarzenberg had been hastily pulled back from Galicia without making the slightest attempt to put up a fight, Napoleon remained convinced that Austria would fight alongside him. Still worse, through a variety of means – including, not least, the letters of Marie-Louise to her father – Vienna was constantly reminded of the strength of France's armies and the great length of her reach. Eventually, the family chit-chat was backed up by the dispatch of a special emissary to Vienna in the person of the Comte de Narbonne. Very much a figure of the *ancien régime*, Narbonne was a clever choice, and, indeed, even a conciliatory one, but his instructions made the reality clear enough:

British gold buys all those in whom hatred or fear are not enough to determine their course ... Play upon the family connection. The emperor, my father-in-law, is intelligent, moderate and sensible: he has felt the full weight of a French invasion, and I have no doubt that today he wishes to continue faithfully to adhere to me. However, the intrigues of the court, the vanities of the *salon*, the bellicose fantasies of certain great ladies, are all working away in their usual base fashion ... The clear-sighted know that such scenes must stop. It should not be difficult for you to show the emperor Francis the need to stay loyal to an alliance that is both more natural and safer for him than the alternative even if it is one that is at the same time superficially somewhat weaker.[60]

As if hinting at violent retribution was not enough, there were also moments of sharp recrimination. Summoned to Paris to see Napoleon, for example, Schwarzenberg was upbraided by Maret who 'provoked him beyond endurance in the course of a private conversation by representing Austria as faithless and even dishonoured'.[61] But to see Austria as a power flirting with war, or, at the very least, one obsessed with curbing France's power, that simply had to be cowed into submission, was a mistake. Francis I remained as pacific as ever; the army was badly equipped and understrength; even the limited intervention in the Russian campaign had exacerbated the effects of the massive devaluation that had been decreed in 1811 of the paper money on which Austria had relied since the 1780s; and relations with Hungary were very tense. As for Metternich, he wanted to check Russian expansion and isolate Britain, the obvious means of doing both being to engineer a peace settlement between France and her continental opponents. That Napoleon would have had to make concessions in Germany and other areas is true enough, but the Austrian chancellor was neither out to overthrow Napoleon, nor bent on getting back all of Austria's lost territories. In his memoirs Metternich speaks of striking 'a decisive blow' against Napoleon when the time was ripe so as to establish 'a real peace, not a mere truce in disguise like all former treaties of peace with the French Republic and with Napoleon', this being something that could 'only be done by restricting the power of France within such limits as . . . establish a balance of power among the chief states'.[62] This sums up Metternich's policy well enough, but there is nothing to suggest that he believed that such a goal could only be attained by military means, and that despite the fact that by the spring of 1813 the army was being readied for battle. Mobilization was essential to back up Austrian diplomacy but the aim was still mediation rather than war, still a compromise peace rather than total victory. Indeed, armed conflict remained both deeply undesirable and lacking in support:

The decided feeling of the different populations of the Austrian imperial states was for the preservation of peace. Austria had borne the burden of all the former wars except that of 1806, which had ended so unfortunately for Prussia; the inner strength of the empire seemed to be exhausted, and the people to have lost all hope of regaining by the force of arms what they had lost. In Austria . . . the expression 'German feeling' had no more meaning than a myth . . . A class not numerous but important from the position of the individuals composing it raised the banner of war in our country . . . [but] their voices died away in space, and their efforts would never have had any effect on the mind of the Emperor Francis, or on the voice of my political conscience. The monarch would not suffer a repetition of those trials which the empire had gone through after the campaigns of 1805 and 1809, and, had he been willing, I should not have been ready to join him.[63]

At the same time, to reiterate a point made in passing above, Metternich was genuinely anxious not to overthrow Napoleon. What he wanted was not just a peace based on a territorial settlement that would keep France in check, but rather an end to all war in Europe. This, he believed, required an arrangement in which the two central facts of European diplomatic life – a powerful France and a powerful Russia – were kept physically apart by a neutral bloc capable of staving off the threats of East and West alike. But if France and Russia were to be kept apart, they also had to be strong, for, if one or the other was ever allowed to think that her alter ego could not keep her in check, then she might well launch such a push for hegemony that nothing could stop it. In the aftermath of 1812, Russian power was clearly enormous, and this therefore required France to be an impressive force as well, and, by extension, one ruled by Napoleon.

Even now, Austria was no enemy, and there is no doubt that, given some constructive diplomacy, Napoleon could still have rescued a great deal from the Russian disaster. And at all events he would have been wise to have striven to keep relations with Vienna on a friendly basis, for within weeks of his forces crossing the frontier Alexander had been joined by Frederick William of Prussia. The Prussian monarch had been placed in an impossible situation. Napoleon's defeat in Russia notwithstanding, his first instinct had been to remain loyal to the alliance of 1812, and he had therefore ordered Yorck's arrest and court martial. Yet Prussia's easternmost territories were now in a state of revolt. Following Tauroggen, Yorck had declared his forces neutral and in effect set up a liberated area around Königsberg. Here, meanwhile, he was joined by Stein, who had been appointed by Alexander I as his commissioner in occupied Prussia, the latter immediately persuading the local estates to decree the formation of a popular militia or *Landwehr*. Terrified of Napoleon, suspicious of Russia, and deeply hostile to the radical military reform now underway in East Prussia, even Frederick William sought to remain on good terms with the French while yet decreeing general mobilization and accepting such measures as the formation of volunteer units from amongst the well-to-do and the abolition of all exemptions from conscription. However, Napoleon's defeat having caused great excitement among the educated classes, the reformers were able to deluge the king with warnings of imminent revolution, while it was also clear that failure to break with France might well be punished by the Russians. Assailed on all sides, and with many of his doubts assuaged by a Russian guarantee that Prussia would be restored to a size equivalent to that of 1806, Frederick William therefore finally agreed to an alliance.

With the French forces, other than a few garrisons, now out of the way across the Elbe, on 16 March 1813 Prussia declared war. With his forces consisting of a mere 65,000 men – the war with Russia had persuaded Napoleon to allow him to recruit 20,000 extra troops – Frederick William now had no option but to adopt the full programme of the reformers. To the accompaniment of a grandiloquent call to arms, on 18 March it was decreed that a *Landwehr* should be formed from all those men aged between seventeen and forty who were not required by the army, and on 21 April that the remainder of Prussia's manpower should serve in the *Landsturm*, an emergency homeguard charged with guerrilla resistance in territories occupied by the French. To say that all this has given rise to a great deal of nonsense in the historiography of the Napoleonic Wars is an understatement. Within three months, the number of Prussians under arms had risen to some 270,000 men, while such enthusiasts for German nationalism as could be found – a very small number – had soon worked themselves up into a frenzy of patriotic enthusiasm. That said, the fact was that few Germans were actually willing to take up arms against the French – volunteers were thin on the ground, conscription unpopular and desertion rife – and the allied rulers were reluctant to raise them in revolt, the most they were prepared to do being to make use of flying columns of volunteers, regulars and Cossacks to harass the French. In a particularly spectacular blow, one such raiding force penetrated as far as Hamburg in the middle of March and in effect left the local authorities with no option but to declare against Napoleon and organize a rebel militia. This, however, was an isolated incident, and one that was in any case of little consequence: retaken by Marshal Davout without difficulty in May, the city was then garrisoned by him until the end of the war in the face of a long siege.

Despite the lack of a popular uprising in Germany, the defection of Prussia (and, with her, little Mecklenburg-Strelitz, which the French had evacuated at the same time) nevertheless gave rise to an entirely new situation. Napoleon was now opposed by not one but two coalitions. At one end of Europe, there stood Russia, Prussia, Sweden and Mecklenburg, and at the other Britain, Spain, Portugal and Sicily. In between the two stood France, Holland, Denmark (whose government had not forgotten the destruction of Copenhagen), the bulk of the Confederation of the Rhine, the Kingdom of Italy, and Naples. Austria, of course, was now neutral and the Grand Duchy of Warsaw had succumbed to Russian occupation, although its army had retreated westwards and was still fighting on with the *grande armée*. Astonishingly enough, it was not until June that the two anti-Napoleonic leagues were fully brought together. In March, Britain signed an alliance with Sweden – a decision that at last brought a Swedish expeditionary force across the Baltic – but only at the cost of considerable wrangling: Britain now agreed that Sweden could have Norway, but Bernadotte was not content with the £1 million he was offered for the rest of the year, and it had eventually to be agreed he would be paid £1 million for the period up to 1 October, after which a new agreement would have to be negotiated. As for the number of men Sweden had to provide in Germany, this was a mere 30,000.

Coming to an agreement with Prussia and Russia was no easier. Although diplomatic relations with Prussia were resumed as soon as the latter declared war on Napoleon, it was not until late April that a new ambassador – Lord Castlereagh's younger brother, Sir Charles Stewart – reached the Prussian government, which was then assembled at allied headquarters in Dresden. In the interim, serious negotiations had been under way with the Russians for some time via the good offices of the British ambassador, Lord Cathcart, but progress had been very slow, and it soon transpired that the talks that now opened with the Prussians would prove no better. Both the eastern powers wanted any subsidy to be paid in appropriate coinage in Europe, whereas the British wanted to issue their payments in London. At stake, of course, were the costs of exchange, and it was only with great difficulty that the British got their way. Also at issue was the size of the contingents maintained in the field: Castlereagh wanted there to be 200,000 Russians, but Alexander maintained that he could only bring forward 150,000, while the Prussians, who were understandably anxious to have as big an impact as possible, wanted Britain to fund 100,000 men, whereas Castlereagh, suspicious of bringing to battle mere mobs of half-armed levies, would only pay for 80,000. And, finally, the initial figure named by Alexander for 1813 was £4 million whereas the British only offered half that sum. In the end all was settled amicably enough – Britain got 240,000 men

(160,000 Russians and 80,000 Prussians) rather than 280,000, but in exchange was asked for no more than the £2 million that had initially been on offer – but the final treaties, which in both cases incorporated a promise not to make a separate peace, were not signed until 14 and 15 June. Thereafter British aid was extensive: counting aid in kind as well as money, as well as payments made under the so-called 'federative paper' scheme agreed in the autumn, by 1814 Prussia had received £2,088,682, Austria £1,639,523, Russia £3,366,334, and Sweden £2,334,992, while a small British expeditionary force was also soon being readied for service in northern Germany. Yet there was still no Sixth Coalition as such. Britain was linked to Russia, Prussia, Sweden, Spain and Portugal by separate treaties, while Russia had agreements with both Prussia and Spain.

Given the problems that the Allies were to face in defeating Napoleon, British aid was vital. Backed by his new *grande armée*, Napoleon was easily able to hold his own against the roughly similar number of Prussians and Russians available for service at this time. Striking east into Saxony (whose monarch had fled into exile in Prague rather than declare for the Allies in the style of Prussia), the emperor overshot the Russians and Prussians, who were advancing westwards on a roughly parallel course in accordance with plans developed by the Prussian chief of staff, Gerhard von Scharnhorst, for a march on the Rhine designed to bring the German people out in revolt and force the princes to change sides. Discovering that there were French troops in their vicinity, the leading allied forces turned on them at Lützen only to find not only that far more of the enemy were in their vicinity than they expected, but also that Napoleon's main body was perfectly poised to fall on their flank. By the end of the day there were 12,000 allied casualties, including Scharnhorst, who was mortally wounded, while the Russians and Prussians had been badly enveloped. Yet Lützen was not the decisive victory for which Napoleon was looking. Want of cavalry ensured that the *grande armée* was not able to deliver the hammer blows of the past, and so its badly shaken opponents were able to retire in good order. Still worse, French losses came to some 20,000 men, the fact being that training and experience were so lacking amongst the new troops that they had no option but to operate in the most clumsy and unsophisticated of styles and, in consequence, suffered casualties that were far worse than should have been the case.

Nor did matters improve as the campaign went on. After the battle of Lützen the Allies abandoned their offensive and fell back to a strong defensive position at Bautzen. Here they were attacked by Napoleon on 20 May. Well protected though their troops were – the front line ran along a line of hills and was studded with entrenchments and redoubts – they were vulnerable to attack from the north as their right flank was open to envelopment. Only a few miles south, meanwhile, lay the Austrian frontier and deliberately so: the allied advance westwards had hugged the northern limits of Moravia so as to ensure that Napoleon could not interpose himself between the Prussians and Russians on the one hand and the Austrians on the other, and thereby deter the latter from joining the war. Napoleon was therefore able to formulate a plan that might well have caused his men to triumph. After Lützen, the *grande armée* had moved east in two columns. Led by the emperor himself, the southernmost column headed straight for Bautzen and struck the enemy more or less head on. The second column, which was commanded by Marshal Ney, had advanced on a more northerly axis, however, and this was now ordered to swing south and take the Allies in the flank and rear. The only line of retreat left to the latter being towards the Austrian frontier, they would face a straight choice of surrender, or violating Austrian neutrality, thereby – or so it was hoped – forcing Vienna to come out in support of Napoleon. Again, however, things went wrong. Arriving on the battlefield on the second day of the battle, Ney misunderstood his orders and sent his troops into action in the wrong direction with the result that the Allies, who had again fought with great determination, got away, the French cavalry being quite unable to break their ranks or make any significant impact upon their retreat. And as at Lützen there were some 20,000 French casualties, although on this occasion they did at least inflict roughly the same number of losses on the Allies.

Following the battle of Bautzen, the Prusso-Russian array continued to fall back, but they were again, for much the same reasons as before, careful to follow the line of the Austrian frontier. To have engineered a retreat north-eastwards in the direction of Breslau, and beyond that central Poland, would have suited the French much better, for the Allies would have been separated from Austria. Driven from their home territory, the Prussians might even have been forced to give up the fight. However, although Alexander and Frederick William were pushed to the point of collapse, the *grande armée* proved incapable of following up its success: without a decent force of cavalry, it could not impose its will on the Allies, while the raw conscripts who had been called up to fill the ranks were unable to endure the forced marching that would have been required of them. One last battle might yet have done the trick. King and tsar alike had been badly shaken by the resilience displayed by Napoleon; Prussia's levies were deserting in droves; and the Russian army was in so bad a state that its new commander-in-chief, Barclay de Tolly (struck down by pneumonia, Kutuzov had died on 28 April) was arguing vehemently for a retreat to Poland. In Silesia, indeed, there were now less than 80,000 Prussians and Russians. The Napoleon of 1805 might yet have kept going and thereby won the war, but, for all his bravado, this was not the Napoleon of 1805. The campaign, it seems, had exhausted him physically, and the euphoria he had displayed in the wake of Lützen, which had been hailed as a great victory, had been replaced by a mood of deep depression. The day after the battle of Bautzen one of his closest confidants, General Duroc, had been mortally wounded observing the retreating Prussians. Much distressed, Napoleon had called a halt to the pursuit:

The emperor ordered the Guard to halt. The tents of the imperial head-quarters were set up in a field on the right side of the road. Napoleon . . . spent the rest of the evening seated on a stool in front of his tent, his hands clasped and his head bent down . . . No one dared go near him: we all stood around with bowed heads.[64]

In this mood even Napoleon was capable of recognizing that all was not well with his army. Aside from the 40,000 battle casualties, 90,000 men had fallen sick or otherwise gone missing, and the men still in the ranks were weary and low in morale. Nor were even senior officers much more encouraging. 'We had done enough to retrieve the honour of our arms after the terrible misfortunes of the preceding campaign,' wrote Marshal Macdonald. 'France and the army earnestly longed for peace.'[65] Only days after Bautzen was fought, an emissary was sent to allied headquarters asking for a ceasefire. This approach was rejected – opinion in the Prussian army was deeply hostile – but on 2 June a message arrived at the headquarters of both armies from Vienna proposing a truce under whose cover Austria could offer her services as mediator. To quote Metternich, 'The emperor left it to me to fix the moment which

I thought most suitable to announce to the belligerent powers that Austria had given up her neutrality, and to invite them to recognize her armed mediation . . . Napoleon's victories at Lützen and Bautzen were the signs which told me the hour had come . . . If Austria showed that she was not inclined to take part in the war against Napoleon, this would give the Russian monarch the excuse to . . . conclude the war.'[66]

With both sides now anxious for a break in the fighting, there followed the temporary suspension of hostilities known as the armistice of Pläswitz (4 June–13 August 1813). This was the turning point of the campaign. For obvious reasons the key player was Austria. In fighting the campaign of Lützen and Bautzen, Napoleon had hoped to produce a change in Vienna's attitude. 'He thought', as Caulaincourt said, 'that a victory would range Austria on his side.'[67] Despite having broken with Napoleon, the Austrian chancellor, Metternich, was desperate to maintain a balance between France and Russia, believing that outright victory for either would spell disaster for the Habsburgs. For war, meanwhile, he had no enthusiasm at all, greatly fearing the nationalistic effervescence Stein and his adherents were attempting to provoke across the whole of central Europe: in March, indeed, he had ordered the arrest of a group of conspirators who had been attempting to organize a fresh insurrection in the Tyrol. To achieve his aims, Metternich would have liked to have arranged a general peace conference, but in the event he was forced to settle for face-to-face discussions with first Alexander and then Napoleon.

Ratified in the convention of Reichenbach of 27 June, the result of his discussions with the Allies was a scheme that would have satisfied most of his objectives. In brief, unless Napoleon agreed to surrender the Illyrian provinces to Austria, recognize the independence of the states of the Confederation of the Rhine, evacuate Germany and Italy, give up the Grand Duchy of Warsaw and leave the Allies to organize the post-war settlement as they chose, Austria would enter the war. As for the future, it was specified that the Papal States, Piedmont and the German possessions of the house of Orange were all to be given back to their previous owners; Hesse-Kassel, Hanover, Hamburg and Lübeck restored as independent states; and Prussia returned to its 1806 frontiers. Confronted with this scheme at Dresden, Napoleon brushed aside Metternich's attempts to present it in a favourable light and swore that he would fight on. Their conversations make up one of the most famous tableaux in the entire history of the Napoleonic Wars. 'Peace and war,' said Metternich, 'lie in Your Majesty's hands . . . Today you can yet conclude peace. Tomorrow it may be too late.'[68] This challenge was met by a torrent of abuse which concluded with the emperor flinging his hat into a corner of the room:

So you, too, want war; well, you shall have it. I have annihilated the Prussian army at Lützen; I have beaten the Russians at Bautzen; now you wish your turn to come. Be it so: the rendezvous shall be in Vienna. Men are incorrigible: experience is lost upon them. Three times have I replaced the Emperor Francis on his throne . . . At the time I said to myself, 'You are perpetrating a folly.' But it was done, and today I repent of it . . . Do they want me to degrade myself? Never! I shall know how to die, but I shall not yield one handsbreadth of soil. Your sovereigns born to the throne may be beaten twenty times and still go back to their palaces; that cannot I – the child of fortune: my reign will not outlast the day when I have ceased to be strong, and therefore to be feared . . . You think to conquer me by a coalition . . . But how many of you Allies are there – four, five, six, twenty? The more you are, so much the better for me. I take up the challenge. I can assure you that . . . next October we shall meet in Vienna; then will it be seen what has become of your good friends, the Russians and the Prussians. Do you count on Germany? See what it did in 1809! To hold the people there in check, my soldiers are sufficient, and, for the faith of the princes, my security is the fear they have of you.[69]

To all this was added a string of observations reminiscent of those that had been lavished on Caulaincourt during the long journey home he had shared with Napoleon in December. The invasion of Russia had only been defeated by 'General Winter'; Francis I would never make war on his own daughter and grandson; the French people were entirely loyal to his rule; the Austrians could not get more than 75,000 men into the field; the common soldiers of the *grande armée* remained devoted to him. Napoleon, then, remained defiant. In the face of this attitude a disappointed Metternich could only state the obvious:

In all that Your Majesty has just said to me I see a fresh proof that Europe and Your Majesty cannot come to an understanding. Your peace is never more than truce. Misfortune, like success, hurries you to war. The moment has arrived when you and Europe both throw down the gauntlet; you will

take it up – you and Europe – and it will not be Europe that will be defeated
. . . You are lost, Sire. I had the presentiment of it when I came; now, in
going, I have the certainty.[70]

Metternich's first efforts to negotiate a settlement, then, had failed. It
is, however, extremely unlikely that he would ever have attained his
aims. In the eyes of all those who observed him, there were serious
doubts that the emperor had ever had any intention of giving way. As
the artillery officer Noël wrote:

Everyone wanted peace, but did the emperor desire it? One would have
thought so. How, otherwise, could he have agreed to an armistice when,
having been victorious in two major battles, he had forced the enemy back
across the Oder and now found himself at the gates of . . . the richest
province in Prussia? Nevertheless, as the negotiations dragged on and the
emperor, so eager when he wanted something, was busy only with preparations for a new campaign, one began to have doubts. Defensive works
covered the left bank of the Elbe from Bohemia to the sea. The ramparts of
Dresden were restored . . . and the fortifications of Torgau were finished . . .
Big hospitals were established at Dresden, Torgau and Magdeburg, huge
warehouses were filled with supplies of every sort . . . The emperor watched
and supervised everything . . . Whole corps arrived to join us at this time . . .
made up of young soldiers full of enthusiasm and goodwill . . . There could
only be one goal for these preparations and deployment of forces; it was to
impress the enemy and so obtain the best possible terms for the peace, or, if
war became essential, to deal such a blow that the struggle would be ended
at once. Yet we knew the emperor well enough to know that, once he found
himself at the head of such a large army, it would indeed be difficult to
extract the least concession from him. Busy as I was . . . I could not be
entirely deaf to the widespread recriminations and complaints that I heard
all around me on the inflexibility of Napoleon's character.[71]

In the circumstances it is difficult to believe that the truce was ever
anything more to Napoleon than an attempt to win time to rest and
recruit his forces. Nevertheless, the emperor did agree to take part in a
conference at Prague and even informally agreed to the principle of
Austrian mediation. But none of this came to anything. Even though
Metternich offered to waive Austria's claim to the Illyrian provinces,
which would presumably have been left as an independent principality,

it soon became clear that Napoleon had no intention of giving way. To the end, he refused point-blank to believe that the Austrians had mobilized in the numbers that were being reported. Caulaincourt was sent to Prague to represent Napoleon in the peace talks, but he was not given the necessary credentials by his master and in consequence, much flattered by the election of Schwarzenberg as allied commander-in-chief, on 12 August Austria finally entered the war. On that very day, the missing papers finally turned up, but Metternich saw clearly that this was simply another of Napoleon's attempts to throw the blame for hostilities on his opponents. He showed Caulaincourt and Narbonne the door: 'I told [him] it would no longer be possible to make use of [the] letters: the die was cast and the fate of Europe was once more left to the decision of arms.'[72] Still he had not completely given up hope that Napoleon could be persuaded to accept a peace settlement. The junior official sent to Metternich to settle the arrangements for the departure of the French delegation from Prague was therefore subjected to an hour-long exposition of the Austrian position which, if a thoroughly implausible piece of diplomatic theatre, was none the less almost pleading in its intensity:

It would be incorrect to say that we talked together, for he was almost exclusively the only one to speak. His eyes were moist, his hands worked nervously, and his forehead was covered with perspiration. He explained to me in detail the designs he had formed, and the efforts he had made since the day of our disasters to preserve peace, to maintain the alliance between Austria and France, and to reconcile the interests of his own country, and the legitimate independence of Germany, with the pride and the real interests of France. He called to mind the attacks to which he had been subjected, the reproaches he had endured, and the efforts he had made, making me, in a measure, a witness of the extremities to which he was now reduced. He then enumerated to me in full the whole military force which was arrayed against us ... the preparations which had been made for the evacuation of Vienna, and the dispositions which had been taken to continue the struggle even though it were after another Austerlitz ... It was the effusion of a soul, full of patriotic and personal anguish, which poured out its innermost feelings even to overflowing without being able to restrain them.[73]

For admirers of Napoleon, the peace terms offered him at Dresden have frequently been regarded as intolerable. Yet in reality they were by no means so bad. With nothing said about Switzerland, the Kingdom of Italy, Naples, Holland, Belgium and Spain, Napoleon would have continued at the head of a France that was only marginally less *grande* than before, and at least potentially backed by a number of clients and satellites. Inherent in the agreement too was a serious diplomatic defeat for London. Britain's envoys were excluded from the negotiations at Reichenbach, and the peace terms left almost all her immediate war aims unresolved. All that the British could do was to go along with the proposals in the hope that Napoleon would reject them, or that Prussia and Russia – who were under no obligation to bring the war to a close even if the emperor accepted the deal – could be persuaded to keep fighting. There was no attempt to renege on the treaties that had been signed so recently with the eastern powers, but Britain's partners were left in no doubt that Reichenbach was not acceptable to London. On 5 July, Lord Castlereagh wrote a long dispatch to Cathcart and Stewart in which he informed them that Spain and Sicily would never be abandoned, that Holland was to be given up by France, and, finally, or at least so it was implied, that the Kingdom of Italy should be restored to its old masters. As for the sort of Europe that Britain wanted the Allies to fight for, this was encapsulated by the plan that had been drawn up in 1805 by William Pitt and was now sent to Russia by Castlereagh: France was to be contained by a much reinforced Holland and a re-constituted Piedmont, backed by Prussia on the one hand and Austria on the other. In taking this stance, Castlereagh's hand was strengthened by the arrival at allied headquarters of news of Wellington's great victory at Vitoria, this allowing the British both to point out that the restoration of Ferdinand VII was no longer even potentially a matter of dispute and to hold out the hope of an invasion of France in Napoleon's rear.

With British subsidies now pouring into the treasuries of the eastern powers, Britain's influence was clearly on the increase. But even with this assistance there was no guarantee that they would be able to attain their objectives. Alexander, in particular, remained hostile to Britain. In September 1812 he had given ample proof of this by offering Russian mediation as a means of ending the conflict between Britain and the United States, and there was therefore little likelihood of him showing much verve in respect of stripping France of Holland and Belgium. And, if some of Prussia's generals were eager for war, Frederick William and

Hardenberg were far less enthusiastic. As a British diplomat on Stewart's staff complained:

One point yielded by Bonaparte to Austria would have turned the scale against us, for throughout the duration of the armistice, considerable political manoeuvring has been carried on for the purpose of furthering the efforts of Austria to prevent a renewal of the war. Hardenberg is not in the best of health, and is quite overwhelmed with the amount of business he has now to transact. He . . . at times, I know, considers us rather as a thorn in his side, and an obstacle to a peaceful settlement of affairs amongst the three powers, than as an ally making the greatest efforts and sacrifices to aid in restoring permanent tranquillity to Europe. The King [i.e. Frederick William III] is as reserved as he has ever been, and not much less apathetic; he is as fond of retirement, varied with a little quiet recreation, as formerly . . . as well as his moody fits when things are not going on smoothly. At times he is indignant at Bonaparte's high-handed ways, and warms up into sharing a little . . . the feeling of his people towards their oppressor. But these are short-lived emotions, for the King has no confidence in himself and the right spirit has rarely strength to assert itself long enough for action to follow its promptings. His Majesty, therefore, cools down rapidly, and sinks back into the same amiable nonentity he has ever been – ruled by those around him, more especially if their influence is exerted in a manner to leave him in the unruffled enjoyment of serenity of mind and the calm, peaceful mode of life he delights in.[74]

One should not push this British view too far. There is no evidence that either Alexander or Frederick William seriously considered peace at this time, and they were, in fact, much irritated when Metternich extended the armistice rather than going to war immediately after Napoleon rejected the peace terms offered at Dresden. So much did the tsar distrust Metternich indeed, that he even sent his sister, the Grand Duchess Catherine, to employ a mixture of bribery and guile to win him over to the allied cause, while at the same time trying to have himself put forward as allied commander-in-chief in place of the Austrian Schwarzenberg. But fighting on until Napoleon was defeated was not the same as insisting on his removal. The series of bipartisan agreements signed at Teplitz on 9 September between Austria, Prussia and Russia to cement the grand alliance said nothing at all about France's political future. Instead they committed the Allies to re-establishing Austria and

Prussia on the frontiers of 1805, maintaining field armies of 150,000 men apiece, ensuring the independence of the states of Germany and settling the fate of Poland among themselves after the war had come to an end. As for the idea of getting rid of Napoleon altogether, of all the allied leaders, in fact, only Bernadotte was now overtly hawkish, and he was driven by nothing more than personal ambition. 'Bonaparte is a rogue,' he told one Russian envoy. 'He must be killed. As long as he is still alive, he will be the scourge of the world. France should not have an emperor. The title is not a French one. What France needs is a king, but he must be a soldier-king. The whole Bourbon race is rotten through and through, and should never be permitted to resume the throne.' That he was the right man for the job, he was certain – 'What man would suit the French more than me?' – but underlying the bluster was also caution: 'A great deal of prudence is required in my position. It is so delicate, so difficult! Setting aside the natural repugnance that I feel in respect of shedding French blood, I have a great reputation to uphold. In this I am under no illusions. My fate hangs on a single battle. If I lose it, I could ask six francs of Europe, and not a single person would give me anything.'[75] With even Britain prepared to sign up to a peace settlement that kept Napoleon in power, all that the French ruler had to do was to stretch out his hand. A solution that preserved his dynasty and left France with significant gains was still available. According to apologists for the emperor, accepting the reduction in his power outlined by Metternich's proposals would not have been borne by the French people. But this is simply nonsense – peace would have seemed cheap at the price. Nor was there much risk of a military coup: surrender might mean many commanders contemplating the loss of prosperous estates in Germany, Italy and Poland, but to fight on was to risk much more. Peace with honour was there for the taking.

Why, then, did the war continue? The answer is devastatingly simple. Rather than accept a compromise peace, Napoleon had elected to gamble on military victory. However, before we look at the campaigns that followed, we must first consider some loose ends elsewhere. At the very time that the guns had fallen silent in Silesia, matters had come to a head in two other theatres of war, namely the Balkans and the Trans-Caucasus. In the Balkans, Russia's disengagement from her war with Turkey had left the Serbs hopelessly vulnerable to an Ottoman counter-attack, while Karadjordje's attempt to set up a centralized state had alienated many key Serbian chieftains. Still worse, the populace were desperately war-weary. In the treaty of Bucharest the Ottomans had been forced to concede both a general amnesty and a guarantee of autonomy if the Serbs would in turn make peace and recognize the suzerainty of Constantinople. But the details of what was meant by autonomy had been left very vague and the Serbs had in effect been left to secure such terms as they could get. These, needless to say, proved to be most unfavourable. Fearing the worst, Karadjordje sought desperately to buy time while secretly appealing to Russia for help. This aid was not forthcoming and Constantinople became more and more impatient. After all, if the matter was still unresolved when the Russians concluded peace with Napoleon, there was an obvious danger of a fresh Russian attack. In late July, then, three Ottoman armies poured into Serbia. Only in a few places was there much resistance, and by early October it was all over, the only bright spot amid the scenes of carnage that followed being that Karadjordje himself managed to reach safety in Hungary.

In the Trans-Caucasus, meanwhile, though fighting had ceased between the Russians and the Ottomans, leaving the former in control of a small amount of additional territory, there was still conflict with the Persians. As will be remembered, Russia had been engaged in a spasmodic war with Persia over the suzerainty of Georgia ever since 1804. A combination of distance and terrain enabled the outmatched Persians to keep up the fight for a considerable time, but in October 1812 they were decisively defeated at Aslanduz on the Araks river, while a second defeat at Lenkoran two months later persuaded them to sue for peace. The result was the treaty of Golestan. Signed on 12 October 1813, this not only confirmed Russian ownership of Georgia, but also handed her what is today Azerbaijan, as well as exclusive rights to navigation on the Caspian Sea.

In terms of Russian expansion in central Asia, the treaty of Golestan was of immense importance, opening the way as it did to the independent khanates of present-day Kazakhstan. In some ways, then, it may be said to have had greater long-term geopolitical effects than anything that happened in Western Europe. In 1813, however, it appeared a sideshow. To return to Napoleon – confronted by the odds that he now faced, even the emperor would have been hard put to survive. Counting the troops of his remaining allies, he could only muster some 335,000 men, despite the fact that the King of Saxony had returned to the fold and mobilized his army. Facing him were a minimum of 515,000 allied troops. Predictably enough, Alexander and Frederick William had derived greater benefit from the truce than Napoleon in terms of getting reinforcements from their home bases, while there also now came forward 40,000 Swedes and 127,000 Austrians. Dividing his forces so that he could strike out in several directions at once, Napoleon succeeded for a while in staving off disaster. Yet France's generals were so used to the emperor's guiding hand that few of them were capable of independent command and several were heavily defeated. Where Napoleon himself was in charge, things were better, but the allied generals had agreed to refuse battle whenever he was present, the result being that all his offensives achieved was to exhaust his own troops. All the time, meanwhile, the supply convoys and communications of the *grande armée* were being constantly harassed by parties of light cavalry and Cossacks. Desperately hungry, the troops were also in severe need of new footwear and clothing, all this being made still worse by the coming of an autumn marked by torrential rains. Confidence in the French camp had been lacking to start with: 'The emperor's *fête* fell on 15 August . . . This was the last time that the French army celebrated its emperor's birthday. There was little enthusiasm, for even the least foreseeing of the officers realized that we were on the eve of great changes, and their forebodings were reflected in the minds of the subalterns . . . Our allies of the Confederation of the Rhine were wavering and the Saxon General Thielmann with his brigade had already gone over to the Prussians. So there was much uneasiness and little confidence among our troops.'[76] As can be imagined, hope was now running out fast.

In the six weeks [Napoleon] spent in and around Dresden, he lost a lot of men. This was as much the result of the want of supplies and the desertion and sickness that began to make themselves felt as of battle. The hospitals were overwhelmed. Our soldiers were lying dead on the roads, having collapsed from hunger, cold and misery . . . After the unfortunate affair on the river Bober, a violent scene took place between Marshal Macdonald and the emperor. Going straight into the marshal's camp, the emperor shouted at the top of his voice, 'Monsieur le Maréchal, what have you done with the army I gave you?' At this, Macdonald indignantly replied, 'You no longer have an army: there is nothing left but a few unfortunates dying of starvation.

Go and have a look in the mountains: you will find plenty of soldiers there all right, but they are all dead of misery. You have lost everything: your only hope is peace.'[77]

Such was the mystique of Napoleon and his army that the emperor's French soldiers continued to show extraordinary levels of devotion, but the subject nationalities began to melt away in large numbers, while in the *grande armée* as a whole morale was clearly very fragile. When Ney was defeated at Dennewitz on 6 September, for example, the day ended in a panic-stricken rout that swept away even formations that were still intact. In addition, there were stirrings behind the lines. After months of procrastination, on 8 October Bavaria, menaced by Austrian invasion, signed a treaty of alliance with Vienna that committed her to uniting her forces with the Allies. With the allied armies closing in, the only solution was either negotiations in good faith or a retreat to the Rhine, but neither of these options was acceptable to Napoleon:

The emperor one morning sent one of his orderly officers to me to ask my opinion of the situation, and what we had better do. We were now in October [and] without rations, except such as could be collected by main force . . . I told the officer plainly that, unless the emperor immediately took the offensive – that is, if he saw any chance of success, which, in my opinion was improbable as we had hitherto failed to force our entrance into Bohemia – he exposed us to serious catastrophes: the army was daily growing weaker by sickness and the ordinary losses of war; that an unsuccessful battle would weaken us still further, and use up . . . ammunition which we could not replace; that the magazines were empty [and] the country ruined; [and] that the prudent course would be to retire . . . and to evacuate those places on the Oder with which we could still communicate, and above all, those on the Elbe . . . He departed, but scarcely had he left me when another orderly officer came to bring me an order not to commence the preliminary execution of my plan, but to advance at once. My reconnaissances and forage parties were already out, and I was consequently very weakened. I told the officer to point out to the emperor that I could not start until they returned . . . It was not long before he returned, saying that the emperor desired me to set out immediately with what troops I had.[78]

Instead of retreating, the emperor adopted a defensive position around Leipzig. The battle that followed was the largest, bloodiest and most dramatic of the Napoleonic Wars, with the 177,000-strong *grande armée* facing an initial total of over 250,000 allied troops. On 16 October Schwarzenberg and Blücher launched simultaneous attacks from north and south, but were successfully repulsed. At this point Napoleon might yet have got away to the west, but he was expecting 14,000 fresh troops to arrive the following day. Why he thought this would make a difference is unclear: setting aside the negligible numbers of men involved, two-thirds of them were potentially unreliable Saxons. But, whatever the reason, he decided to stay put in the expectation that he could secure a genuine victory, while at the same time sending peace terms of his own to the Allies: there would first be an armistice in which France would be allowed to evacuate all her beleaguered eastern garrisons in return for a promise to withdraw to the line of the river Saale, and then a peace settlement whose chief features would be the re-establishment of Spain, Holland, Hanover, Hamburg and Lübeck as independent states in exchange for allied recognition of the Kingdom of Italy and the Confederation of the Rhine. However, to expect that the Allies would accept such terms stretched belief to its very limits. As anyone could see, the result would be to allow Napoleon to regroup his forces and save the thousands of men that even he had now to recognize would otherwise be given up for lost, while reserving the right to fight on at a later date. Among his men there was a much more realistic appreciation of the situation. The artillery officer Noël was now serving at Napoleon's headquarters:

On 17 October we remained in the positions we had occupied on the previous evening. It was a wretched day: the sky hung low and grey and the weather was cold and wet. The battlefield was a terrible sight . . . Our own thoughts were at one with the weather and the scene that met our eyes. Illusions were shattered as everyone began to understand the situation. We saw before us a numerous, courageous enemy determined, at any cost, to regain his independence. We had to start again and in the worst of circumstances . . . Yesterday we had fought two against three; tomorrow we should fight one against two.[79]

To the relief of the French, 17 October proved quiet as the Allies were waiting for the 140,000 reinforcements coming up under Bennigsen and Bernadotte. The fighting was therefore not resumed until the next day when 300,000 men were launched against the French from virtually every point of the compass. Thanks in part to allied bungling and irresolution, at first the *grande armée* held its ground, but then the tide turned. In the very midst of the fighting, the two Saxon divisions which had arrived the previous day changed sides, and in consequence Napoleon ordered a withdrawal. With the only way out of the trap a long and narrow causeway across a marshy river valley, this was an extremely dangerous manoeuvre, and it was not long before complete chaos set in. Among the troops trying to get across the causeway was Marshal Marmont:

My chief of staff and his deputy had been struck down at my side; four of my aides-de-camp were killed, wounded or missing, along with another seven of the officers attached to my staff. As for myself, I had been wounded by a musket ball in the hand and badly bruised on the left arm, while a ball had gone through my hat and another through my coat, on top of which four horses had been killed beneath me ... Disorder reigned on all sides. The blockages caused by wagons in every street and the congestion of the fugitives prevented the maintenance of anything in the way of a formation and impeded the transmission of orders. Terror had taken hold of everyone, and the effects of this may be judged if I tell you that the town is encompassed by a circular boulevard that separates it from its suburbs, and that columns of troops were therefore converging on the Lindenau road – the only way out – from three different directions. So dense was the crowd that, having made my retreat by keeping to the fringes of the boulevard, I found that I could not get into the main stream without assistance. In the end two officers of the Eighty-Sixth opened the way for me. While one of them flung himself into the throng and opened a small space for me with his sabre, the other seized the bridle of the little Arab I was riding and dragged it into the middle of the road. So great was the press that it was lifted off its feet and for some moments literally carried along.[80]

For all the disorder, at first all went well enough. Disorganized and exhausted themselves, the Allies did not react until the retreat had been under way for many hours, and even then they were held at bay by the French rearguard. Many of Napoleon's troops therefore escaped, and even more would doubtless have done so but for the causeway being mistakenly blown up. As a result of this, defeat was converted into catastrophe: at least 30,000 French troops who might have got away were now either killed or captured. Added to the 38,000 casualties the

French had suffered over the previous three days, not to mention the many thousands who had been lost earlier in the campaign, this was a blow from which recovery was simply impossible. On the battlefield lay the wreckage not just of an army, but of an empire. On 21 October, Sir George Jackson rode into Leipzig in company with Metternich:

Part of our way lay over the field of battle, and a more revolting and sickening spectacle I never beheld. Scarcely could we move forward a step without passing over the dead body of some poor fellow, gashed with wounds and clotted in the blood that had weltered from them; another, perhaps, without an arm or a leg; here and there a headless trunk, or it might be a head only, which caused our horses to stumble or start aside, or it might be one of their own species lying across our path, his entrails hanging out, or some part of his body blown away. It made one's blood run cold to glance only, as we passed along, upon the upturned faces of the dead, agony on some, a placid smile on others . . . We got over this 'field of glory' as quickly as we could, and perhaps some of us affected to be less impressed by this terrible scene than we really were. But I know there was many an involuntary shudder, and that many of the glibbest tongues were for the time quite silenced.[81]

Allied casualties had also been very high – at least 50,000 men – but the victory was to prove cheap at the cost, with Napoleonic control of central and northern Europe now evaporating overnight. With the *grande armée* fleeing for the Rhine, Napoleon's German satellites either hastened to come over to the Allies or collapsed. Also lost at this time was Holland, which the French evacuated in the first week of November, leaving a group of influential notables to establish a provisional government. East of the Rhine, all that was left was Denmark, which, though fiercely loyal, had only a small army and was menaced by a Bernadotte determined to conquer Norway. On other fronts things were not much better. In the Pyrenees, Wellington's army had crossed the Spanish frontier, broken through the defensive lines the French had established and advanced to the outskirts of Bayonne. In the Illyrian provinces, the French had been driven out by a combination of a large Austrian army, a rising among the Croats of the old 'military frontier', and a small British naval squadron that took the ports of Trieste and Fiume. And in the Kingdom of Italy, the staunchly loyal Eugène de Beauharnais had rejected an attempt on the part of his father-in-law, King Maximilian of

Bavaria, to get him to change sides, but had none the less been forced to retreat to the Piave river, thereby abandoning large expanses of territory and with them much manpower and revenue. And finally in Naples Murat was supposedly mobilizing his army to assist Eugène, but he was known to be extremely pessimistic and stories were circulating that he was trying to negotiate a deal with the Allies.

The situation, then, was very bleak, but as evidence of Metternich's desire to keep Napoleon on the throne of France, in the wake of the battle of Leipzig there arrived one more peace offer. We come here to the so-called Frankfurt memorandum. Not surprisingly, the triumph of the Allies was viewed with little enthusiasm by the Austrian chancellor. Those in the allied camp who wished to see the overthrow of Napoleon had naturally been encouraged by the results of Leipzig, while Metternich feared that it would whip up support for German nationalism, and all the more so as Stein had come west from Königsberg in the hope of promoting revolution. To deal with this situation, Metternich negotiated a series of bilateral agreements with states such as Baden and Württemberg that safeguarded their independence in exchange for their accession to the allied cause, and at the same time pressurized Alexander into demoting Stein's putative German government to a mere control commission whose authority was restricted to those areas like Saxony (whose monarch paid the price of not going over to the Allies in April) that had no legitimate government. But the crucial issue was to put an end to the war, and this was also the only means of saving Napoleon. What was needed was a new peace offer – and one that was very generous. France, Metternich now suggested, should be offered the frontiers of 1797 complete with Belgium and the Rhineland. In this he was supported by a Nesselrode as alarmed by Stein's 'Jacobinism' as he was, and this in turn produced the agreement of Alexander I. There was a degree of calculation here – the tsar seems to have believed that Napoleon would again reject a deal and thereby legitimize the continuation of the war. Much more surprising was the behaviour of the British ambassador to Austria, Lord Aberdeen. Young and inexperienced, he had been severely shaken by what he had seen at Leipzig and, without consulting any of his fellow envoys, therefore gave his assent to the new terms as well, even though they left several important British goals completely unredeemed.

Whether the proposed settlement would ever actually have been ratified is impossible to say. But in the circumstances it was the best that

Napoleon could hope for. Instead of the prompt agreement that was the most realistic response, however, there came mere temporizing. According to the envoy who brought him the terms, the emperor wanted peace and was prepared to abandon Spain and recognize the collapse of the Confederation of the Rhine on condition of a guarantee of Dutch neutrality and the preservation of the Kingdom of Italy in its present form. However, his written response was much less forthcoming. Napoleon refused to comment on the terms at all, and merely proposed fresh peace talks. This was not enough. The Frankfurt memorandum had caused fury in the British camp – 'Metternich . . . I consider one of our greatest enemies,' wrote Sir George Jackson[82] – and Cathcart and Stewart therefore pressed hard for the terms to be withdrawn or at least for their discussion to be postponed until a special plenipotentiary of real stature could be sent out from London. In practice, then, the proposals lapsed. Such a plenipotentiary was duly sent out in the person of no less a figure than Lord Castlereagh, but by then the allied armies had pushed on to the Rhine, and with every step they advanced the Frankfurt frontiers became more and more unrealistic. But even now by no means all the allied leaders were committed to the overthrow of Napoleon. Frederick William of Prussia, for example, was particularly hesitant:

The king had hoped that peace might be brought about, and he first learned in Frankfurt that, so far from this, the passage of the Rhine had been fixed for the 1st of January. Thrown into the worst possible humour by this news, he sent for Gneisenau and myself to express his dissatisfaction . . . and to reproach us for not having advised against so hazardous an enterprise. We instantly confessed that we had recommended the measure most urgently as Napoleon had rejected the conditions for peace by demanding the most ridiculous conditions. We explained to the king at full length . . . that, of the three great powers, Prussia herself had the greatest interest in seeing this war-loving Napoleon . . . annihilated, if possible by dethroning him, or, if this could not be effected, by driving . . . France back within her old boundaries . . . The king listened to us attentively. Nevertheless, he was not convinced by our reasoning, and persisted in his apprehension that the expedition to Paris would end badly.[83]

The war, then, continued. Back in France Napoleon proceeded to try to rebuild his fortunes. Already a fiction, the French kingdom of Spain was now abandoned: Joseph Bonaparte had already been brusquely sacked in the wake of Vitoria, and, deciding that the moment was ripe to cut his losses, Napoleon now sent a message to Madrid offering to release the imprisoned Ferdinand VII on the understanding that he would make peace with France and expel the Anglo-Portuguese. When these terms were firmly rejected, he decided to release Ferdinand anyway, but while chaos ensued – the result was a military coup that restored absolutism – it was much too late to make any difference. What was left of France's Peninsular army was therefore going to have to keep fighting in the south-west. Nor was it of the slightest account that the emperor also released the Pope and directed him to make his way to Rome. Without the resources of the *grande empire*, the regime's demands soared. Taxes shot up dramatically: land tax rose by 95 per cent and property tax by 100 per cent. As for manpower, in addition to the 350,000 men called up between January and April 1813, and another 30,000 men called up in August, October saw a demand for 120,000 men from the classes of 1809 to 1814 and 160,000 men from the class of 1815, this being followed a month later by a second demand for 300,000 from the classes of 1803 to 1814. And, as if this was not enough, another 180,000 men were mobilized for service as members of the National Guard. This was a *levée en masse* such as France had not seen since 1793. Alongside it, indeed, the 500,000 men raised under the Terror paled into insignificance.

The impact of all this was catastrophic. The war had already been unpopular in France, but the atmosphere produced by the news of Leipzig was one of growing panic. As Pasquier wrote:

There was no longer any hope in anything: every illusion had been destroyed. There were certainly long columns in *Le Moniteur* full of patriotic addresses and expressions of devotion on the part of every corporation, every town council, but this official language had the appearance of a practical joke. It would have been much better by far for the government to have maintained a dignified silence.[84]

If confirmation was needed of the state to which France was reduced, it was the sights that accompanied the arrival of the survivors of the German campaign. 'The army returned in the most dreadful condition,' wrote Lavallette. 'The number of sick and wounded was immense; the hospitals and private houses were not enough to contain them, and that most deadly malady, typhus fever, attacked not only the army, but every village and town through which it passed.'[85] As for fresh recruits, there were scarcely any to be had, still less any will to send them.

France had long since been exhausted, not so much of money . . . but of men. This last scarcity . . . threw whole families into despair and want. They really were bled to the uttermost. The poor man had to give his last son and in him lost his support, and in the fields it was often the women and girls who led the plough . . . And the same disasters occurred in the towns. Numbers of families condemned themselves perpetually to cripple their fortunes in order to save the young man whom other measures ended by reaching . . . The crepe with which the Russian and Leipzig campaigns had covered France had not yet disappeared; bitter tears were still being shed.[86]

Despair, then, was widespread, and to this was added political disaffection. In few parts of the country was royalism much of a force. According to Rochechouart, 'With the exception of the nobility, the clergy and a few wealthy members of the old bourgeoisie, the majority of the populace did not even know the name of Louis XVIII.'[87] But anger at the increased demands of the state inflamed old political antagonisms. Following the Leipzig campaign, for example, Marbot had ended up at Mons in the former Austrian Netherlands. As he wrote, 'I found the spirit of the population changed. There was a regret for the old paternal government of Austria, and a keen desire for separation from France, and the perpetual wars which were ruining commerce and industry. In short, Belgium was only awaiting the opportunity to revolt . . . From my hotel I could see every day 3,000 or 4,000 peasants and artisans assembling in the square and listening to the talk of certain retired Austrian officers . . . All French officials left the department to take refuge at Valenciennes and Cambrai.'[88] At Mons serious trouble was averted by vigorous action on the part of the garrison, but at nearby Hazebrouck there was serious rioting. And even where there was no overt resistance, draft evasion once again became a serious problem, and with it a renewal of brigandage. Almost everywhere there was a mood of barely suppressed fury. 'Observant minds saw plainly that the emperor had already lost his head, and that he would soon lose his crown. Consequently public opinion was violently opposed to him. His military and financial operations were loudly blamed. No longer dreaded, he became the butt of diatribes, satirical songs, lampoons, and all the other offensive weapons employed by French public opinion.'[89] Even attempts to play

on fears of invasion had no effect: 'I was at the Vaudeville,' wrote the
Duc de Broglie. 'The police had given orders for the performance there
of an appropriate play, in which Cossacks plundered a village, pursued
young girls, and set fire to the barns: the piece was outrageously hissed
from the very beginning, interrupted by the noise from the pit, and could
not be terminated.'[90]

Needless to say, the consequent social instability undermined the
loyalty even of the regime's own personnel, who as notables inevitably
had much to lose, as well as no desire to return to the days of Jacobinism
and the *levée en masse* which a desperate emperor now seemed to be
trying to revive. Not only was the rhetoric of the regime increasingly
echoing that of 1793, but Napoleon sent out extraordinary commissioners in the style of the old *députés en mission*, introduced a
number of measures intended to redistribute land to the peasantry, and
decreed the formation of a volunteer militia drawn from unemployed
workers in Paris and other towns of northern France. With a royalist
restoration no longer a serious threat in social and economic terms – on
1 February 1813 Louis XVIII had issued a well-publicized declaration
in which he promised generally to respect the status quo – the political
establishment saw no reason to support a fight to the finish. Already
in December 1813 the *corps législatif* had effectively demanded that
Napoleon make peace immediately. Further signs of disaffection now
appeared in the administration and the propertied classes. The prefects
and their deputies began to refuse to carry out their orders, to connive
at draft evasion and the non-payment of taxes, and even to abscond
altogether, while the bond issue of 200 million francs the regime had
authorized to finance the war effort at the beginning of the year proved
a disaster. Typical enough was the attitude of the former governor of
the Grand Duchy of Berg, Count Beugnot, who in the winter of 1813
was appointed to the prefecture of the department of the Nord: 'I gave
up trying to levy conscripts. More than that, I sent home the young men
from the leading families of the department who had been swept into
the Gardes d'Honneur, and put an end to the persecution that had been
directed against their parents . . . And, finally, loudly proclaiming that,
in the situation that the department might find itself at any moment, all
its people together would not be enough to defend it, I promised that
no one who was called up would be expected to serve outside its limits.'[91]

The new armies, then, were not forthcoming. Asked to provide 5,000 men, for example, Seine Inférieure managed only 1,457, and the country as a whole raised only 63,000. Even had more men appeared, there were few arms. Many of the National Guard, for example, were armed with no more than pikes and fowling pieces. Faced with disaster, the emperor displayed immense energy – 'He goes to bed at eleven o'clock,' his secretary, Baron Fain, told a concerned Lavallette, 'but he gets up at three in the morning and until evening there is not a moment when he is not working.'[92] But no quantity of orders could change matters, and Fain admitted that his master was 'utterly tired out'.[93] Yet there was still no mention of peace. 'Peace! Peace! It's easy enough to say the word,' Napoleon shouted at Beugnot, 'Am I to give up all that I possess in Germany? I have 100,000 men in the fortresses along the Elbe, in Hamburg and in Danzig. If the enemy are foolish enough to cross the Rhine, I will march to meet them . . . and have my garrisons fall on their rear, and then you will see the meaning of the word *débâcle*.'[94] However, in reality, Napoleon's power was on its last legs. In northern Italy, it is true, Eugène de Beauharnais was still holding the line of the Adige, but, having first led his army northwards on the pretext of reinforcing the defenders, Murat suddenly declared against the emperor in a desperate bid to save his throne. In the meantime Bentinck was preparing to set sail for the north from Sicily with an Anglo-Sicilian expeditionary force. Of the Polish strongholds, all had fallen, and in Germany only Hamburg, Wittenberg and Torgau still held out. Still worse, the erstwhile members of the Confederation of the Rhine were all mobilizing large numbers of conscripts, some of them enrolled in popular militias of the same sort as those seen in Prussia. In Denmark and Norway, Danish resistance was being crushed by Swedish troops. Yet another British expeditionary force was being readied for service in Holland. And in France there were only 85,000 men to defend the eastern frontier against an initial total of at least 350,000 Allies, while another 40,000 Frenchmen were facing 90,000 British, Portuguese and Spaniards in the south-west. With reinforcements almost non-existent, it was hardly surprising that many of the emperor's closest confidants were begging him to make peace on whatever terms he could get: 'With a blunt frankness only pardonable for its sincerity, I told him that France was worn out, that the country could not bear much longer the intolerable burden under which it was crushed, and that the people would throw off the yoke in order to surrender themselves, in accordance with their unfortunate habit, to some novelty . . . Particularly I spoke a good deal to him concerning the Bourbons, who would end by inheriting the spoils of his monarchy if ill-luck should overthrow him.'[95]

For the emperor, however, cheer was still to be found in the continued devotion shown by some soldiers. In Paris, one last parade saw Napoleon entrust Marie-Louise and the King of Rome to the garrison prior to his departure for the front: 'The enthusiasm generated by the emperor when he took the young king in his arms . . . can never be forgotten by its witnesses. Frenetic and prolonged cries of "Vive l'empereur!" moved from the Hall of Marshals to the national guard assembled in the Carrousel . . . These demonstrations of so true a love for his son moved the emperor: he kissed the young prince with a warmth that escaped none in the audience.'[96] Instead of listening to the calls for peace with which he was bombarded, Napoleon therefore chose to fight on in the hope of improving his bargaining position, striking hard and fast at a succession of allied commanders as they invaded eastern France. At first it seemed he might succeed. Suffering five major defeats in three weeks, the shaken Allies offered peace on the basis of the frontiers of 1792. But once again Napoleon had been too successful for his own good, electing to fight on in the hope of forcing the resurrection of the Frankfurt proposals. It was his last mistake. Though his improvised armies had performed prodigies of valour, little more could be expected from them, while, recovering their nerve, the Allies now pressed for the frontiers of 1791.

Whether Napoleon could still have achieved anything on the battle-field remains a moot point among historians, but in fact the question is irrelevant. The French state was falling apart. Even the most enthusiastic Jacobins were not fooled by the regime's attempts to evoke the spirit of 1793, while the bulk of the population was furiously hostile to the demands of the regime for yet more men, and angry at the depredations of the half-starved French army. 'Everywhere Napoleon was execrated,' wrote the former member of the Committee of Public Safety, Bertrand Barère. 'A general wish prevailed that the foreigners might be defeated and driven from France, and yet the victories of the emperor were dreaded because they were likely to encourage him in his despotism.'[97] In those areas penetrated by the Austrians, Prussians and Russians, there was much brutality on the part of the invaders, and this produced a few instances of popular resistance, but where the Allies behaved well, as was almost invariably the case in the areas occupied by Wellington, the enemy troops had a friendly welcome. As one of Wellington's officers remembered, 'The English army became popular in time. All the supplies were paid in gold by us, while their own army did not respect property. It was said at the time that Marshal Soult remarked, "I may expect to find by-and-by that the inhabitants will take up arms against us." '[98] In the confusion there were frequent disturbances by the population. 'The peasants in the district of Gourdon . . . endured the execrable and ruin-ous yoke of the customs dues with impatience. They flocked together to Gourdon on market-day to the number of 4,000, piled up the books and registers of the custom-house in the middle of the public square and set fire to them after expelling all the officials.'[99] The elites were no more enamoured of the regime than the people, and expressions of support for the Bourbons began to multiply dramatically. And, last but not least, Napoleon's intransigence had driven the Allies closer together, an agreement reached on 1 March committing all of the powers to total victory over the emperor. 'People realized,' wrote the Duchess of Reggio, 'that, by yielding a certain number of his conquests in preceding years, the emperor might have saved France this invasion; that a little later, the line of the Rhine would at least have been left to him; that, even at the time we had reached, if he would only give the Duke of Vicenza (his representative at the congress of Châtillon) the latitude which that zealous functionary demanded, he would still obtain support-able conditions of peace. Peace! The cry was in every heart, for of glory, the everyday food of the country, France had had a sufficient share.'[100]

As to Napoleon's state of mind as this veritable twilight of the gods unfolded, we have no better guide than the memoirs of Caulaincourt, who had at the last minute been restored as Foreign Minister and sent to represent France at the abortive peace talks that opened at Châtillon:

The break-up of the congress was inevitable. I had long anticipated this, and had foretold it to the emperor, who, deceiving himself with his habitual and unhappy illusions, was doubtless unwilling to believe it. He kept flattering himself that a military success would drive the enemy away from the capital, that after the enemy had had the slightest reverse, the exasperation and courage of the citizens would force a withdrawal from France. He wrote to the Emperor of Austria, and he had the Prince of Neuchâtel write to Prince

Schwarzenberg, as though the negotiations were being held 150 leagues from Paris, as though there were some hope of disuniting powers that had been brought together by a common peril, regardless of any concern other than to escape from the supremacy and sway of the cabinet of the Tuileries . . . For the time being there was but one aim: to subdue France – to chain up Napoleon's power and reach a state of rest . . . But the emperor . . . did not submit to sacrificing for his personal safety the departments which the arms of the Republic had won . . . As I have said already, he gauged everyone's zeal by his own . . . Hoping for a piece of luck, he wished to make time for it to happen, and, instead of answering my dispatches, he sent me nothing but bulletins of victories, so-called . . . as if . . . the winning of a fight against a single corps could change the basis of affairs . . . Dangers crowded upon him, encompassed him, oppressed him, from every side, but he thought to escape from them, and even to hide them from others, by misrepresenting them to himself.[101]

This analysis was confirmed by the reception Caulaincourt received on his return to Napoleon's headquarters. As reported by the unfortunate envoy, the emperor's talk had become even more rambling and incoherent than it had been in the wake of the retreat from Moscow:

To humble us – that is what our enemies wish, but death is better. I am too old a campaigner to hang on to life: I will never sign away France's honour . . . All the high officials are frightened, even the ministers . . . The peasants of Burgundy and the Champagne have more spirit than all the men on my council: you all have the shivers. The word runs that the counter-revolution is complete because the mayor of Bordeaux has turned traitor. No one understands the French but me: indignation will follow on the heels of dejection. You will see what is going to happen before a week is out. The whole population will be under arms; we shall have to come to the enemy's rescue to stop the violence; they will slaughter everything that has a foreign look to it. We will make a fight of it, Caulaincourt. If the nation supports me, the enemy is nearer ruin than I am for anger is running high. I cut the allied communications: they have numbers, but no support. I rally some of my garrisons, wipe out one of their corps, and the slightest reverse can drive them away. They know what their last retreat has already cost them: another move like that and not one of them escapes. If I am beaten, it is better to fall gloriously than subscribe to terms such as the Directory would not have accepted after their Italian reverses. If I have support, I can regain everything.

If fortune deserts me, the country will not be able to reproach me with the breaking of my coronation oath.[102]

The reality, though, was one of misery and horror. The populace of eastern France was not, as Napoleon kept insisting, turning on the invaders, but rather trying desperately to survive. Among them was the writer Charles de Pougens and his niece, Louise de Saint-Léon. Caught in Soissons by the invasion, they first experienced the terrors of siege and assault:

Taking refuge . . . in a ground-level room whose firmly sealed shutters kept us plunged in complete darkness, we listened with many shudders to the explosion of the bombs that rained around us; one shell fell with a terrifying crash in the garden barely a hundred paces from where we were, and reduced a very large tree to dust. Soon afterwards . . . Soissons was taken by assault . . . and the Russians hurled themselves on the ramparts emitting cries, or rather screams, that made us tremble. I won't go into any detail on the terrible events that followed: all that I will say is that the massacre of our poor soldiers and the pillage of the town lasted for a full hour.[103]

Soissons was liberated soon after, but Pougens and his family chose to flee to Louise's home in the nearby village of Vauxbuin. This, however, proved an unfortunate choice. On 2 March, 6,000 Cossacks descended on the village. Pougens managed at first to keep the group safe by persuading the commander that he had been a correspondent of the wife of Paul I, but no sooner had the Cossacks departed than a large group of stragglers appeared and sacked Louise's house. Utterly terrified, left almost without food and constantly threatened by further bands of marauders, Pougens and his family then made their way on foot to Nanteuil, where they managed to board a stagecoach bound for Paris. But in the capital things were little better. Working on the staff of one of the city's main hospitals was the young surgeon, Poumiès de la Siboutie:

Fighting was going on at the gates of Paris. The wounded were brought in in hundreds. We were soon overcrowded. Every available inch of space was filled: the ordinary sick had to be sent to their homes; the pensioners . . . and the incurables were turned out of their wards and herded together in dark corners and attics. Before long even that was not enough, and two patients were assigned to every bed. Each day fresh means had to be devised to house the steadily increasing tide of sick and wounded. The unfortunate fellows dragged themselves to Paris, animated by a feverish desire to obtain shelter and succour. Some fell exhausted on the very steps of the hospital and expired as they reached the haven of a bed. Many had sores and wounds which had not been dressed for days, if ever. Every morning the hospital hearses bore thirty or forty corpses to their long rest. It was the same in all the other asylums and hospitals.[104]

Meanwhile, as even some of Napoleon's most loyal subordinates admitted, the propaganda of the regime had little effect, and was, indeed, counter-productive:

The *Moniteur* was filled with all the complaints, with all the lamentations, of the wretched inhabitants of Montmirail, of Montereau and of Nangis . . . All the towns which had been afflicted with the scourge of war sent deputies to Paris to describe their misery and demand vengeance . . . The great examples of antiquity were invoked; France was reminded of her achievements in 1792 . . . But, it must be confessed, these measures produced at Paris and in all the great towns an effect quite contrary to that which was expected from them. The inhabitants were too civilized to adopt the decisive conduct of the Russians and the Spaniards. The imagination of the citizens was shocked at the violence of the measures suggested to them . . . and peace was loudly demanded as the period of so many horrors.[105]

With matters in such a state, the end came quickly. Though Napoleon continued to fight and manoeuvre relentlessly, he could achieve little. On 9 March Bentinck had landed at Livorno from where, having issued a call for a national revolt against the French that met with no response whatsoever, he marched on Genoa. On 12 March Bordeaux had proclaimed Louis XVIII, its authorities having first made sure that they would be immediately relieved by the Anglo-Portuguese army. As in 1870 and 1940, refugees were streaming west, adding to the confusion. Among those who fled Paris as the enemy closed in was the wife of Marshal Oudinot:

The Versailles road was free . . . We let the empress, her suite and her escort set out, and at about four o'clock in the afternoon we ourselves departed . . . It was almost dark when we arrived. We took possession of two adjacent rooms in an already crowded house in the Rue de l'Orangerie. During the whole night an incessant and confused noise told us of the passage of a large number of men, horses and carriages, and soon the daylight revealed the most astonishing sight that human eyes perhaps have ever looked upon. We stood motionless at our windows. What we saw passing . . . was the empire, the empire . . . with all its pomp and splendour, the ministers . . . the entire council of state, the archives, the crown diamonds, the administrations. And instalments of power and magnificence were mingled on the road with humble households who had heaped up on a barrow all they had been able to carry away from the houses which they were abandoning.[106]

At this point, the army finally broke as well: with the soldiers deserting in droves, at Lyons Augereau simply abandoned his headquarters and in Paris Marmont first surrendered the city, and then led his troops over to the enemy.

It was a climactic moment. With Alexander I and Frederick William III both in the capital, the initiative was now seized by Talleyrand, who had been living there in semi-retirement and now set about persuading the allied monarchs that Napoleon had to go. A rather doubtful Alexander had to be persuaded by some hastily organized demonstrations of support for Louis XVIII, but on 1 April the allied monarchs issued a declaration that they would no longer treat with Napoleon or any of his family, and that France's future government would be decided by the wishes of the French people as expressed by an immediate meeting of the Senate. Stage-managed by Talleyrand, this event could have had but one end. On 2 April the Senate proclaimed Napoleon to be deposed and formally invited Louis XVIII to return to France. Meanwhile, Napoleon was at Fontainebleau with 60,000 men. Though the emperor was still ready to fight on, his remaining commanders could take no more and on 4 April Napoleon was bluntly informed that he must abdicate. The war was not quite over: if only because news of the armistice reached him too late, Wellington fought one last battle at Toulouse on 10 April, while various isolated garrisons also held on for a few more days. But this was a mere detail. Forced to yield to force majeure, on 28 April the emperor sailed for the Elban exile decreed by a treaty negotiated with him at Fontainebleau. The peace of Europe had been restored.

So what finally brought down Napoleon? Certainly not some mythical 'people's war', nor even a general decision to employ the weapons of the French Revolution against him. The answer, of course, is in part to be found in Napoleon himself. Tired, far from healthy, and increasingly living in a world of fantasy, he threw away his only hope of victory in Russia, and then proceeded repeatedly to reject peace offers that would have left him ruler of a country larger than it had been when war began in 1792. In the words of a song popular in the British army of the period, 'Boney was a warrior' and, as such, there could be no peace except one based on the complete subordination of his opponents – that did not, in short, represent the very apotheosis of military glory. Even as late as 1812, this was not a problem in political terms, for Napoleon possessed the resources of an imperium that stretched from the Pyrenees to the Pripet. But pursued in the very different circumstances of 1813 and, still more so, 1814, it was another matter entirely. Forced to make demands of France of a sort which domination of ever greater areas of the Continent had shielded her from ever since 1799, if not 1793, the emperor shattered the acquiescence – often grudging – with which his rule had hitherto been accepted, while at the same time betraying the interests of the propertied elements that were the real bedrock of his regime. Just as damaging, meanwhile, was the impact on the loyalty of Napoleon's satellites: in June 1813, for example, every interest of the 'Third Germany' encapsulated by the Confederation of the Rhine lay in a compromise peace that would have seen a Grand Duchy of Warsaw that the emperor could not protect restored to Austria and Prussia, but compared with the emperor's personal prestige, the interests of Maximilian of Bavaria and the rest were as nothing. Preferring to 'go for broke', he jeopardized every gain they had made in the last ten years and in the process thought nothing of throwing open their peaceful domains to the horrors of war. With their loyalties tested beyond endurance, the princes were therefore thrown willy-nilly into the arms of Metternich, and this, of course, intensified the pressure on France still further.

To a certain extent the emperor's reputation has been shielded from the impact of the complete lack of realism he displayed in the last year of his reign by the extraordinary last-ditch defence which he mounted in the face of the Allies' invasion of France. Even now, in fact, admirers of the emperor still solemnly dream of what might have happened if only Marmont had not surrendered Paris, or the French people had not betrayed their great saviour. Nothing, however, could be more misleading. In the campaign of 1814 – generally agreed to have been one of the most masterly of his entire career – Napoleon certainly achieved much local success, but this was simply the reflection of a situation in which the *grande armée* was no longer *grande*. Able to manoeuvre his army with something of his old celerity, Napoleon was also able to make himself physically visible to far more of his troops than had been the case in either 1812 or 1813: at Arcis-sur-Aube, he even fought sword in hand at the head of his escort and was almost killed when a shell burst directly under his horse. Once again, then, his extraordinary personal magnetism was able to inspire the teenage boys who formed the mainstay of his last army and the result was feats of heroism as great as anything seen in the Napoleonic Wars. Of these perhaps the greatest example was the battle of La Fère-Champenoise (25 February 1814) in which two National Guard divisions fought a desperate rearguard action and in the process lost all but 500 of their 4,000 men. There were therefore advantages to be found in weakness, but in 1814 they were no longer enough to turn the scales in the same way as they had in Italy in 1796, and, if Napoleon thought they could, it is but one more reason to doubt his grasp of the realities of his position.

By contrast, in the allied high command there gradually emerged a structure of authority that succeeded in both containing and channelling the many strains and tensions that beset the Sixth Coalition. One by one the allied rulers, or at least powerful representatives thereof, appeared at a common headquarters; joint strategies were evolved for dealing with the successive stages in the campaign; and, at key moments, major decisions involving all the coalition armies were taken that allowed the Allies to respond effectively to changing circumstances. On 24 March 1814, for example, it was decided to march straight down the river Marne towards Paris irrespective of anything that Napoleon might do to attack the allied rear. Almost to the end there was no unity in terms of war aims – the treaty of Chaumont committed the Allies to fighting on until Napoleon was defeated, but it did not insist on his removal from the throne, still less a Bourbon restoration – but methods were also elaborated that from the start militated against any of the powers reneging on the alliance altogether. From March 1813 onwards none of the powers fighting on the German front ever sent its forces into action in isolation: in the Leipzig campaign, for example, Bernadotte's Army of the North was a mixture of Swedes and Prussians, Schwarzenberg's Army of Bohemia a mixture of Austrians, Russians and Prussians and

Blücher's Army of Silesia a mixture of Prussians and Russians. And when quarrels did erupt in the allied camp, as for example, when Schwarzenberg, for strategic reasons, ordered allied forces to enter Switzerland after Alexander had promised to respect her neutrality, they were at no time allowed to become so bitter as to endanger the future of the war against Napoleon. Time and again, indeed, difficult situations were saved by renewed bouts of negotiation. For all the Allies there was a recognition that in the end the problem of Napoleon could only be resolved through maintaining allied unity. Against hegemony was pitted compromise, and in the end it was compromise that proved the stronger.

I I
The Congress of Vienna

At the beginning of this book, it was asked whether Napoleon had come to constitute, if not the history of the world, then at least the history of Europe, between 1803 and 1814. Following the invasion of Russia, this may be said to have been the case. Long-standing rivalries in Poland, the Baltic and the Balkans were all set aside and even states that had hitherto been bitter enemies such as Austria and Prussia joined forces in a cause represented as that of all Europe. Temporarily suspended, too, was the general suspicion of Britain that had so delayed the construction of the Third Coalition and enabled Napoleon at one time or another to find allies in states as disparate as Denmark, Spain and Russia. Prior to 1813, however, nothing so coherent could be found. For much of the period from 1803 to 1806, Prussia had had her eyes firmly fixed on Hanover, just as from 1807 to 1812 Russia's chief focus of attention had often been Moldavia and Wallachia. Next to the Danubian provinces, St Petersburg had cared most about Poland, but even this was not an interest primarily directed at Napoleon, but rather a reflection of trends in Russian foreign policy visible since at least the 1770s. And, as for the unity that pertained in 1814, in contractual terms it was even more recent in date than the campaigns of 1812 and 1813 from which it stemmed. Indeed, not until 9 March 1814 did the treaty of Chaumont give it formal recognition. No sooner had this document been signed, however, than the conditions which had given birth to the unity of the European Continent were suddenly overturned. Thoroughly defeated, Napoleon abdicated, and Europe, or so it seemed, could at last relax. The fallen emperor was in exile in Elba and the alliance that had toppled him free to settle the Continent more or less as it wished. Resourceful to the end, however, within a few short months the emperor was not only back in Paris but challenging the judgement of 1814. Yet the emperor's resurrection was shortlived: distrust each other though they did, Britain, Prussia, Austria and Russia feared Napoleon even more. No matter how many victories he succeeded in winning, then, the emperor must ultimately have been overwhelmed. Fortunately for Europe, however, the end came sooner rather than later. Thwarted in his efforts to win a great victory at the outset of the campaign, Napoleon was brought to bay near a hitherto obscure Belgian village named Waterloo, and beaten so completely that even he had to concede there was no other option but surrender.

Worried though some of the Allied statesmen were as to what Napoleon might yet do in 1814, the principal attention of the victors was rather concentrated on the peace settlement. In so far as this was concerned, some basic principles – the transfer of Norway to Sweden, the restoration of Austria and Prussia to a position equivalent to that which they had enjoyed prior to Austerlitz and Jena, the retention of a modified version of the Napoleonic state system in Germany, the return of the Bourbons to the throne of Spain, the prevention of further French aggression – had been settled, but many issues had been left unresolved, while much of the detail even of this programme remained extremely vague. Matters were not helped by the fact that there was no consensus as to what the aims of the peacemaking process should be. As a common starting point, it was held that there should be no more war in Europe, or at least a long period of general peace. From Madrid to Moscow governments were all but bankrupt and their peoples were both war-weary and increasingly unwilling to endure the burden of conscription. In many parts of Europe, too, commerce and industry and sometimes even agriculture were all but at a standstill. There was also a serious problem of public order: the hundreds of thousands of deserters, beggars and, in a few areas, irregular combatants of one sort or another proved a fertile breeding ground for brigandage. But most of all, war was equated with revolution. Whereas before 1789 conflict had been a matter of armies, cabinets and dynasties, from the French Revolution onwards it had been associated with frightening levels of social and political change. Setting aside the changes implemented in the territories ruled by France, in Prussia it had proved necessary to emancipate the serfs and, at least in theory, open the officer corps to all classes of society, while in Spain, Sicily and Sweden war had brought political revolution. Only slightly less frightening was the issue of popular revolt, whether it was in Valencia in 1801, Lombardy in 1809 or even England in 1811–12. Clearly, war had to be banished from the scene. How, though, was this to be done? In 1648 and 1713 general peace settlements – the treaties of Westphalia and Utrecht – had been negotiated after periods of near Continent-wide bloodshed, but these had been totally ineffectual when it came to remedying the features in the international system that led to conflict. What was needed, then, was a peace settlement that was very different from anything that had gone before – a revolutionary treaty for a revolutionary age.

The problem was that there was no agreement amongst the powers represented at the international congress that now met at Vienna. The chief positions on a 'systemic' approach to the peace treaty were those of Castlereagh and Alexander I. Let us begin with Castlereagh. The British Foreign Secretary was, as we have seen, a bitter opponent of the French Revolution and, still more so, of Napoleon, and he felt strongly that a restoration of the Bourbons was the best hope for the future. In April 1814 this had duly been achieved, but in a sense the problem had not gone away. There might be another revolution in France, or some new Louis XIV might emerge to challenge the existing order. The chief territorial aim of any settlement therefore had to be the construction of a barrier system that would keep France penned in. Inherited from Pitt, who had seen it as the necessary corollary to any compromise peace with the Republic or Napoleon, this scheme was the central goal of British foreign policy in 1814; but Castlereagh's views were not limited to Western Europe. On the contrary, it was quite clear to him, first, that there would have to be a territorial settlement that took in the Baltic, Poland and the Balkans as much as it did the Rhine frontier; second, that such a settlement would have to rest on a 'balance of power'; and third, that some means would have to be found of ensuring that future disputes were settled by means other than military conflict. Broadly speaking, the idea of an anti-French cordon sanitaire was endorsed by most of the other rulers and statesmen who came to the peace table. However, there were some important variations that were to give rise to many difficulties later on. To avoid provoking her unnecessarily, Castlereagh, for example, wanted France to be treated relatively leniently, whereas the Prussians wanted at the very least massive financial compensation and possibly territory in Alsace-Lorraine as well. Equally, while Castlereagh believed the moment for foreign intervention was the point at which France, or, indeed, any other power, threatened the general peace, Metternich thought in terms of intervention against revolution even when it remained within national boundaries. And, finally, whereas Castlereagh wanted to see a general guarantee that would commit the powers of Europe to maintaining the status quo established in the wake of the Napoleonic Wars against all comers, Alexander wanted to guarantee them against France alone, thereby giving Russia a free hand in Eastern Europe.

This was not the only issue separating Alexander from Castlereagh: in fact the tsar stood for an entirely different solution to Europe's problems. The basic objection to the ideas put forward by the British Foreign Secretary and, for that matter, Metternich, was that they took no account of the idea that revolution might stem from legitimate political, social and economic grievances. In their eyes, revolutionary ideology was self-evidently erroneous – lunatic even – and the men who espoused it little more than unprincipled adventurers. For them to take this line was understandable, perhaps – to recognize the legitimacy of liberal and nationalist aspirations would have been to challenge the very basis of the states which they represented. But it flew in the face of reality: the French Revolution, the Serbian revolt of 1804 and the convulsions which Spain had experienced in 1808, not to mention the enthusiasm felt by many Italians and even more Poles for the Napoleonic satellite states in which they found themselves, had all been the product of genuine grievances against the *ancien régime*. Deeply influenced as he was by a variety of progressive ideas, Alexander insisted that the victors could not remain blind to this problem. Since as early as 1804 he had been advocating a policy designed to lance the revolutionary boil. 'We shall see which shall succeed best,' Alexander had said on his return to Vilna in December 1812, 'to make oneself feared, or to make oneself loved.'[1] Rather than turning the clock back to 1789, the great powers should be building a new Europe in which its different peoples would be given constitutions that would defend them against despotism and aristocratic privilege and at the same time be organized in national states based on the principles of self-determination. This in itself would go a long way to safeguarding the peace, but there would also have to be a variety of institutional safeguards, especially a code of international law and a confederation of Europe.

Various factors had contributed to this programme over the years, including not least Alexander's own vanity, the urgings of Czartoryski in respect of Poland and, more widely, Eastern Europe, and the desire to push the Russian frontier ever further westwards. In the course of the past two years, however, one interest in particular had become ever more important. As we have seen, Alexander had undergone a great conversion experience in the wake of Napoleon's invasion of Russia, and this had played a large part in driving him onwards after the last French troops had staggered over the river Niemen into East Prussia. In the course of 1814 his religious fervour had intensified still further. One reason for this was simple gratitude for divine mercy, but in the course of his journey from the Vistula to the Rhine the tsar had encountered a variety of German mystic and pietist writers with whom he had not previously been familiar. Invited to Britain in the summer of 1814, in addition to being subjected to enough popular adulation to have turned far steadier heads, Alexander then came into contact with representatives of the Quakers, and was deeply moved by their morality and pacifism. Finally, there seems to have been a great feeling of guilt: with Europe devastated by war and disease, the constant round of balls, banquets and receptions that were the staple diet of the allied dignitaries grated upon the tsar and made him all the more convinced something must be done for the future of the Continent.

This thinking had been visible in Alexander's conduct since at least 1812. As we have seen, he had initially been hostile to the restoration of the Bourbons and had instead wanted to give France a ruler more in tune with the feelings of the age – a lesser Napoleon who could recreate the domestic glories of the Consulate without at the same time indulging in dreams of foreign conquest – and it was in fact Alexander who insisted the new France should be given a constitution, just as it was also Alexander who took steps to ensure the Helvetic Confederation did not lose the constitution she had been granted by Napoleon. And finally it was Alexander who played the leading part in securing for both the former emperor and his country the generous terms they were initially accorded. As he later said, 'I have but done my duty. It was frightful to see the evils about me [such as] the Austrians' and Prussians' fury and cupidity, which it was difficult to control. They wanted to use the right of reprisal, but that right has always been revolting to me, for one ought never to take vengeance except by doing good for evil.'[2] Mixed in with all this were the wildest contradictions: full of good intentions when it came to France or Germany, the tsar was to show, at the very least, a considerable capacity for self-delusion when it came to Poland, and was always inclined to exempt Russia from the rules of conduct which he sought to impose on other countries. Nor were there any moves in the direction of political or social reform in Russia, the limit of Alexander's generosity here being the cancellation of all tax arrears and a general release of all prisoners except those guilty of robbery or murder. That Poland did not in the end do very well out of the peace settlement, he did not deny: 'I have not kept all my promises to . . . the Poles, but in working for them I have had great obstacles to overcome . . . The other sovereigns were opposed as much as possible to my projects.'[3] But there was none the less a very different agenda here from the one developed by Castlereagh, and what made this all the more alarming was that in both Germany and Italy there were influential figures whose views chimed with those of the tsar, good examples being Heinrich vom Stein, who continued to favour a united Germany, and Lord William Bentinck, of whom an exasperated Castlereagh complained: 'You will see by Lord William's official dispatches . . . how intolerably prone he is to Whig revolutions everywhere . . . He seems bent on throwing all Italy loose. This might be well as against France, but against Austria and the King of Sardinia, with all the new constitutions which now menace the world with fresh convulsions, it is most absurd.'[4]

Conservatism, then, was set to clash with liberalism. Meanwhile, to complicate matters still further, none of the powers had in any sense abandoned their own particular interests. Britain was determined to exclude the issue of maritime rights from the peace settlement; took care to ensure that the disposition of the colonies of France and her allies was handled by herself alone; and strove hard to keep Belgium out of France's hands, not just to strengthen the buffer state that from the time of Pitt onwards had been envisaged in the Low Countries, but also because the exclusion of France from Belgium had always been deemed central to Britain's security. Equally, beneath the cover afforded by the need to restrain France, Prussia remained bent on the relentless search for territorial acquisitions that had been the mark of its foreign policy in the eighteenth century. As Talleyrand wrote in instructions drawn up for France's conduct at the Congress of Vienna:

In Italy it is Austria who must be prevented from acquiring paramount power by opposing other influences to her. In Germany it is Prussia. The exiguity of her monarchy makes ambition a sort of necessity to her. Any pretext seems good to her. No scruples stop her. Her convenience forms her right. It is thus that, in the course of sixty-three years, she has raised her population from less than four millions of subjects to ten million, and that she has been able to form for herself, if I may so term it, the frame of an immense monarchy, by acquiring here and there scattered territories, which she aims at uniting by incorporating in herself those that separate them. The terrible fall that her ambition brought upon her has not yet cured her of it ... She would have liked to have had Belgium. She would like to have all that lies between the present frontiers of France, the Meuse and the Rhine. She wants Luxembourg. All is lost if Mainz is not given her. She can have no security if she does not possess Saxony.[5]

To single out either Britain or Prussia is unfair, however. As Castlereagh complained, 'Our misfortune is that the powers all look to points instead of the general system of Europe, which makes an endless complication.'[6]

One final key issue was that the rulers and statesmen of 1814 were operating in a very different climate to their predecessors of the eighteenth century. For the first time in history diplomacy had to be conducted in the context of a public opinion that was both aware and aroused. In December 1812 Alexander had complained, 'Under the preceding reign and that of the Empress Catherine nobody troubled himself about the affairs of the state, but today everybody must be initiated into the mysteries of the government. And how can I satisfy all these opinions?'[7] In the Habsburg Empire the aftermath of the French defeat at Kulm had produced a riot: 'The same morning Marshal [sic] Vandamme was brought through Prague on his way to Russia. As soon as he appeared, the excited populace set up such a chorus of yells and hootings, that one would have supposed a whole army of savages or demons had been let loose. He was assailed by every indecent and opprobrious epithet that could be thought of or invented, every insulting gesture, every indignity that circumstances permitted them to heap upon him, and but for the strong guard that surrounded him he would probably have been sacrificed to their fury.'[8] Equally, as events moved to a climax in the campaign of 1813–14, public opinion in London became ever more clamorous for the overthrow of Napoleon. As the Allies closed in, Lord Liverpool specifically warned Castlereagh that any settlement that left the emperor on the throne could lead to serious trouble in London: 'You can scarcely have an idea how insane people are in this country on the subject of any peace with Bonaparte, and I should really not be surprised at any public manifestation of indignation upon the first intelligence of a peace with him being received.'[9]

With Napoleon defeated, however, the first priority was to come to some agreement about France. As we have seen, Louis XVIII had been restored and Napoleon sent to Elba, which a treaty signed on 12 April 1814 at Fontainebleau awarded him in perpetuity, along with a minuscule army drawn from the Imperial Guard, a single frigate, and an annual income of 2 million francs, Marie-Louise and the rest of the Bonaparte family being equally well provided for. But there yet remained the question of France's borders and again the path chosen was one of magnanimity. Signed on 30 May 1814, the treaty of Paris returned her to the frontiers of 1 November 1792 (the one exception was the Principality of Monaco which had been taken over by France in January 1792 and now once again became an independent state) and even awarded her eight border districts which reasons of strategy or geography suggested should really be part of France. Also restored were all France's colonies, apart from Tobago, St Lucia and Mauritius, which went to Britain, and the eastern half of St Domingue which, taken from her in 1795, was given back to Spain. At one time earmarked for Sweden, even Guadeloupe was once more to fly the French flag, though France did have to promise to abolish the slave trade within five years. There was no indemnity, no army of occupation, and no attempt to restore Europe's looted art treasures to their previous owners. And, finally, in one last sop to French dignity, an amnesty was declared for all those foreigners who had served the empire in Germany and elsewhere. There was some grumbling – the impending loss of Belgium, in particular, even led to wild talk of war – but France had got off extraordinarily lightly. If Talleyrand's memoirs ooze self-satisfaction on the matter, it was therefore with some reason:

I think I am justified in recalling with pride the conditions I obtained, no matter how painful and humiliating they were . . . When I think of the date of these treaties of 1814, of the difficulties of every kind that I experienced, and of the spirit of vengeance that I encountered in some of the negotiators . . . I await with confidence the judgement that posterity shall pass upon me. I shall simply call attention to the fact that, six weeks after the king's entrance into Paris, France's territory was secured, the foreign soldiers had quitted French soil, and, by the return of the garrisons of foreign fortresses and of the prisoners, she possessed a superb army, and finally that we had preserved all the admirable works of art carried off by our armies from nearly all the museums of Europe.[10]

If France was thereby contained within a powerful cordon sanitaire, the rest of Europe still had to be dealt with. No sooner had the Congress of Vienna opened in September 1814, however, than the deep-seated tensions that beset the alliance became all too apparent. The problem centred on the linked questions of Poland and Saxony. Motivated by the bizarre mixture of greed and idealism on which we have already commented, Alexander I was proposing the restoration of Poland – interpreted as the Napoleonic Grand Duchy of Warsaw – in the guise of a Russian satellite state ruled by a Romanov prince and provided with a liberal constitution. To this, however, neither Britain, nor Austria, nor Prussia could agree – Britain because it would have left Russia far too strong; Austria because it would have left Russia far too strong, handed Prussia enormous gains in Germany as compensation, and stimulated Polish resentment elsewhere; and Prussia because she would have been left with an indefensible eastern frontier (in which respect she particularly wished to regain the fortresses of Thorn and Posen). All three powers, meanwhile, were supported by France. For this there were several reasons. In the first place it was a good way of reinserting herself into the deliberations of the Allies. In the second, Talleyrand was genuinely much concerned at the potential advance of the Russian frontier to the Oder. And in the third, a further war offered an obvious means of affording employment to the increasingly rebellious army (see below). As the Duke of Wellington wrote in his new capacity as British ambasador to Paris: 'It is quite certain that the internal state of France must give the king most [sic] uneasiness, but this very state may drive him to war if he has a prospect of carrying it on successfully, and that the war will not be protracted to any great length of time.'[11] The result was a serious diplomatic impasse. As Castlereagh lamented,

You will perceive that we make but little way here. As yet I see no real spirit of accommodation: perhaps it is too much to expect that this congress should differ so much from its predecessors. It unfortunately happens that never at any former period was so much spoil thrown loose for the world to scramble for. If Russia had, in the abundance of her territory, been more disinterested, her influence, united with that of Great Britain and France, would have made the settlement comparatively easy. As it is, there is an absence of that controlling authority which is requisite to force a decision upon the ordinary details of business.[12]

Months of confused diplomacy ensued, and the result was a general air of frustration and exhaustion. As a German correspondent of Sir George Jackson wrote:

For the moment stagnation reigns in the council chamber, and from the weariness which naturally ensues from such a state of things, some are likely to die of ennui and the rest to commit suicide. Without the bright presence of the ladies, and the flirtations that naturally result from it, I doubt whether some of the plenipos [sic] would have existed so long.[13]

However, by the end of 1814 the situation was anything but boring. A variety of factors – Russian concessions and suspicion of the British – had caused the Prussians to join the Russians, while Britain, Austria and France were united in opposing them. Chiefly at stake was the fate of Saxony, which was Protestant, exceedingly rich and populous, contiguous to Prussia, under allied administration thanks to her failure to abandon Napoleon in 1813, and in consequence ideally suited to compensate Prussia for her Polish losses. For a brief moment it seemed that war might follow, but almost immediately Alexander backed off: lacking the stomach for more bloodshed, he was also concerned that the end to the War of 1812 brought by Britain's signature of the treaty of Ghent on 24 December 1814 would give her more freedom of manoeuvre in Europe. Nor were the Prussians much more eager for a fight. 'The Prussian generals so conduct themselves in the occupied countries as to make their government hated,' wrote Castlereagh's Under-secretary, Edward Cooke. 'Besides, were a war to take place, Prussia, not Russia, would have the burden, and the former would lose Saxony altogether, if not also the provinces they expect from the Kingdom of Westphalia and on the left bank of the Rhine.'[14] The result was that all parties to the dispute backed down. Very soon a compromise had been agreed whereby most of the Grand Duchy of Warsaw was reconstituted as 'Congress Poland' with Alexander as its monarch, and Prussia awarded Thorn, Posen and some two fifths of Saxony. In one more proof of the new atmosphere in which the statesmen of Europe were operating, the news of the survival of Saxony's independence was greeted with acclaim by the populace. As Sir George Jackson confided to his diary on 26 February 1815:

There was a great patriotic demonstration at Leipzig a few days since. The people assembled in multitudes in the market place, crying, 'Long live our king! Down with the Prussians!' In vain the police tried to disperse them [and] many heads were broken in the attempt, which served only to increase the tumult. At last the Prussian General-Commandant, Bismarck, issued a proclamation calling on the inhabitants to resume 'the wise and prudent attitude that they had maintained until the present moment', as he should be sorry if they compelled him to use harsh measures for maintaining order during the short time he probably had to remain in their country. The latter part of his announcement calmed the populace who after renewed *vivats* for their king and country gradually dispersed.[15]

Given Alexander's constant stress on the importance of constitutionalism in the peace settlement, it is perhaps worth saying something here about the new Polish state. Needless to say, this was constituted to the accompaniment of much official celebration in Warsaw:

The Emperor Alexander arrived at Warsaw on the twenty-sixth of October 1815. He made his entrance on horseback, wearing the Polish uniform and the decoration of the White Eagle. All the windows and streets on His Majesty's route were decorated with flowers, draperies and mottoes. The various deputations met him under a triumphal arch . . . The emperor would not accept the keys of the town, which were offered him by the president of the municipality, and responded thus to the speech of the magistrate, 'I do not accept the keys because I am not come here as a conqueror, but as a protector and friend who desires to see you all happy. But I will accept bread and salt as the most useful gift of God.' The Poles had finally found a king, a father. On the evening of that memorable day the town was illuminated with allegorical transparencies, and an innumerable crowd circulated through the streets shouting the name of their king, Alexander.[16]

Emotional weight was added by the return, under Alexander's auspices, of the 6,000 survivors of the army of the Grand Duchy of Warsaw who had emerged intact from the campaigns of 1813 and 1814. But it was soon clear that Congress Poland possessed little substance. Stripped of the province of Posen – the very heartland of the old monarchy – it was also denied union with the eastern districts seized by Russia in 1792 and 1795. Equally, Austria retained Galicia and regained the district of Tarnopol and, in deference to the wishes of Metternich, Cracow became a free city. Against this, there was a Polish government, a constitution, a Polish army, a separate citizenship for the inhabitants, and a separate code of law from that used in Russia (the Civil Code was retained in full and there was no return to serfdom). Yet in the end all this turned out to be so much show. As Talleyrand wrote cynically, 'Russia does not wish for the re-establishment of Poland in order to lose what she has acquired of it; she wishes it so as to acquire what she does not possess of it.'[17] Real power in the kingdom was held by Alexander's brother, the Grand Duke Constantine, who was commander-in-chief of the army, and the tsar's special envoy, Novosiltsev; Poland was completely tied to Russia in terms of her foreign policy; the Polish parliament proved to have little real power; the constitution's protection of civil liberties was ignored; and as the years passed it became clear that there was no intention of uniting Congress Poland with the eastern provinces. Also dishonoured were the vague references made in the treaty of Vienna to the notion of a Polish commonwealth: hopes for the establishment of a customs union that would enable people and goods alike to travel freely between the various zones of pre-partition Poland proved illusory and the Polish Church was deliberately split up into Prussian, Russian and Polish primatures. Clearly, the freedom on offer from Alexander amounted to very little. As the great resistance leader, Kosciuszko, wrote to Czartoryski as early as June 1815:

We must give thanks to the tsar for having revived the name of Poland, but the name alone does not constitute a nation. The extent of its territory and the number of its inhabitants also count for something. I do not see, unless it is our own desires, on what a guarantee of the promises he has made to us . . . to extend the frontiers of Poland to the river Dvina . . . can rest. By restoring a certain proportion in terms of strength and population between Russia and Poland, such an action would have made for a certain mutual consideration – a stable friendship even – between the Russians and ourselves. Meanwhile, possessed of a liberal constitution and the sort of autonomy for which they hoped, the Poles would have been happy to find themselves ruled alongside the Russians beneath the sceptre of so great a monarch. However, from the very beginning I have perceived a very different order of things. Russians, for example, are filling the leading places in the government alongside us. This certainly cannot inspire much confidence among the Poles: they foresee, not without fear, that over time the word 'Pole' will become a thing of scorn, and that the Russians will soon be treating us as their subjects. Still worse, how will a people so subjugated ever be able to extract themselves from their preponderance?[18]

This gulf between Alexander's rhetoric and the realities of Congress Poland made for one of the weakest points of the Vienna settlement. Far away in London, Lord Liverpool summed up the situation admirably:

The conduct of the emperor of Russia has not surprised me. He is vain, self-sufficient and obstinate, with some talent, but with no common sense or tact. I am strongly impressed with the opinion that this business of Poland will ultimately prove his ruin. If he detaches the Polish provinces incorporated with Russia from that country for the purpose of forming a Polish kingdom, he will never be forgiven by the Russians. If, on the other hand, he annexes the Duchy of Warsaw to Russia, and considers the whole as a mere territorial question, the Poles will justly reproach him as having deceived them, and they will become his bitterest enemies. In short, I see nothing but future commotion out of this Polish arrangement, let it now end as it may.[19]

With Poland and Saxony out of the way, the Congress was able to proceed with other business. Belgium was joined with Holland in a new Kingdom of the United Netherlands (although Holland had to cede the Cape of Good Hope to Britain); the Rhineland was split between Prussia and Bavaria; Genoa added to a restored Piedmont; the Papal States given back to the Pope; and Hanover, Oldenburg, Parma, Modena and Tuscany all restored as independent states. Austria acquired Venetia as well as recovering Lombardy, the Illyrian provinces, Voralberg, the Tyrol, Salzburg and Tarnopol; Bavaria got Würzburg; and Hesse and Prussia split what remained of Westphalia. Last but not least, Britain was given Malta and the Ionian islands. Thus far meanwhile, Naples had continued to be ruled by Joachim Murat, but Louis XVIII had from the start been anxious to remove him in favour of the exiled Ferdinand IV, the result being that Metternich agreed to send an Austrian army against the sometime marshal as a further means of securing French support against Russia.

While the map was thus being redrawn, Germany was also in the grip of a major political reorganization. The Holy Roman Empire had gone forever, but the need for the new Germany to be able to defend itself against French aggression dictated the adoption of some form of federal structure. A special committee having been established to consider the matter, a wide variety of schemes were soon under discussion. Hardly had they been tabled, indeed, than they were lent extra point: in the small hours of 7 March 1815 the stunning news arrived that Napoleon had escaped from Elba. What had happened? In brief, Napoleon had arrived in his new domain on 4 May 1814. Cast down by his downfall, he had initially appeared to accept his new role with equanimity, but it was not long before problems emerged. With incredible lack of foresight, Louis XVIII not only failed to pay Napoleon's annuity, but also confiscated his considerable personal fortune. With the Napoleonic administration inevitably pressing ever harder on the population of Elba, there was also some danger of revolt. Yet would Napoleon have remained quiet even had all been well? According to all accounts, the emperor had rapidly become bored and restless, and it is possible that right from the very beginning he was secretly harbouring dreams of a triumphant return to France. In this respect, the tenor of a conversation that he had in September 1814 with the British commissioner who had been sent to Elba to watch over him is certainly suggestive:

Yesterday I had an audience with Napoleon . . . This audience lasted three hours, during which time there was no interruption. He constantly walked from one extremity of the room to the other, asked questions without number, and descanted upon a great variety of subjects, generally with temper and good nature, excepting when it bore upon the absence of his wife and child, or the defection of Marshal Marmont. He began by asking questions as to . . . Piedmont, Lombardy, Venice and Tuscany. [In his view] the rude manners and different language of the Austrians rendered it impossible for them to become popular with the Italians, who were flattered by the formation of the Kingdom of Italy . . . He enquired with great interest as to the real state of France . . . He appeared to admit the stability of the sovereign and government, supported as the former is by all the marshals . . . but [argued] that the imitation of Great Britain in the government and constitution was absurd . . . After continuing in that strain for a long time . . . he spoke with some warmth of the cessions made by France since his abdication

. . . It was not wise on the part of the Allies to exact them. He spoke as a spectator without any hope or interest . . . But it showed an ignorance of the French character and [the] temper of the present times. Their chief feeling was pride and glory, and it was impossible for them to look forward with satisfaction and tranquillity . . . under such sacrifices. They were conquered only by a great superiority of numbers, [and had not been] humiliated. The population of France had not suffered to the extent that may be supposed, for he had always spared their lives, and expended the Italians, Germans and other foreigners. These observations gradually led him to his own feats in war and the last campaign, [in respect of which] he entered into the details of many operations in which he had repulsed [the enemy] and gained advantages with numbers inferior beyond comparison, and to abuse of Marshal Marmont, to whose defection alone he ascribed his giving up the contest.[20]

Napoleon can only have been encouraged by the stories he was receiving from France, where Bourbon rule had quickly proved unpopular. At the heart of the problem was the old imperial army. In part the issue was one of perception: much of the army had not shared the miseries of 1814, the many thousands of men tied up in isolated garrisons that had held out to the end having come home convinced that they were undefeated. Sharing their sense of betrayal, meanwhile, were the many prisoners of war who now returned from a captivity that had frequently been quite appalling. In part it was a question of economics: whether they had been held in allied prisons, manned the walls of such fortresses as Hamburg, or fought to defend France herself, many veterans now found themselves out of a job or, at best, on half-pay. And, finally, in part it was a question of justice: even those officers and men fortunate enough to have secured a place in the new army had to suffer the humiliation of watching hundreds of Bourbon favourites who had sat out the war in safety being promoted and decorated. Typical of the general feeling are the words of General Thiébault:

Twenty-three years of terrible wars, begun with so much heroism, carried on so unflinchingly and gloriously, ended by blunders so great and disasters so appalling, had produced fatigue, exhaustion, disgust [and] anger. There had been a unanimous wish for peace, and peace had been obtained, but in the calm of repose the sentiment of honour resumed its rights. Having come to ourselves, we could fathom the depth of the abyss into which we had been hurled, and measure the distance from the giant we had lost to the man who took his place. Great errors, doubtless, had . . . brought about the end of his mighty reign, but with him there had been great hopes and a future in view, while those who figured in his place offered neither security nor hope. No one could venture to expect anything from a family . . . who, as Napoleon said, had in five-and-twenty years of deserved misfortune learned nothing and forgotten nothing. They insulted the army; they dismissed all the respectable officials; they snatched away all that could be snatched away from a nation that had already been despoiled. Less than this would have been the ruin of Napoleon at the height of his power and renown.[21]

If veterans of the *grande armée* were prominent in the general grumbling, they were by no means alone. In 1814 the Bourbons had not appeared so bad an option, but perceptions had now changed. In contrast to the moderate views that Louis XVIII had been espousing in 1813, many officials were now sacked, the Church treated with great deference, and the nobility favoured over the bourgeoisie. Many notables, then, were very unhappy, especially as stories began to circulate that the *biens nationaux* might be returned to their previous owners. Nor did such policies do anything to reassure committed liberals, this group having already been alienated by the defects of the constitution drawn up by the Senate in April 1814. The peasantry, too, were concerned for such land as they had acquired during the Revolution, as well as fearful that the tithes and feudal dues were to be restored. Finally, assailed by post-war depression and an influx of cheap British goods, the industrial workers were suffering severe unemployment, and in consequence missed the paternalism that had, however imperfectly, shielded them under the empire.

All this encouraged Napoleon, but by the end of 1814 other issues had begun to push him in the direction of taking action. Setting aside the French government's failure to pay the erstwhile emperor the pension that it had been agreed he should receive, there had always been those who regarded Elba as a place of exile that was not just generous but distinctly injudicious. Both Francis I and Metternich had been violently opposed to the arrangement, all the more so as the treaty of Fontainebleau also gave Marie-Louise and her son the nearby Grand Duchy of Tuscany. Castlereagh, too, was very worried, while Sir Charles Stewart wondered 'whether Napoleon may not bring . . . powder to the iron mines which the island of Elba is so famous for'.[22] According to

Bonapartist sources, from this dissatisfaction there emerged a settled determination to have him murdered. Whether any of this was true, it is hard to say, but by the beginning of 1815 Napoleon's household was in the grip of something that amounted to panic. 'People feared for the emperor's person,' wrote Napoleon's valet, Marchand. 'News arriving from Vienna, via Livorno and Naples, was not reassuring . . . There was talk of St Helena . . . Navy commander Chautard was ordered to keep a vigilant watch on . . . ships cruising near Elba . . . Some defence measures were decided on for the outer gates.'[23] After Waterloo Napoleon claimed that it had been all this that determined him to act as he did, but the sceptic is compelled, first, to observe that Elba was a very small realm for a ruler of Napoleon's energy, and, second, that the optimism that had so sustained him in 1813 and 1814 had once more started to grip him. 'The emperor knew . . . that, outside of a few thousand schemers, the entire nation remained attached to him in spirit, opinion and heart, just as it was attached to the principles of national sovereignty and French honour; that it had only submitted to the necessity imposed by its enemy and the new Judas; [and] that out of 30 million inhabitants, 29.5 million kept alive in their hearts the hope of overthrowing the princes.'[24] And had not his enemies almost just come to blows?

Whatever the truth may have been, by February 1815 Napoleon had resolved on escape. Viewed objectively, the chances of success were slim – in fact it has been claimed that the whole adventure was provoked in an attempt to ensure that 'the monster' could be chained up in some place of exile far from Europe – but on 26 February Napoleon sailed from Elba with his entire army of 750 men. Thus began the most extraordinary adventure of the entire Revolutionary and Napoleonic period. Landing on 1 March near Fréjus, Napoleon was soon on the march for Paris via Grenoble. Such forces of troops as were dispatched against him quickly changed sides, and even in areas far removed from his magnetic presence garrisons declared they would not fight against him. In the eastern city of Toul, for example, Marshal Oudinot summoned his officers to see him:

Not long after, a treble row of officers was crammed in our room, forming a circle with the marshal in the centre. He waited until they had all taken their places in silence, and then expressed himself more or less in the following terms. 'Gentlemen, in the circumstances in which we are placed I wish to make an appeal for your loyalty. We are marching under the white cockade. I am to review you tomorrow before our departure: with what cry will you and your men reply to my "Long live the King!"?' These words were followed by absolute silence. Nothing so striking ever passed before my eyes . . . I saw the storm was about to break; each second was a century. At last the marshal said, 'Well, gentlemen?' Then a young man of inferior rank stepped forward, and said 'Monsieur le Maréchal, I am bound to tell you, and no one here will contradict me: when you cry "Long live the king!", our men, and we, will answer, "Long live the emperor!" '[25]

Trying to rally the garrison of Lyons, Marshal Macdonald had a similar experience:

I was very excited. I finished my speech by saying that I had too good an opinion of their fidelity and patriotic feelings to think that they would refuse to do as I did, who had never deceived them, and that they would follow me along the path of honour and duty; the only guarantee that I asked of them was to join with me in crying, 'Long live the King!' I shouted this several times at the top of my voice. Not one single voice joined me. They all maintained a stony silence: I admit I was disconcerted.[26]

With Louis XVIII fleeing for the Belgian border, by 20 March the emperor was once again in the capital. The scenes that greeted him were extraordinary: 'At least 20,000 persons were crowding the approaches to the Pavilion of Flora, the staircase and the apartments, which last I thought I should never reach . . . Suddenly Napoleon reappeared. There was an instantaneous and irresistible outburst. At [the] sight of him the transports rose to such a pitch that you would have thought the ceilings were coming down.'[27] No sooner had the emperor arrived, meanwhile, than he issued a series of decrees designed to win over the bourgeoisie and to appease the populace. All feudal titles were abolished, the lands of all emigrés were expropriated, and major schemes of public works initiated, while the old electoral colleges that had chosen the Napoleonic legislature were summoned to a giant rally in Paris and charged with the task of approving reforms in the imperial constitution, reforms that would bring freedom of the press and genuine parliamentary government. At the same time, every effort was made to portray the new regime as one of peace, the emperor publicly scoffing at the idea of war and sending ambassadors to Vienna to plead his cause.

Had the emperor really changed? In Paris all was excitement. Crowds filled the streets and squares, and there was much martial enthusiasm amongst certain elements of the population:

Public opinion had indeed changed since 1814. We were eager to join the newly formed companies of artillery, and attended drill twice a day in the gardens of the Luxembourg. We were filled with a fervent desire to blot out all recollection of our pusillanimous conduct in 1814. It was not merely blind passion for Napoleon that animated us. Our susceptibilities had been hurt in every conceivable way under the Restoration, and we really looked upon him as our avenger.[28]

Among the emperor's entourage, then, there was much gloomy speculation. Hortense de Beauharnais, for example, privately urged Napoleon to appoint Caulaincourt as Foreign Minister on the grounds that this might serve as a guarantee of his good faith and so preserve the peace that France so needed. However, the emperor paid no heed: Caulaincourt was 'too much inclined to favour foreigners' and Hortense herself a mere woman who should not concern herself with politics. Encountering Caulaincourt shortly afterwards, Hortense told him of her fears and begged him to act. 'Everyone knows that you are the only one who has always taken the side of peace before the emperor. Your advice is now more necessary than ever. You must oppose ideas of fresh conquests with all your strength.' 'I am sure you are right,' replied Caulaincourt, 'but what can I do if the emperor has not changed and decides that he wants to regain Belgium.' 'My God! He isn't talking of this already?' 'No, but I am concerned that he was received with so much enthusiasm. A little resistance would have been better. How can a man not feel that anything is possible to him after such a welcome? And would he not wish to attempt anything and everything?'[29] Nor was this an end to it, for Napoleon was exhibiting the same sort of delusions as he had in 1813 and 1814. 'The emperor ... was convinced that', as far as the territories of the empire were concerned, 'the people, having been moulded for ten years by institutions similar to our own, would remain on good terms with France; that their common needs and desires would render the decision of their rulers completely irrelevant.'[30]

Within a very short time, however, a number of things had become clear. The first was that war was inevitable: hardly had the Allies heard of Napoleon's escape than they mobilized their armies, declared him to be an outlaw, established a new coalition – the Seventh – and pledged themselves to make war on the emperor until he was finally overthrown. Not a moment was lost. Receiving news that Napoleon had disappeared from Elba early in the morning of 7 March, Metternich hastened to the Emperor Francis:

Before eight o'clock I was with the emperor. He read the dispatch and said to me calmly and quietly . . . 'Napoleon seems to wish to play the adventurer: that is his concern; ours is to secure that peace which he has disturbed for years. Go without delay to the Emperor of Russia and the King of Prussia and tell them that I am ready to order my army to march back to France. I do not doubt that both monarchs will agree with me.' At a quarter past eight I was with the Emperor Alexander, who dismissed me with the same words the Emperor Francis had used. At half-past eight I received a similar declaration from the mouth of King Frederick William III . . . Thus war was decided on in less than an hour.[31]

Such was the anger of the Allies, indeed, that Eugène de Beauharnais, who had taken refuge in Vienna in 1814, was only saved from being imprisoned in some distant fortress by the intercession of his father-in-law, the King of Bavaria. As for Napoleon's envoys, they were in each case sent straight back to Paris.

If Napoleon was spurned in Vienna, things were not much better for him at home. A number of senior dignitaries of the empire had rallied to him, certainly, but otherwise the response was muted. The new constitution was generally scorned by educated people, for example. 'Nobody saw in this association of an old regime with a new one anything other than a concession extracted by the force of circumstance and a means of restoring absolute power in the future. At the same time the . . . venomous criticisms of a number of empassioned writers whipped up violent opposition,' remembered Hortense de Beauharnais.[32] 'It was freely criticized and censured,' wrote the Parisian surgeon, Poumiès de la Siboutie. As for the great assembly of electors to which it was put on 1 June, it did not prove very enthusiastic. To quote the same observer, 'I formed the opinion that the assembly was not favourably disposed towards the emperor. He was very late in coming. When at last he appeared the vast throng rose shouting, "Vive la France! Vive la nation!" The few feeble cries of "Vive l'empereur!" could barely be distinguished . . . Everybody remarked the alteration in his appearance.

He had grown stouter and his fat face was pale and weary, though still impressive.'[33] As even ardent Bonapartists admitted, the old charisma had gone. Seeing him at the same event, Thiébault was deeply shocked, 'His face . . . had lost all expression and all its forcible character; his mouth, compressed, contained none of its ancient witchery; his very head no longer had the pose which used to characterize the conqueror of the world; and his gait was as perplexed as his demeanour and gestures were undecided. Everything about him seemed to have lost its nature and to be broken up; the ordinary pallor of his skin was replaced by a strongly pronounced greenish tinge.'[34] Even the response of the army was muted: 'He had the eagles brought to him to distribute to the army and the national guard. With that stentorian voice of his, he cried to them, "Swear to defend your eagles! Do you swear it?" But the vows were made with little warmth. There was but little enthusiasm: the shouts were not like those of Austerlitz and Wagram and the emperor perceived it.'[35] As for the popular militias – the so-called *fédérés* – that began to appear in the cities and other large towns with the aim of fighting royalism, they failed to reach out beyond the urban poor and petty bourgeoisie and showed signs of considerable ambivalence towards the regime, while they inspired little faith. In the words of one popular song that went the rounds, 'Cobblers, quit your shoes; coalmen, come and join us. If the enemy should come amongst us, at least they won't find any white.'[36]

In short, Napoleon was in desperate trouble. Determined to raise a large army, he could no longer rely on the acquiescence that had permitted the success of the levies of earlier years. On the contrary, in most parts of France the notables who formed the backbone of local government proved singularly uncooperative in the implementation of taxation and conscription alike. Faced by this situation, the Minister of the Interior, Lazare Carnot – the 'architect of victory' of 1793 – dismissed large numbers of officials and attempted to replace them with men who were loyal to the regime, only to find that he could obtain few reliable alternatives. 'As was clearly necessary, there were many changes in the prefects' appointments, but favouritism combined many mistaken selections with some good ones. There were appointed many young men who were zealous, but who could not inspire much confidence. On all sides it was proclaimed that the law should prevail, and yet the majority of the emperor's special commissioners who were sent to the departments everywhere dismissed underlings in order to find room for men who had formerly held the appointments or for those who in past days had given proof of patriotism. Not only did that procedure hinder the transaction of official business . . . but it added a further increase to the number of the discontented.'[37] As for the lower classes, there had in some areas been demonstrations of popular support for Napoleon – in Metz, for example, an angry crowd besieged the headquarters of the governor and raised the tricolour on the tower of the cathedral; at Nevers the governor was chased out of the town when he tried to hold it for Louis XVIII; and at Grenoble, Lyons and, finally, Paris, Napoleon had been greeted by cheering multitudes.

However, whether such events were indicative of feelings in France as a whole was another matter, for they were most often to be found either in districts ravaged by the enemy in 1814 or in places which had some particular reason to remember the empire with gratitude. If the *lyonnais* turned out in strength to greet Napoleon, it was in part because the city's silk industry had consistently been protected by him, while Paris, too, had consistently been favoured. Elsewhere the picture was very different. From large parts of the country came reports of rioting and draft evasion, and the Vendée erupted in a fresh revolt. In the strongly Catholic north the fleeing Louis XVIII was greeted in such towns as Lille by crowds of inhabitants begging him not to leave France. In Marseilles, Lady Bessborough, whom the Hundred Days had caught on holiday in France, reported that the news of the emperor's landing had led to 'strong dissensions between the soldiers and the people'.[38] 'Even in our peaceful valley of the Saulx,' wrote Madame Oudinot, 'the population were becoming both suspicious and hostile . . . The emperor cannot have long retained his illusions on the chances of power which remained to him, because in 1815 it was much less the wish of the nation than of the army that had brought him back from Elba.'[39] Not surprisingly, then, there was considerable confidence amongst the Allies. As Castlereagh wrote to Sir Charles Stewart on 26 March 1815:

The accounts received today speak favourably of the public spirit in the western departments and [announce] that a considerable force is forming there in support of the king's cause. The south, also, is represented as extremely well disposed. Should these reports be confirmed, we may hope that Bonaparte will not be enabled to draw much in men and money from the country beyond the Loire.[40]

Popular enthusiasm for Napoleon in 1815 therefore centred very much on a domestic agenda. As even the enthusiastic Bonapartist Lavallette, put it, 'The wish to have Napoleon was less insistent than the desire to get rid of the Bourbons.'[41] No sooner was a new war on the agenda than enthusiasm fell away. In these circumstances it did not help in the slightest that both Joseph and Jerome appeared once more in Paris. 'It was feared,' wrote Hortense de Beauharnais, 'that they still entertained pretensions to their old kingdoms, and did not believe that it would cost France anything to get them back.'[42] In these circumstances, it was amazing that Napoleon succeeded in raising a fresh army at all, but, for many veterans of the *grande armée*, the eagles continued to represent the only life they knew, the same going for the 200,000 troops whom Louis XVIII had taken into his service in 1814. In consequence, by early June at least 280,000 regular troops were available for service, many of them hardened veterans who were as devoted to the emperor as they were enthusiastic about his return. As British officers were later to discover, they were to remain defiant even in defeat:

The French wounded are almost all quartered in the city hospitals, or in those houses whose owners may have shown a lukewarmness in the present contest. Their constant cry was, and still is, 'Vive l'empereur!' Some of them brought in from the field the other day, extremely weak from loss of blood and want of food ... vented the same exclamation. Louis XVIII sent an officer the other day to inquire if they were in want of anything and to afford assistance to those who required it. He visited every one of the hospitals, but I believe he could not prevail on one to accept assistance from him in the name of his sovereign. They had no king but one.[43]

At the very least, then, Napoleon was in a position to put up a fight. With relatively few allied troops ready to take the field, the emperor could now either wait for the massive invasion that the Seventh Coalition was certain to mount as soon as it had brought up sufficient men, or take the offensive and secure a dramatic victory that might win time for his regime to consolidate its hold on France or even shatter his enemies' resolve. Faced by this choice, the emperor did not hesitate. Nor did it take much time to work out that the obvious targets at which to strike were the Anglo-Dutch-German army of the Duke of Wellington and the Prussian army of Field Marshal Blücher, both of which were cantoned in southern Belgium. The temptation was all the greater as relations between the two leaders were poor. There had been bitter quarrels as to who should take command of the various German contingents that had been sent to Belgium and the quality of neither force was especially good. Even Wellington's British troops were largely composed of raw recruits: 'The British army in Belgium is not numerous . . . A considerable proportion of the army . . . consists of young men who have seen no service whatever.'[44] As for Wellington's Dutch, Belgians and Germans, they were for the most part not only just as inexperienced but also singularly unenthusiastic. According to the rifle officer John Kincaid, 'Our foreign auxiliaries, who constituted more than half of our numerical strength, with some exceptions were little better than a raw militia – a body without a soul.'[45] And, finally, Blücher was having to contend with wholesale disaffection in the many Saxon regiments that had been forcibly incorporated into the Prussian ranks. Among the visitors to his headquarters was a British officer who brought him some dispatches from Wellington: 'It was at the time when the Saxon troops had mutinied because Blücher wished to incorporate them in the divisions of the Prussian army in place of leaving them to act in a body as he had no great opinion of them. This they resented, [and so they] mutinied and compelled Blücher to leave Liège and retire to the village where I found him . . . Blücher disarmed the mutinous Saxons and sent them to the rear.'[46]

To return to the emperor, by early June Napoleon was concentrating as many troops as he dared on the Belgian frontier, his plan being to get between Wellington and Blücher, force them apart, and then defeat them in detail. However, the first shots of the War of the Seventh Coalition were not those fired by his troops as they streamed across the Belgian frontier south of Charleroi on 15 June, as fighting had already erupted in Italy. Here Murat had felt increasingly under siege, the government of Ferdinand IV having spent the months that had passed since the abdication of Napoleon doing all that it could to harass him. Irregular bands were sent over from Sicily to form the nucleus of a fresh revolt in Calabria; traditional patterns of labour migration were exploited as a means of spreading disaffection on the mainland; and everything possible was done to facilitate the operations of the numerous smugglers active around the southern coasts of Italy. When Murat got wind of Metternich's plan to depose him, it was therefore the last straw. Mobilizing his army, he proclaimed a war of Italian liberation, and marched north to attack the Austrians. The latter, however, were ready for him: any man who fled to the Austrian camp having been promised grants of land, large numbers of Neapolitan soldiers deserted, and on 1–2 May Murat was beaten at Tolentino. As Bentinck had already discovered, Italian nationalism was in its infancy and it was a weapon Murat simply could not use to any effect. Among those members of the elite who had served the Napoleonic administration, the new British ambassador to Tuscany, Lord Burghersh, conceded there was much support for a unified Italy: 'In Tuscany to belong to an army which may amount to 3,000 or 4,000 men cannot flatter the pride of any man; in a civil line, the service required by the government is necessarily on so small a scale, and . . . the rewards so limited that neither the ambition of the rich man nor the wants of the poor man with talents will find their reward in devoting themselves to the service of their country.' But the populace as a whole was a different matter. Wherever the Austrians had appeared, Burghersh admitted, 'the manner in which their officers, as well as men, have behaved themselves, as also the heavy contributions which have been raised by the generals, have given universal dissatisfaction, and, I fear, have totally alienated from them the minds of the Italian people'. But that did not equate to nationalism. As he continued:

The glory of the ancient Italian name would excite some ardour in certain sections of the lower orders. It would, however, be confined to those who are exasperated against the German troops. For I am persuaded that, with the people of Italy, no measure could be so hurtful or unpopular as the forming of the country into one kingdom. The different states into which it has so long been divided have separated the feelings and interests of the people. The inhabitants of no separate country hate each other more thoroughly than those of the neighbouring states of Italy . . . The people are, besides, attached to their different capitals. They glory in the privileges they enjoy, and the inhabitants of Naples, Rome and Florence would be most unwilling to see their cities reduced to the state of provincial towns. With feelings such as I have described, the project of an Italian kingdom . . . might for a moment be established, but I doubt its being popular with the mass of the people: its after-details would encounter the greatest difficulties.[47]

To prove the point, it is only necessary to conclude the story of Joachim Murat. An adventurer to the last, having escaped Tolentino and gone into exile in France, in October 1815 he landed in Calabria with a handful of followers and in the marketplace of Pizzo again proclaimed a crusade for a united Italy. Initially, the response was stupefaction – the people really did not seem to have any conception of what he meant – but then an old woman recognized him for who he was. Screaming that he had had four of her sons shot, she fell upon him with fists flailing, and it was only with the greatest difficulty that he escaped being lynched on the spot.

Within hours Murat had been court-martialled and executed. No sooner had the fighting begun in Belgium than the emperor's dreams were revealed to be just as empty. Despite a series of extraordinary mistakes on the part of Wellington, on 16 June Napoleon failed decisively to defeat either of the two armies facing him in the twin battles of Ligny and Quatre Bras. In the first instance this was the result of faulty staff work and the stupidity of the commander of the French left wing, Marshal Ney. Yet Napoleon himself cannot be exonerated: not only could his own orders have been clearer, but, never very bright at the best of times, Ney had not been quite right in the head since the retreat from Moscow and should never have been given an independent command. After 16 June, the situation of the French army grew still more dire. Thanks to a series of misconceptions and, possibly, a renewed bout of ill-health on the part of Napoleon, the French failed to follow up such advantages as they had gained, and allowed the two allied armies to retreat towards Brussels on parallel roads that took them to Waterloo and Wavre. Reaching Waterloo – or rather a prominent ridge known as Mont St Jean that crossed the Brussels–Charleroi highway at right angles two miles to the south – Wellington turned to fight, and thus the stage was set for what turned out to be the decisive battle of the campaign.

If Wellington had made serious mistakes at the beginning of the campaign, he now more than made up for them. Conscious of the many deficiencies of his troops, the position that he took up was extremely strong. Not only did the ridge that was its basis provide cover from the French artillery, but it was marked by three substantial farm complexes that provided ready-made fortresses for the defenders. So sited were these posts, moreover, that at least one of them would have to be stormed before Wellington's main line could be breached. The position might easily have been flanked to the west, true enough, but such a move would have been futile for it would simply have pushed the defenders closer to the Prussians. Committed to a frontal assault as a result, the French did not even outnumber their enemies by very much: one-third of his men having been ordered to follow Blücher under Marshal Grouchy, the emperor had only 72,000 men to Wellington's 67,000. That said, something might still have been achieved; Napoleon's army was of far higher calibre than Wellington's, had far more cannon and also fought with great courage. 'Those amongst us who had witnessed in the Peninsula many well-contested actions were agreed on one point, that we had never before seen such determination displayed by the French as on this day,' remembered Lieutenant Colonel John Leach of the Ninety-Fifth Rifles. 'Fighting under the eye of Napoleon, and feeling what a great and important stake they contested for, will account for their extraordinary perseverance and valour, and for the vast efforts which they made for victory.'[48]

However, gallantry was not enough, four factors forestalling the tactical victory that was all that was still on offer. In the first place, torrential rain had so soaked the battlefield that the first attacks had to be delayed until nearly midday; in the second, the resistance put up by Wellington's army was much greater than might have been expected; in the third, there were serious mistakes in the handling of the French attacks; and in the fourth, Grouchy failed either to stop Blücher from joining Wellington, or to march to Napoleon's support. As a result, by the time that the French finally broke into Wellington's centre at around six o'clock in the evening, large numbers of Prussians were assailing their right flank. In desperation, the emperor now committed part of the infantry of the Imperial Guard. Hitting some of the best troops in Wellington's army, they were shot to pieces and thrown back in disorder. It was the end. Utterly exhausted, under heavy fire, and unsettled by rumours of treason, the French army disintegrated and Wellington ordered a general advance. With the Prussians pressing in on their flank and rear and killing all who stood in their path, Napoleon's forces were soon jammed together in a panic-stricken flight along the main road. Pursued for miles by allied cavalry, they left behind them 25,000 casualties, though at 21,000 allied losses numbered only slightly fewer. 'I had never yet heard of a battle in which everybody was killed,' wrote one participant, 'but this seemed likely as all were going by turns ... The field of battle next morning presented a frightful scene of carnage: it seemed as if the world had tumbled to pieces, and three-fourths of everything [had been] destroyed in the wreck.'[49] As Blücher famously remarked to Wellington when they encountered one another, 'Quelle affaire!' Caught up in the rout of the French army was Captain Coignet of the Guard: 'We had the greatest difficulty in getting away. We could not make way through the panic-stricken multitude. And it was worse when we arrived at Jemappes. The emperor tried to re-establish some kind of order among the retreating troops, but his efforts were in vain. Men of all units from every corps struggled and fought their way through the streets of the little town . . . The one thought uppermost in the minds of all was to get across the little bridge which had been thrown over the river Dyle. Nothing could stand in the way of them.'[50]

The French were right to take to their heels. As the Prussians came on, they behaved with terrible brutality. To quote the British guards officer Gronow:

We perceived, on entering France, that our allies the Prussians had committed fearful atrocities on the defenceless inhabitants of the villages and farms which lay in their line of march. Before we left La Belle Alliance, I had already seen the brutality of some of the Prussian infantry, who hacked and cut up all the cows and pigs which were in the farmyards . . . On our line of march, whenever we arrived at towns or villages through which the Prussians had passed, we found that every article of furniture in the houses had been destroyed in the most wanton manner: looking-glasses, mahogany bedsteads, pictures . . . and mattresses had been hacked, cut, half-burned and scattered about in every direction, and, on the slightest remonstrance of the wretched inhabitants, they were beaten in the most shameful manner and sometimes shot.[51]

Guerrilla resistance, however, was non-existent. 'From what I have seen of these people,' wrote the Royal Horse Artillery officer, Cavalié Mercer, 'it appears very doubtful whether they care a farthing who reigns over them. Be that as it may, we undoubtedly entered France amidst cheers and greetings of the populace . . . The arrival of strangers attracted a concourse of villagers to our bivouac, many old women and young girls bringing quantities of very fine cherries for sale . . . Nor have we seen any trace of [an enemy], having found the peasantry everywhere as peaceably occupied as if no war existed.'[52]

Here and there a few minor skirmishes persisted, but for Napoleon all was lost, and, in a rare moment of realism, on 22 June he abdicated for a second time. There followed several weeks of confusion in which neither the emperor nor the provisional government that had been formed in Paris seem to have known what to do. But on 15 July the emperor finally surrendered to the British at Rochefort in the hope that he might be able to persuade them to treat him leniently. Far to the east, meanwhile, six allied armies had been pouring over the frontier in the face of scattered resistance. Desperate to end the fighting, the provisional government sued for peace, but the Allies insisted on pressing on until they had captured Paris, which fell on 7 July without the much-vaunted *fédérés* firing a shot: 'The good people of Paris began to pour out of the city and mix among us as if nothing had been the matter ... Refreshments of all sorts came into our camp: it was truly astonishing to see what confidence the inhabitants placed in us.'[53] A few diehard garrisons held on throughout the summer – the very last, Montmédy, did not surrender until 13 September – but the Napoleonic Wars were finally at an end.

There is little left to tell. Undisturbed by the return of Napoleon, the process of peace-making had continued in Vienna, the most important piece of business being the organization of the loose confederation that it had been decided should take the place of Napoleon's Rheinbund. By the time Waterloo was fought, in fact, the final act of agreement was already ten days old. As for France, Napoleon was sent to end his days on distant St Helena, and Louis XVIII forced to accept a new peace settlement which stripped his country of a number of strategic frontier districts – the general frontier adopted was now that of 1790 – temporarily deprived her of a number of important fortresses, enforced the return of many art objects, imposed an indemnity of 700 million francs, and subjected her to military occupation. As for the great powers, on 20 November 1815, Britain, Russia, Prussia and Austria entered into the so-called Quadruple Alliance, whereby they engaged to keep the peace against France and to hold regular congresses to ensure that war did not break out again. Even before that, Russia, Prussia and Austria had signed the much-misunderstood Holy Alliance, the point of this agreement being not so much to crush revolution wherever it raised its head, but to promote international stability. On this Metternich, who regarded it with great scorn, is very clear: 'No very severe examination was required on my part to see that the paper was nothing more than a philanthropic aspiration clothed in a religious garb which supplied no material for a treaty between the powers ... The most unanswerable proof of the correctness of this statement exists in the circumstance that never afterwards did it happen that the Holy Alliance was made mention of between the cabinets, nor indeed could it have been mentioned ... The Holy Alliance was not an institution to keep down the rights of the people [or] to promote absolutism or any other tyranny. It was only the outflow of the pietistic feeling of the Emperor Alexander, and the application of Christian principles to politics.'[54]

Although the peace settlement that resulted from the French Wars has often been criticized, it was by no means the disaster of legend, and particularly not if it is assessed in the context of the world as it was understood in 1815. It undoubtedly met the security concerns of the great powers in respect of France: 'As the treaty is now framed,' wrote Castlereagh, 'especially in the exclusion of the family of Bonaparte, I think it will give a very powerful *appui* to the king ... It will also make the Jacobins – in truth the whole nation – feel that they cannot break loose again ... without being committed with all Europe, and bringing down a million of armed men upon their country.'[55] No attempt was made to turn the clock back to 1789, and, if many territorial changes were made, few were especially objectionable to the populations concerned as, outside France, nationalism was in its infancy as a political force. By the same token there was no great outcry in Germany and Italy at the failure of the Vienna settlement to address the issue of national unity, while even in partitioned Poland the issue was not so much continued foreign domination as the way that that domination was exercised. At the same time, too, the new frontiers were on the whole eminently justifiable, the Europe that emerged from Vienna being, as Paul Schroeder in particular has argued, far more stable than that of 1918 or 1945, let alone those of earlier general peace settlements. Encapsulated in the Congress system was the vital recognition that the powers of Europe could no longer engage in the endless dynastic warfare of the eighteenth century: the stakes were too high and the costs too great. The watchword of the Congress, in fact, was not reaction, but rather peace, and, in the wake of the estimated five to seven million deaths of the French Wars, one can thank God for it.

How, though, are we to assess the role of the Napoleonic Wars in European history? The most obvious effect was political. While the conflict gave birth to neither liberalism nor nationalism as political forces, it did accelerate their development, as witness the constitutions of a recognizably modern nature that had been promulgated in Spain, Sicily and Sweden, and the national movements that emerged in Germany, Italy, Serbia, Greece and Poland. On top of this, officer corps were frequently drawn into the discourse of the day, while the much retouched figure of Napoleon Bonaparte served as a constant beacon for all those who dreamed of glory, were excluded by the Restoration system, or were genuinely fired by the ideology of liberation. With progressive political movements further persuaded that the people had only to take to the barricades to defeat the cause of reaction, 1815 appears very much the dawn of an age of turmoil. To political ferment was added economic development. Thanks to the French Wars, the dominant centres of trade and manufacture were forcibly shifted away from the maritime littoral to such inland areas as Saxony and the Ruhr. With its ports blockaded by the British, it might even be argued that continental Europe was turned from commerce to industry, while it is certainly the case that it was the era of relative peace which followed that allowed it to give full play to its considerable economic advantages. Change, then, seemed very likely, and yet the Vienna settlement was postulated upon the state of affairs that pertained in 1815 remaining unchanged for ever. In short, the stability brought by the Vienna settlement was apparent only – the factors that staved off a general conflict for so long being, first, the association of war with revolution, and, second, the political, social and economic cost of maintaining armies of the size that had fought at Wagram, Borodino and Leipzig.

If Europe faced an age of instability, she did so as a very different entity than she had been in 1803. On the peripheries of the Continent, Sweden had finally lost her long struggle with Russia for control of the Baltic and literally been pushed out of mainstream international relations; Spain had been stripped of most of her empire and reduced to bankruptcy; Denmark and Holland had been neutralized as naval powers; and the Ottoman Empire had been subjected to a series of challenges that may be said to have set it on the road to its eventual disintegration. Another loser had been Austria, which had not only seen herself shorn of the control she had once enjoyed of Germany through the Holy Roman Empire, but also been revealed as a state too weak to realize its pretensions. Britain, Prussia and Russia, by contrast, had all been massively strengthened, the first by the acquisition of fresh colonies, the extension of her rule in India, and the confirmation of her naval superiority; the second by the acquisition of territories in western Germany and Saxony that had the capacity to make her the powerhouse of German industry; and the third by the expansion of her power not only westwards but south-eastwards to the frontiers of central Asia. Inherent in all this lay the origins of fresh struggles – between Britain and Russia in Afghanistan and between Prussia and Austria in Germany – but the most dramatic change of all was to be found in the position of France. In 1800, as in 1700, she had been the greatest power in continental Europe, but under Napoleon she had been tested to destruction. Nor did she ever regain her lead. As the process of social and economic change that we have outlined above set in, so she slipped ever further from the pinnacle of power which she had occupied in 1807.

Not all of this was the fault of Napoleon. His responsibility, for example, for the decline in the birthrate that France experienced in the nineteenth century is tenuous at best. However, it does serve as a convenient moment at which once again to consider the question which opened this book. Were the wars all the doing of the emperor? On one level, of course, this question must be answered in the affirmative. As the present author has argued elsewhere, the wars that beset Europe between 1803 and 1815 were truly 'Napoleonic'. Time and again it was Napoleon who either drove other powers to go to war with France, took the initiative in attacking them himself, engaged in actions that augmented the number of his enemies and increased the chances of war in fresh theatres of conflict, or spurned the possibility of a compromise peace. To argue that peace could have been assured at any time by giving way to Napoleon may well be true, but only at the cost of accepting the legitimacy of an imperium that Europe had not seen since Roman times, and of expecting Britain and the rest to surrender not only their most cherished foreign-policy interests, but also many of the notions – above all, that of the balance of power – that underpinned the very survival of the European states system as it was understood in 1800. However, the Napoleonic Wars cannot just be understood in terms of Napoleon himself. One of the reasons why the emperor survived for so long was that there was no great ideological crusade against France. On the contrary, most of the powers of Europe continued to pursue traditional foreign policy objectives long after Napoleon had emerged as a far greater challenge to the international order than the French Revolution had ever been. In doing so, Russia, in particular, unleashed a series of campaigns that, while intimately connected with the story of Napoleon, would in all probability have happened without his influence, just as we may say that, even had the then First Consul been killed at Marengo, the first decade of the nineteenth century would almost certainly still have witnessed a period of general international conflict. What Napoleon eventually did, however, was to pose such a challenge to the powers that the normal working of international relations had to be suspended and even, in the end, reconsidered altogether. There were exceptions – the chief example is the Sweden of Marshal Bernadotte – but by the end of 1813 specific national interest had almost entirely been set aside in favour of a common cause that was genuinely seen as being that of the whole of Europe. With the coming of peace, that brief moment of unity and self-abnegation was lost, but even so the general principle that there was a common cause was not forgotten, and from this there emerged the embryonic system of collective security and crisis management agreed at Vienna.

To return to the quote from John Holland Rose which began this book, the history of Napoleon did not constitute the history of the world, or indeed, even Europe, between 1803 and 1815. That said, however, it may be said to have foreshadowed the history of the world. In the end, the peace-keeping arrangements evolved at the close of the Napoleonic Wars did not work and, after a long period in which conflict in Europe was both short-lived and confined to relatively limited theatres of war, in 1914 and then again in 1939 first Europe and then the world were plunged into general conflict. In these twentieth-century wars, there were many issues at stake, and the presence of a historiography nearly as copious as that generated by Napoleon should serve as a warning against facile generalizations. Yet the situation that faced Europe in 1914 and 1939 was exactly the same as that which it had faced in 1803, in that it was confronted by a power that united unbridled militarism with military, financial and demographic resources that could not in the short term be matched by any of its rivals – by a power, indeed, that, like Napoleon, aimed, whether from the beginning or at some later moment, to establish what amounted to a colonial empire inside Europe. To this, the answer was much the same as it had been in the Napoleonic era, namely the construction of a grand alliance that was increasingly armed, financed and supplied from the resources of the wider world, while with the coming of peace there were again moves in the direction of collective security and crisis management, although only after 1945 did these secure significant results. Within Europe, meanwhile, the European Community is bidding fair finally to abolish war between states altogether, and this in turn leads us back to Napoleon. On St Helena one of his constant refrains was that he had wanted to build a new Europe in which all its various peoples would enjoy unity and self-government and be united in a great confederation. Since the emperor lost his wars and ended up chained Prometheus-like to a rock in the South Atlantic, it is, of course, impossible to pass judgement on what might have occurred in other circumstances. Though there is much about the nature of his rule that suggests that it would be unwise to take the emperor's claims at face value, all that can be said for certain is that, assuming that he did have dreams of a new order, they were never realized. If Napoleon has had any influence in the making of the European Community at all, then it has been, quite literally, in the role of bogeyman.

Notes

Introduction: The Napoleonic Wars in Historical Perspective

1. J. H. Rose, *The Revolutionary and Napoleonic Era, 1789–1815* (Cambridge, 1907), p. 148.
2. Cited in E. Las Cases, *Mémorial de Sainte Hélène*, ed. G. Walter (Paris, 1956), vol. II, p. 232.
3. Cited in ibid., p. 303.
4. As a term 'Continental Blockade' is preferable to 'Continental System', and in consequence it is this form that will be used for the rest of this book.

1 The Origins of the Napoleonic Wars

1. Cited in P. Fleuriot de Langle (ed.), *Napoleon at St Helena: Memoirs of General Bertrand, Grand-Master of the Palace* (London, 1953), pp. 69–70.
2. Louis F. de Bourrienne, *Memoirs of Napoleon Bonaparte*, ed. E. Sanderson (London, 1903), p. 3.
3. J. A. Chaptal, *Mes Souvenirs sur Napoléon*, ed. A. Chaptal (Paris, 1893), p. 174.
4. E. Las Cases, *Mémorial de Sainte Hélène*, ed. G. Walter (Paris, 1956), vol. I, p. 83.
5. Cited in Bourrienne, *Memoirs*, p. 5.
6. Cited in A. Wilson (ed.), *A Diary of St Helena (1816–1817): the Journal of Lady Malcolm containing the Conversations of Sir Pulteney Malcolm with Napoleon* (London, 1899), p. 87.
7. Cited in V. Cronin, *Napoleon* (London, 1971), p. 31.
8. P. Jones (ed.), *Napoleon: How He Did It – the Memoirs of Baron Fain, First Secretary of the Emperor's Cabinet* (San Francisco, 1998), p. 181.
9. Bourrienne, *Memoirs*, p. 5.
10. Ibid.
11. S. de Morsier-Kotthaus, *Memoirs of the Comtesse de Boigne* (London, 1956), pp. 41–2.
12. Cited in F. Masson, *Napoléon dans sa Jeunesse, 1769–1793* (Paris, 1907), p. 293.
13. Cited in ibid., p. 297.
14. Cited in Wilson, *Diary of St Helena*, p. 88.
15. G. Duruy (ed.), *Memoirs of Barras, Member of the Directorate* (London, 1895), vol. I, p. 143.
16. Cited in S. de Chair, *Napoleon on Napoleon: an Autobiography of the Emperor* (London, 1992), p. 83.
17. Bourrienne, *Memoirs*, p. 16.
18. A. F. L. de Viesse de Marmont, *Mémoires du Maréchal Marmont, Duc de Raguse, de 1792 à 1841* (Paris, 1857), vol. I, p. 60.
19. Duruy (ed.), *Memoirs of Barras*, vol. I, p. 161.
20. Ibid., p. 312.

21. L. Junot, *Mémoires de la Duchesse d'Abrantes*, ed. G. Girard (Paris, 1928–30), vol. I, pp. 198–9.
22. Bourrienne, *Memoirs*, p. 18.
23. L. Aldersey White (ed.), *The Adventurous Life of Count Lavallette, Bonaparte's Aide-de-Camp and Postmaster-General, by Himself* (London, 1936), vol. I, p. 101.
24. Cited in F. McLynn, *Napoleon: a Biography* (London, 1997), p. 87.
25. A. Butler (ed.), *The Memoirs of Baron Thiébault, late Lieutenant-General in the French Army* (London, 1896), vol. I, p. 260.
26. Ibid., p. 267.
27. Bourrienne, *Memoirs*, p. 22.
28. Cited in J. Howard, *Letters and Documents of Napoleon: the Ride to Power* (London, 1961), vol. I, p. 33.
29. Marmont, *Mémoires*, vol. I, p. 94.
30. J. Hanoteau (ed.), *Mémoires de la Reine Hortense* (Paris, 1927), vol. I, pp. 41–2.
31. Duruy, *Memoirs of Barras*, vol. II, p. 78.
32. Cited in Las Cases, *Mémorial*, vol. I, p. 344.
33. Cited in ibid., vol. I, pp. 749–50.
34. Duruy, *Memoirs of Barras*, vol. II, p. 89.
35. Aldersey White, *Life of Count Lavallette*, vol. I, pp. 115–16.
36. Duruy, *Memoirs of Barras*, vol. II, p. 181.
37. Marmont, *Mémoires*, vol. I, p. 86.
38. Duruy, *Memoirs of Barras*, vol. II, pp. 85–6.
39. Marmont, *Mémoires*, vol. I, p. 145.
40. Cited in Las Cases, *Mémorial*, vol. I, p. 98.
41. Cited in McLynn, *Napoleon*, p. 153.
42. Aldersey White, *Life of Count Lavallette*, p. 120.
43. A. L. G. de Staël, *Considérations sur les Principaux Evénements de la Révolution Française* (London, 1819), vol. II, p. 175.
44. Cited in Hanoteau, *Mémoires de la Reine Hortense*, vol. I, pp. 45–6.
45. Duruy, *Memoirs of Barras*, vol. II, p. 128.
46. Butler, *Memoirs of Baron Thiébault*, vol. I, p. 298.
47. Cited in Howard (ed.), *Letters and Documents of Napoleon*, p. 196.
48. Bourrienne, *Memoirs*, p. 55.
49. Cited in A. Schom, *Napoleon Bonaparte* (New York, 1998), p. 63.
50. Cited in H. Parker, 'The formation of Napoleon's personality: an exploratory essay', *French Historical Studies*, VII, No. 1 (Spring 1971), p. 22.
51. Cited in A. Castelot, *Napoleon* (New York, 1971), pp. 90–91.
52. Cited in Parker, 'The formation of Napoleon's personality', p. 22; J. Tulard, *Napoleon: the Myth of the Saviour* (London, 1984), p. 64.
53. Bourrienne, *Memoirs*, p. 57.
54. Junot, *Mémoires*, vol. II, pp. 95–6.
55. Staël, *Considérations*, vol. II, pp. 202–3.
56. L. J. Gohier, *Mémoires de Louis-Jérome Gohier, Président du Directoire au 18 Brumaire* (Paris, 1824), p. 26.
57. Cited in F. Markham, *Napoleon* (London, 1963), p. 58.
58. Cited in P. Jupp, *Lord Grenville, 1759–1834* (Oxford, 1985), p. 208.
59. Cited in Howard, *Letters and Documents of Napoleon*, vol. I, p. 226.
60. Bourrienne, *Memoirs*, p. 68.
61. Cited in C. de Rémusat, *Mémoires de Madame de Rémusat, 1802–1808*, ed. P. de Rémusat (Paris, 1884), vol. I, p. 274.
62. Staël, *Considérations*, vol. I, pp. 207–8.
63. Cited in Junot, *Mémoires*, vol. II, p. 138.
64. Cited in Rémusat, *Mémoires*, vol. I, p. 273.
65. Marmont, *Mémoires*, vol. I, p. 355.

66. Aldersey White, *Life of Count Lavallette*, vol. I, p. 223.
67. A. du Casse (ed.), *Mémoires et Correspondance Politique et Militaire du Prince Eugène* (Paris, 1858), vol. I, p. 75.
68. P. L. Roederer, *Mémoires sur la Révolution, le Consulat et l'Empire*, ed. O. Aubry (Paris, 1942), p. 103.
69. Chaptal, *Souvenirs*, pp. 209–10.
70. Staël, *Considérations*, vol. II, p. 234.
71. Cited in Roederer, *Mémoires*, p. 131.
72. Gohier, *Mémoires*, vol. I, pp. 353–4.

2 From Brumaire to Amiens

1. Cited in E. Las Cases, *Mémorial de Sainte Hélène*, ed. G. Walter (Paris, 1956), vol. I, p. 168.
2. J. A. Chaptal, *Mes Souvenirs sur Napoléon*, ed. A. Chaptal (Paris, 1893), p. 224.
3. Louis F. de Bourrienne, *Memoirs of Napoleon Bonaparte*, ed. E. Sanderson (London, 1903), pp. 132–3.
4. A. Thibaudeau, *Bonaparte and the Consulate*, ed. G. Fortescue (London, 1908), pp. 5–6.
5. A. L. G de Staël, *Considérations sur les Principaux Evénements de la Révolution Française* (London, 1819), vol. II, p. 267.
6. J. Hanoteau (ed.), *Mémoires de la Reine Hortense* (Paris, 1927), vol. I, p. 90.
7. Cited in V. Cronin, *Napoleon* (London, 1971), p. 278.
8. Cited in J. F. Bernard, *Talleyrand: a Biography* (London, 1973), p. 229.
9. Cited in Earl of Rosebery (ed.), *The Wellesley Papers: the Life and Correspondence of Richard Colley Wellesley, Marquess Wellesley, 1760–1842* (London, 1914), vol. I, p. 123.
10. Cited in S. de Chair, *Napoleon on Napoleon: an Autobiography of the Emperor* (London, 1992), pp. 173–4.
11. Cited in ibid. p. 148.
12. Cited in K. Roider, *Baron Thugut and Austria's Response to the French Revolution* (Princeton, New Jersey, 1987), p. 129.
13. Cited in ibid., p. 86.
14. Cited in W. Simon, *The Failure of the Prussian Reform Movement, 1807–1819* (New York, 1971), p. 10.
15. Cited in P. Dwyer (ed.), *The Rise of Prussia, 1700–1830* (London, 2000), p. 247.
16. Cited in Las Cases, *Mémorial*, vol. I, p. 415.
17. Cited in K. Waliszewski, *Paul I of Russia, the Son of Catherine the Great* (London, 1913), p. 81.
18. Bourrienne, *Memoirs*, p. 176.
19. Cited in ibid.
20. H. Carnot (ed.), *Memoirs of Bertrand Barère, Chairman of the Committee of Public Safety during the Revolution* (London, 1896), vol. III, p. 93.
21. Cited in J. Howard, *Letters and Documents of Napoleon: the Ride to Power* (London, 1961), p. 437.
22. Cited in Las Cases, *Mémorial*, vol. I, p. 839.
23. Cited in M. de Klinkowstrom (ed.), *Memoirs of Prince Metternich, 1733–1815* (London, 1880), pp. 31, 38.
24. J. Rambaud, *Memoirs of the Comte Roger de Damas, 1787–1806* (London, 1913), p. 295.
25. Ibid., p. 298.
26. Cited in H. Acton, *The Bourbons of Naples, 1734–1825* (London, 1956), p. 296.
27. Cited in ibid., pp. 437–8.
28. Cited in ibid., pp. 438–9.
29. Cited in ibid., pp. 441–2.

30. Cited in Third Earl of Malmesbury (ed.), *Diaries and Correspondence of James Harris, First Earl of Malmesbury* (London, 1844), vol. IV, pp. 52–3.
31. Cited in Rosebery, *The Wellesley Papers*, vol. I, p. 143.
32. Cited in P. Mackesy, *War without Victory: the Downfall of Pitt, 1799–1802* (Oxford, 1994), p. 209.
33. Cited in P. Jupp, *Lord Grenville, 1759–1834* (Oxford, 1985), p. 313; see also J. Ehrman, *The Younger Pitt, II: the Consuming Struggle* (Stanford, California, 1997), p. 558.
34. Cited in P. Ziegler, *Addington: a Life of Henry Addington, First Viscount Sidmouth* (London, 1965), p. 125.
35. Cited in Malmesbury, *Diaries and Correspondence*, vol. IV, p. 61.

3 The Peace of Amiens

1. Cited in E. Las Cases, *Le Mémorial de Sainte-Hélène*, ed. G. Walter (Paris, 1956), vol. II, p. 302.
2. J. A. Chaptal, *Mes Souvenirs sur Napoléon*, ed. A. Chaptal (Paris, 1893), pp. 225–6.
3. A. Thibaudeau, *Bonaparte and the Consulate*, ed. G. Fortescue (London, 1908), p. 168.
4. Cited in ibid., p. 84.
5. Louis F. de Bourrienne, *Memoirs of Napoleon Bonaparte*, ed. E. Sanderson (London, 1903), p. 219.
6. Marquis de Noailles (ed.), *The Life and Memoirs of Count Molé, 1781–1855* (London, 1923), vol. I, pp. 148–9.
7. L. J. Gohier, *Mémoires de Louis-Jérome Gohier, Président du Directoire au 18 Brumaire* (Paris, 1824), vol. II, pp. 256–7. The English artist Joseph Farington, who met the First Consul in the course of a visit to Paris in the autumn of 1802, makes a similar point in respect of his costume: 'He was dressed in blue, much more plain than his officers, which gave him additional consequence, for the power and splendour of his situation was marked by the contrast, as commanding all that brilliant display.' J. Greig (ed.), *The Farington Diary* (London, 1923), vol. II, p. 7.
8. Cited in J. Tulard, *Napoleon: the Myth of the Saviour* (London, 1984), p. 134.
9. Cited in Thibaudeau, *Bonaparte and the Consulate*, p. 120.
10. Cited in ibid., p. 119.
11. Duc d'Audiffret-Pasquier (ed.), *Mémoires du Chancelier Pasquier – Première Partie: Révolution, Consulat, Empire* (Paris, 1895–1914), vol. I, p. 151.
12. J. Fouché, *Memoirs of Joseph Fouché, Duke of Otranto, Minister of the General Police of France* (London, 1892), pp. 155–9.
13. Cited in D. M. Stuart, *Dearest Bess: the Life and Times of Lady Elizabeth Foster, afterwards Duchess of Devonshire, from her Unpublished Journals and Correspondence* (London, 1955), p. 107.
14. Chaptal, *Souvenirs*, pp. 226–7.
15. Gohier, *Mémoires*, vol. II, p. 106.
16. Noailles, *Life and Memoirs*, vol. I, pp. 79–80.
17. Ibid., pp. 84–5.
18. Fouché, *Memoirs*, pp. 190–91.
19. Cited in Thibaudeau, *Bonaparte and the Consulate*, p. 130.
20. Cited in ibid., pp. 266–7.
21. Cited in ibid., p. 249.
22. C. de Rémusat, *Mémoires de Madame de Rémusat, 1802–1808*, ed. P. de Rémusat (Paris, 1884), vol. I, pp. 103–4, 181–2.
23. Chaptal, *Souvenirs*, vol. I, pp. 333–4.
24. Rémusat, *Mémoires*, vol. I, pp. 105–6.
25. Chaptal, *Souvenirs*, pp. 341–3.
26. Greig, *Farington Diary*, vol. II, pp. 54, 87. In the same extract Farington observes, 'His habitual irritation is also expressed by his cutting the arms of the chair in which he sits

while doing business, scratching on the margin of the book that lies before him, etc., etc.'

27. Cited in Stuart, *Dearest Bess*, p. 105.
28. Cited in Chaptal, *Souvenirs*, p. 299.
29. Thibaudeau, *Bonaparte and the Consulate*, p. 125.
30. Cited in ibid., p. 121.
31. Cited in ibid., pp. 120–21.
32. Cited in H. Deutsch, *The Genesis of Napoleonic Imperialism* (Philadelphia, 1975), p. 77.
33. Cited in J. F. Bernard, *Talleyrand: a Biography* (London, 1973), p. 246.
34. Cited in A. Lobanov-Rostovsky, *Russia and Europe, 1789–1825* (Chapel Hill, North Carolina, 1947), pp. 70–71.
35. Comtesse de Choiseul-Gouffier, *Historical Memoirs of the Emperor Alexander I and the Court of Russia*, ed. M. Patterson (London, 1904), p. 51.
36. Cited in Deutsch, *Genesis of Napoleonic Imperialism*, p. 58.
37. Cited in Countess of Minto (ed.), *Life and Letters of Sir Gilbert Elliot, First Earl of Minto, from 1751 to 1806* (London, 1874), vol. III, pp. 259–60.
38. Cited in Earl of Rosebery (ed.), *The Wellesley Papers: the Life and Correspondence of Richard Colley Wellesley, Marquess Wellesley, 1760–1842* (London, 1914), vol. I, pp. 160–61.
39. H. Carnot (ed.), *Memoirs of Bertrand Barère, Chairman of the Committee of Public Safety during the Revolution* (London, 1896), p. 117.
40. Cited in A. Alison, *History of Europe from the Commencement of the French Revolution to the Restoration of the Bourbons in MDCCCXV* (Edinburgh, 1860), vol. VI, pp. 190–92.
41. Cited in Third Earl of Malmesbury (ed.), *Diaries and Correspondence of James Harris, First Earl of Malmesbury* (London, 1844), vol. IV, p. 219.
42. Cited in Lobanov-Rostovsky, *Russia and Europe*, p. 71.
43. Rémusat, *Mémoires*, vol. I, pp. 118–20.
44. Cited in Alison, *History of Europe*, vol. VI, pp. 193–4.
45. Cited in Minto, *Life and Letters*, vol. III, p. 279.
46. Cited in Malmesbury, *Diaries and Correspondence*, vol. IV, p. 61.
47. Cited in ibid., pp. 63, 85.
48. Cited in ibid., p. 65.
49. Cited in ibid.
50. Cited in ibid., p. 230.
51. Cited in ibid., p. 233.
52. Cited in ibid., pp. 207–9.
53. Cited in ibid., pp. 189–90.
54. Cited in ibid., p. 202.
55. Cited in Rosebery, *Wellesley Papers*, vol. I, p. 164.
56. Greig, *Farington Diary*, vol. II, p. 99.
57. L. Junot, *Mémoires de la Duchesse d'Abrantès*, ed. G. Girard (Paris, 1928–30), vol. IV, pp. 285–6.
58. M. Barrière (ed.), *Mémoires de M. le Comte de Vaublanc* (Paris, 1883), p. 401.
59. Junot, *Mémoires*, vol. IV, pp. 286–7.

4 Towards the Third Coalition

1. Cited in J. D. Markham (ed.), *Imperial Glory: the Bulletins of Napoleon's Grande Armée, 1805–1814* (London, 2003), pp. 10, 23.
2. A. L. G. de Staël, *Considérations sur les Principaux Evénements de la Révolution Française* (London, 1819), vol. II, pp. 351–2.
3. M. de Godoy, *Cuenta dada de su Vida Política por Don Manuel de Godoy, Príncipe de la Paz, o sea Memorias Críticas y Apologéticas para la Historia del Reinado del Señor Carlos IV de Borbón*, ed. C. Seco Serrano (Madrid, 1956), vol. I, p. 124.

4. H. Baring (ed.), *The Diary of the Right Hon. William Windham, 1784 to 1810* (London, 1866), p. 417.
5. Cited in J. Sherwig, *Guineas and Gunpowder: British Foreign Aid in the Wars with France, 1793–1815* (Cambridge, Massachusetts, 1969), p. 130.
6. Cited in A. D. Harvey, 'European attitudes to Britain during the French Revolutionary and Napoleonic era', *History*, LXIII, No. 209 (October 1978), p. 360.
7. J. M. Sherer, *Recollections of the Peninsula* (London, 1825), pp. 66–7.
8. Anon., *Leaves from the Diary of an Officer of the Guards* (London, 1854), p. 279.
9. S. Monick (ed.), *Douglas' Tale of the Peninsula and Waterloo* (London, 1997), p. 99.
10. Cited in Countess of Minto (ed.), *Life and Letters of Sir Gilbert Elliot, First Earl of Minto, from 1751 to 1806* (London, 1874), vol. III, pp. 106–8.
11. Baring (ed.), *Diary of the Right Hon. William Windham*, p. 433.
12. Henry Richard, Lord Holland, *Memoirs of the Whig Party during my Time*, ed. by Henry Edward, Lord Holland (London, 1852), vol. I, p. 57.
13. Cited in Earl of Rosebery (ed.), *The Windham Papers: the Life and Correspondence of the Rt. Hon. William Windham, 1750–1810* (London, 1913), vol. II, p. 246.
14. For these remarks, cf. N. Bentley (ed.), *Selections from the Reminiscences of Captain Gronow* (London, 1977), p. 61.
15. J. Rambaud, *Memoirs of the Comte Roger de Damas, 1787–1806* (London, 1913), pp. 304–5.
16. Holland, *Memoirs of the Whig Party*, vol. I, pp. 154–5.
17. Cited in Marquess of Londonderry (ed.), *Correspondence, Dispatches and other Papers of Viscount Castlereagh, Second Marquess of Londonderry* (London, 1848–53), vol. V, p. 77.
18. Cited in Third Earl of Malmesbury (ed.), *Diaries and Correspondence of James Harris, First Earl of Malmesbury* (London, 1844), vol. IV, p. 66.
19. Cited in ibid., p. 174.
20. J. F. de Bourgoing, *A Modern State of Spain* (London, 1808), vol. II, pp. 71, 75.
21. Rambaud, *Memoirs of the Comte Roger de Damas*, p. 304.
22. Cited in Earl of Rosebery (ed.), *The Wellesley Papers: the Life and Correspondence of Richard Colley Wellesley, Marquess Wellesley, 1760–1842* (London, 1914), vol. I, p. 170.
23. M. K. Oginski, *Mémoires de Michel Oginski sur la Pologne et les Polonais depuis 1788 jusqu'à la fin de 1815* (Paris, 1827), vol. II, pp. 141–2.
24. Cited in Malmesbury, *Diaries and Correspondence*, vol. IV, p. 211.
25. C. de Mazade (ed.), *Mémoires du Prince Adam Czartoryski et Correspondance avec l'Empereur Alexandre Ier* (Paris, 1887), vol. I, p. 335.
26. Cited in Londonderry (ed.), *Correspondence, Dispatches and other Papers of Viscount Castlereagh*, vol. V, p. 81.
27. Cited in C. Fedorak, 'In search of a necessary ally: Addington, Hawkesbury and Russia, 1801–1804', *International History Review*, XIII, No. 2 (May 1991), p. 242.
28. Cited in R. Garner, *The Campaign of Trafalgar* (London, 1997), p. 11.
29. Cited in Rosebery, *Wellesley Papers*, vol. I, p. 170.
30. Cited in ibid., p. 171.
31. Cited in Rosebery (ed.), *The Windham Papers*, vol. II, p. 235.
32. Cited in P. Ziegler, *Addington: a Life of Henry Addington, First Viscount Sidmouth* (London, 1965), p. 197.
33. Cited in Malmesbury, *Diaries and Correspondence*, vol. IV, p. 313.
34. Cited in M. de Klinkowstrom (ed.), *Memoirs of Prince Metternich, 1733–1815* (London, 1880), vol. I, p. 49.
35. Cited in A. Paget (ed.), *The Paget Papers: Diplomatic and other Correspondence of the Right Hon. Sir Arthur Paget, G. C. B., 1794–1807* (London, 1896), vol. II, p. 108.
36. Cited in Minto, *Life and Letters*, vol. III, p. 355.
37. Cited in Malmesbury, *Diaries and Correspondence*, vol. IV, p. 271.
38. Cited in P. Dwyer, 'Two definitions of neutrality: Prussia, the European states-system

and the French invasion of Hanover in 1803', *International History Review*, XIX, No. 3 (August 1997), p. 536.

39. C. von Muffling, *Passages from my Life, together with Memoirs of the Campaign of 1813 and 1814* (London, 1853), pp. 6–7.

40. Cited in Malmesbury, *Diaries and Correspondence*, vol. IV, pp. 246–7.

41. J. Fouché, *Memoirs of Joseph Fouché, Duke of Otranto, Minister of the General Police of France* (London, 1892), p. 178.

42. Mazade (ed.), *Mémoires du Prince Adam Czartoryski*, vol. I, p. 38.

43. Ibid., pp. 385–8.

44. For Napoleon's treatment of Morkov, cf. Earl of Ilchester (ed.), *The Journal of Elizabeth, Lady Holland, 1791–1811* (London, 1909), vol. II, p. 159.

45. Mazade (ed.), *Mémoires du Prince Adam Czartoryski*, vol. I, p. 359.

46. G. S. Hellman (ed.), *Memoirs of the Cmte de Mercy Argenteau, Napoleon's Chamberlain and his Minister Plenipotentiary to the King of Bavaria* (New York, 1917), p. 94.

47. J. Hanoteau (ed.), *Mémoires de la Reine Hortense* (Paris, 1927), vol. I, p. 161.

48. Ibid. General Monk had sealed the fate of the Commonwealth in 1660 by taking his troops over to the cause of Charles II.

49. Duc d'Audiffret-Pasquier (ed.), *Mémoires du Chancelier Pasquier – Première Partie; Révolution, Consulat, Empire* (Paris, 1895–1914), vol. I, p. 179.

50. Cited in R. Johnston (ed.), *In the Words of Napoleon: the Emperor Day-by-Day* (London, 2002), p. 136.

51. Bourrienne, *Memoirs*, p. 247; for Staël's views, cf. *Considérations*, vol. II, pp. 327–8.

52. C. de Rémusat, *Mémoires de Madame de Rémusat, 1802–1808*, ed. P. de Rémusat (Paris, 1884), vol. I, p. 387.

53. So at least goes the traditional version. In Fouché's memoirs, we rather see, 'It is more than a crime; it is a political fault.' See Fouché, *Memoirs*, p. 182.

54. A. du Casse (ed.), *Mémoires et Correspondance Politique et Militaire du Prince Eugène* (Paris, 1858), vol. I, p. 91.

55. Comtesse de Choiseul-Gouffier, *Historical Memoirs of the Emperor Alexander I and the Court of Russia*, ed. M. Patterson (London, 1904), p. 53.

56. Mazade (ed.), *Mémoires du Prince Adam Czartoryski*, vol. I, p. 378.

57. A. Thibaudeau, *Bonaparte and the Consulate*, ed. G. Fortescue (London, 1908), p. 310.

58. Cited in Rémusat, *Mémoires*, vol. I, p. 393.

59. Cited in Malmesbury, *Diaries and Correspondence*, vol. IV, pp. 331–2.

60. Fouché, *Memoirs*, p. 192.

61. Klinkowstrom (ed.), *Memoirs of Prince Metternich*, vol. I, p. 48.

62. Rambaud, *Memoirs of Comte Roger de Damas*, pp. 321–2.

63. Ibid., p. 332.

64. H. Bunbury, *Narratives of some Passages in the Great War with France* (London, 1854), pp. 212, 215.

65. Fouché, *Memoirs*, p. 195.

66. Ibid., pp. 195–6.

67. Cited in Rémusat, *Memoires*, vol. I, p. 384.

68. L. Aldersey White (ed.), *The Adventurous Life of Count Lavallette, Bonaparte's Aide-de-Camp and Postmaster-General, by Himself* (London, 1936), vol. I, pp. 256–7.

5 Austerlitz

1. J. L. Hulot, *Souvenirs Militaires du Baron Hulot, Général d'Artillerie, 1773–1843* (Paris, 1886), p. 92.

2. Cited in P. de Ségur, *Memoirs of an Aide-de-Camp of Napoleon, 1800–1812* (Stroud, 2005), p. 140.

3. R. de Montesquieu-Fézensac, *Souvenirs Militaires de 1808 à 1814* (Paris, 1863), p. 33.

4. Ségur, *Memoirs*, p. 146.

5. Cited in ibid., p. 148.

6. J. Fouché, *Memoirs of Joseph Fouché, Duke of Otranto, Minister of the General Police of France* (London, 1892), p. 201.

7. Duc d'Audiffret-Pasquier (ed.), *Mémoires du Chancelier Pasquier – Première Partie: Révolution, Consulat, Empire* (Paris, 1895–1914), vol. I, pp. 219–20.

8. E. de Saint-Hilaire, *Souvenirs intimes du Temps de l'Empire* (Paris, 1860), vol. I, p. 263.

9. Hulot, *Souvenirs Militaires*, pp. 89–90.

10. Montesquieu-Fézensac, *Souvenirs Militaires*, p. 32.

11. Ibid., pp. 64–5.

12. Hulot, *Souvenirs Militaires*, p. 93; Montesquieu-Fézensac, *Souvenirs Militaires*, p. 46; M. Barrès (ed.), *Memoirs of a French Napoleonic Officer: Jean-Baptiste Barrès, Chasseur of the Imperial Guard* (London, 1955), p. 55.

13. P. Haythornthwaite (ed.), *Life in Napoleon's Army: the Memoirs of Captain Elzéar Blaze* (London, 1995), pp. 2–3.

14. Cited in J. D. Markham, *Imperial Glory: the Bulletins of Napoleon's Grande Armée, 1805–1814* (London, 2003), pp. 9–10.

15. B. T. Jones (ed.), *Napoleon's Army: the Military Memoirs of Charles Parquin* (London, 1987), p. 185.

16. Cited in A. Forrest, *Napoleon's Men: the Soldiers of the Revolution and Empire* (London, 2002), p. 93.

17. A. J. M. de Rocca, *Memoirs of the War of the French in Spain*, ed. P. Haythornthwaite (London, 1990), p. 21.

18. A. Bell (ed.), *Memoirs of Baron Lejeune, Aide-de-Camp to Marshals Berthier, Davout and Oudinot* (London, 1897), vol. I, p. 28.

19. J. Fortescue (ed.), *The Note-books of Captain Coignet, Soldier of the Empire* (London, 1928), p. 122.

20. Cited in Forrest, *Napoleon's Men*, pp. 100–101.

21. Cited in ibid., p. 103.

22. Cited in ibid., p. 26.

23. Haythornthwaite, *Life in Napoleon's Army*, p. 177.

24. Cited in Earl of Stanhope, *Notes of Conversations with the Duke of Wellington, 1831–1851* (London, 1888), p. 9.

25. H. d'Ideville (ed.), *Memoirs of Colonel Bugeaud from his Private Correspondence and Original Documents, 1784–1814* (Worley Publications facsimile edition, 1998), p. 54.

26. Cited in M. de Klinkowstrom (ed.), *Memoirs of Prince Metternich, 1733–1815* (London, 1880), vol. I, p. 56.

27. Cited in Third Earl of Malmesbury (ed.), *Diaries and Correspondence of James Harris, First Earl of Malmesbury* (London, 1844), vol. IV, p. 340.

28. Cited in L. Strakhovsky, *Alexander I of Russia: the Man who Defeated Napoleon* (London, 1949), p. 68.

29. C. de Mazade (ed.), *Mémoires du Prince Adam Czartoryski et Correspondance avec l'Empereur Alexandre Ier* (Paris, 1887), vol. I, p. 410.

30. Whether he actually said this is a moot point – Ehrman, who is Pitt's leading modern biographer, admits that no definite reference can be found for anything of the sort. Cf. J. Ehrman, *The Younger Pitt, II: the Consuming Struggle* (Stanford, California, 1997), p. 822.

31. Cited in R. Eden (ed.), *The Journal and Correspondence of William, Lord Auckland* (London, 1860–62), vol. IV, p. 260.

32. Cited in A. Palmer, *Metternich, Councillor of Europe* (London, 1972), p. 48.

33. C. M. de Talleyrand-Périgord, *Memoirs of the Prince de Talleyrand*, ed. by Duc de Broglie (London, 1891), vol. I, p. 225.

34. Ibid., p. 228.

35. Cited in J. M. Thompson, *Napoleon Bonaparte* (Oxford, 1988), p. 286.

36. Cited in *Correspondance de Napoléon I publiée par ordre de l'Empereur Napoléon III* (Paris, 1858; hereafter *CN*), vol. XI, p. 509.
37. Cited in ibid., vol. IX, p. 345.
38. A. F. L. de Viesse de Marmont, *Mémoires du Maréchal Marmont, Duc de Raguse, de 1792 à 1841* (Paris, 1857), vol. II, p. 228.
39. Cited in *CN*, vol. XII, p. 509.
40. Cited in ibid., p. 291.
41. Cited in ibid., vol. XVI, p. 161.
42. Cited in ibid., p. 474.
43. Sir John Moore to J. W. Gordon, 11 October 1806, British Library, Additional Manuscript 49487, ff. 39–43.
44. Cited in P. K. Grimsted, *The Foreign Ministers of Alexander I: Political Attitudes and the Conduct of Russian Diplomacy, 1801–1825* (Berkeley, California, 1969), p. 143.
45. Cited in A. Bryant, *Years of Victory, 1802–1812* (London, 1944), p. 177.
46. Cited in *CN*, vol. XII, p. 571.
47. Talleyrand-Périgord, *Memoirs of the Prince de Talleyrand*, vol. I, p. 230; Malmesbury, *Diaries and Correspondence*, vol. IV, p. 353.
48. H. Bunbury, *Narratives of some Passages in the Great War with France* (London, 1854), pp. 223, 225.
49. Cited in J. Russel, *The Life and Times of Charles James Fox* (London, 1866), vol. III, p. 377.
50. Cited in E. Las Cases, *Mémorial de Sainte Hélène*, ed. G. Walter (Paris, 1956), vol. II, p. 282.
51. Cited in ibid., p. 494.
52. Cited in *CN*, vol. XII, p. 450.
53. L. de Rochechouart, *Souvenirs sur la Révolution, l'Empire et la Restauration* (Paris, 1933), pp. 114–15.
54. Cited in A. Gerolymatos, *The Balkan Wars: Conquest, Revolution and Retribution from the Ottoman Era to the Twentieth Century and Beyond* (New York, 2002), p. 156.
55. L. Edwards (ed.), *The Memoirs of Prota Matija Nenadovic* (Oxford, 1969), p. 136.
56. Rochechouart, *Souvenirs*, p. 213.
57. Audiffret-Pasquier, *Mémoires du Chancelier Pasquier*, vol. I, p. 290.

6 Zenith of Empire

1. Cited in J. D. Markham (ed.), *Imperial Glory: the Bulletins of Napoleon's Grande Armée, 1805–1814* (London, 2003), p. 173.
2. J. Fouché, *Memoirs of Joseph Fouché, Duke of Otranto, Minister of the General Police of France* (London, 1892), pp. 208–9.
3. Cited in H. Fisher, *Studies in Napoleonic Statesmanship: Germany* (Oxford, 1903), p. 128.
4. O. Williams (ed.), *In the Wake of Napoleon: being the Memoirs of Ferdinand von Funck, Lieutenant-General in the Saxon Army and Adjutant General to the King of Saxony* (London, 1931), p. 73.
5. C. von Muffling, *Passages from my Life, together with Memoirs of the Campaign of 1813 and 1814* (London, 1853), pp. 13–14.
6. C. M. de Talleyrand-Périgord, *Memoirs of the Prince de Talleyrand*, ed. by Duc de Broglie (London, 1891), vol. I, p. 231.
7. Cited in J. M. Thompson, *Napoleon Bonaparte* (Oxford, 1988), p. 290.
8. Cited in E. Henderson, *Blücher and the Uprising of Prussia against Napoleon, 1806–1815* (London, 1911), p. 24.
9. Cited in ibid., pp. 10–11.
10. Cited in R. Aron, *Clausewitz, Philosopher of War* (London, 1983), p. 19.
11. Cited in ibid., p. 15.

12. Cited in Henderson, *Blücher*, p. 12.
13. M. de Marbot, *The Memoirs of Baron de Marbot* (London, 1892), vol. I, pp. 215–16.
14. For Lady Holland's views, cf. Earl of Ilchester (ed.), *The Journal of Elizabeth, Lady Holland, 1791–1811* (London, 1909), vol. II, p. 183.
15. Cited in Third Earl of Malmesbury (ed.), *Diaries and Correspondence of James Harris, First Earl of Malmesbury* (London, 1844), vol. IV, pp. 355–6.
16. J. Greig (ed.), *The Farington Diary* (London, 1923), vol. IV, p. 25.
17. Henry Richard, Lord Holland, *Memoirs of the Whig Party during my Time*, edited by Henry Edward, Lord Holland (London, 1852), vol. II, pp. 112–15.
18. Cited in C. Abbot (ed.), *The Diary and Correspondence of Charles Abbot, Lord Colchester, Speaker of the House of Commons, 1802–1817* (London, 1861), vol. II, pp. 131–2.
19. Ilchester, *Spanish Journal of Elizabeth, Lady Holland*, vol. II, p. 147.
20. M. Barrès (ed.), *Memoirs of a French Napoleonic Officer: Jean-Baptiste Barrès, Chasseur of the Imperial Guard* (London, 1955), p. 88.
21. J. Fortescue (ed.), *The Note-books of Captain Coignet, Soldier of the Empire* (London, 1928), pp. 132–3.
22. Muffling, *Memoirs*, p. 18.
23. Williams, *In the Wake of Napoleon*, p. 129.
24. Cited in Henderson, *Blücher and the Uprising of Prussia*, p. 25.
25. Cited in ibid., p. 16.
26. Duc d'Audiffret-Pasquier (ed.), *Mémoires du Chancelier Pasquier – Première Partie; Révolution, Consulat, Empire* (Paris, 1895–1914), vol. I, pp. 292–3.
27. Williams, *In the Wake of Napoleon*, p. 108.
28. Ibid., p. 293.
29. Fortescue (ed.), *Note-books of Captain Coignet*, pp. 137–9.
30. Ibid., p. 136.
31. Williams, *In the Wake of Napoleon*, p. 142.
32. Ilchester, *Diary of Elizabeth, Lady Holland*, pp. 188–9.
33. R. Wilson, *Brief Remarks on the Character and Composition of the Russian Army and a Sketch of the Campaigns in Poland in the years 1806 and 1807* (London, 1810), pp. 2–3.
34. Greig, *Farington Diary*, vol. IV, p. 26.
35. Cited in B. Francis and E. Keary (eds), *The Francis Letters* (London, n.d.), vol. II, p. 668.
36. J. North, *In the Legions of Napoleon: the Memoirs of a Polish Officer in Spain and Russia, 1808–1813* (London, 1999), p. 39.
37. Cited in H. Butterfield, *The Peace Tactics of Napoleon, 1806–1808* (Cambridge, 1959), p. 59.
38. A. Bell (ed.), *Memoirs of Baron Lejeune, Aide-de-Camp to Marshals Berthier, Davout and Oudinot* (London, 1897), vol. I, p. 38.
39. Ibid., vol. I, p. 38.
40. M. K. Oginski, *Mémoires de Michel Oginski sur la Pologne et les Polonais depuis 1788 jusqu'à la fin de 1815* (Paris, 1827), vol. II, p. 337.
41. Ibid., p. 340.
42. Marbot, *Memoirs*, vol. I, p. 38.
43. Bell, *Memoirs of Baron Lejeune*, vol. I, p. 47.
44. Barrès, *Memoirs of a French Napoleonic Officer*, p. 102.
45. P. Haythornthwaite (ed.), *Life in Napoleon's Army: the Memoirs of Captain Elzéar Blaze* (London, 1995), pp. 175–6.
46. Cited in A. du Casse (ed.), *Mémoires et Correspondance Politique et Militaire du Roi Joseph* (Paris, 1854), vol. III, p. 309.
47. Cited in Markham, *Imperial Glory*, pp. 163–4.
48. Cited in Fouché, *Memoirs*, p. 209.
49. Holland, *Memoirs of the Whig Party*, vol. II, p. 95.
50. Rambaud, *Memoirs of the Comte Roger de Damas*, pp. 410–14 *passim*.

51. Holland, *Memoirs of the Whig Party*, vol. II, pp. 95–6.
52. J. Maurice (ed.), *The Diary of Sir John Moore* (London, 1904), vol. II, pp. 141–6, 188–92 *passim*.
53. Cited in Butterfield, *Peace Tactics of Napoleon*, p. 177.
54. Bell, *Memoirs of Baron Lejeune*, vol. I, p. 66; Fortescue, *Notebooks of Captain Coignet*, vol. I, p. 151; Wilson, *Campaigns in Poland*, p. 157.
55. Cited in Bell, *Memoirs of Baron Lejeune*, vol. I, pp. 66–7.
56. Cited in Butterfield, *Peace Tactics of Napoleon*, p. 198.
57. B. T. Jones (ed.), *Napoleon's Army: the Military Memoirs of Charles Parquin* (London, 1987), p. 71.
58. Cited in Butterfield, *Peace Tactics of Napoleon*, p. 36.
59. G. Troubetzkoy (ed.), *In the Service of the Tsar against Napoleon: the Memoirs of Denis Davidov, 1806–1814* (London, 1999), pp. 58–60.
60. Cited in A. Paget (ed.), *The Paget Papers: Diplomatic and other Correspondence of the Right Hon. Sir Arthur Paget, G. C. B., 1794–1807* (London, 1896), vol. II, pp. 323–4.
61. Cited in R. Parkinson, *The Hussar General: the Life of Blücher, Man of Waterloo* (London, 1975), p. 79.
62. Cited in Butterfield, *Peace Tactics of Napoleon*, p. 234.
63. Cited in ibid., p. 203.

7 Across the Pyrenees

1. C. M. de Talleyrand-Périgord, *Memoirs of the Prince de Talleyrand*, ed. by Duc de Broglie (London, 1891), vol. I, p. 244.
2. Cited in M. de Baudus, *Etudes sur Napoléon* (Paris, 1841), vol. I, p. 105.
3. Conde de Toreno, *Historia del Levantamiento, Guerra y Revolución de España*, ed. L. Augusto de Cueto (Madrid, 1953), p. 1.
4. Earl of Ilchester (ed.), *The Spanish Journal of Elizabeth, Lady Holland* (London, 1910), vol. II, pp. 85–6, 107, 123–4.
5. M. de Godoy to María Luisa, 29 May 1801, Archivo Histórico Nacional (Madrid), Sección de Estado (hereafter AHN. Est.) 2821–1.
6. Ilchester, *Spanish Journal of Elizabeth, Lady Holland*, vol. II, p. 167.
7. Ibid., p. 134.
8. Cited in J. I. González-Aller, *La campaña de Trafalgar, 1804–1805: Corpus documental conservado en los archivos españoles* (Madrid, 2004), vol. I, pp. 104–5.
9. Cited in C. Chastenet, *Godoy, Master of Spain, 1792–1801* (London, 1953), p. 107.
10. Cited in C. Oman, *A History of the Peninsular War* (Oxford, 1902–1930), vol. I, p. 603.
11. O. Williams (ed.), *In the Wake of Napoleon: being the Memoirs of Ferdinand von Funck, Lieutenant-General in the Saxon Army and Adjutant General to the King of Saxony* (London, 1931), p. 116.
12. Cited in ibid., p. 167.
13. Cited in A. Paget (ed.), *The Paget Papers: Diplomatic and other Correspondence of the Right Hon. Sir Arthur Paget, G. C. B., 1794–1807* (London, 1896), vol. II, p. 376.
14. Cited in *Correspondance de Napoléon I publiée par ordre de l'Empereur Napoléon III* (Paris, 1858; hereafter *CN*), vol. XVI, p. 83.
15. Duc d'Audiffret-Pasquier (ed.), *Mémoires du Chancelier Pasquier – Première Partie: Révolution, Consulat, Empire* (Paris, 1895–1914), vol. I, p. 309.
16. M. Barrès (ed.), *Memoirs of a French Napoleonic Officer: Jean-Baptiste Barrès, Chasseur of the Imperial Guard* (London, 1955), pp. 119–20.
17. R. Ledos de Beaufort (ed.), *Personal Recollections of the late Duc de Broglie, 1785–1820* (London, 1887), vol. I, pp. 52–3.
18. Cited in *CN*, vol. XVI, p. 19.

19. Cited in A. Hayter (ed.), *The Backbone: Diaries of a Military Family in the Napoleonic Wars* (Bishop Auckland, 1993), p. 114.
20. J. Fouché, *Memoirs of Joseph Fouché, Duke of Otranto, Minister of the General Police of France* (London, 1892), p. 214.
21. Cited in M. de Klinkowstrom (ed.), *Memoirs of Prince Metternich, 1733–1815* (London, 1880), vol. II, p. 158.
22. Cited in *CN*, vol. XVI, p. 80.
23. H. Carnot (ed.), *Memoirs of Bertrand Barère, Chairman of the Committee of Public Safety during the Revolution* (London, 1896), vol. III, pp. 131–2.
24. Anon., *Inocencia del Rey Nuestro Señor D. Ferdinand VII y tramas del pérfido Godoy* (Seville, 1814), pp. 10–11.
25. Cited in *CN*, vol. XVI, pp. 159–60.
26. A. Butler (ed.), *Memoirs of Baron Thiébault, late Lieutenant-General in the French Army* (London, 1896), vol. II, p. 196.
27. A. Berazaluce (ed.), *Recuerdos de la vida de Don Pedro Agustín Girón* (Pamplona, 1978), vol. I, pp. 190–91.
28. A. du Casse (ed.), *Mémoires et Correspondance Politique et Militaire du Roi Joseph* (Paris, 1854–6), vol. IV, p. 8.
29. Fouché, *Memoirs*, vol. I, p. 315.
30. Henry Edward, Lord Holland, *Foreign Reminiscences* (London, 1850), pp. 130–31.
31. M. Artola (ed.), *Memorias de Juan de Escoíquiz* (Madrid, 1957), p. 57.
32. Cited in *CN*, vol. XVI, pp. 500–501.
33. Cited in A. Alcalá Galiano (ed.), *Memorias de Don Antonio Alcalá Galiano* (Madrid, 1886), vol. I, p. 144.
34. Cited in *CN*, vol. XVI, pp. 418–19.
35. A. Bell (ed.), *Memoirs of Baron Lejeune, Aide-de-Camp to Marshals Berthier, Davout and Oudinot* (London, 1897), vol. I, p. 73.
36. M. Foy, *History of the War in the Peninsula under Napoleon* (London, 1827), vol. II, p. 135.
37. Cited in A. Wilson (ed.), *A Diary of St Helena (1816–1817): the Journal of Lady Malcolm containing the Conversations of Sir Pulteney Malcolm with Napoleon* (London, 1899), p. 141.
38. Foy, *War in the Peninsula*, vol. II, p. 20.
39. R. Brindle, 'A Brief Account of Travels, etc., in Spain' (MS), Real Colegio de San Albano, Valladolid, p. 10.
40. Cited in *Diario de Valencia*, 25 March 1808, p. 338.
41. Alcalá Galiano, *Memorias*, vol. I, p. 146.
42. J. Blanco White, *Cartas de España*, ed. V. Llorens and A. Garnica (Madrid, 1972), pp. 294–5.
43. J. Marcén (ed.), *El manuscrito de Matias Calvo: memorias de un monegrino durante la Guerra de la Independencia* (Zaragoza, 2000), p. 177.
44. M. de Marbot, *The Memoirs of Baron de Marbot* (London, 1892), vol. I, p. 306.
45. Alcalá Galiano, *Memorias*, vol. I, p. 160.
46. Cited in *CN*, vol. XVII, p. 66.
47. Cited in E. Las Cases, *Mémorial de Sainte Hélène*, ed. G. Walter (Paris, 1956), vol. I, pp. 780–81.
48. Cited in P. L. Roederer, *Mémoires sur la Révolution, le Consulat et l'Empire*, ed. O. Aubry (Paris, 1942), pp. 220–21.
49. Anon., *El Tirano de la Europa, Napoleón I: Manifiesto que a Todos los Pueblos del Mundo y principalmente a los Españoles presenta el Licenciado D.J.A.C.* (Seville, 1808), pp. 5–9.
50. Marbot, *Memoirs*, vol. I, p. 320.
51. Cited in Las Cases, *Mémorial*, vol. I, pp. 784–5.
52. Cited in ibid., pp. 783–4.

53. Cited in *CN*, vol. XVII, p. 359; with some minor changes, use has been made of the translation given in J. M. Thompson (ed.), *Napoleon's Letters* (London, 1934), pp. 200–201.

8 From Madrid to Vienna

1. Cited in *Correspondence de Napoléon I publiée par ordre de L'Empereur Napoléon III* (Paris, 1858; hereafter CN), vol. XVII, p. 407.
2. Cited in ibid., p. 428.
3. J. Sarrazin, *History of the War in Spain and Portugal from 1807 to 1814* (London, 1815), pp. 64–6.
4. A. Bell (ed.), *Memoirs of Baron Lejeune, Aide-de-Camp to Marshals Berthier, Davout and Oudinot* (London, 1897), vol. I, pp. 105–6.
5. Cited in A. du Casse (ed.), *Mémoires et Correspondance Politique et Militaire du Roi Joseph* (Paris, 1854–6), vol. VII, p. 84.
6. Though occupied by the French during their pursuit of Sir John Moore, Galicia proved difficult to hold and was given up by them a few months later.
7. L. Suchet, *Memoirs of the War in Spain from 1808 to 1814* (London, 1829), vol. II, pp. 141–2.
8. W. Verner (ed.), *A British Rifleman: the Journals and Correspondence of Major George Simmons, Rifle Brigade, during the Peninsular War and the Campaign of Waterloo* (London, 1899), pp. 137–52 *passim*.
9. C. de Rémusat, *Mémoires de Madame de Rémusat, 1802–1808*, ed. P. de Rémusat (Paris, 1884), vol. III, p. 409.
10. Lord Wellington to Lord Liverpool, 25 July 1813, University of Southampton, Wellington Papers (hereafter US. WP.) 1/373.
11. J. Hanoteau (ed.), *Memoirs of General de Caulaincourt, Duke of Vicenza* (London, 1935), vol. I, p. 236.
12. A. F. L. de Viesse de Marmont, *Mémoires du Maréchal Marmont, Duc de Raguse, de 1792 à 1841* (Paris, 1857), vol. IV, p. 259.
13. J. Maurice (ed.), *The Diary of Sir John Moore* (London, 1904), vol. II, pp. 209–11.
14. W. Thompson (ed.), *An Ensign in the Peninsular War: the Letters of John Aitchison*, (London, 1981), p. 32.
15. Cited in R. Weigall (ed.), *Correspondence of Lord Burghersh, afterwards Eleventh Earl of Westmoreland, 1808–1840* (London, 1912), p. 39.
16. Wellington to E. Cooke, 25 November 1812, US. WP.1/351.
17. Canning to Wellington, 16 September 1809, National Archives, Foreign Office Papers (Hereafter NA. FO.) 72/75, ff. 196–208.
18. Cited in M. Martin (ed.), *The Dispatches and Correspondence of the Marquess Wellesley, K. G., during His Lordship's Mission to Spain as Ambassador Extraordinary to the Supreme Junta in 1809* (London, 1838), p. 119.
19. Cited in Weigall, *Correspondence of Lord Burghersh*, p. 33.
20. T. Graham to Liverpool, 23 April 1811, National Archives, War Office Papers (hereafter NA. WO.) 1/252, f. 291.
21. H. Douglas to Liverpool, 13 September 1811, NA. WO.1/261, f. 446; H. Wellesley to Wellington, 18 July 1811, US. WP.12/2/2.
22. Wellington to H. Wellesley, 10 August 1810, US. WP.12/1/1.
23. G. Larpent (ed.), *The Private Journal of Judge-Advocate F. S. Larpent, attached to Wellington's Headquarters, 1812–1814* (London, 1853), vol. II, pp. 127–8.
24. Wellington to Bathurst, 27 November 1813, US. WP.1/381.
25. Cited in H. Acton, *The Bourbons of Naples, 1734–1825* (London, 1956), p. 606.
26. L. Spring (ed.), *An Englishman in the Russian Army, 1807; the Journal of Colonel James Bathurst during the East Prussia Campaign, 1807* (Woking, 2000), p. 18.
27. Hanoteau, *Memoirs of General de Caulaincourt*, vol. I, p. 67.

28. Cited in ibid., p. 63.
29. Ibid., p. 67.
30. Cited in Talleyrand, *Memoirs*, pp. 300–301, 316.
31. Hanoteau, *Memoirs of General de Caulaincourt*, vol. I, p. 84.
32. Cited in G. Stiegler (ed.), *Memoirs of Marshal Oudinot, Duc de Reggio compiled from the Hitherto Unpublished Souvenirs of the Duchesse de Reggio* (New York, 1897), p. 78.
33. Hanoteau, *Memoirs of General de Caulaincourt*, vol. I, p. 84.
34. C. M. de Talleyrand-Périgord, *Memoirs of the Prince de Talleyrand*, ed. by Duc de Broglie (London, 1891), vol. I, p. 325.
35. Hanoteau, *Memoirs of General de Caulaincourt*, vol. I, p. 71.
36. Cited in M. de Klinkowstrom (ed.), *Memoirs of Prince Metternich, 1733–1815* (London, 1880), vol. I, p. 82.
37. Cited in *CN*, vol. XVII, p. 417.
38. Cited in Klinkowstrom (ed.), *Memoirs of Prince Metternich*, vol. I, p. 80.
39. Cited in Talleyrand, *Memoirs*, pp. 305, 309.
40. Cited in Hanoteau, *Memoirs of General de Caulaincourt*, vol. I, pp. 73–88 passim.
41. E. Rousset (ed.), *Recollections of Marshal Macdonald, Duke of Tarentum* (London, 1892), vol. I, pp. 299–301.
42. P. Haythornthwaite (ed.), *Life in Napoleon's Army: the Memoirs of Captain Elzéar Blaze* (London, 1995), pp. 131–2.
43. Cited in Klinkowstrom (ed.), *Memoirs of Prince Metternich*, vol. I, p. 100.
44. Cited in ibid., vol. II, pp. 364–5.
45. W. Müller, *Relation of the Operations and Battles of the Austrian and French Armies in the Year 1809* (London, 1810), p. 13.
46. Cited in J. Gill (ed.) *A Soldier for Napoleon: the Campaigns of Lieutenant Franz Joseph Haussmann, Seventh Bavarian Infantry* (London, 1998), pp. 72–3.
47. M. de Marbot, *The Memoirs of Baron de Marbot* (London, 1892), vol. II, pp. 22–3.

9 The Alliance that Failed

1. Cited in *CN*, vol. XVIII, pp. 375–6.
2. Cited in R. Soltyk, *Operations of the Polish Army during the 1809 campaign in Poland*, ed. by G. Nafziger (Westchester, Ohio, 2002), p. 153.
3. Cited in ibid. pp. 159–60.
4. M. K. Oginski, *Mémoires de Michel Oginski sur la Pologne et les Polonais depuis 1788 jusqu'à la fin de 1815* (Paris, 1827), vol. II, pp. 370–71.
5. Cited in M. de Klinkowstrom (ed.), *Memoirs of Prince Metternich, 1733–1815* (London, 1880), vol. I, p. 120.
6. Cited in Duc d' Audiffret-Pasquier (ed.), *Mémoires du Chancelier Pasquier – Première Partie: Révolution, Consulat, Empire* (Paris, 1895–1914), vol. I, p. 377.
7. Ibid.
8. Cited in L. Aldersey White (ed.), *The Adventurous Life of Count Lavallette, Bonaparte's Aide-de-Camp and Postmaster-General, by Himself* (London, 1936), vol. II, p. 5.
9. Cited in Audiffret-Pasquier (ed.), *Mémoires du Chancelier Pasquier*, vol. I, p. 378.
10. Marquise de la Tour du Pin, *Recollections of the Revolution and the Empire*, ed. W. Geer (London, 1921), pp. 358–9.
11. P. Jones (ed.), *In Napoleon's Shadow: being the First English-Language Edition of the Complete Memoirs of Louis-Joseph Marchand, Valet and Friend of the Emperor, 1811–1821* (San Francisco, 1998), p. 5.
12. P. Jones (ed.), *Napoleon: How He Did It – the Memoirs of Baron Fain, First Secretary of the Emperor's Cabinet* (San Francisco, 1998), p. 183.
13. Cited in D. Seward, *Napoleon's Family* (London, 1986), pp. 124–5.
14. Cited in A. Brett-James (ed.), *1812: Eyewitness Accounts of Napoleon's Defeat in Russia* (London, 1966), p. 48.

15. C. J. Summerville (ed.), *Napoleon's Expedition to Russia: the Memoirs of General de Ségur* (London, 2003), p. 76.
16. Marquis de Noailles (ed.), *The Life and Memoirs of Count Molé, 1781–1855* (London, 1923), vol. I, pp. 140–41.
17. Comtesse de Choiseul-Gouffier, *Historical Memoirs of the Emperor Alexander I and the Court of Russia*, edited by M. Patterson (London, 1904), p. 60.
18. Cited in *CN*, vol. XVI, p. 161.
19. Cited in Noailles, *Life and Memoirs of Count Molé*, pp. 140–41.
20. J. Hanoteau (ed.), *Mémoires de la Reine Hortense* (Paris, 1927), vol. I, pp. 242–3.
21. Cited in *CN*, vol. XIV, p. 28.
22. Cited in *CN*, vol. XVI, p. 161.
23. Cited in J. M. Thompson (ed.), *Napoleon's Letters* (London, 1934), pp. 230–33.
24. Hanoteau, *Mémoires de la Reine Hortense*, vol. II, p. 58.
25. Cited in N. Gotteri (ed.), *La Mission de Lagarde, Policier de l'Empereur, pendant la Guerre d'Espagne, 1809–1811* (Paris, 1991), pp. 141–2.
26. Cited in ibid., pp. 148–52.
27. Cited in L. Lecestre (ed.), *Lettres Inédites de Napoléon Ier* (Paris, 1897), vol. I, pp. 266–7.
28. Cited in ibid., p. 276.
29. Cited in A. du Casse (ed.), *Mémoires et Correspondance Politique et Militaire du Roi Joseph* (Paris, 1854–6), vol. VII, p. 260.
30. Cited in ibid., p. 272.
31. Earl of Ilchester (ed.), *Spanish Journal of Elizabeth, Lady Holland* (London, 1910), vol. I, pp. 127–8.
32. O. Williams (ed.), *In the Wake of Napoleon: being the Memoirs of Ferdinand von Funck, Lieutenant-General in the Saxon Army and Adjutant General to the King of Saxony* (London, 1931), p. 144.
33. Cited in CN, vol. XVI, p. 166.
34. E. Lecky (ed.), *Un Général hollandais sous le premier Empire: Mémoires du Général Baron de Dedem de Gelder, 1774–1825* (Paris, 1900), pp. 107–11.
35. Cited in Lecestre (ed.), *Lettres inédites*, vol. I, pp. 217–18.
36. Cited in ibid., p. 327.
37. C. Lahovary (ed.), *Mémoires de l'Amiral Paul Tchitchagof, Commandant en chef de l'Armée du Danube, Gouverneur des Principautés de Moldavie et de Valachie en 1812* (Paris, 1909), pp. 370–71, 381.
38. Choiseul-Gouffier, *Mémoires*, pp. 64–5.
39. J. Hanoteau (ed.), *Memoirs of General de Caulaincourt, Duke of Vicenza* (London, 1935), vol. I, p. 96.
40. Ibid., p. 101.
41. Ibid.
42. Ibid., p. 110.
43. Cited in L. Czartoryski (ed.), *Alexandre Ier et le Prince Czartoryski: Correspondance particulière et Conversations, 1801–1823* (Paris, 1865), pp. 87–8.
44. Oginski, *Mémoires*, vol. II, pp. 376–7.
45. Cited in Klinkowstrom, *Memoirs of Prince Metternich*, vol. II, pp. 492–4.
46. Cited in V. Cronin, *Napoleon* (London, 1971), p. 384.
47. Oginski, *Mémoires*, vol. II, p. 375.
48. Cited in Lecky, *Mémoires du Général de Dedem*, p. 192.
49. Cited in ibid., p. 193.
50. A. Branche and A. Dagoury (eds), *Recollections of a Parisian (Docteur Poumiès de la Siboutie) under Six Sovereigns, Two Revolutions and a Republic, 1789–1863* (London, 1911), p. 88.
51. Hanoteau, *Mémoires de la Reine Hortense*, vol. II, p. 147.
52. Cited in Hanoteau, *Memoirs of General de Caulaincourt*, vol. I, pp. 171–2.
53. Ibid., p. 383.

54. A. Beugnot (ed.), *Mémoires du Comte Beugnot, Ancien Ministre, 1783–1815* (Paris, 1868), vol. I, p. 486.
55. Ibid., pp. 309–10.
56. Audiffret-Pasquier, *Mémoires du Chancelier Pasquier*, vol. I, p. 516.
57. J. Fouché, *Memoirs of Joseph Fouché, Duke of Otranto, Minister of the General Police of France* (London, 1892), p. 318.
58. Cited in Klinkowstrom, *Memoirs of Prince Metternich*, vol. I, pp. 152–3.
59. Cited in Noailles, *Life and Memoirs of Count Molé*, vol. I, pp. 148–9.
60. Cited in C. Stryienski (ed.), *Mémoires de la Comtesse Potocka, 1794–1820* (Paris, 1911), p. 284.
61. Cited in A. Villemain, *Souvenirs contemporains d'Histoire et de Littérature* (Paris, 1854), vol. I, p. 175.
62. Cited in ibid., p. 180.
63. Cited in CN, vol. XXIII, p. 26.
64. Cited in ibid., p. 191.
65. D. Dufour de Pradt, *Histoire de l'Ambassade dans le Grand Duché de Varsovie en 1812* (Paris, 1815), pp. 44–56 *passim*.
66. A. Bell (ed.), *Memoirs of Baron Lejeune, Aide-de-Camp to Marshals Berthier, Davout and Oudinot* (London, 1897), vol. II, p. 150.
67. A. Mikaberidze (ed.), *The Czar's General: the Memoirs of a Russian General in the Napoleonic Wars* (London, 2005), p. 131.
68. Choiseul-Gouffier, *Memoirs*, p. 67.
69. D. von Uexküll (ed.), *Arms and the Woman: the Diaries of Baron Boris Uxkull, 1812–1819* (London, 1966), p. 62.
70. Cited in Hanoteau, *Memoirs of General de Caulaincourt*, vol. I, pp. 108–9.
71. Mikaberidze (ed.), *The Czar's General*, pp. 108, 111.
72. R. Wilson, *Narrative of Events during the Invasion of Russia by Napoleon Bonaparte and the Retreat of the French Army, 1812* (London, 1860), p. 25.
73. Cited in Hanoteau, *Memoirs of General de Caulaincourt*, vol. I, p. 155.
74. Cited in ibid., p. 171.
75. J. North, *In the Legions of Napoleon: the Memoirs of a Polish Officer in Spain and Russia, 1808–1813* (London, 1999), pp. 188–9.
76. E. Labaume, *A Circumstantial Narrative of the Campaign in Russia* (London, 1815), pp. 3–4.

10 Downfall

1. Cited in M. de Klinkowstrom (ed.), *Memoirs of Prince Metternich, 1733–1815* (London, 1880), vol. I, p. 153.
2. Cited in CN, vol. XXIII, p. 480.
3. Cited in Duc d'Audiffret-Pasquier (ed.), *Mémoires du Chancelier Pasquier – Première Partie: Révolution, Consulat, Empire* (Paris, 1895–1914), vol. I, p. 525.
4. Cited in M. K. Oginski, *Mémoires de Michel Oginski sur la Pologne et les Polonais depuis 1788 jusqu'à la fin de 1815* (Paris, 1827), vol. IV, p. 18.
5. J. Fortescue (ed.), *The Notebooks of Captain Coignet, Soldier of the Empire* (London, 1989), p. 207.
6. M. Raeff (ed.), *The Diary of a Napoleonic Foot Soldier* (Moreton-in-Marsh, 1991), pp. 41–2.
7. J. North (ed.), *With Napoleon in Russia: the Illustrated Memoirs of Major Faber du Faur, 1812* (London, 2001), n.p.
8. Comtesse de Choiseul-Gouffier, *Historical Memoirs of the Emperor Alexander I and the Court of Russia*, ed. by M. Patterson (London, 1904), pp. 97–9.
9. J. Hanoteau (ed.), *Memoirs of General de Caulaincourt, Duke of Vicenza* (London, 1935), vol. I, p. 169.

NOTES

10. M. de Marbot, *The Memoirs of Baron de Marbot* (London, 1892), vol. II, p. 221.
11. C. Stryienski (ed.), *Mémoires de la Comtesse Potocka, 1794–1820* (Paris, 1911), p. 303.
12. A. Bell (ed.), *Memoirs of Baron Lejeune, Aide-de-Camp to Marshals Berthier, Davout and Oudinot* (London, 1897), vol. II, pp. 153–4.
13. D. Dufour de Pradt, *Histoire de l'Ambassade dans le Grand Duché de Varsovie en 1812* (Paris, 1815), pp. 63–4.
14. D. Chlapowski, *Mémoires sur les Guerres de Napoléon, 1806–1813* (Paris, 1908), p. 251.
15. Dufour de Pradt, *Histoire de l'Ambassade dans le Grand Duché de Varsovie*, pp. 114–16.
16. R. Brindle (ed.), *With Napoleon's Guns: the Military Memoirs of an Officer of the First Empire* (London, 2005), pp. 140–41.
17. C. J. Summerville (ed.), *Napoleon's Expedition to Russia: the Memoirs of General de Ségur* (London, 2003), pp. 27–8.
18. Choiseul-Gouffier, *Memoirs*, p. 100.
19. Raeff, *Diary of a Napoleonic Foot Soldier*, p. 44.
20. Hanoteau, *Memoirs of General de Caulaincourt*, vol. I, pp. 191–2.
21. Cited in C. de la Roncière (ed.), *The Letters of Napoleon to Marie-Louise* (London, 1935), p. 80.
22. Cited in Summerville (ed.), *Napoleon's Expedition to Russia*, p. 36.
23. Ibid., p. 40.
24. R. de Fézensac, *A Journal of the Russian Campaign of 1812* (London, 1812), p. 25.
25. Hanoteau, *Memoirs of General de Caulaincourt*, vol. I, pp. 197–8.
26. Summerville (ed.), *Napoleon's Expedition to Russia*, p. 41.
27. J. North, *In the Legions of Napoleon: the Memoirs of a Polish Officer in Spain and Russia, 1808–1813* (London, 1999), p. 209.
28. J. Clarette (ed.), *From Valmy to Waterloo: Extracts from the Diary of Captain Charles François, a Soldier of the Revolution and Empire* (London, 1906), p. 234.
29. Cited in Roncière, *The Letters of Napoleon to Marie-Louise*, p. 87.
30. A. Mikaberidze (ed.), *The Czar's General: the Memoirs of a Russian General in the Napoleonic Wars* (London, 2005), p. 127.
31. Fézensac, *A Journal of the Russian Campaign of 1812*, p. 59.
32. Bell, *Memoirs of Baron Lejeune*, vol. II, p. 170.
33. W. Wallich (ed.), *With Napoleon in Russia, 1812: the Diary of Lieutenant H. A. Vossler, a Soldier of the Grande Armée, 1812–1813* (London, 1969), p. 59.
34. Chlapowski, *Mémoires*, p. 264.
35. G. Troubetzkoy (ed.), *In the Service of the Tsar against Napoleon: the Memoirs of Denis Davidov, 1806–1814* (London, 1999), p. 85.
36. D. von Uexküll (ed.), *Arms and the Woman: the Diaries of Baron Boris Uxkull, 1812–1819* (London, 1966), p. 75.
37. R. Wilson, *Narrative of Events during the Invasion of Russia by Napoleon Bonaparte and the Retreat of the French Army, 1812* (London, 1860), p. 130.
38. Hanoteau, *Memoirs of General de Caulaincourt*, vol. I, p. 247.
39. Cited in ibid., p. 252.
40. Summerfield, *Napoleon's Expedition to Russia*, p. 119.
41. Mikaberidze, *The Czar's General*, pp. 210–11.
42. H. Roeder (ed.), *The Ordeal of Captain Roeder: from the Diary of an Officer of the First Battalion of Hessian Lifeguards during the Moscow Campaign of 1812–13* (London, 1960), pp. 191, 201–2.
43. Wallich, *With Napoleon in Russia*, p. 45.
44. E. Lecky (ed.), *Un Général hollandais sous le premier Empire: Mémoires du Général Baron de Dedem de Gelder, 1774–1825* (Paris, 1900), p. 212.
45. R. Brindle (ed.), *With Napoleon's Guns: the Military Memoirs of an Officer of the First Empire* (London, 2005), pp. 150–51.
46. Cited in R. Wilson, *The French Invasion of Russia* (London, 1860), p. 366.

47. L. de Rochechouart, *Souvenirs sur la Révolution, l'Empire et la Restauration* (Paris, 1933), p. 222.
48. Choiseul-Gouffier, *Memoirs*, p. 150.
49. Cited in Dufour de Pradt, *Ambassade en Pologne*, p. 119.
50. Cited in in L. Czartoryski (ed.), *Alexandre Ier et le Prince Czartoryski: Correspondance particulière et conversations, 1801–1823* (Paris, 1865), pp. 207–8.
51. Cited in Dufour de Pradt, *Histoire de l'Ambassade dans le Grand Duché de Versovie en 1812*, pp. 181–4.
52. Cited in Hanoteau, *Memoirs of General de Caulaincourt*, vol. II, p. 143.
53. Cited in ibid., p. 315.
54. Hanoteau, *Mémoires de la Reine Hortense*, vol. II, p. 151.
55. Marquis de Noailles (ed.), *The Life and Memoirs of Count Molé, 1781–1855* (London, 1923), vol. I, p. 138.
56. J. Fouché, *Memoirs of Joseph Fouché, Duke of Otranto, Minister of the General Police of France* (London, 1892), p. 332.
57. Marbot, *Memoirs*, vol. II, p. 351.
58. Fouché, *Memoirs*, p. 329.
59. Hanoteau, *Memoirs of General de Caulaincourt*, vol. II, p. 347.
60. Cited in A. Villemain, *Souvenirs contemporains d'Histoire et de Littérature* (Paris, 1854), vol. I, pp. 290–92.
61. Hanoteau, *Memoirs of General de Caulaincourt*, vol. II, p. 352.
62. Cited in Klinkowstrom, *Memoirs of Prince Metternich*, vol. I, pp. 158–9.
63. Cited in ibid., p. 166.
64. Fortescue, *Notebooks of Captain Coignet*, p. 248.
65. E. Macdonald, *Recollections of Marshal Macdonald, Duke of Tarentum*, ed. E. Rousset (London, 1892), p. 50.
66. Cited in Klinkowstrom, *Memoirs of Prince Metternich*, vol. I, pp. 167, 176.
67. Hanoteau, *Memoirs of General de Caulaincourt*, vol. II, p. 353.
68. Cited in Klinkowstrom, *Memoirs of Prince Metternich*, vol. I, pp. 185–6.
69. Cited in ibid., pp. 185–7.
70. Cited in ibid., pp. 187, 192.
71. Brindle, *With Napoleon's Guns*, p. 163.
72. Cited in Klinkowstrom, *Memoirs of Prince Metternich*, vol. I, p. 200.
73. R. Ledos de Beaufort (ed.), *Personal Recollections of the late Duc de Broglie, 1785–1820* (London, 1887), vol. I, pp. 228–9.
74. Cited in Lady Jackson (ed.), *The Bath Archives: a Further Selection from the Diaries and Letters of Sir George Jackson, K. C. H., from 1809 to 1816* (London, 1873), pp. 204–5.
75. Cited in Rochechouart, *Souvenirs*, p. 293.
76. Marbot, *Memoirs*, vol. II, p. 361.
77. Lecky, *Mémoires du Général Baron de Dedem*, pp. 332, 337.
78. Macdonald, *Recollections of Marshal Macdonald*, vol. II, p. 66.
79. Brindle, *With Napoleon's Guns*, p. 182.
80. A. F. L. de Viesse de Marmont, *Mémoires du Maréchal Marmont, Duc de Raguse, de 1792 à 1841* (Paris, 1857), vol. XVIII, pp. 295–300.
81. Cited in Jackson (ed.), *The Bath Archives*, p. 314.
82. Cited in ibid., p. 361.
83. C. von Muffling, *Passages from my Life, together with Memoirs of the Campaign of 1813 and 1814* (London, 1853), pp. 92–3.
84. Audiffret-Pasquier, *Mémoires du Chancelier Pasquier*, vol. II, pp. 100–101.
85. L. Aldersey White (ed.), *The Adventurous Life of Count Lavallette, Bonaparte's Aide-de-Camp and Postmaster General, by Himself* (London, 1936), vol. II, p. 25.
86. Cited in G. Stiegler (ed.), *Memoirs of Marshal Oudinot, Duc de Reggio compiled from the Hitherto Unpublished Souvenirs of the Duchesse de Reggio* (New York, 1897), pp. 252–3.

87. Rochechouart, *Souvenirs*, p. 328.
88. Marbot, *Memoirs*, vol. II, pp. 441–2.
89. H. Carnot (ed.), *Memoirs of Bertrand Barère, Chairman of the Committee of Public Safety during the Revolution* (London, 1896), vol. III, p. 168.
90. R. Ledos de Beaufort (ed.), *Personal Recollections of the late Duc de Broglie*, vol. I, pp. 241–2.
91. A. Beugnot (ed.), *Mémoires du Comte Beugnot, Ancien Ministre, 1783–1815* (Paris, 1868), vol. II, p. 68.
92. Cited in Aldersey White (ed.), *Life of Count Lavallette*, vol. II, p. 26.
93. Cited in ibid.
94. Cited in Beugnot, *Mémoires du Comte Beugnot*, vol. II, p. 57.
95. Aldersey White (ed.), *Life of Count Lavallette*, vol. II, pp. 26–7.
96. Jones, *In Napoleon's Shadow*, pp. 34–5.
97. Carnot (ed.), *Memoirs of Bertrand Barère*, vol. III, p. 171.
98. G. Bell, *Rough Notes of an Old Soldier*, ed. B. Stuart (London, 1956), p. 123.
99. Ibid., p. 179.
100. Cited in Stiegler, *Memoirs of Marshal Oudinot*, p. 253.
101. Hanoteau, *Memoirs of General de Caulaincourt*, vol. III, pp. 7–9, 16–17.
102. Cited in ibid., pp. 38–9.
103. L. B. de Saint-Léon, *Mémoires et Souvenirs de Charles de Pougens* (Paris, 1834), pp. 261–2.
104. A. Branche and A. Dagoury (eds), *Recollections of a Parisian (Docteur Poumiès de la Siboutie) under Six Sovereigns, Two Revolutions and a Republic, 1789–1863* (London, 1911), pp. 122–3.
105. A. J. F. Fain, *Memoirs of the Invasion of France by the Allied Armies and of the last Six Months of the Reign of Napoleon* (London, 1834), pp. 161–2.
106. Cited in Stiegler, *Memoirs of Marshal Oudinot*, pp. 254–5.

11 The Congress of Vienna

1. Cited in Comtesse de Choiseul-Gouffier, *Historical Memoirs of the Emperor Alexander I and the Court of Russia*, ed. M. Patterson (London, 1904), p. 148.
2. Cited in ibid., pp. 212–13.
3. Cited in ibid., p. 212.
4. Cited in Second Duke of Wellington (ed.), *Supplementary Despatches, Correspondence and Memoranda of Field Marshal Arthur, Duke of Wellington, K.G.* (London, 1858–62; hereafter *WSD*), vol. IX, p. 64.
5. Cited in C. M. de Talleyrand-Périgord, *Memoirs of the Prince de Talleyrand*, ed. Duc de Broglie (London, 1891), vol. II, p. 177.
6. Cited in *WSD*, vol. IX, p. 357.
7. Cited in Talleyrand, *Memoirs*, vol. II, pp. 133–4.
8. Lady Jackson (ed.), *The Bath Archives: a Further Selection from the Diaries and Letters of Sir George Jackson, K. C. H., from 1809 to 1816* (London, 1873), vol. II, p. 240.
9. Cited in C. Webster, *The Foreign Policy of Castlereagh, 1812–1815* (London, 1931), p. 237.
10. Talleyrand, *Memoirs*, vol. II, pp. 135, 149.
11. Cited in *WSD*, vol. IX, p. 326.
12. Cited in ibid., pp. 465–6.
13. Cited in Jackson, *Bath Archives*, vol. II, p. 464.
14. Cited in *WSD*, p. 493.
15. Cited in Jackson, *Bath Archives*, vol. II, pp. 474–5.
16. Choiseul-Gouffier, *Memoirs*, pp. 206–7.
17. Talleyrand, *Memoirs*, vol. II, p. 179.
18. Cited in M. K. Oginski, *Mémoires de Michel Oginski sur la Pologne et Les Polonais depuis 1788 jusqu'à la fin de 1815* (Paris, 1827), vol. IV, pp. 213–14.

19. Cited in *WSD*, vol. IX, pp. 467–8.

20. Cited in ibid., pp. 268–73.

21. A. Butler (ed.), *Memoirs of Baron Thiébault, late Lieutenant-General in the French Army* (London, 1896), vol. II, pp. 408–10.

22. Cited in Webster, *Foreign Policy of Castlereagh*, p. 249.

23. P. Jones (ed.), *In Napoleon's Shadow: being the First English-Language Edition of the Complete Memoirs of Louis-Joseph Marchand, Valet and Friend of the Emperor, 1811–1821* (San Francisco, 1998), pp. 126–30.

24. Ibid., p. 138.

25. Cited in G. Stiegler (ed.), *Memoirs of Marshal Oudinot, Duc de Reggio compiled from the Hitherto Unpublished Souvenirs of the Duchesse de Reggio* (New York, 1897), p. 296.

26. E. Macdonald, *Recollections of Marshal Macdonald, Duke of Tarentum*, ed. E. Rousset (London, 1892), vol. II, p. 248.

27. Butler (ed.), *Memoirs of Baron Thiébault*, vol. II, p. 419.

28. A. Branche and A. Dagoury (eds), *Recollections of a Parisian (Docteur Poumiès de la Siboutie) under Six Sovereigns, two Revolutions and a Republic, 1789–1863* (London, 1911), p. 147.

29. J. Hanoteau (ed.), *Mémoires de la Reine Hortense* (Paris, 1927), vol. II, p. 338.

30. Ibid., p. 355.

31. Cited in M. de Klinkowstrom (ed.), *Memoirs of Prince Metternich, 1733–1815* (London, 1880), vol. I, pp. 254–5.

32. Hanoteau (ed.), *Mémoires de la Reine Hortense*, vol. II, p. 354.

33. Branche and Dagoury, *Recollections of a Parisian*, pp. 148–9.

34. Butler (ed.), *Memoirs of Baron Thiébault*, vol. II, p. 421.

35. J. Fortescue (ed.), *The Notebooks of Captain Coignet, Soldier of the Empire* (London, 1989), pp. 272–3.

36. Cited in Branche and Dagoury (eds), *Recollections of a Parisian*, p. 148. Ostensibly used here to mean cleanliness, 'white' is, of course, also a reference to royalism.

37. L. Aldersey White, *The Adventurous Life of Count Lavallette, Bonaparte's Aide-de-Camp and Postmaster-General, by Himself* (London, 1936), vol. II, p. 97.

38. Cited in Lady Granville (ed.), *Lord Granville Leveson Gower, First Earl Granville: Private Correspondence, 1781 to 1821* (London, 1916), vol. II, p. 526.

39. Cited in Stiegler, *Memoirs of Marshal Oudinot*, pp. 307–9.

40. Cited in *WSD*, vol. IX, p. 625.

41. Aldersey White, *Life of Count Lavallette*, vol. II, p. 94.

42. Hanoteau, *Mémoires de la Reine Hortense*, vol. II, p. 355.

43. S. Monick (ed.), *The Iberian and Waterloo Campaigns: the Letters of Lieutenant James Hope, 92nd (Highland) Regiment, 1811–1815* (Heathfield, 2000), p. 272.

44. Ibid., p. 214.

45. Cited in J. Kincaid, *Adventures in the Rifle Brigade in the Peninsula, France and the Netherlands from 1809 to 1815*, ed. I. Fletcher (Staplehurst, 1998), p. 345.

46. R. N. Buckley (ed.), *The Napoleonic War Journal of Captain Thomas Henry Browne, 1807–1816* (London, 1987), p. 281.

47. Cited in R. Weigall (ed.), *Correspondence of Lord Burghersh, afterwards Eleventh Earl of Westmoreland, 1808–1840* (London, 1912), pp. 94–5.

48. J. Leach, *Rough Sketches in the Life of an Old Soldier during a Service in the West Indies, at the Siege of Copenhagen in 1807, in the Peninsula and the South of France in the Campaigns from 1808 to 1814 with the Light Division, [and] in the Netherlands in 1815, including the Battles of Quatre Bras and Waterloo* (London, 1831), pp. 393–4.

49. Kincaid, *Adventures in the Rifle Brigade*, pp. 342, 347.

50. Fortescue (ed.), *Notebooks of Captain Coignet*, p. 280.

51. N. Bentley (ed.), *Selections from the Reminiscences of Captain Gronow* (London, 1977), p. 53.

52. C. Mercer, *Journal of the Waterloo Campaign kept throughout the Campaign of 1815*, ed. J. Fortescue (London, 1927), pp. 200–212 *passim*.

53. B. Liddell Hart (ed.), *The Letters of Private Wheeler, 1809–1828* (London, 1951), p. 178.

54. Cited in Klinkowstrom, *Memoirs of Prince Metternich*, vol. I, p. 262.

55. Cited in Webster, *Foreign Policy of Castlereagh*, p. 387.

Glossary of Place Names

Åbo – Turku
Aboukir – Abu Qir
Acre – Akko
Alle, river – Lyna, river
Austerlitz – Slavkov

Breslau – Wrocław

Castelnuovo – Herzegnovi
Cattaro – Kotor
Constantinople – Istanbul
Corfu – Kerkira

Danzig – Gdansk

Ewe – Ewia
Eylau – Bagrationovsk

Finkenstein – Illawa
Frederikshamn – Hamma
Friedland – Pravdinsk

Galatz – Galati
Glogau – Glogow
Golestan – Gulistan

Heilsberg – Lidzbark Warminski

Kolberg – Kolobrszeg
Königsberg – Kaliningrad
Kovno – Kaunas
Kronstädt – Kronshtad
Kulm – Chlumec
Kustrin – Kostrzyn

Lemburg – Lvov

Memel – Klaipeda

Nicopolis – Nikopol
Niemen, river – Neman, river
Novogrodek – Novgrudok

Ouja, River – Uzh, River

Posen – Poznan
Pressburg – Bratislava

Raab – Györ
Ragusa – Dubrovnik
Reichenbach – Dzorzoniow
Reval – Talinn
Rosetta – Rashid
Rustchuk – Ruse

Shumla – Shumen
Silistria – Silistra
Slobosia – Slobozea
Stettin – Szczecin
Sveaborg – Suomenlinna

Tauroggen – Taurage
Teplitz – Teplice
Thorn – Torun
Tilsit – Sovetsk

Vilna – Vilnius
Vistula, river – Wisla, river

Zante – Zakynthos
Znaim – Znojmo

Bibliography

1 Primary Sources

a) Official publications, documentary collections, etc.

Abbot, C. (ed.), *The Diary and Correspondence of Charles Abbot, Lord Colchester, Speaker of the House of Commons, 1802–1817* (London, 1861)

Baring, H. (ed.), *The Diary of the Right Hon. William Windham, 1784 to 1810* (London, 1866)

Bickley, F., *Historical Manuscripts Commission Report on the Manuscripts of Earl Bathurst preserved at Cirencester Park* (London, 1923)

Brotonne, L. de, *Dernières Lettres Inédites de Napoléon* (Paris, 1903)

Casse, A. du (ed.), *Mémoires et Correspondance Politique et Militaire du Prince Eugène* (Paris, 1858)

Casse, A. du (ed.), *Mémoires et Correspondance Politique et Militaire du Roi Joseph* (Paris, 1854–6)

Chair, S. de, *Napoleon on Napoleon: an Autobiography of the Emperor* (London, 1992)

Chuquet, A., *Ordres et Apostilles de Napoléon, 1799–1815* (Paris, 1911)

Correspondance de Napoléon I publiée par Ordre de l'Empereur Napoléon III (Paris, 1858–69)

Czartoryski, L. (ed.), *Alexandre Ier et le Prince Czartoryski: Correspondance particulière et Conversations, 1801–1823* (Paris, 1865)

Francis, B., and E. Keary (eds), *The Francis Letters* (London, n.d.)

González-Aller, J. I. (ed.), *La Campaña de Trafalgar, 1804–1805: Corpus documental conservado en los Archivos españoles* (Madrid, 2004)

Granville, Lady (ed.), *Lord Granville Leveson Gower, First Earl Granville: Private Correspondence, 1781 to 1821* (London, 1916)

Greig, J. (ed.), *The Farington Diary* (London, 1923)

Gurwood, J., *The Dispatches of Field Marshal the Duke of Wellington during his various Campaigns in India, Denmark, Portugal, Spain, the Low Countries and France from 1789 to 1815* (London, 1852)

Hargreaves-Mawdesley, W. (ed.), *Spain under the Bourbons, 1700–1833: a Collection of Documents* (London, 1973)

Hayter, A. (ed.), *The Backbone: Diaries of a Military Family in the Napoleonic Wars* (Bishop Auckland, 1993)

Howard, J., *Letters and Documents of Napoleon: the Ride to Power* (London, 1961)

Jennings, L. (ed.), *The Croker Papers: the Correspondence and Diaries of the Right Honourable John Wilson Croker, LL.D, F.R.S., Secretary to the Admiralty from 1809 to 1830* (London, 1884)

Johnston, R. (ed.), *In the Words of Napoleon: the Emperor Day-by-Day* (London, 2002)

Lecestre, L. (ed.), *Lettres inédites de Napoléon Ier, an VIII–1815* (Paris, 1897)

Londonderry, Marquess of (ed.), *Correspondence, Despatches and other Papers of Viscount Castlereagh, Second Marquess of Londonderry* (London, 1848–53)

Malmesbury, Third Earl of (ed.), *Diaries and Correspondence of James Harris, First Earl of Malmesbury* (London, 1844)

Markham, J. D. (ed.), *Imperial Glory: the Bulletins of Napoleon's Grande Armée, 1805–1814* (London, 2003)

Martin, M. (ed.), *The Dispatches and Correspondence of the Marquess Wellesley, K. G., during His Lordship's Mission to Spain as Ambassador Extraordinary to the Supreme Junta in 1809* (London, 1838)

Minto, Countess of (ed.), *Life and Letters of Sir Gilbert Elliot, First Earl of Minto, from 1751 to 1806* (London, 1874)

Paget, A. (ed.), *The Paget Papers: Diplomatic and other Correspondence of the Right Hon. Sir Arthur Paget, G. C. B., 1794–1807* (London, 1896)

Roncière, C. de la (ed.), *The Letters of Napoleon to Marie-Louise* (London, 1935)

Rosebery, Earl of (ed.), *The Wellesley Papers: the Life and Correspondence of Richard Colley Wellesley, Marquess Wellesley, 1760–1842* (London, 1914)

Rosebery, Earl of (ed.), *The Windham Papers: the Life and Correspondence of the Rt. Hon. William Windham, 1750–1810* (London, 1913)

Stuart, D. M., *Dearest Bess: the Life and Times of Lady Elizabeth Foster, afterwards Duchess of Devonshire, from her Unpublished Journals and Correspondence* (London, 1955)

Thompson, J. M. (ed.), *Napoleon's Letters* (London, 1934)

Thompson, W. (ed.), *An Ensign in the Peninsular War: the Letters of John Aitchison,* (London, 1981)

Weigall, R. (ed.), *Correspondence of Lord Burghersh, afterwards Eleventh Earl of Westmoreland, 1808–1840* (London, 1912)

Wellington, Second Duke of (ed.), *Supplementary Despatches, Correspondence and Memoranda of Field Marshal Arthur, Duke of Wellington K. G.* (London, 1858–72)

b) Diaries, memoirs, personal reminiscences

Alcalá Galiano, A. (ed.), *Memorias de Don Antonio Alcalá Galiano* (Madrid, 1886)

Aldersey White, L. (ed.), *The Adventurous Life of Count Lavallette, Bonaparte's Aide-de-Camp and Postmaster-General, by Himself* (London, 1936)

Anon., *Leaves from the Diary of an Officer of the Guards* (London, 1854)

Artola, M. (ed.), *Memorias de Juan de Escoíquiz* (Madrid, 1957)

Audiffret-Pasquier, Duc d' (ed.), *Mémoires du Chancelier Pasquier – Première Partie: Révolution, Consulat, Empire* (Paris, 1895–1914)

Barrès, M. (ed.), *Memoirs of a French Napoleonic Officer: Jean-Baptiste Barrès, Chasseur of the Imperial Guard* (London, 1955)

Barrière, M. (ed.), *Mémoires de M. le Comte de Vaublanc* (Paris, 1883)

Baudus, M., *Etudes sur Napoléon* (Paris, 1841)

Bell, A., *Memoirs of Baron Lejeune, Aide-de-Camp to Marshals Berthier, Davout and Oudinot* (London, 1897)

Bell, G., *Rough Notes of an Old Soldier*, edited by B. Stuart (London, 1956)

Bentley, N. (ed.), *Selections from the Reminiscences of Captain Gronow* (London, 1977)

Berazaluce, A. (ed.), *Recuerdos de la vida de Don Pedro Agustín Girón* (Pamplona, 1978)

Beugnot, A. (ed.), *Mémoires du Comte Beugnot, Ancien Ministre, 1783–1815* (Paris, 1868)

Blanco White, J., *Cartas de España*, edited by V. Llorens and A. Garnica (Madrid, 1972)

Bourgoing, J. F. de, *A Modern State of Spain* (London, 1808)

Bourrienne, Louis F. de, *Memoirs of Napoleon Bonaparte*, edited by E. Sanderson (London, 1903)

Branche, A., and A. Dagoury (eds), *Recollections of a Parisian (Docteur Poumiès de la Siboutie) under Six Sovereigns, Two Revolutions and a Republic, 1789–1863* (London, 1911)

Brett-James, A. (ed.), *1812: Eyewitness Accounts of Napoleon's Defeat in Russia* (London, 1966)

Brindle, R. (ed.), *With Napoleon's Guns: the Military Memoirs of an Officer of the First Empire* (London, 2005)

Buckley, R. N. (ed.), *The Napoleonic War Journal of Captain Thomas Henry Browne, 1807–1816* (London, 1987)

Bunbury, H., *Narratives of some Passages in the Great War with France* (London, 1854)

Butler, A. (ed.), *The Memoirs of Baron Thiébault, late Lieutenant-General in the French Army* (London, 1896)

Carnot, H. (ed.), *Memoirs of Bertrand Barère, Chairman of the Committee of Public Safety during the Revolution* (London, 1896)

Cases, E. Las, *Mémorial de Sainte Hélène*, edited by G. Walter (Paris, 1956)

Chaptal, J. A., *Mes Souvenirs sur Napoléon*, edited by A. Chaptal (Paris, 1893)

Chlapowski, D., *Mémoires sur les Guerres de Napoléon, 1806–1813* (Paris, 1908)

Choiseul-Gouffier, Comtesse de, *Historical Memoirs of the Emperor Alexander I and the Court of Russia*, edited by M. Patterson (London, 1904)

Clarette, J. (ed.), *From Valmy to Waterloo: Extracts from the Diary of Captain Charles François, a Soldier of the Revolution and Empire* (London, 1906)

Clausewitz, K. von, *On War*, edited by A. Rapoport (London, 1968)

Clausewitz, K. von, *The Campaign of 1812 in Russia* (London, 1943)

Coignet, J. R., *The Notebooks of Captain Coignet, Soldier of the Empire* (London, 1985)

Doppet, F. A., *Mémoires Politiques et Militaires du Général Doppet* (Paris, 1824)

Dufour de Pradt, D., *Histoire de l'Ambassade dans le Grand Duché de Varsovie en 1812* (Paris, 1815)

Duruy, G. (ed.), *Memoirs of Barras, Member of the Directorate* (London, 1895)

Fain, A. J. F., *Memoirs of the Invasion of France by the Allied Armies and of the last Six Months of the Reign of Napoleon* (London, 1834)

Fézensac, R. de, *A Journal of the Russian Campaign of 1812* (London, 1812)

Fleischmann, W. A. von, *Mémoires du Comte Miot de Melito, Ancien Ministre, Ambassadeur, Conseilleur d'Etat et Membre de l'Institut, 1788–1815* (Paris, 1858)

Fleuriot de Langle, P. (ed.), *Napoleon at St Helena: Memoirs of General Bertrand, Grand-Master of the Palace* (London, 1953)

Fortescue, J. (ed.), *The Note-books of Captain Coignet, Soldier of the Empire* (London, 1928)

Fouché, J., *Memoirs of Joseph Fouché, Duke of Otranto, Minister of the General Police of France* (London, 1892)

Foy, M., *History of the War in the Peninsula under Napoleon* (London, 1827)

Gill, J. (ed.), *A Soldier for Napoleon: the Campaigns of Lieutenant Franz Joseph Haussmann, Seventh Bavarian Infantry* (London, 1998)

Godoy, M. de, *Cuenta dada de su Vida Política por Don Manuel de Godoy, Príncipe de la Paz, o sea Memorias Críticas y Apologéticas para la Historia del Reinado del Señor Carlos IV de Borbón*, edited by C. Seco Serrano (Madrid, 1956)

Gohier, L. J., *Mémoires de Louis-Jérome Gohier, Président du Directoire au 18 Brumaire* (Paris, 1824)

Gotteri, N. (ed.), *La Mission de Lagarde, Policier de l'Empereur, pendant la Guerre d'Espagne, 1809–1811* (Paris, 1991)

Hanoteau, J. (ed.), *Mémoires de la Reine Hortense* (Paris, 1927)

Hanoteau, J. (ed.), *Memoirs of General de Caulaincourt, Duke of Vicenza* (London, 1935)

Hellman, G. S. (ed.), *Memoirs of the Cmte. de Mercy Argenteau, Napoleon's Chamberlain and his Minister Plenipotentiary to the King of Bavaria* (New York, 1917)

Holland, Henry Edward, Lord, *Foreign Reminiscences* (London, 1850)

Holland, Henry Richard, Lord, *Memoirs of the Whig Party during my Time*, edited by Henry Edward, Lord Holland (London, 1852)

Hulot, J. L., *Souvenirs Militaires du Baron Hulot, Général d'Artillerie, 1773–1843* (Paris, 1886)

Ideville, H. d' (ed.), *Memoirs of Colonel Bugeaud from his Private Correspondence and Original Documents, 1784–1814* (Worley Publications facsimile edition, 1998)

Ilchester, Earl of (ed.), *The Journal of Elizabeth, Lady Holland, 1791–1811* (London, 1909)

Ilchester, Earl of (ed.), *The Spanish Journal of Elizabeth, Lady Holland* (London, 1910)

Jackson, Lady (ed.), *The Bath Archives: a Further Selection from the Diaries and Letters of Sir George Jackson, K. C. H., from 1809 to 1816* (London, 1873)

Jones, B. T. (ed.), *Napoleon's Army: the Military Memoirs of Charles Parquin* (London, 1987)

Jones, P. (ed.), *Napoleon: How He Did It – the Memoirs of Baron Fain, First Secretary of the Emperor's Cabinet* (San Francisco, 1998)

Jones, P. (ed.), *In Napoleon's Shadow: being the First English-Language Edition of the Complete Memoirs of Louis-Joseph Marchand, Valet and Friend of the Emperor, 1811–1821* (San Francisco, 1998)

Jonnes, M. de, *Adventures in the Revolution and under the Consulate*, edited by J. Fortescue (London, 1929)

Junot, L., *Mémoires de la Duchesse d'Abrantès*, edited by G. Girard (Paris, 1928–30)

Kincaid, J., *Adventures in the Rifle Brigade in the Peninsula, France and the Netherlands from 1809 to 1815*, edited by I. Fletcher (Staplehurst, 1998)

Klinkowstrom, M. de (ed.), *Memoirs of Prince Metternich, 1733–1815* (London, 1880)

Labaume, E., *A Circumstantial Narrative of the Campaign in Russia* (London, 1815)

Lahovary C. P., (ed.), *Mémoires de l'Amiral Paul Tchitchagof, Commandant en chef de l'Armée du Danube, Gouverneur des Principautés de Moldavie et de Valachie en 1812* (Paris, 1909)

Larpent, G. (ed.), *The Private Journal of Judge-Advocate F. S. Larpent, attached to Wellington's Headquarters, 1812–1814* (London, 1853)

Leach, J., *Rough Sketches in the Life of an Old Soldier during a Service in the West Indies, at the Siege of Copenhagen in 1807, in the Peninsula and the South of France in the Campaigns from 1808 to 1814 with the Light Division, [and] in the Netherlands in 1815, including the Battles of Quatre Bras and Waterloo* (London, 1831)

Lecky, E. (ed.), *Un Général hollandais sous le premier Empire: Mémoires du Général Baron de Dedem de Gelder, 1774–1825* (Paris, 1900)

Ledos de Beaufort, R. (ed.), *Personal Recollections of the late Duc de Broglie, 1785–1820* (London, 1887)

Liddell Hart, B. (ed.), *The Letters of Private Wheeler, 1809–1828* (London, 1951)

Macdonald, E., *Recollections of Marshal Macdonald, Duke of Tarentum*, edited by E. Rousset (London, 1892)

Marbot, M. de, *The Memoirs of Baron de Marbot* (London, 1892)

Marcén, J. (ed.), *El Manuscrito de Matias Calvo: Memorias de un Monegrino durante la Guerra de la Independencia* (Zaragoza, 2000)

Maurice, J. (ed.), *The Diary of Sir John Moore* (London, 1904)

Mercer, C., *Journal of the Waterloo Campaign kept throughout the Campaign of 1815*, edited by J. Fortescue (London, 1927)

Mikaberidze A., (ed.), *The Czar's General: the Memoirs of a Russian General in the Napoleonic Wars* (London, 2005)

Monick, S. (ed.), *Douglas' Tale of the Peninsula and Waterloo* (London, 1997)

Monick S. (ed.), *The Iberian and Waterloo Campaigns: the Letters of Lieutenant James Hope, 92nd (Highland) Regiment, 1811–1815* (Heathfield, 2000)

Montesquieu-Fézensac, R. de, *Souvenirs Militaires de 1808 à 1814* (Paris, 1863)

Morsier-Kotthaus, S. de, *Memoirs of the Comtesse de Boigne* (London, 1956)

Muffling, C. von, *Passages from my Life, together with Memoirs of the Campaign of 1813 and 1814* (London, 1853)

Müller, W., *Relation of the Operations and Battles of the Austrian and French Armies in the Year 1809* (London, 1810)

Noailles, Marquis de (ed.), *The Life and Memoirs of Count Molé, 1781–1855* (London, 1923)

North, J., *In the Legions of Napoleon: the Memoirs of a Polish Officer in Spain and Russia, 1808–1813* (London, 1999)

North, J. (ed.), *With Napoleon in Russia: the Illustrated Memoirs of Major Faber du Faur, 1812* (London, 2001)

Oginski, M. K., *Mémoires de Michel Oginski sur la Pologne et les Polonais depuis 1788 jusqu'à la fin de 1815* (Paris, 1827)

Raeff, M. (ed.), *The Diary of a Napoleonic Foot Soldier* (Moreton-in-Marsh, 1991)

Rambaud, J. de (ed.), *Memoirs of the Comte Roger de Damas, 1787–1806* (London, 1913)

Rémusat, C. de, *Mémoires de Madame de Rémusat, 1802–1808*, edited by P. de Rémusat (Paris, 1884)

Rocca, A. J. M. de, *Memoirs of the War of the French in Spain*, edited by P. Haythornthwaite (London, 1990)

Roeder, H. (ed.), *The Ordeal of Captain Roeder: from the Diary of an Officer of the First Battalion of Hessian Lifeguards during the Moscow Campaign of 1812–13* (London, 1960)

Roederer, P., *Mémoires sur la Révolution, le Consulat et l'Empire*, edited by O. Aubry (Paris, 1942)

Saint-Hilaire, E. de, *Souvenirs intimes du Temps de l'Empire* (Paris, 1860)

Saint-Léon, L. B. de, *Mémoires et Souvenirs de Charles de Pougens* (Paris, 1834)

Sarrazin, J., *History of the War in Spain and Portugal from 1807 to 1814* (London, 1815)

Sherer, J. M., *Recollections of the Peninsula* (London, 1825)

Soltyk, R., *Operations of the Polish Army during the 1809 Campaign in Poland*, edited by G. Nafziger (Westchester, Ohio, 2002)

Spring, L. (ed.), *An Englishman in the Russian Army, 1807; the Journal of Colonel James Bathurst during the East Prussia Campaign, 1807* (Woking, 2000)

Staël, A. L. G. de, *Considérations sur les Principaux Evénements de la Révolution Française* (London, 1819)

Stanhope, Earl of, *Notes of Conversations with the Duke of Wellington, 1831–1851* (London, 1888)

Stiegler, G. (ed.), *Memoirs of Marshal Oudinot, Duc de Reggio compiled from the Hitherto Unpublished Souvenirs of the Duchesse de Reggio* (New York, 1897)

Stryienski, C. (ed.), *Mémoires de la Comtesse Potocka, 1794–1820* (Paris, 1911)

Suchet, L. G., *Memoirs of the War in Spain from 1808 to 1814* (London, 1829)

Summerville, C. J. (ed.), *Napoleon's Expedition to Russia: the Memoirs of General de Ségur* (London, 2003)

Talleyrand-Périgord, C. M. de, *Memoirs of the Prince de Talleyrand*, edited by Duc de Broglie (London, 1891)

Thibaudeau, A., *Bonaparte and the Consulate*, edited by G. Fortescue (London, 1908)

Tour du Pin, Marquise de la, *Recollections of the Revolution and the Empire*, edited by W. Geer (London, 1921)

Toreno, Conde de, *Historia del Levantamiento, Guerra y Revolución de España*, edited by L. Augusto de Cueto (Madrid, 1953)

Troubetzkoy, G. (ed.), *In the Service of the Tsar against Napoleon: the Memoirs of Denis Davidov, 1806–1814* (London, 1999)

Uexküll, D. von (ed.), *Arms and the Woman: the Diaries of Baron Boris Uxkull, 1812–1819* (London, 1966)

Verner, W., *A British Rifleman: the Journals and Correspondence of Major George Simmons, Rifle Brigade, during the Peninsular War and the Campaign of Waterloo* (London, 1899)

Viesse de Marmont, A. F. L. de, *Mémoires du Maréchal Marmont, Duc de Raguse, de 1792 à 1841* (Paris, 1857)

Villemain, A., *Souvenirs contemporains d'Histoire et de Littérature* (Paris, 1854)

Wallich, W. (ed.), *With Napoleon in Russia, 1812: the Diary of Lieutenant H. A. Vossler, a Soldier of the Grande Armée, 1812–1813* (London, 1969)

Williams, O. (ed.), *In the Wake of Napoleon: being the Memoirs of Ferdinand von Funck, Lieutenant-General in the Saxon Army and Adjutant General to the King of Saxony* (London, 1931)

Wilson, A., (ed.), *A Diary of St Helena (1816–1817): the Journal of Lady Malcolm containing the Conversations of Sir Pulteney Malcolm with Napoleon* (London, 1899)

Wilson, R., *Brief Remarks on the Character and Composition of the Russian Army and a Sketch of the Campaigns in Poland in the years 1806 and 1807* (London, 1810)

Wilson, R., *Narrative of Events during the Invasion of Russia by Napoleon Bonaparte and the Retreat of the French Army, 1812* (London, 1860)

2 Secondary Sources

Acton, H., *The Bourbons of Naples, 1734–1825* (London, 1956)

Adams, A. *Napoleon and Russia* (London, 2006)

Adkins, L. and R. Adkins, *The War for all the Oceans: from Nelson at the Nile to Napoleon at Waterloo* (London, 2007)

Adkins, R., *Trafalgar: the Biography of a Battle* (London, 2004)

Aftalion, F., *The Revolution: an Economic Interpretation* (Cambridge, 2000)

Alexander, R., *Bonapartism and Revolutionary Tradition in France: the Fédérés of 1815* (Cambridge, 1991)

Alexander, R., 'The *fédérés* of Dijon in 1815', *Historical Journal*, XXX, No. 2 (June 1987), pp. 367–90

Alexander, R. S., *Napoleon* (London, 2001)

Alison, A., *History of Europe from the Commencement of the French Revolution to the Restoration of the Bourbons in 1815* (London, 1840)

Amini, I., *Napoleon and Persia: Franco-Persian Relations under the First Empire within the Context of the Rivalries between France, Britain and Russia* (Richmond, Surrey, 1999)

Arnold, E., 'Some observations on the French opposition to Napoleonic conscription, 1804–1806', *French Historical Studies*, IV, No. 4 (Autumn 1966), pp. 452–61

Arnold, J., *Marengo and Hohenlinden: Napoleon's Rise to Power* (Barnsley, 2005)

Aron, R., *Clausewitz, Philosopher of War* (London, 1983)

Askenazy, S., *Napoléon et la Pologne* (Paris, 1925)

Aston, N., *Christianity and Revolutionary Europe, c. 1750–1830* (Cambridge, 2002)

Atteridge, A. H., *Joachim Murat, Marshal of France and King of Naples* (London, 1911)

Barnett, C., *Britain and her Army, 1509–1970: a Military, Political and Social Survey* (London, 1970)

Bartlett, C. J., *Castlereagh* (London, 1966)

Bemis, S., *A Diplomatic History of the United States* (New York, 1936)

Bergeron, L., *France under Napoleon* (Princeton, New Jersey, 1981)

Bernard, J. F., *Talleyrand: a Biography* (London, 1973)

Best, G., *War and Society in Revolutionary Europe, 1770–1870* (London, 1982)

Black, J., *European International Relations, 1648–1815* (London, 2002)

Black, J., *From Louis XIV to Napoleon: the Fate of a Great Power* (London, 1999)

Black, J., 'Napoleon's impact on international relations', *History Today*, XLVIII, No. 2 (February 1998), pp. 45–51

Blanning, T. C. W., *The French Revolutionary Wars, 1787–1802* (London, 1996)

Blanning, T. C. W., *The Origins of the French Revolutionary Wars* (London, 1986)

Blaufarb, R., *The French Army, 1750–1820: Careers, Talent, Merit* (Manchester, 2002)

Bond, G., *The Grand Expedition: the British Invasion of Holland in 1809* (Athens, Georgia, 1979)

Boycott-Brown, M., *The Road to Rivoli: Napoleon's First Campaign* (London, 2001)

Brittin Austin, P., *1812: the March on Moscow* (London, 1994)

Brittin Austin, P., *1812: Napoleon in Moscow* (London, 1995)

Brittin Austin, P., *1812: the Great Retreat* (London, 1996)

Brittin Austin, P., *1815: the Return of Napoleon* (London, 2002)

Broers, M., *Europe under Napoleon, 1799–1815* (London, 1996)

Bruce, E., *Napoleon and Josephine: an Improbable Marriage* (London, 1995)

Bryant, A., *The Years of Endurance, 1793–1802* (London, 1942)

Bryant, A., *Years of Victory, 1802–1812* (London, 1944)

Bryson, T., *Tars, Turks and Tankers: the Role of the United States Navy in the Middle East, 1800–1979* (Metuchen, New Jersey, 1980)

Buckland, C., *Friedrich von Gentz's Relations with the British Government during the Marquess Wellesley's Foreign Secretaryship of State from 1809 to 1814* (London, 1933)

Buckland, C., *Metternich and the British Government from 1809 to 1813* (London, 1932)

Burrows, S., 'The struggle for European opinion in the Napoleonic Wars: British francophone propaganda, 1803–1814', *French History*, XI, No. 1 (March 1997), pp. 29–53

Bury, J., 'The end of the Napoleonic senate', *Cambridge Historical Journal*, IX, No. 2 (1948), pp. 165–89

Butler, I., *The Eldest Brother: the Marquess Wellesley, 1760–1842* (London, 1973)

Butterfield, H., *Napoleon* (London, 1939)

Butterfield, H., *The Peace Tactics of Napoleon, 1806–1808* (Cambridge, 1959)

Carrington, D., 'The achievement of Pasquale Paoli (1755–1769), and its consequences', *Consortium on Revolutionary Europe Proceedings*, XVI (1986), pp. 56–69

Cate, C., *The War of the Two Emperors: the Duel between Napoleon and Alexander, Russia 1812* (New York, 1985)

Chandler, D. G., *The Campaigns of Napoleon: the Mind and Methods of History's Greatest Soldier* (London, 1966)

Chandler, D. G., 'To lie like a bulletin': an examination of Napoleon's re-writing of the history of the battle of Marengo', *Proceedings of the Annual Meeting of the Western Society for French Historical Studies*, XVIII (1991), pp. 33–44

Chastenet, J., *Godoy, Master of Spain, 1792–1801* (London, 1953)

Clayton, T. and Craig, P., *Trafalgar: the Men, the Battle, the Storm* (London, 2004)

Chuquet, A., *La Jeunesse de Napoléon*, (Paris, 1893)

Connelly, O., *Blundering to Glory: Napoleon's Military Campaigns* (Wilmington, Delaware, 1987)

Connelly, O., *Napoleon's Satellite Kingdoms* (New York, 1965)

Connelly, O., *The Wars of the French Revolution and Napoleon, 1792–1815* (London, 2006)

Connolly, J., 'Bonaparte on the bridge: a note on the iconography of passage', *Consortium on Revolutionary Proceedings*, XV (1985), pp. 45–65

Cookson, J., *The British Armed Nation, 1793–1815* (Oxford, 1997)

Cooper, R., 'Wellington and the Mahrathas in 1803', *International History Review*, XI, No. 1 (February 1989), pp. 31–8

Corrigan, G., *Wellington; a Military Life* (London, 2001)

Cronin, V., *Napoleon* (London, 1971)

Crowhurst, P., *The French War on Trade: Privateering, 1793–1815* (London, 1989)

Dallas, G., *The Final Act: the Roads to Waterloo* (New York, 1996)

Dard, E., *Napoleon and Talleyrand* (London, 1937)

Deutsch, H. C., *The Genesis of Napoleonic Imperialism* (Cambridge, Massachusetts, 1938)

Dickinson, H. T. (ed.), *Britain and the French Revolution, 1789–1815* (London, 1989)

Dorpalen, A., 'The German struggle against Napoleon: the East German view', *Journal of Modern History*, XLI, No. 4, (December 1969), pp. 485–516

Driault, E., *La Politique Orientale de Napoléon* (Paris, 1904)

Duffy, C., *Borodino and the War of 1812* (London, 1973)

Dwyer, P., 'From Corsican nationalist to French revolutionary: problems of identity in the writings of the young Napoleon, 1785–1793', *French History*, XVI, No. 2 (June 2002), pp. 132–52

Dwyer, P. (ed.), *Napoleon and Europe* (London, 2001)

Dwyer, P., 'Prussia and the Armed Neutrality: the invasion of Hanover in 1801', *International History Review*, XV, No. 4 (November 1993), pp. 661–87

Dwyer, P., 'The politics of Prussian neutrality, 1795–1805', *German History*, XII, No. 3 (July 1994), pp. 351–68

Dwyer, P. (ed.), *The Rise of Prussia, 1700–1830* (London, 2000)

Dwyer, P., 'Two definitions of neutrality: Prussia, the European states-system and the French invasion of Hanover in 1803', *International History Review*, XIX, No. 3 (August 1997)

Ehrman, J., *The Younger Pitt, I: the Reluctant Transition* (London, 1983)

Ehrman, J., *The Younger Pitt, II: the Consuming Struggle* (Stanford, California, 1997)

Ellis, G., *Napoleon* (London, 1997)

Ellis, G., *The Napoleonic Empire* (London, 1991)

Emsley, C., *British Society and the French Wars, 1793–1815* (London, 1979)

Emsley, C., *The Longman Companion to Napoleonic Europe* (London, 1993)

Englund, S., *Napoleon: a Political Life* (Cambridge, Massachusetts, 2004)

Epstein, R., *Napoleon's Last Victory and the Emergence of Modern War* (Lawrence, Kansas, 1994)

Epton, N., *The Spanish Mousetrap: Napoleon and the Spanish Court* (London, 1973)

Esdaile, C. J., *Fighting Napoleon: Guerrillas, Bandits and Adventurers in Spain, 1808–1814* (London, 2004)

Esdaile, C. J. (ed.), *Popular Resistance in Napoleonic Europe: Patriots, Partisans and Land Pirates* (London, 2004)

Esdaile, C. J., *The Duke of Wellington and the Command of the Spanish Army* (London, 1990)

Esdaile, C. J., *The French Wars, 1792–1815* (London, 2001)

Esdaile, C. J., *The Peninsular War: a New History* (London, 2002)

Esdaile, C. J. and Muir, R., 'Strategic planning in an age of small government: the wars against Revolutionary France, 1793–1815' in C. Woolgar (ed.), *Wellington Studies, I* (Southampton, 1996), pp. 1–90

Esdaile, C. J., 'Latin America and the Anglo-Spanish alliance against Napoleon, 1808–14', *Bulletin of Hispanic Studies*, LXIX, No. 3 (July 1992), pp. 55–70

Espitalier, A., *Napoleon and King Murat* (London, 1912)

Eyck, F. G., *Loyal Rebels: Andreas Hofer and the Tyrolean Uprising of 1809* (Lanham, Maryland, 1986)

Fedorak, C., 'Maritime vs. continental strategy: Britain and the defeat of Napoleon', *Consortium on Revolutionary Proceedings*, XX (1990), pp. 176–83

Fedorak, C., 'The French capitulation in Egypt and the preliminary Anglo-French treaty of peace in October 1801: a note', *International History Review*, XV, No. 3 (August 1993), pp. 525–34

Fedorak, C., 'In search of a necessary ally: Addington, Hawkesbury and Russia, 1801–1804', *International History Review*, XIII, No. 2 (May 1991), pp. 221–45

Feldbaek, O., 'The foreign policy of Tsar Paul I, 1800–1: an interpretation', *Jahrbücher für Geschichte Osteuropas*, XXX (1982), pp. 16–36

Finley, M., *The Most Monstrous of Wars: the Napoleonic Guerrilla War in Southern Italy, 1806–1811* (Columbia, South Carolina, 1994)

Fisher, H, *Napoleon* (London, 1912)

Fisher, H., *Studies in Napoleonic Statesmanship: Germany* (Oxford, 1903)

Flayheart, W., *Counterpoint to Trafalgar: the Anglo-Russian Invasion of Naples, 1805–1806* (Colombia, South Carolina, 1992)

Fletcher, I., *The Waters of Oblivion: the British Invasion of the Río de la Plata, 1806–1807* (Tunbridge Wells, 1991)

Forrest, A., *Napoleon's Men: the Soldiers of the Revolution and Empire* (London, 2002)

Fortescue, J., *A History of the British Army* (London, 1910–30)

Fregosi, P., *Dreams of Empire: Napoleon and the First World War, 1792–1815* (London, 1989)

Fremont-Barnes, G., *The French Revolutionary Wars* (Botley, 2001)

Fremont-Barnes, G. (ed.), *The Encyclopedia of the French Revolutionary and Napoleonic Wars: a Political, Military and Social History* (Santa Barbara, California, 2006)

Fugier, A., *Napoléon et l'Espagne* (Paris, 1930)

Furet, F., *Revolutionary France, 1770–1880* (London, 1992)

Gagliardo, J. G., *Reich and Nation: the Holy Roman Empire as Idea and Reality, 1763–1806* (Bloomington, Indiana, 1980)

Garner, R., *The Campaign of Trafalgar* (London, 1997)

Garnier, J. P., *Murat, Roi de Naples* (Paris, 1959)

Gash. N. (ed.), *Wellington: Studies in the Military and Political Career of the First Duke of Wellington* (Manchester, 1990)

Gates, D., *The Napoleonic Wars, 1803–1815* (London, 1986)

Gerolymatos, A., *The Balkan Wars: Conquest, Revolution and Retribution from the Ottoman Era to the Twentieth Century and Beyond* (New York, 2002)

Geyl, P., *Napoleon For and Against* (London, 1949)

Gill, J. H., *With Eagles to Glory: Napoleon and his German Allies in the 1809 Campaign* (London, 1992)

Glenny, M., *The Balkans, 1804–1999: Nationalism, War and the Great Powers* (London, 1999)

Glover, R. *Peninsular Preparation: the Reform of the British Army, 1795–1809* (Cambridge, 1963)

Grab, A., 'Army, state and society: conscription and desertion in Napoleonic Italy', *Journal of Modern History*, LXVII, No. 1 (March 1995), pp. 25–54

Grab, A., *Napoleon and the Transformation of Europe* (London, 2003)

Gregory, D., *Sicily, the Insecure Base: a History of the British Occupation of Sicily, 1806–1815* (London, 1988)

Gregory, D., *The Ungovernable Rock: a History of the Anglo-Corsican Kingdom and its Role in Britain's Mediterranean Strategy during the Revolutionary War, 1793–97* (London, 1985)

Griffith, P., *The Art of War of Revolutionary France, 1789–1802* (London, 1998)

Grimsted, P. K., *The Foreign Ministers of Alexander I: Political Attitudes and the Conduct of Russian Diplomacy, 1801–1825* (Berkeley, California, 1969)

Grunwald, C. de, *Baron Stein, Enemy of Napoleon* (London, 1940)

Grunwald, C. de, *Metternich* (London, 1953)

Guy, A. (ed.), *The Road to Waterloo: the British army and the Struggle against Revolutionary and Napoleonic France, 1793–1815* (London, 1990)

Hagemann, K., 'Francophobia and patriotism: anti-French images and sentiments in Prussia and northern Germany during the anti-Napoleonic Wars', *French History*, XVIII, No. 4 (December 2004), pp. 404–25

Hales, E., *Napoleon and the Pope* (London, 1962)

Hall, C. D., *British Strategy in the Napoleonic War, 1803–1815* (Manchester, 1992)

Hall, C.D., *Wellington's Navy: Seapower and the Peninsular War, 1808–1814* (London, 2004)

Hamilton Williams, D., *The Fall of Napoleon: the Final Betrayal* (London, 1994)

Hartley, J., *Alexander I* (London, 1994)

Harvey, A. D., *Britain in the Early Nineteenth Century* (London, 1978)

Harvey, A. D., 'European attitudes to Britain during the French Revolutionary and Napoleonic era', *History*, LXIII, No. 209 (October 1978), pp. 356–65

Hecksher, H., *The Continental System: an Economic Interpretation* (Oxford, 1922)

Henderson, E., *Blücher and the Uprising of Prussia against Napoleon, 1806–1815* (London, 1911)

Herold, J. C., *Bonaparte in Egypt* (London, 1963)

Hibbert, C., *Napoleon: his Wives and Women* (London, 2002)

Hilt, D., *The Troubled Trinity: Godoy and the Spanish Monarchs* (Tuscaloosa, 1987)

Hinde, W., *George Canning* (London, 1973)

Hitchens, K., *The Romanians, 1774–1866* (Oxford, 1996)

Hofschroer, P., *1815: the Waterloo Campaign – Wellington, his German Allies and the Battles of Ligny and Quatre Bras* (London, 1998)

Hofschroer, P., *1815: the Waterloo Campaign – the German Victory* (London, 1999)

Holsti, K. J., *Peace and War: Armed Conflicts and International Order, 1648–1949* (Cambridge, 1991)

Hopton, R., *The Battle of Maida: Fifteen Minutes of Glory* (London, 2002)

Horgan, J., 'Restoration of the Bourbon monarchy, 1813–1814: a matter of great-power self-interest', *Consortium on Revolutionary Europe Proceedings*, XXI (1991), pp. 43–55

Horsman, R., *The War of 1812* (London, 1969)

Howarth, D., *Trafalgar: the Nelson Touch* (London, 1969)

Howarth, D., *A Near-Run Thing: the Day of Waterloo* (London, 1969)

James, L., *The Iron Duke: a Military Biography* (London, 1992)

Johnson, P., *Napoleon* (London, 2002)

Jorgensen, C., *The Anglo-Swedish Alliance against Napoleonic France* (London, 2004)

Jupp, P., *Lord Grenville, 1759–1834* (Oxford, 1985)

Kastor, P., *Nation's Crucible: the Louisiana Purchase and the Creation of America* (New Haven, Connecticut, 2004)

Kauffmann, W., *British Policy and the Independence of Latin America* (London, 1967)

Kenney, J., 'Lord Whitworth and the conspiracy against Tsar Paul I', *Slavic Review*, XXXVI, No. 2 (June 1977), pp. 205–19

Kraehe, E., *Metternich's German Policy* (Princeton, New Jersey, 1963)

Kukiel, M., *Czartoryski and European Unity, 1770–1861* (Princeton, New Jersey, 1955)

Kurtz, H., 'Napoleon in 1815: the second reign', *History Today*, XV, No. 10 (October 1965), pp. 673–87

Lambert, A., *Nelson: Britannia's God of War* (London, 2004)

Lavery, B., *Horatio, Lord Nelson* (London, 2003)

LeDonne, J. P., *The Russian Empire and the World, 1700–1917: the Geopolitics of Expansion and Containment* (Oxford, 1997)

Lee, C., *Nelson and Napoleon: the Long Haul to Trafalgar* (London, 2005)

Lefebvre, G., *The Directory* (London, 1965)

Lefebvre, G., *Napoleon: from 18 Brumaire to Tilsit, 1799–1807* (New York, 1969)

Lefebvre, G., *Napoleon: from Tilsit to Waterloo, 1807–1815* (New York, 1969)

Leggiere, M., *Napoleon and Berlin: the Napoleonic Wars in Prussia, 1813* (London, 2002)

Lobanov-Rostovsky, A., *Russia and Europe, 1789–1825* (Chapel Hill, North Carolina, 1947)

Lovett, G., *Napoleon and the Birth of Modern Spain* (New York, 1965)

Lynch, J., *Bourbon Spain, 1700–1808* (Oxford, 1989)

Lynch, J., *The Spanish-American Revolutions, 1808–1826* (New York, 1973)

Lynn, J., 'Toward an army of honour: the moral evolution of the French army, 1789–1815', *French Historical Studies*, XVI, No. 1 (Spring 1989), pp. 152–73

Lyons, M., *Napoleon Bonaparte and the Legacy of the French Revolution* (London, 1994)

Macartney, C., *The Habsburg Empire, 1790–1918* (London, 1969)

Mackenzie, N., *The Escape from Elba: the Fall and Flight of Napoleon, 1814–1815* (Oxford, 1982)

Mackesy, P., *Statesmen at War: the Strategy of Overthrow, 1798–1799* (London, 1974)

Mackesy, P., *The War in the Mediterranean, 1803–1810* (London, 1957)

Mackesy, P., *War without Victory: the Downfall of Pitt, 1799–1802* (Oxford, 1994)

Madelin, L., *Talleyrand: a Vivid Biography of the Amoral, Unscrupulous and Fascinating French Statesman* (London, 1948)

Mahan, A. T., *The Influence of Seapower upon the French Revolution and Empire, 1793–1812* (London, 1891)

Mahan, J. K., *The War of 1812* (Gainesville, Florida, 1972)

Mansel, P., 'How forgotten were the Bourbons in France between 1812 and 1814?', *European Studies Review*, XIII, No. 1 (January 1983), pp. 13–38

Mansel, P., *Louis XVIII* (London, 1984)

Markham, F., *Napoleon* (London, 1963)

Marshall, P., *Problems of Empire: Britain and India, 1757–1813* (London, 1968)

Martin, A., *Napoleon the Novelist* (Cambridge, 2000)

Masson, F., *Napoleon and his Coronation*, translated by Frederic Cobb (London, 1911)

Masson, F., *Napoléon dans sa Jeunesse, 1769–1793* (Paris, 1907)

Masson, F., *Napoléon et sa Famille* (Paris, 1897–1919)

McGrew, R., *Paul I of Russia, 1754–1801* (Oxford, 1992)

McKay, D. and Scott, H. M, *The Rise of the Great Powers, 1648–1815* (London, 1983)

McLynn, F., *Napoleon: a Biography* (London, 1997)

Meriage, L., *Russia and the First Serbian Insurrection, 1804–1813* (New York, 1987)

Mowat, R., *The Diplomacy of Napoleon* (London, 1924)

Muir, R., *Britain and the Defeat of Napoleon, 1807–1815* (London, 1996)

Murphy, O. T., 'Napoleon and French old-régime politics and diplomacy', *Consortium on Revolutionary Europe Proceedings*, XX (1989), pp. 97–103

Nicholson, H., *The Congress of Vienna: a Study of Allied Unity, 1812–1822* (London, 1948)

O'Dwyer, M., *The Papacy in the Age of Napoleon and the Restoration: Pius VII, 1800–1823* (London, 1985)

Oeschli, W., *History of Switzerland, 1499–1914* (Cambridge, 1922)

Oman, C., *A History of the Peninsular War* (Oxford, 1902–1930)

Oman, C. M. A., *Napoleon's Viceroy: Eugène de Beauharnais* (London, 1966)

Palmer, A., *Alexander I, Tsar of War and Peace* (London, 1974)

Palmer, A., *Bernadotte: Napoleon's Marshal, Sweden's King* (London, 1990)

Palmer, A., *Metternich, Councillor of Europe* (London, 1972)

Palmer, A., *Napoleon in Russia* (London, 1967)

Palmer, M., *Stoddert's War: Naval Operations in the War against France, 1798–1801* (Columbia, South Carolina, 1987)

Paret, P., 'Napoleon as enemy', *Consortium on Revolutionary Europe Proceedings*, XIII (1983), pp. 49–61

Parker, H., 'Why did Napoleon invade Russia? A study in motivation, personality, and social structure', *Consortium on Revolutionary Europe Proceedings*, XX (1989), pp. 86–96

Parker, H., 'The formation of Napoleon's personality: an exploratory essay', *French Historical Studies*, VII, No. 1 (Spring 1971), pp. 6–26

Parkinson, R., *The Fox of the North: the Life of Kutuzov, General of War and Peace* (Abingdon, 1976)

Parkinson, R., *The Hussar General: the Life of Blücher, Man of Waterloo* (London, 1975)

Parra, E. la, *Godoy: la Aventura del Poder* (Barcelona, 2002)

Pivka, O. von, *Armies of the Napoleonic Era* (Newton Abbot, 1979)

Pivka, O. von, *Navies of the Napoleonic Era* (Newton Abbot, 1980)

Pocock, T., *Stopping Napoleon: War and Intrigue in the Mediterranean* (London, 2004)

Puryear, V. J., *Napoleon and the Dardanelles* (Berkeley, California, 1951)

Ragsdale, H., 'A continental system in 1801: Paul I and Bonaparte', *Journal of Modern History*, XLII, No. 1 (March, 1970), pp. 70–89

Ragsdale, H., *Détente in the Napoleonic Era: Bonaparte and the Russians* (Lawrence, Kansas, 1980)

Ragsdale, H., 'The case of Paul I of Russia: an approach to psycho-biography', *Consortium on Revolutionary Europe Proceedings*, XIX (1989), ii, pp. 617–24

Ragsdale, H., 'Russia, Prussia and Europe in the policy of Paul I', *Jahrbücher für Geschichte Osteuropas*, XXXI (1983), pp. 81–118

Ragsdale, H., 'Russian influence at Lunéville', *French Historical Studies*, V, No. 3 (Spring 1968), pp. 274–84

Ragsdale, H., *Tsar Paul and the Question of Madness: an Essay in History and Psychology* (New York, 1988)

Reddaway, W., et al. (eds), *The Cambridge History of Poland, II: From Augustus II to Pilsudski, 1697–1935* (Cambridge, 1951)

Riehn, R., *1812: Napoleon's Russian Campaign* (London, 1991)

Riley, J. P., *Napoleon and the World War of 1813: Lessons in Coalition Warfighting* (London, 2000)

Roberts, A. *Napoleon and Wellington* (London, 2001)

Robertson, W., *France and Latin-American Independence* (Baltimore, 1939)

Robson, M., 'British intervention in Portugal, 1792–1807', *Historical Research*, LXXXVI, No. 191 (February 2003), pp. 93–107

Rodger, A. B., *The War of the Second Coalition, 1798 to 1801: a Strategic Commentary* (Oxford, 1964)

Roider, K., *Baron Thugut and Austria's Response to the French Revolution* (Princeton, New Jersey, 1987)

Roider, K., 'The Habsburg Foreign Ministry and political reform, 1801–1805', *Central European History*, XXII, No. 2 (June 1989), pp. 160–82

Rolo, P., *George Canning: Three Biographical Studies* (London, 1965)

Ros, M., *Night of Fire: the Black Napoleon and the Battle for Haiti* (New York, 1994)

Rose, J. H., *The Revolutionary and Napoleonic Era, 1789–1815* (Cambridge, 1907)

Rose, J. H., 'British West-India commerce as a factor in the Napoleonic War', *Cambridge Historical Journal*, III, No. 1 (1929), pp. 34–46

Rose, J. H., 'Napoleon and seapower', *Cambridge Historical Journal*, I, No. 2 (1924), pp. 138–57

Roselli, J., *Lord William Bentinck: the Making of a Liberal Imperialist, 1774–1839* (London, 1974)

Ross, M., *The Reluctant King: Joseph Bonaparte, King of the Two Sicilies and Spain* (London, 1976)

Ross, S., 'The military strategy of the Directory: the campaigns of 1799', *French Historical Studies*, V, No. 2 (Autumn 1967), pp. 170–87

Rothenberg, G., *The Emperor's Last Victory: Napoleon and the Battle of Wagram* (London, 2004)

Rothenberg, G., *Napoleon's Great Adversaries: the Archduke Charles and the Austrian Army, 1792–1814* (London, 1982)

Rothenberg, G., *The Napoleonic Wars* (London, 2000)

Rowe, M. (ed.), *Collaboration and Resistance in Napoleonic Europe: State-Formation in an Age of Upheaval, c. 1800–1815* (Macmillan, 2003)

Rydjord, J., 'British mediation between Spain and her colonies, 1811–1813', *Hispanic American Historical Review*, XXI, No. 1 (February 1941), pp. 29–50

Saul, N., *Russia and the Mediterranean, 1797–1807* (Chicago, 1970)

Schama, S., *Patriots and Liberators: Revolution in the Netherlands, 1780–1813* (London, 1977)

Schmitt, H., '1812: Stein, Alexander I and the crusade against Napoleon', *Journal of Modern History*, XXXI, No. 4 (December 1959), pp. 325–8

Schneid, F., *Napoleon's Italian Campaigns, 1805–1815* (Westport, Connecticut, 2002)

Schneid, F., *Napoleon's Conquest of Europe: the War of the Third Coalition* (Westport, Connecticut, 2005)

Schneid, F., *Soldiers of Napoleon's Kingdom of Italy: Army, State and Society, 1800–1815* (Boulder, Colorado, 1995)

Schom, A., *Napoleon Bonaparte* (New York, 1998)

Schom, A., *One Hundred Days: Napoleon's Road to Waterloo* (London, 1993)

Schroeder, P., 'Napoleon's foreign policy: a criminal enterprise', *Consortium on Revolutionary Europe Proceedings*, XX (1990), pp. 104–11

Schroeder, P., *The Transformation of European Politics, 1763–1848* (Oxford, 1994)

Schroeder, P., 'An unnatural "natural alliance": Castlereagh, Metternich and Aberdeen in 1813', *International History Review*, X, No. 4 (November 1988), pp. 522–40

Schur, N., *Napoleon and the Holy Land* (London, 1999)

Seeley, J. R., *Life and Times of Stein, or Germany and Prussia in the Napoleonic Age* (Cambridge, 1978)

Semmel, S., *Napoleon and the British* (New Haven, Connecticut, 2004)

Severn, J., 'Spain, the Wellesleys and the politics of war: the Anglo-Spanish alliance, 1808–1812', *Consortium on Revolutionary Europe Proceedings*, XXV (1995), pp. 380–91

Severn, J., *A Wellesley Affair: Richard Marquess Wellesley and the Conduct of Anglo-Spanish Diplomacy, 1809–1812* (Gainesville, Florida, 1991)

Seward, D., *Napoleon's Family* (London, 1986)

Sheehan, J., *German History, 1770–1866* (Oxford, 1989)

Shelah, Y., *Napoleon, 1813* (London, 2000)

Sherwig, J., *Guineas and Gunpowder: British Foreign Aid in the Wars with France, 1793–1815* (Cambridge, Massachusetts, 1969)

Showalter, D., 'Hubertusberg to Auerstädt; the Prussian army in decline', *German History*, XII, No. 3 (July 1994)

Simms, B., 'The road to Jena: Prussian high politics, 1804–6', *German History*, XII, No. 3 (July 1994)

Simms, B., *The Struggle for Mastery in Germany, 1779–1850* (London, 1998)

Simon, W., *The Failure of the Prussian Reform Movement, 1807–1819* (New York, 1971)

Smith, D., *1813, Leipzig: Napoleon and the Battle of the Nations* (Leipzig, 2001)

Smith, D., *The Decline and Fall of Napoleon's Empire* (London, 2005)

Sprout, H. and M., *The Rise of American Naval Power, 1776–1918* (Princeton, New Jersey, 1946)

Sutherland, D. M. G., *France, 1789–1815: Revolution and Counter-Revolution* (London, 1985)

Sweet, P., *Friedrich von Gentz, Defender of the Old Order* (Madison, Wisconsin, 1941)

Sydenham, M. J., *The First French Republic, 1792–1804* (London, 1974)

Tapié, V., *The Rise and Fall of the Habsburg Monarchy* (London, 1971)

Thompson, J. M., *Napoleon Bonaparte* (London, 1952)

Tuck, P. J. N. (ed.), *The East India Company, 1600–1858, V: Warfare, Expansion and Resistance* (London, 1998)

Tulard, J. (ed.), *L'Histoire de Napoléon par la Peinture* (Paris, 1991)

Tulard, J., *Napoleon: the Myth of the Saviour* (London, 1984)

Turnbull, P., *Napoleon's Second Empress* (London, 1971)

Uffindell, A., *The Eagle's Last Triumph: Napoleon's Victory at Ligny, June 1815* (London, 1994)

Vandal, A., *Napoléon et Alexandre I: l'alliance russe sous le premier empire* (Paris, 1896)

Vincent, E., *Nelson: Love and Fame* (New Haven, Connecticut, 2003)

Vucinich W. S., (ed.), *The First Serbian Uprising, 1804–1813* (New York, 1982)

Waliszewski, K., *Paul I of Russia, the Son of Catherine the Great* (London, 1913)

Wandycz, P., *The Lands of Partitioned Poland, 1795–1918* (Seattle, Washington, 1974)

Watson, G., 'The United States and the Peninsular War, 1808–1812', *Historical Journal*, XIX, No. 4 (December 1976), pp. 859–76

Watts, S., *The Republic Reborn: War and the Making of Liberal America, 1790–1820* (Baltimore, Maryland, 1987)

Webster, C., *The Congress of Vienna, 1814–1815* (London, 1934)

Webster, C., *The Foreign Policy of Castlereagh, 1812–1815* (London, 1931)

Whitaker, A., 'The retrocession of Louisiana in Spanish policy', *American Historical Review*, XXXIX (1934), pp. 454–76

Wilson Lyon, E., 'The Franco-American convention of 1800', *Journal of Modern History*, XII, No. 3 (September 1940), pp. 305–33

Woloch, I., 'Napoleonic conscription: state power and civil society', *Past and Present*, No. 111 (May 1986), pp. 101–29

Woolf, S., *A History of Italy, 1700–1860: the Social Constraints of Political Change* (London, 1979)

Zawadzki, W. H., *A Man of Honour: Adam Czartoryski as a Statesman of Russia and Poland, 1795–1831* (Oxford, 1993)

Zawadzki, W., 'Prince Adam Czartorysky and Napoleonic France, 1801–1805: a study of political attitudes', *Historical Journal*, XVIII, No. 2 (June 1975), pp. 245–77

Zawadzki, W., 'Russia and the reopening of the Polish question, 1801–1814', *International History Review*, VII, No. 1 (February 1985), pp. 19–44

Ziegler, P., *Addington: a Life of Henry Addington, First Viscount Sidmouth* (London, 1965)

Zulueta, J. de, 'Trafalgar: the Spanish view', *Mariners' Mirror*, LXVI (1980), pp. 293–317

Index

Belgium 44, 156, 206, 246, 412
and Austria 81
and Britain 47, 315, 79
and France 50, 67, 79, 95, 294, 520
and the campaign of 1813 508, 516
and the Congress of Vienna 537–9, 544
and the War of the Seventh Coalition 554–5
Belgrade 251–2
Bellegarde, Heinrich 96
Belmonte, Prince of 380–81
Bennigsen, Levin August von 278, 282–4, 291–3, 514
Bentinck, Lord William 175, 379–82, 522, 527, 537, 556
Berah, Rajah of 173
Berbice 102
Beresford, Sir William 355, 368
Berg, Grand Duchy of 228, 232–4, 299–300, 320, 521
Berlin, decree of 1806 276
Bernadotte, Jean-Baptiste 81, 93, 114–15, 222, 273, 278, 286, 392
King of Sweden 415–16, 440, 449–50, 480, 500, 564
and Napoleon Bonaparte 510
and the campaign of 1813–14 514, 516, 530
Berthier, Louis Alexandre 52, 103, 120, 220, 471–2
Berthollet, Claude 120
Bertrand, Henri 285
Bessarabia 449
Bessborough, Lady 553
Bessières, Jean-Baptiste 52, 301, 329
Beugnot, Jacques 521–2
Bialystok 433
Blauewberg, battle of 262
Blaze, Elzéar 219, 393

Blenheim, battle of 209
Blücher, Gebhard von 182–3, 258–9, 272–3, 299, 514, 530
and the War of the Seventh Coalition 554–5, 558–9
Boaden, James 278
Bohemia 12, 287
Bokhara, khanate of 89
Bolivia 262, 272
Bonaparte, Caroline 230, 320
Bonaparte, Charlotte 330, 332
Bonaparte, Elise 16, 25, 199, 232, 320, 335
Bonaparte, Jerome 232, 234, 236, 284, 299, 320, 326, 554
King of Westphalia 428–32, 451, 468, 495
Bonaparte, Joseph 24–5, 27, 30–31, 33–4, 120, 149, 330, 415, 554
relations with Napoleon 17, 22, 38, 425–8
King of Naples 228–30, 236, 243–4, 253, 320, 322, 382, 395, 417
King of Spain 3, 425–8, 448, 518–9
and the Peninsular War 348, 351, 357, 359, 425–7
and the campaign of 1812 462
Bonaparte, Josephine 35–7, 39, 55, 116, 127, 131, 140, 143–4, 192–3, 389, 395, 408
Bonaparte, Louis 143, 191, 332
King of Holland 229–31, 320, 419–23, 427–8
Bonaparte, Lucien 25, 35, 99, 120, 232, 236, 330, 332, 428
Bonaparte, Napoleon 1–6, 563–5
abdication 528, 532, 559–60

biography of 15
brigadier 28
Corsican affiliation 17–20, 22, 69
captain 25
character 445–6, 460–61, 506, 529
comparison to historical figures 6–7, 94
corps system 10
domestic policy 114–5, 120–24, 398, 521
early life 16–18
economic policy 122–4
education 19–21
Emperor 193–4, 197, 273–4, 321
exile 13, 528, 532, 539, 560, 565
fall from favour 29–32
First Consul 71–6, 87–8, 93–4, 96–101, 111–18, 125–6
health 413–15, 522, 528–9, 551, 557
major–general 34
marriage to Josephine 35–6, 131, 389, 395
marriage to Marie-Louise 409–13
parents, see Buonaparte, Carlo and Remolino, Letizia
personality 128–30, 178
popularity 56–8, 67–8, 126, 148, 220–21, 441–2, 520, 523, 548–52
propaganda 112, 125–6, 286
public opinion 125, 193–4, 520, 538–9, 551–2
return from exile 545–54
rise to prominence 33–8, 50–58
sub–lieutenant 22
'Twenty–Ninth Bulletin' 492
and Alexander I of Russia 295–8, 335–7, 345–7, 385–91, 402–3, 441–5, 456–7

Frederick II 'the Great',
King of Prussia 9, 12,
23, 42, 44, 274
Frederick VI, King of
Denmark 312
Frederick Augustus I,
Elector (later King) of
Saxony, 256, 299, 512
Frederick William II, King
of Prussia 44–5, 83
Frederick William III, King
of Prussia 83–5, 106,
137, 162, 233
neutrality 182–3, 189,
195, 198, 202, 239–40
and Alexander I 416–17,
440
and Bonaparte 255,
274–5, 291–2, 296,
383–5, 487
and the campaign of
1812 487
and the campaign of
1813–14 498–9,
502–3, 508–10, 512,
518, 528
and the Seventh Coalition
551
and the Third Coalition
222, 224
and the War of 1806
255–8, 260–61,
270–72, 277, 279–81,
285–6, 299, 314
Fréjus 66–8, 548
French Revolution 5–6, 12,
23–4, 33–4, 39–40, 46,
54, 534–5
reception in Europe
79–80, 85–6
French Revolutionary Wars
12, 39
course 47–50, 58–66,
92–6
origins 44–7
number of combatants 9
disruption of trade 159
Frere, John Hookham 368
Fréron, Louis 34
Friedland, battle of 6, 9,
292–3, 295, 313, 486,
491
Fructidor 54, 59–60, 191

Fuentes de Oñoro, battle of
357
Funck, Ferdinand von 256,
271, 277–8, 428

Galatz 404
Galib Efendi 298
Galicia 193, 199, 351, 359,
365–6, 393, 402,
405–6, 437–8, 447, 543
Gamonal, battle of 348
Ganteaume, Honoré 201
Garay, Martín de 370
Gardanne, Claude 298, 446
Genoa, Republic of 18, 30,
81, 90, 164–5, 199,
204, 544
Gentz, Friedrich von 180,
227
George, Prince of Wales
224, 317
George III, King of England
75, 104, 107, 145, 147,
198, 241–2
madness 162, 223, 316
and Hanover 166, 223,
279
Georgia 89, 248–9, 298,
433, 449, 511
Germany 3–4, 7–8, 13, 46,
49–50, 58–9, 89, 91–2,
155, 562
division of 95–6, 108,
134–9
French interest in 302
French occupation 105,
108, 204–5, 195,
232–5, 243, 252–3,
294, 297, 300, 504, 522
Prussian interest in 84–5,
194, 255–6, 299, 563
Russian interest in 88,
187, 489
and Britain 166
and the campaign of
1809 392–6
and the campaign of
1813 499, 510, 516–17
and the Congress of
Vienna 536–7, 540–41,
544, 561
and the Continental
Blockade 424

and the Seven Years War
43
and the Thirty Years War
42
and the War of the Third
Coalition 223, 227, 280
and the War of the
Seventh Coalition
554–5
Ghent, treaty of 541
Gibraltar 63, 289, 330,
339, 360, 362, 364, 371
Giurgiu 404
Goa 140
Godoy, Diego de 341
Godoy, Manuel de 99, 100,
156, 213–15, 268,
324–5, 347–8
and France 322, 331,
337–9
and the Spanish Army
340
background 305–6
domestic policy 305
enemies 306–7, 327–8
fall from power 341–3
foreign policy 307–10
military reforms 304–5,
340
Gohier, Louis 57, 112, 117
Golestan, treaty of 511
Golitsyn, Prince Dmitri 402,
405, 437
Goree 102
Göteborg 361–3
Gourdon 524
Graham, Sir Thomas 365,
373
Granada 303
Gravina, Federico 213, 307
Greece 61, 88, 187, 247,
334, 336, 562
Grenoble 548, 553
Grenville, Lord 78–9, 106,
159, 242, 260, 263–5,
279, 353
Grenvillites 86, 147
Grey, Lord 317, 353
Gronow, Howell 559
Gros, Antoine 126
Grouchy, Emanuel 558
Guadelupe 370, 539
Guastalla 335